MODELS OF CAPITALISM

This volume is the result of a project

sponsored by the Joint Committee on Latin American Studies

of the Social Science Research Council

and the American Council of Learned Societies.

MODELS OF CAPITALISM

LESSONS FOR LATIN AMERICA

EDITED BY

EVELYNE HUBER

THE PENNSYLVANIA STATE UNIVERSITY PRESS
UNIVERSITY PARK, PENNSYLVANIA

Library of Congress Cataloguing-in-Publication Data

Models of capitalism : lessons for Latin America /
 [edited by] Evelyne Huber.
        p.   cm.
    Papers presented at conferences held at the
University of North Carolina, Chapel Hill,
May 1997, and at CEPAL, Nov. 1997.
    Includes index.
    ISBN 0-271-02176-4 (cloth : acid-free paper)
    1. Latin America—Economic policy—
Congresses. 2. Economic policy—Case
studies—Congresses. 3. Comparative
Economics—Congresses. 4. Labor policy—Latin
America—Congresses. 5. Latin America—Social
policy—Congresses. 6. Labor policy—Case
 studies—Congresses. 7. Social policy—Case
studies—Congresses. I. Huber, Evelyne, 1950- .

HC125 .M63 2002
338.98—dc21
                                    2001055299

Copyright © 2002 The Pennsylvania State University
All rights reserved
Printed in the United States of America
Published by The Pennsylvania State University Press,
University Park, PA 16802-1003

It is the policy of The Pennsylvania State University
Press to use acid-free paper for the first printing of all
clothbound books. Publications on uncoated stock
satisfy the minimum requirements of American
National Standard for Information Sciences—Perma-
nence of Paper for Printed Library Materials, ANSI
Z39.48–1992.

CONTENTS

ACKNOWLEDGMENTS

This volume is the product of the efforts and contributions of many people and institutions. It originated in a discussion initiated by Barbara Stallings in the Joint Committee on Latin America of the Social Science Research Council and the American Council of Learned Societies. The project survived the organizational changes at the Social Science Research Council and continued to receive the support of the Council's Regional Advisory Panel for Latin America. A first round of papers was presented at a conference at the University of North Carolina, Chapel Hill, in May 1997, and a second round at a follow-up workshop at CEPAL in Santiago, Chile, in November 1997.

Cosponsors with the Social Science Research Council for the Chapel Hill conference were the University Center for International Studies, the Office of the Vice Provost for Research and Graduate Studies, and the Department of Political Science at UNC, as well as the Duke-UNC Program in Latin American Studies and the Duke-UNC Program in West European Studies.

At the Chapel Hill conference, we benefited greatly from the participation and insightful comments of a number of colleagues: Gao Bai, Jonathan Hartlyn, Herbert Kitschelt, Peter Lange, Gary Marks, Joan Nelson, David Soskice, Kees van Kersbergen, John Weeks, James White, Michael White, Meredith Woo-Cumings, and John Zysman. In Santiago, Osvaldo Rosales provided helpful ideas. Excellent staff support at both conferences was provided by Susana Espasa, and the manuscript was assembled by Mara Goldwyn.

Four colleagues graciously agreed to read the introduction and conclusion to the collection and offered many helpful suggestions: Victor Bulmer-Thomas, Paul Drake, Barbara Stallings, and John Stephens. John Sheahan read the entire manuscript, and his suggestions significantly shaped and improved its final form. Barbara Stallings was centrally involved in the project; she not only provided the initial impetus but also helped plan both conferences and was a highly perceptive critic. Finally and essentially, this book would never have seen the light of day without the leadership role and unfailing organizational follow-through of Eric Hershberg, program director at the Social Science Research Council. He not only took charge of conference organization but also helped shape the agenda and identify the contributors, was an insightful critic, and mustered all the diplomacy needed to get the contributions in more or less on time. All these individuals and institutions deserve thanks and credit for bringing this truly collective and international effort to fruition.

Introduction: Posing the Question

EVELYNE HUBER

Latin American societies have undergone fundamental changes in the past two decades, moving from economies with very wide-ranging state intervention toward more market-driven systems. After a prolonged period of recession these changes produced some successes in the area of economic growth in the 1990s, but also many problems, particularly in the area of poverty and inequality. Moreover, there are underlying problems, such as low saving and investment rates and sluggish export growth, that are reason for concern regarding future economic growth (see, e.g., Fishlow 1995), and events like the Mexican peso crisis in 1994–95, the financial crises of 1998, and particularly the Brazilian crisis in early 1999 forcefully demonstrate the vulnerability of Latin American economies to developments in international financial markets. As the perception of a need for continuing changes in economic and social policies is widely shared, the search for solutions to the challenge of growth with equity has intensified. In this period of globalization, the experiences of countries in different parts of the world are becoming more and more accessible for comparative study, and policymakers increasingly look to a variety of experiences as potential reference points.

In comparative perspective, societies with market economies exhibit great diversity, at every level of economic development, in terms of their capacities to produce growth and equity. The obvious question is why some societies are more successful than others in achieving growth and social integration. During the 1980s, the dominant answer to this question in the debate in international financial institutions, private banking circles, and a number of powerful member governments of the Organisation for Economic Co-operation and Development (OECD) was that success varies positively with the extent to which economies are governed by markets and inversely with the extent of government intervention in the economy. Many economists studying the EANICs (the newly industrialized countries of East Asia) and most social scientists studying social policy in a wide variety of countries challenged this view throughout (e.g., Amsden 1989, Wade 1990, Esping-Andersen 1990), and by the 1990s the view that proper regulation, supervision, and—if necessary—correction of markets, along with public investment in human capital, are pivotal for sustained economic

1

growth and social integration, asserted itself even among the international financial institutions and the more conservative OECD governments.[1]

Here we approach the question of reasons for success in growth and equity from the policy angle, asking which types of economic and social policies governments in the more successful societies pursued. We attempt to identify different models of capitalism, understood as sets of core economic and social policies in the context of market economies. We are choosing this approach because we intend to draw lessons for political action, and policies are action relevant. Geography and resource endowments did affect growth and distribution in different countries, both directly and indirectly by making certain policies likely to be successful. Certainly, a large part of the success story of the South East Asian newly industrialized countries before their financial crises was the investment from Japan, Korea, and Taiwan (Welsh's contribution to this volume; Stallings 1995). However, policymakers in charge of promoting growth and equity can rearrange neither geographic locations nor natural resource endowments, but they can use successful policy models as guides to designing policies for their own societies. Thus we attempt to understand the policy models themselves, the institutional and political conditions under which they operated, and the extent to which the effectiveness of these models is bounded by time and space.

Policies are designed and implemented by actors in given institutional configurations and thus in part depend on particular institutional prerequisites. Institutions themselves are shaped by historical legacies, past power distributions, and policy choices. Accordingly, they are to be regarded as limiting to some extent the range of present policy choices but as being malleable in the medium and longer run. It is crucial to point out here that political power distributions and political choices fundamentally shape institutions. Radical versions of the globalization thesis paint a picture of inexorable pressures toward institutional and policy convergence, toward state retrenchment in both the economic and social policy realm. Empirically, however, few if any signs of such convergence can be demonstrated. Common external pressures are filtered through domestic institutions and power distributions and thus evoke different responses. Despite some policy changes in the same direction of state retrenchment, there is little conver-

---

1. Wade (1996) makes clear that not only dissenting economists but also the Japanese government disagreed with the World Bank's interpretation of the experience of the East Asian NICs. For a discussion of the changes in the debate about development strategies for Latin America among multilateral institutions and supranational development agencies, see Korzeniewicz and Smith 2000.

gence, since typically the states with a more restricted role in economic and social policies to begin with contracted their role further than states with more extensive involvement in these areas. This is true for advanced industrial democracies (Kitschelt et al. 1999) and to a lesser extent also for Latin America, even though greater institutional weakness and stronger international pressures produced radical state retrenchment in some previously highly interventionist states like Chile and Argentina (Filgueira and Filgueira's contribution to this volume; Huber 1997). Thus, while we recognize the importance of pressures from international markets and financial institutions, we are interested precisely in differential responses to these pressures.

The starting point for our investigation is the basic recognition of the need to understand the relationship between the system of production of goods and services and the distribution of life chances in a society. What is produced and how it is produced is heavily related to how material goods are distributed. The "how" refers to both the technological and the social aspects of production, that is, the relationships among capital, labor, and the state. Conceptually, models of capitalism have two essential components, growth-oriented strategies and equity-oriented strategies. The growth-oriented strategies are conventionally identified with economic policies, and the equity-oriented strategies with social policies and labor market policies. It has long been accepted that different growth strategies have different consequences for equity. By now social scientists have also come to recognize that there need not be a trade-off between growth-oriented and equity-oriented strategies, but rather that they can be compatible and that some equity-oriented strategies may actually have positive effects for economic growth. Specifically, scholars are increasingly recognizing that excessive inequality is a barrier to growth.[2] The overlap between pro-growth and pro-equity policies is perhaps most obvious in the area of labor market policy. The creation of employment to a significant extent depends on economic growth, and improvement of the qualification of the labor force supports economic growth.

Accordingly, we combine a disaggregated focus on specific policies with a systematic attempt to capture interrelationships between economic and social structures and policies. We investigate economic policies designed to stimulate growth; labor market policies designed to promote employment, a qualified labor force adequate for these employment opportunities, and labor relations allowing for improvements in productivity and wages; and

---

2. Birdsall and Jaspersen (1997, 4) state that "there is growing evidence that countries with the least inequality grow fastest."

social policies designed to improve general human capital and to distribute life chances among the population in an equitable way. We understand "equitable" to mean working in the direction of eliminating poverty or the exclusion of social strata from full participation in economic, social, and cultural life, and of reducing the differential in life chances between the most and the least privileged strata in a society.

Among the many economic policies that are arguably crucial for economic growth, we focus on three key policy areas: competitiveness, investment promotion, and trade. On the labor market side, we pay particular attention to active labor market policies in the form of training and placement programs, to legal parameters governing labor relations, and to measures for the general upgrading of the qualification of the labor force. Our treatment of social policies includes the entire complex of social policies subsumed under the label of welfare states, as well as education.

As noted, the selection of cases for comparison with the Latin American experience is governed by the criteria of successful performance in growth and equity. We choose Northeast and Southeast Asian countries because of their spectacular growth records, particularly in the two decades from 1975 to 1995 when Latin America was confronting enormous economic problems. In order to understand these countries' favorable performance in equity we also investigate the main characteristics of their labor market and social policies. In choosing these cases as successful examples, we clearly reject the view that the spreading financial crisis of the second half of the 1990s indicates that these growth models were inherently flawed all along. Rather, we side with those who argue that the crisis was a result of rapid financial liberalization (and thus a certain deviation from the traditional models), the rapid growth of financial markets, and panic behavior on the part of investors (e.g., Chang et al. 1998; Radelet and Sachs 1998; Chang 1999).

Additional reference cases for labor market and social policies are advanced industrial democracies, some of which have been highly successful in eliminating poverty and reducing inequality whereas others have not, despite similarly high levels of income per capita. In a parallel fashion, these countries show great differences in the maintenance of full employment both across cases and over time, in the creation of a highly qualified labor force, and in the presence of a dual labor market. These differences among countries at roughly the same levels of affluence and similar levels of competitiveness in world markets should yield important policy lessons.

We are approaching the analysis of these comparative cases with the intention to draw lessons that could help answer the following questions confronting policymakers in Latin America. At a general level, how far and how fast should the opening to foreign goods and capital proceed? What options are available to promote domestic savings and attract foreign capital and channel them into productive investments? How can governments promote the competitiveness of firms and a move up the commodity chain? What can governments do to promote employment and improve the qualifications of the labor force and the distribution of wages? What are the most effective social policies to combat poverty, and how can they be financed in fiscally responsible ways? In all of these policy areas, what are the appropriate roles of the state and the private sector?

To approach the issues in this way is not to imply that all of these questions are being asked openly by Latin American policymakers, but it is to say that these questions are worth asking from a comparative point of view and from the point of view of appropriate policy responses to emerging problems and challenges. For instance, comprehensive and far-reaching tariff reductions have been undertaken by Latin American countries and are not being openly questioned by policymakers at this time. On the other hand, there have been voices warning of a possible backlash against the entire neoliberal project, including trade liberalization. Thus, it is appropriate for an academic project to attempt to elucidate the costs and benefits of different patterns of trade policies. Most of the other policy areas we are looking at here are being debated widely in Latin America and other parts of the world. The possibilities for designing competitiveness and technological upgrading policies that remain viable under the new world trade regime resulting from the Uruguay Round are preoccupying policymakers in a wide variety of countries. After about a decade of uncritical embrace of financial liberalization, the debate about the desirability of controls over national and international financial markets has intensified greatly in the wake of the financial crises spreading in the second half of the 1990s from East Asia to Russia and Latin America. The debate about the desirable degree of flexibility versus protection of labor rights in labor market policies is intense both in OECD countries and in Latin America. There is considerable consensus concerning the need for upgrading the skills of the labor force, but not concerning the responsibility and sources of financing for this task.

In the area of social policy, opinions differ very widely; one model assigns to the state the responsibility for providing, in partnership with employers and employees, a comprehensive social safety net and universalistic free or heavily subsidized social services, whereas a diametrically opposed model assigns only a residual role to the state, to support those who have no chance of insuring themselves through the market or of purchasing services from private providers. Moreover, the traditional conservative view has posited a trade-off between growth-oriented and equity-oriented policies, whereas the social democratic view has held that the two can be mutually reinforcing. In Latin America, the trade-off view has been dominant, and the reform debate in the past two decades has predominantly focused on growth strategies and on how to keep social and labor market policies from being barriers to growth. This book aims to shift the debate by offering insights into other existing models of capitalism, in East Asia and in advanced industrial societies, some of which have done much better than others in making economic, labor market, and social policies compatible or even mutually supportive in the dual quest for growth and equity.

We begin with six papers on Latin America. The first offers an overview of alternative models of capitalism that have been pursued in different historical periods. The next three discuss experiences with economic policies central to the promotion of growth: competitiveness policies, trade policies, and the promotion of investments. The final two analyze social and labor market policy patterns. We then turn to the experiences with models of capitalism in newly industrialized countries of Northeast and Southeast Asia. The first of this group of chapters focuses on growth-oriented policies, the second takes a more integrative view and looks at growth- and equity-oriented policies and their interaction, and the third situates social and labor market policies in the larger context of the East Asian models of capitalism. The final set of chapters analyzes social policy and labor market policy in Western Europe, the United States, and Canada. All four of these chapters ask explicitly about the impact of policy configurations on equity, and some ask about their relationship to growth as well.

In his overview of models of capitalism in Latin America (Chapter 1), John Sheahan points out that they suffered from much greater instability than models of capitalism in advanced industrial societies. None of these models had much staying power in Latin America; rather, economic and social policies were characterized by rapid and radical changes. None of them worked well in the equity dimension, and growth over the entire period since World War II has been only moderate. Sheahan classifies models of capitalism according to the degree of economic interventionism and the degree of concern with inclusion. He argues that the economically interventionist models failed largely because they were used in a predominantly protectionist fashion, rather than in a dynamic fashion to promote industrial diversification and technological upgrading. The models where the concern with equity was apparently greatest were the populist ones, but these models failed in the medium to longer run because of reckless macroeconomic policies in the form of high deficit spending and excessive monetary expansion.

Sheahan demonstrates that regional averages show no association between any particular model and a reduction in poverty. Nevertheless, countries where inclusion was pursued over relatively extended periods of time, such as in Costa Rica, Uruguay (before 1973 and after 1985), and Chile (before 1973 and after 1989), show better performance in levels or trajectories (in the case of Chile in the 1990s) of poverty rates than others. They also perform better in basic indicators of quality of life and human capital, such as basic health indicators and literacy rates. Liberal, noninterventionist models of economic and social policy do not perform well in Latin America because of several underlying structural conditions, most prominently high inequality in the distribution of human capital, weak employment in high productivity sectors, high concentration of ownership of land and capital, high economic instability resulting from reliance on primary exports and external capital, and weak democratic institutions. The general trend over the past two decades, of course, has been toward liberal models, but Chile and Brazil show traits of an emerging new model, one that combines liberal economic policies with more interventionist social policies. As Sheahan emphasizes, the advantage of the concept of models of capitalism is precisely that it overcomes the constraint of thinking in simple dichotomies of old-style, inward-looking interventionism versus new outward-oriented neoliberalism, or populism versus neoliberalism, but instead opens up other alternatives, such as outward-oriented interventionism concerned with inclusion, that is, linked to activist but fiscally responsible social policies.

Renato Baumann, in his discussion of the changes in trade policy in Latin America (Chapter 2), documents the great extent and speed of these changes, with the average tariff level having fallen from 45 percent in the 1980s to 13 percent in 1995. He argues that it is very difficult to isolate the effects of trade liberalization, because this liberalization was undertaken in the context of an entire package of structural reforms. Moreover, the first half of the 1990s was a period of favorable variation in the terms of trade of most Latin American countries. Certainly, the reform process was not smooth and involved considerable costs in the short term. In the 1990s, the share of imports and exports as a percentage of GDP increased significantly, though imports increased at a faster rate than exports. Trade policies then contributed to lowering inflation by way of greater import penetration. The 1990s also saw renewed output growth and an increase in investment levels, the latter in part caused by a greater availability of foreign resources. Again,

Baumann argues that it is difficult to pinpoint what role trade liberalization played in this. If we assume that trade liberalization is responsible for export growth, we can detect an indirect effect on growth insofar as firms with higher export/output ratios tend to perform better in productivity and other indicators of competitiveness. The distributive effect of trade liberalization is even more difficult to assess. If we look at general trends, there was no movement toward a lowering of inequality. On the contrary, the disparity between professional staff and workers in low productivity sectors increased in the 1990s in the seven major Latin American countries Baumann analyzes. In addition, the most dynamic sector from the point of view of employment creation has been the informal sector, which is not affected much by export growth.

Baumann makes two additional important points. First, he argues that the agreements of the Uruguay Round leave Latin American countries some important room in which to maneuver in that (1) subsidization may be accepted as part of development programs, and (2) quantitative restrictions still may be imposed to protect a balance of payments in difficulties. Second, he points to the strong efforts at subregional integration and to the increase in importance of intraregional trade in the total foreign trade of Latin American countries. The most dynamic area is clearly Mercosur, both in trade growth and in the inflow of foreign capital, particularly foreign direct investment.

Wilson Peres traces the development of competitiveness policy in Latin America (in Chapter 3), showing that—after a decade of being banned from policy discourse under the weight of neoliberal doctrine—it has reemerged in modified form. He ascribes this renewed interest in competitiveness policy to unfulfilled promises of exclusive reliance on markets. Neoliberalism still shapes official conceptions of competitiveness policies in that they are supposed to work only horizontally, rather than targeting specific sectors as traditional industrial policy used to do, though in practice there is more direct and selective involvement, including sectoral policies. The key differences between the new and some versions of the old policies are the orientation toward accelerating rather than retarding industrial transformation, the context of adherence to orthodox macroeconomic policies, and the tendency to increase the competitiveness of already existing industries rather than creating new ones. The currently dominant policies are export promotion, support for innovation and technology diffusion, human resource development, and support for small and medium enterprises. Less accepted though still in some use are subsidized credits, direct fiscal incentives, protectionist trade management, and public sector procurement.

The main weakness of competitiveness policy as currently practiced in Latin America is deficient implementation and lack of evaluation of programs, rooted in lack of coordination among state agencies. The ministries of industry, typically in charge of elaborating the plans, do not control the policy instruments necessary for their implementation, most of which tend to be under the control of the ministries of finance. In addition, after years of budget cuts for state agencies, these agencies have lost capacity to handle complexity. A promising feature is the use of boards with representatives from both the public and private sectors, which gives legitimacy to the designs of competitiveness policy.

Robert Grosse notes (in Chapter 4) that foreign direct investment (FDI) into Latin America has grown substantially in the 1990s, but he cautions that this is probably more a result of the growth of the U.S. economy and the resumption of growth in Latin America than of specific policies to attract FDI. Still, he presents a regression which shows that FDI promotion policies did have an effect; in other words, countries that pursued such policies received more FDI than countries that did not do so. He argues that three policy areas have crucial effects on FDI: (1) policies aimed directly at FDI, such as barriers to the operation of foreign corporations or incentives provided to them; (2) macroeconomic stabilization policies that reduce the country risk for investors, such as stable monetary policy, liberalization of interest rates, privatization of state-owned enterprises, deregulation of sectors traditionally dominated by state enterprises, and conservative fiscal policies; and (3) policies that stabilize a country's international financial position, such as debt reduction, including debt-equity swaps, liberalization of international capital flows, and a stable exchange rate or access to instruments for protection against exchange rate risk. In an overview of changing policies toward foreign investment in Latin America since the 1970s he shows that liberalization has spread since the second half of the 1980s, in tandem with supportive macroeconomic and financial policies, thus providing a supportive environment for the inflow of FDI.

At the same time, Grosse points out that the average savings rate in the region actually declined somewhat from the period 1983–86 to 1993–96, from 21 percent of GDP to 19 percent, despite successful economic stabilization and the return of higher growth rates. On the positive side, he argues that the privatization of pension funds in many countries contributed to the growth of domestic long-term capital markets and thus facilitated the channeling of savings into productive investment. Still, the continued comparatively low savings rate suggests that Latin America remains highly vulnerable to external developments, particularly a downturn in the U.S. economy, which might reduce the inflow of FDI regardless of the policies pursued by Latin American governments. Moreover, a very simple regression model of unemployment with GDP growth and a dummy variable for FDI promotion policy (0 before, 1 after), for the eight largest Latin American economies, shows that FDI promotion policies are actually positively related to unemployment, though the coefficient does not reach statistical significance. Grosse interprets this result as being consistent with the critiques that policies designed to open the Latin American economies and attract FDI have a tendency to aggravate the unemployment problem rather than ameliorate it.

In their analysis of models of capitalism and welfare in Latin America, Carlos and Fernando Filgueira point out (in Chapter 5) that the dominant trend has been toward a retrenchment of welfare state expenditures and at least partial privatization of social insurance and social services. They draw our attention to the great heterogeneity of social policy regimes in Latin America as of 1980, with vast differences in public expenditures and in the proportions of the population covered by social insurance, health care, and education, and in the quality of these various programs and services. They also emphasize the structural problems of high population growth, particularly among the lower socioeconomic strata, high dependency ratios, low educational levels particularly in intermediate education, low labor force participation rates, and the high proportion of low productivity employment. They argue that the root causes of the failure of states to deal effectively with these problems were less the faulty designs of social policy than the underlying structural factors of centralizing authoritarianism, general inequality, rent-seeking political elites, and the bureaucratic weakness of the state.

Filgueira and Filgueira do point to a fundamental problem in the traditional design of social policies, though—the close link of the provision of pensions and health care to formal employment, which left vast sectors of the population uncovered in most countries and became increasingly less viable as the economic adjustment programs of the 1980s and 1990s let formal sector employment shrink even more. This situation, along with the fiscal crisis of social security programs, forced reforms, but the reforms did not result from national debates about desirable models of society to be achieved by social policy regimes; rather, they were subordinated to the goals of economic reform. Under the influence of the international financial institutions, policy shifted toward privatization of social insurance, greater reliance on private providers of services, increasing self-financing of services, and concentration of state efforts on targeted compensatory programs, many of them based on temporary external financing. The policy debate centered around making policy instruments recommended by international organizations more efficient, not around long-term and comprehensive social policy strategies to reduce poverty and inequality.

Víctor E. Tokman's chapter on recent experiences with labor market policy in Latin America (Chapter 6) brings out clearly how intimately economic growth policies are related to labor markets and distribution. He points out how economic objectives have been given priority over social objectives like full employment and systemic solidarity, with the result that the spread of low-quality employment and decreasing wages, particularly minimum wages, have dominated the scene. Economic growth, and thus savings and investment, is crucial for employment creation but has been insufficient in the 1980s and 1990s to achieve significant job creation. Tokman suggests that a more favorable financial environment and stable rules of the game would be needed, along with industrial policies in the targeted forms of sectoral and local policies and support for small and micro enterprises, including the informal sector, and in the more general form of investment in education and training. He also emphasizes the importance of an improvement in productivity and thus a change in the culture of productivity among both entrepreneurs and workers, a change which could be fostered by changes in labor organization within enterprises.

The dominant trend in legislation on labor relations in Latin America has been to make contracts and bargaining more flexible. Whereas this change has certainly helped enterprises become better able to adapt to changing demand conditions, it has also created more unemployment and job instability in the short run and arguably has constituted a disincentive for improving productivity. Similarly, decentralization of bargaining improves local flexibility but bears the danger of weakening the capacity of central actors to promote solidarity and social integration. Tokman points to policy measures that could have a very favorable impact on the situation of workers in the changed environment, but so far these measures have not really reached the implementation stage. They include an expansion of unemployment insurance and recurring training, as well as an extension of protection to part-time workers and those in subcontracting and seasonal employment.

In Chapter 7 Ha-Joon Chang nicely puts into relief some major differences between the experiences of Japan, Korea, and Taiwan and those of the countries of Latin America in the three policy areas discussed in the chapters by Baumann, Peres, and Grosse. Maybe the difference most discussed in the literature is that between the Latin American strategy of import substitution industrialization (ISI) accompanied by reliance on raw material exports and the Northeast Asian strategy of infant industry protection tied to the promotion of the export of manufactured goods. Chang goes beyond this conventional distinction by highlighting how the link between infant industry protection and export promotion was used in part to address the problem of the unavailability of economies of scale for protected industries. Trade policy was used to complement industrial policy and vice versa. Other central elements of industrial policy were controls on entry and capacity in infant industries, the management of competition to avoid the waste of resources without removing the incentive for raising productivity, the regulation of the inflow of technology and of foreign direct investment, and support for domestic technology absorption capability. Chang argues that the distinction between selective versus general (or horizontal) industrial policy is misleading in that even general industrial policy is necessarily selective in some ways when resources are finite.

In discussing Northeast Asian savings and investment policy, Chang first points to the debate in the literature about the direction of causality between high savings and high investment rates and puts primary emphasis on investment rates. Northeast Asian governments, in stark contrast to most Latin American countries, promoted domestic investment by imposing very strict controls on capital flight. At the same time they controlled capital inflows. In addition, they limited luxury consumption through high tariffs, taxes, and outright bans, a policy with important implications, not only for the investment rate, but also for the creation of a sense of national community and national purpose.

Finally, Chang addresses two aspects of the crucial question of replicability of the Northeast Asian model. First, he argues against the view that their specific historical and cultural legacy endowed the Northeast Asian countries with uniquely capable bureaucracies, pointing instead to the possibility of national adaptation and innovation in institutions. Second, like Baumann, he challenges the view that the Uruguay Round of GATT eliminated all possibilities for interventionist trade and industrial policies, pointing to the balance of payments clause and a range of other policy instruments that are still viable. He ends by rejecting an interpretation of the current economic problems in Japan and the financial crisis in Korea as evidence of any inherent weakness of the Northeast Asian model, pointing to the fact that a large part of the problem stems precisely from deviations from the traditional model.

Bridget Welsh explains (in Chapter 8) the late-late developmental success of Indonesia, Malaysia, and Thailand in terms of both regional factors and specific policies, and the ethnic and political factors motivating and enabling these policies. The regional context was crucial insofar as first Japanese firms and then Taiwanese and Korean firms began to invest massive amounts of capital in these countries, in part in order to take advantage of preferential access to the U.S. market, and in part to keep their production costs low in the face of rising wages in their own countries. Moreover, Japan, Taiwan, and Korea served as models for the later developers in the region, and some of these later developers pursued a deliberate strategy of learning from them.

The policies pursued, like those in the newly industrialized countries of Northeast Asia, were highly interventionist, at least until the late 1980s. The comparatively favorable performance in reducing poverty and keeping inequality from rising during the industrial spurt was the result of several factors: (1) strong investment in the agricultural sector, particularly from 1965 to 1975, such as in irrigation schemes and the production of fertilizers and other agricultural inputs, which greatly strengthened the peasant economy; (2) the creation of large numbers of jobs in the rapidly growing industrial sector; (3) price controls and subsidies for food and petroleum; and (4) investment in education, particularly at the primary level. In industry, the governments promoted light industry from the 1950s to the 1970s, with high protective tariffs for infant industries. The governments also expanded the public sector by investing in infrastructure and public sector enterprises. Still, they remained committed to fiscal conservatism and low inflation. In the 1970s, they embarked on an export-led growth strategy in both light and heavy industries. One component of this strategy was the introduction of export processing zones. Another was the selective attraction of foreign technology for heavy industry. A third was a gradual liberalization of the trade regime.

From the 1960s on, these countries were very open toward FDI, and FDI accelerated greatly in the 1980s along with the acceleration of export production. This openness did not entail total reliance on the market, however; rather, the governments selectively promoted certain sectors and built partnerships with foreign capital. Domestically, the governments aligned themselves with sectors of the capitalist class, creating favorable conditions for investment by these groups. The state bureaucracies performed an important developmental role, and at least initially resembled the bureaucracies of their Northeast Asian counterparts in that they were based on meritocratic criteria. Another similarity to the newly industrialized countries of Northeast Asia was the tight control on labor and the left, thus providing capital not only with a stable environment regarding property rights but also with cheap labor.

As Welsh points out, the very success of these policies in terms of growth of production, exports, and FDI led to a partial move away from their pursuit in the 1980s. The trade regime was liberalized, public enterprises were privatized, agriculture did not receive the same attention as before, and political criteria came to replace merit in recruitment and promotion in the bureaucracies. In addition, what had been an asset in the promotion of economic growth in earlier stages became a liability later, once the alliances between governments and sectors of the capitalist class provided growing opportunities for rent-seeking behavior on the part of the latter. Similarly, as the role of the private sector in the economy grew and the state retrenched, the concern with promoting equity declined and inequality increased. Finally, Welsh argues that the enormous expansion of the financial markets in the 1990s, enabling the inflow of massive amounts of short-term capital, combined with the long-standing reliance on FDI, made these countries highly vulnerable to financial crises.

The East Asian experience with labor market and social policies contrasts rather sharply with the Latin American and the European and North American ones. Whereas labor was politically incorporated to varying degrees at least in the larger Latin American countries (Collier and Collier 1991) and in North America and Europe by the middle of the twentieth century, Japan, Korea, and Taiwan built their models of capitalism on the social basis of coalitions between the state, large and small business, and agriculture, with virtually total exclusion of labor. As T. J. Pempel points out (in Chapter 9), it was only in response to democratization and increasing labor militancy and electoral challenges that these countries established any significant welfare state programs. Japan, having democratized after World War II, responded to such challenges in the 1960s and 1970s with the encouragement of company unions and company-based welfare on the one hand and national-level welfare state programs on the other. Korea and Taiwan embarked on social policy reforms, particularly in the area of medical care, as a result of political liberalization in the 1980s. Still, welfare state expenditures remained very low in comparative perspective. In Japan, the consolidation of the electoral dominance of the Liberal Democratic Party (LDP) was followed by a retrenchment of welfare state programs in the 1980s.

Japanese labor market policy was primarily proactive, focused on market-oriented labor training with cooperation between the government and the private sector. In response to the first oil shock, unions in the large companies were incorporated into a de facto bargain under which they moderated wage demands in exchange for business commitments to job security and retraining, and government promises of support for industrial restructuring and labor retraining programs, low taxes, and low inflation. What, then, accounts for the comparatively low degree of inequality and poverty in these countries despite the absence of significant redistributive tax and transfer programs? Pempel points to the land reforms in all three countries, to virtually full employment, to heavy investment in human resources, and to the distribution of company and public welfare through the extended family. However, he raises doubts about the replicability of these experiences by drawing attention to the fact that the very high growth rates achieved by these three countries have to be seen at least in part as a result of favorable international conditions, particularly the pattern of bilateral relations with the United States.

John D. Stephens elaborates (in Chapter 10) the contrasts between the different types of welfare state regimes of advanced industrial countries in terms of their basic program characteristics, their relationships to specific labor market and production regimes, their distributive outcomes, and their resilience in the new international economic environment. With the exception of Britain and Ireland, the European welfare states are of either the social democratic or the Christian democratic type. They rely much more on public funding of welfare state goods and services and accordingly provide more generous benefits than the liberal regimes, but they differ from one another in the extent of provision of universal basic transfer benefits, the public delivery of social services, and the provision of support for women's labor force participation, all of which are significantly higher in social democratic regimes. The labor market regimes associated with social democratic welfare states are characterized by high union density and union centralization, very wide contract extension, and high centralization of collective bargaining, the combination of which results in comparatively low wage inequality and the absence of a dual labor market, in stark contrast to the labor market regimes in countries with liberal welfare states, which have the opposite characteristics and outcomes. Labor market regimes in countries with Christian democratic welfare states occupy intermediate positions in union density and centralization, contract extension, and centralization of collective bargaining, as well as in wage dispersion; the countries in northern continental Europe are much closer to the social democratic than the liberal types of labor market regimes.

The different welfare state and labor market regimes are embedded in different production regimes, understood as patterns of relationship among employers and between employers, the government, banks, and labor that shape financial relations, macroeconomic and trade policy, vocational training, and industrial relations. In coordinated market economies, the various actors work together to design and implement policies oriented toward medium- and longer-term favorable results in investments, industrial competitiveness, productivity, and so on; in uncoordinated market economies these actors work largely individually according to shorter-term market logics. Liberal welfare state regimes are embedded in uncoordinated market economies, social democratic and Christian democratic welfare state regimes in coordinated market economies.

The different labor market and welfare state regimes effect markedly different degrees of redistribution and thus significant differences in poverty levels. The social democratic welfare state regimes are most redistributive and have the lowest poverty rates, followed closely by the Northern European Christian democratic welfare state regimes. The most redistributive policy design is a combination of public universal basic flat rate with public income-related benefits in transfer programs (simply because all private alternatives are more inegalitarian), and the main factor accounting for differences in poverty rates among the elderly is the level of minimum pensions. The key policies to protect another highly vulnerable group from falling below the poverty line, single mothers, are universal child allowances and policies supportive of mothers' employment.

Since the 1980s European welfare state and labor market regimes have clearly come under pressure, and all of them implemented some cuts in major programs. Higher levels of unemployment and thus lower contributions to social security schemes accompanied by greater demand for unemployment benefits simply forced either increases in taxes or cuts in benefits. However, in none of the social democratic or Christian democratic regimes can we speak of a real welfare state regime shift. Deregulation of national and international financial markets made the pursuit of a number of policies to maintain full employment more difficult, and the internationalization of production shifted bargaining power from governments and labor to capital, but the basic parameters of the coordinated market economies and labor market regimes remained in place as well. In fact, it was in the liberal welfare state and labor market regimes that cuts were most severe.

Stephens points to two important lessons: First, the European experience shows that it is possible to pursue growth and equity in the context of highly open, export-dependent economies. Second, welfare state and labor market regimes that invest in youth, labor mobilization including female labor, and human capital, and that promote cooperation between labor and capital at a variety of levels are better able to maintain a competitive position in world markets, high levels of employment, and thus a generous social safety net. He ends with a caution against too holistic and deterministic interpretations of the connection between welfare state, labor market, and production regimes. Production regimes do not exert inexorable pressures toward given welfare state regimes; rather, and here his argument squares fully with John Myles's (in Chapter 11), within these basic regimes there is room for choice of social policy designs that offer more or less generous and redistributive benefits.

The comparison between the United States and Canada, two cases of liberal welfare state regimes, in John Myles's chapter nicely underscores the importance of welfare state policy designs for distributional outcomes. Both countries have comparatively highly inegalitarian labor market outcomes, but whereas poverty and inequality have risen in the United States, income distribution and poverty rates have remained relatively stable in Canada. The liberal welfare state regimes of the United States and Canada are characterized by heavy reliance on the market for social insurance and by low welfare spending. Myles argues that the overall amount of spending on welfare state programs clearly matters for poverty and inequality, but in addition the type of design of welfare state programs is of importance. Compared to Europe, welfare state spending in both Canada and the United States has been low, but Canada has universal coverage in health care and predominantly public delivery of health care, as well as a strong tradition of universal basic benefits based on citizenship for children and the elderly. This tradition of universalism favored the reorientation of all cash transfer programs toward a negative income tax (NIT), beginning in 1978, and this new system proved comparatively resilient in the period of welfare state retrenchment. This NIT system provides subsidies to poor and low income households at a rate that declines with rising incomes, but—in stark contrast to traditional social assistance schemes—it declines at less than 100 percent so that it preserves a substantial incentive to increase earnings. A similar program was established in 1973 in the United States, the Earned Income Tax Credit for working poor families with children, but it is much more restricted in scope and the bulk of spending for the poor of working age continued to follow the traditional means-tested social assistance model.

Social assistance, or "welfare as we know it," of course came under heavy attack, and benefits were severely limited in duration in the United States in the 1990s, in contrast to the Canadian NIT program, which continued to grow in a political context that was similarly oriented toward budgetary austerity. Myles offers several reasons to account for the different fate of these two types of programs. First, the support coalitions for the NIT programs are broader, including those interested in controlling public expenditures by turning all transfer programs into targeted programs, those interested in increasing labor market flexibility and having work incentives for low income recipients, and those interested in increasing the incomes of poor and low income households. Traditional social assistance programs tend to have very narrow support coalitions, largely confined to the last of the three groups mentioned. Second, politicians prefer NIT programs because of their comparatively low transparency, which makes it easier to disguise cutbacks and avoid blame. Cutbacks in universal, flat-rate benefits for instance, such as basic pensions and child allowances, are much more visible. Nevertheless, Myles does end on a note of caution, pointing out that the savings achieved from a reduction of benefits to upper and middle income earners due to the transition, savings that were allocated to lower income families, have come to an end, and the future capacity of the NIT program to keep poverty and inequality from rising will depend on the willingness of politicians to put the program on a permanent and adequate financial basis.

Thomas Janoski and Antonio Alas's chapter on labor market policies in Europe (Chapter 12) further underlines the extreme status of U.S. labor market policies. The chapter begins with an overview of the wide variety of labor market policies, both active and passive, that have been pursued in different countries, and it points out that hardly any of them have been pursued in the United States. It then goes on to a comparison of active and passive labor market policies in Britain and Germany, the former close to the noninterventionist/weak labor market policy pole, the latter close to the interventionist/strong labor market policy pole. Essentially, active labor market policies are aimed at preventing or reducing unemployment through job placement, job training, and job creation, whereas passive labor market policies are aimed at protecting workers through a variety of measures, among them unemployment insurance, job protection, and minimum wage legislation. In the 1980s and 1990s, the amount of money spent on passive labor market policies has been roughly double the amount spent on active labor market policies in the OECD / European Community area, but there have been significant differences among countries in this ratio. As Stephens points out in Chapter 10, social democratic governments have emphasized active labor market policies, whereas Christian democratic governments have relied more on passive ones.

To some extent, both varieties of labor market policy require strong labor market institutions, primarily strong unions and employer organizations, capable of representing and coordinating the actions of their constituents to be effective, but active labor market policies require such institutions to a greater extent. Unions have been of moderate strength in Britain if measured by union density, but they have been highly decentralized and incapable of extending contract coverage to a very large part of the nonunionized labor force, in contrast to Germany. There is no tradition of centralized tripartite negotiation; Conservative governments have consistently opposed such corporatist practices, along with other kinds of government intervention into the labor market. Accordingly active labor market policies have been weak, poorly funded and coordinated, and of generally short duration. In contrast, in Germany unions and employer organizations have been stronger and have long been involved in coordinated bargaining. Both the Social Democratic Party and the labor wing of the Christian Democratic Party have supported active labor market policies, which resulted in strong emphasis on such policies in the early 1950s and then again after the return of the Social Democrats to power in the late 1960s. The initial job training system in Germany is extremely strong, but the government also supports retraining for redundant workers and advanced training, as well as job placement and employment creation. The high unemployment in the former East Germany after unification has greatly strained resources for both active and passive labor market policies, and some cutbacks in unemployment insurance benefits have been imposed, but the basic commitment to active labor market policy remains.

Janoski and Alas end with a discussion of the effectiveness of active labor market policies. They point out that there are problems with evaluation research because of different assumptions regarding the displacement and substitution effects of job creation policies, and because of the fact that spending on labor market policies automatically goes up with unemployment, as long as the rules governing policies remain unchanged. However, there are two solid results. First, countries that do pursue active labor market policies have lower levels of unemployment than similarly situated countries that do not pursue such policies. Second, increasing the ratio of spending on active to spending on passive labor market policies has a strong negative effect on long-term unemployment rates and a smaller positive effect on short-term unemployment rates, which indicates that maintaining a high ratio of active to passive labor market policy expenditure supports flexibility and labor mobility. Finally, the policies that seem to work specially well are those targeted at particular kinds of unemployed people.

Among the developed countries, the U.S. experience with labor market policies is closest to the East Asian one in terms of the restrictions imposed on organized labor. As David Robertson makes clear in Chapter 13, employers in the United States have unusual freedom to hire, fire, and control the terms of employment. U.S. trade union law helps to fragment and decentralize union power and makes it costly and difficult for workers to act collectively. As a result, collective bargaining agreements covered less than 20 percent of American workers at the beginning of the 1990s, compared to more than double this rate in Canada (Myles, this volume) and 60–95 percent in Europe (Stephens, this volume). The legislature has let the minimum wage fall in real terms since the 1960s by regularly delaying adjustments to inflation. American expenditures on passive and active labor market policies are extremely low compared to European expenditures, and private employment agencies play a much more important role than public ones. Federalism plays a major role in keeping rights and benefits for labor low, because companies can put state governments under competitive pressure to provide a "favorable business climate" as a precondition for investment and thus job creation in the state. For instance, unemployment and work injury insurance are the responsibility of the states and have been kept very low by pressures to reduce tax burdens on employers.

U.S. labor market policies have been held up as a model by international institutions, including the OECD, as supposedly responsible for very strong total employment growth in the United States, reaching 40 percent between 1970 and 1990, compared for instance to 10 percent in Germany. However, Robertson raises some serious doubts about this interpretation. First, there are other reasons that may account for the difference in employment growth between the United States and Western Europe, such as the rate of growth of the labor force, which was twice as high in the United States, and the expansionary fiscal policy of the 1980s. Second, there are serious issues about the quality of employment, such as the fact that more than 7 million Americans held more than one job by the end of the 1980s, wage dispersion is the highest among the advanced industrial democracies, and the number of working poor has been comparatively very large. Third, the difference between American and European unemployment levels disappears when the American prison population is included in the calculations.

The conclusion attempts to answer the question whether an identifiable new model of capitalism is emerging in Latin America, and it attempts to pull the insights from the different chapters together in order to extract some guidelines for designing policy patterns and constructing institutions that could improve Latin America's performance in both growth and equity. It offers some reflections about the interconnectedness of policy patterns and about path dependency versus room for choice in policy design, accepting the importance of both dynamics but emphasizing the need to concentrate on the latter. Then it proceeds to review debates and establish lessons from the various experiences in the individual policy areas that are the focus of this volume. After this exercise in analytical separation, the discussion of transferability of policies comes back to a more holistic view of models of capitalism and argues for the superiority of production, labor market, and social policy regimes that integrate all major actors and social strata.

As noted earlier, it is in this emphasis on growth-oriented and equity-oriented policies as the two essential components of models of capitalism, or on the connection of labor market and social policies to growth policies, that the specific contribution of this volume lies. Studies of East Asian development and comparisons of East Asian and Latin American development have attracted considerable attention since the 1980s when the divergence in the experiences of the two areas became particularly pronounced. Several conferences and volumes have been dedicated to these issues, such as Gereffi and Wyman 1990, World Bank 1993, Stallings 1995, and Birdsall and Jaspersen 1997. However, all of them focused on growth patterns and policies, offering some comments on different patterns of distribution, but without a systematic examination of the causes of the latter. This volume, then, is innovative in two respects. First, it explicitly connects the discussion of growth policies with an analysis of labor market and social policies, and second it introduces a new set of comparisons by including Western European and North American experiences with labor market and social policies. We have only begun to develop an understanding of the systematic interrelationships between production, labor market, and social policy regimes. There are collective efforts under way to improve our understanding in this area for advanced industrial democracies and their more stable policy regimes;[3] for newly developed or developing countries, even more research is needed on concrete experiences with their labor market and social policy regimes before we can more systematically connect them to growth patterns and policies. Here we are making a step in this direction by introducing into the discussion of Latin American models of capitalism examples of policy patterns from East Asia and advanced industrial democracies that were successful in reducing poverty and inequality while promoting growth.

REFERENCES

Amsden, Alice H. 1989. *Asia's Next Giant: South Korea and Late Industrialization.* New York: Oxford University Press.

3. For instance, one such project is being coordinated by Jelle Visser and Philip Manow at the Max Planck Institut für Gesellschaftsforschung in Cologne, another one by Paul Pierson at Harvard University.

Birdsall, Nancy, and Frederick Jaspersen. 1997. "Lessons from East Asia's Success." In Nancy Birdsall and Frederick Jaspersen, eds., *Pathways to Growth: Comparing East Asia and Latin America*. Washington, D.C.: IDB, Johns Hopkins University Press.

Chang, Ha-Joon. 1999. "Industrial Policy and East Asia—the Miracle, the Crisis, and the Future." Paper presented at the World Bank Workshop "Rethinking the East Asian Miracle," San Francisco, February.

Chang, Ha-Joon, H.-J. Park, and C. G. Yoo. 1998. "Interpreting the Korean Crisis." *Cambridge Journal of Economics* 22, no. 6.

Collier, Ruth Berins, and David Collier. 1991. *Shaping the Political Arena*. Princeton: Princeton University Press.

Esping-Andersen, Gøsta. 1990. *The Three Worlds of Welfare Capitalism*. Princeton: Princeton University Press.

Fishlow, Albert. 1995. "Future Sustainable Latin American Growth: A Need for Savings." *Review of Black Political Economy* 24, no. 1:7–21.

Gereffi, Gary, and Donald L. Wyman, eds. 1990. *Manufacturing Miracles: Paths of Industrialization in Latin America and East Asia*. Princeton: Princeton University Press.

Huber, Evelyne. 1997. "Welfare Reform in Latin America: Comparative Perspectives." Paper delivered at a conference on welfare reform in Latin America, University of Notre Dame.

Kitschelt, Herbert, Peter Lange, Gary Marks, and John Stephens, eds. 1999. *Continuity and Change in Contemporary Capitalism*. Cambridge: Cambridge University Press.

Korzeniewicz, Roberto P., and William C. Smith. 2000. "Poverty, Inequality, and Growth in Latin America: Searching for the High Road to Globalization." *Latin American Research Review* 35, no. 3:7–54.

Radelet, Steven, and Jeffrey Sachs. 1998. "The Onset of the East Asian Financial Crisis." Cambridge: Harvard Institute for International Development. Draft manuscript.

Stallings, Barbara. 1995. *Global Change, Regional Response: The New International Context of Development*. Cambridge: Cambridge University Press.

Wade, Robert. 1996. "Japan, the World Bank, and the Art of Paradigm Maintenance: The East Asian Miracle in Political Perspective." *New Left Review* 217:3–36.

———. 1990. *Governing the Market: Economic Theory and the Role of the Government in East Asian Industrialization*. Princeton: Princeton University Press.

World Bank. 1993. *The East Asian Miracle: Economic Growth and Public Policy*. New York: Oxford University Press.

PART ONE

An Emerging Model of Capitalism in Latin America?

Alternative Models of Capitalism in Latin America

JOHN SHEAHAN

Capitalism has not worked as well in Latin America as it usually has, at least since the 1930s, in the industrialized countries. All countries have had a plentiful variety of problems with it: the same forces that can make capitalism so dynamic at its best inescapably bring with them considerable potential for damage. The industrialized countries have developed a variety of institutions intended to limit the damage, though they are always under debate. Latin American societies have more strains to cope with and more intense conflicts over what to do about them.

The studies of contrasts among different models of contemporary capitalism that form the background of the present volume have been centered on the experiences of the industrialized countries.[1] This approach is well exemplified by John Stephen's chapter "European Welfare State Regimes" (Chapter 10), the chapters that contrast labor market policies in the United States and Western Europe (Chapters 12 and 13), and John Myles's chapter on the contrasts between Canada and the United States (Chapter 11). The models used by these authors help organize discussion of important distinctions but their application to Latin American countries raises three problems. The first is that they do not cover enough of the range of possibilities to take adequate account of the more dramatic differences in this region. The second is the instability of economic strategies in Latin America: these countries change their versions of capitalism more frequently, and more radically, than European countries do.

Of course, capitalism keeps evolving in the industrialized countries too, toward greater state activism when capitalism seemed to be falling apart in the 1930s and through the period of early postwar recovery, then back to increasing reliance on the private sector. But within the general postwar trend toward lessening state intervention, the countries which follow highly liberal

I would like to thank Evelyne Huber and Efraín Gonzales de Olarte for very helpful comments on drafts of this chapter.

1. Andrew Shonefield's classic *Modern Capitalism* (1965) focuses on differences among England, France, Germany, and the United States. The more recent *Continuity and Change in Contemporary Capitalism* (Kitschelt et al. 1999) includes more European countries and Japan, as well as Australia and New Zealand, but not developing countries.

versions and those with more activist models have remained on their clearly separate tracks (Soskice 1999, 122–23). Statistical comparisons between social democratic and Christian democratic models in the industrialized countries can safely rely on long-term stable links between each country and its economic model (Stephens et al. 1999). In contrast, many Latin American countries have moved from liberal versions of capitalism through different varieties of populism or state-led development, some through fiercely repressive systems, and then most to differing forms of liberalism. They don't stay put. That characteristic is a reflection of the fact that their versions of capitalism have not been convincingly successful.

The third and most fundamental problem with the application of eurocentric models to Latin America is that the structural characteristics of the region, both economic and political, still differ greatly from those of the industrialized countries. These differences mean that even formally similar models cannot be expected to have consistently similar consequences. The interactions of instruments and context are crucial. Some of these never-ending questions are discussed in this chapter, following consideration of the models themselves.

If analysis of contrasts within capitalism started from Latin American experience, its variety would call for several different models of both liberalism and activist state intervention. The most frequent forms of the latter have been directed toward industrialization and economic growth; others have been more concerned with questions of inclusion. Both sets of objectives have wide support and both have frequently been frustrated. Through the last half-century Latin America achieved considerable industrialization but the rate of growth of GDP per capita remained relatively low, at about 1.4 percent a year (IDB 2000, 1–6). Problems of reducing instability remain critical but the greater difficulty has been on the side of persistent poverty and inequality, of leaving too many people out of the growth process.

This chapter emphasizes questions of inclusion. Does the economic and social system provide decent education and opportunities for personal mobility and productive employment, or does it leave out a great many people? If the structure of the economy is such that even good periods of economic growth leave weak employment conditions and fail to generate rising real wages, does the society accept such failures or try to do something about them?

The first section explains a wider set of criteria and models than those usually applied to the industrialized countries, in the belief that different lines of analysis can provide a better fit for Latin American experience. The second section uses these models to review changes in the orientations of a sample of countries and to explore possible connections between differences in models and trends in the incidence of poverty. The third section examines the other side of causation: how structural conditions shape the consequences of different models. The fourth concludes with a question: does the concept of "models of capitalism" illuminate Latin American experience?

CRITERIA FOR DIFFERENTIATION AMONG MODELS OF CAPITALISM

Distinctions among models in other chapters in this volume make good use of both two-way and three-way contrasts: either between passive and active systems, or alternatively between liberal models on the passive side and two different paths on the active: more egalitarian ("social democratic") models and more conservatively oriented ("corporatist" or "Christian democratic") systems. These current distinctions leave aside one of the central concerns of Andrew Shonefield's earlier analysis of postwar capitalism: the great variety of forms of intervention in Europe that were aimed at stimulating more dynamic systems of production, with better employment conditions, than had been achieved with prewar liberalism. With the strong growth and high employment of the 1950s and 1960s that appeal of promotional intervention lost its urgency in the industrialized countries. In Latin America, where comparably successful transformation was not achieved, activist models remained dominant much longer.

No framework of models can take account of more than a fraction of the rich confusions of reality. Logically consistent categories may provide useful bases of reference but the kinds of capitalism that countries actually follow are eclectic compromises in response to conflicting pressures. Table 1.1 suggests a possible framework of models based on Latin American experience, parallel to those of the industrialized countries but modified to take account of major differences.

Liberal Models

The general concept of liberal capitalism, in the sense of primary reliance on private ownership of the means of production and on market forces, with a basic premise against extensive state intervention, can itself take different forms. When it is associated with well-established democracy, liberalism is always modified in many ways by pressures of public preferences. They include preferences for wide access to education, unemployment insurance, protection of the right of labor to organize, attempts to reduce discrimination in hiring and lending practices, consumer and investor protection

Table 1.1 Proposed Distinctions Among Models of Capitalism in Latin America

1. Liberal

Regime type	Characteristics
a. Traditional liberal	Primary reliance on market forces and private investors, though with frequent use of protection against imports, special favors, and other forms of moderate intervention; Labor organization usually discouraged if not repressed; Typically low taxes and weak social services; Predominantly either authoritarian governments or limited democracies with narrow range of public influence.
b. Neoliberal, or "the new economic model"	Extreme version of liberalism with low protectionism and efforts to reduce all kinds of interference with markets; Emphasis on "flexibility" in labor markets; More use of targeted as opposed to universal type social programs; Unregulated capital movements and great concern for approval by the international financial community; Initially associated with repressive governments but in most current cases with at least moderately open democracies.
c. Mixed liberal with selective activism	Combinations of neoliberal orientation in some dimensions (usually in trade policies, privatization, and fiscal restraint), with more activist and inclusionary social policies, and with acceptance of an important role for organized labor. In other words, on the liberal side but not neoliberal as that term is usually understood.

2. State-led attempts to promote change

Regime type	Characteristics
a. Activist developmentalism centered on industrialization	State promotion of sectoral change and growth, mainly through support of private sector but also with extensive regulation and use of public enterprise; Labor organizations often manipulated or controlled; Social programs sometimes important but usually clientalistic; Governments often authoritarian ("bureaucratic authoritarian"), though some have been democratic. This model shares many characteristics of early postwar French promotion of structural change, and of Japan, South Korea, and Taiwan in their periods of rapid transformation.
b. Activist and relatively inclusive	Partially liberal in allowing markets to guide buyers and sellers but qualified by social efforts to promote wide participation and by some use of selective incentives to

Table 1.1 Proposed Distinctions Among Models of Capitalism in Latin America (*continued*)

	promote changes in structures of production (distant cousins of European social democracy and of neostructuralism as proposed by CEPAL). Consistently democratic.
c. Populist, in terms of economic criteria	Extensive intervention usually intended to favor inclusion, with some cases of genuine achievements but with self-destructive disregard of the constraints necessary for a functional economic system; Frequently authoritarian though sometimes a clientalistic type of democracy.

against fraud, protection of the environment, and so on through an ever-evolving list of limits on the damaging consequences of unrestricted liberalism. As any conservative observer can rightly say, the government intervenes in the economy in countless ways. In a crucial sense, democratic pressures to limit capitalism are what protect its positive functions by holding its potentially destructive forces within acceptable bounds.

While economic liberalism in the industrialized countries usually presumes restraints imposed by democratic institutions, that has not been the common version in Latin America. In the first three decades of the twentieth century Latin American countries followed liberal economic models almost without exception, but some with political systems that made no pretense of democracy and others with formal democracies that allowed at most a narrow circle of effective participation. Model 1a of Table 1.1 should be understood as parallel to, but not the same as, economic liberalism in contemporary Europe.

Similarly, the neoliberal model 1b has been associated with both highly repressive authoritarian governments and with democracy. The worst-case version in postwar Latin American experience was the experience of the three Southern Cone countries, starting in 1973, under what might be called market authoritarianism: a version of economic liberalism disdainful of human rights and public preferences (Sheahan 1987, 125–28, 188–89, and 221–33). In the 1990s, Peru also came disturbingly close to this model, with an aggressively neoliberal economic orientation enforced by a government that had little patience with democracy (Gonzales de Olarte 1998).

From the 1930s to the 1990s the economic models of Latin American countries changed a great deal, with many though not all adopting nonliberal, activist versions. Then the wave of reversals that started in the 1970s and culminated in the 1990s brought most of them back to liberalism, in many cases to a different version: neoliberalism, or "the new economic model" (Bulmer-Thomas 1996; Reinhardt and Peres 2000).

Neoliberalism can be seen as a more nearly total rejection of state intervention, insistence on "flexible" labor markets with little protection for workers, greater use of targeted social programs as opposed to universalist methods such as food subsidies, opposition to the use of fiscal policy to counter depressed conditions of demand, and acceptance of unregulated capital flows. That acceptance of freely moving capital dictates a preoccupation with any possible conflict with investors, foreign or domestic.

While the changes of the 1980s and 1990s clearly moved the region toward greater economic liberalism, neoliberalism did not become the rule for all countries. At present, it applies reasonably well to Argentina, Colombia, Mexico, and Peru; less well, with more reservations, to Brazil, Chile, Costa Rica, Uruguay, or—*ni hablar*—Venezuela. Costa Rica and Uruguay retain characteristics closer to model 2b, to be discussed, and Venezuela closer to model 2c, populism. Brazil and Chile present more complicated examples of a kind of liberalism that does not readily fit either model 1a or 1b.

Brazil became much more liberal in the 1990s than in preceding decades, though with reservations that argue against calling the system neoliberal. Among the reservations are the continued use of selective protection (notably for the automobile industry), avoidance of the punitive approach to labor organization that has been common in neoliberal regimes, and greatly increased social programs that include serious efforts at inclusion (Helwege 2000; Stallings and Peres 2000). This mixed version of liberalism in some dimensions with intervention in others is not unlike the balance in Chile since its return to democracy. It may become a common result in the future and could be considered a separate, much moderated, version of liberalism on the lines proposed as model 1c.

Chile's revised economic and social strategy in the 1990s could be regarded as nearer to liberalism than to a social democratic model (Hershberg 1997; Roberts 1997; Korzeniewicz and Smith 2000). On the liberal side, it has been consistently open to international competition, avoided extensive intervention, privatized many firms (though not the dominant copper producer), and accepted a high degree of management autonomy to determine conditions of employment. On a more activist side, the democratic regime has made great efforts to improve the quality and the distribution of human resources, restored basic rights for labor organization, implemented social negotiation with the private sector and labor on basic questions of taxation and labor policy, and used mild forms of capital controls and exchange rate management to favor export competitiveness despite criticism from the inter-

national financial community (Pizzaro et al. 1995; Raczynski 1995; Sheahan 1997). That balance is not neoliberal: it has been more of an assertion
of independent national choice, not wholly dominated by the international
financial community but accepting the need for an open, competitive economy. It calls for a mixed category like 1c, for reasons similar to Brazil.

Activist Developmentalism

The first of the three activist branches of Latin American capitalism in Table
1.1 refers to the many regimes that have tried to promote industrialization,
or modernization in general, with at most a secondary concern for inclusion. They have used widespread intervention, high protection, considerable
public ownership, and usually a corporatist-style control of urban labor.
Some of the leading examples include Mexico under the PRI from 1940 to
1970 (Lustig 1992; Middlebrook 1995; Shadlen 2000), Argentina in the
second half of the 1960s (Mallon and Sourrouille 1975, 28–30 and 116),
and Brazil both under the regime of Getulio Vargas, effectively extended
from 1930 to 1954, and those of the generals who ruled the country from
1964 to 1985 (Bergsman 1970; Hewlett 1980; Baer 1989).[2]

The Argentine case and Brazil from 1964 are examples of high state
activism linked to political repression—Guillermo O'Donnell's "bureaucratic
authoritarianism" (O'Donnell 1973). But active state intervention is not
necessarily linked to military repression. Colombia managed to maintain
democratic institutions under a series of elected governments while promoting industrialization, using active exchange rate management to promote
export diversification, from 1968 to the late 1980s. Its intervention was
milder and more indirect than that in Argentina and Brazil; the model could
be considered almost equally well as a relatively active form of liberalism or
a relatively liberal style of developmentalism.

The activist model used in Argentina, Brazil, and Mexico in the periods
cited had many similarities to both the promotional version of capitalism in
early postwar France and to those of Japan, South Korea, and Taiwan in
their periods of rapid economic transformation. From 1945 into the 1960s

---

2. Rabello de Castro and Ronci characterize the Vargas period as one of "classic populism"; namely, the use of economic policies "intended to acquire and maintain authoritarian
power" (1991, 151 and 153–58). That political criterion is valid but this regime did not follow
the common populist practice of short-run macroeconomic stimulation at the cost of creating
unsustainable disequilibria; its economic policies had more the character of efforts to promote
structural change. Bresser Pereira concludes that this regime "was politically populist; economically, it was not" (1993, 55).

France used extensive intervention, including public ownership of financial institutions and firms in competitive industries, selective lending by public financial institutions guided by a mild form of central planning, and administrative pressures to push private investment in desired directions, in a successful drive to convert one of the weakest of the industrialized economies into one of the more dynamic (Sheahan 1963; Shonefield 1965). Similarly, the larger East Asian economies used models that shared many characteristics with Argentina, Brazil, and Mexico. On both sides, the state was an active promoter and participant in economic change. On both sides, the governments repressed or manipulated labor movements, gave selective support to those private investors who carried out projects consistent with the governments' goals, and in general rejected the main themes of economic liberalism.

Why did the East Asians make so much more rapid headway than the Latin American countries using such a similar model? Many studies have made good suggestions, of which at least two seem to command wide agreement: access to decent education for practically everyone, creating an economically mobile labor force with high learning capacity, and the orientation of government intervention toward support for firms capable of competing in world markets, rather than for firms dependent on protected domestic markets (Amsden 1989; Ha-Joon Chang, this volume).[3] Several Latin American countries turned model 2a toward export diversification in the 1960s: Mexico through administrative pressures; Brazil and Colombia, from 1968, more through exchange rate management. These changes proved helpful but their consequences were weakened, compared to the East Asians, by poor development of human resources.

Activist Inclusionary Models

Either liberalism or activist developmentalism could in principle bring the whole labor force into increasingly productive employment, with rising earnings. In Latin American experience, neither has had much success in this respect. Employment conditions have weakened rather than strengthened. Access to education, skills, land, and capital have remained highly unequal. Capitalism emphasizes individual initiative and choice based on

3. T. J. Pempel emphasizes "labor exclusion" as one of the keys of rapid development in the East Asian experience (see Chapter 9 of this volume). That practice is familiar in Latin America too but it has not been dependably associated with dynamic growth. More central factors in East Asian success included wide access to education and the outward, competitive orientation of the policies used to promote industrialization.

abilities; leaving a substantial share of the population without access to decent education distorts capitalism at its core.

A few countries have traditionally done more than most of the region at promoting inclusion, in the past through wider access to education and in more recent years through programs to help people prepare for productive employment, to find it, and to keep it. These experiences remain a long distance from social democracy in the European style but could be considered as steps in that direction.

As of 1960, adult literacy rates in the three countries of the Southern Cone ranged from 84 to 91 percent; as of 1970 they were 88 percent in Costa Rica and 87 in Cuba. In twelve other countries, less than two-thirds of the adult population was considered literate in 1960 (World Bank 1983; Sheahan and Iglesias 1998, 9). These five countries had established a necessary condition for an inclusionary kind of capitalism (though one of them happened to be determinedly anticapitalist). Other Latin American countries had not, and in that crucial sense had little chance of escaping high inequality.

A notable feature of the Southern Cone countries and Costa Rica was that they emphasized education for rural areas as well as urban much earlier than the others. One of the most promising trends in the rest of the region has been that the other countries have been catching up, at least in terms of coverage. The problem has become more the contrast between the persistently low quality of public education, that of the majority, and the higher quality education available to upper income families.

In their chapter in this volume, Carlos and Fernando Filgueira identify three examples of countries with relatively inclusive welfare programs, as of 1970: Argentina, Chile, and Uruguay. Costa Rica might well have been added. They consider Brazil and Mexico as intermediate "dual regimes," and give dismal indicators for seven others considered, with good reason, to be "excluding" systems. Unhappily, greater inclusion did not ensure stability: all three of the Southern Cone countries were forced off that path by military repression, opposed to inclusion, in the decade following this picture. After their returns to democracy their paths differed. Uruguay resumed much of its earlier orientation, Argentina turned more to neoliberalism, and Chile to the mixed model 1c, combining serious efforts at inclusion through social policies with a less activist, more liberal, economic orientation.

Costa Rica and Uruguay have such strong social programs, as well as some activist economic policies, that even after partial liberalization they still deserve to be considered activist-inclusionary. They stand out from the rest of the region as the two countries in which social spending as a share of

GDP is far higher, relative to their levels of income per capita, than expected by worldwide standards (IDB 1999, 181–82).[4] Although Costa Rica's welfare state was pulled more toward liberalism in the 1990s (Trejos 1995), it maintains strong concern for universal education and social welfare and has braved a good deal of external criticism by keeping selective incentives for export diversification. Uruguay has always been in the forefront of promoting access to education and had perhaps the most advanced welfare state in the region before the bitter repression forced on it in 1973. With democracy restored, it has accepted some liberalization of trade policies and decentralization of government but its strongly entrenched institutional support for political and social participation remains fundamentally intact (Filgueira and Papadópulos 1997). Organized labor still has strong economic and political roles. Even a relatively liberal administration in the 1990s allowed a referendum on privatization and accepted the overwhelming public vote against it.

The missing model of inclusion has been any close approach to social democracy. Costa Rica and Uruguay, and at a greater remove Chile, have some of its characteristics, especially on the social side. What they lack is the kind of dynamic coordination on the economic side, guided by wide consensus on goals and methods, that characterized European social democracy at its best. Kenneth Roberts makes a strong case against the likelihood that Latin American countries can repeat this model, given the constraints of globalization and a marked shift in the balance of political strength between capital and labor (Roberts 1997). But it may still be possible, as he suggests, to find a helpful Latin American alternative. The main lines of a possible Latin American version have been explained and advocated as a "neostructuralist" model (CEPAL 1992; Ramos 1996; Ffrench-Davis 1998). It emphasizes strong social policies to develop human resources on a more nearly equal basis, an active economic strategy intended to reshape the structure of production through promotional measures rather than protection, support for organized labor as a participant in social negotiation, and careful macroeconomic management. That vision allows for many variations in detail. It may be beyond reach in the near term but it could at the very least serve as a promising guide.

Populism

Populism—in the sense of impossible promises for political purposes, direct intervention to raise wage rates without concern for productivity, and

---

4. They also stand out as the two countries with the highest percentages of popular approval of democracy (IDB 1999, 22–23).

manipulation of fiscal and monetary policies for short-run stimulation at the cost of unsustainable disequilibria—has never worked well and never will. It has had possibly more than enough effective criticism (Sachs 1989; Dornbusch and Edwards 1991). The criticism may be more than enough in the sense that long-victimized Latin Americans now seem to recoil at almost any suggestion of intervention, however mild. That mistaken identification of modest economic activism with hopeless populism will probably be overcome soon, though a good many people seem determined to maintain the confusion.

Models with populist characteristics can, in the best of cases, accomplish changes that favor inclusion. The regimes of Lázaro Cárdenas in Mexico from 1934 to 1940 and of General Velasco in Peru from 1968 to 1975, both usually considered populist, proved able to implement inclusionary changes (Collier 1982; Gonzales de Olarte and Samamé 1994, 28–30; Sheahan 1999, 133–38). They included major land reforms, recognition for labor organization as legitimate, and in Velasco's regime support for broader access to education. In countries with such drastically concentrated land ownership and badly treated rural labor as Mexico before Cárdenas and Peru before Velasco, these changes were significant improvements.

MOVEMENT AMONG MODELS AND CHANGES IN POVERTY

Naturally, attempts to identify individual country experiences with specific models leads to uncertainty about borderlines and an urge to stretch definitions to fit particular cases. It immediately becomes necessary to add qualifying phrases. Still, the main differences among models seem sufficiently stable to permit at least a provisional examination of how they may be related to degrees of success in reducing poverty. Table 1.2 gives a small sample, for six countries, of movement among these models.

Table 1.2 may exaggerate the instability of country orientations, with Argentina perhaps the champion. Another group, including many Central American and Caribbean countries, remained much longer under authoritarian versions of traditional liberalism. They were more stable but serve as a reminder that stability isn't everything. They were blocked from change either by their own rulers or by intervention from the United States when actual or likely changes seemed disturbingly radical. Experiments in Argentine style, however unhelpful as most proved to be, require a degree of independence. A happier exception has been the long-term stability of activist-inclusionary models in Costa Rica and Uruguay, not because of repression but because of relatively successful inclusion.

Table 1.2 Examples of Movement Among Different Models: Argentina, Brazil, Chile, Colombia, Mexico, and Peru

Argentina

Period	Regime type (see Table 1.1)	Remarks
1946–55	2c	Populism with inclusionary content
1958–62	2a	Activist developmental
1966–70	2a	Activist developmental under military control: bureaucratic authoritarian
1970–76	2c	Populism with no clear direction
1976–82	1b	Neoliberal under military rule: "market authoritarian"
1983–90	2c	Populism with transition to liberalism
1990–2000	1b	Neoliberal democratic

Brazil

Period	Regime type (see Table 1.1)	Remarks
1930–58	2a	Activist developmental
1958–64	2c	Populism
1964–85	2a	Developmental under military: bureaucratic authoritarian
1993–2000	1c	Mixed liberal with selective activism

Chile

Period	Regime type (see Table 1.1)	Remarks
1965–70	2b	Activist inclusive
1970–73		Marxist
1973–90	1b	Neoliberal, market authoritarian, though with two variants:
1975–82		Neoliberal without qualification
1983–90		Promotional within liberal model
1990–2000	1c	Mixed liberal with selective activism

Colombia

Period	Regime type (see Table 1.1)	Remarks
1958–68	1a	Basically liberal though with weak element of developmentalism
1968–90	2a	Activist developmental in moderate democratic version
1990–2000	1b	Neoliberal

Table 1.2   Examples of Movement Among Different Models: Argentina, Brazil, Chile, Colombia, Mexico, and Peru (*continued*)

	Mexico	
Period	Regime type (see Table 1.1)	Remarks
1934–40	2c	Populist with genuine inclusive element
1940–70	2a	Activist developmental
1970–82	2c	Populist
1982–2000	1a	Liberal, though close to neoliberal after 1985

	Peru	
Period	Regime type (see Table 1.1)	Remarks
1950–62	1a	Traditional liberal
1963–68	2a	Developmental in intent but so indecisive that the term "activist" would be misleading
1968–75	2c	Populist under military government, with inclusionary features and some promotion of structural change
1980–85		Hybrid model: populist with some liberalization
1985–90	2c	Populist to chaotic degree
1990–2000	1b	Neoliberal, originally democratic but then corrupted by government turned authoritarian

Viewed in terms of regional averages it does not look likely that changes in models have been related in any systematic way to reduction of poverty. Table 1.3 makes clear that, through all the turmoil of the last three decades, the incidence of poverty has not greatly changed.

By the first measure in Table 1.3, 40 percent of households were below the CEPAL poverty line in 1970 and 41 in 1990, though the incidence then came down to 36 percent by 1997. As these modest changes imply, the number of people living in poverty increased greatly. By the third measure, World Bank estimates of the percentage of people with levels of consumption less than a third of the averages in their countries in 1993, the incidence of poverty remained practically constant from 1987 to 1998, a period in which many countries changed to more liberal economic models.

Although these regional estimates do not suggest any remarkable progress in reducing the incidence of poverty, individual countries have had considerably different experiences. Admittedly, emphatically, it is a treacherous business to relate differences in levels of poverty to particular models. Comparable observations of poverty are few, their timing is not closely related to that of different models, and in any case it is always doubtful to

Table 1.3 Indicators of Poverty for Latin America as a Whole, 1970 to 1998

1970	1980	1987	1990	1997	1998
Percentage of households below the poverty line as defined by CEPAL					
40	35	—	41	36	—
People with incomes below $1 per day (millions)					
—	—	63.7	73.8	—	78.2
Percent of population with consumption less than one-third national average for 1993					
—	—	50.2	51.5	—	51.4

SOURCES: CEPAL 1995, 146; CEPAL 2000, 270; World Bank 2000, 23–24.

read anything about causation from parallels in timing. This does not mean that comparisons are impossible but that they are always subject to questions about the specific historical context.

Table 1.4 gives estimates of the percentages of households in poverty for six countries during periods of specified models, relying primarily on CEPAL measures of the incidence of poverty. The estimates used are for national samples, excluding those with urban coverage only, and are restricted to cases in which at least two reasonably comparable estimates can be associated with a particular model. The limitation to national measures unhappily means leaving out Argentina and Uruguay, the two countries with the lowest urban poverty. Despite that loss, it would seem essential to include rural poverty in such comparisons, because disregard of rural poverty has been a central aspect of failures to achieve inclusion.

Comparisons are possible across countries for the initial year, 1970, and in later years for different models within each country. For 1970, Chile and Costa Rica stood out for having much less poverty than the others; Brazil, Colombia, and Peru for having much more. Chile and Costa Rica were the only two examples of model 2b at the time. Brazil and Colombia were following the developmentalist model 2a, as was Mexico, with its intermediate level of poverty. The populist model in Peru at the time had the highest level of poverty but this was a clear case of misleading association: high poverty had been inherited from preceding liberal regimes, in a country which had stayed close to liberalism longer than any of the others in this sample.

Observed differences in levels of poverty reflect all the factors of each country's historical experience but perhaps the first systematic explanatory variable that could be expected to have high importance is the level of income: richer countries normally have less poverty. A simple regression of

these poverty levels against GDP per capita for 1970 indicates that the relationship holds, but not strongly: the coefficient of correlation is only 0.30.
An alternative variable, directly related to the concept of inclusionary model
2b, is the rate of literacy in each country. A simple regression of poverty levels against differences in literacy rates gives a distinctly closer fit: the coefficient of correlation is 0.77.[5] At least for this small sample, differences in
models seem to have been more directly relevant than differences in levels of
income per capita.

Considering changes in levels of poverty within individual countries, the
most dramatic case of worsening poverty after 1970 is associated with Chile's
experience under its market authoritarian version of neoliberalism. The incidence of poverty almost doubled between 1970 and 1987 (even after allowing for upward revision of the estimate for 1970 as noted in Table 1.4). It
then fell back slightly in the last three years of that regime. After Chile's
return to democracy in 1990 it came down swiftly; by 1998 it was back
close to the level of 1970 (or below if compared to the adjusted estimate for
1970). The nature of the model under which poverty came down so well
could be debated. In this table it is cited as model 1c, mixed liberal with
inclusive social dimensions, for the reasons discussed earlier.

Costa Rica has the best claim to a steady path of inclusionary, if modest,
activism (despite a rocky time from 1978 to 1982 when one government
veered more toward a neoliberal model). Its incidence of poverty remained
relatively low from 1970 to 1990, without improvement, but then came
down slightly in the 1990s. In marked contrast, Peru's singularly unsuccessful version of populism in the period from 1985 to 1990 greatly raised an
initially high incidence of poverty. It should be noted that the measure given
for 1991, in the absence of comparable estimates for 1990, exaggerates the
damage attributable to model 2c because it includes the first year of the following neoliberal strategy. Still, steep decreases in GDP and in real wages in
the last years of the populist model make clear that poverty increased
greatly during the period of that model. Under the new model 1b, it then
came down moderately, as the economy recovered from prior chaos.

Mexico's populist interval from 1970 to 1982, followed by two years of
partial liberalization before the next measure of poverty, left the incidence of
poverty unchanged for this period as a whole. But further movement to a
neoliberal model was followed by higher incidence of poverty through 1998.
This weak record might be blamed on the interruption of growth during the

5. Estimates of GDP per capita for 1970 are from IDB 1990, 4; estimates of literacy from
World Bank 1983, vol. 2. For Colombia, the literacy rate for 1970 was estimated by interpola-
tion between measures for 1961 and 1973; for Costa Rica, the measure used is for 1973.

Table 1.4 Estimates of the Percentages of Households Below Poverty Lines for Dates Associated with Different Models of Capitalism: Brazil, Chile, Colombia, Costa Rica, Mexico, and Peru

Brazil					
	1970	1979	1990	1993	1996
Model of capitalism (see Table 1.1)					
Activist-developmental (2a)	49	39	—	—	—
Mixed liberal with selective activism (1c)	—	—	41	37	29

Chile				
	1970	1987	1990	1998
Model of capitalism (see Table 1.1)				
Activist-inclusionary (2b) in 1970, then neoliberal (1b), market authoritarian	17	39	33	—
Mixed liberal with selective activism (1c)	—	—	33	18

Colombia				
	1970	1986	1994	1997
Model of capitalism (see Table 1.1)				
Activist-developmental (2a)	45	38	—	—
Neoliberal (1b)	—	—	47	45

Costa Rica			
	1970	1990	1997
Model of capitalism (see Table 1.1)	—	—	—
Activist-inclusionary (2b)	24	24	—
Activist-inclusionary (2b)	—	24	20

Mexico					
	1970	1977	1984	1989	1998
Model of capitalism (see Table 1.1)					
Populist (2c) until 1982, then liberal (1a)	34	32	34	—	—
Neoliberal (1b)	—	—	34	39	38

Peru					
	1970	1979	1985	1991	1994	1997
Model of capitalism (see Table 1.1)						
Populist (2c)	50	46	—	—	—	—
Populist (2c) until 1990	—	—	38	55	—	—
Neoliberal (1b)	—	—	—	—	54	49

SOURCES: For Brazil (2a), Chile (1b), Colombia (2a), Costa Rica (2b, 1970 and 1990), Mexico (2c then 1a), and Peru (2c, 1970 and 1979), the source is CEPAL 1995, 145–46. For Brazil (1c), Chile (1c), Colombia (1b), Costa Rica (2b, 1990 and 1997), and Mexico (1b), the source is CEPAL 2000, 269–70. For Peru (2c, 1985 and 1991), the source is Instituto Cuanto and UNICEF 1995, 30. For Peru (1b), the source is World Bank 2000, 281.

Table 1.4   Estimates of the Percentages of Households Below Poverty Lines for Dates Associated with Different Models of Capitalism: Brazil, Chile, Colombia, Costa Rica, Mexico, and Peru (*continued*)

NOTE: Estimates as read horizontally on each line are from the same source and should be comparable in most cases; except for 1970, estimates on different lines are not readily comparable. The published estimate of 17 percent for poverty in Chile in 1970 is not fully comparable to later figures because of a definitional change: a comparable estimate would be about 20 to 22 percent (Sheahan 1997, 13). Estimates for Colombia suggest a major increase in poverty between the last measure for model 2a and the first for model 1b; it surely increased somewhat but comparisons are uncertain because coverage of the surveys was considerably extended from 1993.

peso crisis of 1994–95, but then the crisis itself was in large measure a result of the neoliberal model (Sheahan 1997, 20–25). The best periods of sustained improvement came, somewhat disconcertingly, under two different models: 1c in both Brazil and Chile in the 1990s, and 2a both in Brazil in the 1970s and Colombia from 1970 to 1986. In the last three of these cases, a major reason for the improvement was that these countries successfully maintained long periods of economic growth allied with export diversification: they succeeded in raising employment steadily while avoiding the steep external deficits that have stopped growth so often in Latin America. It should also be noted that the authoritarian government of the 1980s in Chile adopted much the same employment-generating export orientation after its initial neoliberal model led to deep depression in the early years of the decade: the second phase of market authoritarianism noted in Table 1.2 included sufficiently strong growth of employment to begin reducing poverty from 1987 on (Labán and Larraín 1995, 118).

The improvement in Brazil between 1990 and 1996 is more surprising. Output growth was very weak in the first half of this period, though better in the second. Urban unemployment went up slightly. The fall in poverty might in some measure be attributed to increased and improved social programs, as noted above. But a less positive contributing factor was a rising external deficit in the period of the more marked decrease in poverty, associated with the kind of currency appreciation that has so often accompanied liberalization (Franco 2000).[6] Appreciation and excess imports can do a good deal to raise real wages and reduce poverty temporarily: the practice has been a standard feature of the first years of populist governments (Sachs 1989). It can lead to sharp reversals and worsening poverty when

6. Measured in constant 1990 dollars, exports of goods and services exceeded imports by $6 billion in 1993 but by 1996 Brazil had an import surplus of $27 billion, 5 percent of GDP (IDB 1999, 209 and 211). By an alternative estimate, the current account fell from a balance in 1993 to a deficit equal to 3.1 percent of GDP by 1996 (Stallings and Peres 2000, 57).

the financial sector begins to doubt that loans can be repaid, and the resulting capital flight causes a currency crash.

That repeated scenario of financial collapse after current account deficits have risen greatly caught up with Brazil in January 1999. Poverty must have risen considerably as the whole economy was set back. But the following consequences of such episodes can go in different directions, for different structures of production and trade. For countries dependent on primary exports, the initial effects of devaluations can be negative. Although a competitive exchange rate is essential for sustained growth, the stimulus of devaluation for exports may work slowly at best, and the overall impact can be a prolonged contraction. In contrast, in a country with a fairly strong base of industrial exports, devaluation can be an almost immediate stimulus to rising production of exports and early macroeconomic recovery. When Mexico was hit by the peso crisis of December 1994, its industrial exports responded powerfully; the economy was set back badly at first but a sustained recovery began within a year. Much the same seemed to be the case with Brazilian recovery during the year after its currency fell in January 1999. Does all this have anything to do with models of capitalism? Probably, yes. Countries that have managed to transform their structures of production and trade in the direction of competitive industrial exports—by carrying through an effective version of model 2a in the first place—can better afford to adopt liberal models, and gain from them, than countries that have not yet accomplished such transformations.

UNDERLYING STRUCTURAL CONDITIONS: CONTEXTS AND INSTRUMENTS

The consequences of any given set of institutions or economic policies depend jointly on their own characteristics and on the contexts in which they operate. Capitalism in liberal versions under which state intervention is limited may be consistent with good economic growth and relatively low degrees of poverty and inequality if basic economic conditions are favorable, or may fail badly if they are not. Liberal systems have not functioned consistently well in Latin America because common structural conditions bias their consequences against inclusion. To degrees much more pronounced than in the industrialized countries, they can reinforce inequality. But more activist systems have often failed at least as badly, because their methods have raised so many problems of their own. It is not activism per se that gives better results: it is, or could be, the kinds of activism appropriate for the specific context.

At least five characteristics of the Latin American context can turn liberal models in unhelpful directions: (1) inequalities in access to effective education and more generally in the distribution of human capital; (2) persistently weak employment conditions, even in periods of good economic growth; (3) unmeasured but beyond doubt extremely high concentration in the ownership of capital; (4) constraints on economic growth, and high instability, imposed on many countries by dependence on primary exports and external capital; and (5) weakness of democratic institutions and consequently of the kinds of corrective intervention that could make liberal capitalism less inequitable. None of these characteristics is either exclusive to Latin America or immutable. They are all questions of degree; many countries have been able to change some of them for the better. Access to education has been greatly broadened everywhere, though the quality of public education remains weak. Even good periods of economic growth may not do much for people discouraged by lack of education. Still, employment conditions improved sufficiently in Brazil and Colombia during the 1970s to bring poverty down notably in both countries. They improved in Chile as well, with even stronger effect on poverty, after its neoliberal economic strategy was modified in 1982. It would seem unlikely that the concentration of capital ownership, other than land, has changed for the better anywhere. A much wider distribution of land ownership was achieved in Peru under the Velasco government at the end of the 1960s, and somewhat better distribution in other countries in that period, but the trend since has been toward greater concentration (Stallings and Peres 2000, 180–81). Dependence on primary exports has been gradually lessening, most notably through rising industrial exports from Brazil and Mexico. Even the share of exports by labor-intensive industries within manufacturing increased, strongly for Mexico and slightly for others as well (Stallings and Peres 2000, 155–60).

The most hopeful improvement has been the spread, however uncertain so far, of democracy. The chances that it will take firmer hold, with greater meaning, could surely be improved if the majority of the Latin American people gain from the kinds of economic policies followed by newly democratic governments. If the economic results turn out to be as weak as those under Peru's restored democracy in the 1980s, public support of democracy itself could wither away.

Living with weak employment conditions for many years has made that issue central for most people in Latin America. A recent survey of what people consider to be the most important problem of their country puts unemployment in first place, education in second, and low wages in third (IDB 2000, 3). Poverty and economic instability, which might well be added to the same set of preoccupations, follow closely. None of these problems originated with economic liberalization in the 1990s: they have been persisting structural conditions for a long time. But some have grown worse under liberalization, notably in Argentina. Liberalization has clearly not been a remedy.

Open unemployment is a serious concern but perhaps not as significant as the growing numbers of people who survive only through occupations with extremely low productivity and earnings. Both problems are discussed in Víctor Tokman's chapter in this volume. Open unemployment in the relatively prosperous year of 1980 is estimated (see Table 6.1) at 6.7 percent. It rose to 8.0 percent in 1990 and 8.8 by 1999. Meanwhile, the share of the labor force working in the informal sector—doing something, if only standing on the sidewalk all day trying to sell coat hangers—increased from 40.2 percent in 1980 to 44.4 percent in 1990 and 48.5 by 1999.

The informal sector includes many people who prefer to work either by themselves or in small family firms, some independent workers with good incomes, and many others trying to survive in the absence of opportunities for productive employment (Tokman 1992). Some indication of what the trend in size of the informal sector might be under relatively good employment conditions can be observed from measures for Chile, where open unemployment came down steadily after the country modified its neoliberal model to promote export growth from 1982: the share of informal employment came down from 29.1 percent in 1982 to 23.6 percent by 1990 (García 1993, 103). The contrary rising trend for the region as a whole, from 40 percent of the nonagricultural labor force working outside the formal sector in 1980 to nearly 50 percent in 1999, is evidence of a fundamental economic failure.

In the context of such an overwhelming excess of labor relative to opportunities for productive employment, a liberal model that remains committed to a sink-or-swim approach is bound to leave many people in chronic poverty. But could more activist models of capitalism be expected to do much better? It would not be easy in the best of cases. The region has come to share the trend of the industrialized countries toward increasing relative demand for skilled labor. That works against equality everywhere but especially so when those with skills are small minorities. Better education, training for skills in demand, and help in placement of workers can reduce the scale of the problem under either liberal or nonliberal models. But such programs are not likely to provide an adequate answer without powerful support from the side of demand for workers. That is where more activist models have a potential advantage, provided they avoid the traps of the past.

The activist model 2a followed for so many years in Latin America could have been a considerable help. Promotional intervention using similar methods was a key to successful conversion of the French economy in the early postwar years and to the dynamic transformations in East Asia. The truly unfortunate error in Latin America was to use it mainly in a protectionist style rather than as a force to propel the industrial sector toward a competitive, technologically dynamic path. That may have been a politically determined choice. The private sector in Latin America, with its traditional preference for protection, maintained a more influential voice than its counterparts in early postwar France (where the private sector had fallen into disgrace from prewar weakness and wartime collaboration), or in East Asia (where wartime dislocations also left weak industrial sectors dependent on government help). These differences were important, though clearly not the whole story. The economics of comparative advantage, given Latin America's relative wealth of natural resources, made it doubly difficult to establish an activist strategy centered on promoting competitive industrial sectors. It still does.

The populist model 2c, the frequent alternative to model 2a, proved consistently to be an unfortunate kind of activism. Its appeal is evident: the reality of high inequality and persistent poverty creates strong pressures to try quick remedies through public spending programs and monetary expansion. Alongside such mistakes, many programs included promises that could, if fulfilled, have changed the operation of the economy toward greater inclusion. A few of them left genuine achievements, notably the land reforms of the Cárdenas and Velasco governments. It was the common curse of pushing spending past any limits consistent with restraint of inflation and external deficits that usually did them in. The costly consequences of the model did a great deal to change the balance of public preferences away from any kind of intervention, toward liberal and even neoliberal models.

The social side of the new economic model has usually included serious efforts to improve the human and productive potential of the poor. If these efforts could be combined with means to promote more rapid and more stable growth of demand for workers, the future could become much more promising. The major hope on the demand side would be to find ways to stimulate investment and exports jointly, to change the structures of production and trade on parallel lines so that growth is not cut off as frequently by rising external deficits. If exports consist mainly of primary products, and worst of all if they are capital-intensive mining products that create few employment opportunities, the chances of success will remain as low as in the past. An adequate answer needs to include systematic efforts to promote change in comparative advantages. But that is exactly contrary to the intent and effect of a fully neoliberal model.

Most of the region lacks anything like Mexico's success in developing a competitive export sector. Conversely, Mexico lacks Chile's relative success in promoting rapid growth of employment combined with rising real wages for more than a decade. Change on the external side is necessary but not sufficient. The problems differ among countries but the region as a whole remains a great distance from the basic conditions under which economic liberalism can be expected to generate widely shared gains in opportunities for productive employment and rising incomes.

DOES THE CONCEPT OF "MODELS OF CAPITALISM" ILLUMINATE LATIN AMERICAN EXPERIENCE?

To reconsider familiar issues from a different angle can be illuminating, or it can be disorienting. Or both, as it was with dependency theory. The concept of multiple models of capitalism does not have either the powerful sweep or the seductive determinism of dependency analysis. It does not concentrate on conflicts between developing and industrialized countries; it promotes attention instead to parallels across regions and to contrasts within them.

An extended study of such models would need to develop quantitative controls, tighten definitions, and examine the causes for adoption and rejection of different models. This provisional inquiry is focused on their nature and consequences, as distinct from the forces that determine what models are adopted. Still, it may serve as a framework to consider two relevant questions. Why has capitalism been so much less successful in Latin America than it has usually been in the industrialized countries? What model or models might reasonably be expected to give better results?

In terms of the proposed models, three differences between capitalism in the industrialized countries and in Latin America are evident. The first is that traditional liberalism in Latin America was not in most cases associated with democracy, at least in any sense of wide participation by an informed population. The second is that Latin America has not had any experience of the European model of social democracy, the model that has been most successful in combining emphasis on equality with effective economic management. The third is that the model of liberalism that the international financial community has urged on Latin America, the neoliberal model 1b, is more regressive, more adverse to equality and to structural transformation, than acceptable to any industrialized country.

This bleak picture—two unfavorable versions of liberalism and the absence of the most egalitarian model of the industrialized countries—surely has a good deal to do with the weakness of capitalism in Latin America. It should, of course, be modified to take account of the exceptions that have come close to escaping this pattern. The few Latin American countries that have maintained long-term versions of widely participatory democracy—Chile, Costa Rica, and Uruguay (except for the periods of military repression in Chile and Uruguay)—have done better than the rest of the region in holding down poverty. In Costa Rica and Uruguay that relative success has been associated with the activist-inclusionary model 2b. That model is the region's closest approach, so far, to European social democracy.

Chile's version of capitalism during its period of improving employment conditions and decreasing poverty in the 1990s was a more liberal model, though more the mixed liberal model 1c, with activist characteristics in some dimensions, than a neoliberal one. The same mixed model fits Brazilian experience in the 1990s. It may be that a combination of liberalism in the dimensions of trade policies and fiscal restraint, along with selective promotion of structural change and strong social programs, can give distinctly better results than past alternatives. Where the structure of production has been reoriented to favor the growth of competitive industrial sectors, as in Mexico and in Brazil, more nearly liberal solutions could be promising. Where they have not, or that kind of change has just barely begun, more active intervention in both economic and social domains is still needed to open up any adequate solutions for conditions of excess unskilled labor and high inequality.

These relationships among models may help clarify alternatives but they are clearly insufficient in themselves as explanations of Latin America's economic problems. The structural conditions of these economies, summarized in the preceding section, are the core determinants. The most important negative factors have been the inequality of human resources and personal mobility, the growth of unskilled labor relative to opportunities for productive employment, the low capacity for innovation and competition of the industrial sector, and the common problem of dependence on primary exports and external capital. These conditions would damage performance under any model of capitalism. But then the question is, why has so little has been done to change them? Why haven't social choices been more helpful?

A possible answer is that the historical weakness of democracy contributed to the persistence of adverse economic structures. The preferences of the low income majority could not be brought to bear on public decisions in the ways that they could, at least much of the time, in the better-functioning European versions of capitalism. In particular, they could have exerted pressure to correct failures to provide anything like equal opportunities for education, access to skills, or social and economic mobility.

In its turn, the weakness of democratic institutions may be explicable in part by the ways that capitalism has functioned in the region. Liberal models that supported the long-term dominance of landowner interests were prone to oppose the taxation needed to build egalitarian systems of public education, and to oppose intervention to change structures of production and trade. The regional change to model 2b was not just a matter of industrialization; it was also an attempt to shift the political balance. It did, but that model also favored a strong role of the private sector in deciding public policies, gave special advantages and monopoly power to privileged firms, and exerted a pronounced pull toward authoritarian government. When public opposition seemed to become seriously troublesome, as the private sector and the military thought it did in Brazil in the early 1960s, and again in the Southern Cone in the next decade, the private sector helped promote authoritarian solutions. Again in Peru in 1992, the private sector rallied without hesitation behind the authoritarian measures adopted by a government promising to protect neoliberalism. Latin American capitalists have not been consistent enthusiasts for democracy. Nor have North American investors in the region.

As a way of organizing the productive system, capitalism has a lot to be said for it. In terms of human relations, of encouraging concern for others as opposed to pure selfishness, or for values beyond consumerism, it has a lot to be said against it. To restrain its destructive side requires strong social institutions and a never-ending struggle, in the United States as everywhere.

It took many years of effort, and the decisive help of the medical profession, to slow down the tobacco industry's drive to promote adolescent addiction. The absurdly inefficient and inequitable system of health care analyzed by John Myles in this volume is testimony to the power of the lobbying and campaign contributions of those who benefit from its weaknesses, perhaps most notably the pharmaceutical industry. When the Microsoft Corporation loses an antitrust suit—a heartening reminder of historical concern for competition—it moves on to lobby Congress to cut the budget of the antitrust division, and then to the presidential campaign to put on its payroll one of the leading advisers to the candidate most likely to drop the suit. The integrity of legislators, of administrative agencies, and of the conditions of competition are undermined in the interest of protecting profits. These are not the kinds of market forces that Adam Smith had in mind.

If such perversions can go on in a country with well-established institutions designed to favor competition and to limit corruption of the political process, it is not hard to see that Latin American countries need to build up stronger protections against destructive forms of profit-seeking. Activist intervention in this sense is essential both for well-functioning markets and for meaningful democracy.

Capitalism could have worked more constructively in Latin America if it had been restrained by stronger democratic institutions and by social choices favoring wider inclusion. It could also have worked better if it had not been distorted by misdirected protectionism, erratic intervention, and frequent disregard of the necessary conditions for macroeconomic balance. If it is ever to offer adequate opportunities for productive employment, the structures of production of most of these countries will need to be transformed. Capitalism could accomplish that, without waiting forever, if given the right incentives within a coherent model. That could be done under democratic governments either by combining effective versions of models 2a and 2b, or through the mixed liberal-activist model 1c. They all have much in common, though with variable degrees of liberalism and activism, and room for different emphasis among multiple goals. More paths than one are open.

REFERENCES

Amsden, Alice. 1989. "Why Isn't the Whole World Experimenting with the East Asian Model to Develop?" *World Development* 22:627–33.

Baer, Werner. 1989. *The Brazilian Economy: Growth and Development.* 3d ed. New York: Praeger.

Bergsman, Joel. 1970. *Brazil: Industrialization and Trade Policies.* London: Oxford University Press.

Bresser Pereira, Luiz Carlos. 1993. "Economic Reform and Economic Growth: Efficiency and Politics in Latin America." In José Maria Maravall and Adam Przeworski, eds., *Economic Reform in New Democracies: A Social-Democratic Approach,* 15–76. Cambridge: Cambridge University Press.

Bulmer-Thomas, Victor, ed. 1996. *The New Economic Model in Latin America and Its Impact on Income Distribution and Poverty.* New York: St. Martin's Press.

CEPAL (Comisión Económica para América Latina y el Caribe). 1992. *Equidad y transformación productiva: Un enfoque integrado.* Santiago: CEPAL.

———. 1995. *Social Panorama of Latin America, 1995.* Santiago: CEPAL.

———. 2000. *Panorama Social de América Latina, 1999–2000.* Santiago: CEPAL.

Chalmers, Douglas A., Carlos M. Vilas, Katherine Hite, Scott B. Martin, Kerianne Piester, and Monique Segarra, eds. 1997. *The New Politics of Inequality in Latin America: Rethinking Participation and Representation.* Oxford: Oxford University Press.

Collier, Ruth Berins. 1982. "Popular Sector Incorporation and Political Supremacy: Regime Evolution in Brazil and Mexico." In Sylvia Ann Hewlett and Reichard Weinert, eds., *Brazil and Mexico: Patterns in Late Development.* Philadelphia: Institute of the Study of Human Issues.

Dornbusch, Rudiger, and Sebastian Edwards, eds. 1991. *The Macroeconomics of Populism in Latin America.* Chicago: The University of Chicago Press for the National Bureau of Economic Research.

Ffrench-Davis, Ricardo. 1998. "An Outline of a Neo-Structuralist Approach." *CEPAL Review,* no. 34:37–44.

Filgueira, Fernando, and Jorge Papadópulos. 1997. "Putting Conservativism to Good Use? Long Crisis and Vetoed Alternatives in Uruguay." In Chalmers et al., 360–87.

Franco, Gustavo H. B. 2000. "The Real Plan and the Exchange Rate." Princeton Essays in International Finance. No. 217.

García, Norberto E. 1993. *Ajuste, reformas y mercado liberal: Costa Rica (1980–1990), Chile (1973–1992), Mexico (1981–1991).* Santiago: Programa Regional del Empleo en América Latina y el Caribe.

Gonzales de Olarte, Efraín. 1998. *El neoliberalismo a la peruana: Economía política del ajuste estructural, 1990–1997.* Lima: Instituto de Estudios Peruanos.

Gonzales de Olarte, Efraín, and Lilian Samamé. 1994. *El Pendulo Peruano: Política Económica, gobernabilidad y subdesarrollo, 1963–1990.* 2d ed. Lima: Instituto de Estudios Peruanos.

Helwege, Ann. 2000. "Trends in Social Spending in Argentina, Brazil, and Mexico." Paper presented at the Latin American Studies Association meeting, Miami, March.

Hershberg, Eric. 1997. "Market-Oriented Development Strategies and State-Society Relations in New Democracies: Lessons from Contemporary Chile and Spain." In Chalmers et al., 337–59.

Hewlett, Sylvia Ann. 1980. *The Cruel Dilemmas of Development: Twentieth-Century Brazil.* New York: Basic Books.

IDB (InterAmerican Development Bank). 1990. *Economic and Social Progress in Latin America, 1990 Report.* Washington, D.C.: IDB.

———. 1999. *Facing up to Inequality in Latin America: Economic and Social Progress in Latin America, 1998–1999 Report.* Washington, D.C.: IDB.

———. 2000. *Development Beyond Economics: Economic and Social Progress in Latin America, 2000 Report.* Washington, D.C.: IDB.

Instituto Cuánto y UNICEF. 1995. *Retrato de la familia peruana: Niveles de vida.* Lima: Instituto Cuánto.

Kitschelt, Herbert, Peter Lange, Gary Marks, and John D. Stephens, eds. 1999. *Continuity and Change in Contemporary Capitalism.* Cambridge: Cambridge University Press.

Korzeniewicz, Roberto Patricio, and William C. Smith. 2000. "Poverty, Inequality, and Growth in Latin America: Searching for the High Road to Globalization." *Latin American Research Review* 35, no. 3:7–54.

Labán, Raúl, and Felipe Larraín. 1995. "Continuity, Change, and the Political Economy of Transition in Chile." In Rudiger Dornbusch and Sebastian Edwards, eds., *Reform, Recovery and Growth: Latin America and the Middle East,* 115–48. Chicago: University of Chicago Press.

Lustig, Nora. 1992. *Mexico: The Remaking of an Economy.* Washington, D.C.: The Brookings Institution.

Mallon, Richard, and Juan Sourrouille. 1975. *Economic Policy Making in a Conflict Society: The Argentine Case.* Cambridge: Harvard University Press.

Middlebrook, Kevin J. 1995. *The Paradox of Revolution: Labor, the State, and Authoritarianism in Mexico.* Baltimore: Johns Hopkins University Press.

O'Donnell, Guillermo. 1973. *Modernization and Bureaucratic-Authoritarianism: Studies in South American Politics.* Berkeley and Los Angeles: University of California, Institute of International Studies.

Pizzaro, Crisóstomo, Dagmar Raczynski, and Joaquin Vial, eds. 1995. *Políticas económicas y sociales en el Chile democratico.* Santiago: CIEPLAN and UNICEF.

Rabello de Castro, Paulo, and Marcio Ronci. 1991. "Sixty Years of Populism in Brazil." In Rudiger Dornbusch and Sebastian Edwards, eds., *Reform, Recovery and Growth: Latin America and the Middle East,* 151–74. Chicago: University of Chicago Press.

Raczynski, Dagmar, ed. 1995. *Strategies to Combat Poverty in Latin America.* Washington, D.C.: IDB, distributed by Johns Hopkins University Press.

Ramos, Joseph R. 1996. "Poverty and Inequality in Latin America: A Neostructural Perspective." *Journal of Latin American Studies and World Affairs* 38, no. 2/3:141–57.

Reinhardt, Nola, and Wilson Peres. 2000. "Latin America's New Economic Model: Micro Responses and Economic Restructuring." *World Development,* no. 28–29:1543–66.

Roberts, Kenneth M. 1997. "Rethinking Economic Alternatives: Left Parties and the Articulation of Popular Demands in Chile and Peru." In Chalmers et al., 313–36.

Sachs, Jeffrey D. 1989. "Social Conflict and Populist Policies in Latin America." National Bureau of Economic Research, Working Paper 2897.

Shadlen, Kenneth C. 2000. "Neoliberalism, Corporatism, and Small Business Activism in Contemporary Mexico." *Latin American Research Review* 35, no. 2:73–106.

Sheahan, John. 1963. *Promotion and Control of Industry in Postwar France.* Cambridge: Harvard University Press.

———. 1987. *Patterns of Development in Latin America: Poverty, Repression, and Economic Strategy.* Princeton: Princeton University Press.

———. 1997. "Effects of Liberalization Programs on Poverty and Inequality: Chile, Mexico, and Peru." *Latin American Research Review* 32, no. 3:7–37.

———. 1999. *Searching for a Better Society: The Peruvian Economy from 1950.* University Park: Pennsylvania State University Press.

Sheahan, John, and Enrique Iglesias. 1998. "Kinds and Causes of Inequality in Latin America." In Nancy Birdsall, Carol Graham, and Richard H. Sabot, eds., *Beyond Tradeoffs: Market Reform and Equitable Growth in Latin America,* 29–60. Washington, D.C.: The Brookings Institution and IDB.

Shonefield, Andrew. 1965. *Modern Capitalism: The Changing Balance of Public and Private Power.* New York and London: Oxford University Press.

Soskice, David. 1999. "Divergent Production Regimes: Coordinated and Uncoordinated Market Economies in the 1980s and 1990s." In Herbert Kitschelt, Peter Lange, Gary Marks, and John D. Stephens, eds., *Continuity and*

Change in Contemporary Capitalism. New York: Cambridge University Press.

Stallings, Barbara, and Wilson Peres, 2000. *Growth, Employment and Equity: The Impact of Economic Reform in Latin America and the Caribbean.* Washington, D.C.: The Brookings Institution and the Economic Commission for Latin America and the Caribbean.

Stephens, John D., Evelyne Huber, and Leonard Ray. 1999. "The Welfare State in Hard Times." In Herbert Kitschelt, Peter Lange, Gary Marks, and John D. Stephens, eds., *Continuity and Change in Contemporary Capitalism.* New York: Cambridge University Press.

Tokman, Víctor E., ed. 1992. *Beyond Regulation: The Informal Economy in Latin America.* Boulder, Colo.: Lynne Rienner.

Trejos, Juan Diego. 1995. "Costa Rica: The State's Response to Poverty." In Dagmar Raczynski, ed., *Strategies to Combat Poverty in Latin America.* Washington, D.C.: IDB, distributed by Johns Hopkins University Press.

World Bank. 1983. *World Tables.* 3d ed. Vol. 2. Washington, D.C.: World Bank.

———. 2000. *World Development Report, 2000/2001: Attacking Poverty.* Washington, D.C.: World Bank.

2

Trade Policies, Growth, and Equity in Latin America

RENATO BAUMANN

Latin American countries have since the mid-1980s experienced unprecedented movements toward more liberal trade policies, in many cases as part of a broader package of policy reform that often includes the adoption of price stabilization measures, the privatization of public enterprises, and fiscal and financial reforms.

When a current account problem developed in a Latin American country, the typical response from the 1960s up through the mid-1980s was to tighten quantitative restrictions, usually by shifting items from a free to a restricted list (Rajapatirana 1996). Furthermore, countries that had access to external funds tended to finance the deficit rather than attempt to adjust their macroeconomic policies. Since the mid-1980s, however, Latin American countries have responded to unfavorable macroeconomic situations, not by restricting trade, but by liberalizing it.

At the same time most of the countries in the region intensified their efforts to foster economic integration. Regional negotiations of unprecedented magnitude often included a number of issues, ranging from the institutional apparatus of each subregional experiment to common investment policies, but have typically been centered on the conditions for preferential market access.[1] The rather impressive figures for trade performance in recent years are therefore the net result of both processes, and isolating the specific consequences of regional trade on a preferential basis from the overall stimuli stemming from trade liberalization is not an easy task.

RECENT TRADE POLICIES

A Brief Regional Overview

The years since 1985 have seen significant changes in policymaking in Latin America and the Caribbean. Trade liberalization has become a common

The views expressed here do not necessarily correspond to those of UN/ECLAC and Universidade de Brasilia.
    1. See, in this regard, ECLAC 1994.

feature, as part of packages of structural reforms that include price stabilization and privatization and reform of the financial sector, the labor market, and the fiscal and the social security systems.

As far as trade reforms are concerned, for Latin America and the Caribbean as a whole the average tariff level has changed from a level of 44.6 percent in the years prior to the reforms (mid- to late 1980s)[2] to 13.1 percent by 1995. Maximum tariff rates have been lowered from 83.7 percent to 41 percent, and import permit and other nontariff barriers have been mostly dismantled (BID 1996).

Another characteristic of the process of liberalization is the gradual adoption of more uniform tariff schedules. As a result, trade and exchange rate regimes are now more open in Latin America than at any time since the Great Depression, with the important consequence that taxes on foreign trade, which corresponded on average to 29.9 percent of fiscal revenue in 1980, have by 1995 reduced their participation to only 16.6 percent of total revenue (BID 1996).

This movement raises a number of questions. First and foremost, one might ask whether this policy approach has fostered improved trade performance or GDP and industrial growth. Latin America is well known for its regressive pattern of income distribution. A second important issue is therefore the role of the trade policy in the improvement of asset and income distribution.

A third set of questions has to do with the very process of reforming trade policy. How was it done, what differences stem from the experiences of the various countries, and what lessons can be derived from these experiences? A last set of issues follows from the process of trade policy reform and its relation to the new international environment for trade policy. Of particular importance here are the conditions determined by the Uruguay Round and the implications for policymaking.

The Experience of Seven Selected Countries

For the purposes of the present work we shall focus on the experience of seven Latin American countries. This group includes the largest economies—

2. It is often conceded that trade reforms for the region as a whole started by 1989. The first experience of a broad trade reform took place in Chile, in 1973–79, with some reversal in the early 1980s. The years between 1985 and 1988 have witnessed trade liberalization in Chile, Mexico, Bolivia, Costa Rica, Jamaica, Guatemala, and Guyana. Fourteen other countries in the region started their liberalization process after 1989 (BID 1996).

Argentina, Brazil, and Mexico—and therefore some of the most diversified productive and trade structures in the region (Brazil, Mexico). It also includes two of the less dynamic economies in Latin America—Bolivia and Venezuela—as well as medium regional powers such as Chile and Colombia, known for their comparatively lower inflation rates (by regional standards) as well as for a higher than (regional) average degree of geographic diversification of their trade flows.

All seven economies have gone through significant processes of trade reform since the mid- to late 1980s. Maximum tariff levels have gone down sharply (Table 2.1)—in some cases, as in Bolivia, falling to less than one-tenth of the original level—and by 1996 most of the countries in Table 2.1 had maximum nominal tariff rates of 20 percent. Average tariffs were also significantly reduced. According to figures in Table 2.1 the typical Latin American country could be said to have in the late 1990s an average tariff rate of about 13 percent. This is still much higher than the single-digit nominal rates often found in industrial countries, but there is little questioning about the extent of the reduction in comparison to the average protection levels traditionally adopted by Latin American countries.

It is worth noting that the process of tariff reduction in these countries was not as smooth as this table seems to suggest, especially in consumer goods, but there is little doubt that the speed and degree of the reduction itself was without precedent in Latin America.

As an outcome of this process most countries now have most of their tariff lines in the range of 0–10 percent (all items, in the case of Bolivia), and in this group of countries only Brazil and Mexico presented in 1996 tariff rates over 35 percent for some products (Table 2.2).

The process of liberalization has also led to a more homogeneous and less distorted structure of trade barriers, as theory would suggest. Consider, for instance, some indicators of effective tariff protection in Brazil (Pinheiro and Almeida 1995): in 1980 effective rates were as high as 36 percent for consumer goods, 42 percent for intermediate goods and 72 percent for capital goods. In 1993 the corresponding rates were 29 percent, 19 percent, and 23 percent.[3]

This increased homogeneity of the tariff structure conceals some significant differences at the national level in the protection margins provided for

3. Kume (1996) estimates that for all the traded goods the (nonweighted) average effective tariff rate was further reduced from 19 percent in July 1993 to 14 percent in December 1994 (although increasing once again to 23 percent in December 1995, mostly because of the renewed protection of the automobile sector). Weighting by value-added the corresponding figures would be 14, 12, and 13 percent.

Table 2.1   Selected Latin American Countries: Indicators of Recent Tariff Reform

Country	Program started	Maximum tariff level (%)		Average tariff level (%)	
		Previous	1996	Previous	1996
Argentina[a]	1989	65	30	39	14
Bolivia	1986	150	10	12	10
Brazil[b]	1987	105	35	51	10
Chile[c]	1984	35	11	35	11
Colombia	1990	100	20	44	11
Mexico[d]	1985	100	20	24	14
Venezuela	1989	135	20	35	12

SOURCE: CEPAL 1998.
[a] Tariffs for Argentina include an additional 3 percent tax.
[b] Estimates for Brazil in 1996 do not include the temporary increase in tariff rates for some 109 items (automobiles and durable consumer goods), which would lead the average rate to 12.7 percent.
[c] Chile's first tariff reduction took place between 1973 and 1979, leading to a uniform rate of 10 percent; this was raised to 35 percent in 1984 and gradually reduced thereafter.
[d] Estimates for Mexico do not consider the temporary increase in tariff rates in 1995 for some 65 items (with rates as high as 260%), which would have led to an average level of 13.5 percent in 1995.

certain types of products. Witness, for example, the experience of defining the structure of the Common External Tariff in Mercosur, in 1990–92. The only precedent the four countries had as a reference was the corresponding process that took place in the European Community: there, the common tariff was set—for most products—as the average of the national tariff schedules. The four Mercosur members had, however, such different tariff schedules—Brazil had higher rates for consumer goods, whereas Uruguay and Paraguay had higher rates for primary products, and lower ones for manufactures—that the Common Tariff had to be entirely redesigned without immediate resemblance to the previous national schedules.

In spite of the intensity of recent trade reform in Latin America, a number of nontariff barriers are still in operation. The most common practices are technical requirements, requirements for previous authorization in the case of sensitive products, and the prohibition of sensitive products, among several others. The tariff equivalents of such barriers have yet to be estimated. Whatever the equivalence, however, this trend is found in several industrial countries: low nominal tariff rates coupled with the use of nontariff barriers.

Such policy changes are bound to have had some effect on the aggregate indicators of these economies.

Table 2.2   The Basic Tariff Structure of Seven Latin American Countries (number of positions by tariff range as of mid-1996)

	0–10	11–25	26–35	Over 35
Argentina	3430	5496	262	0
Bolivia	6778	0	0	0
Brazil	6259	5286	201	49
Chile	22	5790	0	0
Colombia	3932	3288	45	1
Mexico	4386	4789	437	66
Venezuela	3466	3121	13	0

SOURCE: ECLAC 1997.

THE OUTCOME

Trade Performance

It is difficult to isolate the effects of trade liberalization on the economies of Latin America and the Caribbean for several reasons: the effects caused by a change in trade policy are often naturally slow to emerge; this change in trade policy was made at the same time as other structural reforms that affected the whole economy; this change in trade policy also occurred at the same time as important changes in the international scenario. The direction and magnitude of trade flows following trade liberalization are therefore only in part an outcome of the trade reforms.

Whatever the determining factors, Latin American economies have become significantly more open in relation to foreign trade, as illustrated by Table 2.3. The rates of growth both of exports and imports surpassed that of GDP for every country, quite significantly in some cases.

Table 2.3 also shows that in general the more liberal trade policies have done more to allow imports to penetrate the domestic markets of these countries than they have to improve the export/GDP ratio.

This is not to say that the impact on the export sector has been insignificant. As a matter of fact, one of the characteristics of the early 1990s in the export sector of Latin America was the change in the trade structure for some countries of the region, as shown in Table 2.4. Witness, for instance, the direction of the variation in the relative participation of primary products in total Argentine and Chilean exports, as well as Mexican exports of products intensive in technical progress. The causes for such changes vary in each case (as well as their domestic effects) but the existence of subregional agreements and of financing mechanisms has certainly played a role.

Table 2.3   The Average Annual Growth Rate (%) of GDP, Exports, and Imports
of Goods and Services in Seven Latin American Countries, 1991–1999

	1991–1994			1995–1999		
	ΔGDP	ΔExp	ΔImp	ΔGDP	ΔExp	ΔImp
Argentina	7.9	3.8	45.4	2.3	10.3	6.2
Bolivia	4.1	7.2	5.3	4.1	1.6	6.6
Brazil	2.8	6.9	16.7	1.9	4.1	8.1
Chile	8.3	10.3	13.3	5.5	9.0	7.5
Colombia	4.3	6.0	26.6	1.3	7.7	0.4
Mexico	3.6	9.0	14.5	2.9	17.0	12.0
Venezuela	3.5	5.6	12.7	0.6	3.3	6.6

SOURCE: ECLAC 2000.

Table 2.5 shows that imports of products intensive in technical progress
and in some cases also durable consumer goods have risen and those of primary products have fallen. This is the outcome of at least three complementary effects: (1) wealth effects accruing from stabilization programs, coupled
with the existence of repressed domestic demand for importables because of
long periods of import repression; (2) the effects of regional integration
processes—preferential trade margins plus the existence of less sophisticated
consumers as compared to, say, those from OECD countries, which have
led Latin American countries to concentrate in regional markets most of
their exports of elaborated products; and (3) the easier access to imported
producer goods in a new economic environment with lower price increases
and positive output growth rates, which has often stimulated new, modernizing investment. (See the subsection titled "Output Growth" below.)

The outcome has been an increasing import component of domestic production. For instance, in Brazil it has been estimated that the share of the
external demand increased from 8.8 percent of total industrial production
in 1989 to 15 percent in 1998, while the import/output ratio increased from
4 percent to 20 percent in the same period, according to figures presented in
Moreira 1999.[4]

Part of the export growth achieved in the early 1990s was made possible
by favorable foreign demand conditions. As shown in Table 2.6, all the countries considered here experienced more favorable variation in their terms of

4. With very different sectoral intensity: the import/output ratios for natural resource-
intensive industries increased from 3 to 8 percent between 1989 and 1998, but the corresponding figures for technology-intensive sectors were 7 and 44 percent.

Table 2.4 Seven Latin American Countries: Selected Products as a Percentage of Total Exports

	Primary products[a]	Traditional industrial products[b]	Products with scale economies[c]	Durable goods[d]	Products intensive in technical progress[e]
Argentina					
1990	29	33	31	2	5
1997	31	29	21	10	6
Bolivia					
1990	67	16	17	0	0
1997	48	35	16	0	1
Brazil					
1990	20	29	31	7	13
1997	20	30	24	10	14
Chile					
1990	27	16	53	1	1
1997	31	20	44	1	2
Colombia					
1990	63	21	13	0	1
1997	59	19	15	2	4
Mexico					
1990	47	9	17	13	14
1997	14	19	9	23	35
Venezuela					
1990	83	3	11	1	1
1997	58	3	37	1	1

SOURCE: CEPAL 1999.

[a] Primary products: Vegetables, fruits, wood, minerals, petroleum.

[b] Traditional industrial products: Dairy products, oil, textiles, tools, furniture, shoes, printed matter.

[c] Products with scale economies: Pulp, cement, basic metals.

[d] Durable goods: Durable consumer goods, automobiles.

[e] Products intensive in technical progress: Machinery, instruments, chemical products.

trade in 1991–94 as compared to the previous decade,[5] although in the second half of the decade the outcome was mixed, with exporters of oil and natural gas (Venezuela, Mexico, Bolivia) benefiting from favorable oil market conditions, in parallel with sharp price deterioration for the other countries.

In summary, the early 1990s were remarkable years in Latin America as a period of unprecedented openness to foreign trade, although the paths to

5. Another important determining factor is the reduced volatility of the real exchange rate, achieved by both the higher commitment to the external sector and the greater price stability. Gavin (1997) estimates that volatility to have been much lower in 1990–96 than in the 1980s.

Table 2.5 Seven Latin American Countries: Selected Products as a Percentage of Total Imports

	Primary products[a]	Traditional industrial products[b]	Products with scale economies[c]	Durable goods[d]	Products intensive in technical progress[e]
Argentina					
1990	16	9	37	8	29
1997	5	17	23	17	37
Bolivia					
1990	4	21	24	20	32
1997	5	15	27	20	34
Brazil					
1990	33	11	22	4	30
1997	15	13	24	10	38
Chile					
1990	16	14	22	12	35
1997	11	20	20	16	32
Colombia					
1990	6	8	42	8	35
1997	7	16	29	10	33
Mexico					
1990	9	21	22	16	33
1997	5	23	18	10	40
Venezuela					
1990	8	14	31	9	38
1997	7	18	25	17	34

SOURCE: CEPAL 1999.
[a] Primary products: Vegetables, fruits, wood, minerals, petroleum.
[b] Traditional industrial products: Dairy products, oil, textiles, tools, furniture, shoes, printed matter.
[c] Products with scale economies: Pulp, cement, basic metals.
[d] Durable goods: Durable consumer goods, automobiles.
[e] Products intensive in technical progress: Machinery, instruments, chemical products.

more open economies differ among countries, reflecting among other things the very differences among their productive structures.

Other Indicators

Price Stabilization   One of the most remarkable achievements of the Latin American economies in recent years has been the sharp decline in the rate of price increase.

Latin America became well known for having experienced some of the highest inflation rates in the world, especially since the debt crisis of the

Table 2.6 Terms of Trade in Seven Latin American Countries, 1981–1999 (annual averages, percent change in terms of trade)

	1981–1990	1991–1994	1995–1999
Argentina	−4.2	1.8	−1.2
Bolivia	−2.9	−2.0	1.5
Brazil	−1.8	8.8	0.8
Chile	−2.1	0.6	−1.8
Colombia	−1.5	8.8	0.8
Mexico	−4.0	−0.8	−0.2
Venezuela	−4.9	−4.8	3.5

SOURCE: CEPAL 2000.

early 1980s. Four-digit annual inflation rates were observed in Argentina, Bolivia, and Brazil in different moments of that decade.

This scenario has changed significantly since the mid-1980s. Most countries have adopted stabilization programs that have been quite successful in reducing the pace of price increase. Table 2.7 shows some basic information in this regard for the seven countries considered here.

Price stabilization is an undisputed achievement for these countries, with the sole exceptions of Colombia—with a long peculiar performance of "steady" annual price increases around 20 percent—and Venezuela, with an opposite (increasing) trajectory. Argentina, Bolivia, and Chile have even obtained single-digit annual rates for consumer price increases, whereas Brazil and Mexico present clear reducing trends in their inflationary processes.

Trade policies (together with other reforms) have played a significant role in this process. As shown earlier, the reduction of trade barriers has led to an increase in the import component of domestic supply, and this actually contributed to a large extent to reduce the pace of price increase. As a matter of fact, an IDB analysis has found that for the region as a whole "67% of the trade liberalization programmes and 45% of the financial reforms have started at the same year when price stabilization was achieved" (BID 1996), an indication that these reforms were often both part of the same policy package and that they contributed to price stabilization.[6]

Output Growth The period of analysis is one of resumed growth, after what has been called "the lost decade" of the 1980s. Table 2.8 shows indications of

---

6. Baumann, Rivero, and Zavattiero (1997) indicate that in Brazil this use of trade reform for purposes of price stabilization has actually led to unclear price signals, because import tariff rates varied sharply within a limited period of time with no clear economic logic.

Table 2.7 Consumer Prices in Selected Latin American Countries, 1985–1999 (average annual percentages, increase in consumer prices)

	1985–89	1990–93	1994–99
Argentina	262	363	0.8
Bolivia	42	13	7.2
Brazil	283	1425	162.6*
Chile	14	18	6.1
Colombia	19	27	17.9
Mexico	62	17	22.2
Venezuela	28	36	53.0

SOURCE: CEPAL 2000.
* Stabilization plan adopted in July 1994 led to increases in consumer price indexes of 22 percent in 1995 and 9.3 percent in 1995–99.

positive growth rates in all seven countries, although performance was far more impressive in the first half of the decade.

These higher output growth rates have led to a recuperation of investment rates,[7] but—according to Table 2.8—in only a few cases have these rates returned to the levels obtained in the early 1980s.

There is hence a correspondence between the years of higher output growth and the years when Latin American economies were more open to foreign trade. What is less clear is the specific contribution of trade to such growth performance. It is beyond the scope of this chapter to investigate the precise causality between trade and output growth, but one can rely upon some available indirect evidence to illustrate such a relationship for Latin America in recent years.

A process of trade liberalization is expected to lead to export expansion, and contributes to improving productive efficiency via the reallocation of resources, the increase in the scale of domestic production, the reduction in X-inefficiency, and the increase in total factor productivity.

For Brazil Bonelli found a positive association in 1975–85 between export growth and the increase in total factor productivity in industry (in accordance with Verdoorn's Law) and positive links between the export/output ratio and labor productivity for several industries in 1980–85 (Bonelli 1991, 1994). Baumann (1994) found for a sample of 200 firms responsible for

---

7. Part of it made possible by the availability of foreign resources. For instance, for most of the seven countries considered here the Current Account / GDP ratio was much higher in 1990–94 than in 1980 or 1995. In turn, this inflow of resources—coupled to stabilization programs that emphasized exchange rates as nominal anchors—has led to exchange rate appreciation in relation to parity equilibrium levels estimated to have in most cases surpassed 10 percent in 1990–96, when measured in terms of consumer prices (see CEPAL 1996).

Table 2.8 GDP Growth and Investment Ratio in Seven Latin American Countries, 1980–1999 (annual average percentage from 1990 constant values)

	GDP		Investment/GDP (%)			
	1991–94	1995–99	1980	1990	1995	1999
Argentina	7.9	2.3	26	14	20	20
Bolivia	4.1	4.1	13	13	16	21
Brazil	2.8	1.9	34	23	23	20
Chile	8.3	5.5	21	23	28	19
Colombia	4.3	1.3	21	17	25	14
Mexico	3.6	2.9	25	19	17	28
Venezuela	3.5	0.6	29	14	15	16

SOURCES: CEPAL 1996a and 2000.

about one-fourth of Brazilian manufactured exports that the external market provided a cushion against recession in the years 1990–92, and that firms with higher export/sales ratios performed better in terms of several indicators of efficiency and competitiveness than those firms which concentrated their sales in the domestic market.

The process has been, however, neither instantaneous nor linear nor painless. For instance, Meller (1993) shows that following trade reform in Chile in the early 1970s there was a marked process of adjustment of the productive sector, with firms increasing the use of imported inputs, a sharply rising number of firms disappearing from the market (four times as many firms closed in 1980–81 as in 1975–76), and industrial jobs being reduced by 24 percent between 1974 and 1981.

Similar outcomes in terms of a rather modest impact on growth following trade reform are found in Mexico's post-1985 experience—between 1985 and 1993 there was no increase at all in per capita GDP and investment remained below historical levels—as well as in Bolivia, where in the eight years following reform per capita GDP grew by only 1.2 percent annually, a rate barely sufficient to bring it to a mere 87 percent of its level before the crisis of the early 1980s (Agosin and Ffrench-Davis 1995). Ros (1993) also emphasizes the fact that in the five years following trade reform in Mexico industrial labor productivity remained as low as in the five years that preceded it.

Another element following a process of trade reform is that its actual impact is differentiated by sectors, as theory would suggest. For instance, Meller (1993) shows that in Chile natural-resource–intensive export sectors grew by approximately 2 percent of GDP between 1980 and 1990,[8] whereas

---

8. The number of exporting firms doubled between 1986 and 1991 (Meller 1993).

import substituting industries shrank by almost 8 percent of GDP in the same period.

Whatever the precise timing between the reform and its actual effect on output performance or in spite of the costs that might be expected from the transition period, the evidence points in general to a positive (but occasionally qualified) relation between trade and output growth. As a matter of fact, for Latin America as a whole Lora and Barrera (1997) found that recent trade reform is the most important single contributor to output growth and factor productivity.

DISTRIBUTIVE ASPECTS

The analysis of the effects of foreign trade on the factor market for Latin American countries has to take into account a number of regional characteristics.

To start with, Latin America is well known for presenting very regressive income distribution patterns and high concentration of asset ownership. For the 1990s as a whole Morley (2000) estimates average Gini coefficients for Latin America as high as 0.49, compared to corresponding figures of 0.34 for OECD countries and 0.47 for sub-Saharan Africa.[9] In the seven countries considered here on average only 15 percent of urban income accrues to the poorest 40 percent of the urban population, while the richest 10 percent absorb 30–40 percent (CEPAL 1997).

The relation between trade and income distribution is varied and comprises several aspects, ranging from employment effects stemming from Hecksher-Ohlin type of approaches[10] to effects associated with net export income and reduction of the cost of the basic consumer basket, and to the domestic impact of competition with imported goods and services.

Latin American exports are clearly intensive in the relatively cheaper production factor—labor—at the same time that they are determined by the abundance of natural resources. For instance, tests of the Hecksher-Ohlin theorem in the 1970s in Brazil (Tyler 1976) and more recently for the early 1980s (Lafetá 1995) indicate trade specialization according to the presumed

9. According to figures in Morley 2000, ever since the 1970s Latin America has presented the highest indicators of income concentration in the world. Morley indicates that income distribution in this region improved in the 1970s, worsened in the next decade and remained relatively stable during the 1990s.

10. Where trade benefits more intensively the income accruing to the abundant factor (i.e., labor).

factor endowment, even when labor skills are taken into account. Also, Table 2.4 shows a predominance of exports of primary products and products with scale economies.

Be that as it may, however, it is clear that—because of the limited weight of foreign trade in Latin American economic activity, and for other major reasons—trade cannot be seen as a panacea for the distributive problems in the region. Firms producing or reselling for export must be large enough to take advantage of economies of scale, to market their products, to provide technical support to their customers, and to gain access to financing. This means that trade activity is associated with a good deal of systematic formal relationships in the labor market, as different from other activities oriented toward the domestic market.

This in itself leads to some qualifications to the links between the export activity and the factor market in the region.

The impact of trade performance is likely to be largely—although not fully—transmitted to the labor market. In these seven countries, for instance, a high proportion of the employed, economically active population consists of wage earners. Figures vary from a minimum of 54 percent in Bolivia to 75 percent in Mexico. The relevant point for the appraisal of the distributive impact of exporting is, however, that non-wage earners account for a significant share of the workforce. For the region as a whole, self-employed workers comprise 25–30 percent of the workforce (CEPAL 1996).

Furthermore, the informal sector is not only important in magnitude. Evidence indicates that in Latin America as a whole the most dynamic part of the labor market is the one associated with the informal sector. According to ILO estimates, in the 1990–95 period 84 percent of the new jobs created in the region were in the informal sector (CEPAL 1997a), and presumably were only indirectly—if at all—related to foreign trade.

This means that conventional appraisal of the Stolper-Samuelson type for the domestic distributive impact of trade in Latin America requires some qualification: it is not quite clear how the factors employed in the informal sectors benefit from trade performance.

Moreover, Table 2.4 shows that the export sector in several Latin American countries has experienced sharp modifications in recent years. A number of countries have seen their export composition become increasingly concentrated in natural-resource–intensive products. While labor-intensive products such as light manufactures are expected to have a direct positive impact on the labor market, the larger scale required for the production of natural-resource–intensive goods might have a different impact on the factor market.

A final qualification of the tentative decision to relate aggregate figures to trade performance is that for most countries in the region foreign trade still corresponds to a very limited share of domestic product, so even a composition of trade flows in accordance with comparative advantages is likely to have reduced effects on the domestic factor market.

Whatever the specific impact of trade, some indicators corresponding to the period of most intense trade growth are sufficient to add strong qualifications to associating the external sector to the main outcomes in the domestic factor market.

For instance, during the 1990s—when it has been shown that trade growth was quite intense for Latin American countries—urban unemployment for the seven countries in 1990–99 varied from 2.7 percent in 1989 to 3.7 percent in 1997, whereas in Argentina and Colombia, figures surpassed 14 percent in 1999, being twice as high as those for the 1980s, according to CEPAL 2000b.

Furthermore, the disparity between professional staff and blue-collar workers has actually increased in a systematic way in each one of the seven countries considered here, as shown in Table 2.9. This would seem to be consistent with the figures in Table 2.4, which show that a second trend in the changes of recent export composition in Latin America has to do with some countries exporting relatively more durable goods as well as technology-intensive products, by and large an outcome of preferential concessions accruing from regional integration agreements.

This means an actual worsening of the distributive profile among employed personnel. The increasing gap between earnings of highly qualified employees and relatively unskilled workers goes against expectations based on a Hecksher-Ohlin type of approach.

Notwithstanding the positive impact the unprecedented growth of foreign trade in Latin America might have had on income distribution, the figures in Table 2.9 indicate that the scenario has actually worsened: even in a period of intense involvement with the external market these economies have presented increasingly concentrated distributive patterns.

There is by now a large and increasing literature about the reforms undertaken by Latin American countries in the 1990s and their actual outcomes. It is often conceded that inequality has increased during these years, and likely explanations are apparently associated with differences in access to education facilities, repressive wage policies required for export performance, accumulation of physical capital ownership, and other factors not directly related to external trade (Morley 2000; Neri and Camargo 2000).

It is beyond our present purposes to go any deeper into that discussion. In any case, concern with the distributive aspects of trade and trade policy

Table 2.9 Average Income of Employers, Professional, and Nonprofessional
Workers in Seven Latin American Countries, 1989–1998 (in multiples of poverty lines)

Country	Year	Employers	Professional workers	Nonprofessional workers[a]
Argentina[b]	1990	20.6	9.4	4.5
	1997	24.2	—	—
Bolivia	1989	16.2	7.7	3.6
	1997	10.1	8.8	3.2
Brazil	1990	16.1	8.2	3.8
	1996	19.1	10.7	3.9
Chile	1990	24.8	7.4	3.5
	1998	33.8	11.7	4.3
Colombia	1991	17.1	8.3	2.2
	1997	10.9	6.9	2.7
Mexico	1989	21.7	6.9	3.1
	1998	18.2	6.9	3.1
Venezuela	1990	11.9	6.6	3.6
	1997	11.2	5. 8	2.4

SOURCE: CEPAL 2000b.
[a] In establishments with more than five employees.
[b] Buenos Aires.

leads us to consider the way trade policy has been designed and implemented in these countries.

TRADE POLICYMAKING

Recent episodes of trade reform in Latin America are an important subject
of analysis not only for their effects. The peculiarities of each process of
trade policymaking might determine its overall results.

The move toward more liberal trade policies in the region has often
been associated with stabilization packages as well as with the need for
raising investment rates. For instance, the 1985 reform in Mexico was
motivated by the dismal performance of non-oil exports together with the
perception by the government that part of the failure to achieve price stabilization was caused by the failure to achieve rapid import liberalization
(Ros 1993). In Colombia trade reform was justified on the basis of the
slow growth, even after the basic macroeconomic disequilibria had been
controlled. The diagnosis was that this was an outcome of low investment
rates and low industrial productivity, associated with the high protection
against imports (Ocampo 1993). Similar reasoning can be found in the
trade reforms of Chile in the early 1970s: slow growth coupled with basic

macroeconomic disequilibria were associated with static inefficient allocation of resources. In Brazil the overall perception since the mid-1980s was
that barriers and overall distortions in trade policy had lost momentum as
stimuli for tariff jumping investment, as in the previous decades.

From a theoretical standpoint the optimum timing for a trade reform
would be when (1) the economy is at a peak of the business cycle (so no
additional pressure can be reasonably expected to jeopardize the trade balance); (2) the country has considerable foreign reserves (for protection
against speculative movements on the exchange rates); and (3) export expansion surpasses import expansion.[11]

It is rare, however, that every one of these three conditions can be met.
As a matter of fact, domestic disequilibria, say, on the fiscal side, and/or
slow output growth rates have often led multilateral organizations to push
for trade reform even under less than ideal conditions. One peculiar aspect
of recent reforms in Latin America is, however, that—although they have
been designed in accordance to orthodox prescriptions—it is not quite clear
what role these institutions have actually played in the process. The reforms
seem to have been mostly an outcome of domestic policymakers' decisions.
As an illustration of that, in reviewing Colombian trade reform in the mid-
1980s, Ocampo (1993) refers to the World Bank having manifested surprise
about the rhythm of the reforms.

The foregoing does not mean that the reforms always reflected consensus
among economic agents. Every trade reform involves different perceptions
of the gains and losses: resistance arises in the sectors that are affected
(entrepreneurs and workers react via political pressure), whereas potential
beneficiaries often remain silent. But in some cases potential reactions were
avoided via specific mechanisms. For instance, in Mexico sectors that would
be potentially affected by trade liberalization could initially count on high
exchange rates, which provided a protective cushion that reduced the conflicts of objectives. Later on, further acceleration of trade liberalization took
place in the context of the Solidarity Pact, a stabilization program adopted
in accordance with the unions and entrepreneurs' syndicates (Ros 1993).

This raises the important issue of the new tariff schedules following
reform being determined in a centralized way, following the designs of policymakers, or being the outcome of negotiated positions. The Brazilian experience is quite illustrative in this regard.

11. Other conditions refer to the credibility of government intentions and the exchange
rate policy at the time of the trade reform, among others. See, in this regard, Rodrik 1996 and
Edwards 1990.

The tariff schedule determined by law in 1957 remained in operation for thirty years, until its first reform in 1987. During those three decades provisional modifications in the nominal tariff rates were granted through a tariff policy council, comprised of representatives from several government agencies as well as representatives of the private sector. It goes without saying that the outdated tariff structure could only survive thanks to provisional adaptations. This is illustrated, for instance, by the fact that in 1980–88 the council authorized 1970 cases of tariff reduction plus 526 cases of tariff exemption (in both cases, based on the argument of nonexistent similar domestic production), as compared to only 169 tariff increases in the same period. From these, 1059 cases were formally demanded by producers' syndicates and 886 by official institutions (Baumann 1993).

Whatever the inadequacies of such a system, it might be argued that it allowed for some transparency, since the decisions were formal and openly taken, considering the arguments from both consumers and producers of import-substituting products. This system was abolished in 1990 on the grounds that such mechanisms actually allowed for the operation of lobbies and led to the long survival of an inadequate tariff schedule. Since then, tariff rates have been determined by specialized government agencies.

In reviewing the experience since 1990, Baumann, Rivero, and Zavattiero (1997) found this to have been a period of systematic tariff reduction—the average tariff rate fell from 32 percent in 1990 to 13 percent in 1996—but also that the criteria for tariff policy determination are not as transparent as one might have expected. For the period from July 1994 to September 1996 the number of episodes of tariff reduction amounted to some 10,000 cases, whereas the increases of tariff rates totaled 6449. Furthermore, for some products (at the 10-digit classification) there were up to seven changes in tariff rates during those twenty-seven months, with variations corresponding in some cases to up to 19 percentage points.

What these developments indicate is that the actual *process* of tariff policymaking might be as important as the *design* of the overall tariff policy itself. This leads to a final set of considerations, related to the present possibilities for trade policy, after the most recent round of multilateral negotiations.

AFTER THE URUGUAY ROUND

The Uruguay Round of multilateral negotiations in the GATT has led to achievements as far as the economic relations among countries are concerned, unprecedented for their scope and depth.

The main outcomes from the Uruguay Round can be summarized as follows (Rego 1996):

1. Average tariff cut of 37 percent. Industrial countries have agreed to cut their tariffs in manufactures from 6.3 percent to 3.8 percent and increase tariff exemptions from 20 percent to 44 percent. After a five-year period only 5 percent of their imports will have tariffs above 15 percent.

2. Negotiations on agricultural products have resumed at a multilateral level. Non-tariff barriers for more than 30 percent of the traded products were translated into tariff levels and the resulting tariffs are to be reduced by 36 percent for developed countries within six years and by 24 percent for developing countries within ten years. New norms and new commitments were agreed on in relation to trade in agricultural goods.

3. Textile products were also negotiated on a multilateral basis, with the Multifibre Agreement to be eliminated within ten years from January 1995.

4. Binding of tariff lines at the WTO, reflecting an unprecedented approach from several developing countries in regard to the multilateral trading system.

5. Creation of a General Agreement for Trade in Services—GATS.

6. Adoption of a General Agreement on Trade-Related Property Rights.

7. Improvement of trade mechanisms, with the negotiation of an agreement on safeguards as well as the codes on subsidies and antidumping measures.

8. Creation of a new system of dispute settlement.

Some of these outcomes have direct consequences for developing countries. First and foremost, developing countries should benefit from the expected expansion of global trade (estimated at 1 percent per year over the next ten years) that will result from the achievements of the Uruguay Round.

Other positive effects follow from the temporary exceptions and longer periods granted to developing economies for the implementation of the obligations that have been negotiated. Also, a number of specific clauses were established by which developed countries should give differentiated treatment to less developed ones (via, for instance, transfer of technology). Furthermore, it was agreed that technical assistance is to be given to these countries in areas related to commerce, sanitary measures, and others.

Four other topics are particularly important for developing countries in general, as a result of the Uruguay Round. First, the reduction and binding of tariffs for such important export items as shoes, textile products, pulp and paper, steel, wood products, ceramics, and others.

Second, the gradual replacing of the Multifibre Agreement by multilateral negotiations has important consequences to the extent that trade in these products changes from almost bilateral negotiations to multilateral forums, with specific rules and conditions to deal with unfair practices. Third, the gradual reduction of export subsidies to trade of agricultural products will (if it can be achieved) effect a similar significant change of the opportunities open to developing countries.

Fourth, the revision of the antidumping code and the subsidies code as well as the regulation of the use of compensatory rights are of particular importance for several countries in the region, be it for the abusive use of such mechanisms by some of these countries or for their being the object of specific investigations following accusations of unfair practices.

The agreements achieved at the Uruguay Round are a guarantee of greater transparency and predictability in several areas of trade policy, be it for the number of consolidated tariff positions or the need to publish the changes in the import regime (Tussie 1996). Latin American countries have kept some degrees of freedom by consolidating tariffs with maximum levels of 30–35 percent, markedly higher than the corresponding level for developed countries. Table 2.10 illustrates the point. Notice that for Latin America the increase in the number of bound positions was significant in regard to both primary and industrial products, whereas for the industrial countries the movement was far more intense in the primary sector.

Some other points should be of specific concern to Latin American countries.

To start with, the Treaty on Intellectual Property has raised costs for Latin American countries, which will have to make important changes in their legal regimes in order to conform to it. But they have also kept some room for maneuver by maintaining transition periods, by the clause that makes patents non-retroactive, and so forth (Tussie 1996).

The Agreement on Subsidies and Compensatory Measures has actually reduced the margin for the adoption of traditional forms of trade policy adopted by countries in the region. On the positive side, however, for the first time a rather precise definition of subsidy has been reached, and there is formal reference to the fact that subsidization can be part of a development program.

Developing countries in general (Latin American countries in particular) have often justified the adoption of protective devices on the grounds of difficulties with the balance of payments. In spite of strong pressure during the negotiations, the possibility of using Article XVIII.b (capacity to impose

Table 2.10 Tariff Positions Fixed by the Uruguay Round (expressed as percentages of total traded product categories)

	Latin America	Industrial countries
Industrial products		
Percentage of Fixed Tariff Lines		
before	38	78
after	100	99
Primary products		
Percentage of Fixed Tariff Lines		
before	36	58
after	100	100

SOURCE: BID 1996, Cuadro 2.2, p. 101.

quantitative restrictions for protecting BOP fragility) has been maintained, which provides a significant room for maneuver.

In general, the creation of the WTO is seen as an opportunity to increase transparency and focus of trade policies. But it will certainly require a great effort on the part of the countries of Latin America to adapt domestic norms and institutions to the conditions set by the Agreements.

As Tussie (1996) puts it, under the new scenario developing-country governments will have to confine their support of export activities to external measures, such as providing market information. Direct support through the transfer of public monies will no longer be permitted, a measure that was vulnerable to retaliation anyway.

THE ROLE OF REGIONAL INTEGRATION

Latin American and Caribbean countries have in the late 1980s and in the 1990s not only experienced unprecedented trade liberalization. They have also intensified efforts toward greater regional integration than ever before.[12]

The new economic scenario allowed for resuming output growth and some gains in terms of social welfare: for Latin America as a whole GDP increased 3 percent in the first half of the 1990s, as compared to only 0.9 percent during the previous decade. An evaluation in terms of regional groupings shows that the results achieved by Mercosur countries in terms of per capita GDP growth surpassed that of all other subregional groups in the hemisphere, as shown in Table 2.11.

12. See ECLAC 1994 for a discussion of the basic features of that process.

Table 2.11   Per Capita GDP in Selected Areas (in 1990 U.S. dollars)

	Per capita GDP		
Area	1990	1998	Variation(%)
Mercosur	3222	3767	16.9
Andean Group	1734	1982	14.3
Central America Common Market	934	1048	12.2
Caribbean Community	2748	2871	4.5
NAFTA	17510	19649	12.2

SOURCE: BID 1999.

The dynamism of external sales that contributed to that outcome is clearly associated with the broader access to subregional markets, thanks—among other factors—to a number of preferential trade agreements. This has led to an increased importance of intraregional trade in total foreign trade of Latin American countries in general. Table 2.12 illustrates the point.

Little doubt remains as to the recent period being one of sharp intensification of trade flows within each country group. In every Latin American and Caribbean country group the subregional market increased its importance with respect to total exports in the first half of the 1990s. Preferential trade concessions played a significant role, but part of this outcome was due to the overall business facilitation that belongs to the trade reform implemented in these countries, as well as to the increased access to the international capital markets and the exchange rate policies adopted during this period.

The latter leads to discussing the perception of such integration processes from the viewpoint of economic agents external to the region.

A first indicator of the reaction of such agents is the performance of foreign direct investment flows. As shown in Table 2.13, the 1990s were characterized by a remarkable increase in the inflow of risk capital in Latin America as a whole. Figures in that table also show that no other area in the hemisphere experienced as great an increase in the inflow of risk capital as the Mercosur countries did: FDI inflow in 1998 was some twenty-three times higher than in 1990.

Such performance was remarkable even in international terms. The share of Mercosur countries in total FDI flows into developing economies increased from an average of 7.6 percent in 1990–93 to 21.2 percent in 1997–99, and in terms of total world flows in the same period the corresponding figures are 2.1 percent and 5.9 percent respectively (Chudnovsky and Lopez 2000), indicating the confidence of investors in this group of countries.

As important as these figures is the fact that FDI *among* Mercosur countries also increased significantly in this period: according to CEPAL (1997b)

Table 2.12 Participation of Intra-Area Exports in Several Country Groupings in Latin America, 1990 and 1998

	Percentage of total exports	
	1990	1998
LAIA	10.8	17.2
Andean Group	4.0	12.0
Mercosur	9.0	25.0
Central America Common Market	15.0	13.0
CARICOM	8.0	15.0

Source: BID 1999.

the number of Brazilian firms with productive plants or subsidiaries in Argentina increased from fewer than twenty to more than four hundred firms, whereas more than eighty Argentine firms started to invest in the Brazilian market in the same period. A significant share of these bilateral investments is related to processes of merger and acquisition of existing firms, including those linked to the privatization of public enterprises.

A second aspect linked to the external perception relative to the integration process has to do with the impact of this process on the existing trade flows. This leads to the discussion of whether the recent integration process in Latin America is trade-creating or trade-diverting.

This discussion has focused on Mercosur for two reasons: (1) the dramatic increase in importance of intraregional trade blocs in terms of total exports, and (2) the types of goods being traded between the Mercosur countries themselves.

Some critics (such as Yeats 1997) reckon that external trade policy in Mercosur is less biased than the policies adopted previous to the formation of Mercosur, and represents therefore an improvement in terms of efficiency. But these critics consider trade policy as a major factor responsible for the observed changes in trade flows. As most of intrabloc trade consists of capital-intensive products[13]—in which the four member countries are not internationally competitive—this would mean that countries that do not belong to the group are being negatively affected by significant trade diversion.

The argument against such criticism is that whatever trade deviation the formation of Mercosur might have caused has been by and large compensated for by a significant increase in the total value of the goods imported from outside Mercosur by its member states. Between 1990 and 1995 intra-

---

13. Data presented in Yeats 1997 show that in intra-Mercosur trade, food and other primary products accounted for only 29 percent of total regional exports in 1994.

Table 2.13   Net Foreign Capital Inflow in Selected Areas ($U.S. billions)

	1990	1998
Mercosur	2.3	46.7
Andean Group	0.3	9.4
CACM	1.0	3.1
Caribbean Community	0.1	2.0
Total Latin America	16.5	82.7
NAFTA	101.5	275.4

SOURCE: BID 1999.

regional imports increased their share in total imports from 15 percent to 19 percent, but at the same time the value of total imports increased threefold. One of the consequences is that the trade balance for Mercosur as a whole fell sharply from U.S.$14 billion in 1991 to only U.S.$0.5 billion in 1995 (IDB 1996).

Winters (1997), Laird (1997), and Serra et al. (1997) emphasize the probable association between the growth of intrabloc exports and the margins of preference given to partner countries: intrabloc exports increased from 11 percent of total exports by the four countries in 1991 to 21.5 percent in 1996. As a consequence—and given the fact that Mercosur members are internationally competitive in primary products and that intra-area trade is predominantly in manufactured goods—consumers in the four countries are being forced into purchasing locally produced products of lower quality than those that could be obtained from nonmember countries.

The argument against such critics is that the composition of trade flows mirrors a "learning effect" involving a non-static perspective of the comparative advantages of each country. Furthermore, it is not correct to say that there is excess intrabloc trade in Mercosur when 80 percent of Mercosur trade is extra-area, as compared to 60 percent in the case of NAFTA and 40 percent in the case of the European Union.

Burki (1997) and Serra et al. (1997) also argue that the incentives provided by Mercosur countries attract investors, possibly at a cost to neighboring countries. The argument against such criticism is that empirical evidence shows that incentives are not all that matters. Market size, expectations regarding future performance, macroeconomic stability, and other elements are even more determining of investment flows. It is therefore reasonable to expect that the relative size of Mercosur economies, as well as their recent macroeconomic adjustment processes, coupled to the privatization of public enterprises in its member states, would naturally lead to more significant inflows of foreign capital than elsewhere in the region.

There are, therefore, arguments that the countries in the region should pursue a strategy of deepening their economic integration process, to the extent that such a process is consistent with fair multilateral treatment, that is, in accordance with an "open regionalism" strategy.[14]

What is less clear is the extent to which the project of a Free Trade Area for the Americas—a project comprising thirty-four Latin American and Caribbean countries—is likely to affect such a trajectory.

It is still rather premature for any affirmative statement in that regard, since by the time of writing the actual negotiations leading to the FTAA have not formally started,[15] and it is not quite clear what form these negotiations will take. Furthermore, there are marked differences among the countries involved in the process, with some of them pressing for a faster negotiating process, and others preferring more cautious approaches, consistent with the consolidation of the present subregional integration experiments.

A number of other considerations could be presented with relation to the FTAA project at its present stage, such as the readiness of the countries in the region to negotiate trade in services, labor regimes, investment regulations, and several other aspects, like the differences among individual countries in their interest to have a broader access to the U.S. market.

Be that as it may, the negotiations of preferential trade concessions at a hemispheric level have to take into account that (1) the scenario in which such negotiations will take place is unprecedented for the intensity of the integration experiments as well as for the fact that such experiments are being conducted at the same time as multilateral concessions are being made by all countries involved;[16] (2) economic agents and governments in the region have an increasingly clear perception that there are gains to accrue from regional integration, and hence the cost of not considering such gains by opting for alternative schemes might be quite significant in some cases; and (3) there is an increasing perception also that the integration processes (and trade flows in general) could be far more extensive if resources were available to overcome a number of specific infrastructural constraints, so that the potential agenda for the negotiations should comprise not only specific trade issues, but also the criteria for business facilitation in several aspects of investment policy.

14. Or, to put it in another way, subregional preferences have to be "WTO-consistent."

15. There are still some doubts whether the U.S. Congress will provide the "fast track" authority required for the negotiations.

16. There are no indications that Latin American and Caribbean countries are likely to change their present open trade policy orientation.

In other words, it is hard to see how an eventual FTAA could by itself change such important characteristics of the present Latin American and Caribbean economies as those listed above. It is more likely that a hemispheric initiative would more than anything else supplement present policies by allowing for the additional reduction of barriers to the flow of goods and services.

LESSONS FROM THE SEVEN EXPERIENCES

The 1990s will become known as the time when Latin American economies had to adapt to the macroeconomic difficulties by resorting to trade liberalization and more intense regional integration.

More open trade policies in most cases were adopted as part of price stabilization packages, which included as well reforms of the financial sector, reforms of the labor market, and changes in the fiscal and social security systems.

In reviewing the experiences of seven countries of the region with their trade policy reforms it turned out that at least eight lessons can be derived from these experiences, as follows.

Lesson 1 is that trade reform is not a smooth process for every country. The more diversified the productive structure the higher the probability of differentiated tariff rates for some products (consumer goods in particular) and the more likely the process of tariff reduction will follow a stop-and-go path.

Lesson 2 is that, as suggested by theory, the more liberal scenario allowed for changes in the composition of trade flows, a movement that might be related to an accommodation to the (static) comparative advantages of each economy.

Lesson 3 is that external conditions have been very helpful in determining these results. The period of intense changes in the trade flows was also one of favorable variation of the terms of trade for these countries.

Lesson 4 is that more open systems allowed for higher output growth rates, but in a nonlinear and painful way. Import/output ratios tended to surpass export ratios at the early stages of the process, leading in some cases to very significant adjustment of the whole productive structure.

Lesson 5 follows from the difficulty in isolating the actual impact trade liberalization has had on income distribution in the region. Be it for the relatively limited weight trade has in the overall economic activity of these countries or any other reason, the fact is that the period of more intense growth of trade flows is characterized by a corresponding worsening of several indicators of distribution.

Lesson 6 is that the process of trade policymaking matters. The outcome of a trade reform will vary according to whether the economic agents likely to be affected by the reform have participated in the process and/or have been granted conditions to live with the new, higher degree of exposure to imports. This is particularly important when—like the recent processes in Latin America—the reform of trade policy is not imposed from outside, but rather results from domestic decisions.

Lesson 7 following from these experiences is that the new scenario determined by the agreements achieved at the Uruguay Round reduces the margin for a number of instruments that have traditionally been adopted by the countries in the region, at the same time that it preserves a number of advantages in terms of differentiated treatment for developing countries and involves some challenges from the need to adapt to the need to deal with a number of new issues.

Finally, Lesson 8 is that experience has shown that there are gains in terms of greater productive complementarity to be achieved from subregional integration, whenever the preferences are consistent with multilateral concessions.

REFERENCES

Agosin, M., and R. Ffrench-Davis. 1995. "Trade Liberalization and Growth: Recent Experiences in Latin America." *Journal of Interamerican Studies and World Affairs* 37, no. 3.

ALADI. 1997. *ALADI—A Nova Realidade da Integração*. Montevideo.

Alcorta, L., and W. Peres. 1996. "Sistemas de Innovación y Especialización Tecnológica en América Latina y el Caribe." CEPAL, *Desarrollo Productivo No. 33.*

Baumann, R. 1993. "A Political Economy Analysis of Import Policy in Brazil: 1980–1988." *Série Reformas de Política Pública,* no. 3. Santiago: CEPAL.

———. 1994. "A Saga da Competitividade das Exportações Industriais Brasileiras—1992." *Pesquisa e Planejamento Econômico* 24, no. 2 (August).

Baumann, R., J. Rivero, and Y. Zavattiero. 1997. "As Tarifas de Importações no Plano Real." *Pesquisa e Planejamento Econômico* 27, no. 3 (December).

BID. 1996. *Progreso Económico y Social en America Latina, Informe 1996, Tema Especial—Cómo Organizar Con Éxito los Servicios Sociales.* Washington, D.C.: IDB.

———. 1999. *Integración y Comércio en América.* Nota Periódica, October, Washington, D.C.

Bonelli, R. 1991. "Crescimento e Produtividade na Indústria Brasileira: Impactos da Orientação Comercial." *Pesquisa e Planejamento Econômico* 21, no. 3 (December).

———. 1994. "Produtividade, Crescimento Industrial e Exportações de Manufatu-
rados no Brasil: Desempenho e Competitividade." IPEA, *Texto para Discussão* no. 327, Janeiro.

Burki, S. J. 1997. "Trade Open Regionalism in LAC." Speech at the Third Annual
Conference on Development in Latin America and the Caribbean, June 30,
Montevideo, mimeographed.

CEPAL (Comisión Económica para América Latina y el Caribe). 1996. *Balance Preliminar de América Latina y el Caribe.* Santiago: CEPAL.

———. 1997a. *La Brecha de la Equidad.* Santiago: CEPAL.

———. 1997b. *La Inversión Extranjera en América Latina y el Caribe—Informe
1996.* Santiago: CEPAL.

———. 1998. *América Latina y el Caribe—Políticas para Mejorar la Inserción en la
Economía Mundial.* Santiago: CEPAL/Fondo de Cultura Económica.

———. 1999. *Panorama de la Inserción Internacional de América Latina y el
Caribe—1998.* Santiago: CEPAL.

———. 2000a. *Estudio Económico de América Latina y el Caribe—1999–2000.*
Santiago: CEPAL.

———. 2000b. *Panorama Social de América Latina, 1999–2000.* Santiago: CEPAL.

Chudnovsky, D., and J. Lopez. 2000. "El 'Boom' de Inversión Extranjera Directa en
el Mercosur en los Años 1990: Características, Determinantes e Impactos."
Buenos Aires.

ECLAC. 1994. *Open Regionalism in Latin America and the Caribbean—Economic
Integration as a Contribution to Changing Patterns with Social Equity.* Santiago: United Nations Commission for Latin America and the Caribbean.

Edwards, S. 1990. "The Sequencing of Economic Reform: Analytical Issues and
Lessons from Latin American Experiences." *The World Economy* 13, no. 1
(March).

Gavin, M. 1997. "A Decade of Reform in Latin America: Has It Delivered Lower
Volatility?" Paper presented at the IDB Annual Meeting in Barcelona, March.

Inter-American Development Bank (IDB). 1996. *Integration and the Americas—A
Preliminary Estimate of 1996 Trade.* Periodic Note.

Kume, H. 1996. "A Política de Importação no Plano Real e a Estrutura de Proteção
Efetiva." IPEA, *Texto para Discussão* no. 423.

Lafetá, D. 1995. "A Qualificação da Mão-de-Obra no Comércio Internacional
Brasileiro: Um Teste do Teorema de Hecksher-Ohlin." Master's thesis,
Department of Economics, Universidade de Brasilia.

Laird, S. 1997. "Mercosur: Objectives and Achievements." Paper presented at the
Third Annual Conference on Development in Latin America and the
Caribbean, Montevideo, June 30.

Lora, E., and F. Barrera. 1997. "Una Década de Reformas Estructurales en América
Latina: el Crecimiento, la Productividad y la Inversión ya no Son Como
Antes." Paper presented at the IDB Annual Meeting in Barcelona, March.

Meller, P. 1993. "Economia Política de la Apertura Comercial Chilena." CEPAL,
Serie Reformas de Política Pública, no. 5.

Moreira, M. M. 1999. "A Indústria Brasileira nos anos 90: O Que Já se Pode
Dizer?" In F. Giambiagi and M. M. Moreira, eds., *A Economia Brasileira nos
Anos 90.* Rio de Janeiro: BNDES.

Moreira, M. M., and P. G. Correa. 1996. "Abertura Comercial e Indústria: O Que se Pode Esperar e o Que se Vem Obtendo." BNDES/AP/DEPEC, *Texto para Discussão*, No. 49.

Morley, S. 2000. *La Distribución del Ingreso en América Latina y el Caribe.* Mexico City: CEPAL, Fondo de Cultura Económica.

Neri, M., and J. M. Camargo. 2000. "Efeitos Distributivos das Reformas Estruturais no Brasil." In R. Baumann, ed., *Brasil: Uma Década em Transição.* Rio de Janeiro: CEPAL, Ed. Campus.

Ocampo, J. A. 1993. "Economia y Economia Política de la Reforma Comercial Colombiana." CEPAL, *Serie Reformas de Política Pública*, no. 1.

Pinheiro, A. C., and G. B. Almeida. 1995. "Padrões Setoriais da Proteção na Economia Brasileira." In E. Teixeira and D. Aguiar, eds., *Comércio Internacional e Comercialização Agrícola.* Viçosa: FINEP, FAPEMIG.

Rajapatirana, Sajath. 1996. "Trade Policies, Macroeconomic Adjustment, and Manufactured Exports: The Latin American Experience." *Weltwirtschaftliches Archiv* 132, no. 3.

Rego, E. C. L. 1996. "Do GATT à OMC: O Que Mudou, Como Funciona e Para Onde Caminha O Sistema Multilateral de Comércio." BNDES, *Texto para Discussão*, no. 51.

Rodrik, D. 1996. "Understanding Economic Policy Reform." *Journal of Economic Literature* 34 (March).

Ros, J. 1993. "La Reforma del Régimen Comercial en México Durante los Años Ochenta: Sus Efectos Económicos y Dimensiones Políticas." CEPAL, *Serie Reformas de Política Pública*, no. 4.

Serra, J., et al. 1997. *Reflections on Regionalism—Report of the Study Group on International Trade.* Washington, D.C.: Carnegie Endowment for International Peace, The Brookings Institution.

Tussie, D. 1996. "Políticas Comerciales y Compromisos en la Organización Mundial del Comercio." CEPAL, Doc. LC/R.1672, July.

Tyler, W. 1976. *Manufactured Export Expansion and Industrialization in Brazil.* Kieler Studien 134. Tübingen: J. C. B. Mohr.

Winters, L. A. 1997. "Assessing Regional Integration Arrangements." Paper presented at the Third Annual Conference on Development in Latin America and the Caribbean, Montevideo, June 30.

Yeats, A. 1997. "Does Mercosur's Trade Performance Raise Concerns About the Effects of Regional Trade Arrangements?" *Policy Research Working Paper No. 1729.* World Bank, February.

3

Industrial Competitiveness Policies in Latin America and the Caribbean in the 1990s

WILSON PERES

Industrial competitiveness policies, after being largely ignored during the second half of the 1980s,[1] are very much back on the table in Latin America and the Caribbean in the 1990s.[2] This return has taken place in countries that differ greatly in size and economic structure, and over the optimal extent of government intervention in the economy. Outstanding examples of this comeback are the industrial policy programs launched in Brazil, Mexico, and Jamaica in 1996, the continuity of the efforts initiated two years before in Colombia, and an increase in the amount, as well as the intensity, of the policy measures implemented in Chile since the beginning of the 1990s. Discussions about the importance to be assigned to competitiveness policies also have an outstanding position in public and private debates in Bolivia, Costa Rica, Peru, Uruguay, and Venezuela. Indeed, most of the governments in this region have entered the debate about the need to implement industrial competitiveness policies and the emphasis they should give to policy measures that impact on industry structure and dynamism.

The decline of traditional industrial policy that started in the early 1980s was the result of an ideological change that emphasized the role of the private sector as a development agent, reducing the role that the governments in this region have traditionally played in development. This was an effect, not only of an ideological change in the same direction occurring in the

A Spanish version of this chapter has appeared as the first chapter of Wilson Peres, ed., *Políticas de Competitividad Industrial. América Latina y el Caribe en los años noventa* (Mexico City: Siglo XXI Editores, 1997). Carmen Carril and Rosalía Manchego from ECLAC prepared the current translation.

1. At a formal level, the main exception was Brazil, where in 1988 the so-called New Industrial Policy (Nova Politica Industrial) was elaborated. In fact, however, that policy was minimally implemented.

2. Although the terms "industrial policy" and "competitiveness policy" are used interchangeably in the literature, it is better to use "industrial policy" to refer to those policies aimed at increasing the density of the industrial structure through the creation of new manufacturing industries, and "competitiveness policy" to refer to those policies centered on efforts to raise the competitiveness of existing sectors to international levels (Gassmann 1994). Naturally, industrial competitiveness policies would be those specially directed to the industrial sector of an economy. These semantic distinctions could help to clarify the discussions that employ either term.

United States and the United Kingdom toward the late 1970s, but also, and probably mainly, of the failure of past industrial policies to adapt to a new context determined by the current technological revolution in the world and trade liberalization in the region.

Nevertheless, the return of competitiveness policies has not meant, practically in any case, going back to the past. This renewed interest operates in an economic, institutional, and policy context fundamentally different from that prevailing less than a decade before. The substance of the policy itself has changed, as well as the method used to link it to the behavior of economic agents. The aim of this chapter is to analyze the causes of this renewed interest in industrial competitiveness policies, the changes they present regarding traditional industrial policies in the region, and the opportunities this reappearance opens. To accomplish these objectives, this chapter is based on studies prepared by the ECLAC/UNDP Regional Project on Competitiveness and Innovation Policies (RLA/88/039), which show the main contents of the industrial competitiveness policies in Brazil, Chile, Colombia, Costa Rica, Jamaica, Mexico, and Uruguay as of mid-1996 (Peres, forthcoming). Furthermore, the experiences of other countries of the region will also be incorporated when useful.

The new interest on industrial competitiveness policies in Latin America and the Caribbean operates in a context characterized by a few important facts.

1. At an international level, there exists a clear trend toward the consensus that, at least in theory, industrial policies—when accepted in spite of recommendations by the prevailing economic theory—must essentially have a horizontal scope and be aimed at "leveling the playing field" by correcting clearly identified market failures and giving support to industry as a whole through improvement of the operation of markets for its production factors. Particularly, these policies should include the prevention of monopolistic structures and practices, the strengthening of property rights, improvements in the access to information and training, and the supplying of physical, and in some cases technological, infrastructure (OECD 1992).
2. The previous approach is much less accepted in practice than in theory for two reasons. On one side, for many governments, including those of developed countries, it is politically unacceptable not to be involved in industrial matters that have negative impacts on employment in specific regions, and on some sectoral performances that may affect the public's perception about national competitiveness and technological

dynamism.[3] On the other hand, lessons from the experiences of successful East Asian economies are still present, at least for those who estimate that such success was strongly based on highly interventionist industrial policies. Those lessons have not been wiped out, in spite of important policy changes in those countries in the last decade, and in spite of the fact that these policies were formulated and carried out in an international context that no longer exists.

3. In the Latin American and Caribbean policy arena, there is a clear theoretical and practical predominance of policies directed to achieve or preserve *macroeconomic* stability. The new industrial competitiveness policies have not been designed as an alternative to the prevailing macroeconomic policies—which would not be possible—but only as a complement to achieve competitiveness and economic growth at a rhythm not provided by macroeconomic actions. On the other hand, at least in theory, industrial competitiveness policies accept the irreversibility of structural changes that have led to stabilization: trade liberalization, privatization of most of the manufacturing industries previously owned by the state, economic leadership by the private sector, and increasingly stronger regional integration schemes. In this framework, industrial competitiveness policies have adjusted to a general context, which tends to consider them, at best, as a "necessary evil" (De Band 1994).

4. Economic growth in the region during the 1990s has been mediocre,[4] in spite of the hopes aroused by progress made in resolving the problem of the external debt toward the end of the 1980s. In this context, the industrial sector's performance has been inferior to the total GDP: 2.2 percent and 2.9 percent annually respectively during 1990–94, that is, before the second Mexican crisis (CEPAL 1996b). This is the basis for positions that suggest that industry is no longer the engine of growth, as it clearly was during the import substitution industrialization stage (Katz et al. 1996). The industrial sector has also lost importance as a source of new jobs; and everything suggests that—in the medium term, while the current technological revolution is under way— employment creation will most probably be very small or even negative, as in recent years.

3. This is extremely clear in the United States, as well as the European Union, especially with regard to their textile, steel, automobiles, and aerospace industries (Ferguson and Ferguson 1994).

4. The good performance of countries like Chile and Colombia, although important for policy lessons, is not large enough to change the overall figures for the region.

5. The industrial structure in the region has experienced important changes regarding five variables: (a) a strong increase in the production and exports of large capital-intensive commodities, such as petrochemicals in Mexico and Venezuela, steel in Brazil, vegetable oils in Argentina, and cellulose in Chile (Katz et al. 1996); (b) an increasing importance of assembly operations in export processing zones in northern Mexico, Central America, and the Caribbean; (c) a renewed leadership of the automobile industry in a context of an almost general decline in the remaining metal-mechanic industries; (d) scant development of the most modern industries, such as, for example, those related to the production of sophisticated electrical and electronic goods, which continue to be, in most countries, only assembly operations with low local content of key components; and (e) a breakdown in the importance of traditional labor-intensive industries, such as textiles, garments, and footwear. These changes have led industrial competitiveness policies to consider (a) and (b) as activities with revealed comparative advantages, (c) as a sector deserving a special policy regime, (d) as sectors to be promoted at least in theory, and (e) as activities that must be restructured or rescued because of the social impact their breakdown could cause.

6. The region's industry has increased its export competitiveness and is learning to operate in an open and extremely dynamic international market. Nevertheless, this improvement is concentrated in a rather reduced group of firms, usually large ones, which have efficiently adjusted their strategies to the new reality. Productivity in the region continues to be much below the international technological frontier, and there is no indication that this gap is being closed (Ramos 1996). This concentration of technical progress and its benefits has increased the dualism in the region's industrial structure, as well as strengthened the need for policies to foster the integration of small and medium-sized firms into the dynamism of the modern sector.

7. Even though there is very little research on the structure of industrial agents, everything points out that subsidiaries of multinational corporations continue to be leaders in industrial sectors that produce durable consumer goods and modern nondurable consumer goods. Conglomerates (holdings) of large private domestic firms continue to dominate sectors that produce industrial commodities and traditional capital-intensive consumer goods. This structure has been minimally modified by the privatization of state-owned enterprises because of the relatively small state ownership of manufacturing industries and also because they have been acquired by national as well as foreign enter-

prises, although in shares that vary from country to country. The strengthening of the national conglomerates is evident in the dynamism with which they have undertaken strategic alliances and joint ventures with foreign enterprises and their incipient internationalization through foreign direct investment, first in Latin America and later in the United States and Western Europe. Small and medium-sized enterprises continue to operate in their traditional areas (labor-intensive consumer goods), although they face increasing difficulties caused by foreign competition.

8. The Latin American and Caribbean countries have privatized most of their manufacturing activities. In spite of the reduction in the size and number of public sector agencies and enterprises, governments continue to be the largest economic agents in the region. The weakness usually ascribed to them is more the result of an ideological defeat of state interventionism and the loss of qualified workers because of their salary policy, than of a significant reduction of their capability to collect resources via taxes and tariffs, to direct their procurement power toward national and local policy goals, and to manage the largest enterprises in the region (for example, PETROBRAS in Brazil, PEMEX in Mexico, PDVSA in Venezuela, ECOPETROL in Colombia, and CODELCO in Chile).[5]

The revival of industrial competitiveness policies has taken place in this framework and has basically been a reaction to it. However, beyond those general determinants, such policies have essentially responded to national demands. Therefore, to understand them properly it is necessary to analyze policy dynamics at the country level, which requires an understanding of the region's diversity.

CURRENT POLICIES

Leaving aside many country characteristics, industrial competitiveness policy initiatives in the seven Latin American and Caribbean countries analyzed in this chapter can be divided into three groups. Each one of those groups shares some basic policy characteristics and methods, despite the big economic differences among the countries included.

5. PEMEX, PETROBRAS, PDVSA, and ECOPETROL are oil companies. CODELCO is a copper mining firm.

The first group consists of those countries which have a formal industrial strategy that is integrated in a specific industrial program that is part of a general economic development strategy. This group—Brazil, Mexico, and Jamaica—is also the only one that takes the region's industrial policy tradition fully into account, despite the important differences of their current policy approaches from those prevailing in the past. This was to be expected, given the fact that these countries have a long experience in policy design.

The contents of the policy documents issued in 1996 reveal the approach shared by the countries of this group: "Política Industrial, Tecnológica y de Comercio Exterior" (Industrial, Technological and Foreign Trade Policy in Brazil), "Programa de Política Industrial y Comercio Exterior" (Industrial and Foreign Trade Policy Program in Mexico), and National Industrial Policy in Jamaica. In this group, predominant policies have a horizontal scope, that is to say, they do not discriminate between different industries. However, in every document, considerations are included, although not always precise, about vertical or sectoral policies, as in the case of the promotion of specific industrial clusters in Mexico or strategic activities with revealed competitive advantages in Jamaica. In this context the most surprising element has been recognition, by Mexico, of the importance of strengthening production chains that have been weakened by trade liberalization, in spite of the benefits trade liberalization implied regarding productivity and quality improvement in the industrial sector in general.

The second group is made up of the Central American and Andean countries, where progressively general *competitiveness* policy approaches tend to predominate; those policy perspectives being directly or indirectly based on the methodology of Michael Porter's *The Competitiveness Advantage of Nations* (see Porter 1993). An outstanding example of policies originated from this approach is that developed in Colombia since mid-1994. In this case, strategy is not based on a vision of industrial development, but on the pursuit of an increasing competitiveness of industries, agriculture, and services through the creation of competitiveness advantages in specific clusters, which are materialized at the subregional or local levels. Examples of this approach are the proposals for increasing competitiveness of economic activities clustered around five Colombian cities (Barranquilla, Bucaramanga, Cali, Cartagena, and Medellín), Arequipa in Peru, and Santa Cruz de la Sierra in Bolivia, as well as more traditional sectoral proposals oriented toward activities such as textiles and garments, graphic industries, chemicals and petrochemicals, tourism, and agriculture.

Most of the recent policy perspectives in this group of countries are based, sometimes even by opposition, on the proposals of a consulting firm linked to Michael Porter's Monitor Company, which has designed, since 1992, policies and actions to increase enterprise competitiveness in Colombia, Peru, Bolivia, and Venezuela. Those proposals are directed at increasing the awareness of the political and economic agents of the need to develop competitive advantages based on a competitiveness vision shared by private and public sectors. From this starting point, they design specific actions, generally very precisely defined, for the development of production factors, increasing linkages within industry clusters, improving the quality of domestic demand, and strengthening strategy design and rivalry among competitors.

Although not always accepted and very seldom implemented in the mentioned countries, Monitor's proposals have increased the attention business sectors pay to competitiveness and opened a space for competitiveness policies in governments as different in their approaches to state intervention as those of President Samper in Colombia and President Fujimori in Peru. On the other hand, Monitor's principal shortcoming has been to overestimate the abilities of the governments in question to implement its policy recommendations, even taking into account that their proposals include policies and actions that cost little and are rather easy to execute.

In Central America, similar policy perspectives have been present, mostly based on the results of a project on the competitiveness of the region's production chains developed by the Federation of Private Sector Organizations of Central America and Panama, with financial support from the Inter-American Development Bank (FEDEPRICAP 1994). After the project was complete, the main industrial chambers of the countries in the region fostered the idea of designing an agenda for industrial modernization in Central America,[6] to promote greater capital accumulation, a more efficient allocation of resources, more productivity, and stronger linkages among industrial firms (CEPAL and ONUDI 1996). Beyond this proposal, the *Strategy for Industrial Modernisation in Costa Rica* of September 1994 establishes policy commitments to increase competitiveness through instruments of horizontal and sectoral impact. The strategy proposed in this document is intended to combine a global approach to attain "dynamic competitive advantages" with actions designed to improve the "competitive diamond" of specific industrial chains (MEIC-MICIT 1996).

Finally, a third group of countries (Chile and Uruguay) are implementing actions to increase competitiveness, starting not from an analysis of

---

6. The leader in this process was the Federation of Central American Industry Chambers and Associations (FECAICA). The *Agenda* has obtained support from the ministers in charge of industrial policy in the region and from the Permanent Secretariat of the General Treaty of Central American Economic Integration (SIECA).

overall industrial policy or competitiveness, but from an emphasis on policy instruments of only horizontal impact. These actions progressively tend to focus their attention on business demands of technological and training assistance, which also tend to be provided through "mediating" non-governmental organizations. In their most advanced stage, as in the case of Chile, these policies increasingly seek, at least in theory, the creation of an "industrial atmosphere" leading to development of "associative" endeavors through the establishment of "local networks of innovators" (Bianchi and Bellini 1991; Dini 1995).

In those countries, governments do not aim actions at specific industries, except in the very special cases of activities with serious problems, to help these industries carry on their restructuring process in the current context of economic integration, for example, the creation of the Southern Common Market (MERCOSUR). In these cases, sectoral policies are the result of focusing already existing policy instruments on specific geographical areas, particularly those affected by negative sectoral dynamics.

ANALYTICAL PERSPECTIVE

A preliminary analysis of the policies presented in this chapter indicates a predominance of policies that seek to accelerate the operation of markets ("accelerative" industry policies, according to Ferguson and Ferguson 1994) over those directed to stop or retard it. In other words, current policies are progressive, as long as their goal is not to avoid technological and structural change, but to implement instruments that allow such change to take place swiftly and efficiently. This is important because the revival of industrial competitiveness policies could have had the purpose of avoiding changes, or at least retarding them; however, this does not seem to be the case, even in countries like Colombia and Mexico where current competitiveness policies strongly diverge from those of governments in office at the beginning of the 1990s.

The survival of the belief that governments are able, through their policies, to accelerate and reduce costs of a process of change—by making it more efficient—was not obvious five years ago, when everything suggested that *neutral* policies, which only try to improve the operation of markets, would be dominating. The most common laissez-faire policies (protection against unfair competition, clear allocation of intangible property rights, reduction of transaction costs, for example) have played a minor role in comparison to policies directed to replace or correct market mechanisms in order to speed up changes (export promotion, technology diffusion, human resources development, and small-enterprise modernization). But resistance to a strict laissez-faire regime has not implied a return to the sort of industrial planning intervention that prevailed in the region up to the late 1970s.

From a general perspective, several trends can be identified underlying the policies of the three groups of policy approaches previously analyzed.

1. Policies no longer stress the development of new industries, but the efforts to increase the efficiency of industries already existing in each country. This means that countries are actually designing industrial competitiveness policies, not industrial policies as they were traditionally understood.[7]

2. Closely related to (1), and to the increasing importance of industrial commodities producers in the region already mentioned, policies have tended to strengthen the existing pattern of comparative advantages, more than the creation of new competitive advantages. Although in many countries the expression "transform comparative advantages into competitive advantages" has been fully incorporated into business and political language, actual concentration of policy actions in the promotion of efficiency of existing industries—that is to say, the industries that survived the adjustment process—has made such a transformation a secondary priority.[8]

3. In spite of the importance of formal political definitions issued by many of the countries in the region, the contents and the timing of most important policies of the decade (stabilization, trade liberalization, privatization, and negotiation of trade agreements, including the World Trade Organization) have determined the approach to competitiveness policies and, much more important, the region's industrial structure and dynamism. These structural change policies have actually been *implicit* industrial competitiveness policies, generally with a clear sectoral impact. What has been previously called the revival of industrial competitiveness policies actually has been mostly the revival of *explicit* policies, once the package of *implicit* policies was accepted.

7. Definitions of industrial policy are innumerable; but, at the end they can be summarized as policy actions that try to change the production vector of the industrial sector. A recent revision of different definitions and scopes of such policy may be seen in Ferguson and Ferguson 1994, chap. 7, or in Bianchi et al. 1994.

8. This is especially clear in the low priority currently given to policy objectives such as "to move into a second export stage" (that is to say, one more intensive in manufactures of high value added), which was widely accepted in Chile at the beginning of the 1990s.

4. Regional integration processes have had opposite impacts on policy design. Although the opening-up to larger world markets has increased competition and, therefore, improved the efficiency of market mechanisms, it has also granted new strength to sectoral policies for at least two reasons. First, it has forced relatively noninterventionist governments, such as Chile's, to confront the sectoral dimension because of the heterogeneous impacts of integration over the different regions of the country. Second, as it began to be appreciated when the North American Free Trade Agreement (NAFTA) was negotiated, international trade agreements are negotiated on a sectoral or product basis. Therefore, such negotiations make governments pay attention to the sectoral dimension, even those governments that would prefer not to discriminate among industries.[9] This is clearly shown in the reversal of the previous trend toward a flat tariff structure in most countries of the region. At least for the mid-term such a trend has been reversed as a result of reciprocal or unilateral concessions between countries negotiating trade agreements.

5. Policy action in the region is strongly concentrated in four different types of policy instruments: export promotion (definitely the most important), support innovation and technology diffusion, human resources development, and small and medium enterprise development. Less developed, but equally pervasive, are policies oriented toward deregulation and reduction of bureaucratic requirements for the setting-up or operation of industries. These efforts try to reduce this important component of what has been called "country cost," which degrades the competitive position of firms.

6. Similar policy perspectives and instruments in countries as different as Brazil and Costa Rica or Mexico and Jamaica give rise to two questions. First, what is the origin of such similarities and have they been caused by a successful international transfer of policy experiences or by the imitation, based on fast readings, of a set of instruments generally accepted in the specialized literature? Second, to what extent have trade liberalization and globalization of some relevant markets reduced the importance of structural differences among countries, such as domestic market size? Probably the best answer (although an optimistic one) is that structural changes have forced firms and regions to

---

9. This is particularly outstanding in the case of the automobile industry, which always obtains advantages that imply that free trade is once again postponed for a significant period. This is so, from the NAFTA to the MERCOSUR, including Chile's negotiations with this latter group as well as with Mexico.

compete in world markets, eliminating the advantages previously provided by a trade regime that allowed a privileged access to their national markets. More open markets, therefore, have reduced the impact of national economic differences, allowing policy experiences disseminated by international organizations and consulting firms to be reasonably imitated.

7. International transfer of policy experiences may explain why there are so few *new* policy instruments in the region. Such a transfer rapidly disseminates new policy lines and instruments and tends to generate a common sense about what is a modern and viable package of instruments. One of the few exceptions in this situation are the projects to promote the development of association among small enterprises (PROFOS), which have been implemented in Chile since 1991.

8. Industrial policies are increasingly being designed and implemented at a decentralized level, particularly in the largest countries. This is shown by the competition for new investment among different Brazilian states, as well as in the designing of new industrial development programs at the subnational level in Colombia and Mexico. Even in smaller countries, the local dimension is gaining strength.[10] Three mechanisms are frequently used in the competition for new investment projects: fiscal incentives, the creation of an economic and institutional environment favorable to business, and the creation of production factors needed for stronger firm competitiveness. The results of those instruments have not yet been evaluated, but it is clear that they may lead either to negative- or to positive-sum games. Thus, incentive-based competition ("fiscal war") will probably result in negative-sum games, while rules-based or factor-creation competition may have much better results.

9. In contrast to the emphasis on some policy instruments, others have lost presence and, more important, acceptance. Such is the case of subsidized credit, direct fiscal incentives (although they are currently used to support technological research in Brazil, for example, and workers' training and the opening of new markets or new exports in Chile), the *ad hoc* management of tariff and nontariff barriers to trade (despite the almost permanent readjustments of the common external tariff by Brazil and Argentina during the implementation of the MERCOSUR) and public sector procurement (despite its significant return in the 1996 Mexican industrial policy).

10. For example, the Araucania region in Chile designed a policy proposal in 1996 to foster its development in the context of a closer integration with the MERCOSUR.

10. On the other hand, there is only an incipient development of industrial decentralization policies, competition policies, which, with very few exceptions, currently exist only in the law; environment protection, which is more a subject for speeches than for action; and gender discrimination reduction or prevention in the industry, which rarely are considered even in speeches.

11. Sectoral policies continue to be in a rather ambiguous situation; countries still do not know how to tackle them, despite their growing acceptance in policy discourse (industrial clusters in Mexico, leading activity groups in Venezuela, sectoral policy agreements in Colombia). These policies have been the most damaged when protection, direct fiscal incentives, and subsidized credit were eliminated. Sectoral policies tend to be understood in two different ways. Sometimes a sector or industry is the focus for preexisting horizontal instruments, as in the case of the restructuring of coal mining in Chile. In other cases, a sector is the object of ad hoc policies exceptionally implemented because of its economic or political importance, as in the case of the automobile industry in most of the producer countries of the region. In brief, neither Latin America, nor the Caribbean (as shown by Jamaica), nor the rest of the world (De Band 1994) knows how to implement industrial targeting without protection and direct subsidies.

12. Finally, it is necessary to emphasize that in spite of progress made to narrow the focus of industrial competitiveness policies, they still tend to look like answers to long lists of conditions necessary to improve competitiveness (*laundry lists*). This situation makes it rather difficult for governments to make sound policy decisions. As indicated in a previous work (Peres 1994), the best contribution that policy analysts and economic agents could make to the improvement of policy design in the region would be to move from the conceptualization of numerous *necessary* conditions to the selection of a few conditions which they consider to be *sufficient* for industrial competitiveness.

IMPLEMENTATION FAILURES

The previous analysis shows that the Latin American and Caribbean countries have improved significantly their capabilities to design industrial policies and have also adjusted such policies to the new characteristics of the international marketplace; however, implementation capabilities in the region are still meager, as is shown by programs that are never implemented or by programs that have not had any relevant impact in spite of, or perhaps because of, their ambitious objectives. This poor implementation capability, which has become a real bottleneck to the strengthening of the impact of industrial competitiveness policies in the region (Peres 1994), is the result of several determinants which combine to produce such an effect.

1. The major problem is the gap between design and implementation, which is a characteristic in most of those countries. This gap has at least two dimensions. On one hand, ministries responsible for the design of industrial policy do not normally control the policy instruments necessary for their execution. This is especially clear in the cases related to tariffs, fiscal incentives, and industrial or export financing, which tend to be in the orbit of the Treasury, while policy design lies within the Ministry of Industry. This gap explains why programs in the region are so ambiguous and why often they read more like research reports than actual policy documents.[11] Similar problems related to poor coordination and bureaucratic rivalry emerge also in other areas, such as science and technology, international economic negotiations, and competition policies.

2. Besides the bureaucratic inefficiency caused by these conflicts, their major cost is that the necessary balance between objectives and constraints is only considered after the fact. This allows policymakers to present highly ambitious objectives (for example, competitive integration into the world markets) at the same time that the agencies which implement policies face budgetary restrictions that allow only insignificant levels of expenditures to achieve these objectives. This problem is particularly evident in policy designs that include many objectives, but no goals, as is too frequently the case in the region.

3. Institutional failures in policy implementation are also caused by the lack of a policy *operator*, that is to say, an institution (not necessarily a state agency) able to lead the policy process. It is quite usual in the region to overestimate the importance of systemic or structural determinants, thus neglecting the role of leaders, either individuals or institutions. To improve policy implementation it is necessary to promote the development of the leadership capabilities and the political will of people and institutions that are in charge of policymaking or have to apply policy instruments.

11. Often such documents are filled with considerations like "mechanisms will be studied for. . . ." Sometimes, we find more considerations of this type than actual policy commitments.

4. Moreover, policy implementation is always more difficult and complex than policy design, and naturally more expensive. This greater complexity is caused by the fact that it is precisely during the implementation process when problems such as uncertainty, lack of information, and the operator's bounded rationality have to be faced. Thus, it is relatively easy to "pick winners" when designing policies and extremely difficult to use that selection as a sound basis for actual policy implementation. After more than a decade of budget reductions and in a context where government policy agencies have lost a significant part of their technical capabilities, policy complexity is particularly difficult to handle.

The progress the region has made regarding the transfer of successful policy design experiences seldom can be extended to institutional development, which plays an essential role in policy implementation. While it is relatively easy to replicate a successful policy design, it is far more difficult to replicate the institutional learning necessary to carry it out. Sometimes, even in the same country, it is difficult to replicate successful experiences in order to extend their impact beyond more than a few dozen enterprises.[12]

In general, implementation bottlenecks may be understood as a governance problem, that is to say a problem related to the power and the rules used in the management of economic resources for development. Implementation, as well as governance, is determined by several factors: (1) the degree of social consensus behind the policies; (2) the transparency and fairness of the rules of the game; (3) the quality of the government's actions; and (4) the responsiveness and accountability of those actions (Lahera 1996). In the particular case of industrial policies, lack of consensus, poor design of the rules, and absence of impact evaluations diminish the quality of the government's actions.

In this field, the most important improvements have been the agreements reached between the private and public sectors in the area of policy design. These agreements have been reached through different institutional arrangements. The following two are among the most significant ones.

First, there are the mechanisms for negotiation between business chambers (generally at their highest level) and the public agencies in charge of the industrial policies. Two recent examples are (1) the collaboration between

---

12. This is particularly true regarding the most successful institutions of the national systems for innovation in the region. Many countries are interested in replicating the experiences of such entities as the Chile Foundation, the Brazilian technological parks, and the Electric Research Institute of Mexico. However, it has been extremely difficult to reproduce these experiences, despite the fact that their most relevant features are well known (Dini and Peres 1995).

the Ministry of Trade and Industrial Promotion (Secretaría de Comercio y Fomento Industrial) and the Mexican Confederation of Industrial Chambers (Confederación de Cámaras Industriales de los Estados Unidos Mexicanos) in the elaboration of the *Programme of Industrial Policy and Foreign Trade* of May 1996; and (2) the cooperation between the Ministry of Industry and Trade (Ministerio de Fomento) and the Venezuelan Confederation of Industry (Confederación Venezolana de Industriales) in the design of *New Guidelines for a Negotiated Industrial Strategy*, announced in June of the same year. It is too early to evaluate the impact on policy implementation produced by these collaborative experiences, but it is already evident that the dialogue they implied has made it possible for the private sector—or at least a part of it, the large enterprises—to feel and present as their own a policy design that in the past would have been considered as governmental and strange.

Second, the creation of formal organizations—councils or boards—for policy negotiation is another mechanism used to generate agreements. These organizations have different institutional arrangements, but they always respond to the need of an arena to negotiate competitiveness issues, particularly regarding the industrial sector. Examples of these organizations which have developed since 1992 are the Brazilian industry negotiation boards (*camaras sectoriais*), the Industrial Policy Council in Costa Rica (Consejo Superior de Concertación de la Política Industrial), the National Competitiveness Board in Colombia (Consejo Nacional de Competitividad), and the Chilean Production Development Board (Foro de Desarrollo Productivo). Other examples are some current initiatives such as the creation of an Industrial Competitiveness Council in Bolivia (Consejo de Nacional de Competitividad) and an Industrial Development Council in Venezuela (Consejo de Desarrollo Industrial), as well as the implementation of a Competitiveness and Productivity National Council in Ecuador (Consejo Nacional de Productividad y Competitividad).[13]

A brief review of these experiences shows the variety of conditions that policy implementation must face in the region. The boards are different in their functions, institutional insertion, membership, and their members' power. In the case of Chile and Colombia, the functions of the boards are those of a consulting organization. In Brazil, the industry negotiation chambers are oriented toward decision making. Naturally, in the first case their

13. The National Agreement for the Advancement of Productivity and Quality (Acuerdo Nacional para la Productividad y la Calidad) in Mexico in 1992 could also have been included in this list, but lack of implementation made it almost irrelevant.

members can be individuals with no formal representation of business or labor organizations, while in the second case such representation is essential, since the agreements reached should be binding on all the members of those organizations.

Even when the boards of different countries may have similar functions, their institutional insertion and membership composition differ. Thus, for example, the Chilean Production Development Board is under the Industry Ministry, while the National Competitiveness Council of Colombia is integrated into the Presidency of the Republic. The boards always include as main actors the private and public sectors, while labor participation differs remarkably (from strong engagement as in Brazil to a reluctant participation as in Chile). The academic sector (universities) is formally included only in Colombia.

Although the private sector considers the competitiveness boards as adequate channels of communication with the authorities and also as a good source of information, it is still too early and very difficult to reach general conclusions from the experiences of the boards.

From an organizational perspective, it is possible to suggest that it seems to be more efficient to have rather small boards or councils (which can create working committees for specific tasks) so that they can meet frequently, have clearly defined missions within a predetermined time frame, and are connected to the highest decision-making level possible.[14] This last point prevents those boards from being seen as initiatives that favor the actions of particular ministries.

In relation to the incorporation of the academic and labor sectors, there are two aspects that deserve to be described. On the one hand, the incorporation of intellectuals is very useful in organizations that must constantly compare different experiences, present conclusions, and prepare documents. On the other, labor participation, although essential in competitiveness matters, has faced two types of problems: (1) lack of representatives with technical capability, and (2) the difficulty during labor conflicts of maintaining its representatives in a council that also includes employers' delegates. Finally, the advantage of having boards with a decision-making capability or just a consulting one strictly depends on the disposition and possibilities of the different national governments in sharing part of their power. Nevertheless, it is clear that granting decision-making capability motivates the private sector to assume a shared responsibility in policy management.

14. The National Competitiveness Council of Colombia has these characteristics. This entity seems to be the most efficient and has the lowest conflict level of the ones here analyzed.

A final mention of the driving forces behind these boards is useful to understanding their actual dimensions and implications. While in Colombia the private sector, particularly the large enterprises, was the force that promoted the creation of the National Competitiveness Council, in Brazil the sectoral chambers were answers to government initiatives strongly supported by proactive business and labor sectors. In the Chilean Production Development Board, the government has been the initial and permanent force, facing difficulties to obtain a stable labor presence and spontaneous business participation.

The operation of the competitiveness boards has had a significant impact on competitiveness policy design in the region; however, such operation has also shown that the social agreements required for policy design are not always sufficient for its implementation. The assumption that the policies are not always implemented, which is quite often made in the region, facilitates the process of negotiation to reach social agreements at the policy design level, since these tend to be supported by only very weak implementation commitments. The well-known management rule that indicates that a usual procedure to advance in the *quasi* resolution of conflicts is through nonoperational agreements that postpone difficult operational decisions is largely applied. This is a real problem: ambitious competitiveness policies often tend to be based on formal (empty) social agreements even if they are nonoperational. Therefore, in this framework frequent new negotiations of policy design agreements are much more the rule than the exception.

The competitiveness policy boards have fully operated as a way to legitimize those policies and at least partially as mechanisms to improve their efficiency. This combination of legitimacy and efficiency is the boards' most important contribution to policy implementation and, therefore, to economic governance. Actually, the boards have supported the substitution of a *substantive* rationality approach to policy decisions—which is very difficult to achieve because of the dynamism and uncertainty prevailing in the market place previously mentioned—by a *procedural* approach to rationality (De Band 1994). Thus, the application of the *right* policymaking mechanism becomes a means to reach a *right* decision, that is to say a decision that may be implemented. This logic may not be perfect, but it seems to work efficiently.

Another dimension of this *procedural* rationality that tends to be extensively accepted is that of the *decentralization* of competitiveness policies to return managerial capabilities and power to the states, provinces, and counties. In this case, the *rightness* of the policies is a result, not only of their *substantive* contents, but also of the fact that their implementation agents and direct beneficiaries have participated in their design. There are important reasons to promote the idea that competitiveness policies should no longer be limited to the national dimension, but should become authentically decentralized. Two of those reasons are (1) to facilitate a country's adaptation to a new international trade environment by fostering a set of comparative advantages different than the one prevailing in the past, and (2) to be able to grant subsidies that are admissible (*green*) for the World Trade Organisation (WTO). However, the potential impact of decentralization on the policies' legitimacy and efficiency, in the sense previously used, must not be underestimated.

This might not be the ideal approach to the subject; but it implies a real progress from past approaches to industrial decentralization—or industrial deconcentration without any transfer of power to the local levels—which were no more than instruments to correct or reduce economic concentration in a few development poles.

The mechanisms to foster policy consensus and promote decentralization open a real possibility to progress in policy implementation. Moreover, they can be efficiently combined with another characteristic that policies in the region are acquiring: to be efficient parts of a *work agenda* (or road map) instead of being an element of a formal plan or program. Such agendas specify strategies and open the possibility of applying instruments and policy lines—some of which are not even defined in the policy documents— that will be determined by negotiation during implementation, sometimes at a decentralized level. The 1996 industrial policies of Brazil and Mexico may adequately be defined as *work agendas,* and are considered as such by their public and private authors.

PROGRESS, OBSTACLES, AND OPPORTUNITIES

The revival of industrial policies in the 1990s is a clear advance from when it was believed that the operation of the market mechanisms, developed by the radical and necessary structural changes of the 1980s, would be sufficient to assure economic growth, as well as social justice.

Industrial competitiveness policies reappeared with great strength in most of the Latin American and Caribbean countries because the economic context generated by the laissez-faire approach to policies did not fulfill the expectations it had raised, or, at least, not with the speed that some analysts and politicians had ingenuously expected. In this sense, one of the most important lessons from the Chilean experience had not been understood;

that is to say, the long period of business and institutional learning needed to get positive results regarding growth and employment once the structural changes began. Moreover, the 1996 industrial and foreign trade program of Mexico shows very clearly that it is feasible to make important changes in the main competitiveness policies of the country while keeping within the framework of orthodox macroeconomic policy. Thus reality has proved wrong the assumption that, given an orthodox macroeconomic policy, there was only one possible industrial strategy: no policy at all.

The strengthening of the competitiveness policies in Chile *also* deserves special mention. In this case, the policies did not emerge as a reaction to slow growth, but from the government's perception that the factors behind fast growth from the late 1980s through the mid-1990s could not be replicated in the future and that, in some cases, they are already being exhausted. Among the forces difficult to replicate are all those that had a "once and for all" impact, for example, the opening up of the economy from a previous situation in which extreme protectionism prevailed or a fast and radical privatization process. Among the factors that are being exhausted, the most relevant one is the possibility of maintaining a strongly undervalued exchange rate in the long term, as well as low real wages. So, the Chilean government decided to put in place competitiveness policies in the fields of technology promotion and human resource development to accelerate new competitive advantages of the country, beyond those derived from relatively abundant natural resources and cheap labor. Moreover, export promotion policies in Chile are mostly the result of a persistent belief, prevailing since the late 1970s, that the new external markets—particularly for nontraditional products—are not already opened, but that they *should* be opened in a joint effort of private entrepreneurs with governmental support (Macario 1996).

The most important weakness of policy design in the region is how to make compatible the new policy context with the will of several countries to develop sectoral (industry level) policies. It is difficult to imagine a mid-term scenario where *comprehensive* sectoral programs—with goals, action lines, and financial resources directly attached—will be again designed in the region. However, progress in this field is still possible if future policy design recognizes that horizontal policy lines have heterogeneous sectoral impacts, since not all industrial sectors require new technologies and qualified human resources with similar intensity. Thus the design of instruments of horizontal scope should incorporate an estimate of their potential sectoral impact, or conversely, those instruments may be designed with the purpose of supporting the industrial sectors that use them most intensively and frequently.

It is important to emphasize that although competitiveness policies are stronger in those countries where no fast results were obtained from structural changes, they are not aimed at reversing those changes or slowing their speed. In spite of this fact, there has been a strong tendency to subordinate competitiveness policies to macroeconomic stabilization policies, in terms of their perceived relevance and in the timing of their implementation.

To accept this perspective is a mistake, since stabilization itself is only feasible in the mid-term if structural change also takes place, which involves several *implicit components of competitiveness policy*. Without ignoring the political impacts on the legitimacy of the governments associated with every success or failure in each stabilization effort, competitiveness policies must be complementary to and simultaneous with each stabilization effort. This should be so because a stabilized environment has a strong impact on competitiveness, as well as the fact that only strong and sustained productivity growth in the long term makes the results of the stabilization process structurally feasible and sustainable. To advance in this field it is necessary to integrate microeconomic and macroeconomic perspectives (Katz 1996), despite the complexity of the theoretical and analytical task involved. To focus on the institutional changes required to materialize the results of the competitiveness policies—the reform of the savings and investment system, for example—may be an efficient way to reduce this complexity.

The progress of policy design in the region must be accompanied as soon as possible by progress in the implementation and evaluation of policy impacts. Concentration of the best human resources of government in planning and designing policies has already given its results. In most countries of the region, it is necessary to seriously face the possibility of transferring those resources toward the implementation and evaluation areas, where the government's actions are weakest.

The equivalent of this proposal for the private sector is to continue strengthening business chambers as intermediate-level organizations capable of participating in the policy implementation process. A modern competitiveness policy is one that provides information, supports business efforts regarding technology diffusion and human resources development, and facilitates the export process. And as a modern business chamber is one that provides services to its members in the same areas, the possibilities of achieving synergy in both efforts are very high.[15] However, it is necessary to

15. The experiences of the Association of Manufacturing Exporters (Asociación de Exportadores de Manufacturas) in the implementation of projects to promote small enterprises in Chile, and the Colombian Association of Plastic Industries (Asociación Colombiana de Industrias Plásticas) in establishing a sectoral technology and training center, are lessons that should be taken into account. On the other side, the experience of the Brazilian confederation of labor

strengthen the technical capabilities of these chambers, so that they may become organizations that provide useful services to their members, overcoming their traditional role in the region, which up until now has been to lobby for trade protection and public contracts for their members (León 1995).

The combination of public efforts to make more efficient the policy implementation and evaluation processes with private efforts to strengthen its chambers in order to actively participate in materializing competitiveness policies will help overcome several situations in which consensus about policies does not result in actions. In other words, it will help to close the enormous gap between *theoretical* strategies and *applied* strategies that prevails in the region (Monitor Company 1994 and 1995).

Finally, it is important, at least for those who defend the idea that competitiveness policies are necessary, particularly for developing countries (Ramos 1996), to be aware that a *window of opportunity* has been opened but that it will not remain open forever. For just as these policies were revived because the promises of laissez-faire were not kept, fast and concrete results will also be expected from them; all the more so when they are still considered by many analysts and politicians as a "necessary evil." To keep this window of opportunity open demands impact and action; once again implementation is of the essence.

REFERENCES

Bianchi, P., and N. Bellini. 1991. "Public Policies for Local Networks of Innovators." *Research Policy* 20.
Bianchi, P., K. Cowling, and R. Sugden, eds. 1994. *Europe's Economic Challenge: Analyses of Industrial Strategy and Agenda for the 1990s*. London: Routledge.
CEPAL (Comisión Económica para América Latina y el Caribe). 1996a. *América Latina y el Caribe: 15 años de desempeño económico*. Santiago: CEPAL.
———. 1996b. *Balance Preliminar de América Latina y el Caribe*. Santiago: CEPAL.
CEPAL and ONUDI. 1996. *Centroamérica: Agenda para la modernización industrial*. San José, Costa Rica, and Mexico City: CEPAL.
De Band, J. 1994. "Policy Mix and Industrial Strategies." In P. Bianchi, K. Cowling, and R. Sugden, eds., *Europe's Economic Challenge: Analyses of Industrial Strategy and Agenda for the 1990s*. London: Routledge.
Dini, M. 1995. *Dalle politiche guidata dalla domanda alle politiche per le articolazione: Il caso del Cile*. Santiago: CORFO.

unions CUT (Central Unica de Trabalhadores) indicates that it is possible to expect a similar synergy if labor is also integrated into the national efforts toward competitiveness.

Dini, M., and W. Peres. 1995. "Sistemas de innovación en América Latina: Experiencias locales y apoyo institucional." In Pontificia Universidad Javeriana, ed., *Política Industrial y Desarrollo Tecnológico: Lecciones para el caso colombiano.* Bogota: Centro Editorial Javeriano.

FEDEPRICAP. 1994. *Competitividad de los sectores productivos de Centroamérica y Panamá.* San Jose, Costa Rica: FEDEPRICAP.

Ferguson, P. R., and G. J. Ferguson. 1994. *Industrial Economics. Issues and Perspectives.* 2d ed. London: Macmillan.

Gassmann, H. 1994. "From Industrial Policy to Competitiveness Policies." *OECD Observer,* no. 187 (April-May).

Katz, J. 1996. "Interacciones entre lo micro y lo macro y su manifestación en el ámbito de la producción industrial." In J. Katz, ed., *Estabilización macroeconómica, reforma estructural y comportamiento industrial: Estructura y funcionamiento del sector manufacturero latinoamericano en los años 90.* Buenos Aires: ECLAC/IDRC and Alianza Editorial.

Katz, J., J. M. Benavente, G. Crespi, and G. Stumpo. 1996. *Nuevos problemas y oportunidades en el desarrollo industrial de América Latina.* Santiago: ECLAC, Division of Production, Productivity and Management.

Lahera, E. 1996. *Aspectos económicos de la gobernabilidad.* Santiago: ECLAC.

León, L. V. 1995. *Fortalecimiento de gremios empresariales en América Latina.* Serie Desarrollo Productivo, 29. Santiago: ECLAC.

Macario, C. 1996. *Experiencias exitosas de exportación: Las principales lecciones de Brasil, Chile, Colombia y México.* Santiago: ECLAC, Division of Production, Productivity and Management.

MEIC-MICIT. 1996. *Política de modernización industrial. Un pueblo en marcha. Informe de la Gestión 1994-1996.* San José, Costa Rica: Ministerio de Economía, Industria y Comercio, June.

Monitor Company. 1994. *Creando la ventaja competitiva de Colombia, Resumen Ejecutivo.* Medellín: Cámara de Comercio de Medellín.

———. 1995. *Construyendo las ventajas competitivas del Perú: Región Arequipa.* Boston: Monitor Company.

OECD (Organisation for Economic Co-operation and Development). 1992. *Industrial Policy in OECD Countries. Annual Review, 1992.* Paris: OECD.

Peres, W. 1994. "Policies for Competitiveness." *CEPAL Review* (Santiago) 53.

———, ed. Forthcoming. *Políticas de competitividad industrial en América Latina y el Caribe en los Años Noventa.*

Porter, Michael. 1993. *The Competitive Advantage of Nations: The New Paradigm for Company Competitiveness and Global Strategy.* Boston: Harvard Business School Management Programs.

Ramos, J. 1996. *Política industrial y competitividad en economía abiertas.* Santiago: ECLAC, Division of Production, Productivity and Management.

Investment Promotion Policies in Latin America

ROBERT GROSSE

The Latin American experience with foreign direct investment (FDI) has been quite a rollercoaster ride over the past four decades. Before the arrival of inward-looking direct investment policies in the 1960s, Latin American countries generally offered foreign companies relatively unrestricted opportunity to bring in their capital, skills and technology. In exchange for these inflows, the foreign companies were largely allowed to remit their after-tax profits, pay royalties for technology and skill transfers, and generally operate similarly to local companies.

This policy environment and outlook changed dramatically during the 1960s, when the so-called *Cepalista* influence took hold through the region. The influence of the United Nations Center on Latin America (CEPAL) was disproportionately large, given the small resources mobilized by the UN in the region. However, the policy recommendations coming from the CEPAL analysts (led by Raul Prebisch) were consistent with the countries' attempts to gain greater control over their economic destinies. These policies called for strict regulation of foreign multinationals, especially limiting foreign ownership of local affiliates and placing restrictions on payments for technology and other services.

This period was ended by the external debt crisis of the 1980s, when governments throughout the region were faced with inadequate foreign exchange resources, domestic economic recession, and a shortage of policy alternatives. It became clear that the multinationals were a potential source of foreign exchange and other needed inputs. This crisis spawned a range of policies aimed at attracting foreign capital, technology, and management skills. Over the course of this decade, the policy environment in Latin America changed 180 degrees from restrictive to welcoming toward foreign companies.

By the beginning of the 1990s the policy environment had moved almost completely toward *apertura*,[1] with open capital markets, relatively free trade,

I would like to acknowledge the excellent research assistance provided by Megan Gallagher on this project.
   1. With the exception of Brazil, which consistently has remained more inward-looking than the other countries of the region. Brazil's government did begin a major program of economic

and access for foreign multinationals virtually throughout the region. When the alternative of Soviet communism declined with the fall of the Berlin Wall in 1989, and then disappeared completely with the breakup of the Soviet Union in 1991, the *apertura* process was cemented in for the long haul. Appendix Table 4.3 describes some of the key policies in larger Latin American countries during the 1970s, 1980s, and 1990s.

It is this environment during the late 1980s and 1990s that is the focus of the present analysis. What policy alternatives have the Latin American countries used to implement the *apertura* model? How have these policies performed in terms of producing increased (foreign) capital investment in the region? What other impacts have accompanied the expected growth of trade, capital flows, and national income? The following sections seek to answer these questions. Before entering the current decade, some additional historical review may be useful.

THE POSTWAR PERIOD

The period immediately after World War II was characterized in Latin American economic policy by a broad interest in obtaining the up-to-date products and technology that could be made available from U.S. and European multinational enterprises. Large firms such as Exxon and the oil majors, General Motors and the other auto companies, and many consumer goods companies such as Colgate-Palmolive and Nestlé invested in local sales subsidiaries and increasingly in the local production of some of their products.

Most of the direct investment in Latin America at that time was in (1) raw materials ventures such as oil exploration and production, along with similar activity in copper, tin, bauxite, iron ore, and other minerals and metals; (2) agricultural production of crops such as bananas and pineapples; and (3) infrastructure operation such as telephone and telegraph service, air transportation, and railroads.[2] Manufactured goods were largely imported, often through sales offices of the multinationals in Latin America. In this last instance, the actual production took place mostly outside the region.[3]

---

opening in 1994, with the Real Plan, as discussed later in the text. See also Manuel da Fonseca, "Brazil's Real Plan," *Journal of Latin American Studies* 30 (1998): 619–39.

2. Although the railroads throughout Latin America were built and initially operated by British and U.S. investors, many in the late 1800s, by the 1950s most of them had been sold to local (government) investors.

3. Exceptions include products such as soap, cheese, and a range of other consumer products where the lack of important scale economies in production and relatively high transportation

By the end of the 1950s the economic infrastructure and the available managerial skill in Latin America were sufficiently advanced to encourage governments in the region to begin pushing for more local autonomy from the multinationals. That is, they began looking for ways to better control their own destinies, including control over production of goods and services. A policy framework consistent with this development context was precisely what the CEPAL analysts proposed (Prebisch 1950, 1959). They argued that the multinationals could be dealt with as suppliers of inputs such as technology and capital, rather than as owners and controllers of business activity. (A key missing link in the analysis here was that the multinationals needed control over their affiliates in order to take best advantage of their skills and scale economies. The multinationals also largely controlled access to foreign markets, which their Latin American exports served.)[4]

One clear institutional outgrowth of this policy perspective was the Andean Pact, a regional grouping of countries in the Andean region (initially comprising Bolivia, Colombia, Chile, Ecuador, and Peru; Venezuela later joined and Chile dropped out), which sought to channel foreign company activities into desired sectors and forms. This group required foreign multinational companies to sell at least 51 percent ownership of local affiliates to local investors over a period of time, thus trying to assure local control.[5]

Similarly, Mexico's 1973 foreign investment law limited foreign multinationals to a maximum of 40 percent ownership of local affiliates (with some exceptions permitted). Brazil's policy on foreign ownership prohibited FDI in the computer industry, for any products that were available locally, and particularly for PCs in the 1980s.[6] In general the policy environment was highly restrictive and in some cases really anti-multinational.

---

costs made them less competitive with similar products produced locally. Firms such as Colgate-Palmolive and Nestle were in Latin America at that time producing some products locally and importing others from the United States and Europe.

4. And perhaps fundamentally as well: the multinationals had other target countries where they could utilize their skills and resources; so if the Latin American countries did not want to "play ball," there were plenty of other opportunities available elsewhere.

5. The Andean Foreign Investment Code (Decision 24 of the Andean Pact) was launched in 1971 and remained in force until 1987. This rule required fade-out of foreign ownership to a maximum of 49 percent over ten years, elimination of royalty payments for intracompany technology transfers, and other limitations on multinational company activities. Some exceptions were granted, and the least-developed countries (Ecuador and Bolivia) were given extra time to meet the goals of the code. See Grosse 1983.

6. See, for example, Anne Piorkowsky, "Brazilian Computer Import Restrictions: Technological Independence and Commercial Reality," *Law and Policy in International Business* 17 (1985): 619–45.

In this environment the world experienced the OPEC cartel's successful effort to raise oil prices and producing countries' revenues. Interestingly, though the bulk of the OPEC oil was produced in the Middle East, it was Venezuelan president Carlos Andres Perez who led the effort to take control of the industry and raise prices.[7] Venezuela nationalized the foreign oil companies in 1975 and remained a staunch supporter of inward-looking development (generally labeled import-substituting industrialization, ISI) for the following fifteen years.[8]

Interestingly, Chile rejected this policy once the leftist Allende regime had been overthrown by the military led by Augusto Pinochet in 1973. Chile was a founding member of the Andean Pact in 1969, but it rejected Decision 24 (the foreign investment code) and withdrew from the group in 1976, largely because it had decided to follow an outward-looking industrialization policy.

The rollercoaster was, so to speak, moving uphill in the 1960s and 1970s. Government regulation on foreign multinationals was increasing, and the environment was relatively hostile. This all changed once the region fell into a massive economic crisis during the 1980s, launched by the external debt crisis in 1982.

THE DEBT CRISIS PERIOD

In August of 1982 the Mexican government announced its inability to meet its commitments on foreign commercial bank debt. That is, the Mexican government declared that it would not pay the interest and principal due on its loans from foreign commercial banks. This declaration was followed by similar statements from governments throughout Latin America, crucially those of Argentina and Brazil, but also from those of Chile, Venezuela, and many other countries.

The debt crisis began at this point, and then when it became clear that it was a crisis of solvency rather than of liquidity, both Latin American and outside countries and businesses started looking for systemic solutions. The solution process began with a financial strategy of recycling the defaulted

7. See Cesar Baena, *The Balance Between Politics and Corporate Strategy: PDVSA's Internationalization Strategy* (London: Ashgate, 1999).

8. Ecuador followed suit with the nationalization of Texaco's affiliate in 1977 and assignment of all oil exploration and production to the national oil company, CEPE (now Petroecuador). Mexico, the region's final major oil producer, had nationalized the oil industry in 1938, so there was no change in this sector in Mexico during the Cepalista period.

loans into tradable instruments (loan packages, multiyear restructuring agreements, and ultimately, Brady bonds) and continued with a search for means to enable governments to cope with future foreign debt payments.

As part of the effort to push toward a solution to the debt overhang, industrialized-country governments argued in favor of the economic opening of the debtor economies. Such a policy environment could be used to attract foreign investment and to alleviate some of the pressure on Latin American governments to drop some of the restrictions on domestic financial and product markets. It signified a move to end the ISI policy framework in favor of what has often been called an export-led industrialization framework. Though the reality did not have to be export-led, it did have to permit foreign firms access to domestic markets, and domestic firms access to foreign markets.

An early example of a country that undertook this policy shift was Bolivia.[9] In 1984 Bolivia had reached an impasse with foreign lenders to supply funds to the government. The economy was in a depression, with export prices (particularly of tin and agricultural products) remaining very low and debt-servicing costs very high. Bolivia's government formally initiated a policy of nonpayment of both interest and principal on the foreign bank debt at that time.

Beginning in 1985, Bolivia undertook a process of dramatic restructuring, beginning with the opening of the economy to foreign trade and investment. Tariff barriers were dropped precipitously, and the Andean Pact rules limiting FDI were suspended. This process was followed by the negotiation of a settlement on the external debt in 1987, in which the foreign bank lenders agreed to receive 11 cents on the dollar for their outstanding, nonperforming loans to Bolivia. The money to buy back the loans was donated by a number of foreign governments, including several European and even Latin American ones. The banks were forced either to accept the buy-back or to convert their loans into twenty-five-year, collateralized bonds at the same conversion rate. This creative but obviously costly debt strategy was an excellent solution for a small country such as Bolivia, with a total foreign debt of less than U.S.$4 billion, but it could not serve as a model for the larger countries of the region.

The depths of the debt crisis could be defined as occurring in the year 1989, when secondary market prices for foreign bank debt dropped to their lowest levels of the decade (see Fig. 4.1).

9. This section draws on Jaime Delgadillo, "Bolivia's Debt Repurchase Operation: Lessons for the Future," in Grosse 1992, 103–37.

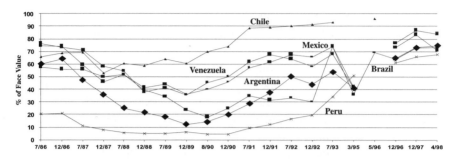

Fig. 4.1   Debt Prices for the Six Major Latin American Debtors

As the crisis was bottoming out, the beginnings of a broad economic policy shift were starting to be felt throughout Latin America. The Bolivian example above was a precursor, but the Mexican policy changes of 1986–89 really crystallized this sea change.

POLICIES TO REVERSE THE ISI MODEL

The policies used by governments across the region to dismantle the ISI frameworks can be categorized into three types that influence FDI:

1. Policies aimed at influencing FDI directly
2. Macroeconomic stabilization policies that also affect FDI
3. International financial policies that affect direct investors' activities

First, there are *policies directly aimed at FDI,* such as limits on foreign ownership and remittance of profits and other financial flows within multinational firms. The policies may also be on other activities of the multinationals, such as the transfer of technology (e.g., patent protection and limits on royalty payments). They also include incentives to attract investors such as auto manufacturers to produce locally. As barriers are reduced, and/or incentives to FDI offered, the costs of investing are reduced and the attractiveness of investing rises.

Second, there are *policies that aim to stabilize the macroeconomic environment,* thus reducing the country risk faced by direct investors and making the market more attractive. These policies include slow and stable growth of the money supply, liberalization of interest rates, privatization of state-owned enterprises and deregulation of those sectors, and government spending policies that reduce corruption and overspending. These policies, if successful, create a more attractive investment environment for domestic as well as foreign investors. In our context the key point is that successful stabilization policy does serve to attract FDI, and macroeconomic instability tends to discourage it.

And third there are *policies that put a country on a stable international financial footing*. These include such policies as agreements to resolve external debt arrears, rules that stimulate incoming financial investment flows (such as permitting foreigners to buy local financial instruments and to carry out debt-equity swaps). These policies were enacted largely to deal with the 1980s external debt crisis. Such policies also include regimes that offer either exchange rate stability or access to instruments for protection against exchange rate volatility. The opening up of Latin American countries' capital accounts (i.e., portfolio investment flows and trade in financial instruments, in addition to FDI) has produced much greater capital flows in the 1990s, but one could not argue that it has been completely stabilizing, as seen in the Tequila crisis of Mexico in 1994–95 and the Brazilian crisis of 1999.

All of these types of policy are discussed in the context of country and policy examples.

COUNTRY EXAMPLES

The most striking policy changes to occur as a result of the debt crisis were those implemented by the country whose default defined the onset of the crisis, Mexico. Under unrelenting pressure to reform from international lending organizations, Mexico's government ultimately agreed to economic liberalization policies in the late 1980s. In 1986 Mexico joined the General Agreement on Tariffs and Trade, effectively agreeing to reduce tariff barriers to imports from other member countries of the GATT (i.e., well over one hundred countries).

Mexico reversed its 1973 policy on FDI, replacing it with a 1989 policy[10] permitting full foreign ownership of firms in most sectors (other than a few, such as domestic television and radio broadcasting, petroleum, and nuclear energy). The 1989 law was a striking rejection of the CEPAL model and an explicit recognition of the interdependence of Mexico with foreign companies, markets, technology, and funds.

---

10. Government of Mexico, "Reglamento de Ley para promover la Inversión Mexicana y Regular la Inversión Extranjera," *Diario Oficial*, May 16, 1989.

This opening to FDI was reinforced with the debt-equity swap program that Mexico initiated in 1986. The debt-equity swap program permitted foreign investors to buy nonperforming commercial bank loans of foreign banks to Mexican official borrowers, and then convert those (dollar-denominated) loans into pesos for direct investment in Mexico. Beginning with investments by Chrysler and Nissan in auto assembly, Mexico's government participated in a wide range of swaps, reducing the total foreign bank debt by several billion dollars in the first three years of the program.

And in 1990 Mexico was the first country to agree to a broad external debt restructuring under the so-called Brady Plan, in which the bulk of government foreign bank debt was transformed into long-term bonds whose principal was guaranteed by thirty-year U.S. Treasury bonds. This final step enabled Mexico to regain creditworthiness in international financial markets—though this creditworthiness was largely limited to private-sector borrowers for several years, before the government itself was able to enter international capital markets successfully.

The process of *apertura* in Mexico was followed increasingly throughout Latin America, beginning in 1989. *Argentina*'s newly elected government of Carlos Menem broke with previous inward-looking policies and moved boldly to sell off state-owned companies (beginning with the national airline and the national telephone company), as well as negotiating a Brady Plan debt restructuring.

The Argentine case was possibly even more striking than Mexico's turnabout on policy toward foreign firms and the foreign sector in general. Argentina had followed an inward-looking development policy since the early years of the twentieth century. Just prior to the First World War, Argentina's economy had been the seventh largest in the world. For various reasons, including the desire to control national resources and economic activity, successive Argentine governments had put increasing restrictions on foreign (and domestic) business and had taken ownership control of many business activities, from provision of utilities such as electric power and telecommunications to operation of an airline, the national oil monopoly, and many others.

Although the blame is generally placed on the military regimes (and sometimes popularly elected generals' regimes) of leaders in Argentina, starting with Juan Perón in 1945, the ISI policies really began earlier in the century. In any event, the military governments did not alter this policy, and with it the Argentine economy fell further and further behind the industrial leaders in Europe and North America.

By the end of the 1980s, Argentina had slipped to the sixteenth-largest economy in the world, behind such upstarts as Korea and rival Brazil. In three successive waves of macroeconomic policy in that decade, Argentina experienced more than 100 percent annual inflation, along with the huge additional burden of the external debt crisis. As a reaction to these overwhelming economic pressures, the government of President Raúl Alfonsín[11] tried to begin a process of reducing barriers to private sector development. Some steps succeeded, but the efforts were hindered by a policy inertia and congressional opposition, such that it required the election in 1989 of an opposition party government to really open the door to major policy change.

This government, headed by President Carlos Menem, took office in May 1989 and immediately began to change the policy landscape. Privatization of state-owned enterprises began with the sales of Entel (telecom) and Aerolineas Argentinas (airline). A Brady Plan was negotiated in 1992 that transformed the foreign commercial bank debt into a more manageable bond structure and enabled Argentine borrowers to return to international capital markets for the first time since 1982. Debt-equity swaps were permitted and even recommended as partial means of paying for the purchase of companies in privatizations.

The best-known policy undertaken early in the Menem regime was the decision to fix the Argentine currency to the U.S. dollar, and to decree that the money supply would only be increased as additional dollars were brought into the country (e.g., to pay for exports or for incoming foreign investment)—the Cavallo Plan. Argentina's creation of a Monetary Board, and the strict link to the U.S. dollar has been credited with breaking a decade-long mentality of hyperinflation and stabilizing the domestic economy. Indeed, the Cavallo Plan may be the most successful stabilization program in post–World War II Latin America.[12]

Argentina moved much further than any other country in Latin America with its privatization program, selling off almost every state-owned company, including the "crown jewel," YPF, the national oil company. In retrospect, with low oil prices through the 1990s, this strategy brought the government billions of dollars in income from the sale of the company and passed the losses during the last few years of severely depressed oil prices on to private

---

11. Alfonsín was popularly elected as president in 1983. His Radical Party regime was largely unable to make the break with the economic policies of the preceding military governments in terms of economic stabilization, privatization, debt relief, and so on. It fell to the government of Carlos Menem, of the opposition Peronist Party beginning in 1989, to really achieve the break and forge a broad array of *apertura* policies. Interestingly, the Peronists were traditionally an inward-looking, nationalistic party as well; Menem did not by any means campaign for election on the basis of pursuing free-market policies; but once elected he and his government moved rapidly and successfully in that direction.

12. The Cavallo Plan did indeed achieve the economic stabilization of Latin America's most inflation-wracked economy, and the stable growth path has endured now for a decade.

owners (i.e., thousands of individual and institutional investors in Argentina, New York, and London). Regardless of the timing of that sale, the policy has been to put virtually all economic activity into the private sector, with even public services such as street cleaning and repair passed on to private contractors.

The case of *Brazil* provides a dramatic counterpoint to the previous examples. Brazil was the last of the Latin American countries to begin a process of economic opening and has progressed the least of all of them. Brazil faced the same debt crisis and hyperinflation problems that Argentina did, and successive governments went through repeated efforts to stabilize the economy. The Cruzado Plan (1986), the Bresser Plan (1987), the Summer Plan (1989), and the Collor Plan I (1990) and II (1991) all resulted in initial positive outcomes, but were followed soon by additional instability and weak economic growth or recession.

It was not until 1994 that Brazil's government negotiated a Brady Plan to deal with its foreign commercial bank debt. In the same year Brazil's government launched the Real Plan, along with a new currency, the real. This time the stabilization policy did work, and up to late 1998, the economy grew robustly with low inflation.

Another counterexample to the previous ones is *Chile*. While Brazil was the laggard in moving its policy to economic opening, Chile led the other countries by more than a decade with its liberalization. Under the military government of Augusto Pinochet, Chile adopted a policy framework significantly influenced by the free-market "Chicago Boys" (principally Arnold Harberger and Milton Friedman), beginning in 1976. As noted, Chile rejected the interventionist Andean Pact and followed that move with the installation of an open regime toward FDI (in Decision 200). In the same vein Chile began to sell off state-owned firms and to open up the economy to private-sector participation. Chile's foreign exchange market was largely open to capital flows from the late 1970s onward, though repatriation of capital investment was not permitted for one year after the initial investment until that rule was dropped in 1998.

Chile encountered a severe recession and a run on the peso in 1981, when copper prices plummeted and foreign exchange earnings thus dropped pre-

---

However, an additional result of the dollar-linked economy was a slower growth rate than in several others Latin American countries in the late 1990s, a comparatively high level of unemployment, and ultimately a maxi-devaluation in 2002. Thus it would be incorrect to say that the plan was a success in this longer time frame—whereas it clearly was a huge success for its first several years (i.e., for Menem's first term of office).

cipitously. In addition, domestic credit grew excessively during 1981, to the point where many banks were highly overexposed, and with the weak macroeconomic conditions several of them failed.[13] The debt crisis beginning in 1982 only exacerbated the problem, but by about 1984 Chile had turned the corner and was growing positively again. From that point on, the economic model of Chile has served as a primary example of the good points of *apertura* in Latin America. Chile's economic growth from 1984 through 1998 averaged about 4.8 percent per year in real terms, by far the best in the region. The impact of the Mexican "tequila" crisis at the end of 1994 and the Asian crisis of 1997–99 have been less in Chile than elsewhere in the region. In short, the export-led industrialization and general *apertura* model of Chile offers a noteworthy success story in Latin America, and it began long before the other countries of the region began to seriously consider such a direction.

DEBT-EQUITY SWAPS AS A MECHANISM TO PROMOTE INWARD FDI

The use of debt-equity swaps to promote inward FDI is a concept with quite an interesting history. The idea of exchanging something of value for a nonperforming loan is as old as the use of loans. Typically, the lender wants to take something of value that can be sold to recuperate the original loan principal; this is the purpose of collateral on many loans. In the late 1800s, bonds issued for construction of railroads in Central America defaulted, and the lenders (bond purchasers) took ownership of the railroad in more than one case. This is a simple debt-equity swap. Many other similar instances have occurred through the history of bank lending and bond issuance.

Since governments historically have not been forced to provide collateral for their loans (although they sometimes have, even in earlier centuries), lenders are left with a weak position in sovereign loans. In response to their lack of access to international capital markets during the 1980s, a number of governments accepted the idea of allowing dollar-denominated foreign debt to be received back, in exchange for either local currency to use for buying a local company, or alternatively in direct exchange for shares in a local company.

---

13. The excessive credit expansion has been blamed on poor or corrupt management of some of the banks, but the extent of bad management versus wrongful actions by managers was never fully explained. The weak economy in 1982 led to a generalized banking crisis, and Chile was among the hardest-hit countries at the onset of the external debt crisis in Latin America that year (Barandiaran and Hernández 1999).

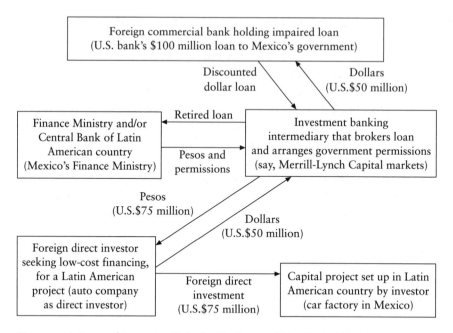

Fig. 4.2   A Swap of Sovereign Debt for Equity in a New Capital Project

The structure of a simple debt-equity swap appears in Figure 4.2.

The original bank lender whose loan is not being paid by the Latin American government borrower agrees to sell the loan at a discount under face value. The purchaser of the loan previously agrees with the Latin American government to exchange the loan for local currency (say, pesos), which in turn can be used for investment in a business in that country. The first transaction is for the loan buyer to pay the loan seller in cash some dis-counted value for the loan (say, 50 percent of face value). The lender leaves the scene with cash, plus a book loss of 50 percent of the loan value.[14]

Next, the investor takes the loan document to the Latin American gov-ernment and requests local currency, to be used in equity investment in that country. In some cases the government sells a state-owned company's shares directly to the investor at this point. In most cases, the investor receives pesos to use in buying a company or starting a new one. The amount of local currency, in order for the swap to be attractive, must be above the original 50 percent discount of the loan and below the 100 percent face

14. Assuming that the loan had not already been partially written down on the lender's book. If the loan loss had already been partially taken, then the selling bank would receive less current tax benefit from selling the loan.

value that the government would pay otherwise. A payment of 75 percent of face value would not be uncommon in this context.

Once the investor turns in the loan document, the loan is canceled and eliminated. The government remains with only the obligation to honor the new pesos as they are used in the economy. The result may be somewhat inflationary, as the new money "chases" the existing goods. Assuming some unemployment, the investment being made may generate more output in the economy and thus more jobs, etc. Critics argue that many investors would have invested anyway, without the benefit of the swap. Allowing the investors to, in effect, buy pesos at a discount certainly offers them an incentive to invest. Whether or not they would have invested otherwise is a moot point, under the circumstances.[15]

PRIVATIZATION AND ITS RELATION TO INWARD DIRECT INVESTMENT

One of the major policy prescriptions of the International Monetary Fund in the context of its loans to Latin American governments during the debt crisis was that the countries put much more of their economies into the private sector, that is to say, out of state hands. This move included the major demand to sell off ownership of state-owned companies to private investors (allowing for some exceptions such as the petroleum industry and the media).

Privatizations began to occur in response to the debt crisis in 1985 and 1986, approximately at the time that debt-equity swaps took hold. The two phenomena were quite related, as strategies for reducing the burden of foreign debt. The privatizations began (to be sure, in Chile in the 1970s) in Mexico with the sales of Aeromexico and Mexicana de Aviacion, but they did not really take off as a widespread phenomenon until 1989, when Argentina joined the process.

Then, by 1993, privatizations accounted for perhaps one-third of all FDI in Latin America, with sales of enormous telephone monopolies, electric power companies, airlines, and even some oil companies.

Some of the major early privatizations in several countries are listed in Table 4.1. Notice that the sectors tend to focus on public utilities and other

---

15. The debate over whether or not debt-equity swaps provided a net benefit to the host country was quite acrimonious in the mid-1980s. It was argued that swaps were inflationary, that they gave foreigners privileged access to local currency relative to local investors, and that the investments would have been made even without the swap opportunity. In the event, over U.S.$50 billion of debt-equity swaps took place in Latin American between 1985 and 1990.

infrastructure. Many commercial banks likewise were privatized during 1989–95. Manufacturing and commercialization had been in private hands throughout, and crown-jewel–type natural resource firms were not privatized for the most part until later in the 1990s.

Of course, it must be recognized that privatization is a policy that can only be used once: after a firm is sold to private-sector investors, it cannot be reprivatized (unless, of course, it is first renationalized!). Thus, the enormous impetus to FDI in Latin America provided by privatization during the 1990s will fade away over the next few years, as the remaining number of state-owned companies dwindles.

THE USE OF FREE TRADE ZONES TO STIMULATE DIRECT INVESTMENT

Free-trade zones are typically industrial parks near ports or airports, which enable firms using them to avoid paying tariffs or taxes on goods imported into the zone or exported from the zone—as long as the products do not enter the local, domestic market. These zones have been established in industrial and emerging markets, with the usual intent to attract jobs and business activity to locations that otherwise would not attract such business on their own. Panama's free trade zone at Colon, for example, has long flourished as a location to which U.S. and European products are shipped, for subsequent transshipment to other destination countries in the Americas or elsewhere.

One particular kind of zone that is important in the context of FDI in Latin America is the Export Processing Zone (EPZ). This kind of free trade zone gives tax and tariff exemption to assembly operations that import some of their inputs from abroad and export their final products. The most important industries involved in this activity in Latin America are automobile, clothing, and electronics manufacture. In Mexico alone, this type of business (called *maquila*) employed close to one million people in 1998 and produced about U.S.$56 billion of annual output.[16]

The establishment of EPZs is not recent, with many of them existing from the 1970s and early 1980s. The use of the zones has jumped in the 1990s, as trade barriers fell in Latin America, and more importing has been possible.

As a policy to attract FDI, export processing zone legislation has been quite successful, although the viability of such zones varies widely among countries. For example, the amount of EPZ production in Venezuela is minis-

16. This situation is changing, as Mexico complies with the North American Free Trade Agreement, which allows Mexican goods tariff-free access to the U.S. and Canadian markets. The maquiladora companies have been subject to corporate profit and asset taxes since 1995, and their output may now be sold in the domestic Mexican market.

cule relative to the size of the economy; while in Panama EPZ production is a very significant percentage of total GDP.

SOME OUTCOMES OF THE EFFORTS TO ATTRACT FDI

The results of these policies to open up Latin American economies to competition and to the entry of foreign firms appear to have been very positive. Economic growth returned to the 3–6 percent per year range for most countries in the region during the 1990s, with the exceptions of Mexico's 1994–95 crisis, which dragged down growth in several countries in 1995, and the Asian crisis of 1997–99, which contributed to lowering Latin American growth in 1998.

Of course, it is very difficult to separate out the impact of the specific policies from the overall global economic conditions, and most important for Latin America, the health of the U.S. economy. With the U.S. economy growing in boom conditions for most of the 1990s, Latin America has been very well positioned for solid economic growth. With the demise of the communist alternative, the policy choices have narrowed substantially, so most countries have been moving to more open markets, not just in Latin America.

A simple correlation model between FDI promotion policies and FDI into the countries of the region, also accounting for market size, gives an initial idea of the impact of this part of economic opening. A regression model of the form:

$$\text{FDI flow} = -467.41 + 1434.36 \text{ (FDI promotion policy)} + 0.01 \text{ (GDP)}$$
$$(t = -2.22, \alpha = .01) \quad (t = 5.86, \alpha = .001) \quad (t = 10.13, \alpha = .001)$$
$$R^2 = 0.49 \ F = 65.74 \ (\alpha = .001)$$

produces significant results (at the $\alpha = .001$ level) showing a positive impact of the policies on their target.[17] The policy variable is simply a 0/1 dummy variable, equal to one beginning in the year that the major policy opening toward FDI took place.[18]

---

17. In this model, GDP is defined as GDP minus FDI, since FDI is by definition part of GDP.

18. This is consistent with Wells and Wint 1990 and other studies of direct investment policy. The decision as to which policy changes constitute the appropriate ones for assigning the year of the change is somewhat arbitrary. Even so, revising the model with alternative years for Colombia and Peru, where changes accumulated in 1990 and 1991, produced no change in significance of the results. Likewise, in Argentina, the policy change could be defined as occurring in 1989 or 1990, but either way the statistical results remained the same.

Table 4.1 Early Privatizations in Latin America

Privatized enterprise	Industry	Foreign participation	Price of sale (in U.S.$ millions)	Year
	Argentina			
Aerolíneas Argentinas	Air transport	Yes	660	1990
Empresa Nacional de Telecomunicaciones (ENTEL)	Telecommunications	Yes	1594	1990
Gas del Estado	Energy	Yes	2380	1992
Servicios Eléctricos del Gran Buenos Aires (SEGBA)	Electricity	No	1121	1992
Teléfonica Argentina	Telecommunications	No	849	1991
Yacimentos Petroliferos Fiscales (YPF)	Petroleum	Yes	1846	1993
	Brazil			
Compañia Asos Expeciais Itabira (ACESITA)	Steel	No	465	1992
PETROFLEX	Chemicals	No	234	1992
Usinas Siderúrgicas de Minas Gerais (USIMINAS)	Steel	No	1530	1991
	Chile			
Compañia de Teléfonos de Chile (CTC)	Telecommunications	Yes	114	1986–1988
Empresa Nacional de Electricidad (ENDESA)	Energy	No	590	1986–1989
Línea Aérea Nacional de Chile (LAN Chile)	Air transport	Yes	42	1989
	Mexico			
Banamex	Finance	No	3131	1991
Banca Serfin	Finance	No	912	1992
Bancomer	Finance	No	2515	1991
Sidermex	Steel	No	340	1992
Teléfonos de México (TELEMEX)	Telecommunications	Yes	2227	1990–1992

Table 4.1 Early Privatizations in Latin America (*continued*)

Privatized enterprise	Industry	Foreign participation	Price of sale (in U.S.$ millions)	Year
	Peru			
Hierro Peru	Mining	Yes	120	1992
	Venezuela			
Compañia de Teléfonos de Venezuela (CANTV)	Telecommunications	Yes	1900	1991
VIASA	Air transport	Yes	145	1991

SOURCE: ECLAC/UNCTAD 1992.

Another simple correlation model between FDI promotion policies and unemployment gives some additional insight into the possible impacts of these policies. A regression of unemployment for the eight largest Latin American economies on GDP growth and the same dummy variable equal to zero before FDI promotion and 1 since that time produces the following results:

Unemployment rate = .07 + −0.01(GDP growth) + 0.01(FDI promotion policy)

$$(t = 16.9, \alpha = .001) \quad (t = -1.51) \quad (t = 1.61)$$
$$R^2 = 0.02 \ F = 2.46 \ (\alpha = .1)$$

While unquestionably a crude measure, this model shows that a more open policy toward FDI is *positively* related to unemployment. That is, once GDP growth is accounted for, ignoring the many other factors that were varying, the more open regimes toward FDI correlate with higher unemployment in the Latin American countries. While the coefficient is not significant, still the direction of the impact seems accurate and consistent with recent criticisms of the *apertura* model and higher unemployment in many countries.

POLICIES THAT PROMOTE DOMESTIC SAVINGS

While there may not be a "savings promotion policy" *per se,* the idea of increasing domestic savings has long been a target of policymakers in Latin America. With savings rates of about half of those in Asia (15–20 percent of GDP, vs. 30–35 percent in Asia) during the 1980s and 1990s, the Latin American countries have a large opportunity to increase investment by boosting savings.

The most important policies that have been implemented in Latin America toward this end are economic stabilization policies, which make it more secure for investors to hold their wealth in domestic financial instruments and other investments. As Latin American governments have undertaken policy reforms, and as external conditions have changed, the success of stabilization policies has been quite impressive during the 1990s. Nevertheless, savings rates have not responded consistently to this stability, as shown in Table 4.2. While some countries such as Chile and Colombia have experienced dramatic increases in their savings rates since the debt crisis, the region as a whole has seen a slight downward trend in savings relative to GDP.[19]

19. Evan Tanner (1996) explains this phenomenon as possibly reflecting a permanent income hypothesis kind of behavior, in that savers may save less currently in expectation of

POLICIES TO PROMOTE INWARD FINANCIAL INVESTMENT FROM ABROAD

Although the focus of this analysis has been on real capital investment (namely, FDI), the overall perspective can usefully be expanded to financial or portfolio investment as well. This kind of investment is generally not promoted via policies to subsidize or assist investors, but rather it may be encouraged simply by the opening up of regulations on capital flows.

Just as with the opening of FDI rules, Latin American governments across the board have reduced restrictions on financial capital flows during the 1990s. These policies have come under heavy fire since the Mexican "tequila" crisis of 1994, and even more with the Asian crisis of 1997 and subsequent Brazilian crisis in 1998–99.

Ignoring for the moment the concern with the appropriateness of policies to liberalize financial capital flows, the fact remains that such flows have been less restricted under the *apertura* policy frameworks around the region. Most countries of the region have largely eliminated capital controls, thus allowing domestic and foreign portfolio investors the opportunity to move funds internationally as they choose. Likewise, exchange rates have become much more stable in the 1990s than they were in the 1980s, although that fact will not assuage the Mexican and Brazilian savers who saw their wealth depleted by 50 percent or more in dollar terms during the tequila crisis and the more recent Brazil crisis.

CHANNELING SAVINGS INTO PRODUCTIVE INVESTMENT

In addition to the broad macroeconomic policies (and reasonable good luck) that have enabled the Latin American countries to achieve stabilized growth in the 1990s, an additional specific policy initiative has gained wide acceptance and usage in the region. This is the policy on pension fund management, in which many countries have "privatized" their social security systems and allowed private-sector pension management companies to manage the long-term funds involved. Starting with Chile's private pension management plan of 1980 (see Haindl 1997), several countries, including Argentina, Peru, and Colombia, have joined the trend.

This means that they have put into private hands the problem of holding onto the retirement funds of each country's citizens, and of finding financially attractive uses for these funds. One major use of the funds has been to build

---

higher incomes in the future. Once stabilization succeeds, the savings rate may decline as optimism about the future increases.

Table 4.2   Savings Rates in Latin America, the 1980s versus the 1990s

Country	Savings/GDP 1983–86 average (%)	Savings/GDP 1993–96 average (%)
Argentina	21	19
Brazil	27	19
Chile	10	33
Colombia	14	26
Mexico	19	16
Peru	19	24
Venezuela	25	17
Latin America and the Caribbean	21	19

SOURCE: United Nations Center 1996.

long-term capital markets in the countries of the region. And one investment category in this long-term category is shares of stock, or direct investment. Thus, national governments have encouraged the development of stock markets in the region, and they have simultaneously attracted foreign along with the domestic investment into this segment of the financial market.

Although the costs and benefits of private pension fund management may be debated, it cannot be doubted that this shift has produced a boom in Latin American capital markets. During the 1980s it was virtually impossible to find medium- or long-term investment instruments other than government bonds in Latin America. With the spread of private pension management companies, as well as the lifting of restrictions on foreign investors, Latin American countries from Mexico to Argentina are finding a new source of funding for long-term capital users.

CONCLUSIONS

FDI into Latin America boomed during the 1990s. This phenomenon was due largely to the rapid growth of the U.S. economy, from which a large percentage of the investment originated. It was also due to the recoveries of the Latin American economies from the 1980s debt crisis. Positive real economic growth in the region made investment there much more attractive than in the previous decade. And finally, this boom was partly attributable to government policies in the region that attracted FDI.

The government policies that attract FDI are not all aimed at that specific purpose. To be sure, the policies of giving national (that is to say, equal) treatment to foreign companies and offering incentives to entice auto production are aimed at foreign direct investors, as are a number of other policies. But also important, general macroeconomic policies that have stabilized the economies and liberalized capital flows have also stimulated FDI by reducing barriers to activities of the multinational firms. The lower inflation and interest rates that exist because of more stable monetary policies in the 1990s have reduced the level of country risk dramatically. The exchange rate regimes, from Argentina's currency board and fixed exchange rate (fixed to the U.S. dollar) to Mexico's floating exchange rate accompanied by hedging instruments (forwards, futures, and options between pesos and dollars), provide multinationals the tools to deal with exchange rate risk and to thus reduce their overall risks.

In sum, the government policies in place in Latin America today clearly promote FDI into the region, and they are having exactly that impact across the region. Policies vary from one country to another, and Brazil and Argentina present almost polar opposites in this sense—but the net result is that both of these countries and their neighbors throughout the region are operating policy frameworks that may be classified as following the *apertura* model, with limits on direct investors being the exception rather than the rule.

In the aftermath of the Asian financial crisis, Brazil was hit with speculation against the real, a major devaluation in January of 1999, and subsequent uncertainty for several months. It appears that, by mid-2000, that crisis has been survived, and Brazil has returned to a positive growth path with reasonably low and stable inflation. In spite of this turn of events, the FDI flows into Brazil remain high and growing in the early twenty-first century. The same is likely to hold for the Latin American region overall in the next few years. The risk accompanying this investment flow is that the level of global interdependency existing today means that any major downturn in the United States or Europe is likely to have a strong impact on Latin America and FDI there, regardless of government policies in the region.

Appendix
Table 4.3   Foreign Direct Investment Regulations in Latin America

Country	1976	1986	1996
Argentina		Approval needed for FDI over $20 million; utilities and banking generally limited to local firms	No restrictions; national treatment of foreign firms
Brazil		FDI banned in airlines, media, energy, PCs; fx controls on remittances; JVs only in telecom, banking, mining	FDI banned in airlines, media, fishing, gasohol; other sectors fairly open
Chile		No restrictions; national treatment of foreign firms	No restrictions; national treatment of foreign firms
Colombia	Ancom Decision 24 rules*	Ancom Decision 24 rules*	Few restrictions; mostly national treatment of foreign firms
Ecuador	Ancom Decision 24 rules*	Ancom Decision 24 rules*	Some limits on fishing, airlines, energy, and telecom; other sectors open
Mexico		Majority Mexican ownership required; 40% max foreign ownership in some sectors; no foreign ownership of banks, oil, media; no fx controls	Restrictions on oil, power, and media; elsewhere national treatment of foreign firms
Peru	Ancom Decision 24 rules*	Ancom Decision 24 rules*	Some border-area limits; otherwise, national treatment of foreign firms
Venezuela	Ancom Decision 24 rules*	Ancom Decision 24 rules*	Restrictions on oil, media, other natural resources; other sectors open

SOURCE: Economist Intelligence Unit/Business International Corporation, *Business Latin America*, various issues.
*Ancom Decision 24 is the Andean Pact's Foreign Investment Code. It requires fade-out of foreign ownership to a maximum of 49 percent in ten years, disallows royalty payment to parent companies, limits intrafirm loans, limits profit remittance to 20 percent of registered capital.

Appendix
Table 4.4 Global FDI Flows (in millions of $U.S.)

	Direct investment abroad			Direct investment inflows		
	1977	1987	1997	1977	1987	1997
United States and Canada	15003	38786	135888	4826	62338	100580
Japan	1701	19520	26059	24	1170	3200
Europe (industrialized)	7485	73287	207295	9969	39902	116558
Eastern Europe	2	17	4022	328	198	22939
Asia	35	1889	17021	1305	8150	79981
Latin America	357	203	4274	3263	4342	61544

REFERENCES

Barandiaran, Edgardo, and Leonardo Hernández. 1999. "Origins and Resolution of a Banking Crisis: Chile 1982–86." Banco Central de Chile *Documentos de Trabajo,* no. 57 (December).

Bergsman, J., and W. Edisis. 1988. *Debt-Equity Swaps and Foreign Direct Investment in Latin America.* Washington, D.C.: International Finance Corporation, 1988.

Bradford, Colin, ed. 1993. *Mobilizing International Investment for Latin America.* Paris: OECD.

CEPAL (Comisión Económica para América Latina y el Caribe). 1998. *Foreign Investment in Latin America and the Caribbean.* Santiago: United Nations. [E.98.II.G.14]

Contractor, Farok. 1995. "Promoting Foreign Direct Investment in Developing Countries." *International Trade Journal* 9, no. 1 (Spring): 107–41.

ECLAC/UNCTAD. 1992. "Inversión extranjera directa en America Latina y el Caribe, 1970–1990, Volumen I: Panorama regional." Programme on Transnational Corporations Joint Unit, Documento de la Sala de Conferencia DSC/l, 14 September.

Ganitsky, J., and G. Lema. "Foreign Investment Through Debt Equity Swaps." *Sloan Management Review* 29, no. 2 (1988): 21–29.

Grosse, Robert. 1983. "The Andean Foreign Investment Code's Effect on Foreign Direct Investment." *Journal of International Business Studies* (Winter): 121–33.

———. 1997. "Foreign Direct Investment in Latin America." In Robert Grosse, ed., *Generating Savings for Development in Latin America,* 135–53. Coral Gables, Fla.: North/South Center, November.

———, ed. 1992. *Private Sector Solutions to the Latin American Debt Problem.* Coral Gables, Fla.: North/South Center.

———, ed. 1995. *Government Responses to the Latin American Debt Problem.* Coral Gables, Fla.: North/South Center, November.

Grosse, Robert, and Juan Yañes. 1998. "The Privatization of YPF." *Academic of Management Executive* 12, no. 2 (Spring): 51–63.

Haindl, Eric R. 1997. "Chilean Pension Fund Reform and its Impact on Savings." In Robert Grosse, ed., *Generating Savings for Development in Latin America,* 113–34. Coral Gables, Fla.: North/South Center, November.

Larrain, F., and A. Velasco. 1990. "Can Swaps Solve the Debt Crisis?" In *Princeton Studies in International Finance*. Princeton: Princeton University Press.

OECD (Organisation for Economic Co-operation and Development). 1997. *Investment Policies in Latin America and Multilateral Rules on Investment*. Paris: OECD.

Prebisch, Raul. 1950. *The Economic Development of Latin America and Its Principal Problems*. New York: United Nations, 1950. Reprinted as "The Economic Development of Latin America and Its Principal Problems," *Economic Bulletin for Latin America* 7, no. 1(1962): 1–51.

———. 1959. "Commercial Policy in the Underdeveloped Countries." *American Economic Review* 69 (May): 251–73.

Rojo, Pablo, and Jeffrey Hoberman. 1994. "Deregulation in Argentina: A Policymakers' View." *Quarterly Review of Economics and Finance* 34 (Summer): 151–77.

Tanner, Evan. 1997. "Savings, Stabilization, and Reform in Latin America: Patterns and Policies in the 1990s." In Robert Grosse, ed., *Generating Savings for Development in Latin America*, 13–34. Coral Gables, Fla.: North/South Center, November.

United Nations Center on Latin America and the Caribbean. 1996. *Economic Survey of Latin America and the Caribbean*. Santiago: CEPAL.

Wells, Louis T., Jr., and Alvin Wint. 1990. *Marketing a Country: Promotion as a Tool for Attracting Foreign Investment*. Washington, D.C.: World Bank.

5

Models of Welfare and Models of Capitalism: The Limits of Transferability

CARLOS H. FILGUEIRA AND FERNANDO FILGUEIRA

Over the last two decades, Latin American countries have implemented significant reforms in a variety of social policy domains, including social security, pension and retirement systems, health care, education, and public assistance and antipoverty programs. The region has become a veritable laboratory for experimenting with strategies previously unknown anywhere else in the world. Thanks in part to the decisive action of multilateral agencies, these developments fostered a new generation of policy instruments: creation of a variety of safety nets (e.g., means-tested safety nets, universal work-fare safety nets, etc.); social security systems based on individual capitalization and savings; decentralized and targeted programs to combat poverty; social investment funds; and various approaches to ensuring citizenship income or citizenship entitlements. There have also been important institutional innovations in education and health care. The new reforms emphasize three types of arrangements: decentralization, autonomous management, and a public-private mix.

From various perspectives, the region has made considerable advances. The social question has received increasing attention in the public agenda of Latin American governments, achieving priority akin to that of economic and state reform. At the same time, traditional institutional arrangements have given way to a broader spectrum of policy alternatives and strategies. Many of Latin America's most underdeveloped countries, with the most severe social inequities and with the worst public benefits systems, became for the first time more institutionally effective. Meanwhile, in relatively advanced countries with more extensive social coverage, reforms have sought to replace highly centralized, unequal, and inefficient public benefits systems. Throughout, reforms have prompted a reassessment of the potential for civil society to participate in the management of social policy.

The intersection of innovative and traditional approaches brings to the fore urgent problems concerning the relevance and viability of new policy instruments and frameworks. This is particularly noteworthy in two respects.

This chapter draws on eight case studies carried out through the Latin American Program on Social Policies, sponsored by the CIID/IDRC of Canada, from 1992 to 1994.

First, the objective of reform has not always been clear. Beyond the generic goals of "social improvement" or "compensatory measures" to address the vulnerability caused by adjustment and stabilization policies, discussions of the aims of social policy lack complexity. There is, for example, no debate about the implications of different welfare state models (Esping-Andersen 1991), classified in the literature as liberal, conservative, and social democratic.

Second, the relevance, viability, and efficiency of such strategies differ depending on the sociopolitical context. Policy instruments are not important in and of themselves, but rather for the function they perform in a given system. This means, simply, that the transfer and adaptation of strategies across countries or regions is not guaranteed by purely technical criteria or social engineering. At the same time, it is unlikely that certain kinds of social policies will flourish or be implemented properly in the absence of the necessary sociopolitical actors in the political arena. Though there is room for debate and precise linkages are difficult to identify, a comparison of Europe and the United States, or in the Latin American context, of Uruguay and Bolivia, suggests more than coincidental linkages between the broader sociopolitical context and the presence of strong or weak welfare states.

Social security as protection against risks of individuals can be based on the market (individual capitalization), the state (welfare regimes), or on civil society (precapitalist protection). But the prevalence of one approach or another is no mere epiphenomenon. Rather, it is constitutive of the social order and is influenced by long-established traditions. While the horizontal solidarity of the English or the communitarian traditions of Scandinavia form the basis of a strong civil society that makes certain policies viable, this does not assure their successful transfer to societies where the state, rather than the community, is central to social order. Similarly, Japan's incipient and late social security system organized around productive enterprises and the family is part of, indeed an extension of, primordial social institutions, and not the result of ad hoc arrangements that can easily be replicated in other societies.

Naturally, this does not mean that countries cannot learn from other experiences or that there exists a perfect determinism between welfare strategies and sociopolitical contexts. The point is simply that we must evaluate critically the realistic possibilities for transferring approaches across countries. We shall examine this in greater detail.

The transfer of welfare state strategies implies certain risks at the point where one seeks to identify concrete public policy instruments. Technical logics clash with political and social limitations, and with actors in the political and social sphere; this can render the model unworkable or limit or distort the anticipated effects of technical advice. In addition, failure to consider the social and political underpinnings of systems of public assistance—treating them solely as technical matters—invites limited progress, or excessive optimism, about prospects for institutionalizing such systems. A third point to keep in mind is that a narrow approach, by its very nature, ignores the multiple functions of social policy. Yet as Esping-Andersen (1991) has noted, these policies play latent critical functions with regard to social cohesion, participation, and democracy. The uncritical transplantation of models from other societies without consideration of these latent functions can yield results that on the surface appear positive, but that obscure deeper effects that have consequences for the social and political order. At the same time, to assume that the *instruments* are neutral is the most inefficient and naive way to modify the ultimate *goals* of social protection systems, without doing so explicitly.

STRUCTURAL TRENDS IN LATIN AMERICA

Latin America has been known throughout its history for its extremely high levels of inequality despite its relatively advanced modernization. It has often been assumed that the move from a model of highly stratified, corporatist-inspired social policy to a liberal model with a residual nature or the creation of such a system where none existed would presumably improve the distributive and, by some accounts, the integrative effects of welfare programs. We argue that this assumption is incorrect.

The shortcomings of the social policies of the traditional model of development were a partial product of the unequal character of the model itself and its more general structural tendencies. Whether social policies reinforced these patterns is a separate question.

But the effects of these development models on the objectives of social integration and greater equality cannot be attributed solely to social policy. In other words, the problems of social policy in Latin America were not exclusively the result of centralism, the pretension of universalism, or statist and sectoral approaches. Thus, decentralization, privatization, and targeting are not their automatic solution. The problem in the region has been centralized authoritarianism, general inequality, rent-seeking political elites, and the bureaucratic weakness of states in coordinating and distributing services.

These problems have not disappeared, and their structural bases seem more present than ever.

Income Distribution

The persistence of inequality is evident in patterns of income distribution that have not been overcome despite profound economic and productive transformations. In this sense, inequality in every country has tended to evolve only slightly, despite the constant pressures of the industrialization process, urbanization, and the radical transformation of the social structure brought about by the rise of middle classes and the industrial proletariat as well as by the extraordinary expansion of the state. It is surprising, then, to note the remarkable stability of differences in the degree of inequality across countries over the past thirty-five years.

With the exceptions of Honduras, for which recent information is unavailable, and Paraguay, for which information is unreliable, the ranking of the majority of the countries in terms of levels of inequality as measured by the Gini index, has remained constant between 1960 and 1995. Considering four categories of the Gini index (greater than 0.50, between 0.50 and 0.45, between 0.45 and 0.40, and between 0.40 and 0.35), we find that of the eight Latin American countries, five have maintained the same level of inequality (Brazil, Chile, Colombia, Venezuela, and Uruguay), two have dropped to one level less of inequality (Costa Rica and Mexico), and one has increased (Argentina) over these thirty-five years.[1] Naturally, none of this evidence suggests that there has not been some variation in the concentration of income or significant fluctuations in certain subperiods in certain countries, owing above all to the ups and downs of the economy or to changes in regime (Londoño and Székely 1997). Nonetheless, what is important to emphasize is the relative rigidity of distributive patterns in a region where it is difficult to find even relative movements between categories within the Gini index range of variation.

To the extent that the analysis only covers a few countries and does so by following a UN Economic Commission for Latin America (ECLA) methodology for estimating income concentration, it is useful to add evidence derived from more recent studies conducted by the InterAmerican Development Bank (IDB) and the World Bank. Some of these studies confirm the

1. This is derived from information contained in annual reports of CEPAL, Panorama Social de America Latina, 1991–99, and national-level studies. The data cover the urban population in almost all countries, but in some include only the capital city and the larger urban centers. The series for each country are comparable, however.

tendencies we have identified, though they are not unanimous, while those covering the 1990s help to determine more recent trends.

Analyzing the persistence of inequality in Latin America during the 1990s, Székely and Hilgert (1999) examine forty-nine household surveys in fourteen countries and conclude that the region has followed the global trend toward greater inequality. They find that six countries have maintained a constant level of inequality (Bolivia, Colombia, Ecuador, Chile, Costa Rica, and Mexico), while in the remaining eight countries (Brazil, Honduras, Nicaragua, Paraguay, Panama, El Salvador, Venezuela, and Uruguay) inequality has increased. These results are not without problems: coverage is imperfect, and for most countries the trends correspond to different subsets of the decade rather than for the entire ten-year period. Nonetheless, the findings are consistent with other approaches to the measurement of inequality, including those anticipated by ECLA's analysis of the previous period. When we separate variation in the Gini index into four categories, (more than 0.56; between 0.56 and 0.52; between 0.52 and 0.48, and less than 0.48), we find that twelve of the fourteen countries have maintained their ranking even though most experienced an increase in inequality, while only two countries (El Salvador and Paraguay) moved into the next higher category of inequality. Rather than changes in the relative distance between countries, the new model of capitalism in Latin America is characterized by a generalized movement toward a higher level of income concentration.[2]

Population and Demographic Transition

In comparison with developed countries, Latin America exhibits population patterns that indicate a demographic transition at its intermediate and advanced stages. Thus, indicators of mortality, birthrates, fertility, population growth, dependency rates, and life expectancy at birth are typical of processes that occurred much earlier in developed countries.

The Latin American population is growing at a rate that is four times faster than that of developed countries (annual growth rate of 1.9 percent vs. 0.5 percent). The fertility and birthrates are double those of developed countries (3.3 percent vs. 1.7 percent and 27 percent vs. 13 percent respectively). But the most pronounced differences are found in infant mortality rates (47.2 in Latin America and the Caribbean in contrast with 8 in developed

2. This is not the place to discuss multiple difficulties in the measurement of income distribution. Owing to the variety of sources of data and approaches, Gini index scores vary widely (in general studies by the World Bank and IDB they reach indices higher than those of CEPAL) (Székely and Hilgert 1999).

countries), and in life expectancy at birth, which is thirteen years lower in the region than in the developed world.

Finally, as a consequence of reproductive behavior, 68 percent of the population is comprised of dependents, compared to 49 percent in core countries. This essentially can be attributed to the different age structure of the populations: the high rate of dependence found in Latin America is determined by the predominance of younger generations relative to those of retirement age (World Bank 1994; CEPAL 1990–95).

The preceding information suggests that despite advances in the process of demographic transition, the region will continue to grow at an accelerated rate in the years to come. The 1990 projections for the year 2000 predicted an increase in population of 82 million inhabitants, reaching a total of 515 million, an increase of approximately 22 percent. Despite a projected decrease in fertility rates, the relative youth of the population will have an inertial effect sustaining high birthrates. At the same time, the growth of the population will continue to reflect the reproductive habits of the most disadvantaged social classes: almost half of all births in the region take place in families living in extreme poverty (UNDP 1990).

In the last two decades, the Latin American population has become predominantly urban and better educated. Overall indicators of both dimensions now approximate those of developed countries. Nonetheless, significant quantitative and qualitative differences persist. The rapid urbanization process has made for great urban concentrations and the well-known phenomenon of the emergence of mega-cities. Urbanization in the region was characterized by limited incorporation of the labor force into the urban formal sector, a weak capacity for social integration, and increases in poverty. High rates of urbanization, only slightly lower than those of developed countries (75.3 percent compared to 78.3 percent), have therefore not been accompanied by a growing social incorporation.

The predominance of rural over urban poverty was a historic trait of the region through the mid-1980s. This relationship has been inverted, to the point where poverty is now a predominantly urban phenomenon.

Education and Employment

Much of the educational advance of the adult population in the region during the 1980s was a consequence of growing coverage achieved during the two preceding decades. In the majority of countries, average years of schooling increased among youth, though there were signs of regression and stagnation in some urban areas of Chile, Mexico, and Brazil and in rural areas of other countries (CEPAL 1990–95).

Despite these advances, educational coverage remains considerably below that of developed countries. This is particularly noteworthy at the secondary level, where coverage in developed countries is practically double that of Latin America, at 91.6 percent and 42.7 percent, respectively. In primary education, the similarity of coverage hides significant differences in achievement and learning across social strata. The cultural level and structure of the household, access to resources, and the sociocultural milieu in which schools operate show that levels of inequality are not diminishing, and in some cases have increased. As a consequence educational results vary widely, diverse forms of discrimination are growing, and there is an unequal development of skills and social capacities.

To the extent that new sectors incorporated into the educational system belong to the lowest social strata, inequality within the educational system expanded owing to the sociocultural disadvantages of these groups. During the last decade, educational progress was accompanied by different rates of advance across social strata: the highest strata increased their levels of education more than the rest of the population. Moreover, coverage has been subjected to another sort of pressure: not only did it have to expand to absorb a growing demand at all levels, but it has had to do so under significant pressure provoked by absolute demographic growth (CEPAL 1990–95). Not only does this pattern of growth differ from that of the core countries, but most of these characteristics contrast as well with those that predominate in many of the Asian newly industrialized countries (NICs).

Finally, labor force participation rates, measured as a percentage of the population, are 42 percent higher in the developed countries than in Latin America. Taking the entire population as a referent, little more than a third (35.2 percent) participate in the labor force, and the participation of women does not surpass 18.6 percent. Female labor force participation in the region is half that of developed countries.

According to CEPAL (1993, in CEPAL 1900–1995), the high rate of low-skilled jobs is one of the most conspicuous characteristics of the urban employment structure. These consist of nonprofessional, nonspecialized employees, as well as those employed in microenterprises and self-employed unskilled workers. The share of such workers in the economically active population varies between roughly 30 percent, in countries where the phenomenon is less frequent, to 50 percent in the smaller, poorer countries.

Analysis of the occupational structure created in the last few years shows an increase in this trend. During the three years from 1990 to 1992, eight of every ten new nonagricultural jobs that were created were concentrated in the informal sector or in small enterprises. From 1980 to 1990, the tendency was similar: large firms and the public sector absorbed only two of every ten employees (PREALC 1993). During the last three years, the structure of formal sector employment of newly hired workers also underwent relevant changes: as a result of adjustment policies, the relative weight of public employment fell, that of the medium-sized enterprises declined, and that of big business increased.

To the extent that the most salient characteristic of Latin American societies resides in the close tie between welfare and formal employment, the weak absorptive capacity of the formal productive sector, combined with high indices of poverty and social exclusion, has weakened or impeded broad coverage of traditional social benefits systems. As a consequence of the application of adjustment policies and the deregulation of the labor market, during the 1980s social protection systems were incapable of countering the inequalities that resulted from those policies.

MODELS OF DEVELOPMENT AND SOCIAL POLICIES

Import Substitution and Stratified Social Citizenship

A particular mode of Keynesian policy influenced a good part of the development models in Latin America between 1930 and 1970–80. We refer to the import substitution models (ISI) articulated theoretically in the ECLA paradigm and in the contributions of Raul Prebisch. In this model, the state assumes a central role in the process of economic and social development. Supported by hard currency generated by primary product exports, the state apparatus in the region was able to finance the growth of industries oriented toward domestic production with subsidies and a variety of protectionist measures. At the same time, the state played a role absorbing excess labor and provided the capital for basic works of economic and social infrastructure.

This model made possible, in a particular historical context, a significant process of social and economic modernization. It did so, however, with systematic biases in the distribution of benefits. Particularly with regard to welfare policies, it introduced a limited development, strongly oriented toward the urban sectors, with preferential or exclusive coverage for those sectors integrated in the formal labor market. Rural workers, domestic workers, and those sectors of the informal and secondary markets were excluded. The sectors effectively protected in these systems were themselves marked by clear patterns of stratification in terms of access, range of coverage against risks, and quality of benefits (Mesa-Lago 1994). State employees and those in key services gained early access to comprehensive coverage, while blue-collar workers received later and limited forms of protection.

Beyond the general review of the development model in the region and its impact on the models of social policy, it is imperative to note that enormous variations existed and continue to exist in the welfare systems in the various Latin American countries. The development of welfare policies must be understood in the context of the peculiar economic and political development of the region and in light of heterogeneity across countries. Different degrees of expansion of the import substitution model, distinct types of export-oriented production, and variations in the political power of different sectors of capital and labor must all be taken into account in constructing typologies of welfare state development in Latin America (Huber 1995).

A Tentative Typology of Welfare States in
Latin America, from 1930 to the 1970s

The first challenge for the student of Latin American social policy is the immense variety of models and degrees of development of welfare systems in different countries.[3] This variety is evident in the resource levels destined for social services; in the demographic coverage of the protection systems; in the range, variation, and quality of services; and in the sectoral distribution of social spending.

Stratified Universalism (Uruguay, Argentina, Chile)   Uruguay, Argentina, and Chile are among those Mesa-Lago defines as "pioneer" countries. In accordance with that criterion Brazil should also be included, but as we argue in the pages that follow, it fits in a different category.

The first crucial aspect of this group of countries is that, in one way or another, around 1970 they protected the majority of the population through systems of social security and health care while simultaneously extending primary and secondary education to all of the population. In other words, they all offered extended levels of decommodification both of service provision outside the market and in monetary benefits for various situations of employment interruption.

Other central characteristics of these systems include a sharp stratification of benefits, conditions of eligibility, and levels of protection in social security and in health care. State workers and professionals, and those in

---

3. A discussion of the conceptual guideposts for the discussion that follows is found in Filgueira 1998.

Table 5.1 Social Policy Indicators for Stratified Universal Countries, 1970 to 1980

	Social security (% of worforce covered)	Social security (% of total population covered, 1980)	Social spending (as % of 1980 GDP)	Immunization (% of population under 1 year old)	Percentage of age group enrolled in primary school	Percentage of age group enrolled in secondary school
Argentina	68.0	78.9	16.2	93	105	44
Uruguay	95.4	68.5	17.0	97	112	59
Chile	75.6	67.3	13.7	98	107	39

SOURCES: Mesa-Lago 1991; World Bank 1994; Miranda 1994; Cominetti 1994.

Table 5.2   Social (Outcome) Indicators for Stratified Universal Countries, to 1970

	Households below the poverty line (%)	Households below indigence line (%)	Illiteracy (%)	Infant mortality (per 1,000 live births)	Life expectancy at birth
Argentina	8	1	7.4	41	68.4
Uruguay	10	4[a]	10.2	47	68.6
Chile	17	6	11.0	62	64.2

SOURCE: CEPAL 1995; CEPAL Anuario Estadístico de América Latina 1980.
[a] Urban areas only.

urban services and urban manufacturing—in that order—accessed protections and benefits, and also in that order experienced stratified quality and access. The self-employed, the informal sector, the chronically unemployed, and rural workers did so later and with less success in terms of both access and benefits. However, it is important to emphasize the point, the stratification of social services cushioned rather than reinforced the prevailing pattern of social stratification. Stated more simply, if we were to calculate the Gini coefficients of primary income and income after transfers, the latter would be more egalitarian than the former. Moreover, the development of different social protection systems had a significant impact on variables related to social welfare. These gains cannot simply be attributed to the level of economic development, since cases like Brazil and Mexico with similar levels of per capita GDP exhibit notoriously inferior social indicators.

The explanation for the peculiar development of these social systems must be sought, not in their early development, but in the political economy of national development and in its political administration. The cases of Uruguay and Argentina presented a version of ISI anchored in the export of primary materials with very low demand for labor and high international profitability. Strong migratory processes toward the urban centers created pressure for the incorporation of subaltern sectors. The state promoted this incorporation through extending public employment and supporting domestic industry. The strength of the state vis-à-vis domestic capital—the anti-Schumpeterian alliance described by Evans (1979)—combined with the early unionization of subordinated sectors made it possible to negotiate and implement extensive social protection programs, with tripartite financing (in the case of social security) or unilateral financing (in the case of education as well as certain areas of health care). Chile is a more complicated case. Also a country with a significant development of ISI, the latter was based in this instance on mining and a diversified agrarian export economy with greater demand for labor. It exhibited, like the other cases, a significant rural-urban migration, though the process took place later. The first groups to be incorporated into the social protection system were the same as in Uruguay and Argentina—the public workers and professionals. Utilizing resources generated by foreign trade, state elites developed the first social service programs (education and, to a lesser extent, health care) and social security. In turn, strongly unionized miners, enjoying close ties to political parties in the urban centers, were able to exert pressure and achieve incorporation into the systems of social protection and services.

These three cases represent, as Huber indicates with regard to Chile and Argentina, the model closest to the corporatist-conservative system Esping-Andersen identifies for industrialized countries. The conditions in which they confronted reforms of the social policy systems of the 1970s and 1980s were particularly difficult, since they had to contend with change, having achieved significant levels of protection in predominantly recessionary contexts marked by contractions of public spending in general and social spending in particular. To this must be added the fact that, given the nature of their development, the groups best situated to defend their benefits were those that received the majority of resources, so that reforms aiming to foster equality through spending adjustments could easily result perversely in heightened stratification. Targeting and decentralization, just like the privatization of a good part of their social services, should be evaluated with this in mind. The viability, sustainability, and desirability of these reforms depends on their capacity to respond appropriately to this context.

Dual Regimes (Brazil, Mexico) Until the 1970s Brazil and Mexico exhibited an almost universal development of primary education and a significant though stratified degree of health coverage. With regard to social security, coverage accentuated the stratified aspects of mature systems, without the universalized coverage of stratified universal systems. It is in these countries where the problem of territorial heterogeneity can be seen most clearly. This is not because their rates of differential development were greater than those of the exclusionary systems we will analyze later. Rather, what is clear is a significant development of the formal labor market, the state, and benefits in certain states and regions and a virtual absence of benefits and low incorporation (through the market or the state) of the majority of the population in other regions. These countries have been characterized by a form of ISI supported by rents derived from primary sector activities with high labor intensity and significant regional heterogeneity in levels of economic and social development. In both cases, this pattern is structurally evidenced and reproduced by a comparatively high degree of federalism.

Politically, control and incorporation of the popular sectors has rested on a combination of clientelism and patrimonialism in the zones of least economic and social development, and on vertical corporatism in more developed areas. The short duration and low intensity of electorally competitive democratic regimes has permitted this dual form of incorporation, increasing power differentials separating popular sectors in core and peripheral areas. In contrast to stratified universalist countries, social protection systems cushion social segmentation only for those sectors incorporated into modern frameworks of protection. These systems exacerbate stratification between the latter and those not fortunate enough to be part of such frameworks.

Exclusionary Regimes (Dominican Republic, Guatemala, Honduras, El Salvador, Nicaragua, Bolivia, Ecuador) With the exception of Costa Rica, the Central American countries—and Bolivia and Peru—exhibit elitist systems of social security and health care and dual systems in education. Measured by income, poverty in all of these countries exceeds 50 percent. Except for Guatemala (27 percent), less than 20 percent of the population had basic benefits programs or social security around 1970, and the figures for healthcare coverage are similar. Education was different, for the expansion of primary enrollments, with sharp differences in quality, reached more than half of the population, almost reaching the point of universal coverage in some countries.

These cases approximate what Peter Evans (1995) labels "predatory states." Elites appropriate the state apparatus and, supported by the export of primary goods in enclave economies, employ the fiscal capacity of these states to extract profits without providing collective benefits in return, either through infrastructure, regulation, or social services. Systems of social protection and social security of this type for the most part consist of elitist policies that grant additional privileges to privileged populations. Professionals, a greatly reduced number of formal sector workers, and public sector functionaries are those who typically are favored by these models. The majority of the population located in the informal sector, agriculture, and secondary labor markets are excluded.

It is worth noting that the social structures of these countries are characterized by high degrees of inequality, evident in the distribution of national wealth between the urban and rural sectors and between different rural areas, as well as between the urban center and the periphery. In other words, the market has generated clusters of negative and positive social configurations.

Table 5.3 Social Policy Indicators for Dualist Countries, 1970 to 1980

	Social security (% of worforce covered	Social security (% of total population covered, 1980)	Social spending (as % of 1980 GDP)	Immunization (% of population under 1 year old)	Percentage of age group enrolled in primary school	Percentage of age group enrolled in secondary school
Brazil	27.0	96.3	9.3	66	82	26
Mexico	28.1	53.4	8.0	80	104	22

SOURCES: Mesa-Lago 1991; World Bank 1994; Miranda 1994; Cominetti 1994.

Table 5.4   Social (Outcome) Indicators for Dual Countries up to 1970

	Households below the poverty line (%)	Households below indigence line (%)	Illiteracy (%)	Infant mortality (per 1,000 live births)	Life expectancy at birth
Brazil	49	25	33.6	95	59.8
Mexico	34	12	25.8	60	62.7

SOURCE: CEPAL 1995; CEPAL Anuario Estadístico de América Latina 1980.

For its part, the extent to which the state has intervened to correct imbalances, in effect by pooling risk, has been minimal. State bureaucracies also reflect this reality, with marked differences in their efficiency and productivity, meaning that in some urban areas the state functions effectively, while in rural outposts it may be virtually absent. Finally, at the political level, organized participation of subaltern sectors in decision-making spheres has been historically low, given their limited organizational capacity and the largely repressive character of political regimes. The incorporation and co-optation of socially subaltern sectors has been achieved through clientelistic and patrimonialist mechanisms of local elites, or through sui-generis forms of repression and political policing. Consistent with this simplified description, social indicators in this type of country systematically present extremes of exclusion, as well as the highest difference among regions of different levels of development.

Globalization and Structural Transformations   The central dilemmas of social policy in Latin America can only be understood by taking into consideration the sociopolitical and economic contexts in which they develop. Among these aspects, emphasis must be placed upon the macrostructural transformations that have occurred recently in the region and in the world, and their impact on the possibilities and limits of social policies.

Propelled by changes in the international system, Latin American countries are experiencing profound and accelerated transformations. As a consequence of globalization and of the virtual shrinking of the world, countries strive to insert themselves into a new, increasingly competitive and open international system.

These developments have a clear impact in Latin America: they demand the difficult transformation from highly protected economic systems—models of inward development or of import substitution—to open and export-oriented economies. Countries thus have had to internalize external vectors of change and process their responses to the new challenges in an endogenous

Table 5-5   Social Policy Indicators for Exclusionary Countries, 1970/1980

	Social security (% of worforce covered)	Social security (% of total population covered, 1980)	Social spending (as % of 1980 GDP)	Immunization (% of population under 1 year old)	Percentage of age group enrolled in primary school	Percentage of age group enrolled in secondary school
Bolivia	9.0	25.4	5.9	70	76	24
Ecuador	14.8	9.4	9.3	61	97	22
Dominican Republic	8.9	—	0.7/2.3[a]	40	100	21
Nicaragua	14.8	9.1	2.3/—[a]	90	80	18
El Salvador	11.6	6.2	1.3/1.7[a]	—	85	22
Guatemala	27.0	14.2	1.6/3.7[a]	—	57	8
Honduras	4.2	7.3	0.9/12.2[a]	75	87	14

SOURCES: Mesa-Lago 1991; World Bank 1994; Miranda 1994; Cominetti 1994.
[a] Social Security spending / health spending.

Table 5.6   Social (Outcome) Indicators for Exclusionary Countries 1970 to 1989

	Households below the poverty line (%)	Households below indigence line (%)	Illiteracy (%)	Infant mortality (per 1,000 live births)	Life expectancy at birth
Bolivia	50[a]	22[ab]	37.3	157	46.7
Ecuador	—	—	25.8	100	57.1
Dominican Republic	—	—	33.1	72	57.9
Nicaragua	—	—	42.1	109	52.9
El Salvador	—	—	42.9	92	59.1
Guatemala	65[c]	33[c]	53.8	104	54.6
Honduras	65	45	40.5	110	54.1

SOURCE: CEPAL 1995; CEPAL Anuario Estadístic de América Latina 1980.
[a] 1989.
[b] Urban areas.
[c] 1980.

manner. For this reason it is not surprising that the external vectors of change are the same for all countries, yet their responses differ.

Scientific and technological change cannot be disassociated from the process of globalization. The use of new technologies has contributed to the alteration of the structural and institutional bases of social security programs prevailing in the region because they modify the flows of capital and inter-firm relations (the distribution of contracting and subcontracting firms in chains organized at a national and international level), while transforming patterns of international trade (growth of exchange between industrial firms) and the organization of labor and labor markets give rise to the emergence of new modalities of labor informality and to increasing flexibility of employment.

A growing process of bloc formation (e.g., NAFTA, MERCOSUR, etc.) has redefined long-standing scenarios. In the area of social policies, to the extent that processes of regional and subregional integration continue, new problems are emerging as a result of the different degrees of maturity of national social security programs, their relative incompatibility, and the possible paths of adjustment of labor legislation across countries.

As a consequence of the change in the development model we are witnessing a reorganization of relations between state and society and of public-private space, in a mixture that recognizes multiple possible arrangements. Social security and social protection programs that in the past had operated almost exclusively from the public sphere and were organized institutionally around principles of centralization and sectoral specialization are now subjected to transformations that seek to reorient them toward privatization, decentralization, and integration.

Policies designed to promote industrial restructuring have caused new forms of social vulnerability to emerge in the region, while exacerbating traditional ones. The greatest impact has been brought about by trends in employment. For the younger generations, entry into the labor market has become more problematic, while the stability of adult male employment has diminished in a context already marked by precariousness. Instead of decreasing, informal employment has increased, while female employment, considered from certain points of view as a positive advance for gender equality, has proven to have ambiguous consequences. The high percentage of married women with children at an active age who are entering the workforce contrasts clearly with tendencies of the past, when working women were generally single. These new patterns of employment combine with demographic tendencies—like marriage rates, frequency of divorce, free unions, and so on—to configure new forms of social vulnerability: they reinforce patterns of disintegration and incompleteness in family organization (growing illegitimacy of children, single mothers, absence of fathers, incomplete households headed by women).[4]

Weak traditional systems of social protection are proving incapable of confronting emergent problems in the new globalized scenario. In those countries that were able to develop relatively advanced systems of social protection, the equity-oriented strategies that were still valid in the 1960s were already showing signs of exhaustion. Social security systems, in particular, had gone through actuarial and financial crises (Mesa-Lago 1994).

Meanwhile, some of the expectations placed both on full employment and on the increasing formalization of the labor force in order to sustain stable, long-term benefits systems (especially pensions and health coverage) have proven to be unfulfillable in the face of tendencies in the labor market that run precisely counter to this logic.

It is for these reasons that to this point social protection and benefits systems have exhausted all possibilities for reform inside a dominant paradigm. There has been no shortage of attempts to effect partial reform, but each of them only served to leave the systems in deeper crisis and to deprive the paradigm of that much more legitimacy. The need for reform was imposed as a

---

4. The breakdown of the classic "breadwinner" family structure triggered by the growing participation of women in the work force has significant implications for social vulnerability that cannot be developed here. Of particular import is its impact on social integration and on the socialization of children in urban popular sectors.

consensual fact, and the brief history that social policies then followed is well known. In terms of social security, Chile led a process of neoliberal reform that later was extended—totally or in part—to a large part of the region. Meanwhile, in terms of policy options, targeted approaches to combating poverty and the privatization of social security were affirmed with noteworthy conviction.

ON THE IMPLEMENTATION OF NEW SOCIAL POLICIES: SOCIAL SECURITY AND EMERGENCY FUNDS, DECENTRALIZATION, AND TERTIARIZATION

Evaluating the result of social policies is not a simple task. Besides the shortage of information, the objectives that social policies pursue present complicated problems. The climate in which implementation of social programs takes place can often be compared to that in which an experiment takes place: as a result, changes in context have consequences far beyond their impact on individuals involved directly in those programs. Yet we need not worry greatly about this point, for the reality is that studies evaluating social programs in Latin America are few and far between. Multilateral development agencies, in particular, recently have begun to encourage greater availability of information, as they have incorporated evaluation as an additional criterion for the approval of projects. Yet little can be said about what was implemented in the past. The following discussion presents partial results derived from the handful of experiences that are well known.

National-level studies conducted through the "Social Policies Network Program" coincide in identifying a model common to all countries before the 1980s. Economic programs received priority, with the focus on policies of stabilization, adjustment, economic reconversion, and efficiency-maximizing state reforms. Even when the economy was not the priority of the public agenda, social policy remained subordinated to other goals. In Peru, during the period of Alan García, social policy was subordinated to the more general objective of national pacification. An examination of the National Solidarity Program in Mexico shows that during that period social policy was part of the PRI's strategy to recover part of its social bases of support in response to the erosion of its legitimacy within labor unions. As a consequence, it tended to favor potentially disruptive groups, those facing greater social tensions though not necessarily the most deprived social sectors (Molinar and Weldon 1994).

Until the 1970s, social policy occupied a back seat to other priorities. Influenced by various programs, actions, and loans of multilateral agencies, many governments launched new social programs. It is impossible to affirm, however, that these reflected priorities of key political actors being translated into state policy.

A good part of these programs continue to be financed by external resources, and indeed were supplements to national accounts devoted to traditional service provision. Thus transformations in social policy have sought to compensate for problems of inequity, social integration, and lack of benefits that grew as a result of economic opening and adjustment policies, or have involved institutional and regulatory reforms of a partial and sectoral character, operating within the existing logic of public benefits provision.

In this last case, the principle of self-finance took priority in certain countries. The golden rule of social policies was that users should pay, though this would mean a progressive privatization of collective services. As the National Studies on Social Policy Brazil Report (CEBRAP 1994) noted with regard to education and health:

> Finally, the logic of self-finance helped to privilege investment in physical infrastructure, installations, and equipment without corresponding reinforcement of the capacities of states and municipalities to assume the financial responsibility for the subsequent operation of services. This magnified the debt of local governments and diminished the social efficacy of large investments. Excessive administrative centralization and the accelerated pace of growth surpassed managerial capacities, a problem that was aggravated by the absence of any type of public control. Social policies were thus captured easily by private interests, lobbies, etc. In addition, we must point out that a good part of the expansion of the government's social services took place through partnerships with the private sector, principally in the supply of goods and services.

During the last few decades, a multiplicity of unprecedented institutions, actions, plans, and social measures were generated in the region. The sole exception has been Colombia, in which social policy retained a low profile, and effective social policies have been limited in number.

The other three countries—Argentina, Mexico, and Chile—have experienced more radical policy changes, aspiring to nationwide coverage in some programs. For its part, Argentina decentralized its social programs to the point that the majority of public spending comes from the provinces. Meanwhile, there has been a marked shift toward a public-private mix in service delivery, with state functions declining and an opening of spaces for participation by the private sector. In Mexico, the National Solidarity Program, targeted toward the poor and elaborated on the basis of the experiences of PIDER and COPLAMAR, constitutes an innovative program, financed by the state but superimposed on traditional institutional arrangements for social services.

Finally, Chile is the country that has been transformed the most. Since the military came to power in 1973, it has drastically reduced resources and imposed structural reforms diminishing the size of the state by transferring functions to the private sector and decentralizing ministries and services. Chile also has implemented concrete measures for reducing or eliminating universal programs, targeting state efforts to the poorest sections of the population.

Until the 1970s, social policies in Chile basically aimed to stimulate community participation and incorporate organized institutions of the poor rather than to orient policy exclusively toward the individual or family unit; replace assistance with efforts to orient production and investment in human capital; balance programs directed toward the poor with initiatives aimed at the middle class; and implement measures attending to emergent problems such as quality of education, stratification of technical-professional education, and increasing investment in the healthcare system, housing subsidies, and broadened coverage of social assistance programs.

Despite being the three countries that have advanced furthest in constructing a national policy or integrated social programs, Chile, Mexico, and Argentina have experienced a variety of "compatibility" problems that have limited their efforts to achieve fully integrated social policies. Analyses of these countries coincide in pointing out:

1. Problems of deviation from original objectives, sectoral bias in coverage toward sectors enjoying privileged influence.
2. Inefficiencies in implementation caused by low administrative capacity and poor management of units that assume decentralized functions.
3. Problems of compatibility, duplication of services, and contradictions between the central and regional levels.
4. Difficulties of implementation derived from the effects of political party machines and their behavioral logics.

In social security, the extension of experiences to other countries shows, more than in any other area of reform, the importance of endogenous effects for the ways in which external changes are processed internally. In Chile, the process of reform carried out during the dictatorship constituted

the most complete application of neoliberal principles. In Uruguay, following an initial proposal and later a plebiscite and extensive social mobilization, there came an eclectic reform that combined an individual private
capitalization system with a solidarity component. Argentina followed the
same path, while Peru adopted a social security system closer to that of
Chile. In Brazil, social security reform seems to be advancing slowly, but
there are still no concrete results.

Beyond the well-known evaluations of the region's social security reform
models (Mesa-Lago 1994), what appears to be new in the mixed models of
solidarity and capitalization is that implementation of reforms inspires problems that affect the realization of the solidarity component. Some reforms—
like the Uruguayan—opted for the noncompulsive choice of capitalization
system, allowing contributors to choose the system they prefer. Since the
goal of the reform was for people to opt for the capitalization system, significant incentives and rewards were offered, and obligations to contribute
resources to the solidarity system were reduced. The results proved, however, that policymakers underestimated the preferences of the contributors.
The proportion of those who preferred to contribute less to the solidarity
system has been much higher than anticipated. As a consequence, the most
likely risk of such an approach is a decline in resources and an eventual
financial collapse of the solidarity component, though as with any policy
with effects deferred over the long term, it is impossible to make definitive
predictions about studies that analyze alternative hypotheses of contributors' behavior.

A second core of transformations for which we have systematic evaluations involve social investment funds designed to combat poverty (Wurgaft
1993). The performance of the region since it began to implement the first
programs (around 1990) is positive in terms of learning and experience, but
evaluations show scant and contradictory results.[5] The programs do not
affect the poorest and neediest sectors, while the effects on investment are
scant. It is also unlikely that such effects will last beyond the active period
of the programs. In addition, the programs have not had aggregate effects
and do not reflect general tendencies concerning poverty and need.

When programs are evaluated in aggregate terms, alongside changes in
the scale of poverty, we see that the absolute number of people living below
the poverty line increased from 136 million in 1980 to 196 million in 1990,

5. Transitional funds were implemented in six countries by 1990, and in Ecuador in
1993. Among the permanent funds implemented in these six countries, Costa Rica stands out
as an early case (1974), along with Bolivia in 1988 and Mexico in 1989.

despite continued economic growth in Colombia, Costa Rica, Chile, Mexico, and Uruguay. The growth of poverty was accompanied by an increase of the extremely poor population from 19 percent to 22 percent, representing 31 million more people with economic resources that were inadequate to ensure subsistence. The scandalous landscape of poverty in the region, despite some recent encouraging tendencies, cannot obscure the fact that in 1992 only one of eleven countries for which information was available experienced lower poverty rates than in 1980 (CEPAL 1998).

According to the most recent data from CEPAL (1995), in the three years between 1992 and 1994 poverty experienced a slight decline. However, estimates over the very short term cannot overlook the structural character of poverty, nor can they identify a reliable relationship between the application of policies and behavior on a macro level. In reality, despite the vast resources allocated to social investment funds during the period under consideration, there is little hope for any significant reduction in poverty.

As to inequality, analysis of data covering these years shows that recession, adjustment policies, and restructuring accentuated the regressive features of income distribution. Medium- and low-income groups disproportionately bore the weight of adjustment, while the top 5 percent maintained or increased its share of the total national income.

In the first years of the 1990s, there was a slight improvement in income redistribution, but only a minority of the countries showed values in the Gini index less than those of the 1980s. The most recent information from CEPAL shows that the concentration of wealth between the first five years of the 1980s and 1992—in some cases 1994—continued to grow in six of the twelve countries for which there is available information. Among these, the highest growth in the Gini coefficient was registered in the three largest countries in the region—Argentina, Mexico, and Brazil.

Despite sustaining high economic growth for more than ten years, Chile fell in the group of countries with the highest level of overall inequality. It has the same level of urban inequality as Guatemala—Gini coefficient 0.479 for 1994—and is only surpassed by Brazil, the most unequal country in the region, and maybe in the world, with a value of 0.535 in 1990 (CEPAL 1995, table 11).

If these trends continue, the combination of economic policies and antipoverty social policies will manage, in the best of cases, to partially compensate for some of the effects of the market on employment and wages in a handful of regions or localities. But the levels of poverty and indigence, like the deterioration in quality of life for vast sectors of the middle and lower classes, exhibit a stubborn persistence.

ON THE TRANSFER OF MODELS AND STRATEGIES

In this section we address the viability of efforts to apply strategies and institutional approaches across country and regional contexts. The rationale for this exercise is not only theoretical or conceptual. Indeed, Latin America has been literally bombarded with technical advice citing the Asian model and the strategies of the U.S. welfare state as examples one should aspire to emulate.

The analysis that follows attempts to make three points. First, the model furthest from the concerns of the region is probably that of the Southeast Asian countries. Second, comparison between both groups of countries suggests a series of complicated problems that undermine the utility of transferring social policies. And third, the model (or models) of greatest relevance to the region cannot be found in the U.S. experience but rather in the conservative-corporatist tradition of Europe.

The key to understanding the particularities of social policies in Latin America lies in a series of historical features peculiar to the region. In particular, Latin America experienced an early process of decolonization, more than a century before most of Asia; the region became involved in the international market at an early stage; and in cultural terms it has long formed part of the West. From its Iberian roots, however, Latin America inherited a particular set of Western traditions: strongly patrimonialist structures with their correlates of aristocratic-military power, sustained by the privileges of land ownership and centralized and bureaucratic political power.[6]

The trajectory of the region corresponds most closely to the "conservative modernization" model in which, despite social modernization, traditional upper classes remained stagnant and/or resisted economic modernization. Thus powerful tensions between aspirations and legitimate expectations have long characterized Latin American social structures. This is all the more relevant in light of educational achievements and traditional liberal professions of higher prestige, the expansion of urbanization, and the growth of middle-class employment in the tertiary sector or in the state, all without a corresponding unleashing of productive forces and equitable income distribution.

6. In making such gross simplifications, it is essential to point to significant differences within the region. In particular, Argentina and Uruguay, known in the literature of the last century as countries of "recent settlement," or "white settler colonies," to distinguish them, along with New Zealand, Australia, and Canada, from other colonial situations. A favorable insertion in the global system, with primary export economies in semitemperate zones linked to the metropolitan core of England, with ample flows of capital investment and infrastructural development, combined with widespread availability of land and a limited indigenous population, tended to generate a relatively modern and urbanized class structure, comprised of an upper class of native-born landowners and nascent urban middle- and lower-class sectors.

And despite the travails of democracy, many countries of the region experienced the creation of union and corporatist structures that emulated European models, and which were often led by European immigrants of anarchist or socialist inclinations. This was common from the beginning of the century in the Southern Cone, though union structures arose later and at an unequal rate across the region. Political parties in the region sought for better or worse to play a role of intermediary akin to that of their counterparts in Europe. While in most countries none of these processes encompassed the majority of the population—Argentina and Uruguay are the only truly middle-class Latin American societies—there always existed, to a greater or lesser extent, a significant core of social and political actors capable of organizing themselves and articulating their demands.[7] It is for precisely this reason that these countries are best described as highly mobilized societies.[8]

Consideration of newly industrializing countries (NICs) in Asia suggests the presence of some core characteristics similar to those of Latin America. The persistence of semi-absolutist structures, characterized by the label of "oriental despotism," are key to understanding Asian systems.

But if it makes little sense to apply historical models to the present in an oversimplified fashion, it is nonetheless the case that there are legitimate grounds for questioning the generalized relevance of political rights as understood in Western liberal democracies. Recognition of such structures is not just a question of the relationships between economic development and political regime. If that were all that was involved, our conclusions would be simple enough: history offers sufficient examples of economic development both in democratic societies and under authoritarian regimes. But analyses of political processes frequently commit the conceptual error of ignoring systematic characteristics and examining public policies independently of political constraints, as if they were pieces of a puzzle that could be attached to any circumstance.[9] To be sure, the strategies pursued by

7. It is well known that populism and clientelism were among the predominant forms of political articulation and economic redistribution in Latin America. Combined with labor movements and unions with varying degrees of power and influence, these constituted the basis for significant social and political mobilization in the region.

8. Huber (1995) notes crucial differences in terms of alliances and the formation and development of European welfare states based on the relatively early appearance of middle classes vis-à-vis the industrial working class in European industrial development.

9. This is evident, for example, in claims that reduce the problem of governability and efficiency to the capacity of a totalitarian authority to implement programs (World Bank 1994). "While it is true that governments of the eight countries have tended to be authoritarian or paternalist, they have been prepared as well to give opportunities to express opinion and exercise true autonomy for a technocratic elite and portions of the private sector. Unlike authoritarian rulers in many other countries, leaders of this group of countries realized that economic development was not possible without cooperation." Or when it is affirmed that

many Asian countries, such as the quest to maintain autonomy of civil servants, promoting cooperation with the private sector, and the establishment of highly prestigious administrative career ladders, are valid in themselves. However, what accounts for the economic success of the Asian NICs is not the aggregation of such strategic elements but rather a particular form of articulation of total public authority with some—and not all—actors in civil society. Hence, for example, the exclusion and repression of labor organizations in these settings.

It is equally clear that Asian civil society is distinguished by patterns of inclusive familiar relations, traditional community networks, and different modalities of active religious communities, through all of which flow immeasurable reservoirs of social capital. For the most part, Asian societies only recently emerged from a fundamentally peasant base. Neither social mobilization, nor the explosion of consumption expectations, nor the high degrees of individuation typical of developed societies and of Latin America have been salient characteristics of Asian societies. The exceptional growth of technically oriented education contrasts with traditional Latin American educational systems, which are geared toward the humanities and toward the construction of citizenship, and which thereby serve as sources of legitimacy for political, social, and civil rights. These are certainly not mobilized societies.[10]

Other critical differences are equally noteworthy. In Asian societies, high levels of equality have been maintained throughout much of the process of industrialization, partly because of the complete or partial destruction of the traditional upper classes, for a variety of reasons, but typically through imperial conquest or the impact of war. Moreover, modern middle classes consolidated late and expanded slowly.

For its part, the United States, with the important exception of the South, consolidated at an early stage social structures comprised of free workers and farmers, for whom the frontier offered the advantage of an individual and entrepreneurial alternative to purely wage-earning conditions. The important role of political parties in this society was not in terms of mediation among class interests, as in Europe, but as a constraint on capitalist advance by delimiting the rights of property. Rooted in Anglo-Saxon law, common

---

"the first step consisted in contracting independent and honest technocrats and isolating them from everyday political pressures."

10. Clearly, one cannot explain the remarkable delay of Asian countries in establishing social security systems, and their doing so eventually with highly limited coverage, without keeping in mind the assets available to families with an accumulated stock of social capital (Pempel, this volume).

law contributed fundamentally to establishing rights and duties that define citizenship across multiple dimensions, encompassing civil, social, and political incorporation. The relative abundance of work joined with the strong regulatory role of the political and judicial systems to configure a country in which social order is constructed upon strong axes of law and market.

If the United States has as its core law and market, a risky stretch of the metaphor is irresistible: Southeast Asia achieves order through a core of "family and bureaucracy," and Europe and Latin America do so through "parties and state." The role of social policies in each of these forms will vary, and has varied, in these different types of societies. Transplanting a model of social policy or welfare brings with it serious disruptive effects when it entails abandoning latent functions that social policy models fulfilled or ceased fulfilling in specific contexts of social production and reproduction.

CONCLUSIONS

The relative lack of analysis of social policy in the context of new economic conditions reflects a critical problem. While economic activity globalizes alongside international debates and regulations, social policies remain confined to the national level or strictly within the sphere of influence of international agencies. It is thus no surprise that these policies are being discussed within constraints posed by the transnational economic arena. It appears unlikely that the emerging discourse at the international level will have the capacity to counteract the primacy of economic constraints if it is unable to effect accountability at the regional level with regard to social policy.

During the last few years, a worldwide discourse about policy and social development has been consolidating within and among global institutions and multilateral organizations that, in practice, set the agenda for social reform in the contemporary world (World Bank, IMF, ILO, Inter-American Development Bank, Council of Europe, OECD, European Union, Unicef, ECLAC, and others).

Between and within these agencies, the discourse emphasizes distinct aspects of the functions and ultimate objectives of the welfare state. In the past, for some agencies the primary objective of welfare policies was social cohesion and maintaining existing patterns of social stratification (a conservative version of the European Union or the corporate version of the ILO or World Bank). For other organizations, if those policies really intended to become a means for social-economic investment through the development of human resources (Southeast Asia, OECD, ECLAC, IDB), they also emphasized the importance of their commitment to democracy (as in the discourse of the ILO). For other international institutions, by contrast, welfare practices were considered a weight or obstacle that should be removed, since they were perceived to be an incentive for unproductive investments and relatively undemocratic forms of administration.

Today, discussions of post-Fordist patterns of economic growth remain loyal to the old paradigm of well-being (social cohesion, investment, and redistribution), despite recognizing that regulated labor markets were no longer appropriate frameworks for approaches to social security. A particular set of prescriptions and recommendations about types of welfare policies, among which figured prominently such concepts as safety nets, universal work-fare safety nets (IMF), and so on, have become part of the spectrum of alternatives included in today's global discourse (Deacon 1995).

The greatest challenge to social reform in Latin America is to design a set of instruments for social action and regulation that better distribute wealth and opportunities, reduce levels of poverty and indigence, and augment the general well-being of the population while guaranteeing the security of the most vulnerable sectors. There is a consensus in the region that these objectives offer a path toward social cohesion, sustainable economic development, and the strengthening of democracy. Such altruistic intentions have long formed part of Latin American discourse and rhetoric, though none of these objectives have been realized. A final consideration of these themes requires reflection, analysis, and empirical study of the formation of social policy in the region. It is particularly necessary to concentrate on the ends of social policy, and not solely on the most appropriate means or instruments for carrying out such policies. In this regard, several points deserve special emphasis.

The first concerns crucial problems in the definition of "policy space" and "policy options": what is the perception of actors concerning the economic constraints and policies that determine the potential scope of social policies? The second point concerns issues of "policy alternatives" as perceived by decision-makers: what are their models, where do they come from, and what social effects are attributed to these policy packages? Third, there are problems of policy design—how to construct specific strategies of action and regulation for delivering, directing, and realizing policy objectives; and how appropriate are existing institutional structures, can their efficiency be improved, and how might they be transformed? A final point refers to aspects of control and learning: how can we evaluate the fulfillment of program objectives, extract lessons from policies that are implemented, and communicate those lessons to decision-makers?

National-level studies conducted during the first phase of the Latin American Program on Social Policy revealed a wide spectrum of activities and the broad coverage of studies devoted to strategies of policy design and, to a lesser degree, evaluation. This is not the case with regard to the area of "policy alternatives" or to the analysis of "policy space," where levels of information and debate are quite low. In this context, naturally there is a tendency to attribute policy failures or shortcomings exclusively to the greater or lesser degrees of efficiency of alternative strategies, rather than to the appropriateness of these strategies to the ends they purportedly seek.

A second set of problems is closely related to this last one. Both the ends and the means for social policy coincide with, contradict, or complement other aspects of social life, in particular, those represented by the spheres of economics and politics. In Latin America, there are no comprehensive studies of social policies as systems that are defined in relation to economic processes and policies, political systems, or social structures.

It is well known that the region has progressed from a stage of economic adjustment to adjustment with a "human face" and "social adjustment." Nonetheless, after a long period of experimentation, we still lack integrated studies of the social effects of economic policy, the economic effects of social policy, and the political factors that determine the options of policy and implementation. To evaluate programs it is not sufficient to depend only on evaluations that divorce the social from the economic and political logics with which it interacts. Nor is it enough to consider political factors as interferences or anomalies that impinge on achievement of project objectives and social programs. It is worth recalling that the complexity of decision-making processes lies precisely in the fact that policies emerge from different rationalities—economic, social, political, and technical—and that what can be good for one of these aspects is not necessarily good for the others.

This point derives its relevance from several factors. It helps us to understand the particular configuration of the majority of countries of the region in the broader context of the problems specific to Third World societies. Under the import substitution model the region had two important moments of industrial growth: one in the first decades of the century and another during the 1950s and 1960s. The social structure was modernized through the expansion of the tertiary sector, while the growth of the middle class and the expansion of education and urbanization contributed to the modernization of the state. The hopes and expectations of the population traditionally had as points of reference the lifestyles and consumption patterns of the most developed societies. At the same time, in the political sphere, the countries of the region experienced, to greater or lesser degrees, the presence of workers' organizations, stable political parties, and institutional and constitutional frameworks that partially reflected certain characteristics of Western European countries.

These characteristics have had consequences for the structure of necessities and demands. Whether because of the growth and legitimacy of aspirations or the proliferation of agencies charged with organizing and steering demands, the countries of the region can be conceptualized as having been mobilized and politically complex for a long time. In contrast, a common characteristic of all countries of the region has been the difficulty of creating egalitarian societies while covering the basic needs of the entire population. For these reasons, historically, the prevailing model of development in the region has corresponded to what can be labeled a conservative and exclusionary modernization.

REFERENCES

CEPAL (Comisión Económica para América Latina y el Caribe). 1980. *Anuario Estadístico de América Latina*. Santiago: CEPAL.
————. 1990–95. *Anuarios Estadísticos de América Latina*. Panorama Social de América Latina. Santiago: CEPAL.
————. 1995. *Panorama Social de América Latina, Chile, 1994*. Santiago: CEPAL.
————. 1996. *Panorama Social de América Latina, Chile, 1995*. Santiago: CEPAL.
————. 1998. *Panorama Social de América Latina, Chile, 1997*. Santiago: CEPAL.
————. 2000. *Panorama Social de América Latina, Chile, 1999*. Santiago: CEPAL.
CEBRAP. 1994. *Políticas Sociais no Brasil*. São Paulo: Centro Brasileiro de Anàlise e Planejamento.
Deacon, B. 1995. "Global Institutions, Social Policy and Social Development." UNRISD, Occasional Paper, U.N. World Summit on Social Development.
Esping-Anderson, G. 1990. *The Three Worlds of Welfare Capitalism*. Princeton: Princeton University Press.
Evans, Peter. 1979. *Dependent Development*. Princeton: Princeton University Press.
————. 1995. *Embedded Autonomy: States and Industrial Transformation*. Princeton: Princeton University Press.
Filgueira, Fernando. 1998. "El nuevo modelo de prestaciones sociales en América Latina." In Brian Roberts, ed., *Ciudadanía Políticas Sociales*. Serie Centroamérica en Reestructuración. San Jose, Costa Rica: FLACSO/SSRC.
Huber, Evelyne. 1995. "Options for Social Policy in Latin America." In Gøsta Esping-Andersen, ed., *Welfare States in Transition*. London: Sage Publications.
Londoño, J. L., and M. Székely. 1997. "Sorpresas distributivas después de una década de reformas." Working Paper. Washington, D.C.: Inter-American Development Bank.
Mesa-Lago, C. 1994. *La reforma de la seguridad social y las pensiones en América Latina*. Quito: INCAE.

Molinar, Juan, and Jeffrey A. Weldon. 1994. "Electoral Determinants and Conse-
quences of National Solidarity." In Wayne A. Cornelius, Ann L. Craig, and
Jonathan Fox, eds., *Transforming State-Society Relations in Mexico*. San
Diego, Calif.: University of California, Center for U.S.-Mexican Studies.

PREALC. 1993. *Boletín PREALC Informa, No. 32*. Santiago: PREALC.

Székely, M., and M. Hilgert. 1999. *The 1990s in Latin America: Another Decade of
Persistent Inequality*. Washington, D.C.: IDB.

UNDP. 1990. *Development Report, United Nations Development Program*. New
York: UNDP.

World Bank. 1994. *World Development Report, International Economics Department*. New York: Oxford University Press.

Wurgaft, José. 1993. *Fondos de Inversión Social en América Latina*. Santiago: PRE-
ALC, OIT (Organización Internacional de Trabajo = ILO).

———. 1994. *Políticas Sociais no Brasil*. São Paulo: Centro Brasileiro de Anàlise e
Planejamento.

6

Jobs and Solidarity: Challenges for Labor Market Policy in Latin America

VÍCTOR E. TOKMAN

This chapter deals with the search for a new generation of employment policies to respond to the current needs for jobs and solidarity. These two objectives were at the foundations of the socioeconomic order prevailing in most Latin American countries up to the recent period of intensive adjustments to the debt crisis and to the transformation of the world economy. What began as a traditional short-term stabilization adjustment in the early 1980s evolved into a full structural transformation affecting, not only some of the foundations of the economic system, but also its social ordering.

I open with a brief review of the main trends in employment and incomes to identify the issues that have emerged during the process of adjustment. In particular, I find it necessary to observe whether jobs are being created quickly enough and whether these new jobs are good enough and pay well enough to be considered socially acceptable. Poverty and equity outcomes are largely determined by this evolution in employment.

Those who make policy and establish priorities should take into account the transformation of the international economy and how that transformation has affected the functioning of the economies and, particularly, the labor markets of Latin America. I identify the main processes of change in order to set the scene in which the new generation of policies will have to perform.

I then identify the policy areas that pertain to employment creation. I establish priorities and analyze the redesigning of policy instruments. Some of these instruments have proven themselves as means for employment creation, but still must be adapted to these new circumstances; others are innovative responses to emerging issues. It should come as no surprise that after several years of trial and error in policy innovation, some of the new policies have already become widely acknowledged as accepted best practices. This, of course, leaves some policy areas still subject to different approaches. This chapter distinguishes between these two sets of policies to contribute to the clarification of the *new conventional wisdom* and to the advancement of the discussion about the controversies that remain.

Finally, I take a comprehensive look at the emerging economic and social system. Despite the fact that the adjustment is still recent and there is little hard evidence available, it is still possible to identify how the old socioeconomic order has changed, and the goals that any emerging substitute must strive to realize. In particular, jobs and solidarity are envisaged as the basis of social inclusion in the old system, but also as guiding principles that need to be recovered in any emerging substitute.[1] The new generation of policies is then analyzed in a context where economic progress should bring about social inclusion through job creation and increased equity through the reduction of income disparities.

JOBS AND INCOMES: PERFORMANCE AND MAIN EMERGING ISSUES

The data pertaining to economic performance, employment, and incomes during the last decade and a half in Latin America are well known. For my purposes here it will suffice to review them in general terms to identify the issues that must be addressed when seeking a new generation of development policies. These issues relate to the dynamics of job creation and to poverty and equity outcomes during and after adjustment.

Table 6.1 presents the main trends of a set of indicators for Latin America as a whole during the 1980–99 period. The 1980s were characterized by adjustment to the debt crisis and to the new economic environment. The immediate effects of the adjustment were mainly concentrated in the first half of the decade, although as we will see below, this was different from country to country. Total output was stagnant up to 1984 and recuperated at a slow pace after that year. The recovery continued in the 1990s, although the pace of that recovery slowed in 1995 and 1999 because of major adjustments. The first hesitation in this recovery, the so-called tequila crisis, occurred primarily in Mexico, Argentina, and Uruguay in 1995; the second, which was more widespread, occurred in 1999 as an effect of the financial crisis in Asia. This faltering raised the question of whether growth could be sustained, even at such a modest pace. The 1980s saw slow or no growth and rapid inflation; the late 1980s and the 1990s, continuous progress in reducing inflation in all countries. These trends took place in a context of an accelerated reduction of fiscal deficits and an important opening of the economies, as expressed by the rapid expansion of export and import coefficients.

---

1. This is not to claim that the goals of job creation and solidarity were realized on a large scale under the old system, but simply that they were emphasized as goals over long periods and under many governments. Indeed, weakness of employment creation has been a persistent structural problem.

The supply of labor was affected by two opposing dynamics. On one hand, as a result of the advanced stage of demographic transition of most of the countries, the rate of growth of the population and thus the labor force began to decelerate. On the other, the process of migration from rural areas to the cities continued and by 1999 more than 75 percent of the labor force was in urban areas as compared to 67 percent in 1980. In spite of the lower supply pressure, the employment and incomes situations deteriorated. In short, not enough jobs were created; those that were created were of poor quality; and overall wages fell, particularly during the period of adjustment.

Low growth during the first half of the 1980s made it impossible to absorb the newcomers into the labor market. This led to an expansion of open unemployment, which reached its peak in 1985. Although the levels reached were not high by international standards, this is partly explained by the accelerated expansion of low-quality employment, mostly in informal activities. Employment in the informal sector expanded as a percentage of non-agricultural employment from 40 to around 50 percent between 1980 and the end of the 1990s. In fact, during the 1980s and 1990s, eight out of every ten new jobs created were in the informal sector. As a result of adjustment and privatization, the role played by public employment in job creation, particularly after 1985, fell. And finally, wages, both minimum and in manufacturing, decreased during the 1980s so much that the 1999 minimum wage was 26 percent lower than the 1980 minimum wage, and the 1999 manufacturing wage was only 3 percent higher than its 1980 counterpart in real terms.

The poor performance of the 1980s resulted in an increase in urban poverty. The overall percentage of households below the poverty line increased from 35 to 41 percent, reversing the declining trend shown previous to the crisis. A better performance was registered during the 1990s when poverty decreased to 36 percent, which was, however, still higher than the 1980 level. Rural poverty, however, remained constant. Sixty-three percent of poor households are located in urban areas. In addition, 88 percent of the 60 million new poor are urban. It is also the case that it is the formerly nonindigent poor who account for more than 80 percent of the new poor. The situation of middle income groups has deteriorated because of changes in the job market and the reduction of social expenditure combined with the processes of privatization and targeting. Middle income groups, many of them public employees, have suffered job losses or reduction of wages on the one hand, while on the other, they have had to start paying for public services previously received either free or at subsidized prices.

Taking the region as a whole, however, makes it difficult to see how each country has performed. Table 6.2 describes the performance in various

Table 6.1 Latin America: Economic Activity, Employment, Wages, and Poverty,
1980–1999 (percentage of annual rates of growth and index)

	1980	1985	1990	1995	1998	1999
Economic activity						
GNP[a]	—	0.6	1.9	2.9	3.7	0.0
GNP per capita	—	−1.6	−0.1	1.1	1.9	−1.8
Inflation[a]	—	134.8	487.5	287.5	13.2	9.8
Population and employment						
Population growth	—	2.1	1.9	1.8	1.8	1.8
EAP total growth	—	3.5	3.1	2.6	2.6	2.6
EAP urban[b]	66.9	70.0	72.8	75.3	76.6	76.6
Nonagricultural EAP growth	—	3.5	4.4	3.0	2.8	2.8
Rate of open unemployment[c]	6.7	10.1	8.0	7.2	8.2	8.8
Informality	40.2	47.0	44.4	46.5	47.9	48.5
Public employment	15.7	16.6	15.5	13.4	13.0	13.0
Wages[d]						
Real wage	100.0	93.1	86.6	92.9	102.3	102.9
Minimum real wage	100.0	86.4	68.4	70.8	71.9	73.8
Poverty						
Percentage	35.0	37.0	41.0	38.0	36.0	36.0
Urbanization[e]	71.4	—	85.4	84.2	83.3	83.3

SOURCE: ILO on the basis of national statistics.
[a] Annual rate of growth during the period.
[b] As percentage of total EAP.
[c] As percentage of nonagricultural employment.
[d] Index 1980 = 100.
[e] Increase of urban poor in relation to the increase of all poor.

areas of nine countries for which data are available during the adjustment, recovery, and postadjustment subperiods. As can be seen, the years of each subperiod are not the same in all countries, but clearly the bulk of adjustment is concentrated in the first half of the 1980s. The evolution of output, employment, and poverty shows homogeneity during adjustment and more diversity in the successive periods.

Adjustment meant a reduction of income per capita and a deterioration of the employment and income situations. Unemployment increased, the quality of jobs deteriorated, and wages fell. Poverty, as a result, expanded. By and large, this evolution was common to all countries; the intensities were, however, different. The adjustment in the labor market affected mostly unemployment in Argentina and Chile, while employment in the informal sector expanded only moderately. In Brazil, adjustment concentrated in expansion of low-quality jobs, which helped keep unemployment low. Real wages in manufacturing deteriorated in most countries except Argentina and Colombia.

The recovery period, which followed the most intensive adjustment, was also similar from country to country, although not as homogeneous across the region as adjustment had been. Output expansion allowed for a recovery of income per capita and a reduction of unemployment levels except in Argentina and Mexico. The recovery was not strong enough to reduce or even contain the informal sector, which continued to grow in all countries except Uruguay, while real wages recuperated in most countries except in Venezuela. The data show important reductions of unemployment, but mostly as a result of an expanded level of employment of low productivity. As a result, poverty continued to grow. The exceptions were Chile and Uruguay, which showed a reduction in poverty levels.

The postadjustment period is difficult to identify in most countries, since only Chile and Colombia have been able to maintain a high and sustained rate of growth for a significant number of years. The rest of the countries registered growth during varying periods, but this growth was affected by successive macroeconomic adjustments of high intensity. Indeed, only Argentina, Brazil, Colombia, Chile, and Uruguay were able to recuperate the precrisis output per capita level (see the last panel of Table 6.2). Only Argentina and Uruguay failed to both reduce unemployment and increase real wages, but only Chile managed to keep the share of informal jobs in nonagricultural employment from rising. The results in terms of poverty and equity are mixed. Chile and Uruguay were able to reduce poverty, while Argentina, Brazil, Colombia, and Costa Rica were not. However, equity only improved significantly in Uruguay and Colombia, and to a lesser extent, in Chile.

To sum up, while it is clear that adjustment damaged the employment situation and increased poverty and inequity, the effects during postadjustment were not as homogeneous. In particular, it is difficult to tell whether after adjustment a new behavior is emerging. Several issues can, however, be identified for policy formulation. The first is that growth is a necessary condition for reducing unemployment, but its rhythm and stability also matter. The second is that wages were determined more by the degree of success in controlling inflation than by the evolution of the labor market. The third is that despite recovery, job creation continues to be concentrated in the informal sector. The result is that productivity remains low and seems to be growing very slowly. This harms both external competitiveness and internal social equity. Finally, although a strong recovery seems to reduce poverty, it does not necessarily improve equity. Only in Uruguay do we see a correlation between strong recovery and improved equity, while in Chile, in spite of a significant reduction of poverty, income distribution remained highly unequal. The data suggest that an increase in the level of

Table 6.2 Adjustment and Postadjustment (indexes)

Countries	Period	Income per capita	Unemployment	Informality	Real wages in manufacturing	Urban poverty	Income concentration
Adjustment period (compared to the precrisis level)							
Argentina	1980–83	86.1	180.8	102.0	103.9	144.4	100.0
Brazil	1979–83	91.7	104.7	130.3	81.9	127.3	109.3
Chile	1981–83	83.5	211.1	107.5	87.0	120.3	103.8
Colombia	1980–83	98.8	120.6	104.8	109.8	100.0	104.0
Costa Rica	1980–83	85.1	141.7	109.3	86.5	125.0	95.0
Mexico	1981–84	91.8	135.7	101.4	69.5	106.3	100.0
Peru	1982–84	90.2	134.8	100.0	69.9	110.2	114.7
Uruguay	1981–86	90.8	159.7	117.3	97.9	155.6	—
Venezuela	1981–86	86.7	177.9	130.2	93.7	138.9	108.0
Recovery period (compared to the level at the beginning of the recovery = 1985)							
Argentina	1991–95	115.0	269.2	108.0	104.0	111.7	—
Brazil	1993–95	106.5	88.9	101.5	104.4	—	—
Chile	1987–95	149.5	44.5	101.4	139.2	61.5	98.8
Colombia	1980–95	133.5	89.7	117.3	124.3	105.6	100.0
Costa Rica	1985–95	118.7	85.1	122.9	115.4	109.7	103.0
Mexico	1991–94	101.4	233.3	102.2	116.1	107.1	—
Peru	1992–95	121.9	75.5	102.8	111.6	92.5	—
Uruguay	1985–95	133.7	80.0	95.9	118.2	57.1	61.2
Venezuela	1989–95	106.7	97.9	115.5	70.9	122.2	101.0
Postadjustment (compared to the precrisis level = 1980)							
Argentina	1991–97	113.2	496.2	—	74.9	171.4	144.3
Brazil	1987–96	105.5	120.6	173.8	135.7	104.4	124.7
Chile	1987–98	174.0	59.0	96.8	149.9	78.1	91.4
Colombia	1986–97	132.4	153.0	103.7	129.1	107.4	73.6
Costa Rica	1988–97	99.6	90.0	132.6	130.7	118.8	117.3
Uruguay	1989–97	121.0	137.8	118.9	116.7	88.9	65.8

employment contributes to poverty reduction, reinforced in the cases of Chile and Uruguay by a significant increase in social expenditure targeted at the poor. However, the majority of the new jobs for the poor were informal, and their incomes grew at a slower pace than average income and clearly more slowly than those received by high income groups. Hence, income differentials tended to widen and consequently, inequality increased.

THE NEW STRUCTURAL SCENARIO

The performance during and after adjustment is not, however, transitory, since the changes in the international economy and those introduced internally as a result of the adjustment process generated a different structural scenario. Any initiative to create new development policies must start by identifying the main changes in the old scenario. Three main processes characterize the emerging scenario: globalization, privatization, and deregulation.

Globalization means that the national economies are today more integrated into the international economy and that goods, capital, communications, and people are closer than ever before in the past. This has been the result of the opening of the national economies and rapid technological change. Trade and financial liberalization has been the result of the reduction of tariff and nontariff barriers by multilateral agreements in GATT and the creation of its successor, the WTO; by new or reactivated integration schemes, such as NAFTA and Mercosur; by an explosion of bilateral trade agreements during recent years; and most important, by a unilateral tariff reduction as a key component of the adjustment policy. The tariff for Latin America decreased from 35–100 percent on average for minimum and maximum levels in 1985 to 14–22 percent in the early 1990s, while diversification of the tariff structure was greatly reduced, being limited in most countries to three or fewer categories.

Globalization creates new opportunities for growth and job creation, but at the same time affects the determinants of employment and wages and requires regulation to avoid spurious international competition. On one hand, given the differences in factor endowments, it is expected that trade from developing to developed countries will be concentrated in goods that are unskilled-labor intensive and could reduce the demand for this type of jobs and decrease the relative wages of the affected group in developed countries.

This expected result could also be combined with the prevailing differences of remuneration and labor regulations between countries, which could generate a trade expansion that rewards unfair labor practices and the increased exploitation of workers. This has led to international discussion about how to avoid this outcome and whether there is need for additional regulation. While there are no general agreements on how to proceed, it is clear that nobody is proposing that wages be made uniform worldwide, since this would affect the competitive position of developing countries, nor is trade expansion based on labor exploitation being considered as an acceptable alternative. Trade sanctions for those who do not comply with minimum international standards have also been discussed, but so far the danger of abusing such sanctions for the purpose of perpetuating protectionism in the developed countries has prevented its acceptance. There is, however, a more general agreement that international and national monitoring will be needed to ensure that economic progress is accompanied by social progress and, particularly, that all trading partners will respect basic labor standards.

Globalization also affects the determinants of job creation and wages, because in open economies the capacity to compete becomes a major factor constraining wage adjustments, since unlike in closed (preglobalization) economies, there is a closer link between wages and productivity. If wages grow faster than productivity in a closed economy, the result is inflation; but if wages grow faster than productivity in an open economy, the result is a loss in competitiveness. In addition, under globalization the fluctuations in demand require the processes of production and labor to be more adaptable and flexible than they were before.

Privatization is the second feature of the new scenario, that is, the decrease of size and functions of government and the increasing importance of the private sector and markets in the management and allocation of resources. Public employment falls, and public enterprises are transferred to national or international capital. Both changes are mainly the result of the need to reduce fiscal deficits during adjustment. In addition, and this is a subject to which due attention has not been paid, the responsibility for investment is increasingly transferred to the private sector, limiting public investment to basic infrastructure and social sectors and even in these with increasing participation of the private sector in the execution and management.

Deregulation is the third process introduced in the new scenario. This has meant reducing protection and government intervention in trade, finance, and labor markets. As mentioned earlier, trade and financial liberalization are leading to increased globalization, while protection in product and labor markets is reduced to increase economic efficiency and to allow for a greater role for markets in the allocation of resources. The process of deregulation has led to substantial legal reforms, but there has also been an important de facto flexibilization caused by the freer operation of markets.

The triple process of globalization, privatization, and deregulation is occurring in an international environment, characterized by a universalization of economic and social problems, and by a growing ideological homogeneity. Today, the employment and social exclusion problems are no longer concentrated in developing countries, but constitute a major problem even in the more developed economies of the world. Unemployment in the OECD countries is high and does not decrease, affecting more than 30 million people, while 10 million are no longer actively searching for jobs (OECD 1994a; ILO 1996). The average rate of unemployment exceeds on average 10 percent and in some vulnerable groups, such as younger workers, 20 percent in most countries. The end of the cold war broke ideological barriers, and present conflicts are led less by ideological divergence and more by local interests or natural reaction against the social cost of adjustment.

It is in this new scenario that the search for new policies for job creation should be focused. The substantial changes in the functioning of the international socioeconomic order and its increased universality require fundamental changes in instruments and strategies, but beyond that, they also require a systemic change that could offer an alternative to the old ways of doing business. In the following sections we will first review the policy areas for employment creation where there is an emerging consensus; second, those in which different views and approaches still prevail.

EMERGING CONSENSUS ON NEW POLICIES FOR EMPLOYMENT CREATION

Growth

Job creation is mainly determined by what is happening outside the labor market. This is an issue on which there is general agreement, and that highlights the dependency of job creation on economic growth, which in turn depends on investments and savings.

A clear lesson learned from the recent adjustment experience is that without growth there is no new productive employment.

There are fundamental changes in the process of growth associated with the new economic scenario. Growth possibilities in a globalized world are increasingly associated with trade and international finances, since the opening of the economies means enlarged access to world markets and increased mobility of capital. In addition, privatization transfers an increasing responsibility for investments from the government to the private sector. Public employment is no longer the main and, in most cases, not even a significant source of new jobs as it was in the past in Latin America. These processes have at least three important effects on the relationship between economic and social policies.

First, as private entrepreneurs assume more responsibility for the creation of new jobs, they will have to invest more, and this requires adequate incentives and, in particular, a sound macroeconomic policy, attractive returns on investment, and stability. Stability refers not only to low inflation, but also more comprehensively to the rules of the game. And that is closely related to the degree of social commitment with ongoing policies. Such commitment requires a perception of "fairness" by all social groups, in the sense that everybody receives a fair share of economic progress (Solow 1989). And this is difficult to achieve when there is widespread poverty, very low wages, inadequate working conditions, or a skewed balance of bargaining power. In fact, the new socioeconomic order requires a strong interaction between economic and social policies for ensuring its sustainability.

Second, labor policies can also contribute to economic growth and, particularly, to savings creation and stability. Recent reforms in social security have introduced new mechanisms for savings mobilization; national tripartite consultations can contribute to the achievement of macroeconomic balances by wage moderation and by explicitly committing a country to economic reforms. This will diminish country-risks and will attract investments.

And third, a more competitive international environment requires a closer monitoring of the labor dimensions of trade. As it is presently discussed in many instances, trade expansion cannot be based on exploited labor, since this will increasingly affect not only the country where exploitation takes place, but also its trading partners. That is the justification for the introduction of new regulatory mechanisms that can safeguard against labor abuses as an instrument for trade gains. The discussions on this issue in the ILO and the WTO, as well as in the integration agreements, such as NAFTA and Mercosur, recognize this emerging link and are designing new machinery to ensure that the benefits of globalization are fairly shared by all at international and national levels.

There is also agreement on the instruments that should be used to accelerate the growth of the world economy, which will automatically facilitate economic expansion in most countries: a better macroeconomic policy coordination between major countries; a reduction of interest rates and a better balance and sequencing between fiscal and monetary policies; and a reduction in currency exchange market fluctuations and capital volatility.

A crucial issue still under debate is the inadequacy of present macroeconomic policy management to contribute to any move toward full employment. The necessary rate of growth generally exceeds that which ensures sound macroeconomic management, particularly because of the postadjustment features of financial and exchange markets. These are high interest rates and overvalued rates of exchange, both of which restrict growth. Under this framework, the burden of employment creation is shifted to labor policies, which by themselves can have only a limited influence on employment; moreover, overshooting in other markets transfers an exaggerated burden of adjustment to the labor market. Unless some policy interventions ensure a friendlier financial environment for growth and employment creation, labor policy reforms will not create jobs.

The Return of "Industrial Policies"

After a period of relying mainly and, in some cases, exclusively on macroeconomic policies, the policymakers of Latin American have come to acknowledge more and more the need to introduce additional dimensions in economic management. Three of these dimensions are crucial for employment creation: the sectoral, the local, and the size of enterprises.

Governments recognize, first, that *different sectors* require specific policies, in particular, the rural sector, both in the traditional and agribusiness segments. The traditional rural sector has the highest poverty rates, the poorest jobs, and in some countries, the highest concentration of vulnerable ethnic groups, particularly indigenous populations. Solutions to the problems of the rural sector cannot be found in simple economic management; they require the extension of basic infrastructure to physically integrate the territory, the redistribution of land to alleviate land restriction, the establishment of ownership to avoid precariousness and encourage investment, and the creation of access to resources and markets. In addition, a special effort in social investment is also needed, since deficiencies in education, health, and nutrition are at their greatest in these areas. Modernization of agriculture, which in most countries has meant the introduction of agribusinesses for export, is introducing new occupational problems, which also require particular attention. The use of child labor, the widespread discrimination against women, the lack of protection from occupational hazards, and the lack of protection of labor rights, particularly the right of collective bargaining for seasonal workers are the most pressing problems.

A second dimension is the *local or regional*, which although related to the sectoral, refers particularly to the concentrated impact of economic restructuring on local labor markets. Indeed, the economic restructuring of major industries in mining, manufacturing, and some basic services has affected big enterprises that directly or indirectly were the main pillars of local labor markets. Restructuring has meant downsizing and privatizing. This has also resulted in increased unemployment at the local level that is exacerbated by the lack of alternative opportunities for generally highly specialized workers in their most productive years. Heading off this negative outcome will require policies for labor reconversion to adapt the affected workers to new opportunities, additional investment to generate such opportunities, and protection and indemnities to compensate for transitional costs, to diminish vulnerability, and to encourage mobility, both occupational and geographical.

A third dimension of utmost importance from an employment perspective is the *size of establishments* and, particularly, the policies to support small and microenterprises and, in general, the informal sector. More than half of nonagricultural employment in Latin America is informal, and eight out of every ten new jobs created in the last fifteen years were in these small and microenterprises (ILO 1995). In addition, productivity levels of microenterprises are very low, and the gap in productivity between them and modern sector enterprises is large and growing. This explains the concentration of underemployment and low incomes in these enterprises. In addition, given the constraints envisaged for a sufficient expansion of employment in modern sectors, there is need to improve the economic and social situation of those presently working in the informal sector.

Policies for the informal sector are well known and widely applied, at least at pilot levels. They include the provision of a friendly regulatory environment, productive support, and new forms of protection from social risks, such as illness, death, and accident. The regulatory environment includes not only an adequate regulatory framework but also a friendlier administrative processing to allow for compliance with this framework. Administrative simplification, automatic processing, and reduction of regulations make up the policy package needed to facilitate growth. Deregulation, however, cannot mean withdrawing protection from matters in the public interest (such as the environment) or from vulnerable groups, since enterprise growth should be placed in an acceptable social framework. In addition, the regulatory environment by itself will not solve the structural deficiencies related to lack of access to resources and markets. This requires another set of policies to facilitate access to capital, skills, technology, and more dynamic markets. Finally, social and labor protection should be redesigned or supplemented to incorporate those today excluded, since the ongoing forms of protection were conceived for those occupying jobs in modern activities (Tokman 1994).

These specific or sectoral policies are well known, and there is an increasing amount of experience to deal with the specific requirements and to identify best practices. There are, however, at least two general aspects that should be considered. First is the need to increase the hierarchization of these policies. This, in turn, requires a unified strategic orientation and an adequate institutional level. The strategic orientation should concentrate on the incorporation of small and microenterprises into the modernization process without confusing this incorporation with support for their survival, which is also a valid objective, but more related to social compensation than to productive development objectives. In practice, these two objectives are sometimes difficult to separate, but there is a need to allocate priority to capitalization and access to dynamic markets to ensure more productive jobs in these enterprises. In relation to the adequate institutional level, there is a need to avoid the present fragmentation and build up a national and unified program. This will require not governmental or centralized control, but rather a system with clear guidelines that functions in a decentralized manner with a high level of private participation, since this is the only feasible way to attend to the needs of a sector where the units are small, many, and dispersed.

Second, there is a need to graduate from successful pilot projects to systemic results. The more general the coverage of the programs and the more automatic their effects, the larger will be the number of microenterprises supported. The coverage should be targeted on those informal units that can be potentially supported, which generally are only a fraction (around 35 percent) of the universe. More general measures, such as providing a friendly regulatory environment or easing the access to credit, have greater potential scope, but their effect will depend on the automatic availability and longevity of these measures. To promote such responses, there is a need to combine general with selective interventions. This should be, perhaps, the main objective of the programs supporting microenterprise development: to contribute to the functioning of the microenterprise being supported for a limited period of time in order to create economic behavior which neither the market nor the characteristics of the enterprise itself would spontaneously give rise to. This will require, among other policies, to provide an adequate regulatory environment, decreasing the discrimination emerging from imperfections in the products and the market, and allocating priority to indirect rather than direct forms of intervention.

Investing in People

A third area of consensus is the need to invest in people, particularly in education and training. This is an old area, but its priority and the way to approach it are affected by the changing world conditions.

The experience of recent decades is clearly showing that growth is increasingly knowledge-intensive and that the more successful countries are those which have invested in educating and training their people. It is also becoming clear that those who do not have access to adequate education are becoming the new marginals. Investing in education and training, while always necessary, is then becoming a requirement for progress at all levels in a globalized world.

The renewed priority of this area is accompanied by the need to adapt the traditional model of training. This, as described by Gallart (1999), has been organized in two layers. The first layer is incorporated into the formal educational system as technical secondary education, mostly geared toward the children of the working class. The other is based on big public institutions that cater to workers to be trained in the skills demanded by manufacturing expansion. This form of delivery is showing its limitations, particularly in relation to the relevance of training and its effective demand in the labor market, but also in relation to the interactions with the educational system at the primary level.

Changes in the skill profile and job contents associated with the new wave of technological change are creating a demand for competencies more than for specialized skills. These competencies are associated with abilities mainly provided at the primary level; hence, the reform has to go beyond the technical or training sphere. These basic abilities are developed in the early stages of education and constitute a prerequisite and a base for adaptation of skills, according to needs emerging from a more dynamic system. There is then room for a new alliance between primary education on the one hand and technical secondary education and skills training on the other.

The emerging model also has several additional characteristics that differentiate it from the prevailing one. The first is a shift from supply- to demand-driven instruction to better respond to the needs of the labor market. This requires closer links between training and the enterprises. The second is an increased emphasis on the redesigning of secondary levels, since as argued by Tillet (1995), that level has proven to be important for those countries successfully experiencing productivity increases. It is also clear that there are vulnerable groups that will require special public attention: in particular, these are the youth from poor families, workers in need of labor reconversion, usually associated with privatization, and those already working in informal activities.

Two comments should be made in relation to the configuration of the new educational system. The first refers to the priority allocated to secondary education, particularly at the technical level, since this can be read as contradicting the prevailing wisdom about giving preferential attention to the primary level. For the Latin American countries with almost universal coverage at the primary educational level, the challenge is one of increasing quality and eliminating the differences between schools attended by the children of the wealthy and those attended by the children of the poor. But, as argued before, the technical capacities demanded by modern enterprises are closely linked to an adequate secondary level education.

The second comment refers to the institutional redesigning that is taking place. There is an increasing role for enterprises in the training system to ensure a closer link with demand. There is also agreement that externalities are important and justify public programs. The enterprises cannot do all this training themselves, and they are not interested in investing in an unstable labor market. Small and microenterprises are also unable to deliver training by themselves; this training will also have to be accomplished in the public sphere. However, there is, finally, agreement that the private sector should participate in training delivery. All these changes challenge the existing training institutions developed in the framework of the previous strategy. Should these institutions be closed or can they perhaps adapt? Indeed, some of them are already adapting to the new form of operation and, particularly, trying to respond to the needs of the vulnerable groups. In addition, although training policies should probably be decentralized in their execution, there will be a need for orientation and monitoring to ensure quality levels. This monitoring role is a public function and will have to be performed at a more centralized level by creating a space in the public administration, or by converting the existing training institutes.

Increasing the Capacity of Growth to Create Employment

In an open economic environment there is a need to increase productivity because this is the only way to compete internationally and, at the same time, to create adequately remunerated jobs. Labor productivity in Latin America is on average low. Recent studies show that in manufacturing branches such as food processing and steel and in banking in the most industrialized countries of the region (Argentina, Mexico, Brazil, Colombia, and Venezuela) the productivity of labor is around one-quarter to one-third the prevailing level in the same sectors in the United States. In telecommunications the differences are smaller, around 20 percent, because of the transnational characteristic of this sector (McKingsley Global Institute 1994). The same can be said when average labor productivity for the manufacturing sector as a whole is compared to that of more developed countries or to that of the countries of Southeast Asia.

In addition, productivity differentials have increased during the last four and a half decades. Total factor productivity differentials with Japan tripled, with Asia more than doubled, with the rest of OECD countries increased by 180 percent (Hoffman 1995). During the 1980s productivity differentials between sectors and within sectors also tended to increase. Labor productivity in the service sector decreased on average, resulting from an expansion of low productivity employment that not even the fast expansion of modern services such as telecommunications and financial services could offset. A similar trend was observed in manufacturing, where the accelerated productivity growth during the 1990s was concentrated in medium and big enterprises, while productivity increases in small enterprises have been lower or nonexistent.

To sum up, in Latin America productivity is low by international standards and productivity differentials have expanded, not only on the international level, but also within countries, which has created a more and more heterogeneous productive structure. There is then a need to increase productivity and to diminish differentials. For this it is necessary to invest in and to adopt specific labor policies. There is a need, as argued above, to invest in the people to improve their skills, to better organize the labor process, and to generate a favorable labor environment, both within enterprises and at the national level. Investment in human development is generally low, and little attention is paid to improving labor relations. There is a need to introduce a productivity culture, not only among entrepreneurs but also among workers. Apart from investing in the people, there is a need to improve labor organization within the enterprises. There have been improvements to respond to the challenge of increasing flexibility and reducing costs. There have been changes in labor legislation related to firing, allowing enterprises to adjust more rapidly and in a less costly way to fluctuations in demand; new labor contracts have been introduced to permit a more flexible use of labor with lower costs; and it is now possible in most countries to hire workers under atypical contracts for training and apprenticeship. All these measures are cost reducers and increase flexibility. However, very little advance has been made on strategies geared toward value-added increases that would benefit the enterprise, create jobs, and raise wages.

These productivity strategies are related to changes in the organization of work within enterprises such as the introduction of group work and the diversification enrichment of tasks. They are also the result of labor legislation and bargaining practices prevailing in each country. In fact, most big corporations at the world level have moved from cost-reducing strategies to productivity strategies designed to better exploit technology that requires an improvement of the labor environment within the enterprises. Fiat, for instance, fired 20,000 workers in the 1980s, but in the 1990s was searching for strategic alliances with its unions to introduce product innovation, which constituted its major constraint for competition. Increasingly, there is a strategic change from cost reduction to the search for total quality.

The experience in OECD countries shows that, in spite of the different adjustment strategies followed, there are at least four common trends that can be identified. First, there is a trend to decentralize to increase the autonomy of the enterprise in adopting human resources and industrial relations policies and in collective bargaining. Second, there is a trend toward greater flexibility, which includes reducing preestablished standards and allocating more autonomy to employers. Within enterprises, this manifests itself as a trend toward greater flexibility in the organization of the labor process, to include the introduction of group work, "total quality" production, job rotation, and increased complementarity and coordination of tasks. Third, there is an increase in training and higher remunerations for more skilled work or for better performance. Finally, there is a fall in unionization rates (Locke et al. 1995).

The experience also shows that the promotion of productivity strategies poses several dilemmas. In spite of the coexistence of cost-control and value-added strategies, the former become more frequent when unions and institutions are weak and when government plays a limited role in labor markets. Flexibility leads to polarization because of differences in wages, type of occupations, and career opportunities, and this makes it more difficult to introduce value-added strategies. Finally, the fall in unionization rates confronted with the need for greater worker participation requires the introduction of new mechanisms to facilitate such participation.

Another important factor related to the introduction of a productivity culture is the widening of the collective bargaining agenda to include issues beyond wage adjustments. There has been an almost absolute concentration on wages, while there has been no attention paid to productivity, its implications, the ways to increase it, and the sharing of the eventual benefits. This widening of the collective bargaining agenda will require a cultural change, since labor and management will have to abandon their mutual antagonisms to move together to expose the constraints that hinder productivity expansion and to adopt measures to confront them.

An adequate institutional framework can also be created outside collective bargaining to avoid mixing productivity issues with, for example, wage negotiations, which would allow work on productivity issues to continue even during times of labor conflict. In the case of Canada, for example, bipartite councils at the branch level have proven effective in the effort to identify productivity problems, solve them, and retrain workers to carry them out. In other countries there are tripartite councils created with the same objective.

It is, finally, equally important to promote a change in the culture of the small entrepreneur. The policies just discussed should be sufficient to increase productivity, but in addition there is the opportunity to mobilize the flexibility and closeness to clients that small enterprises enjoy, characteristics that are key components of modern strategies of productivity and competitiveness at all levels of production. At the level of the small entrepreneur, however, the producer-client relationship is not fully commercial, and the employer-employee relationship is not formal, since they are mostly family members. The market requires quality and dates of delivery, and expansion is accompanied by a formalization of labor relations. This exposes the small entrepreneur to a new world of social relations. From a self-sufficient individualism, he or she will have to establish relations with the government to benefit from programs, with banks to obtain credit, and with larger enterprises to obtain access to more dynamic markets.

This will not be easy, but recent experience has shown that it is possible. Economic liberalization in Latin America has demonstrated that the entrepreneurial capacity to penetrate international markets and to compete at home exists. This economic liberalization has been the result of globalization and the change in macroeconomic management, but it has also been the outcome of public actions to support this effort through free trade agreements and reciprocal investment guarantees at the international level and, internally, by fiscal and promotional instruments. The lessons learned by the larger entrepreneurs can be adapted for the smaller ones and should serve to mobilize their individual and collective support. Doing so would be good business for all parties involved. The small will gain, but also the big, individually, by improving the economic efficiency of their enterprises and, collectively, by increasing their representation and hence, their social legitimacy.

Targeting Vulnerable Groups

There is also consensus that additional policies will be needed to support and protect particularly vulnerable groups. A priority case, which illustrates this need, is the younger workers from low income families. This group suffers twice the unemployment rate, on average, of other groups. They tend to join the workforce too young because their families need the income.

Thus they miss the training that could have saved them from a vicious circle of unemployment or deadend jobs and have little chance of acquiring marketable skills or improving their incomes during their working lives.

Public programs are needed that will give these young people access to education and skill acquisition. Additional measures are needed to improve their employability and facilitate their entry into the workforce in jobs that lead to careers. A growing number of programs of this type have been introduced in several countries, constituting interesting examples of a new generation of policy design, because although using public funds, there is a substantial involvement of the private sector both in providing training to the youth and in accepting them for apprenticeships in their enterprises. Governments still manage, guide, control, and evaluate these programs, but they have become an innovative way to respond to specific needs of vulnerable groups.

As argued by Tendler and Freedheim on the basis of their analysis of direct programs for vulnerable groups, programs executed by governments have been fairly successful when the design and, particularly, the attitudes toward those working in the programs follow the best practices of innovative enterprises. In particular, there is higher commitment when public work is valued and recognized. This is the case when government helps in building such positive public images without too obviously making political use of the programs. Diversity of tasks on a voluntary basis has also proven to be more adequate to clients' demands; and although this makes supervision more difficult, civil society is able to play a more active control role. Finally, decentralization is more effective, not when central government disappears, as it is usually thought, but rather when it plays an active role to improve local government and empower civil society (Tendler and Freedheim 1994).

THE POLICY AREAS UNDER DISCUSSION: LABOR POLICIES FOR EMPLOYMENT CREATION

There are several policy areas where there is as yet no agreement on what the accepted best practices are. They tend to be mostly in the sphere of labor policies. Three of these areas are flexibility, how and what to protect, and the importance of labor costs in international competitiveness.

Increasing Flexibility and Strengthening Social Actors

Economic changes require that enterprises become better able to adapt to demand fluctuations and the increased competitiveness of the new socioeconomic order. This has led to the search for flexibility in the production process and in labor organization. The main challenge is how to achieve this flexibility without severely reducing worker protection. Two usual ways to meet this challenge have been to facilitate the process of firing and hiring labor and to decentralize collective bargaining. The first reduces the costs and makes it easier to adapt the level of employment, and the latter tends better to bring wages in line with economic conditions prevailing at the firm level.

Changes in labor contracts and the diversification of the types of contracts have been the main objectives of the many labor reforms introduced recently in several Latin American countries. The indefinite contract assumed in most national laws has been increasingly replaced by contracts with less stability and lower commitments. The main changes have concentrated in the introduction of atypical contracts to favor hiring generally for fixed periods without the costs involved in long-term contracts to promote employment of special groups, like young people, or to encourage training practices, or to subcontract labor or enterprises to reduce fixed costs. In addition, firing practices have been eased by increasing the number of reasons that can justify letting a worker go and by reducing the obligations of employers to separated workers. Finally, employers have been granted greater flexibility in how they distribute the hours and days of work so that they can better adapt to fluctuations in demand. The expected long-term result is an increased level of employment, but the usual short-run impact is an expansion of unemployment and job instability. Another downside to these changes is the reduced incentive for employers and employees alike to invest in training and the reduced motivation of workers to increase productivity.

A second major trend, although less important so far in Latin America, is the decentralization of collective bargaining at the firm level. This practice allows enterprises to negotiate wages closer to productivity conditions and ensures wage flexibility according to economic possibilities. Decentralizing wage negotiations has also been followed by increasing the share of variable wages on total remunerations, linking them to economic results and providing at the same time more flexibility in wages and increased commitment to the enterprise. The process of decentralization has been a universal one and has adopted a gradual form by moving away from more centralized forms of collective bargaining. National negotiation has been replaced by negotiation by sector; and negotiation by sector is being replaced or supplemented by negotiation at the firm level. Several countries—notably, the United Kingdom, New Zealand, and Chile—have in fact made the firm the only level of wage bargaining (OECD 1994b).

More generally, there has been a change in how labor is regulated, which, in fact, has redefined the relations between government, the markets, and civil society. In labor law in particular, this move is known as the passage from heteronomy to autonomy. The first term, "heteronomy," refers to a process where the state defines, sanctions, implements, and monitors the law; whereas the second, "autonomy," refers to a condition in which society has more space for agreements, given a more general regulatory environment. This move toward social autonomy will enhance the capacity to respond to economic challenges. Societies moving toward social autonomy cannot, however, afford to ignore the prevailing imbalance in power between labor and management, since this imbalance can perpetuate itself. Labor legislation has been passed to protect workers in recognition of their weaker bargaining position in relation to employers. Unfortunately, the situation remains out of balance, and the move to autonomy might reinforce the power of the powerful at the expense of the relatively powerless. The answer, however, is not to postpone or delay the process of change, but rather to supplement this strategy with other measures.

To start, there is a need to invest in developing collective actors, such as unions, and to improve their capacity to represent their members and their technical capacity to intervene or participate in decision making on economic and social matters. The issue under discussion is not whether to protect the workers but how to protect them. How the state intervenes on behalf of workers can promote autonomy or it can result, as it unfortunately has in many instances in the past, in subordination of social actors to governments or ruling political parties. Government should not replace social actors by, for instance, fixing wages by decree or forcing unionization. In doing so, it will weaken, not reinforce, union autonomy, and thus union bargaining power. This redefined form of intervention has been happening in many countries where, in the last ten years, nine constitutional reforms and six labor legislation reforms were introduced across Latin America to reestablish the rights of freedom of association and collective bargaining, which are prerequisites for trade union development and which were severely restricted during the long authoritarian period in the recent Latin American past (Bronstein 1995).

It is also important to note that the decentralization of collective bargaining to the enterprise level can affect the capacity of unions to influence national decisions, since organized labor's power base is partly derived from collective bargaining at the sectoral and national levels. This, again, should not be the necessary outcome, provided that the unions can adapt to the new industrial relations scenario. There is room in the new setting for national actors and collective action, since only at the national level can they contribute to ensure worker solidarity and social incorporation into the economic system. Decentralization of collective bargaining should not be taken as synonymous with decentralization of collective action, nor should the firm become the only level at which negotiations occur. There is a role to be played by federations and confederations of workers in supporting negotiations at different levels, and there are new areas that open possibilities for action at such levels, such as training and social security, areas that recent reforms have displaced from the governmental to the private sector.

The transformation of industrial relations must go even further. If the social dialogue is to be meaningful, it must include the unrepresented, whether through existing corporations or through other means. Unions and employers' organizations are approaching the informals more and more; NGOs are becoming active participants and, particularly on specific issues, key actors in bringing the informals into the process of transformation. The agenda for discussion must go beyond wages into training, productivity, and the reorganization of the labor process. Decentralization should not be restricted to the enterprise, since the local community is also becoming a more important space for dialogue and policy implementation, particularly in the social field (Reilly 1998; Raczynski 1998; Hansenne 1996).

There are then new rules and new possibilities for collective action. It is clear that decentralization will contribute to an improved responsiveness to economic challenges, but it is also recognized that collective action at the national level can provide unique contributions to economic stability with social progress. The challenge is how to ensure consistency between them.

Redesigning and Enlarging Social Protection

Another key issue in policy formulation is how to adapt social protection to the new order and how to protect the emerging job categories. Life-long employment will have to give way to the need for flexibility; changing jobs will become the rule rather than the exception. For this new behavior to prove socially viable, the workers must remain employable throughout their working lives (Chirac 1996); that means that a way must be found to help them learn to adapt to new job requirements without affecting social protection. A combination of active and passive labor market policies will be needed to ensure a continuous adaptation of capacities and competencies and, simultaneously, compensate for income losses during the transitions between jobs. This, in fact, will mean protecting mobility rather than building up protection on the basis of the present, and assumed to be permanent, occupation. Unemployment insurances combined with recurrent training are instruments that will be central to the new generation of protection policies.

A parallel problem emerges that concerns extending protection to workers occupied in part-time, subcontracted, and seasonal labor, particularly in agribusiness. At present social protection and more general labor rights presume the traditional full-time occupation. Expanding the definition of what constitutes a job worthy of protection will entail extending protection to workers whose positions are more precarious. This will require adapting protection without destroying the economic advantages to the employer of this more flexible way of occupation but, at the same time, ensuring that workers in these categories can exercise basic labor rights, such as freedom of association or collective bargaining, and have access to certain levels of protection related to their particular job situation. This would mean, for example, allowing workers to form unions, to act collectively, and to be protected against work accidents.

To the above-mentioned new challenges for protection should be added those workers who have not been covered by present systems of protection, particularly those working in the informal sector. Universal coverage against work risks and age is a task that will become ever more important, especially because of the recent expansion of the informal sector, since recent reforms in social security and health regulations, although they will contribute to economic efficiency, have done little to improve coverage. To sum up, protection should be redesigned to accommodate a more mobile labor market and extended to include both the new categories of workers and those who have traditionally been excluded from such protection.

Labor Costs and International Competitiveness

A third and final policy area under discussion is that of labor costs and international competitiveness. It is usually argued that overpriced labor can affect access to international markets. Indeed, in a more competitive environment costs do matter. Overpriced labor can be the result of higher wages or high nonwage labor costs or both. The situation in most Latin American countries does not seem to justify the priority allocated to this issue, but the discussion itself sheds light on related issues beyond the labor market not so frequently emphasized.

Wages in most countries, in spite of the recent tenuous recuperation, are still lower than in 1980. Minimum wages on average are 27 percent lower in 1995 than in 1980 and wages in manufacturing industry are 8 percent below the 1980 level. Nonwage labor costs vary according to countries between 40 and 60 percent of wages, being higher than in Korea and the United States, but much lower than those prevailing in European OECD members. In addition, labor costs per hour in manufacturing are between two and five dollars (U.S.), between one-quarter and one-eighth of the U.S. level and even lower than the level of the Southeast Asian countries. Labor cost differences per unit of output are smaller because of higher productivity in competing countries. This, as elaborated above, demonstrates that one becomes more competitive by raising productivity rather than by lowering costs (Martínez and Tokman 1996). This does not mean, however, that there are no adjustments to be made in the labor cost structure that could reduce costs, particularly the cost of unskilled labor. Labor taxes on unskilled labor tend to reduce employment, while some of the existing taxes on the wage bill would be more efficient if they were transferred to other sources of revenue, particularly those which finance housing or other investments.

Changes in labor costs in the 1990s raise additional policy questions. Labor costs have not increased beyond productivity—for instance, in Argentina, Brazil, Mexico, or Peru—and hence were not constraints to increased access to international markets. However, when stated in terms of foreign currency or when observed in relation to producer prices, the situation shows decreased gains and, in most cases, a loss of competitiveness (see Table 6.3). This is due to the effects of macroeconomic policy during the period, which in most countries was based on national currencies, which had become overvalued both in an attempt to reduce inflation and because of the liberalization of capital flows. Part of the loss is explained by the delay in adjusting the rates of exchange. On the other hand, internal prices adapt at differing speeds to the more competitive economic environment; traded goods tend to adapt rapidly, whereas consumer goods, whose prices are more influenced by nontraded goods and services, tend to be slower in adjusting. The result is that while labor costs expressed as a percentage of consumer prices did not grow, they did, in fact, grow very fast when considered as a percentage of producer prices. This outcome of changes in relative prices, while beyond labor markets, did influence the dynamic of wage determination because it generated different perspectives for workers (based on acquisition power of wages) and entrepreneurs (based on profit margins).

JOBS AND SOLIDARITY REDEFINED: THE BASIS FOR A NEW GENERATION OF POLICIES

We have reviewed in this chapter the main trends during and after adjustment, focusing on the identification of emerging labor and incomes problems. We also identified the main features of the new structural context that

Table 6.3 Evolution of Labor Costs and International Competitiveness in Manufacturing, 1990–1995 (average annual changes in percentages)

	Argentina	Brazil	Chile	Mexico	Peru
Annual changes in real labor costs deflated by the consumer price index	−1.6	2.9	4.3	1.2	5.1
Annual changes in real labor costs deflated by the producer price index	9.1	12.5	6.9	4.3	17.2
Annual changes in real labor costs in U.S. dollars	14.4	8.5	9.4	1.5	11.6
Productivity	7.0	7.5	3.2	5.2	6.6
Difference between productivity changes and the annual changes in real labor costs deflated by the consumer price index	8.5	4.5	−1.1	4.0	1.4
Difference between productivity changes and the annual changes in real labor costs deflated by the producer price index	−1.9	-4.4	−3.5	0.9	−9.0
Difference between productivity changes and the annual changes in real labor costs in U.S. dollars	−6.5	−0.9	−5.7	3.6	−4.5

SOURCE: Martínez and Tokman 1996.

should be taken into account when designing policies to confront these problems. Globalization, privatization, and liberalization were the three main processes shaping the new economic and social order. Policy instruments already in place must be adapted to these changes if they are to be effective. New policies are required, since the structural transformation has brought about new problems. The goals of job creation and social cohesion remain unchanged, but they cannot be achieved if the substantial transformation that has taken place during recent years is ignored.

This we have done by identifying policy areas for employment creation and their required specification for the new context. Some of these areas are increasingly accepted, others are still in dispute. In fact, establishing social priorities and redesigning the policy instruments are both necessary steps in the creation of a new generation of policies for job creation. Priorities are necessary because not all the instruments of the past are still applicable; redesigning them is necessary because they do not work as they used to; they do not necessarily have the effects they once had.

A more fundamental question, which would embrace this new generation of policies, refers to whether as a result of adjustment a new paradigm in terms of equity is emerging in the postadjustment period. Although it is too soon to tell whether or not such a paradigm is emerging, the very possibility is central to the policymaking project.

Labor and Incomes in the Postadjustment Period

Only five countries in Latin America (Brazil, Chile, Colombia, Costa Rica, and Uruguay) enjoyed a higher per capita income in the 1990s than in the 1970s. In addition, some of these were late reformers, and hence, it is still too early to tell whether their recent economic gains will prove stable in the longer run.

The available evidence suggests that two unsolved problems characterize the postadjustment period. The first is the decline in job quality. Unlike more developed countries, the countries of Latin America have seen, not jobless growth, but rather the rapid expansion of low productivity employment. The data for the region as a whole since 1990 show that the employment elasticity was 0.83. However, this figure hides three trends. The first trend is that most of the new jobs created were of low quality. Employment in the informal sector (including microenterprises) accounted for more than eight of every ten new jobs. The second trend is the declining power of public employment to balance fiscal accounts. The third trend is that employment in large private enterprises has grown, but with an elasticity that was lower than that for total employment (0.47). The situation varies according to countries.

In addition to these three trends in the employment structure, there has also been an increase in open unemployment, particularly in Argentina and Mexico, starting in 1994 but reaching high levels in 1995. The stage in which each country is in the reform process seems also to influence the employment outcome. If early reformers (Chile, Colombia, Costa Rica) are separated from late reformers (Argentina, Brazil, Peru), it is apparent that the latter group records a lower employment expansion (elasticities of 0.2–0.4 as compared to 0.7–1.0).[2] With the exceptions of Brazil and Chile, most countries reduced or maintained public employment levels. The poor quality of the new jobs is fairly uniform throughout the region, with the exceptions of Argentina where it is worse and Chile where less than 40 percent of the new jobs were informal.

2. Mexico is also included in the table and can be considered as a late reformer. Since the data go up to 1994 the results are misleading, for they show a situation of low growth and high employment creation both informally and in large private companies. The story of 1995 is well known and has resulted in doubling the rate of unemployment and a contraction of both output and employment in large enterprises.

Table 6.4   Growth and Employment in the Postadjustment Period (percentage change from previous period)

GNP growth (annual rates)	Total urban employment	Employment in large private enterprises	Informal employment as a percentage of new employment (%)	Public employment growth (annual rates)
		Latin America (1990–94)		
3.6	0.83	0.47	84.1	−0.4
		Early reformers		
		Chile (1987–94)		
6.7	0.7	0.9	39.0	3.3
		Costa Rica (1988–94)		
4.8	0.9	1.3	51.0	0.2
		Colombia (1986–94)		
4.1	1.0	0.8	75.0	0.1
		Late reformers		
		Argentina (1991–94)		
7.4	0.2	0.2	142.0	−0.6
		Brazil (1993–94)		
5.8	0.4	−0.1	89.0	3.8
		Peru (1992–94)		
9.2	0.4	0.5	74.0	−7.0
		Mexico (1991–94)		
2.3	1.6	2.0	68.0	0.7

SOURCE: ILO, on the basis of official data for each country.

The second unsolved problem is that poverty has not declined and equity has not improved in the postadjustment period. Only Chile and Uruguay show decreases in poverty levels, but in Chile despite a substantial decrease in poverty, there was little change in the significant income differences prevailing between different social groups.

A Successful Adjustment Story Without Increased Equity: The Case of Chile

A case that deserves further study is Chile, since it is the only country in the region that has registered eight years of sustained growth in the postadjustment period and has managed to reduce poverty from 38 to 24 percent. In addition to sustained and rapid growth, Chile has also decreased inflation, increased employment and real wages, decreased unemployment, and substantially increased social expenditure. However, income differentials between the top and the bottom 20 percent remain constant around 12 and the share of the top 20 percent at around 56 percent (see Table 6.5). The question is why in this favorable scenario in terms of growth and poverty reduction there has been no increase in equity?

It is interesting to contrast the Chilean case with those of other successful countries, such as the NICs Malaysia and Indonesia, which also sustained growth and reduced poverty, but unlike Chile increased equity. Poverty decreased in Malaysia from 49 to 17 percent between 1970 and 1990, while income differentials between the top and the bottom 20 percent diminished from 17 to 12. A similar record is observed in Indonesia from 1980 to 1990 when poverty decreased from 39 to 16 percent and income differentials from 7.5 to 5 percent.[3] What did Indonesia and Malaysia do that Chile did not?

Another, perhaps more interesting, comparison is with the United States, since in spite of the differences in levels of development, Chile tends to share strong commonalties with the United States in terms of institutions and policy orientations, particularly during the postadjustment period. It is surprising to find that the share of the bottom 20 percent is similar in both countries, around 4–5 percent, and has remained at that level for decades. The comparison also shows that the upper 20 percent in the United States at present share around 40 percent of national income, as compared to 55 in Chile.[4] A share at the Chilean level can only be found in the United States before the Great Depression of the 1930s. This suggests that Chile is moving toward a twenty-first-century capitalism with a distribution of income of the period before the Second World War.

The expectation had been that inequality would fall over time, as shown by Tinbergen in 1975 and in the pioneer studies of Kuznets, after a period of increased concentration in the early stages of development. In fact, the data available for developed countries show such a trend in the 1970s for countries other than the United States. It fell in the United Kingdom in the first half of the 1970s and for the period up to 1981 in Sweden. In Finland, France, and Italy there was a fall in the Gini coefficient between 1970 and mid-1980s of some 5 percentage points or more. However, this trend has been interrupted. Since roughly the mid-1980s these countries have shown

3. There has also been a narrowing wage gap between higher and lower skill groups in Indonesia, while wage differentials in Chile have increased.

4. The data on income distribution in the United States for 1994 show a smaller share for the lowest quintile and a larger one for the top quintile. Hence income differentials are at present larger, but still both the share of the higher income groups and the differential are lower than in Chile. In addition, it should be noted that the share of the top quintile, in spite of the recent rise, is still lower than it was three decades ago.

Table 6.5 Evolution of Poverty and Income Distribution in Chile, Malaysia, Indonesia, and the United States

	Chile		Malaysia		Indonesia		United States		
	1987	1994	1970	1990	1980	1990	1929	1970	1985
Poverty[a]	38.1	24.1	49.3	17.3	39.1	15.8			
Share of lowest quintile	4.556	4.656	3.356	4.653	6.649	8.742	4.054	4.542	4.741.
Income differentials[b]	12.4	12.2	17.0	12.0	7.5	5.0	13.6	9.5	8.9

SOURCE: For Malaysia, Indonesia, and the United States, the sources are World Bank, *World Development Report*, various issues; U.S. Department of Commerce, Bureau of the Census, *Historical Statistics of the United States, Colonial Times to 1970* (1979). For Chile the source is the Ministerio de Planificación, *Encuestas Cassen 1987 and 1992*. If the World Bank report had been used as a source, the income differential would have increased to 11.7 and 18.3 between 1988 and 1992, and the figure for the share of the top quintile would have increased from 51.4 percent to 60.4 percent between the two years.

[a] Percentage of poor households.
[b] Income differentials between the top and bottom quintiles.

either no change or a decline in income equality. Inequality showed an upward trend in the United States from the end of the 1960s; in the United Kingdom there was a marked rise of income inequality from 1979 to 1989 and the same happened in Sweden between 1988 and 1991 (Atkinson 1996; Krugman 1995). In the light of this empirical evidence it could be also argued that Chile is presently following a path similar developed countries as a result of the new and more universal orientation of economic policies, without having passed through the stage of increased equity registered in those countries.

Even in the case of Chile where job quality did not deteriorate over the course of the adjustment, it is important to note the differences between income groups in relation to access to education and employment. The first and second quintiles at the bottom register a decrease of formal occupation and an expansion of more than 20 percent of informal employment between 1992 and 1994; while for the upper quintile the reverse happened (formal occupation rose 13.5 percent and informal employment fell 2.7 percent).[5] The segmented access to new jobs is closely linked in the case of Chile to differences in education. The expansion of employment in the two bottom quintiles is concentrated in jobs occupied by people without education, which grew by 30 percent between 1992 and 1994, and those with secondary technical and professional training institute levels, which grew by 11 percent. At the other end, the upper quintile population had access to jobs requiring university and postgraduate levels of education or training at professional institutes,[6] which expanded by 13 percent. More than half of the new jobs with high educational level content went to the upper income families, while the lower 40 percent took jobs requiring only secondary or technical-level educations. Essentially, the poor have poor jobs, and the wealthy have good ones.

This is closely related to differential access to the quantity and quality of education. Chile had reduced its average rate of illiteracy by 1994 to 4.4 percent, while the coverage of basic education is almost universal. However, illiteracy rates among the poor families double those of the nonpoor. Participation in the school system by the children of the poor families is lower than in the upper income quintile. They enter school at a later age. Eighty-

5. In fact, the better jobs go to those from the third to the fifth quintile, but the rates of growth of the two upper quintiles are around 13 percent, while that of the third is 6.7 percent.

6. It must be noted that professional institutes in Chile have a different content for families of different incomes. For the lower income groups, they are mostly training institutes; while for the richer they are private universities which have not received official authorization to call themselves such. In fact, this latter group has grown very rapidly in recent years.

five percent of the children younger than five in the two first quintiles do not attend any school; whereas 62 percent of the children under five in the upper income quintile do. The differences widen when they refer to other levels of education, since the non-school attendance at the primary level is 4.4 times larger for the children of the poor, and at the secondary level, is almost 7 times. Differences in school attendance are reinforced by quality differentials, since the evaluation of academic achievement in primary education in grammar, mathematics, history, and natural sciences shows that those students of private paid schools scored 81.9 points out of 100 on a standardized achievement test, whereas those attending private subsidized schools scored only 67.4 points, and those attending free public schools, who tend to be from lower income groups, scored only 61.2 points.

Jobs and Equity in the Emerging System

A crucial question that should still be answered is whether these features are inherent in the emerging model or whether they constitute transitory stages. In this chapter, only preliminary comments can be offered to contribute to this discussion. The first conceptual issue to be clarified is the identification of the pillars of the old system and how the new arrangements are affecting them. This will contribute to policy guidance in a broader sense.

The two pillars of the old system are under severe questioning and, in many cases, as the result of the process of reform, de facto abandoned. The first one is the search for full employment, and the second is systemic solidarity. The first was the most important instrument to provide the people access to good jobs and to upward channels of mobility, resulting in greater societal homogeneity. Systemic solidarity was geared to correct social imbalances that could not be taken care of through productive insertion, mostly through labor and welfare policies.

The goal of full employment has been progressively abandoned, because of the overriding priority on stabilization leading to more restrictive policies, and because technological changes are making it possible to increase productivity without creating jobs. This is the present discussion labeled as "jobless growth" or "the end of jobs," which refers to the acceptance of the fact that the search for full employment is no longer a feasible strategy.

Systemic solidarity has also been affected by several factors, particularly by the predominance of economic over social objectives. Globalization and privatization are leading to the adoption of more flexible labor policies, which are intended to protect entrepreneurs as the main sector responsible for job creation. This affects the capacity to implement redistributive fiscal policies, since increasingly they are envisaged as antiproductive interventions. Social policy changes also affect systemic solidarity, both because public transfers become easy targets in times of priority concern about balancing the budget, and because targeting, while justified on efficiency grounds, implies a redistribution from the middle to the bottom.

Individual action is overtaking collective action. In the labor field, decentralization to the level of the firm means weaker instruments for social mobilization; and at the enterprise level, new technologies are reducing labor solidarity, since job diversity makes it more difficult for workers to identify the interests they have in common. Changes in the economic environment have also forced firms to become more competitive in order to survive both internationally and at home. In addition, the expansion of informal activities also implies greater competition among individuals and family firms for survival. Similarly, social solutions to risk situations are increasingly transferred to the individuals or the family, while collective action is concentrated on the very poor. Indeed, economic efficiency considerations are important to make the system workable in the new environment, but unless compensatory mechanisms are introduced, social disintegration cannot be ruled out in the future.

Does it matter? Large and even growing differences can coexist with successful policies of poverty reduction and with more efficient social targeting protecting the most vulnerable sectors of society. How dysfunctional is inequity and how far can it be tolerated? These are difficult questions to answer, and I will limit my response to three comments.

First, contrary to prevailing economic wisdom that inequality is necessary to foster growth in early stages of development, a recent and rapidly expanding literature suggests that inequality is negatively associated with growth (Perotti 1996; Alesina and Rodrik 1994; Clarke 1995; Bruno, Ravaillon, and Squire 1996; M. Tokman 1996). While growth reduces poverty, its effects on equity are unclear. Furthermore, greater equality generates faster growth because of enlarging markets, diminishing the costs of imperfections in capital markets, reducing needs for public transfers, decreasing political instability, and making property rights more secure. Hence, equality is not only ethical, it is good economic policy.

Second, poverty and equity are not independent. The rhythm of progress in fighting poverty is linked to the capacity to change the distribution of income. If the rich cannot be taxed, there will be fewer resources to transfer to the poor. It is simple arithmetic: the fewer the resources available to transfer to the poor, the longer it will take to eliminate poverty. It is true that the increased efficiency in the use of resources can compensate, but it is also clear that it is becoming more difficult to introduce tax reforms, which means that whenever it is feasible, governments must resort to taxing everyone indirectly instead of collecting revenues from taxes on incomes or capital gains. In addition, globalization concerns more than trade and finance: it also applies to communications. The revolution in communications has meant that people are closer than ever both internationally and within the same country. This leads to a homogenization of consumption. Advertising and communications make everyone a participant in the introduction of new products, a factor that is by itself the main avenue for technological innovation. This phenomenon makes everyone equal in expectations, not actual consumption, which makes the old dilemma of unmet expectations even more acute, even where the incomes of the poor might be growing.

The final reflection is to anticipate what kind of society is emerging. O'Donnell (1998) suggests that polarization is already happening. There is a group that has access to better jobs, but this group is also opting for exit to protect its relative prosperity. The members of this group live in different urban areas, have special schools for their children, and are creating their own police. In part they are reacting to growing urban violence and to the declining quality of public services, but to a great extent they are also exercising an economic and social option. Life is improving for everyone, of course, but very slowly. The relatively rich are getting richer, and the poor are getting less poor, but at nowhere near the same pace. Present differences will probably be not only perpetuated but exaggerated across generations. Of primary importance is the fact that the children whose parents can afford to send them to better schools will be better prepared for the future. Nowadays the children of the elite are no longer attending the leading public schools, where access to a quality education was once independent of socioeconomic background.

The policies suggested in this chapter are geared toward reintroducing the two key objectives of jobs and solidarity in the new context. Job creation is a top priority, as it must be if the economies of Latin America are to be able to compete in the new international environment. However, job creation also raises the issues of job quality and productivity. The principle of full employment, while still valid, must be adapted to the present where a substantial part of employment is not in stable and protected jobs. This, of course, does not mean the acceptance of any kind of job as legitimate, but rather the search for higher productivity and new forms of protection to ensure the social acceptability of this search. Investing in people, changing entrepreneurial strategies from downsizing to productivity expansion, ensuring a friendly industrial relations atmosphere, and redesigning protection are instruments for creation of better jobs. It will also be necessary to target low productivity segments and, particularly, informal activities and microenter-prises, since the bulk of jobs that need upgrading in terms of productivity, incomes, and social protection are and will continue to be for an indefinite period in this sector. At the same time, these policies to support the infor-mal sector and microenterprises will provide an efficient way to decrease poverty and improve equity.

This, however, will not be sufficient, since the bases of systemic solidarity are also under major change. There is need to search, as I have suggested, for new instruments of collective solidarity in a labor field which is moving toward decentralization and individualism and for a redesigning of protec-tion policies to cover the vulnerable, the emerging precarious categories, and the structurally excluded because of their occupational status. Although beyond the scope of this chapter, this aspect relates to the redefinition of social policies, which in their most recent versions improve their economic efficiency while losing their capacity to contribute to social integration. In their extreme versions, they are reduced from social to antipoverty policies, and this cannot be functional in unequal societies like those prevailing in most Latin American countries (Raczynski 1998).

Redistributive measures, especially tax reforms, cannot be ruled out of the agenda. In addition, there is need for recovering public spaces for social coexistence. This will require the creation of an institutional capacity in government, a factor largely ignored during the first stage of adjustment, although not necessarily the return to public intervention. What is impor-tant is to ensure the possibility of establishing free access spaces where peo-ple of different origins can coexist and enrich each other. This is applicable particularly to education at the primary level, but can be extended to public goods such as parks and media spaces, which provide opportunities for sharing. Finally, there is a need to empower the people, since policies cannot be imposed and more equitable policies cannot be adopted without the cooperation of civil society.

The above constitutes a basis for the formulation of a new generation of policies for jobs and solidarity. It aims to contribute to the effort to answer fundamental questions, which require innovative approaches to cope with old problems in a different economic environment.

REFERENCES

Alesina, A., and D. Rodrik. 1994. "Distributive Politics and Economic Growth." *Quarterly Journal of Economics* 109, no. 2:465–90.
Atkinson, A. B. 1996. "Income Distribution in Europe and the United States." *Oxford Review of Economic Policy* 12, no. 1.

Bronstein, A. S. 1995. "Societal Change and Industrial Relations in Latin America: Trends and Prospects." *International Labour Review* 134, no. 2.

Bruno, M., M. Ravaillon, and L. Squire. 1996. "Equity and Growth in Developing Countries: Old and New Perspectives on the Policy Issues." Policy Research Working Paper 1563, World Bank, Washington, D.C.

Chacón, B. 1999. "Calidad del empleo y pobreza en Chile, 1990–1996." In *La calidad del empleo. La experiencia de los países latinoamericanos y de los Estados Unidos.* Santiago: ILO.

Chirac, J. 1996. Speech delivered at the 83d session of the International Labour Conference, Geneva, June.

Clarke, G. 1995. "More Evidence on Income Distribution and Growth." *Journal of Development Economics* 47, no. 2:403–27.

Fukuchi, T. 1998. "Expected Role of Human Resource Development." In V. E. Tokman and G. O'Donnell, eds., *Poverty and Inequality in Latin America, Issues and New Challenges.* Notre Dame: University of Notre Dame Press.

Gallart, M. A. 1998. "Restructuring, Education and Training." In V. E. Tokman and G. O'Donnell, eds., *Poverty and Inequality in Latin America, Issues and New Challenges.* Notre Dame: University of Notre Dame Press.

Hansenne, M. 1996. Address delivered at the "Forum on the Future of the European Society." Economic Social Committee of the European Union, Brussels, May.

Hoffman, A. 1995. *Economic Growth and Fluctuations in Latin America—The Long Run.* Miami: North-South Center, University of Miami.

ILO (International Labour Organisation). 1995. "Labor Overview '95." *ILO News* (Regional Office, Lima).

———. 1996. "Employment Policies in a Global Context." Report 5, 83d session of the International Labor Conference, Geneva, June 1996.

Krugman, P. 1995. *The Age of Diminished Expectations.* Cambridge: MIT Press.

Locke, R., M. Piore, and T. Kotchan. 1995. "Reconceptualizing Comparative Industrial Relations: Lessons from International Research." *International Labour Review* 134, no. 2.

Martínez, D., and V. E. Tokman. 1996. "Costo laboral en el sector manufacturero de América Latina: Incidencia sobre la competitividad en el sector y la protección de los trabajadores." *ILO News* (Regional Office, Lima).

McKingsley Global Institute. 1994. "Latin American Productivity." *Latin American Weekly Report,* June.

O'Donnell, G. 1998. "Poverty and Inequality in Latin America: Some Political Reflections." In V. E. Tokman and G. O'Donnell, eds., *Poverty and Inequality in Latin America, Issues and New Challenges.* Notre Dame: University of Notre Dame Press.

OECD (Organisation for Economic Co-operation and Development). 1994a. *The OECD Jobs Study: Facts, Analysis, Strategies.* Paris: OECD.

———. 1994b. *Perspectivas del empleo.* Madrid: OECD.

Perotti, R. 1996. "Growth, Income Distribution and Democracy: What the Data Say." *Journal of Economic Growth* (June).

Raczynski, D. 1998. "The Crisis of Old Models of Social Protection and New Alternatives for Dealing with Poverty and Vulnerability." In V. E. Tokman and G. O'Donnell, eds., *Poverty and Inequality in Latin America, Issues and New Challenges*. Notre Dame: University of Notre Dame Press.

Reilly, Ch. 1998. "Balancing Development: State, Markets, and Civil Society." In V. E. Tokman and G. O'Donnell, eds., *Poverty and Inequality in Latin America, Issues and New Challenges*. Notre Dame: University of Notre Dame Press.

Solow, R. 1989. *The Labor Market as a Social Institution*. The Royer Lectures. Berkeley and Los Angeles: University of California Press.

Tendler, J., and S. Freedheim. 1994. "Trust in a Rent-Seeking World: Health and Government Transformed in North East Brazil." *World Development* 22, no. 12.

Tillet, A. 1995. Commentary on the paper *Restructuring, education and training* of María Antonia Gallart (IDRC, Montevideo, October).

Tinbergen, J. 1975. *Income Distribution*. Amsterdam: North Holland.

Tokman, M. 1996. "Inequality, Institutions and Growth." Manuscript (University of California, Berkeley).

Tokman, V. E. 1994. "Informalidad y pobreza. Progreso y modernización productiva." *Trimestre Económico* (Mexico City), no. 241 (January-March).

———. 1995. "Pobreza y equidad. Dos objetivos relacionados." *ILO News* (Regional Office, Lima).

PART TWO

Models of Capitalism in East Asia

The East Asian Model of Economic Policy

HA-JOON CHANG

HA-JOON CHANG

BELATED INTEREST IN THE DIVERSITY OF CAPITALISM

The last two decades have witnessed the rise of neoliberalism as the dominant vision of how our economies should be organized (for some critical reviews of the neoliberal doctrine, see Chang 1994a, chaps. 1–2, and essays in Chang and Rowthorn 1995).[1] In this revival of the old doctrine of laissez-faire, the early postwar consensus that capitalism has to be "tamed" in order to be saved from itself (Shonfield 1965 is a classic statement of this early consensus) has been overturned, and the virtues of the "invisible hand" are endlessly praised. Countries that do not conform to this doctrine are constantly chastised for being "backward-looking," and the (idealized version of) Anglo-Saxon capitalism, characterized by reactive (if not completely noninterventionist) governments and arms-length contractual relationships, is promoted as the "best practice" model.

During the same period, however, there have been a number of debates that focused on the differences between different "models" of capitalism with different goals, institutional structures, and policy tools. These debates were prompted by the very divergent economic performances of different economies, both developed and developing, all of which can be described as "capitalist" in the sense that they rely heavily (although by no means exclusively) on private property, profit motives, and market-type coordination of activities. Prominent debates in this vein include (1) the debate on financial systems and corporate governance, especially contrasting the Anglo-Saxon and the German-Japanese models;[2] (2) the debates on industrial relations, which include the debate on (mainly) Scandinavian social corporatism and the debate on the Japanese employment system;[3] (3) the

I thank Evelyne Huber, Eric Hershberg, and Barbara Stallings for their useful comments.

1. The first two chapters of Chang and Rowthorn 1995 appear in Spanish translation in Chang 1996b.

2. Zysman 1983 and Cox 1986 are important earlier works in this literature. More recent influential works include Albert 1991 and Dore 1993.

3. On social corporatism, see Goldthorpe 1984, Schott 1984, Bruno and Sachs 1985, and Pekkarinen et al. 1992. On the Japanese employment system, see Dore 1987, Koike 1987, Aoki 1990, and Aoki and Dore 1994.

debate on industrial policy, especially, although not exclusively, in relation to the East Asian experience;[4] and (4) the debate on industrial districts, especially based on the experiences of Central Italy (Emilia-Romagna) and Southern Germany (Baden-Württemberg).[5]

Collectively, these debates have demonstrated how there are many different ways to organize production and distribution even within a basically *capitalist* institutional framework, and how these differences matter for economic performance. The common message from these debates is that economies which have the institutional mechanisms to generate more effective long-term-oriented cooperative arrangements regarding (technological and organizational) learning and investments (in human and physical assets) are likely to outperform the countries that predominantly rely on classic free market mechanisms, which depend on short-term-oriented, individualistic competitive forces that work through arm's length contracts (for a theoretical discussion on the institutional diversity of capitalism, see Chang 1997a).

It is interesting that this diversity in the institutional structure of capitalism has been there ever since "late development" began, that is, when the then "backward" nations like France, Germany, and the United States started trying to adapt British institutions to their own economic, political, and social conditions in order to industrialize (Gerschenkron 1966 is the classic work on this). The institutional diversity of capitalism persisted even through the heyday of laissez-faire, namely the period between 1870 and 1913, and has increased in many ways throughout the postwar period, although more recently there are increasing questions about the corroding effect of globalization on it (see essays in Berger and Dore 1996). However, it is only recently that the issue has received proper attention. What are the reasons for this?

First, during the first three decades of the postwar period, all advanced capitalist economies performed very well by historical standards, thus bestowing the name of the "Golden Age of Capitalism" on the period (Marglin

4. It was not just in East Asia where industrial policy played an important role. Before the 1980s, France conducted a very "East Asian style" industrial policy (Cohen 1977, Hall 1986). Some other European economies, especially Austria and Finland, are also known to have emphasized sectoral industrial policy (Vartiainen 1995). However, it is true that the debate of the 1980s was largely prompted by the success of East Asia. Summaries of the debate can be found in Johnson 1984, introduction; Thompson 1989, introduction; and Chang 1994a, chap. 3. The more recent phase of the debate revolved around the so-called East Asian Miracle Report by the World Bank (1993). See "Trade Policy: Infant Industry Programs and Export Promotion" (this chapter) for further details on the debate surrounding this report.

5. For example, see Brusco 1982, Piore and Sabel 1984, Murray 1987, Castells et al. 1989, and Dei Ottati 1994.

and Schor 1990; Cairncross and Cairncross 1992). Certain countries did so well that their performance was called miraculous (such as Japan and Germany), but even those underperformers, such as the United States and the United Kingdom, did well enough to prevent their underperformance from becoming a matter of serious political concern. Accordingly, there was relatively little interest in explaining why some countries were doing better than others, and consequently finding out how the better-performing countries organized their economies, until the "Golden Age" ended (in the mid-1970s).

Second, at least until the onset of their stagnation in the 1970s, the socialist economies seemed to pose a serious competitive threat to capitalism, and in the face of such a challenge, the differences between capitalist economies probably seemed less important. And given the cold war, there was a certain political interest on the part of the advanced capitalist economies in underplaying the perceived differences between themselves.[6]

Third, its vast economic superiority during the early postwar years made it possible for the United States, the standardbearer of laissez-faire doctrine in the postwar world order (although not before the War when it was itself a "catching-up" economy relying heavily on infant industry protection; see Chang, 2002, for details), to ignore what it later perceived as the canted playing fields created by the "abnormal" institutions of its trading partners (normality here being defined by the U.S. model of that particular historical moment). Various recent attempts led by the United States to standardize the institutional structure across different countries in the name of securing a level playing field, and all the intellectual trappings that go with such attempts, can be seen as a belated and somewhat pathological acknowledgment that such "abnormal" institutions have been important competitive assets of its trading partners.

Last, the underdevelopment of institutionally conscious economic theories until the 1980s may have been one reason behind the neglect of the institutional diversity of capitalism. The orthodox, that is neoclassical, economic theory is a theory about (very narrowly and peculiarly defined) markets, and is not able to adequately deal with other economic institutions of modern capitalism, such as firms, unions, and government regulatory regimes. This made it naturally difficult to discuss the institutional diversity of capitalism

---

6. So, for example, the early postwar attempt by the United States to remold the German institutional structure in its own image (or the propagandistic version of it) was quickly watered down, and consequently the German model allowed to develop, as soon as the cold war became serious in the 1950s. However, American-style "free market" rhetoric remained very strong in German political discourse, especially during the early postwar years (Shonfield 1965).

in a way that was acceptable to the academic establishment. The rise of institutional economics during the last two decades has prompted a wide range of empirical studies of diverse economic institutions, utilizing better analytical tools, and thus bestowing more "respectability" to comparative institutional analysis (e.g., Langlois 1986 and Aoki et al. 1990).

Whatever the exact weight that we assign to each of the above-mentioned factors in apportioning the blame for the relative absence of interest in the diversity of capitalism until recently, it is clear that now, compared to even, say, ten years ago, there is a much more widespread recognition of the issue. Moreover, there are now much richer theoretical and empirical literatures to draw upon in discussing it. Perhaps more pertinent for this collection, there is a growing interest in the application of certain successful "models" to less successful countries. Needless to say, such desire to learn from the successful countries has been the essence of "late development" efforts since the last century, but what makes this current phase interesting is that, for the first time in many years, the "best-practice" status of the Anglo-Saxon model is being seriously challenged—although the current crisis in Asia has generated a degree of Anglo-Saxon triumphalism (which I discuss later in the chapter). It is in this context that I want to place my discussion of the East Asian model of economic policy.

IS THERE AN EAST ASIAN MODEL?

The spectacular economic performance of certain East Asian countries after the Second World War, first that of Japan and then those of the first-tier NICs (namely, Korea, Taiwan, Singapore, and Hong Kong), has naturally generated a lot of interest in an East Asian "model." Since the war these countries have grown at roughly 6 percent per annum in per capita terms, which puts the growth rates of the first industrial nations during the "Industrial Revolution" (1–1.5 percent p.a.) to shame and even overshadows their records during the "Golden Age" (around 3 percent p.a.), thus making their postwar experience *literally the fastest economic transformation in human history*. And given the (belatedly acknowledged) differences in the institutions and policies of many East Asian countries from those found in the Anglo-Saxon economies, which (rightly or wrongly) have set the international norms, the model has been regarded by many as providing an obvious, and probably superior, alternative to the dominant Anglo-Saxon model.

As is well known, the talk of an East Asian model has generated many heated debates. And as in the case of debates involving other economic models, such as Scandinavian corporatism or Latin American import-substitution industrialization, these debates have involved questioning the desirability, sustainability, and replicability of the model. What makes the debate on East Asia unique, however, is that it also has involved questioning of the very *existence* of the model.

The classic example of this is the early mainstream argument that the East Asian countries succeeded on the basis of free market, free trade policies, namely, the kinds of policies and institutions that constitute the Anglo-Saxon model. If we adopt this interpretation, there is no point in talking about an East Asian model, because it is essentially the same as the Anglo-Saxon one. Although the fallacy of this interpretation has been widely exposed recently, it still has a remarkable staying power in popular policy discourse.

Later, other commentators have questioned the existence of an East Asian model from a different angle, namely, from the assertion that because the East Asian countries differ from each other in terms of their institutions and policies, it makes no sense to talk of a region-wide model. This is at one level correct, since the East Asian countries do differ among themselves in important ways. However, at another level, it is not very useful, because if we accept this line of reasoning, we will never be able to talk about a model that applies to more than one country. At least when we exclude the two city-states (Hong Kong and Singapore) and look only at the Big Three (Japan, Korea, and Taiwan), we can identify enough commonalities between them to warrant a talk of a model.

The World Bank (1993) has recently muddied the water in this debate even further by lumping the second-tier NICs (Malaysia, Indonesia, and Thailand) together with the Original Five (Japan plus the first-tier NICs) and arguing that there are really two East Asian models—the Northeast Asian one (the Original Five) and the Southeast Asian one (the second-tier NICs). The Bank then goes on to argue that the Southeast Asian model is more suitable for other developing countries because it is more market-oriented and therefore institutionally less demanding. Although the differences between the two groups are less than what the Bank makes them out to be, it is true that there are considerable differences in terms of institutions and policies between the Original Five (or more pertinently the Big Three) and the second-tier NICs. However, this is really diverting our attention from the real issue, because the original usage of the term "East Asian model" essentially referred to the Big Three, and certainly did not imply that all the countries in (the very broadly defined) East Asia are practicing one model (for further criticisms of this point, see Akyüz et al. 1998).

So when we talk about the East Asian model in this chapter, we are referring to the economic model of capitalism as practiced by the Big Three, that is, Japan, Korea, and Taiwan. Since it is an "ideal type," not all the details of the model match the real-life experiences of even these three countries, but that is no reason to reject it; some degree of generalization is necessary in any social science discourse. We will try to bring out the differences between these countries whenever they bring out important points, but will ignore them when they do not.

INVESTMENT POLICY

The first area of economic policy that we want to look at is investment policy. The role of physical investments as one of the main determinants of growth is theoretically central in many economic models and is empirically very well established by now. And it is well known that the East Asian countries have maintained very impressive investment ratios during their high growth period. Less well understood is how this has been possible.

The most conventional explanation of high investments in the East Asian countries is that they could invest a lot because they saved a lot. As for the cause of high savings, some believe that it was due to their Confucian culture, which emphasizes frugality and abstinence from instant gratification, but the critical limitation of this interpretation is that, like many other simplistic "cultural" explanations, it attributes a recent phenomenon (i.e., high savings) to a millennium-old cause (Confucian culture) (on the criticism of the simplistic version of "cultural" explanations of the East Asian success, see Dore 1987). Alternatively, it has been argued that high savings in these countries were encouraged by high real interest rates, but by now there is a rather widespread consensus that this explanation is not supported by evidence (e.g., see Stiglitz 1998).

In the end, it is doubtful whether it is high savings that is causing high investments, rather than the other way around. Although there is an ongoing theoretical dispute on the relationship between savings and investments, there is a growing opinion that investment, rather than savings, is the prime mover in the savings-investment-growth dynamic (see Studart 1995). Therefore, while we should not dismiss the important role that certain "savings policies" played in raising savings in East Asia (e.g., tax benefits for savers, a postal savings system that gave access to banking facilities to those in rural areas), we wish to concentrate our attention on how high and productive investments were made possible.

Maintaining "Stability," East Asian Fashion

Many commentators emphasize the importance of political and economic stability in encouraging investments, a position that probably has a particularly strong appeal in Latin America. Political and/or economic instabilities obviously shrink the potential investors' time horizon and discourage commitments of resources to projects whose returns are far in the future and often uncertain but which may be crucial for modern industrial development. The Keynesian notion of "animal spirit" and the notion of "investors' confidence" frequently used in policy discussions (if not in academic debates) reflect such concerns.

More recently, however, there has been a tendency among the mainstream economists to interpret this issue of stability very narrowly and basically reduce it to the achievement (or otherwise) of very low inflation (say, below 5 percent).[7] And in this context the East Asian countries have been often paraded as examples of the investment-boosting effect of low inflation.

However, the East Asian experiences, especially those of Japan and Korea during their earlier periods of development, do not lend much support to this argument. At least until the late 1970s, the Japanese and the Korean states have pursued what can be called a "pro-investment macroeconomic policy" (the term is from Chang 1993), which puts emphasis on maintaining high levels of investment, if necessary at the cost of moderate inflation.[8] For example, average rates of inflation (measured by the average annual growth of the consumer price index) in Korea were 17.4 percent in the 1960s and 19.8 percent in the 1970s, which were higher than the inflation rates found in many Latin American countries, for whose "troubles" inflation is often blamed, during the same period.[9] Even when they pursued "stabilization" programs (e.g., Korea in the early 1980s), their macroeconomic policy was fine-tuned to ensure that it did not kill off investor confidence (and thus investments), if necessary at the cost of allowing more inflation— a policy pattern that has obviously been broken in Korea recently by the

7. Some recent studies show, however, there is no statistical correlation between growth and inflation rate if the latter is moderate (say, less than 40 percent; see Bruno and Easterly 1994).

8. The Kuomintang government that has ruled Taiwan since 1949 has had a much greater aversion to inflation, since it has regarded its failure to control inflation as one reason why it lost the mainland to the Communists.

9. In the 1960s, the Korean inflation rate was higher than those of Venezuela (1.3%), Bolivia (3.5%), Mexico (3.6%), Peru (10.4%), and Colombia (11.9%), and was not much lower than that of Argentina (21.7%). In the 1970s, it was higher than those found in Venezuela (12.1%), Ecuador (14.4%), and Mexico (19.3%), and was not much lower than those found in Colombia (22.0%) or Bolivia (22.3%). See Singh 1995, table 5, for further information.

IMF's insistence on low inflation and budget balancing (for some criticisms of this policy, see Stiglitz 1998, Wade and Veneroso 1998, and Chang 1998a).

Controlling Capital Outflows and Inflows

In any country, especially in the early stages of development, capital flights have to be prevented in order to ensure that whatever investable surplus that is generated in the economy at least stays in the country, before one can contemplate making sure that it is reinvested in productive projects. However, capital flight was an even more serious problem for the East Asian countries, because of the constant (real and imagined) threats from their Communist neighbors. So until recently the East Asian states maintained very strict regimes of capital control. Every economic transaction involving foreign exchange had to be made through the banks under government ownership and/or control; indeed, in Korea those who attempted major capital flight risked actual capital punishment.

How important it can be to have an effective means of preventing capital control is particularly dramatically demonstrated by the case of Korea during the 1980s. In the buildup to the debt crisis of the early 1980s, there was virtually no capital flight out of Korea, which was then the fourth-largest debtor country in the world, while many other major debtor countries in Latin America suffered from massive capital flight, which was estimated by Sachs (1984) to have been sometimes as big as the total debt of the country. While strict capital control did not save Brazil from a downward macroeconomic spiral after the debt crisis (there was also very little capital flight from Brazil during the period), thus showing that capital control is only part of the story, it would be hard to deny that it was central to Korea's escape from a similar fate.

However much a government controls capital outflows, if it cannot control capital inflows, its control over the direction and pattern of investment will be diminished. In terms of their relations with foreign capital, the experiences of the East Asian countries during their high growth years diverged considerably, except that, contrary to some popular perception, none of them have relied heavily on foreign direct investment (more on this later). Japan during this period did not rely on any form of foreign capital inflow—little aid, no loans, virtually no FDI. Taiwan received a relatively large amount of foreign aid in the earlier stages of development (but not as much as Korea did), but did not borrow very much from abroad. While its reliance on FDI was higher than that of Japan or Korea, it was rarely above the international average (see Table 7.1). Korea received a lot of aid in the 1950s and the 1960s (but much less than countries like Chile did) and borrowed a lot (but only under strict government control), but strictly controlled FDI. Although more recently these countries have relaxed many of these controls (with disastrous consequences in the case of Korea), it is important to note that controls on capital inflows constituted a main pillar in the East Asian country's investment policy (see Chang et al. 1998, and Chang and Yoo 2000 for further details on the role of capital account liberalization in the current Korean crisis).

Luxury Consumption Control

Securing the maximum possible amount of investable surplus by controlling capital inflows and outflows may be the first step toward guaranteeing its reinvestment, but there is still a long way to go before it is actually invested. One obvious hurdle is that the potential investor classes who control such surplus may consume it in "luxury" goods, rather than investing it—a problem that has been an exceptionally emotional issue in the Latin American development discourse, at least until recently.

Of course, the economics behind luxury consumption is not so simple as to allow us to say that higher luxury consumption necessarily reduces investments (think about Malthus or Keynes) or that restraint of such consumption necessarily requires government intervention,[10] but the issue is more than a "moralistic" one, contrary to what many mainstream economists believe (for a more detailed discussion, see Chang 1997b). Especially in many developing countries where imports of luxury goods (or the parts and components needed to produce them) usually have to chase after scarce foreign exchanges in competition with the capital goods that are necessary for investment (given the lack of a viable capital goods sector), control of luxury consumption becomes even more important for investment.

The East Asian countries, accordingly, imposed heavy tariffs and domestic taxes on, and sometimes even banned the domestic production as well as the imports of, certain "luxury" products, especially in the earlier stages of their development. For example, Korea and Japan have had literally the two lowest numbers of passenger cars per capita of any of the advanced and developing countries at the comparable levels of development.[11] For another example, in Korea, travel abroad for tourism was banned until the early

10. For example, following Max Weber's classic work, it is widely accepted that the Protestant ethic restrained luxury consumption by the entrepreneurial class in the early phases of capitalist development in Western Europe. I thank Chung H. Lee for reminding me of this important point.

11. For example, when their per capital GDP in 1985 international dollars reached $3,000, both Japan (in 1960) and Korea (in 1978) had five passenger cars per 1,000 people. In contrast,

Table 7.1 The Ratio of FDI Inflows to Gross Domestic Capital Formation for Various Regions and Selected Countries, 1971–1998 (annual averages)

	1971–75	1976–80	1981–85	1986–90	1991–95	1996–98
All countries	n.a.	n.a.	2.3	4.1	4.3	8.2
Developed	n.a.	n.a.	2.2	4.6	3.7	7.4
European Union	n.a.	n.a.	2.6	5.9	6.0	10.2
United States	0.9	2.0	2.9	6.9	4.2	9.7
Canada	3.6	1.7	1.0	5.8	5.8	12.7
Japan	0.1	0.1	0.1	0.0	n.a.	n.a.
Developing	n.a.	n.a.	3.3	3.2	6.4	10.1
Africa	n.a.	n.a.	2.3	3.5	5.8	8.3
LatinAmerica	n.a.	n.a.	4.1	4.2	7.5	15.1
Argentina	0.1	2.1	5.0	11.1	15.8	12.1
Brazil	4.2	3.9	4.3	1.7	2.2	12.5
Chile	−7.3	4.2	6.7	20.6	13.6	26.8
Mexico	3.5	3.6	5.0	7.5	11.8	14.5
Asia	n.a.	n.a.	3.1	2.8	5.9	8.4
China	0.0	0.1	0.9	2.1	11.1	13.8
Hong Kong	5.9	4.2	6.9	12.9	8.0	17.0
India	0.3	0.1	0.1	0.3	1.2	3.3
Indonesia	4.6	2.4	0.9	2.1	4.7	5.1
Korea	1.9	0.4	0.5	1.2	0.7	2.9
Malaysia	15.2	11.9	10.8	11.7	19.3	12.8
Pakistan	0.5	0.9	1.3	2.3	4.5	7.2
Philippines	1.0	0.9	0.8	6.7	7.4	8.9
Singapore	15.0	16.6	17.4	35.0	30.7	22.7
Taiwan	1.4	1.2	1.5	3.7	2.4	2.5
Thailand	3.0	1.5	3.0	6.5	3.9	11.7
Eastern Europe	n.a.	n.a.	0.0	0.1	8.4	10.2

SOURCES: UNCTAD, *World Investment Report (WIR)*, 1993, Annex Table 3 (1971–80); *WIR*, 1995, Annex Table 5 (1981–92); *WIR*, 1999, Annex Table B.5 (for 1993–97); *WIR* 2000 (for 1998).

1980s, and was since then heavily controlled, until it was (almost) fully liberalized in 1988 (there are still restrictions on the amount of money that one can take abroad for tourism purposes) (for more details, see Chang 1997b). The interesting thing is that, after the liberalization in 1988, Korea's foreign tourism expenditure increased fivefold in three years, thus suggesting that

at the same level of income, the corresponding numbers were 21 for Thailand (in 1989), 29 for Brazil (in 1973), and 65 for South Africa (in 1979). At the $5,000 level, Japan had 29 (in 1966) and Korea 20 (in 1987) passenger cars per 1,000 people. The corresponding numbers were 49 for Mexico (in 1977) and 104 for Malaysia (in 1990). Unfortunately, comparable data on Taiwan are not available after the mid-1960s, but until then it showed a similar, although somewhat milder version, of the Japanese and Korean pattern.

the low expenditure before the liberalization was not really caused by a "cultural" aversion to spending, as it is sometimes asserted, but was a result of government control.

One important, and usually ignored, function of control on luxury consumption is in the realm of politics. By restraining the extent to which the elite could enjoy their wealth for their personal pleasures, luxury consumption control in the East Asian countries helped to create the sense that there was a national "community" with a common project (in this case, economic development), whose burdens and fruits all the citizens were sharing in "fair" (if not equal) measures. Such sense of common project has contributed to the political stability of these countries, which then contributed to investment growth by shoring up investor confidence. Thus the political and economic stability of the East Asian countries was as much an outcome of deliberate government policy as it was because of the lack of distribution conflicts consequent to "equal income distribution," as it is frequently argued in the current literature (for a review of the literature propagating such view, see Alesina and Perotti 1994).

Disciplining the Recipients of State-Created Rents

Once the governments of the East Asian countries ensured that any invisible surplus was not wasted in luxury consumption, they still faced the problem of ensuring that the investments are made productively, since "bad" investments will simply waste resources and reduce the amount of surplus available for investment in the next round. Some would argue that the market signals will direct the investors into the right areas, but we know that this is simply not true as a general proposition. Especially in the context of late-development, industrial development requires the creation of rents by the state to induce investments in "infant" industries when there are already established producers abroad. However, the fact that the creation of rents by the state is necessary for development does not mean that it is sufficient. This is because, once they are awarded the state-created rents, the investors may have little incentive to raise productivity, as the market discipline has been temporarily weakened (or sometimes eliminated altogether). So it becomes crucial for the state to play the disciplinarian role.

The subject of state discipline has been rather extensively discussed elsewhere (and I discuss it later in this chapter as well), and thus does not require an elaboration here, but let us summarize what we regard as the main points that have emerged from the debate up to now (for further discussions see Toye 1987, Amsden 1989, Chang 1993, and Evans 1995).

The success of the East Asian states in disciplining the recipients of their rents can be attributed at one level to the famously (or notoriously, depending on one's position) enormous power that they have wielded over corporations through their control over bank credit and other financial sources. However, if it is to be used productively, this power has to be exercised with a commitment to productivity growth. In the East Asian case, such commitment largely stemmed from its brand of developmentalist ideology, which was strengthened in the cases of Korea and Taiwan by the necessity to compete with their Communist neighbors.

At a more practical level, state discipline in East Asia also owes its success to a number of factors. First of all, the choice of "strategic" industries was made with a high degree of realism (i.e., there was no Indian-style attempt to catch up across all sectors), although sometimes the choice seemed too risky to many people (e.g., Korea's forays into steel and shipbuilding in the 1970s). Second, the emphasis on exports made it possible for the state to judge enterprise performance relatively "objectively" by watching their performances in the world market, although it was by no means blindly accepting them as the only performance criterion. Third, the state policies were designed on the basis of detailed information on the state of the domestic and the international economies, which were collected from mandatory reporting by the state-supported enterprises and from various public and semipublic agencies (e.g., state trading companies, embassies), thus making them sensitive to the developments in world markets.

TRADE POLICY: INFANT INDUSTRY PROGRAMS AND EXPORT PROMOTION

In the early days of international fascination with the East Asian "miracle," that is, during the 1970s and the early 1980s, the export successes of the East Asian countries were often touted as living proofs for the validity of the doctrine of comparative advantage and free trade to deal with this problem (classic examples include Ranis and Fei 1975 and Balassa 1982). When subsequent researches showed that the trade regimes of these countries were full of tariff protections and quantitative restrictions and therefore could not be described as "free trade" regimes, some orthodox trade economists invented the notion of so-called virtual free trade (Little 1982; Lal 1983; World Bank 1987). It was argued that the anti-export biases of protectionist policies in the East Asian countries were canceled out by export subsidies, thus resulting in a "neutral" incentive regime which "simulated" the free trade outcome. There are numerous problems with this argument, which we do not have time to go into (for a more detailed criticism, see Chang 1993; also see Yusuf and Peter 1985 and Wade 1990), but there are two main problems. The first is that the relative prices found in the trade regime of protection-cum-export-promotion are not necessarily the same as those under a genuine free trade regime, and therefore that it is not possible to say that the former trade regime "simulates" the latter.[12] Second, the argument ultimately relies on the doctrine of comparative advantage, which had been already rejected in the earlier round of the debate.

Our argument against the doctrine of comparative advantage, which lies behind the neoclassical justification for free trade, is not that it is logically flawed, but that it has very little to say about the relationship between trade, trade policy, and economic development. Let us explain why.

Economic development in a developing country requires importing technologies from more advanced countries and adapting them to local needs and capabilities, unless it is willing to reinvent the wheel, so to speak. And this is the process through which all countries after the first industrial nation, that is, Britain, industrialized. This gives the follower countries an opportunity to grow faster than the leader countries, since they can draw on the knowledge stock accumulated by the latter.

However, being a follower also has its drawbacks. The trouble is that, when a follower country tries to move into a new industry, it finds that its firms have to compete with the already well established firms from developed countries. In the face of such competition, it is necessary for the follower country to violate the principle of comparative advantage *deliberately* and protect the new, or "infant," industry from international competition until their national firms can attain internationally competitive levels of productivity. The success of the East Asian countries in effectively promoting their infant industries is too well known to require documenting in any detail (Amsden 1989; Wade 1990; Chang 1993), but at this point it is worth noting that this is how most other now-developed countries developed in the first place—including the United States, which was the most protected economy in the world in the late nineteenth and early twentieth centuries (see Table 7.2; also see Kozul-Wright 1995).

But then why have many developing countries failed to make their infant industry programs work? I argue that this is at least partly because they

---

12. The point is that it is the variance in the rates of protection across industries that matters rather than the average rate of protection. Following the logic of the "virtual free trade" argument, we would recommend a Londoner who is moving to New York to bring the same clothes that he used to wear in London, because New York has a "virtually mild weather," because its average temperature is similar to that in London, which has a genuinely mild weather.

Table 7.2   Tariff Rates for Selected Developed Countries in Their Early Stages of Development (the rates are for manufactured goods except for Japan, which are for all goods)

	1820	1875	1913	1925
Austria	n.a.	15–20	18	16
Belgium	7	9–10	9	15
France	n.a.	12–15	20	21
Italy	n.a.	8–10	18	22
Japan	n.a.	4[a]	20	13
Sweden	n.a.	3–5	20	16
United Kingdom	50	0	n.a.	5
United States	40	40–50	25	37

Source: World Bank, World Development Report, 1991, p. 97, Box Table 5.2.
[a] Before 1899, Japan was made to keep low tariff rates through a series of "unequal treaties" with the European and North American countries.

lacked an export promotion strategy that was well integrated with the infant industry programs, the need for which was emphasized by the early proponents of Latin American import substitution such as Raul Prebisch but was subsequently ignored for various political and economic reasons. The development of infant industries requires the ability to export to earn enough foreign exchange to acquire new technologies (mainly by buying the machinery that embodies such technology but also by paying for technical licenses and technical consultancies).[13] Without a stable supply of the foreign exchange and hence of new technology, a developing country that has no independent R and D capability is likely to end up reproducing the obsolete technologies that it imported in the past—the most extreme case being North Korea. In other words, export success is a vital element in successful infant industry promotion, rather than some antithesis of it as depicted in the conventional criticisms of the infant industry doctrine. Given these considerations, the importance of export in a late-developing context cannot be overemphasized.

At this point, it is important to point out that, unlike in the conventional wisdom, the importance of export success does *not* mean that the country should adopt a "free trade" policy. As the experience of East Asia shows, achieving export growth in the earlier stage of development can be greatly helped by appropriate government policies.

To begin with, it is widely acknowledged that the export successes of the East Asian countries were greatly helped by the policies that kept their currencies slightly undervalued until the 1985 Plaza Accord, which drove their

13. Needless to say, there are sources other than exporting for foreign exchange, such as foreign aid and foreign direct investments. However, past experience tells us that, except for a small number of exceptionally placed countries, neither of these will be sufficient in the long run.

currency values up (Dornbusch 1996)[14]—a contrast to the early Latin American experiences where overvalued exchange rates hindered export growth. As important as exchange rate policy may be in the short run, a continued export success in the long run requires the emergence of enough new industries to ensure that newly emerging competitor countries do not compromise the country's foreign exchange earning capability. Hence the importance of infant industry promotion for export success, which completes a two-way feedback loop between infant industry promotion and export promotion.

In addition, financial support and critical "intelligence" from the government can be crucial in helping a firm export. The East Asian governments provided export subsidies (which, we should not forget, also violate the principle of comparative advantage). These subsidies took the forms of subsidized loans for exporters, tariff rebates on export inputs, or generous "wastage allowances" to the exporters using domestically scarce inputs (to permit them to sell some of the "wastes" in the domestic market at a premium). The East Asian governments also provided information on foreign markets, usually through the government trading agency (such as JETRO in Japan and KOTRA in Korea) but sometimes even through the diplomatic service. There were also efforts to promote the development of private sector organizations to perform these functions (such as exporters' associations, various industry associations, and general trading companies).

So if catching-up by developing countries requires violating the doctrine of comparative advantage (infant industry programs *and* export promotion), is there any place for this doctrine in designing trade policy for developing countries? I think there is.

The doctrine of comparative advantage helps us quantify the sacrifices a country is making in order to develop its infant industries, and therefore helps us avoid infant industry promotions of excessive magnitude and duration. However, that is just about it. The doctrine is a static framework, which tells us how much we can gain by specialization, *given* our current factor endowments, but not very much about what we have to do in order to improve our position over time, even as some leading neoclassical trade economists admit (Krueger 1980). To put it slightly differently, it can help us to know what sacrifices we are making *now* by protecting certain industries, but it does not help us predict what good (or bad) will come out of it *in the long run*. The whole point about infant industry protection is *not* to ignore the principle of comparative advantage altogether, but to violate it

---

14. A departure from such exchange rate policy stance contributed to the outbreak of the current Korean crisis. See Chang 1998a.

strategically, knowing that this will result in a loss in current income, but will make it possible, if properly done, to develop new industries which can put the country on a higher growth trajectory in the longer run.

To summarize, the secret of East Asian trade policy is its simultaneous and coordinated pursuit of infant industry protection and export promotion (sometimes the same industry was subject to both at the same time). These two goals are, contrary to the conventional wisdom, *not* mutually incompatible but interdependent. A successful infant industry program needs continued export success if it is to be sustained by a continued inflow of advanced technologies. In turn, a continued export success needs successful infant industry programs which can sustain the continued upgrading of export industries, as well as other state interventions in areas of exchange rate management, trade credit provision, marketing information service, and product quality control. In designing a successful infant industry program, the principle of comparative advantage can help, since it can give the policymakers some sense of what price their economy is paying in protecting certain new industries. However, the usefulness of the principle of comparative advantage stops just about there, since it does not tell us much about how an economy can maximize its "returns" from such protection.

INDUSTRIAL POLICY

The role of industrial policy—to be more precise, "selective industrial policy"—has been the most controversial dimension of the debate on the East Asian experience (for an updated review of the debate, see Chang 1999). As late as the late 1980s, many mainstream economists tried to simply ignore this issue by arguing that there was very little selective industrial policy practiced in East Asia. For example, as late as in 1988, one of the leading neoclassical trade economists, Bela Balassa, argued that the Korean state's role, "apart from the promotion of shipbuilding and steel . . . has been to create a modern infrastructure, to provide a stable incentive system, and to ensure that government bureaucracy will help rather than hinder exports" (Balassa 1988, S286).

Later, when the weight of the emerging evidence on the breadth and the depth of selective industrial policy in East Asia was just too great to ignore,[15] the mainstream economists grudgingly acknowledged its existence,

---

15. Details of the East Asian practices can be found in Magaziner and Hout 1980, Johnson 1982, Dore 1986, and Dosi et al. 1989 on Japan; Jones and Sakong 1980, Luedde-Neurath

but tried to insist that, perhaps except in Japan, it was at best irrelevant and at worst a failure—the so-called East Asian Miracle Report is the best example (World Bank 1993). However, the verdict on selective industrial policy in the "East Asian Miracle Report" has been subject to severe criticisms (e.g., see articles in *World Development 1994*, no. 4; Fishlow et al. 1994; and Chang 1995a, appendix),[16] and now many people accept that selective industrial policy has been on the whole successful in East Asia and may be applicable to other countries. Even the World Bank itself is now willing to acknowledge that selective industrial policy makes theoretical sense and can often be successful, although it still shows great reservation regarding its replicability in other developing countries, on the grounds that it is administratively too demanding (World Bank 1997, chap. 4; I discuss this point at greater length later in the chapter).

As the debate on the East Asian selective industrial policy is now fairly well known, I do not want to summarize it here. What I will try to do in the following will be to look at the East Asian experience in industrial policy in three areas that in my opinion need further attention. But before doing that, let me make some remarks on the most controversial theoretical issue in the industrial policy debate, namely, the relative merits of "selective" and "general" industrial policies.

Selective versus General Industrial Policies

In various debates on industrial policy, the contrast between "selective" (or "targeted") and "general" (or "functional") industrial policies has been frequently drawn. Those who are skeptical about state activism argue that "selective" industrial policy, which targets specific sectors or even firms, does not work because it often "distorts" market signals, is technically difficult to manage, and is liable to interest group capture and corruption. Therefore, they argue that industrial policy should be of a "general" kind, providing those "general" resources that all industries use but which are underprovided by the market, such as technology, skills, and the infrastructures for transportation and information transmission. Thus recommended are policies like investment in education, R and D, and infrastructure (see, e.g., Price 1980, Lindbeck 1981, and World Bank 1993).

1986, Amsden 1989, Chang 1993, and Evans 1995 on Korea; and Amsden 1985 and Wade 1990 on Taiwan.

16. A Spanish translation of Chang 1995a appears in Chang 1996b.

However, in a world of limited financial resources and limited administrative capabilities, there is always going to be some degree of "selectivity" in the conduct of industrial policy. For example, it may be thought that a generalized support for R and D, unlike, say, a subsidized R and D fund for a designated industry, does not involve selectivity. However, unless there are unlimited financial and administrative resources, devoting more resources to support R and D activities means that R and D intensive industries are now *implicitly* being favored over other industries. In this way, the so-called general industrial policy may end up targeting certain sectors without acknowledging it, with the consequent risk of policy incoherence.

Moreover, to be successful, many types of "general" interventions in the end have to entail explicit targeting. Let us take the case of human resource development. While supporting primary education involves relatively little targeting (but even here there could be some targeting in terms of ethnic groups or geographical locations), supporting science and engineering education in universities or even some types of "technical education" at secondary schools will require explicit targeting of the industries that are going to benefit from such supports, given the highly specialized nature of such education—for example, there is no point in producing too many electronics engineers in a country when the industry is still very underdeveloped, unless, that is, there is an explicit policy to develop the industry in the medium term (which is exactly what Korea did during the 1970s).

All in all, what is clear is that selectivity is not something that we can wish away. It has been with us all along, and it will always be. While there may be a "public relations" case for not explicitly using terms like "targeting" or "selective industrial policy," the practice itself is an issue that has to be, and in fact is being, routinely confronted by the practitioners of industrial policy. Indeed, it may be far better to explicitly acknowledge the inevitability of selectivity and openly discuss which sector to target in which ways, rather than try to pretend that there is no targeting going on, thereby increasing the danger of incoherence between different targeting exercises. Moreover, in countries with weak administrative capacities, policies that are more precisely targeted may in fact have a better chance of success because they conserve administrative resources. The crucial question, in conclusion, is *not* whether or not industrial policy should be selective, *but* how to be selective in the right areas in the right manner, given the overall industrial policy objectives.

Raising Infant Industries: Discipline, Economies of Scale, and Exports

Earlier we pointed out that, like in all the other stories of late development, industrialization in East Asia required protecting the domestic firms in infant industries from international competition through tariff protection and other, nontariff barriers. However, in many other developing countries, similar exercises have produced unimpressive, and sometimes even very negative, results, and naturally the successes of the East Asian countries in raising infant industries have attracted a lot of attention.

Many commentators, including myself, have attributed the East Asian success in infant industry promotion to the ability of the state to impose discipline on the recipients of state-created rents, and by now this argument is widely accepted as the most important difference between East Asia and other developing countries (see, e.g., Toye 1987, Amsden 1989, Wade 1990, and Chang 1993).[17] However, there is a hitherto neglected element in the logic of infant industry programs that needs to be brought out more clearly, if we are to better understand the difficulties involved in designing the disciplinary measures—that is, the problem of economies of scale.

Many modern industries are subject to significant economies of scale, and if that economy is not exploited, it becomes difficult to achieve international competitiveness. However, the late-developing countries normally have small domestic markets, which seriously limits their firms' ability to exploit economies of scale. Moreover, at the earlier stages of development, many of the products from these industries fall into the "luxury" category, and allowing a rapid expansion of domestic demands for them may hurt capital accumulation, for as was mentioned earlier, luxuries are basically consumed by the investing classes. While the control of luxury consumption may be necessary in the earlier stages of development in promoting capital accumulation (as was done in the East Asian countries), such control restricts the domestic market size for many industries even further.

All this means that infant industry programs in the late-developing countries will have to operate under severe constraints on the ability of the domestic firms to exploit economies of scale. Faced with this problem, many late-developing country governments have imposed controls on entry (and exit) and capacity expansion in the industries concerned, and the East Asian countries have not been exceptions in this regard. Their governments have managed extensive regimes of regulation regarding entry and capacity in many industries with scale economy. The problem, however, is that, even with such controls, many domestic markets in many developing countries are still too small to fully realize an economy of scale. Given this, even when the hoped-for technological learning by the protected firms happens (as in the "ideal" infant industry promotion scenario), it is very difficult for them

---

17. Evans (1995) emphasizes that such discipline will be most successfully applied when the autonomy of the state is "embedded" in the concrete social structure in which it exists.

to achieve internationally competitive levels of productivity, since they operate well below the minimum efficient scale.

As a result, the only way to relax this constraint on productivity set by domestic market size is for the firms in the infant industries to export. However, the problem is that these industries were protected in the first place because their firms could not compete with the already established producers from the advanced countries, whether at home or in the export markets. So the developing countries trying to promote infant industries with scale economy are faced with a dilemma. They cannot become competitive in the world market without exporting, which will enable them to exploit scale economy, but they cannot export before they become competitive by raising their productivity.

The typical response by a developing country government to this dilemma has been to give up the export option but keep the protection. The problem with this solution is that this way the firms never "grow up" and remain "infants" for life. Needless to say, this has happened in certain East Asian industries—the Taiwanese passenger car industry being the best-known example. However, the East Asian policymakers often took different courses of action. Occasionally, they would "gamble" by encouraging, or even forcing, the domestic firms to build world-class capacities from the beginning so that they would be able to exploit the scale economy, with the positive side-effect that they were forced to enter the world market very early to avoid being stuck with an enormous excess capacity (the Korean steel and shipbuilding industries are the best examples). More typically, however, they initially accepted suboptimal production scales, but used a range of policy measures to bring forward the day when these firms could export and thus produce at more than the minimum efficient scales.

Some of these policies were precisely the export promoting policies that we discussed earlier, but the others were what are typically known as "selective" industrial policy measures aimed at raising the productivity of specific industries. They included (1) organizing mergers and negotiated market-segmentation in industries with too many producers with suboptimal scale so that maximum possible scale could be achieved; (2) subsidizing capital equipment upgrading through "rationalization" or "modernization" programs aimed at specific industries; (3) subsidizing R and D or training in specific industries directly or indirectly through the operation of public research or training institutes; and (4) spreading information on best-practice technologies in particular industries by various public or semipublic agencies.

The above discussion shows that the ways in which the state in a late-developing context can discipline the recipients of the rents that it has created are significantly affected by the context of late development itself. The need to achieve scale economy compels the government to control entry into many industries, but frequently even this is not sufficient to raise the productivity of a domestic firm to international levels. The logical solution to this problem will be either to abandon the industry altogether, as the mainstream economists argue, or to make the firms start exporting as soon as possible, as the East Asian policymakers attempted to do (often successfully). Needless to say, export success by infant industries cannot be achieved under a "free trade" policy, and requires policy interventions that will raise productivity of the firms as well as policies to help them export.

Managing Competition: Allocative Efficiency versus Productivity

If economies of scale are taken seriously by the policymakers of a late-developing country with small domestic markets and thus a restricted number of producers in each industry, an obvious problem that its government faces is the existence of oligopolistic, or even monopolistic, markets. While there is no one-to-one relationship between the number of firms in an industry and the intensity of competition between them (in fact East Asia provides many examples of fierce competition in oligopolistic markets), oligopolistic markets pose greater challenge to the designers of competition policy. And in countries with serious infant industry programs, the resulting absence of competition from imports makes competition policy even more challenging.

In the mainstream competition policy discourse, the allocative inefficiencies created by the market powers of oligopolistic firms are regarded as the most serious problem facing the competition policymakers, and thus a vigorous Anglo-Saxon (or rather American) style antitrust policy is recommended to deal with the problem. Thus, even many neoliberal supporters of far-reaching deregulation would concede that antitrust policy is one area where government activism is legitimate and necessary (Chang 1997c). Restricting the abuse of power by the dominant firms through antitrust action has been certainly an issue in East Asia, but it was only a minor part of its competition policy, and its focuses were elsewhere.

First of all, as we pointed out earlier, the East Asian governments have deliberately created oligopolistic, or even monopolistic, market structures, in order to exploit scale economy as much as possible, if that was regarded as important in the particular industry concerned. Mainstream economists frequently ignore this point, but many estimates of the allocative inefficiencies arising from "noncompetitive" markets suggest only modest figures (1–2 percent usually), whereas the cost increase that follows from suboptimal scale of production is known to be very significant in many industries. To put it differently, under the East Asian competition policy regime, economies of scale are more important than issues of market power.

Second, the East Asian governments have been deeply concerned with "excessive," "wasteful," or "destructive" competition. The notion of "excessive" competition has often been dismissed as a notion based on "irrational" fears of competition by ignorant bureaucrats, but it makes perfect sense once we acknowledge the importance of dedicated physical and human assets in modern industries (or what Williamson would call "specific assets"; see Williamson 1985). Given the existence of such "specific" assets, any failed project that follows an "excessive" entry (compared to what is warranted by the demand condition) leads to a "waste" of resources in the sense that the "specific" assets employed in the project may not be transferred to other activities without significant losses in their economic values (for further details, see Chang 1994a, chap. 3). As a result, the East Asian governments have tried to coordinate investments *ex ante* in order to prevent excess entry, but when excess entry materialized for whatever reason (e.g., erroneous projection, sudden changes in world market conditions, some firms defying the government plan, etc.), it organized (explicit and implicit) recession cartels, negotiated capacity-scrapping arrangements, or even forced merger and market-sharing programs, to reduce the "wastes" from excessive competition.

Third, the East Asian governments have willingly suspended antitrust actions and allowed firms to collude, when they thought that a suspension of competition was necessary for raising productivity (for a more detailed theoretical account, see Chang 1994a, chap. 3).[18] For example, the Japanese state has frequently allowed, and often taken the initiative in organizing, various types of cartels—to weather recession, to coordinate capacity expansion, to encourage joint R and D, to allow collusion in export markets, to promote technological upgrading by small firms, to phase out declining industries, just to name a few (Magaziner and Hout 1980; Dore 1986). In Korea, there existed no antitrust legislation until 1981, and even after that collusive behaviors were explicitly allowed in "promising industries" which needed to "increase R and D, improve quality, and attain efficient produc-

18. The German antitrust legislation, which has served as a model for the Japanese legislation since the latter's 1953 amendment away from the Anglo-Saxon elements imposed earlier by the American Occupation Authority, also provides many similar "escape" clauses to cartel and other collusive behaviors, especially by the small firms, when they are related to aims like "rationalization," "specialization" (i.e., negotiated market segmentation), joint export activities, and structural adjustments (Shin, 1994, 343–55).

tion scale," and in "declining industries," which needed to "scale down their capacities" (the quotations are from the Sixth Five Year Plan [1987–91] document; for further details, see Chang 1993). In Taiwan, where many large firms have been public enterprises, antitrust policy has had a different dynamic, but the Taiwanese state did not hesitate to promote mergers it deemed necessary for exploiting scale economy (see Wade 1990, 186–87). The above-mentioned policies frequently ossified the cartels and resulted in industrial stagnation in other countries, but the East Asian countries avoided such danger, because the suspension of competition was regarded as a temporary measure to achieve relatively well specified goals that were deemed necessary for productivity enhancement (although it can sometimes last quite long), and thus did not result in a general suspension of competition.

Many commentators have criticized the "lax" attitude by the East Asian governments toward antitrust policy as an evidence for the prevalence of corrupt collusion between the state and big business—or "crony capitalism," to use the currently popular terminology. However, the discussion here suggests that it resulted more from a (non-neoclassical) view of competition held by the East Asian policymakers that is very different from the one held by mainstream economists.[19] The emphasis of their (broadly defined) competition policy was on raising productivity in sunrise industries and managing smooth resource transfer out of sunset industries without the "wastes" that can result from unrestrained competition. And if it was necessary for those purposes, these governments were quite willing to restrict entry and capacity expansion (thus creating oligopolistic markets) and allow collusive behaviors among the firms, although these actions were taken with a clearly defined productivity-related goals and with a relatively clear time limit.[20]

Technology Policy: Controlling the Inflows and Raising Capabilities

The importance of technology in determining the competitiveness of a country needs no further mention. And recent developments in the literature on

19. Broadly, the view of competition held by the East Asian policymakers is close to what I call the "Continental" (mainly Germanic) view of competition, which is represented by some politically unlikely bedfellows such as Marx, Schumpeter, and Hayek, and which contrasts with the Anglo-Saxon view that is epitomized in neoclassical economics (for some classic works on this contrast, see Hayek 1949 and McNulty 1968; Chang 1994a, chap. 3, provides a more up-to-date discussion of this issue).

20. An added benefit of such a "managed competition" regime has been to slow down the competitive process to a pace that is economically and politically acceptable to the "losers" in the process, so that they would not block the necessary structural changes (Chang 1994b, 1996b). For a discussion of this point in the East Asian context, see Chang 1996a.

the economics of technology have shown that policy actions matter greatly for technological development (see essays in Dosi et al. 1988, Lundvall 1992, and Nelson 1993). For the more advanced countries, the importance of R and D policies has been emphasized (e.g., see Fargerberg 1996), but for the late-developing countries, technology policy needs to take a somewhat different form. Given the need of late-developing countries to import and assimilate technologies, policies that regulate the inflows of technology and that enhance the abilities to absorb the technology, rather than R and D policy, become crucial.

Unlike some other developing countries, which ostensibly pursued "technological self-sufficiency" only to end up reproducing obsolete technologies imported decades ago in the absence of independent R and D capabilities, the East Asian countries have always been keen to gain access to the most advanced technologies that they could handle. However, they have also been acutely aware of the need to regulate technology inflows in line with the broad industrial strategy and with the specific sectoral needs. So, for example, the government allowed or restricted the import of a certain piece of machinery, depending on whether the industry producing that machine was being promoted as a strategic industry, whether the sector using the machine could meet the urgent need for technological upgrading only with the imported machines, and whether the machine did not embody overly obsolete technology. Technology licensing was also carefully controlled in order to ensure that the right kind of technologies were imported on the right terms. Investments by TNCs (transnational corporations) were also heavily regulated, in the belief that accepting a "package" of finance, technologies, managerial skills, and other capabilities offered by TNCs is not as good for long-term industrial development as encouraging the national firms to construct their own packages, using their own managerial skills—obviously with some necessary outsourcing (on this point, see Helleiner 1989, Lall 1993, and Chudnovsky 1993).

East Asian policies toward TNCs deserve a special mention, given the current enthusiasm about globalization and the role of TNCs in it (for criticisms of the globalization thesis, see Hirst and Thompson 1996, Wade 1996, and Chang 1998c). The restrictive attitude of Japan toward TNCs is well known, but it should be noted that Taiwan and especially Korea also maintained rather restrictive regulatory regimes vis-à-vis TNCs (see Chang 1998b for details)—although Korea was compelled to abandon its under the terms of the recent IMF bail-out. Thus the East Asian governments imposed restrictions on the areas where TNCs could enter. And even when entry was allowed, they encouraged joint ventures, preferably under local majority ownership, in an attempt to facilitate the transfer of core technologies and managerial skills.[21] Policy measures other than the ones concerning entry and ownership were also used to control the activities of TNCs. For example, the technology that was to be brought in by the investing TNCs was carefully screened, and checked to ensure that it was not overly obsolete and that the royalties charged on the local subsidiaries, if any, were not excessive. For another example, in order to maximize technology spillover, those investors who were more willing to transfer technologies were preferred (unless they were technologically too far behind), and local contents requirements were quite strictly imposed.[22]

Policies that regulate the inflows of technology in East Asia would not have been so effective without the policies to enhance the capabilities of the domestic firms to absorb the imported technologies. Obviously, these included some policies that do not involve industry-specific measures, such as government funding and management of general education. For the purpose of more specialized skill formation, the East Asian governments also employed a range of measures (with certain country variations). They included (1) deliberate channeling of funding into science and engineering departments in universities, especially those related to "strategic" industries (e.g., electronics engineering); (2) public provision of specialized industrial training; (3) introduction of compulsory training schemes for large industrial firms (which are generally in those industries that were promoted as "strategic"); and (4) introduction of (German-style) skill certification systems that

21. For example, in the case of Korea, even in sectors where FDI was allowed, foreign ownership above 50 percent was prohibited except where FDI were deemed to be of "strategical" importance, which covered only about 13 percent of all the manufacturing industries (EPB 1981, 70). These included industries where access to proprietary technology was deemed essential for further development of the industry, and industries where the capital requirement and/or the risks involved in the investment were very large. The ownership ceiling was also relaxed if (1) the investments were made in the free trade zones; (2) the investments were made by overseas Koreans; or (3) the investments would "diversify" the origins of FDI into the country—namely, investments from countries other than the United States and Japan, which had previously dominated the Korean FDI scene. For details, see EPB 1981, 70–71. As a result of such policies, as of the mid-1980s, only 5 percent of TNC subsidiaries in Korea were wholly owned, whereas the corresponding figures were 50 percent for Mexico and 60 percent for Brazil, countries which are often believed to have had much more "anti-foreign" policy orientations than that of Korea (Evans 1987, 208). Because of the scarcity of large private sector domestic firms, the Taiwanese government had to be more flexible on the ownership question (33.5 percent of the TNC subsidiaries were wholly owned as of 1985; Schive 1993, 319), but Taiwan's reliance on FDI on the whole was for most of the time below the developing country average (see Table 7.1).

22. One thing to note, however, is that the targets for localization were set realistically, so that they would not seriously hurt the export competitiveness of the country—it was in fact the case that in some industries they were less strictly applied to the products destined for the export market than those destined for the domestic market.

encourage the workers to acquire specialized skills whose possession cannot be easily verified.[23]

Even before a late-developing country reaches the world's technological frontier, there comes a stage when it becomes necessary for it to be engaged in some R and D, because as the imported technologies become more and more sophisticated, even mere absorption of a technology may require some independent R and D. And as is well known, when they reached this stage, the East Asian countries all engaged in highly organized efforts to promote R and D (for the details, see the country chapters in Nelson 1993).[24] What is notable is that even when they started spending significant amounts in R and D, the efforts were concentrated in "applied" areas, often very precisely targeted by the government at particular end products with clear marketability, rather than in "basic" areas. Although this practice attracted criticisms from certain quarters for not leading to "genuinely creative" R and D, others argue that such a "goal-oriented" nature is a strength, rather than a weakness, of the East Asian R and D policies, since it means that R and D spending gets directly and quickly translated into advantages in product markets.

The importance of enhancing the level of technology in order to enhance the competitiveness of a country cannot be overemphasized. However, the kinds of things that a late-developing country has to do in order to increase its technological level are rather different from what the countries on the frontier have to do. They need to put more efforts into monitoring and controlling what kinds of technologies are imported by whom on what terms, and need to put more emphasis on enhancing skills on the shop floor. Technology policies in East Asia were neither aimed at achieving some imaginary technological self-sufficiency nor blindly following the market forces. They were based on a clear notion of gradual technological upgrading, which involved a careful control over the paths of technological evolution through controls over technology inflow and over the formation of the capabilities to absorb imported technologies.

---

23. Needless to say, many studies have emphasized the role of certain labor institutions, such as lifetime employment and company unionism, in the East Asian countries in encouraging specialized skill formation. However, except for pointing out the fact that the evolution of some of these institutions has been heavily influenced by their governments, the issue need not detain us here. On the role of labor institution in skill formation in East Asia, see Dore 1987, chaps. 2, 5, 7, and 8, for Japan; and You and Chang 1993 for Korea.

24. Given the absence of large private sector firms, the Taiwanese government has accounted the bulk of R and D expenditure, whereas in Japan and Korea, R and D spending by the private sector has been larger than that by the public sector except in the earlier stages of their development.

THE QUESTION OF REPLICABILITY

The question of replicability has been a persistent theme in the debate on East Asia. In the early days of the debate, when the mainstream economists recommended the supposedly "free market, free trade" model of East Asia to other developing countries, many Dependency theorists pointed out that there were too many historical, geopolitical, and perhaps cultural idiosyncrasies that made the model generally inapplicable, although they did not question the mainstream characterization of the model itself (on the curious similarities between the early mainstream and the Dependency interpretations of the East Asian experience, see Chang 1990; for criticisms of the "idiosyncrasy" arguments, see Chang 1995b, whose Spanish translation appears in Chang 1996b). Later, when it became clear that the East Asian countries were not succeeding on the basis of a "free market, free trade" policy, the mainstream economists adopted the Dependency style argument they had disparaged so much earlier and argued that the East Asian model could not be replicated, because its success was based on certain unique conditions which other countries do not possess (World Bank 1993 is the best example).

In the following, we examine two arguments in this vein that have recently become especially popular. The first emphasizes the importance of competent bureaucracy in successfully administering the kinds of "sophisticated" industrial and trade policies that the East Asian countries have used. The second emphasizes the difficulty of using the East Asian–style "non-market-conforming" trade and industrial policy instruments in the new international trading regime that came out of the Uruguay Round. How plausible are these arguments?

In response to the first, it should be admitted that a competent bureaucracy is certainly needed for an effective administration of East-Asian-style industrial and trade policies. However, it is not clear whether administering such policies necessarily requires more bureaucratic capabilities than other, supposedly "easier" policies such as macroeconomic policy. This would certainly depend on the extent of intervention and the sophistication of policy tools employed—for example, a deft management of exchange rates or interest rates may be more difficult than running a few industry-specific technological upgrading schemes.

More important, those who make this argument mistakenly assert that the well-developed bureaucracies of the East Asian countries were part of their historically determined "initial conditions." These countries had to spend a lot of time and energy in reforming their bureaucracies and training their bureaucrats before they could establish the kind of bureaucracies that they have now (Cheng et al. 1998). It is instructive to note in this context that Korea was sending its bureaucrats for training to the Philippines and Pakistan until the late 1960s.

Anyway, since many Latin American countries were much more advanced than the East Asian countries until the early 1980s, it would be difficult to argue that they could not adopt at least some of the "sophisticated" policies practiced in East Asia because they lack the (bureaucratic and other) "capability." For example, as we can see in Table 7.3, in 1961, even the least developed of the Latin American countries in the sample, namely, Brazil ($129), had per capita income 1.6 times that of Korea ($82), manufacturing value added (MVA) 2.5 times that of Korea, and had only slightly lower ratio of literacy (61% vs. 71%). Even when we compare it with Taiwan, whose per capita income was essentially at the same level ($121 vs. $129), we find that Brazil had somewhat higher literacy ratio (61% vs. 54%) and 2.5 times the MVA. When we compare the East Asian countries with the other Latin American countries in the sample (Ecuador, Mexico, Chile, and Argentina), we find that the latter were all much more advanced than the former. If we accept that the bureaucratic capability of a country would be strongly correlated with the level of its economic development and broad human capital endowment, we find it difficult to agree with the argument that the Latin American countries cannot, or could not, adopt the East Asian style policy because of the lack of "capability."

More generally, we should point out that the view that countries need to have some "special" (bureaucratic and other) capabilities before they can adopt some economic "model" that is not predominantly "market-based" (such as the East Asian model) is based on the mistaken mainstream belief that while markets, as "natural" phenomena, can be transplanted anywhere, "institutions" (including the modern bureaucracy), as man-made things, cannot. However, recent developments in institutional economics have persuasively demonstrated, first, that the conventional dichotomy between markets and institutions is misleading, since markets themselves are institutions, and second that markets are *not* natural phenomena that develop spontaneously, but (like other institutions) have to be deliberately constructed. Indeed, if the market-based Anglo-Saxon model is so easy to replicate, why is it the case that most of the "success stories," be they German, Japanese, or Scandinavian, were based on some "deviant" model? The difficulty that many developing and transitional economies are currently experiencing with their neoliberal reforms is just another testimony to how hard it actually is to replicate the predominantly market-based Anglo-Saxon model. In fact, the establishment of market institutions required a lot of government interven-

Table 7.3   Initial Conditions

	1961 per capita income (current $)	1961 per capita MVA (1958 $)	Literacy rate circa 1960 (%)	1938 per capita MVA (1958 $)	Literacy rate circa 1945 (%)
Indonesia	49	3 (1958)	47	4	n.a.
Tanzania	50	4 (1958)	17	n.a.	n.a.
Pakistan	54	9	16	n.a.	18 (1951)
Zaire	67	11	31	n.a.	n.a.
India	69	11	24	6	19 (1951)
Kenya	72	12 (1958)	20	n.a.	n.a.
Korea	82	22	71	9	22 (1945)
Thailand	88	9	68	6	53 (1947)
Sri Lanka	122	18	61	16	n.a.
Taiwan	122	23	54	12	50 (1950)
Brazil	129	50	61	16	43 (1940)
Ecuador	143	26	67	19	n.a.
Ghana	179	8 (1958)	27	n.a.	n.a.
Philippines	200	16	72	13	52 (1948)
Malaysia (Malaya)	215	27	23	n.a.	38 (1947)
Mexico	279	83	62	45	57 (1950)
Chile	377	82	84	72	77 (1940)
Argentina	378	114	91	98	86 (1947)
South Africa	396	138	57	62	n.a.
Singapore	n.a.	n.a.	n.a.	n.a.	46 (1947)
Japan	402	227	98	75	n.a.
United States	2308	926	98	375	n.a.

SOURCES: The source for the MVA (manufacturing value added) figures is United Nations, Growth of World Industry, 1938-61 (1965). The sources for the 1945 literacy figures are UNESCO, Statistical Yearbook, UN, Statistical Yearbook, various years; and McGinn et al., Education and Development in Korea (1980), Table 17. The source for the 1960 literacy figures is World Bank, World Development Report, various years. The income figures for 1961 are from Kindleberger, Economic Development (1965), Table 1.1, except the one for Korea, which is from the Korean National Account Statistics.

tion even in the Anglo-Saxon economies in their early days (see Polanyi 1957 on Britain, and Kozul-Wright 1995 on the United States).

The argument that the East Asian model cannot be replicated elsewhere because of the uniqueness of their institutions sees those institutions as something immutable and thus underestimates the possibility of institutional adaptation and innovation. Like technologies, institutions (and indeed "culture" as a set of informal institutions) are subject to adaptation and innovation, and therefore should not be seen as something immutable that a country inherits from its past. Especially from the point of view of the late-developing countries, adapting imported institutions to the local conditions is as important as, if not more important than, adapting imported technologies, and the East Asian countries themselves show how important and feasible such institutional adaptation can be.[25]

In response to the second argument citing the highly "liberal" post-Uruguay-Round world trading regime as a major constraint on adopting some of the East Asian policy tools, three points must be made (the following details are from Akyüz et al. 1998; also see Amsden 2000).

First, the conventional wisdom overestimates the policy "freedom" that existed in the pre-WTO international trading system. However, even the old GATT system imposed many restrictions on the kinds of policy tools. And as a result, the East Asian countries had to exercise a considerable amount of policy ingenuity and administrative and diplomatic skill to maintain some of their policies even under the pre-WTO system.

Second, while the WTO system does put more constraints on the scope of policy tools that can be used, the constraints are not as widespread and binding as they are usually argued to be. For example, the "balance of payments" clause, which, rather than the "infant industry" clause, had been the most frequently evoked justification for quantitative restrictions under the pre-WTO regime by the East Asian countries (and other developing countries), still exists under this new regime. Also, subsidies may be more strictly sanctioned against in the WTO system, but there are still "nonactionable"[26] subsidies such as basic research, agriculture, and regional development. And in the case of the poorest countries, some subsidies prohibited in other countries, notably export subsidies, are still allowed. Last, the agreements on so-called TRIPs (trade-related intellectual property rights) and TRIMs (trade-related investment measures) do constrain the scope for things like local contents requirements or compulsory technology licensing, but exceptions can be made (although not easily),[27] and a wide range of other measures that can serve similar purposes are not affected by these agreements (e.g., export performance requirements on TNC subsidiaries).

Finally, it needs emphasizing that the new trading regime does not prohibit many policy measures that have been used in the East Asian policy

25. The early Japanese experience is particularly instructive here. When the Japanese first embarked on the industrialization process, they had to import a lot of foreign institutions, picking what they though were the most suitable among the "best practices." So if we look at the early Meiji period, we find an institutional patchwork. The commercial law system was from France, their criminal law from Germany, the central bank from Belgium, the navy from Britain, the army from Germany, the education system first from America but later from Germany, and so on (for some more details, see Westney 1987).

26. This means that retaliatory action cannot be taken against these subsidies.

27. Local content requirements can be invoked under the balance of payments clause. Compulsory licensing is also allowed under special circumstances.

regime. Strategic credit rationing by the state, the use of domestic taxes to encourage or discourage particular activities, dissemination of information on export markets and best-practice technology by state agencies, direct and indirect controls on competition in strategic industries, and policies to encourage the formation of specialized skills are only some of the more important examples.

I would agree with those who express skepticism about the replicability of the East Asian model, if all they mean is that countries with different conditions may have to find different solutions to similar problems (for some theoretical discussion, see Chang 1997a). However, they often have a very exaggerated view about the superiority of the "initial conditions" of the East Asian countries (Chang 1998d), and have an unduly pessimistic view about other countries changing their conditions. So they believe that initial institutional (and cultural) conditions are almost perfectly binding and therefore countries which do not start with the East Asian sort of initial conditions cannot emulate them. One curious thing here is that most of these people do not seem to believe that the "initial conditions" may be equally binding when countries aim to imitate the Anglo-Saxon model that they typically recommend. The same sort of exaggeration, narrowness of view, and prejudice dominate the discussions on the effect of WTO trading regime. The pre-WTO trading regimes are described as somehow very permissive, the constraints imposed by the new regime are highly exaggerated, and the role of policy ingenuity in getting around these constraints is completely ignored.

THE END OF THE EAST ASIAN MODEL?

With the recent crisis in Korea and the prolonged recession in Japan, now there is a widespread talk of the end of the East Asian model. In contrast, the recent strengths of the American and the British economies are taken as proof that the Anglo-Saxon model is the best economic model there is.

While it is perfectly understandable why there is such a sentiment, we need to put things into perspective. To begin with, not all the East Asian economies are equally in trouble. Korea may have experienced a deep crisis, but Taiwan and Singapore did not. Indeed, it is interesting to note that the Asian countries that have recently experienced problems were either the ones that did not follow the "East Asian model" (the Southeast Asian countries and Hong Kong) or the ones that moved away from such a model (Japan and Korea).

Moreover, although the Japanese performance may have been inferior to those of the Anglo-Saxon economies during the second half of the 1990s, the performance difference is a lot smaller than what is normally assumed. During the 1990s as a whole, the Japanese per capita GDP growth rate, at 1.4 percent, was only a fraction lower than that of the United States at 1.6 percent and superior to those of Switzerland (-0.4%), Sweden (0.8%), Canada (0.8%), Italy (1.1%), and France (1.3%) (data from the World Bank and the *Financial Times*). Also, according to the data from the *Economist* published in April 1999, in terms of productivity growth rate (that is, the rate of growth of GDP per worker), the United States, at 0.9 percent, was behind Japan, which was at 1.2 percent, between 1989 and 1998.

Moreover, the current economic troubles in Japan, and especially Korea, came about because those countries *departed* from the "traditional" East Asian model, not because they *adhered* to it. The current recession in Japan started when the asset bubble that built up following the financial liberalization in the late 1980s finally burst in the early 1990s. The recession that followed from it owed a lot to the refusal by the Japanese government to intervene quickly and decisively in the financial sector to clean it up in the manner that the ostensibly less interventionist U.S. government had with a similar problem, namely, the S&L crisis during the 1980s.

The recent crisis in Korea is a result of the rapid buildup of short-term foreign debts that had fed the investment boom between 1994 and 1996 that was made possible by the abandonment of traditional industrial policy measures (e.g., investment coordination, control on "excessive competition") by the Kim Young Sam government, which took power in 1993—although the Korean industrial policy had been weakening since the early 1990s. And what made this debt buildup possible was the ill-designed financial liberalization program that was started in 1993 by the same government. The departure from the traditional exchange rate policy also added to the problem (for further details on the Korean crisis, see Chang 1998a, Chang et al. 1998, and Chang and Yoo 2000; for the Asian crisis in general, see Wade and Veneroso 1998, Stiglitz 1998, Chang 2000, and Chang et al. 2001).

With Korea (voluntarily and involuntarily) deregulating its economy with an alarming speed to restore "international confidence" in it and with Japan accelerating its financial deregulation (if not deregulation in other areas) in response to its current recession, it seems that the East Asian model will be significantly watered down, if not abandoned, in the coming years. However, the evolutionary dynamics of economic institutions are too complex for us to say with full confidence that these economies will become "Anglo-Saxon" in the near future. After all, it was out of the very American institutional frameworks that were imposed by the U.S. Occupation Authorities after the Second World War that the famous "idiosyncratic" Japanese and

German models emerged. In addition, the changing fortunes of the major OECD economies in the coming years will deflate the overconfident Anglo-Saxon triumphalism and put the whole debate on a more sensible footing. It will be very interesting to watch what happens in Korea and Japan, as well as the United States, over the next several years.

LESSONS FOR LATIN AMERICA?

During the last twenty years or so, a number of attempts to explain the differential performances across different capitalist countries have generated a belated interest in the institutional diversity of capitalism. Such interest naturally makes us question the wisdom of neoliberal economics, which claims that there is only one efficient way of organizing a capitalist economy, namely an idealized version of the Anglo-Saxon economic model based on unconstrained markets with minimal state intervention—a view which is in the ascendancy at the moment. Among the "models" that challenge the dominant Anglo-Saxon model is the East Asian one, whose "economic" (as opposed to "social") dimension we examined in this chapter.

We have examined three broad areas of the East Asian model of economic policy—investment policy, trade policy, and industrial policy (including technology policy). We have emphasized how the constraints (and opportunities) imposed by the imperatives of late development shaped such policies in these countries, and how they overcame these constraints. In the process, we highlighted some policies which we regard as important but which have received inadequate attention even by those who are sympathetic to the East Asian model. These included, among others, (1) the pro-investment, rather than anti-inflationary, macroeconomic policy; (2) the control on luxury consumption, which served both economic *and* political functions; (3) the strict control on FDI, which is contrary to the popular impression that these economies (perhaps except Japan) have had an "open" FDI policy; (4) the integrated pursuit of infant industry protection and export promotion; (5) the use of export as a tool to exploit scale economy and thus to accelerate the maturation of infant industries; and (6) the productivity-oriented (as opposed to allocation-oriented) view of competition.

Then we discussed whether replicating the East Asian model in other countries is feasible. Noting that a wholesale replication of any socio-economic model, and not just the East Asian model, is impossible, we examined two "impossibility of learning from East Asia" arguments that are especially popular these days—one related to bureaucratic institutions, and the other related to changes in the international trading regime—and found them both wanting. We pointed out that while both of them have a point, they are misinformed, exaggerated, and biased in their outlook. This discussion was followed by a short commentary on whether the current economic troubles in some (but not all) East Asian countries signify the end of the East Asian model. We argued that, first, the relative performances of the East Asian countries and the Anglo-Saxon economies need to be put into perspective, and, second, that the troubles in the East Asian countries mainly owe to their departures from the traditional model, rather than to their adherence to it. We also pointed out that the process of institutional evolution is difficult to predict, and therefore that it is not obvious that countries like Japan and Korea will emerge as truly Anglo-Saxon economies out of their recent troubles that have prompted them to adopt many Anglo-Saxon institutions.

The East Asian model of economic policy may look very different from some other models, especially the Anglo-Saxon one (but perhaps not their earlier reincarnations—e.g., the early U.S. model). However, they also share many characteristics with other models, especially those of many continental European countries and Latin American countries, not least because they all had to develop their policies under the constraints of late development. The interesting question, however, is not what these similarities are, but what are the crucial differences between the East Asian model of economic policy and those of continental Europe and Latin America.

With a view to drawing lessons for Latin America, I may point out some likely candidates: luxury consumption control (conspicuously missing in Latin America); an active use of export as a part of infant industry program (an especially big contrast with Latin America); a skillful management of domestic competition, based on a productivity-oriented view of competition; and active policies to promote technology absorption (policies toward TNCs being the biggest difference with Latin America in this area). However, my personal knowledge about most non–East Asian countries is too inadequate to make much progress here. A series of more systematic comparative studies will be needed before we can distill some useful policy lessons, and I regard the present volume to be a very useful launching pad for such efforts in the future.

REFERENCES

Akyüz, Y., H-J. Chang, and R. Kozul-Wright. 1998. "New Perspectives on East Asian Development." *Journal of Development Studies* 34, no. 6.

Alesina, A., and R. Perotti. 1994. "The Political Economy of Growth: A Critical Survey of the Recent Literature." *The World Bank Economic Review* 8, no. 3.

Albert, M. 1991. *Capitalism vs. Capitalism.* New York: Four Walls Eight Windows.

Amsden, A. 1985. "The State and Taiwan's Economic Development." In P. Evans, D. Rueschemeyer, and T. Skocpol, eds., *Bringing the State Back In.* Cambridge: Cambridge University Press.

———. 1989. *Asia's Next Giant: South Korea and Late Industrialization.* New York: Oxford University Press.

———. 2000. "Industrialisation under New WTO Law." A paper for the UNCTAD X meeting, February 12–19, Bangkok.

Aoki, M. 1990. "A New Paradigm of Work Organisation and Coordination?—Lessons from Japanese Experience." In S. Marglin and J. Schor, eds., *The Rise and Fall of the Golden Age.* Oxford: Oxford University Press.

Aoki, M., and R. Dore, eds. 1994. *The Japanese Firm.* Oxford: Oxford University Press.

Aoki, M., B. Gustafsson, and O. Williamson, eds. 1990. *The Firm as a Nexus of Treaties.* London: Sage Publications.

Balassa, B. 1982. "Development Strategies and Economic Performance." In B. Balassa et al., *Development Strategies in Semi-Industrial Economies.* Baltimore: Johns Hopkins University Press.

———. 1988. "The Lessons of East Asian Development: An Overview." *Economic Development and Cultural Change* 36, no. 3 (April, Supplement).

Berger, S., and R. Dore, eds. 1996. *National Diversity and Global Capitalism.* Ithaca: Cornell University Press.

Bruno, M., and W. Easterly. 1994. "Inflation Crises and Long-run Growth." Policy Research Department, Macroeconomic and Growth Division, World Bank. Mimeographed.

Bruno, M., and J. Sachs. 1985. *Economics of Worldwide Stagflation.* Cambridge: Harvard University Press.

Brusco, M. 1982. "The Emilian Model: Productive Decentralisation and Social Integration." *Cambridge Journal of Economics* 6, no. 2.

Cairncross, F., and A. Cairncross, eds. 1992. *The Legacy of the Golden Age—The 1960s and Their Economic Consequences.* London: Routledge.

Castells, M., A. Portes, and L. Benton, eds. 1989. *The Informal Economy.* Baltimore: Johns Hopkins University Press.

Chang, H-J. 1990. "Interpreting the Korean Experience—Heaven or Hell?" Research Paper Series, no. 42, Faculty of Economics and Politics, University of Cambridge.

———. 1993. "The Political Economy of Industrial Policy in Korea." *Cambridge Journal of Economics* 17, no. 2.

———. 1994a. *The Political Economy of Industrial Policy.* London: Macmillan.

———. 1994b. "State, Institutions, and Structural Change." *Structural Change and Economic Dynamics* 5, no. 2.

———. 1995a. "Explaining 'Flexible Rigidities' in East Asia." In T. Killick, ed., *The Flexible Economy.* London: Routledge.

———. 1995b. "Return to Europe?—Is There Anything That Eastern Europe Can Learn From East Asia?" In H-J. Chang and P. Nolan, eds., *The Transformation of the Communist Economies—Against the Mainstream.* London and Basingstoke: Macmillan.

———. 1996a. "Understanding the Recent Regulatory Changes in Japan and Korea." A paper prepared for the Project "Regulatory Policy and Regulatory Reform for Sustainable Development," Economic Development Institute, World Bank, Washington, D.C.

———. 1996b. *El Papel del Estado en el Cambio Económico.* Mexico City: Editorial Planeta Mexicana.

———. 1997a. "Markets, Madness, and Many Middle Ways: Some Reflections on the Institutional Diversity of Capitalism." In P. Arestis, G. Palma, and M. Sawyer, eds., *Essays in Honour of Geoff Harcourt—Volume 2: Markets, Unemployment, and Economic Policy.* London: Routledge.

———. 1997b. "Luxury Consumption Control and Industrialisation in East Asia." A background paper prepared for *Trade and Development Report 1997,* UNCTAD, Geneva. Mimeograph.

———. 1997c. "The Economics and Politics of Regulation." *Cambridge Journal of Economics* 21, no. 6.

———. 1998a. "Korea: The Misunderstood Crisis." *World Development* 26, no. 8.

———. 1998b. "Globalisation, Transnational Corporations, and Economic Development—Can the Developing Countries Pursue Strategic Industrial Policy in a Globalising World Economy?" In D. Baker, G. Epstein, and R. Pollin, eds., *Globalisation and Progressive Economic Policy: What Are the Real Constraints and Opportunities?* Cambridge: Cambridge University Press.

———. 1998c. "Transnational Corporations and Strategic Industrial Policy." In R. Kozul-Wright and B. Rowthorn, eds., *Transnational Corporations in the World Economy.* London: Macmillan.

———. 1998d. "Initial Conditions of Development—Comparing the East Asian and the Sub-Saharan African Experiences." A background paper for *UNCTAD Trade and Development Report, 1998.*

———. 1999. "Industrial Policy and East Asia—the Miracle, the Crisis, and the Future." A paper presented at the World Bank workshop "Rethinking East Asian Miracle," San Francisco, February.

———. 2000. "The Hazard of Moral Hazard—Untangling the Asian Crisis." *World Development* 28, no. 4.

———. 2002. *Kicking Away the Ladder—Development Strategy in Historical Perspective.* London: Atheneum Press.

Chang, H-J., G. Palma, and H. Whittaker, eds. 2001. *Financial Liberalization and the Asian Crisis.* Basingstoke: Palgrave.

Chang, H-J., H-J. Park, and C-G. Yoo. 1998. "Interpreting the Korean Crisis: Financial Liberalisation, Industrial Policy, and Corporate Governance." *Cambridge Journal of Economics* 22, no. 6.

Chang, H-J., and B. Rowthorn, eds. 1995. *Role of the State in Economic Change.* Oxford: Oxford University Press.

Chang, H-J., and C-G. Yoo. 2000. "Triumph of the Rentiers?" *Challenge,* January-February.

Cheng, T., S. Haggard, and D. Kang. 1998. "Institutions and Growth in Korea and Taiwan: The Bureaucracy." *Journal of Development Studies* 34, no. 6.

Chudnovsky, D., ed. 1993. *Transnational Corporations and Industrialisation.* London: Routledge.

Cohen, S. 1977. *Modern Capitalist Planning: The French Model.* 2d ed. Berkeley and Los Angeles: University of California Press.

Cox, A., ed. 1986. *State, Finance, and Industry in Comparative Perspective.* Brighton: Wheatsheaf Books.

Dei Ottati, G. 1994. "Trust, Interlinking Transactions, and Credit in the Industrial District." *Cambridge Journal of Economics* 18, no. 6.

Dore, R. 1986. *Flexible Rigidities: Industrial Policy and Structural Adjustment in the Japanese Economy, 1970–80.* London: The Athlone Press.

———. 1987. *Taking Japan Seriously—A Confucian Perspective on Leading Economic Issues.* London: The Athlone Press.

———. 1993. "What Makes the Japanese Different?" In C. Crouch and D. Marquand, eds., *Ethics and Markets.* Cambridge: Polity Press.

Dornbusch, R. 1996. "The Effectiveness of Exchange-Rate Changes." *Oxford Review of Economic Policy* 12, no. 3.

Dosi, G., C. Freeman, R. Nelson, G. Silverberg, and L. Soete, eds. 1988. *Technical Change and Economic Theory.* London: Pinter Publishers.

Dosi, G., L. Tyson, and J. Zysman. 1989. "Trade, Technologies and Development: A Framework for Discussing Japan." In C. Johnson, L. Tyson, and J. Zysman, eds., *Politics and Productivity.* New York: Harper Business.

EPB (Economic Planning Board). 1981. *Oegoogin Tooja Baeksuh* (White paper on foreign investment; in Korean). Seoul: The Government of Korea.

Evans, P. 1987. "Class, State, and Dependence in East Asia: Lessons for Latin Americanists." In F. Deyo, ed., *The Political Economy of the New Asian Industrialism.* Ithaca: Cornell University Press.

———. 1995. *Embedded Autonomy: States and Industrial Transformation.* Princeton: Princeton University Press.

Fargerberg, J. 1996. "Technology and Competitiveness." *Oxford Review of Economic Policy* 12, no. 3.

Fishlow, A., C. Gwin, S. Haggard, D. Rodrik, and R. Wade. 1994. *Miracle or Design?—Lessons from the East Asian Experience.* Washington, D.C.: Overseas Development Council.

Gerschenkron, A. 1962. *Economic Backwardness in Historical Perspective.* Cambridge: Harvard University Press.

Goldthorpe, J., ed. 1984. *Order and Conflict in Contemporary Capitalism.* Oxford: Oxford University Press.

Hall, P. 1986. *Governing the Economy: The Politics of State Intervention in Britain and France.* Cambridge: Polity Press.

Hayek, F. 1949. "The Meaning of Competition." In F. Hayek, *Individualism and Economic Order.* London: Routledge and Kegan Paul.

Helleiner, G. 1989. "Transnational Corporations and Direct Foreign Investment." In H. Chenery and T. N. Srinivasan, eds., *Handbook of Development Economics,* vol. 2. Amsterdam: Elsevier Science Publishers.

Hirst, P., and G. Thompson. 1996. *Globalisation in Question.* Cambridge: Polity Press.

Johnson, C. 1982. *MITI and the Japanese Miracle: The Making of Industrial Policy, 1925–75.* Stanford: Stanford University Press.

————, ed. 1984. *The Industrial Policy Debate*. San Francisco: Institute for Contemporary Studies.

Jones, L., and I. Sakong. 1980. *Government, Business and Entrepreneurship in Economic Development: The Korean Case*. Cambridge: Harvard University Press.

Koike, K. 1987. "Human Resource Development and Labour-Management Relations." In K. Yamamura and Y. Yasuba, eds., *The Political Economy of Japan*, vol. 1. Stanford: Stanford University Press.

Kozul-Wright, R. 1995. "The Myth of Anglo-Saxon Capitalism: Reconstructing the History of the American State." In H-J. Chang and B. Rowthorn, eds., *Role of the State in Economic Change*. Oxford: Oxford University Press.

Krueger, A. 1980. "Trade Policy as an Input to Development." *American Economic Review* 70, no. 3.

Lal, D. 1983. *The Poverty of Development Economics*. London: The Institute of Economic Affairs.

Lall, S., ed. 1993. *Transnational Corporations and Economic Development*. London: Routledge.

Langlois, R., ed. 1986. *Economics as a Process*. Cambridge: Cambridge University Press.

Lindbeck, A. 1981. "Industrial Policy as an Issue in the Economic Environment." *The World Economy* 4, no. 4.

Little, I. 1982. *Economic Development*. New York: Basic Books.

Luedde-Neurath, R. 1986. *Import Controls and Export-Oriented Development: A Reassessment of the South Korean Case*. Boulder, Colo.: Westview.

Lundvall, B-Å., ed. 1992. *National Systems of Innovation: Towards a Theory of Innovation and Interactive Learning*. London: Pinter Publishers.

Magaziner, I., and T. Hout. 1980. *Japanese Industrial Policy*. London: Policy Studies Institute.

Marglin, S., and J. Schor, eds. 1990. *The Golden Age of Capitalism*. Oxford: Clarendon Press.

McNulty, P. 1968. "Economic Theory and the Meaning of Competition." *Quarterly Journal of Economics* 82, no. 4.

Murray, F. 1987. "Flexible Specialisation in the 'Third Italy.'" *Capital and Class* (Winter).

Nelson, R., ed. 1993. *National Innovation Systems*. New York: Oxford University Press.

Pekkarinen, J., M. Pohjola, and B. Rowthorn, eds. 1992. *Social Corporatism*. Oxford: Oxford University Press.

Piore, M., and C. Sabel. 1984. *The Second Industrial Divide*. New York: Basic Books.

Polanyi, K. 1957. *The Great Transformation*. Boston: Beacon Press.

Price, V. 1980. "Alternatives to Delayed Structural Adjustment in 'Workshop Europe.'" *The World Economy* 3, no. 2.

Ranis, G., and J. Fei. 1975. "A Model of Growth and Employment in the Open Dualistic Economy: The Cases of Korea and Taiwan." In F. Stewart, ed., *Employment, Distribution, and Development*. London: Frank Case.

Sachs, J. 1984. "Comment on C. Diaz-Alejandro, *Latin American Debt: I Don't Think We Are in Kansas Anymore*." *Brookings Papers on Economic Activity*, no. 2.

Schive, C. 1993. "Foreign Investment and Technology Transfer in Taiwan." In S. Lall, ed., *Transnational Corporations and Economic Development*. London: Routledge.

Schott, K. 1984. *Policy, Power and Order*. New Haven: Yale University Press.

Shin, K. 1994. *An International Comparison of Competition Policy: USA, Japan, and Germany* (in Korean). Seoul: Korea Development Institute.

Shonfield, A. 1965. *Modern Capitalism: The Changing Balance of Public and Private Power*. Oxford: Oxford University Press.

Singh, A. 1995. "How Did East Asia Grow So Fast?—Slow Progress Towards An Analytical Consensus." UNCTAD Discussion Paper No. 97, United Nations Conference on Trade and Development (UNCTAD), Geneva.

Stiglitz, J. 1998. "Sound Finance and Sustainable Development in Asia." Keynote address to the Asia Development Forum, jointly organized by the World Bank and the Asian Development Bank, Manila, March 9–12.

Studart, R. 1995. "The Efficiency of Financial Systems, Liberalisation, and Economic Development." *Journal of Post-Keynesian Economics* 18, no. 2.

Thompson, G., ed. 1989. *Industrial Policy: USA and UK Debates*. London: Routledge.

Toye, J. 1987. *Dilemmas of Development*. Oxford: Blackwell.

Vartiainen, J. 1995. "The State and Structural Change: What can be Learnt from the Successful Late Industrializers?" In H-J. Chang and B. Rowthorn, eds., *Role of the State in Economic Change*. Oxford: Oxford University Press.

Wade, R. 1990. *Governing the Market*. Princeton: Princeton University Press.

———. 1996. "Globalization and Its Limits: Reports on the Death of the National Economy Are Greatly Exaggerated." In S. Berger and R. Dore, eds., *National Diversity and Global Capitalism*. Ithaca: Cornell University Press.

Wade, R., and F. Veneroso. 1998. "The Asian Crisis: The High Debt Model vs. The Wall Street-Treasury-MIF Complex." *New Left Review* (March-April).

Westney, E. 1987. *Imitation and Innovation: The Transfer of Western Organisational Patterns to Meiji Japan*. Cambridge: Cambridge University Press.

Williamson, O. 1985. *The Economic Institutions of Capitalism*. New York: The Free Press.

World Bank. 1987. *World Development Report, 1987*. New York: Oxford University Press.

———. 1993. *The East Asian Miracle: Economic Growth and Public Policy*. New York: Oxford University Press.

———. 1994. *World Development Report, 1994*. New York: Oxford University Press.

———. 1997. *World Development Report, 1997*. New York: Oxford University Press.

You, J., and H-J. Chang. 1993. "The Myth of Free Labour Market in Korea." *Contributions to Political Economy* 12.

Yusuf, S., and R. Peters. 1985. "Capital Accumulation and Economic Growth: The Korean Paradigm." World Bank Staff Working Paper no. 712.

Zysman, J. 1983. *Governments, Markets, and Growth*. Oxford: Martin Robertson.

Lessons from Southeast Asia: Growth, Equity, and Vulnerability

BRIDGET WELSH

From 1960 through 1996 three Southeast Asian countries—Indonesia, Malaysia, and Thailand—managed to beat the odds, rapidly expanding their economies while reducing poverty.[1] This was a remarkable achievement. Beginning in 1997, however, the fortunes of these countries were reversed with the onset of the Asian financial crisis.[2] This crisis not only undermined their economies, but also discredited their performance. In my view it is too early to dismiss the lessons we can learn from these "late, late developers" (Gershenkron 1962). I argue that there were important factors that promoted growth and greater equality in these countries: specific economic and social policies, the developmental orientation of their states, and a regional proximity to models of success and capital. At the same time, other factors left them highly vulnerable to changes in the international political economy, notably an unchecked dependence on foreign capital; a close, collusive relationship between domestic business groups and states; a dependence on a weakening regional hegemon; and a growing incompatibility between private-sector–led growth and poverty reduction. This chapter describes the unique set of factors that contributed to growth, equity, and vulnerability in Southeast Asia and suggests that there are important lessons from this pattern of economic development for other developing countries.

Until the 1990s the experiences of these Southeast Asian (SEA) countries had been overshadowed by the more prominent Northeast Asian (NEA) success stories, notably Japan, South Korea, and Taiwan. The 1993 World Bank study, however, put these SEA economies on the map. It described how Indonesia, Malaysia, and Thailand had transformed their economies from a dependence on agriculture to industry, while achieving the impressive

The author would like to thank Evelyne Huber, Kellee Tsai, Ann Marie Murphy, Jim Logerfo, Yi-feng Tao, and two anonymous reviewers for their comments on this chapter. The author is solely responsible for any errors the chapter may contain.

    1. The experiences of Indonesia, Malaysia, and Thailand are unique and are not representative of the region as a whole. The use of the term "Southeast Asia" below is used for convenience to distinguish a pattern of economic development in these countries.

    2. The "Asian financial crisis" refers to the economic downturn beginning in July 1997, which began in Thailand and extended throughout the region.

combination of growth and greater equality. The World Bank emphasized the importance of the market and foreign investment for growth of these economies and challenged the "statist" position that highlighted the importance of selective industrial strategies and government intervention (Chang 1994; Johnson 1995). This provoked a debate about the relative importance of market forces and political factors in Southeast Asia (Jomo 1997). The Asian financial crisis continues to draw attention to the region, and the debate has escalated in the wake of attempts to address the economic downturn.

This chapter initially examines the success of the SEA economies through 1996. What becomes evident is that the economic transformation in Southeast Asia did not occur overnight. While these "late, late developers" did develop rapidly, compared to the Western counterparts a century earlier, the changes occurred over three decades and involved periods of relative decline. Compared to their NEA neighbors, development in Southeast Asia was a much slower process.

I identify in this chapter the factors underlying the economic success of these countries. I focus on the commonalities among the SEA countries and compare the similar conditions and policies in these countries with the success stories of Northeast Asia.[3] This discussion builds directly on the earlier chapter by Ha-Joon Chang that focuses on the "Big Three" NEA countries—Japan, South Korea, and Taiwan. The comparison demonstrates that there are important features associated with the success of SEA countries, beyond the market orientation and political factors highlighted by the World Bank. SEA development was the result of a combination of policies *and* government intervention. These policies involved agricultural development, investment in industry, human resource development, infrastructure, and technology transfers. In contrast to the World Bank's interpretation of political institutions in Southeast Asia, these policies would not have been implemented without the development orientation of the countries' political leaders and institutions and their timely intervention to address problem areas. The multiethnic configuration of SEA societies contributed to the developmental orientation of these regimes by providing a rational for reducing poverty.[4] Finally, the location of these countries, with close proximity to models of economic success and foreign capital, further facilitated the development process. What uniquely stands out in the SEA success story

---

3. Unfortunately, important differences in the timing and weight of factors that promoted economic development in these countries are beyond the scope of this chapter.

4. The use of the term "regimes" is intentional and emphasizes the leaders in power as well as the bureaucracies in these countries.

is the importance of foreign capital, the developmental orientation of the regimes, ethnic heterogeneity, and the regional context.

This discussion provides the background for the third goal of this chapter, gleaning important lessons from the SEA experiences on how to achieve economic development. It is here that I incorporate the recent problems in these economies brought about by the Asian financial crisis. Southeast Asia's success came with a price—vulnerability. The sources of this vulnerability were economic, political, and regional; all ironically closely tied to their earlier economic success. These economies would not have expanded without foreign capital. Foreign investment was critical, more so than in Northeast Asia. When the international climate changed in 1997, and foreign investors began to question some of the economic fundamentals in Southeast Asia, their extreme dependence on foreign funds debilitated these economies. The flight of foreign capital set their exchange rates spiraling downward and exposed a pattern of domestic private lending that bankrupted domestic private capitalists and strained local financial sectors; all of which contracted their economies.

On the political side of the equation, the same irony existed. The political support from domestic capitalists for the regimes was narrow and consisted of close relationships among a handful of selected capitalists and political leaders. These alliances promoted rent-seeking behavior that weakened the private financial sectors of these economies and over time encouraged decision making in the state that was not motivated by a desire to generate equity. Ironically, the political source of support that allowed for earlier economic development began to hinder economic prosperity.

Equally important was a change in the attitude of the SEA regimes toward the eradication of poverty. As development occurred in these countries, particularly after the privatization of the state enterprises and reduction of the state in the economy (in turn increasing the role of private sector as the leading force in the economy), social equality became less of a priority. Ethnic heterogeneity no longer promoted equality, but rather served as a potential source of conflict, especially in Malaysia and Indonesia. These changes occurred before the financial crisis began.

Finally, the role of the regional hegemon also contributed to Southeast Asia's problems. Japan's currency had been declining and its economy weakening since 1995. It was not able to offer a model to address the problems of private debt or adequate support to weather the rapid currency devaluations. Again, ironically, the regional context was no longer able to offer the benefits it had earlier. The strengths of the unique pattern of SEA development—dependence on foreign capital, developmental orientation of the regimes, ethnic heterogeneity, and the regional context—had transformed into serious weaknesses.

Table 8.1 Sectoral Contribution to GDP Growth, 1960–1995 (percentage)

	Indonesia		Malaysia		Thailand	
Year	Industry	Agriculture	Industry	Agriculture	Industry	Agriculture
1960	13.4[a]	38.7[a]	8.7[b]	40[b]	7.4	58.3
1970	24.4	27.0	13.4	30.8	10.9	47.5
1980	30.1	20.0	20.0	22.8	13.4	24.3
1990	37.8	13.6	26.9	18.7	19.4	19.4
1995	30.2	10.9	33.1	13.6	17.2	24.3

SOURCES: World Bank, World Tables, 1991; Malaysian Ministry of Finance, Economic Report, various years; Bank of Thailand, Central Bureau of Statistics, Indonesia.
[a] 1961.
[b] 1957.

SOUTHEAST ASIAN ECONOMIC DEVELOPMENT

The story of SEA development began in the 1960s. In 1945 none of these countries had robust industrial sectors. Like most former colonies, they were dependent on the export of a narrow base of agricultural commodities. Malaysia relied on tin and rubber, Thailand rice, Indonesia coffee and oil. Between 1960 and 1995 the share of GNP from agriculture decreased, and was rapidly replaced by manufacturing. The change was the most significant in Thailand, since the largest proportion of its population moved out of agriculture. In 1965 agriculture comprised 55 percent of GDP. By 1995 that figure was cut in half, 24.3 percent of GDP.[5] During the same period, manufacturing had increased from 8.5 percent to 17.2 percent of GDP.[6] Table 8.1 demonstrates that similar changes occurred in Indonesia and Malaysia.

While the transformation of the structure of their economies paralleled the experience of NEA economies, the timing and scope of industrialization differed. With the development of shipbuilding and the promotion of industry by the Japanese in Korea and Taiwan, the NEA economies began significantly to industrialize as early as the 1930s (Cumings 1984; Ito 1993). The SEA economies did not begin to industrialize extensively until the 1970s. In the following decade, the pace of industrialization intensified. This coincided with the growing emphasis on an export-led industrialization strategy to promote economic growth and with the flood of Japanese yen after the 1985 Plaza Accord (Jomo 1997). The emphasis on industry, however,

5. *World Development Report*, 1997–1999.
6. Ibid.

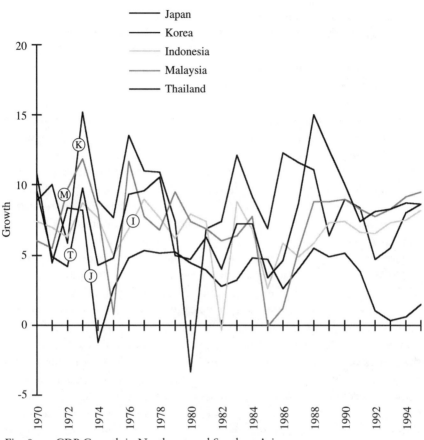

Fig. 8.1   GDP Growth in Northeast and Southest Asia
SOURCE: World Bank 1991; 1997.

obscured a persistent reliance on nonindustrial forms of production. The
scope of industrialization in SEA countries was narrower. Agriculture, mining, and services continued to comprise a comparatively larger share of
these economies than in the NEA countries.

It is important to note that SEA countries did not achieve quite the same
levels of growth as NEA countries. Throughout this transformation, the SEA
economies averaged about 3.5 percent growth a year since 1960 (World
Bank 1993). This is lower than the countries in Northeast Asia, at 5 percent
a year, but considerably higher than the rest of the developing world, at 1.5
percent (World Bank 1993). These rates also changed over time. The SEA
countries achieved high growth rates in the 1960s, slightly lower rates in the
1970s, a sharp drop in the 1980s, and consistently impressive rates from
1986 through 1995. As Figure 8.1 shows, the variation in growth over time

is wider than in NEA countries after 1970, especially Japan. These differences point to the variation in the timing of implementing policies and different resource bases of these countries. They do not, however, obscure the overall common trend: sustained and rapid growth.

Many developing countries have experienced high growth. What makes the SEA experience impressive was that growth was achieved with a more equitable income distribution than that of most developing countries, particularly those in Latin America. Table 8.2 shows that the SEA countries succeeded in improving equality. The Gini coefficients in Malaysia and Indonesia reduced over the three decades. The change in equality in Thailand was less impressive, but the level of social inequality in Thailand remained lower than most of the developing world. These ratios are considerably better than those for Latin American countries, notably Brazil (.59) and Mexico (.53) (Székely 1998).

Greater equality was accompanied by significant reductions in poverty. Indonesia was the most successful of the three countries. In 1965 60 percent of the population lived in poverty, with 67 million people living in absolute poverty. By 1993 this number was drastically reduced to only 14 percent or 24 million people living in poverty (Dasgupta 1997, 209). In Thailand the number of people living in poverty decreased from 16 million in 1965 to less than half a million by 1995 (World Bank 1998). In Malaysia 1.6 million lived in poverty in 1965. By 1995 this figure had been reduced to less than 900,000 (World Bank 1998). These reductions took place while their populations increased, in some cases doubling. In each of these countries this decline in poverty has been concentrated in the rural areas, the center of poverty in Southeast Asia. In Indonesia, for example, the number of rural poor deceased from 40.4 percent in 1976 to 14.3 percent in 1990 (Booth 1997, 128).[7]

Again, the success of the SEA countries did not match the achievement of their NEA counterparts. Tracing poverty rates and Gini coefficients over time, the 1993 World Bank study (31) shows that Japan and Taiwan were the most successful in promoting equality. Indonesia, however, paralleled Korea. With consistently higher inequality Malaysia and Thailand were the least impressive. These rankings need to be understood in the context of these economies, however. Despite Indonesia's comparative success, it remained the poorest country of the three, with a per capita income of $980 in 1995, compared to $2,740 in Thailand in 1995 and $3,890 in Malaysia

7. In the wake of the crisis, the success of poverty eradication programs have been questioned, especially in Indonesia. In my view, these figures should be interpreted as indicators of a trend rather than as concrete numbers. Booth 1999c discusses some of the debate associated with the measurement of poverty.

Table 8.2   Gini Coefficients in East Asia

Economy	Gini coefficient			
	1965[a]	1975	1985	1995[b]
Japan	0.348	0.355	—	—
Taiwan	0.358	0.321	—	—
Korea	0.343	0.355	—	—
Indonesia	0.35	0.34	0.33	0.317
Malaysia	0.498	0.505	0.493	0.484
Thailand	0.423	0.426	0.426	0.462

SOURCES: World Bank 1997, 223; Ikemoto 1991, 72.

[a] Taiwan figures refer to 1966.

[b] Malaysia figures refer to 1989, Thailand 1992, and Indonesia 1993.

(World Bank 1997). These figures are considerably lower than the per capita incomes of the NEA countries, well above $10,000. Yet, on the whole, the SEA countries achieved more income equality than the majority of developing countries in Latin America and Africa. Their achievements are especially significant because of the high level of poverty in each of these countries after World War II.

OUT OF THE SHADOW OF NORTHEAST ASIA: A SOUTHEAST ASIAN MODEL?

To understand these differences in growth and equality promotion, I compare the experiences in Southeast Asia with those in Northeast Asia. Interestingly, there is a unique set of factors associated with SEA development.[8] Because of the weaknesses of these economies and the limited regional scope of these experiences, this is not labeled a "Southeast Asian model" as such, but rather a "Southeast Asian pattern."

Physical, Historical, and Social Setting

A major difference between NEA and SEA countries involves the initial conditions of the two regions and their implication. Foremost, SEA countries were (and still are) rich in natural resources. All three countries have significant

8. The pioneering work in discussing the differences between Southeast Asia and Northeast Asia is Jomo 1997; see especially pages 10–26. This discussion builds on this account, although there are differences in the explanation of political conditions and emphasis of particular factors. More recently, Anne Booth (1999b) has contributed to the debate, by highlighting the differences among the Southeast Asian countries.

Table 8.3   Poverty in Southeast Asia

Number of people in poverty (millions)				
Economy	1965	1975	1985	1995
Indonesia	89	87.2	52.8	21.9
Malaysia	1.6[a]	2.1	1.7	0.9
Thailand	16[b]	3.4	5.1	<0.5

SOURCE: Ahuja et al. 1997, 6.
[a] 1970.
[b] 1962. Muscat 1994, 241; World Bank 1998.

arable land. This has allowed them to maintain robust agricultural sectors. Thailand, for example, has been a leading producer of rice and other agricultural products. Up until the 1970s, Malaysia was one of the world's leading producers of rubber. Indonesia and Malaysia are blessed with oil, timber, and rich mineral deposits. These endowments differ significantly from those of the NEA countries, which lack natural resources.

The effects of these endowments on SEA economic development have been twofold. First, it has created quasi-rentier SEA governments have gained revenue that has allowed them to build infrastructure and fund education and social services without directly taxing their populations. This has contributed to overall economic development without threatening the regimes or creating broader constituencies demanding broader representation for their tax contributions. Second, the resource bases of these countries have dampened the immediate need to develop, at least in the short term. With resources at their disposal, SEA regimes were not pressed to yield immediate results. The abundance of natural resources provided a "resource buffer" against the immediate push to develop and limited the political costs of a delay in economic development. Yet unlike Nigeria or Ecuador, the SEA regimes did not waste this benefit. They did not squander their resource rents, choosing instead to use the "resource buffer" as an opportunity to carefully select their strategies, correct their mistakes, promote economic development, and build support for their regimes.

Extensive resource endowments have perhaps compensated for the advantage that the NEA countries had at the end of World War II (Amsden 1989; Gold 1986). SEA states occupied a less advantageous position in the international political economy; they were producers of primary products for Western economies. In contrast, Korea and Taiwan had begun to industrialize their economies and were closely integrated into Japanese industrial expansion. Colonialism and the Japanese occupation also left SEA countries deeply scarred (Booth 1999b). Rather than cleaning the slates for change as in Northeast Asia, the immediate postwar context in Southeast Asia was rife with domestic conflicts that had been accentuated through the 1940s. Both Malaysia and Indonesia faced civil wars that involved national and class struggles.[9] Thailand, never colonized, was in the comparatively strongest position, but faced a wide rural and urban income gap. This divide imploded in the late 1960s and caused a conflict similar to that in Malaysia. All three countries had to address internal security problems. Unlike Taiwan, and to a lesser extent Japan and Korea, these countries did not have the same external security threat that dissipated domestic conflicts (Woo-Cummings 1998; Stubbs 1999).

The situation was made more difficult by the fact that SEA countries initially faced sharper social inequalities than the NEA countries did. There was a wide gap between the rich and poor throughout Southeast Asia, that mirrored conditions in Latin America. The majority of the poor lived in the rural areas, creating regional distortions as well as a wide income divide. Of the three countries, conditions in Indonesia were perhaps the most difficult. The country had a shortage of land on the most heavily populated island, Java, and numerous landless peasants. Conditions in the outer islands, such as West Papua, were even more difficult. The problem of poverty in Southeast Asia was much sharper than in Northeast Asia, in part, because of the lack of land reform. This difference was compounded by the fact that SEA countries lacked adequate state capacity to address poverty in the years immediately following colonial rule. Wracked by a war with the Dutch and a lack of clear leadership, Indonesia did not have the bureaucratic capacity to implement any redistributive policies through the 1950s (Feith 1962). Indonesia did not attempt land reform until the early 1960s, and this contributed to the downfall of the Sukarno regime (1955–65). While Thailand and Malaysia had more capable bureaucracies and introduced some redistributive measures, these were not widespread. The SEA countries failed to redress poverty in the immediate postcolonial period, which in turn fueled the domestic conflicts in these countries.

Social divisions were accentuated by ethnic differences. With its many islands, Indonesia has hundreds of different ethnic groups. Malaysia is comprised of primarily three groups: Malays, Chinese, and Indians. Thailand,

9. Indonesia fought the Dutch for independence until 1949 and tackled regional rebellions in the late 1950s. A class struggle was an important factor in the downfall of Sukarno in 1965. Malaysia was debilitated by the "Communist Emergency" through the 1950s, which eliminated the left as a political force in that country. In this conflict the Malaysian Communist Party, comprised predominantly of Chinese Malaysians, challenged British rule and the existing class structure.

however, is the most homogenous, and thus similar to the countries in Northeast Asia. Yet even Thailand has a degree of heterogeneity because of regional differences and immigration from China to mainland Southeast Asia. Ethnic differences are common throughout the developing world. What made the ethnic differences in SEA countries sharper was the fact that there was an ethnic group that stood out as the wealthy outsider. The ethnic Chinese dominated SEA domestic capital, although they were more integrated with the local population in Thailand.

The immediate result of SEA's sharp class and ethnic divisions was an intensification of the internal security problems. In later years, income differences among social groups would create a strong distributive incentive for political leaders, particularly in Malaysia and Indonesia. Ethnic income inequalities in particular underscored an emphasis on greater social equality in the 1970s.

Considering the physical, social, and historical setting as a whole, Southeast Asia inherited a more difficult context to promote economic development than Northeast Asia did. Natural resources were a blessing and a curse. Ultimately, the presence of natural resources delayed economic development, although they made the delay more viable politically. The legacy of colonialism and the Japanese occupation stirred up social conflicts and forced these regimes to deal immediately with internal security issues, as opposed to economic development. While NEA countries had their own internal conflicts, SEA countries did not have the same external threat to dissipate internal problems. The social context was perhaps the most difficult factor. Class and ethnic inequalities were sharper in Southeast Asia than in Northeast Asia. The task of poverty reduction was even more pressing in Southeast Asia. Burdened by these obstacles, SEA countries began the development process much later than their NEA counterparts.

Macroeconomic Factors

If we put aside the issue of timing and look at the economic prescriptions these countries adopted to promote growth and equity, we find striking similarities between the two regions. The range of common macroeconomic factors extend from the overall strategies toward economic development and the large role of the public sector in the early stages of economic development to similar fiscal and monetary policies. The differences between the regions involve the degree to which a particular macroeconomic factor influenced economic development. Some of these differences are minor, such as Northeast Asia's greater emphasis on lower inflation. Others are more

Table 8.4 Comparative Initial Conditions, Northeast Asia and Southeast Asia

	Resources	Internal security	Social divisions	Overall consequence
Northeast Asia	Lacked resources	Less conflict	Greater initial equality	More favorable conditions for development
Southeast Asia	Resource buffer	Widespread conflicts	Sharp class and ethnic differences	Less favorable conditions for development

significant. Two factors stand out in the SEA experience: the larger role of foreign capital, particularly private investment, and public spending on rural areas as a result of the domestic conflicts mentioned earlier.

Beginning with the commonalities, both regions adopted similar economic strategies that emphasized industrialization. Early on, leaders in SEA countries recognized the importance of restructuring their economies away from agriculture. Indonesia, Malaysia, and Thailand initially adopted a strategy of import-substitution industrialization (ISI) in the 1950s, although their economies continued to be dominated by the export of agricultural commodities through the 1960s. Each of these countries carved out its own niche in the export sector. Malaysia built on existing resource industries and developed a manufacturing sector around rubber and tin which later expanded to include timber and palm oil (Lim 1973). Thailand similarly built upon its resource foundation, focusing on agricultural exports, particularly fruits and seafood (Warr 1993). Canning and food processing became the foundation of the manufacturing sector. Indonesia, in contrast, failed to develop a diverse industrial sector during the early years of its economic development. Its manufacturing activity was concentrated in the petroleum sector through the 1960s (Hill 1997).

By the 1980s SEA countries had adopted an export-led growth strategy in both light and heavy industries (Ariff and Hill 1985). These countries recognized the difficulties of the import-substitution strategy comparatively early on and were able to change strategies easily because, in part, domestic labor was not as powerful a political actor as it has been in Latin America. SEA countries capitalized on their low labor costs. Malaysia moved toward a combination of export-led growth and ISI as early as 1971 (Jomo and Edwards 1993). It was able to capitalize on its literate and English-speaking workforce to attract electronics firms so that by the 1980s the country had become a center for the fast-growing semiconductor production industry. Thailand adopted export-led growth strategy in the early 1980s (Warr 1993).

Although labor-intensive industries existed in Thailand from the 1970s, it was not until 1981 that Thailand significantly expanded textile and semi-conductor production. Of the three countries, Indonesia was the last to industrialize for export (Hill 1996). In the mid-1980s Indonesia diversified its industrial center around its capital, Jakarta. By the 1990s Indonesia became one of the largest producers of plywood, textiles, and shoes and had ventured into steel and timber-related manufacturing. In contrast to the Latin American response to the debt crisis of the 1980s, the SEA economic downturn in the early 1980s contributed to the region's adoption of export-led growth.

The SEA export-oriented industrialization strategy was not without problems. Success varied across sectors. Unlike Thailand and Indonesia, Malaysia failed to become competitive in textiles. Lacking skilled labor, Indonesia did not develop a large semiconductor sector. The greatest problems involved heavy industry. Echoing Korea's difficulties, Malaysia's launch into heavy industry (automobiles) in the early 1980s had disappointing results; it failed to create robust linkages with the rest of the economy. Similarly, Indonesia's development of aircraft manufacturing encountered problems (Hill 1996). Thailand's automobile sector was more successful, but the scope of heavy industry remained narrow (Doner 1991a). As in Northeast Asia, the prompt recognition and attention to the difficulties maintained growth. SEA leaders often chose to continue to develop the troubled sector, such as the automobile sector in Malaysia, but simultaneously tried to promote other, more competitive, sectors to maintain economic growth, such as semiconductors in Malaysia and textiles in Indonesia.

The manner in which SEA regimes supported export-led industrialization varied from that of Northeast Asia. SEA countries were much more open to foreign capital.[10] Capital from Western and NEA governments *and* investors built Southeast Asia's industrial base (Ramstetter 1991). The 1995 *World Investment Report* calculated the ratio of foreign capital to gross capital formation in these three countries in the early 1990s. The average ratio in Malaysia was very high, at 24.6. In Thailand and Indonesia the ratios were 4.7 and 4.5. These numbers paralleled, and in the case of Malaysia exceeded, the significance of foreign capital in the NEA economies at the early stages of their development (Haggard and Cheng 1987). In contrast to the NEA countries, the high level of foreign capital in these economies persisted throughout the three decades of development.

---

10. Indonesia, before 1966, is the only exception. Sukarno pursued a policy of nonalignment which discouraged Western investment during his leadership.

The composition of foreign capital also varied. Compared to the NEA countries, more capital originated from private investment, rather than foreign aid. This difference grew wider over time. Foreign portfolio capital became more prominent in the 1990s, and foreign investors comprised a larger percentage of overall portfolio capital than in the NEA economies. This reflected the openness of the SEA regimes to foreign investment. Yet since many of the funds went abroad or were invested in short-term ventures, portfolio capital made a limited productive contribution to economic development. In contrast to the NEA economies, where domestic investment took on a more important role, the engine of SEA growth remained foreign private investment in industry.

To maintain their openness to foreign capital, SEA countries reformed their trade policies to support export-led growth (Findley and Garnaut 1986). Trade policy promoted infant industries in early years (1960–70s) through high tariffs on imports, although the level of protectionism was comparatively lower than that in Northeast Asia. With the adoption of export-led growth, SEA economies initiated major steps to open their markets. Malaysia, for example, introduced export-processing zones in the 1970s. By 1980, 70 percent of exports originated from these zones (World Bank 1993, 193). With the exception of the automobile sector, SEA countries lowered tariffs at a faster rate than NEA countries and in larger increments (Matthews and Ravenhill 1994). With greater domestic capital, the NEA economies did not need to make themselves attractive to outsiders. Southeast Asia's greater dependence on foreign investment, however, led to different trade policies.

SEA countries also used fiscal policy to attract capital and maintain international competitiveness. Many of the policies were similar to those of Northeast Asia. SEA governments placed a high premium on curbing inflation. A history of fiscal conservatism in Malaysia and Thailand kept inflation low, averaging 3.4 percent and 5.6 percent from 1961 to 1991 (World Bank 1993, 110). Indonesia's average was much higher, 12.4 percent, but considerably lower than the average, 192.1 percent, for Latin America and the Caribbean during the same period (World Bank 1993, 110). In particular, low inflation was a major priority of Suharto's New Order government (1966–98), where inflation was synonymous with political failure. Throughout Southeast Asia, low inflation accompanied low budget deficits. Although deficits did exist, the governments made concerted efforts to balance their finances. SEA countries also worked to promote exchange rate stability. Malaysia, like Hong Kong, pegged its currency to the British pound until 1973. Thailand and Indonesia, like South Korea, pegged their currencies to the U.S. dollar. From

1954 through 1984 the Thai baht was only devalued once, in 1981. Indonesia maintained a fixed rate from 1971 through 1978, but devalued three times, (1978, 1983, 1986), before it decided to float its currency. The devaluations of the late 1980s only managed to enhance export production and buttressed the export-led industrialization strategy. In the 1990s all three SEA countries "quasi-pegged" their currencies to the U.S. dollar, hoping to attract capital and maintain stability. Yet in the wake of the crisis, these measures were inadequate to offset the contagion effect in currency markets. SEA countries did not have enough reserves to support their perceived overvalued exchange rates (Jomo 1998). Nevertheless, the stability of the exchange rates over the three decades as a whole was instrumental to their success. Overall, SEA countries followed the model of the NEA countries in fiscal and monetary policies.

SEA economies diverged from the NEA experiences in one area: tax incentives and tax rates. SEA countries developed attractive tax incentive packages to promote industrialization, even during the ISI years. This contrasts with NEA countries and reflects the underlying dependence on foreign capital. Moreover, SEA countries lowered direct taxes in the 1980s before the NEA countries, to maintain their competitiveness in the international economy.

Others have described each of these factors—economic strategy, foreign capital, trade, fiscal, and monetary policies—as part of the "East Asian Miracle." Implicit in many of these studies is an emphasis on the role of the market as a catalyst for economic growth. However, one should not confuse specific strategies and policies with an embrace of the free market. If one looks at the pattern of growth in SEA countries over a longer period, from the 1960s instead of from the 1980s, the public sector was a critical dimension of these economies. The scope of state intervention in the economy was significant, paralleling state involvement in Japan, Taiwan, and South Korea (Wade 1988). The expansion of the public sector stimulated growth in the economy in the early years of development and enhanced state capacity to promote growth. Historically, SEA countries have more in common with the NEA experience, and less in common with contemporary free market proponents. What makes the public sector in Southeast Asia sharply different from that in Northeast Asia is the emphasis on public spending in the rural sectors.

The root of the high involvement in the public sector in the economy had to do with the ethnic and internal security issues outlined earlier. Beginning in the 1970s Malaysia adopted an affirmative action policy (NEP) that heavily invested in rural development and expanded state ownership of the economy to reduce poverty among the Malays, the ethnic group that controlled political power. Public spending was a viable economic option because of oil revenue. In this period in which ethnicity was politicized, Malaysia's leaders were more dependent on the public sector and foreign investment than on the domestic private sector, which was comprised of Chinese capitalists (Jesudason 1989). It was not until the late 1980s that Malaysia began to privatize its economy, as a response to deteriorating international conditions (1985–86 recession) and greater economic security among the Malay community within Malaysia.

There was a similar political dimension for broad state investment in the economy in Indonesia. Economic policy in Indonesia from 1966 to 1995 was shaped by four actors: Suharto, the Chinese capitalists, technocrats, and *pribumis* (indigenous Indonesians, largely Muslims) (Bresnan 1993). Throughout the New Order, Suharto and the Chinese capitalists maintained a close relationship, although this alliance loosened in the 1990s, as his family members became increasingly important in the economy. The relationships between "select" businessmen and Suharto's regime would lead to the group of businessmen known as "cronies." Despite their prominence, the "cronies" had little influence over Indonesia's national economic strategy. From 1966 onward, technocrats and *pribumis* fought for supremacy over economic policy, with the former group emphasizing fiscal austerity and the latter promoting spending for rural development of the Muslims and national (state) ownership of resources. In the 1970s, with the huge oil revenue, the *pribumis* dominated economic policy. This led to a significant expansion in public spending, particularly in rural areas (Booth 1992). This would change in the late 1980s after the recession of 1985–86, but public sector expansion comprised a significant part of economic policy for over a decade.

Thailand's economy through the 1970s was based on trade of its agricultural products, notably rice. Public sector spending was promoted by the military government beginning in the late 1970s in response to increasing unrest among the rural sector and students and the need to restructure the economy. The military government relied on economic legitimacy to perpetuate its rule and realized that Thailand's economy was less competitive than in earlier years. This resulted in a similar emphasis on spending in the rural sector and public ownership of companies, although narrower in scope since Thailand lacked the advantage of oil revenues. The level of state involvement in the economy would change with the advent of democracy and economic difficulties in the 1980s, as the state privatized its holdings and reduced spending (Hewison 1989).

This pattern of high public spending stands in stark contrast to free market doctrine. Public spending served to redress poverty and promote growth.

Table 8.5 Comparative Macroeconomic Factors, NEA and SEA

	Northeast Asia	Southeast Asia
Economic Strategy	Emphasis industry	Emphasis industry
	Early transition from ISI to export-led growth	Early transition from ISI to export-led growth
Labor	Limited Freedom	Limited Freedom
Foreign Capital	High early stages development	High early stages development
	Foreign aid important	Foreign investment important
Trade Policy	More protectionism	Less protectionism
	Less reform	More reform
Fiscal Policy I	Low inflation emphasis	Low inflation emphasis
	Less inflation	More inflation (especially Indonesia)
Fiscal Policy II	Limited tax incentives	Broader tax incentives
	Less tax reform	Earlier tax reform
Monetary Policy	Emphasis on stable currency	Emphasis on stable currency
Role of Public Sector	Extensive in early stages	Extensive in early stages
	Less focus on rural communities	Greater focus on rural communities

Natural resources and social conflicts combined to promote focus on the rural communities. While the regimes were repressive, especially in Indonesia, the leaders of these countries recognized the need to have a long-term solution to the problem of poverty.

The overall picture that emerges from the discussion of macroeconomic factors is one of similarity. As the summary in Table 8.5 describes, NEA and SEA countries followed similar strategies to promote development, adopted similar fiscal and monetary policies, and maintained a large public sector to promote growth. The main differences are the greater role of foreign capital in SEA economies, particularly private investment, the accompanying differences in trade and fiscal policies to stimulate foreign investment, and greater public spending in rural areas.

Regional Context of Development

One unique facet of SEA development involves the regional context. In contrast to countries in Latin America and Africa, Indonesia, Malaysia, and Thailand had an "East Asian Model" centered in the regional economic hegemon, Japan. By the 1970s, SEA countries also had the experiences of Taiwan, South Korea, Hong Kong, and neighboring Singapore to learn from. The presence of Asian "successes" inspired many of the SEA regimes. Malaysia, for example, adopted a "Look East Policy" in the early 1980s and worked to replicate the structure of Japanese firms and unions in Malaysia (Jomo 1994). NEA capitalists and bureaucrats became regional consultants throughout Southeast Asia. While Taiwan and South Korea similarly had the example of Japan, SEA countries had a broader set of experiences to emulate.

Another crucial dimension of the regional context involved the relationship between SEA and NEA countries. The regional hegemon, Japan, did not promote militarization, unlike the United States in Latin America. The relationship between SEA and NEA countries was predominantly economic, involving partnerships for mutual profits (Bernard and Ravenhill 1995; Jomo 1997). NEA economies became sources of capital and technology. Japanese investment poured into SEA economies beginning in the import-substitution years, backed by official government aid, which aimed to reduce labor costs for Japanese industry. Japanese investment and aid expanded further in the late 1970s, when SEA countries adopted export-led growth strategies. In the 1980s Japanese firms used the proximity of SEA countries to avoid U.S. tariffs (Pasuk 1990). Since SEA countries still had their GSP (Generalized System of Preferences)[11] status, Japanese firms used Southeast Asia as their base of manufacturing to increase profits. By 1990 Japanese direct investment comprised 39 percent, 24 percent, and 54 percent of overall foreign investment in Indonesia, Malaysia, and Thailand (Jomo 1997, 36).

Not to be left out, Taiwanese and Korean investment became increasingly important in the 1980s (Jomo 1997). Taiwanese investment through the 1970s and 1980s was geared toward increasing access to resources and promoting Taiwan's international image. In the 1990s Taiwanese investment was directed toward maintaining its international competitiveness, primarily in light industry. In 1990 Taiwanese direct investment comprised 27 percent, 14 percent, and 35 percent of overall foreign investment in Indonesia, Malaysia, and Thailand (Jomo 1997, 45). While Japanese and Taiwanese investment focused on industry, including small and medium-sized firms, Korean investment in Southeast Asia initially concentrated on the resource-extracting activities such as mining, fisheries, and forestry (Jomo 1997). It was only in the late 1980s that Korean investors, similarly aiming to maintain their country's international competitiveness, began to focus on industry, particularly labor-intensive products.

The SEA and NEA economies also benefited from Chinese business networks (Hamilton 1991; McVey 1992). These groups, quite diverse in character, became actively engaged in small and medium-sized enterprises and

---

11. By the early 1980s, many of the public sector enterprises were heavily indebted in all of the Southeast Asian countries.

fostered economic partnerships between and among SEA and NEA capitalists. Since each of the SEA countries has a large Chinese business class, these networks increased the vibrancy of domestic capital, especially in Thailand and Indonesia. As the region became more integrated and China became a more prominent player in the economic well-being of the region, these networks took on greater significance, stimulating further development in Southeast Asia.

The fortuitous location of SEA countries worked to their advantage. As Table 8.6 shows, SEA countries were "at the right place at the right time." With models to follow and neighboring investors ready to transfer technology and built-in business networks that tied SEA capitalists with a wider circle of entrepreneurs, SEA economies gained added strength. The advantageous regional context perhaps most distinguishes SEA development from other parts of the world.

Political Factors

The political environment was as important as the regional context. The most obvious similarity between NEA and SEA countries involved political stability. Until 1998, Southeast Asia was extraordinarily stable, paralleling conditions in Northeast Asia. Leaders in Southeast Asia governed for decades. Suharto was in control of Indonesia for thirty-two years, from 1966 to 1998. The coalition led by the United Malay National Organization has controlled Malaysia since independence in 1957. The current Prime Minister Mahathir has been in power since 1981. Thailand has been less stable on the surface. Since 1932 Thailand has had a plethora of leaders. Yet this turnover hides a deeper continuity in the political system. The military, monarchy, and bureaucracy have checked destabilizing forces. The military has done so directly, governing the country for more than half the century. The monarch has indirectly intervened in politics at key junctures to maintain stability. Throughout, the bureaucracy has been fairly well insulated from political pressures, thus assuring policy continuity. SEA stability has allowed technocrats to develop long-term strategies for economic development and made these countries attractive to foreign capital.

Along with the political stability, the SEA structure of power resembled that of Northeast Asia, democracies dominated by a single party and military governments. Indonesia's New Order government controlled by Suharto through 1998 was as authoritarian as the Park government in Korea from 1961 to 1987. UMNO's control of Malaysia closely resembles the LDP

Table 8.6   Comparative Regional Issues, Northeast Asia and Southeast Asia

	Northeast Asia	Southeast Asia
Models of "Success"	Japan model for Korea and Taiwan	More examples to emulate
Source of Capital	U.S. capital more important	Northeast Asian more important
Chinese Business Networks	Important in Taiwan	Important throughout region
Overall Consequence	Greater dependence on domestic capital and own experiences for development	Greater dependence on foreign capital and regional links

dominance in Japan, although the political system has been considerably more closed in Malaysia than in Japan, particularly since 1970. With a variety of military leaders and a liberalization of the polity toward democracy, Thailand and Taiwan are also similar. Despite the parallels among specific NEA and SEA countries, regime type alone does not correspond to a specific pattern of economic development. Despite a prevalence of authoritarian regimes, the political systems varied considerably. Few would equate Japan under the LDP with the New Order period in Indonesia. In contrast to views linking authoritarianism with economic development, there is no such relationship in Souteast Asia. What is perhaps more telling is that the height of economic development did not always occur under authoritarian rule. For example, Thailand's rapid expansion of its economy occurred while the regime was opening up politically in the late 1980s.

Another common political factor among these countries was the conservative ideological outlook of the regimes. In both regions the left was largely excluded from power. Through the protection of property rights, business interests were safeguarded as these countries embraced capitalism and the West in the cold war climate. This is not to say that issues of "social justice" were removed from the political agenda, but that redistribution was secondary to economic growth. Unhindered economic exchange among businessmen was guaranteed. This dimension was especially important for the SEA countries, given their dependence on foreign capital. The reasons for this common outlook differed, however. In Northeast Asia external threats reinforced a more capitalist ideology, whereas in Southeast Asia their commitment to capitalism was more in response to domestic threats by leftist groups.

All of the countries also relied on keeping their labor movements weak. The NEA regimes took steps to minimize the political power of labor and assure profits (Deyo 1989). In Southeast Asia labor was comparatively weaker. Part of this can be explained by the size and composition of the labor force. Since the majorities in these countries were located in rural areas, urban labor made up only a small share of constituents. Since the working class was a minority, SEA political leaders saw no need to mobilize it. Moreover, many of the workers in industry were women, who lacked the same level of political influence as men. In the case of Malaysia before the 1970s, urban labor was predominantly Chinese and thus had a weaker voice in Malaysian politics. Labor's limited influence was further accentuated by its the weakness of the left vis-à-vis state; for example, SEA workers were denied the right to strike. For those unions that were allowed to exist, government leaders co-opted the leadership and prevented workers from forming independent unions. In the 1980s SEA governments, particularly Malaysia, tried to restructure unions altogether by promoting unions organized in accordance with the "Japanese model." In this model laborers were asked to minimize their demands for wages and better working conditions for the good of the company. In contrast to the bargain with labor in Northeast Asia, which usually involved job security, labor in Southeast Asia did not receive the same guarantees. Low labor costs contributed to SEA international competitiveness and made these countries attractive for foreign investors; however, these benefits were attained at the expense of the workers, who were poorly paid and worked in "sweatshop" environments without job security. To ensure the attractiveness of their economies to foreign capital, SEA regimes relied on a passive labor force.

The SEA governments depended on "economic legitimacy" for their political survival. Although NEA regimes also drew legitimacy from economic performance, in Southeast Asia this need took on greater significance. For example, when Suharto (a military general) assumed power de facto in 1966 it was in part due to the incompetence of the previous administration's economic management. Like many of the militaries in Latin America, the prestige of the Indonesia military was intertwined with economic performance. All of the SEA leaders touted economic development as the basis for their continued rule, especially the nondemocratic leaders. As advocates of "Asian values," SEA leaders invoked their economic successes to justify their tenures. Thus it is not surprising that the Asian financial crisis, which has undermined these economies, has precipitated political instability in all three SEA regimes.

Dependence on "economic legitimacy" is closely tied to what Chalmers Johnson (1995) labeled "economic nationalism." In the former economic performance is used to support the regime. In the latter economic performance is tied to a national identity and incorporates a regime's "develop-

mental" outlook. Both regions share a developmental outlook. This story
has been well told in Northeast Asia (Johnson 1995; Amsden 1985, 1990;
Woo-Cummings 1999). In Southeast Asia economic nationalism has been
closely tied to individual leaders. When Mahathir Mohamad came to power
in 1981, for example, he closely identified with social inequalities and had
formulated policies to redress these problems as early as 1970 in his book
The Malay Dilemma. He later went on to formulate the "Vision 20/20"
plan to promote development in Malaysia. While the leaders of Thailand
and Indonesia were not as vocal about economic development, their commitment to national development was ingrained in their ideologies. The militaries in Thailand and Indonesia closely identified with the need to redress
poverty, particularly in the mid-1970s. Economic nationalism played a large
role in SEA development, although not as large as it did in NEA countries.
The Asian financial crisis has shown that there were clear nondevelopmen-
tal dimensions of SEA regimes, evident by the widespread corruption.

What differentiates the two regions is the source of economic nationalism.
This corresponds to the discussion earlier that highlighted the different initial
conditions these countries inherited after World War II. In NEA countries
the international environment accentuated economic nationalism. Security
threats in Korea and Taiwan and the lack of a security arsenal in Japan
forced these countries' leaders to promote economic development. In contrast, SEA economic nationalism was motivated by domestic concerns,
namely a desire for greater national integration and social equity. Economic
development was viewed as the main vehicle for integration and cohesion.
In Indonesia, for example, leaders faced the difficult task of integrating the
different regions of Indonesia and promoting national identity. Without economic development, regionalism in Indonesia would have threatened the
territorial integrity of the country. The same could be said for the regional
differences in Thailand, where the northeast and south are comparatively
less well off and sought greater autonomy, and Malaysia, where East Malaysia sought greater autonomy from the western peninsula. All of the SEA
leaders saw economic development as essential to nation-building.

Economic nationalism was also reinforced by the social cleavages in Southeast Asia, particularly ethnic differences. Through the 1980s the Chinese
comprised the wealthiest minority in Southeast Asia. They were resented by
the local populations in the region. The poorer majorities had greater political clout and pressured leaders to redress economic differences. In Indonesia,
the power of the *pribumis* kept economic distribution on the political agenda.
Similarly, in Malaysia the NEP affirmative-action policy and corresponding
high public spending was motivated by a desire to improve the well-being of

the Malay community. These distributive efforts, which improved social equality, would not have succeeded without economic expansion. Growth was vital for the economy, not only to increase the regime's legitimacy, but also for securing the political support of ethnic majorities. In contrast, Thailand never had as strong an economic nationalist agenda involving ethnic differences. Thai regional and class differences were more important catalysts for economic development. Economic concerns came on the agenda as a result of internal security threats in the late 1960s, namely minimizing communism among the peasantry. Ironically, when SEA regimes proved successful at nation-building and redressing some of the ethnic income disparities, the level of economic nationalism dissipated, especially in Indonesia. Leaders lost sight of their aims to promote equality and focused on perpetuating their power.

The lower level of developmentalism in Southeast Asia can be also attributed to the composition of the SEA state institutions. On one level SEA states shared many of the "developmental" qualities highlighted in Northeast Asia (Hawes and Liu 1993; Mackie 1988; Crone 1988). These qualities include a development-oriented bureaucracy recruited on merit with embedded autonomy, which in turn provided the bureaucrats with the capacity to direct economic development with adequate domestic support of industrialists. Skilled bureaucrats in each of the SEA countries played important roles in economic policymaking. Thailand, for example, was known as the "bureaucratic polity" because of central role the bureaucracy played in the political system (Riggs 1966). Technocrats in Indonesia's Ministry of Finance or in the Economic Planning Unit in Malaysia played significant roles in economic policy in the other SEA countries as well. They were selected based on their knowledge and merit. In matters of tax and industrial policy, they solicited information from business groups in society and became centers of information to stimulate growth and equity.

On the other hand, SEA states were not able to address problems as well as their NEA counterparts (Doner 1991b). First, the bureaucrats in SEA states lacked the same leadership capacity. In Thailand the bureaucrats made decisions based on consensus, often delaying the implementation of critical policies. Muscat (1994) has argued that they reacted (in a timely manner) to conditions, but did not necessarily act as agents to create conditions. In Malaysia and Indonesia, the bureaucracy was largely secondary to the existing political leaderships. The bureaucracy in these countries lacked the power to guide the economy. Bureaucrats in Southeast Asia were often forced to make decisions for the sake of political expediency rather than for sound economic reasons. In other instances, such as in the late 1970s in

Indonesia, bureaucrats were excluded from the decision-making process altogether. SEA bureaucrats had to operate within political constraints and were more a reflection of the leadership than autonomous decision-makers.

Another area that made SEA states less developmental involved the level of meritocracy within these states. In the 1970s, as the public sectors in these economies expanded, the quality of the civil service declined. In part, this was shaped by the immediate need for personnel, who often lacked the training of earlier generations. The increasing ethnic orientation of these states in the 1970s was also responsible. As ethnicity became more central in policymaking, it became a criterion for hiring. Bureaucrats in Malaysia, and to a lesser extent Indonesia, were selected according to their ethnicity, not their qualifications. These states no longer recruited the same quality of personnel that they had done earlier. With growth in these economies in the 1980s, the private sector became even more attractive for the educated elite, further decreasing the quality of personnel.

Finally, SEA states did not have the same level of embedded autonomy as those in Northeast Asia. Domestic capital was not as robust and the spectrum of interaction with domestic business groups and the state was much narrower (Haggard 1997). In Indonesia the main business groups were the Chinese capitalists and other businessmen tied to Suharto or his family (MacIntyre 1992). This group only comprised a small minority. In Malaysia the Chinese were less favored, as a result of the ethnic dynamic in the country. Consequently, the state did not make a concerted effort to reach out toward domestic capital. Those individuals that were regularly consulted were closely tied to the regime (Gomez and Jomo 1997). The Thai state had the broadest relationship with domestic capital (Anek 1992). Yet, even in this case a small minority, specifically the Chinese, controlled the domestic wealth. Throughout Southeast Asia, the relationship with business lacked the depth of the NEA economies. In many cases, domestic capitalists were excluded from the productive sectors of the economy, the industrialization drive. This hampered the capacity of these states to implement broad-based economic policies in small and medium-sized industries.

The narrow business-state alliance also fostered rent-seeking. The relationship between business and the state followed patron-client ties; it was an unequal personal relationship that involved reciprocity. The government provided access to the economy, while the business sector was responsible for expanding the economy and the coffers of individuals in the regime. The fact that the business class was confined to a small group added to the "exclusiveness" of this circle. As the economy expanded, the stakes in the relationship increased as the sums exchanged grew larger. The fact that domestic capital in these countries was made up of a minority ethnic group lacking political power also contributed to rent-seeking. Chinese capitalists were forced to maintain ties to the state through this narrow exclusive alliance relationship because they could not openly lobby for economic policy. With privatization in the mid-1980s, the sale of public companies only added to the general level of corruption. The consequences of the rent-seeking for the economy were both positive and negative. In the short term business was given access to the decision-making process and could articulate policies that promoted and maintained growth. Many of the selected capitalists, particularly in the early years of export-led industrial development in the 1970s, were capable businessmen who provided services and stimulated economic growth. The negative side of corruption, however, was always present. Over time, the negative aspect of rent-seeking took on greater prominence with the consolidation of the power of political cronies. This limited equity promotion and the efficient allocation of resources in the economy.

Table 8.7 summarizes the political factors outlined above. While SEA regimes adopted many similar characteristics, including a developmental regime, the developmentalism was shallower than it was in the NEA countries. This shallowness was shaped by the political environment, especially the ethnic configuration of domestic capital and source of economic nationalism.

Human and Physical Capital

The final major component of the economic development involved the investment in education and infrastructure. Here again, there is an overarching common thread between the two regions, although significant differences in the degree of investment, timing, and policies do exist.

Consider the investment in education: The development in human capital began to expand significantly from the 1970s in the three countries. The percentage of GDP investment in education increased from 1.7 percent to 2.2 percent in Indonesia, 3.4 percent to 4.0 percent in Thailand, and decreased slightly from 6.0 percent to 5.5 percent in Malaysia from 1980 through 1992 (Booth 1999a, 2). The amount of money spent on education in Southeast Asia was far lower than that spent in Northeast Asia. In 1995, for example, 1.5 percent of GDP and 3.3 percent of GDP were spent on education in Indonesia and Thailand respectively, compared to 4.1 percent in Korea (World Bank 1998). This difference is substantial, since SEA countries have lower GDPs than NEA countries (Snodgrass 1997).

The timing of the investment in education also differed. SEA economies began investing in human capital much later than NEA economies did. SEA

Table 8.7   Comparative Political Factors, Northeast Asia and Southeast Asia

	Northeast Asia	Southeast Asia
Similarities		
Stability	Important throughout region	Important throughout region
Regime Type	Varied regime types. No direct tie to economic development	Varied regime types. No direct tie to economic development
Ideology/Legitimacy	Conservative Reliance on economic legitimacy	Conservative Reliance on economic legitimacy
Labor Rights	Limited freedom to mobilize height of economic expansion	Less freedom to mobilize result of size and lower political status
Differences		
Economic Nationalism	Important catalyst for development Fostered by international conditions	Important catalyst for development Fostered by domestic conditions
Developmental State I	Important role for technocrats, state policy selection, and embeddedness	Important role for technocrats, state policy selection, and embeddedness, but less than in NEA
Developmental State II	Greater leadership capacity of bureaucracy	Less leadership capacity of bureaucracy
Developmental State III	Greater meritocracy Less rent-seeking	Less meritocracy Greater rent-seeking

investment in education began in the late 1960s and did not increase substantially until the following decade. The NEA economies expanded education "ahead of demand" in the early 1960s and (Booth 1999a, 8). These differences in timing were the result of the initial conditions in each country, particularly the colonial legacies and the attention to immediate postcolonial domestic conflicts discussed earlier (Booth 1999a; 1999b).

Finally, the structure of education differed between SEA and NEA countries. In SEA countries the focus was on primary education, which had important implications for equity promotion (World Bank 1993). The structure of SEA populations, with younger and rapidly growing populations, contributed to this emphasis on primary education. In Indonesia, for example, between 1970 and the early 1980s the numbers of children in primary schools doubled from 13 million to over 26 million (Dasgupta 1997, 223). By the mid-1980s near-universal primary education was achieved (Dasgupta 1997, 224). Compared to NEA countries, there was less emphasis on education at the higher levels. The expansion of secondary and tertiary education occurred more slowly in Southeast Asia. Even in the 1990s the level of illiteracy was much higher than in Northeast Asia. In Malaysia, for example, over 15 percent of the population was illiterate (World Bank 1997). The end result of these differences between the regions over education point to lower equity promotion in Southeast Asia.

Each of these different dimensions of economic development suggests that there is a unique Southeast Asian pattern of economic development. Overall, there are three major similarities between Northeast and Southeast Asia that differentiate economic development in East Asia from that in many other developing regions: similar emphasis on export-led industrialization supported by fiscal conservatism in conjuction with early expansion of the public sector, investment in human development, and political stability/conservatism. What makes the pattern of economic development in Southeast Asia stand out is the lateness of the growth as a result of the initial conditions in these countries; the ethnic heterogeneity of these societies, which in turn acts as a catalyst for economic nationalism and equity promotion; the regional context, which supported economic development; the lower level of developmentalism of SEA states corresponding to a more prominent role for the political leadership; and the ethnic configuration of these societies.

LESSONS FROM SOUTHEAST ASIA—GROWTH AND EQUALITY

Within the SEA pattern of economic development there are a number of specific measures that promoted the coveted combination of high growth and equity. In most cases, however, these policies tended to promote one dimension of this equation more than the other, so one should look at the policies in combination rather than individually.

Looking at SEA development historically, the first factor that stands out is an early emphasis on agriculture in rural communities. Considering the contemporary emphasis of industrialization in development, this policy seems outdated. Yet perhaps more than any other factor, the early attention to improving agricultural production significantly reduced poverty in Southeast Asia. In Thailand, for example, the number of people living in poverty dropped from 16 million to 3.4 million between 1965 and 1975 (World Bank 1993). What is striking about poverty reduction in these countries is that SEA governments continued to concentrate on the agricultural sector through the 1970s, deepening the poverty reduction effort. The development of land irrigation schemes and fertilizer production, among other agricultural inputs, increased the efficiency of the peasant economy. The immediate consequence of greater food production was an improved standard of living and greater social equality. The fact that land ownership was not as skewed as that of Latin America increased the effectiveness of these efforts. The immediate effects of this policy on growth were minimal, although not insignificant. The attention to the rural areas fostered greater political stability. This, in turn, gave SEA governments more flexibility in selecting and implementing more diversified development policies.

This attention to agriculture contributed directly to the second factor. It allowed for a large public sector at the early stages of growth. Not only did SEA governments invest in agriculture, they established public enterprises to promote industrialization. These measures diversified the industrial base of these countries (Jomo 1997). The success of these ventures was short-lived, but reflected a similar pattern between Northeast and Southeast Asia which built the foundation for economic development.[12]

The third factor that promoted the combination of growth and greater equality was the development orientation of SEA regimes. While SEA states did not have the same level of developmentalism as the NEA states did, SEA countries were led by individuals who focused on development with a purposefulness not usually found in other developing regions. Technocrats played important policymaking roles in all of SEA countries. Whether it was the "Berkeley Mafia" that repaired Indonesia's economy between 1966 and 1970, or the capable bureaucrats in Thailand through the 1970s, or the technocrats who promoted the change toward export-led growth in the 1970s in Malaysia, planning and expertise were vital foundations for economic development in Southeast Asia (Bresnan 1993). These technocrats kept economic development on track and provided institutional momentum to generate growth and greater equality. They also fostered strategic alliances with business groups. For example, in Malaysia from 1977 onward the views of business groups were incorporated into economic planning in the annual budget dialogues, contributing to changes in tax policy (Welsh 1998). Similarly, a Joint Public-Private Consultative Committee was created in Thailand in the early 1980s. While the level of "embedded autonomy" was not equal to that of the NEA experience, the developmentalism of these states was central in SEA development.

To fully comprehend the role of technocrats and political leaders of SEA regimes one has to look closely at the specific policies they advocated. The fourth factor that promoted growth and greater equality was the pro-foreign investment strategy initiated in the 1960s. The 1993 World Bank study is right here; foreign capital was the lifeline of these smaller economies. Leaders

12. "GSP" = "Generalized System of Preferences."

and technocrats in these countries recognized that small economies have three ways to acquire capital to stimulate growth: foreign investment in the private sector, foreign loans for the public sector or domestic capital for both sectors. Southeast Asia relied on the former, although in the 1970s, at the height of the expansion of the public sector, these countries did increase their indebtedness. This indebtedness, however, was balanced by a strong push for foreign capital. The third option was not viable for these SEA countries. Initially, domestic capital was not robust enough to rapidly develop industry. In SEA countries domestic capital was also politically tainted. In Malaysia, and to a lesser extent in Indonesia, broad-based alliances with (Chinese) domestic capital involved political costs the regimes were not willing to assume. Instead they allied with foreign capital. These countries supported this pro-foreign investment strategy by protecting property rights, maintaining a stable exchange rate and low inflation, and offering attractive tax incentives, all measures advocated by technocrats.

The productive allocation of foreign capital was directly tied to the growth of these economies, particularly in the export-led growth industries. The pro-foreign investment and export-led growth strategies also contributed to poverty reduction. The expansion of industry created employment and encouraged migration from rural areas to industrial sites. Dasgupta (1997) argues that it was job creation that did the most to decrease poverty in Indonesia. Between 1985 and 1990, 42 percent of new jobs in Indonesia were in industry. At the height of Indonesia's growth, between 1990 and 1993, this figure reached 62 percent. This change occurred when the labor force was growing on average by 3 percent annually. A similar increase in employment through industrial expansion occurred in Malaysia and Thailand.[13] Despite the weakness of labor politically in SEA countries, these jobs were better paying than the agricultural work these laborers had left behind. In Indonesia, between 1970 and 1991 wages in manufacturing increased by 5.5 percent (Dasgupta 1997, 221). The migration away from the rural areas also reduced rural poverty by creating links between the rural areas and cities and facilitating a greater movement of goods and services.

There is a mistaken impression that these countries lacked clearly defined industrial policies (World Bank 1993). Jomo (1997) convincingly challenges this view, arguing that SEA countries had a defined industrial strategy from the 1970s. He argues that SEA countries moved decisively toward light indus-

---

13. Between 1980 and 1990 the percentage of the workforce employed in industry increased from 19 to 23 percent in Malaysia and 10 to 14 percent in Thailand (World Bank 1997, 221).

try (Indonesia and Malaysia) and were selective in their investment in heavy industry (Thailand and Malaysia). He draws on the stated goals and policy frameworks of the technocrats in these economies. Technocrats were responsive to the success and failures of these efforts and acted accordingly to attract investment and technology in these sectors. In the case of Malaysia's failure with the textile industry, for example, leaders and technocrats responded by deepening electronic production. Moreover, the connection between the SEA economies and NEA capital was carefully nurtured and maintained.

While the scope of public spending was narrower in SEA than in NEA countries, Southeast Asia buttressed the expansion of the economy with the development of human and physical capital. This reduced inequality by leading to higher standards of living.[14] The investment in transportation, electricity production, and telecommunications, directed by SEA regimes, increased the attractiveness of these countries. What distinguished the SEA countries from other developing countries was an early emphasis on infrastructure development, inspired by the success of the NEA economies. As early as the 1960s, Indonesia focused on expanding transportation, increasing the number of cars, roads, and the available wattage of electricity (Hill 1996). Malaysia was perhaps the most successful in this, launching a national program to construct highways. Thailand made similar investments. For example, the U.S. military helped build roads in the northeast in the 1960s. Beyond making these locations more attractive to foreign capital, these changes increased labor mobility within these countries and opened different parts of the country to investment and growth.

To maintain the momentum in economic development, SEA states focused on expanding and allocating their technology (Dahlman and Brimble 1990). In the 1960s the focus was on agriculture. SEA governments invested in rice production, especially in Indonesia and Thailand. Both countries experienced "green revolutions" as yields of rice increased through investment in fertilizer production and seeds. These countries became self-sufficient in rice.[15] Malaysia had similar transfers for rubber production that benefited smaller producers. In the 1970s the focus moved to attracting technology for industry. The government encouraged partnerships with NEA and Western companies in light and heavy industry. In Malaysia the government supported an alliance with Mitsubishi to develop the national car, the Proton

14. Booth (1999a) challenges this view by suggesting that equity promotion is overstated. She is correct, but it is a mistake not to acknowledge that gains were made.

15. This occurred in the 1970s in Thailand and in the 1980s in Indonesia. Indonesia is no longer self-sufficient in rice as a result of a drought in 1997–98 and the turmoil brought about by the Asian financial crisis.

Saga. In Thailand we see similar alliances with Japanese firms (Doner 1991a). The move to acquire technology supported the selective industrial strategy noted above and had a positive impact on economic development.

These governments provided a safety net for their citizens through the mid-1990s through pricing policies and food and petroleum subsidies. SEA governments protected the cost of imported staples of the SEA diet, such as, for example, garlic and onions. It also offered subsidies on oil, fertilizer, and nonstaple food items. Although these were reduced in the 1980s, subsidies continued to comprise a large share of public expenditure through the 1990s. Hill (1996, 54) demonstrates that the subsidy on fertilizer comprised 15 percent of Indonesia's development budget. These subsidies helped to reduce costs and were particularly important for the poorer majorities in these countries located in the rural areas (Ali 1987; Ahuja et al. 1997).

The final factor that stands out in the SEA experience is an emphasis on regional integration. As noted above, the regional context was an integral part of SEA economic development. SEA governments adopted specific initiatives to expand regional integration and foster alliances with foreign capital in Northeast Asia. First, SEA countries promoted growth triangles with their neighbors (e.g., in northern Malaysia and southern Thailand, in southern Malaysia near Singapore and Indonesia). They also created export processing zones with incentives for foreign capital. These initiatives contributed to growth directly, since they led to industrial expansion and indirectly to greater equity. A third, less obvious policy involved the transfer to labor, particularly from Indonesia to Malaysia. Laborers from Indonesia for the service sector and construction industry were allowed to immigrate. This maintained the low cost of labor and contributed to growth in Malaysia and fostered greater social equity in Indonesia because the "guest workers" sent part of their pay home.

LESSONS FROM SOUTHEAST ASIA—VULNERABILITY

The impressive story of SEA development must be put in perspective. The Asian financial crisis has demonstrated the vulnerability of these countries. During the first two years of the crisis, SEA economies contracted sharply, averaging a 9.5 percent decline.[16] Indonesia had the largest reversal in economic fortunes, contracting 13.7 percent in one year. Although these

16. Indonesia's economy contracted by 13.7 percent in 1998, Thailand's by 8 percent, and Malaysia's by 6.8 percent (World Bank Development Report, 1999).

Table 8.8   Summary: Factors Promoting Growth and Equity

	Growth	Equity
Emphasis on agriculture	Minimal effect	Reduced poverty in neediest areas
Early expansion public sector	Supported growth in agriculture and industrial expansion	Contributed to greater distribution
Developmental state	Outlined priorities, gathered information and solidified alliances with business	Maintained recognition of the need to expand the economy to address equity
Pro-foreign investment	Stimulated vital lifeline of foreign capital for investment	Contributed to industrial expansion, which increased employment
Pro-export-led industrialization	Strategy allowed for expansion of light industries	Contributed to industrial expansion, which increased employment
Selective industrial strategies	Facilitated the expansion of light and some heavy industry	Reduced poverty through job creation
Investment in human capital	Increased the skill level of labor	Directly led to the reduction of poverty
Technology transfers	Facilitated the expansion of agriculture and industry	Reduced poverty in rural areas and created greater employment
Pricing thresholds subsidies	Limited effect	Reduced poverty
Regional integration	Growth triangles, export processing zones, and labor transfers all increased growth	Indirect consequence for equity as a result of industrial expansion

economies rebounded in 1999 and 2000, growth and equality promotion have not yet returned to pre-crisis levels. There continues to be a sharp increase in poverty throughout the region. Estimates suggest that poverty had doubled since 1997 (World Bank 2000). In the country worst hit by the crisis, Indonesia, the most optimistic estimate for poverty published by the government claims that the percentage of people in poverty increased from 11.3 percent in 1996 to 39.9 percent in 1998. In other words, the number of people living in poverty increased from 22.5 million to 79.4 million. The most pessimistic estimate, published by the International Labor Organization, puts the figure at 129.6 million people living in poverty in Indonesia by the end of 1999 (Booth 1999c). The Asian financial crisis has seriously undermined SEA economic achievements.

The debate over the causes and solutions to the crisis has become a major focal point of scholars (see McLeod and Garnaut 1998; Jomo 1998; Arndt and Hill 1999; Yoshihara 1999). Most have focused on economic factors. Free-market advocates highlight transparency and financial reform. Others have isolated the problems of exchange rates, adequate reserves, and private sector debt. Some scholars have focused their analyses on international factors, notably the role of currency speculators, the inadequacy of the IMF response in the region, and problems associated with regional contagion. Yet others have concentrated on political factors, namely rent-seeking and the structure of the SEA regimes. I argue that the root of the troubles of these countries can be found in the SEA pattern of development. Ironically, many of the same features that were part of the SEA success have undermined their current economic performance.

The first, and perhaps most controversial, dimension of vulnerability of SEA countries involves the degree of dependence of these economies on foreign capital. Since private investment was vital for industrial expansion, SEA countries needed to open their markets. The measures to attract investment capital had a positive impact on development. Yet the move to attract portfolio capital was not as successful. As part of an effort to be internationally competitive and maintain the inflow of private investment, SEA countries developed their financial sectors beginning in the late 1980s (Masuyama 1999). In Thailand, for example, foreign exchange controls were lifted and the regulations of portfolio management were removed (Yos and Prakorn 1999). These measures stimulated investment in local financial markets. Yet they also deepened the dependence on foreign funds, since the majority of investment originated from abroad. Addicted to foreign funds, SEA governments were blind to the need to distinguish different forms of capital. While SEA leaders were correct in recognizing that foreign capitalists operate with a "herd mentality" and often interpret barriers in one sector as an indication of obstacles in other sectors of the economy, they set themselves up for the rapid capital flight. SEA countries need to protect themselves from the fickleness and shallowness of portfolio investors. The success of capital controls in Chile, China, and Malaysia suggests that regulation of capital flows, particularly portfolio capital, may help prevent a recurrence of the events associated with the financial crisis.

The dependence on foreign capital had a more serious consequence beyond capital flight and the resulting rapid decline in exchange rates. As alluded to earlier, foreign capitalists dominated the productive sectors of the SEA economies. In part because of the ethnic composition of SEA societies, domestic capitalists were largely excluded from industrialization; they were encouraged to invest in other, nonproductive sectors of the economy, namely the property and stock markets. Not only were these riskier investments, they were shorter term and encouraged the expansion of private sector debt in the SEA financial sector. This debt was paid in U.S. dollars to foreign banks. In Malaysia, for example, foreign liabilities more than doubled from 1995 to 1997 (Jomo 1998, 182). The dependence on foreign capitalists created the conditions that encouraged domestic investors to take unnecessary risks that eventually led to a high number of bankruptcies and undermined the financial sectors in SEA countries. Ultimately, the high dependence on foreign capital contributed to SEA vulnerability.

The SEA pattern of development points to a second serious problem, rent-seeking. Rent-seeking in Southeast Asia was tied to the narrow base of support for these regimes and the decreasing developmental orientation of these regimes. By the 1990s, SEA political leaders became embroiled in rent-seeking practices. Of long standing, rent-seeking clearly was not a catalyst for the crisis. Yet as the crisis unfolded, the scope of corruption became more important, the inefficiencies and inequalities of this practice were reevaluated. Rent-seeking was seen ex post facto as a contributing factor to the financial crisis of the 1990s, limiting growth, and increasing inequality in these economies. The opposition to corruption in turn led to political instability, notably in Indonesia and Malaysia. The prevalence of corruption in the region deepened the crisis.

The regional context also played a part in SEA vulnerability. These economies were closely integrated with the regional hegemon, Japan. This relationship was partly responsible for the onset of the crisis and aggravated the crisis once it began. In 1997 the Japanese yen began to appreciate, after a period of decline, and effectively devalued the currencies of the region (Kregel 1998). This placed pressure on the SEA currencies, which later became the target of currency speculators. As the crisis took effect, and bankruptcies increased as a result of the high private sector debt, the fact that most of the debt was due to Japanese banks, which were also failing, only served to make matters even worse (Jomo 1998). Perhaps more significant was the fact that Japan could no longer offer the model or economic support it had at earlier stages of development. Japan's own economic decline, the fragmentation of its leadership, and the weakening of its bureaucracy all undermined Japan's role in Southeast Asia (Pempel 1998). Some scholars even suggest that Japan is no longer as economically competitive in Southeast Asia, which would undermine the relationship between Southeast Asia and Japan even further and potentially lead to the decline of all the economies concerned (Akyüz 1998). It is perhaps too early to tell. What is clear, however, is that the SEA relationship with Japan has not yielded the same positive results it had earlier.

The final point of vulnerability in the SEA model is more complicated and perhaps more tenuous. In my view, the attitudes toward poverty reduction in Southeast Asia have changed, and as a result of that change the efforts to reduce poverty are declining. Buoyed by the creation of middle classes, SEA leaders were not placing the same priority on poverty reduction. In the 1990s SEA governments significantly reduced their public sectors and placed greater emphasis on market forces. As the private sector became more important, concerns with social equality waned. Inequalities brought about by the market were allowed to persist. Consider the effects of education policy in the 1990s (Booth 1999a). Throughout Southeast Asia secondary and tertiary education is limited to a small sector of the population. Many of the secondary schools are private and charge high fees. As populations grew, SEA governments turned over a greater share of higher education to private enterprise, which catered to the wealthier segment of the population. At the same time, SEA governments also increased public school fees. These measures aggravated inequality among young people, who now comprise the majority of the population in the region. The cutbacks in public spending undermined the poverty reduction effort.

In Malaysia, reforms in the NEP affirmative-action policy have had a similar effect. The market has taken the place of the public sector as the means to address social inequalities. After 1990 firms were no longer required to implement the quota system to hire *bumiputeras* (largely Malays), one of the major impoverished sectors of the population (Geoffrey and Stafford 1997). The underlying premise of this change was that the NEP was successful (a group of Malays had arrived), and that poverty reduction was not as urgent a priority. The government simultaneously began scaling back the scope of NEP state distribution, including spending on rural areas, and began to discuss the privatization of its social services, namely health care. Yet many Malays and other social groups, especially Indians and other indigenous minorities, remain impoverished. The Malaysian government felt that it needed to remove the quotas and embrace market forces to become more competitive internationally. The ability to use ethnic differences to address poverty became less viable in Malaysia in the 1990s. The end result was the poverty reduction effort was undermined.

Both examples show that there is a trade-off between social equality and growth when the private sector has more influence over the direction of the economy. The fact that the greatest gains in equity promotion occurred when the public sector had a prominent role in these economies supports this finding. Although not all the poverty figures, to date, capture the negative effect of the reduction of public spending, there are exceptions. A recent study on Thailand suggests increasing social inequality. This study claims that the Gini coefficient rose from 35.74 in 1975 to 45.39 in 1992 (Ahuja et al. 1997, 38). The greatest increase in poverty corresponded to the decline in public spending. Of the SEA countries, the government that introduced the largest cutback in public spending was Malaysia. It is not a surprise that the Gini coefficient in Malaysia is the worst of the case studies and has not declined significantly in the past decade.

The four sources of vulnerability in the SEA pattern of development—too great a dependence on foreign capital leading to the threat of capital flight and a weak domestic private sector, corruption as a result of the dissipated developmental orientation of the regimes, too great a dependence on a weak regional hegemon, and poverty reduction as a result of too close of an embrace with market forces and reliance on ethnic heterogeneity for state distribution—taken together suggest that elements of SEA pattern of development were flawed. It would be a mistake to suggest that these flaws were an integral part of the pattern of development. Rather, they developed out of the choices takes by SEA leaders as these economies evolved. SEA governments need to carefully reexamine why SEA economies became vulnerable and do what is necessary to return to their earlier success.

REFLECTIONS

The first step in this effort is to acknowledge that the SEA countries did make some remarkable achievements. By facing the difficult conditions they inherited after World War II, SEA regimes responded to the greater ethnic and social cleavages and internal security problems by promoting that enviable combination of growth and greater social equality. They did this by relying on regional models and integration, following sound macroeconomic policies, and creating developmental states that were adaptive to economic conditions. They followed their own pattern, which relied more on foreign capital and mutually beneficial partnerships with neighbors and turned problems of social cleavages into a rationale for equity promotion.

This pattern of development was the product of specific factors, which were fostered by SEA leaders. The second step in improving the fate of SEA and other developing countries is to identify these factors. We learn from these countries that there is a set of measures that contributed to that coveted combination of growth and equity. This included an early emphasis on agriculture, early expansion of the public sector, a developmental state, a pro-foreign investment and export-led industrialization development strategy supported by an investment in human capital, promotion of technology transfers, pricing thresholds, and subsidies and regional integration.

Somewhere along the line, SEA countries have lost track of these policies and the aim of economic development. An excessive dependence on foreign capital, less developmentalism, rent-seeking, greater inequality as a result of decreased emphasis on poverty reduction, and too great a dependence on a weakening regional hegemon have all limited the capacity of these economies to sustain growth and equity. SEA regimes need to return to the developmental orientation of earlier years, increase public spending, especially on human development and rural communities, and be more willing to recognize the shortcomings of existing partnerships and dependencies. The responsibility of future development in Southeast Asia will lie with the leaders in the region, who are likely to be more responsive to the electorate, notably in Indonesia and Thailand. Globalization of international finance, however, has made the task of development more difficult.

Writing in 1995 Peter Evans discussed how the developmental states of Northeast Asia may be self-destructive. A similar pattern may have indeed formed in Southeast Asia, as elements in the pattern of development have undermined both equity and growth. This does not mean that the lessons of Southeast Asia should be ignored—quite to the contrary. We need to address the weaknesses and build on the strengths of the Southeast Asian experience. Only then will the pattern become a model.

REFERENCES

Ahuja, V., et. al. 1997. *Everyone's Miracle: Revisiting Poverty and Inequality in East Asia.* Washington, D.C.: World Bank.

Akyüz, Y. 1998. "The East Asian Financial Crisis: Back to the Future." In K. S. Jomo, ed., *Tigers in Trouble: Financial Governance, Liberalisation and Crises in East Asia.* New York: Zed Books.

Ali, I. 1987. "Rice in Indonesia: Price Policy and Comparative Advantage." *Bulletin of Indonesian Economic Studies* 23, no. 3:80–99.

Amsden, A. 1985. "The State and Taiwan's Economic Development." In P. Evans, D. Rueschemeyer, and T. Skocpol, eds., *Bringing the State Back In.* Cambridge: Cambridge University Press

———. 1989. *Asia's Next Giant: South Korea and Late Industrialization.* New York: Oxford University Press.

Anek, L. 1992. *Business Associations and the New Political Economy of Thailand.* Boulder, Colo.: Westview.

Ariff, M., and H. Hill. 1985. *Export Oriented Industrialization: The ASEAN Experience.* Sydney: Allen and Unwin.

Arndt, H. W., and H. Hill, eds. 1999. *Southeast Asia's Economic Crisis: Origins, Lessons and the Way Forward*. Singapore: Institute of Southeast Asian Studies

Bernard, M., and J. Ravenhill. 1995. "Beyond Product Cycles and Flying Geese: Regionalisation, Hierarchy, and the Industrialisation of East Asia." *World Politics* 47, no. 2 (January): 171–209.

Booth, A. 1992. *The Oil Boom and After: Indonesian Economic Policy and Performance in the Soeharto Era*. Singapore: Oxford University Press.

———. 1997. *The Indonesia Economy in the Nineteenth and Twentieth Centuries: A History of Missed Opportunities*. London: Macmillan.

———. 1999a. "Education and Economic Development in Southeast Asia: Myths and Realities." Paper presented at the Second International Malaysian Studies Conference, University of Malaya, Kuala Lumpur, August 2–4.

———. 1999b. "Initial Conditions and Miraculous Growth: Why Is Southeast Asia Different from Taiwan and South Korea?" *World Development* 27, no. 2 (February): 301–22.

———. 1999c. "The Impact of the Crisis on Poverty and Equity." In H. W. Arndt and H. Hill, eds., *Southeast Asia's Economic Crisis: Origins, Lessons and the Way Forward*. Singapore: Institute of Southeast Asian Studies.

Bresnan, J. 1993. *Managing Indonesia: The Modern Political Economy*. New York: Columbia University Press.

Chang, Ha-Joon. 1994. *The Political Economy of Industrial Policy*. London: Macmillan.

Crone, D. 1988. "State, Social Elites, and Government Capacity in Southeast Asia." *World Politics* 40, no. 2.

Cumings, B. 1984. "The Origins and Development of the Northeast Asian Political Economy: Industrial Sectors, Product Cycles, and Political Consequences." *International Organization* 38, no. 1:1–40.

Dahlman, C. J., and P. Brimble. 1990. *Technology Strategy and Policy for Industrial Competitiveness: A Case Study of Thailand*. Washington, D.C.: World Bank.

Dasgupta, D. 1997. "Poverty Reduction in Indonesia." In Henry S. Rowen, ed., *Behind East Asian Growth*. London: Routledge.

Deyo, F. C. 1989. *Beneath the Miracle: Labor Subordination in the New Asian Industrialism*. Berkeley and Los Angeles: University of California Press.

Doner, R. F. 1991a. "Approaches to the Politics of Economic Growth in Southeast Asia." *World Politics* 44, no. 3.

———. 1991b. *Driving a Bargain: Automotive Industrialization and Japanese Firms in Southeast Asia*. Berkeley and Los Angeles: University of California Press.

Evans, P. 1995. *Embedded Autonomy: States and Industrial Transformation*. Princeton: Princeton University Press.

Feith, H. 1962. *The Decline of Constitutional Democracy in Indonesia*. Ithaca: Cornell University Press.

Findley, C., and R. Garnaut, eds. 1986. *The Political Economy of Manufacturing Protection: Experiences of ASEAN and Australia*. Sydney: Allen and Unwin.

Geoffrey, D., and S. D. Stafford. 1997. "Malaysia's New Economic Policy and the Global Economy: The Evolution of Ethnic Accommodation." *Pacific Review* 10, no. 4:556–80.

Gershenkron, A. 1962. *Economic Backwardness in Historical Perspective*. Cambridge: Harvard University Press.

Gold, T. 1986. *State and Society in the Taiwan Miracle.* Armonk, N.Y.: M. E. Sharpe.

Gomez, E. T., and K. S. Jomo. 1997. *Malaysia's Political Economy: Politics, Patronage, and Profits.* New York: Cambridge University Press.

Haggard, S. 1997. "Business, Politics and Policy in East and Southeast Asia." In H. Rowen, ed., *Behind East Asian Growth.* New York: Routledge.

Haggard, S., and T. Cheng. 1987. "State and Foreign Capital in the East Asian NICs." In F. Deyo, ed., *The Political Economy of the New Asian Industrialism.* Ithaca: Cornell University Press.

Hamilton, G., ed. 1991. *Business Networks and Economic Development in East and Southeast Asia.* Hong Kong: Center for Asian Studies, University of Hong Kong.

Hawes, G., and H. Liu. 1993. "Explaining the Dynamics of the Southeast Asian Political Economy: State, Society and the Search for Economic Growth." *World Politics* 45, no. 4:629–60.

Hewison, K. 1989. *Power and Politics in Thailand.* Manila: Journal of Contemporary Asia Publishers.

Hill, H. 1996. *Southeast Asia's Emerging Giant: Indonesia Economic Policy and Development Since 1966.* New York: Cambridge University Press.

———. 1997. *Indonesia's Industrial Transformation.* Singapore: ISEAS, University of Singapore.

Ikemoto, Y. 1991. *Income Distribution in Thailand.* Tokyo: Institute of Developing Economies.

Ito, T. 1993. *The Japanese Economy.* Cambridge: MIT Press.

Jesudason, J. 1989. *Ethnicity and the Economy: The State, Chinese Business, and Multinationals in Malaysia.* Singapore: Oxford University Press

Johnson, C. 1995. *Japan: Who Governs? The Rise of the Developmental State.* New York: W. W. Norton.

Jomo, K. S., ed. 1994. *Japan and Malaysian Development: In the Shadow of the Rising Sun.* New York: Routledge.

———. 1997. *Southeast Asia's Misunderstood Miracle: Industrial Policy and Economic Development in Thailand, Malaysia and Indonesia.* Boulder, Colo.: Westview.

———, ed. 1998. *Tigers in Trouble: Financial Governance, Liberalisation and Crises in East Asia.* New York: Zed Books.

Jomo, K. S., and C. Edwards. 1993. "Malaysian Industrialisation in Historical Perspective." In K. S. Jomo, ed., *Industrialising Malaysia: Policy, Performance, Prospects.* New York: Routledge.

Kregel, J. 1998. "East Asia Is Not Mexico: The Difference Between Balance of Payments Crises and Debt Deflation." In K. S. Jomo, ed., *Tigers in Trouble: Financial Governance, Liberalisation and Crises in East Asia.* New York: Zed Books.

Lim, David. 1973. *Economic Growth and Development in West Malaysia, 1947–1970.* Kuala Lumpur: Oxford University Press.

MacIntyre, A. 1992. *Business and Politics in Indonesia.* Sydney: Allen and Unwin.

———, ed. 1994. *Business and Government in Industrialising Asia.* Sydney: Allen and Unwin.

Mackie, J.A.C. 1988. "Economic Growth in the ASEAN Countries: The Political Underpinnings." In H. Hughes, ed. *Achieving Industrialization in East Asia.* Cambridge: Cambridge University Press.

Masuyama, S. 1999. "Introduction: The Evolution of Financial Systems in East Asia and Their Responses to Financial and Economic Crisis." In S. Masuyama, D. Vandenbrink, and Chia S. Y., eds., *East Asia's Financial Systems: Evolution and Crisis.* Singapore: Institute of Southeast Asian Studies.

Matthews, T., and J. Ravenhill. 1994. "Strategic Trade Policy: The Northeast Asian Experience." In A. MacIntyre, ed., *Business and Government in Industrialising Asia.* Sydney: Allen and Unwin.

McLeod, R., and R. Garnaut. 1998. *East Asia in Crisis: From Being a Miracle to Needing One.* New York: Routledge.

McVey, R. 1992. *Southeast Asian Capitalists.* Ithaca: Southeast Asia Program, Cornell University Press

Mohamad, M. 1970. *Malay Dilemma.* Kuala Lumpur: Pelanduk Publications.

Muscat, R. J. 1994. *The Fifth Tiger: A Study of Thai Development Policy.* New York: M. E. Sharpe.

Pasuk 1990. *See* Phongpaichit 1990.

Pempel, T. J. 1998. "Structural *Gaiatsu:* International Finance and Political Change in Japan." Paper presented at the Annual Meeting of the American Political Science Association, Boston, September 2–6.

Phongpaichit, Pasuk. 1990. *The New Wave of Japanese Investment in ASEAN: Determinants and Prospects.* Singapore: Institute of Southeast Asian Studies.

Ramstetter, E. 1991. *Direct Foreign Investment in Asia's Developing Economies and Structural Change in the Asia-Pacific Region.* Boulder, Colo.: Westview.

Riggs, F. 1966. *Thailand: The Modernization of the Bureaucratic Polity.* Honolulu, Hawaii: East-West Center Press.

Snodgrass, D. 1997. "Education in Korea and Malaysia." In H. Rowen, ed., *Behind East Asian Growth.* New York: Routledge.

Stubbs, Richard. 1999. "War and Economic Development: Export-Oriented Industrialization in East and Southeast Asia." *Comparative Politics* 31, no. 3:337–55.

Székely, M. 1998. *Facing up to Inequality in Latin America: Economic and Social Progress in Latin America 1998–1999.* Washington D.C.: IDB.

Wade, R. 1988. *Governing the Market: Economic Theory and the Role of Government in East Asian Industrialization.* Princeton: Princeton University Press.

Warr, P. 1993. *The Thai Economy in Transition.* New York: Cambridge University Press.

Welsh, B. 1998. "The Political Economy of the Malaysian Tax Regime of the 1980s." Paper presented at the Southeast Asia in the Twentieth Century sponsored by the University of the Philippines, Quezon City, Philippines, January 28.

Woo-Cummings, M. J. 1998. "National Security and the Rise of the Developmental State in South Korea and Taiwan." In H. Rowen, ed., *Behind East Asian Growth.* New York: Routledge.

———. 1999. *The Developmental State.* Ithaca: Cornell University Press.

World Bank. 1993. *The East Asian Miracle: Economic Growth and Public Policy.* New York: Oxford University Press.

———. 1995. *World Investment Report*. Washington, D.C.: World Bank Publications.

———. 1997. *World Development Report*. Washington, D.C.: World Bank Publications.

———. 1998. *Social Crisis in East Asia*. Washington, D.C.: World Bank Publications.

———. 2000. *East Asia: Recovery and Beyond*. Washington, D.C.: World Bank Publications.

Yos, V., and V. Prakorn. 1999. "Thailand's Financial Evolution and the 1997 Crisis." In S. Masuyama, D. Vandenbrink, and Chia S. Y., eds., *East Asia's Financial Systems: Evolution and Crisis*. Singapore: Institute of Southeast Asian Studies.

Yoshihara, Kunio. 1999. *Building a Prosperous Southeast Asia: From Ersatz to Echt Capitalism*. Richmond, Va.: Curzon Press.

9

Labor Exclusion and Privatized Welfare: Two Keys to Asian Capitalist Development

T. J. PEMPEL

Perhaps the most perplexing strategic question confronting political and economic leaders in most countries of the world is "How do we catch up?" Closing down economic gaps requires clear strategic thinking about how best to organize the national polity and the national economy.[1]

Any late industrializer intent on rapid economic improvement faces at least two critical problems. First, there is the domestic problem: how to mobilize the disparate, and often competing, political and economic resources of the nation-state into one relatively cohesive, developmentally positive, direction. It requires turning "national economic growth" into what Gramsci would call a hegemonic project, namely, a broad and coherent thrust or bias within an entire nation's policy behavior (see Mouffe 1987, 223).

Typically this requires that political leaders develop an effective strategy for dealing with, on the one hand, such potentially "antigrowth" domestic sectors as landlords and generals resistant to any form of economic transformation that may undercut their bases of power, while at the same time fending off expanding populist sectors demanding slices of the developmental pie in ways that reduce national extractive and investment capabilities.

No matter how successful this domestic effort, international barriers to economic transformation must also be surmounted. How does a country close the wide gaps in technological sophistication, economic productivity, market access, and lifestyles, rather than simply staying some relatively fixed distance behind, or worse still, falling further behind? How can a country advance its own economic transformation in a competitive world, many of whose powerful actors—both nations and corporations—have interests competitive with, rather than complementary to, those very economic strategies?

Since the early twentieth century, few countries have played this complex catch-up game with much success. By the first two decades of this century, most of the currently industrialized democracies were rather well launched on their respective paths toward economic success. Except for wars it was

1. This is of course the classic argument put forward by Alexander Gerschenkron. See Gerschenkron 1962.

not until the oil shocks of the 1970s that the previously uninterrupted economic growth of the industrialized democracies hit a major snag.

Yet aside from a short-term increase in the wealth of the oil-producing countries, the downturn that followed did little to close the gap between the few relatively rich and the many quite poor nations of the world. Today, the richest 20 percent of the world accounts for nearly 83 percent of global production; the poorest accounts for only 1.4 percent. And the gap between rich and poor is widening. In 1960 the ratio between the richest 20 percent of the world's population and that of the poorest 20 percent was 30:1. In 1970 it had risen to 32:1; by 1980 it was 45:1, ten years later, it was nearly 60:1 (Frieden and Lake 1995, 417).

The most important exception to both the widening gaps between rich and poor countries and also to the prevailing economic downturns of the post-oil shock years took place in Asia. Japan, of course, made tremendous economic progress during the late nineteenth and early twentieth centuries, only to see its positive trajectory blunted by authoritarianism, imperial expansion, Western protectionism, and ultimately, military and economic collapse. But in the first four decades following World War II, Japan led the world in productivity improvements and economic growth by margins of two-to-one. And by the mid- to late 1980s, the so-called Four Tigers (Taiwan, South Korea, Hong Kong, and Singapore) were achieving growth rates even more spectacular than Japan's. Subsequently, Malaysia and Thailand, and then Indonesia and South China all underwent similarly explosive economic transformation.[2] These countries within Asia stood in striking contrast to the languid non-growth in the rest of the nonindustrialized world. Asia was the one geographical area that demonstrated consistent successes in the game of economic catch-up.

The economic stagnation and financial crisis within Japan throughout the 1990s, coupled with the broader Asian slowdown that began in summer 1997 and which engulfed primarily Thailand, South Korea, Indonesia, Malaysia, and the Philippines, have combined to rub the bloom off the rose of Asian economic success. The "Asian miracle" that challenged both economic theory and corporate profits in much of the West was transmogrified into an "Asian contagion" that mired much of the region in economic stagnation. Subsequent problems, however, should not detract from the undeniable absolute and relative improvements that all of these countries made economically over a short period of time. As such, they still remain far

---

2. The literature on East Asian economic growth is overwhelming. Among the more important works, see Johnson 1982, Samuels 1987 and 1994, Wade 1990, and Haggard 1990. For a review of much of the literature on Asian development, see Pempel 1993.

ahead of where they were two or three decades ago; and perhaps more important for the future, most remain far better poised for additional improvement than they would have been had they never enjoyed their catch-up spurts of growth. Most countries of the industrializing world would happily trade places even given Asia's recent downturns.

Various suggestions have been put forward as common explanations for what the World Bank (1993) has labeled "The East Asian Miracle." Among the most prominent have been "Confucian culture," "laissez-faire economics," "the developmental state," "network capitalism," "American empire," and "Japan's embrace." This chapter makes no attempt to assess these alternatives.[3] Its goal is more specific, namely to demonstrate the powerful contribution made to Asia's particular version of capitalist success by the more explicitly socioeconomic factors of labor markets and social welfare. Before doing so however, it is critical to differentiate two very different versions of "Asian capitalism."

TWO ASIAN CAPITALISMS

There are in reality at least two different Asian capitalisms, each rooted in a separate "indigenous capitalist tradition." Both emerged as nineteenth-century responses to the coming of the West. Each offers an important but quite different capitalist impulse with profoundly distinct political implications. On the one hand there was the Japanese tradition of a state-led corporatized political economy; on the other, the Chinese tradition of family-led entrepreneurial deal-making. The first is associated with industrial capitalism; the second with commercial capitalism.

The Japanese pattern grew out of a politically framed domestic economy and the creation of indigenous industrial capacity, most notably in heavy industrial production. This trend is most closely associated with Japan, South Korea, and Taiwan, and more recently with the South China–Hong Kong–Taipei nexus. In contrast, the pattern of commercial capitalism can be traced back to the nineteenth-century efforts by Chinese heads of households to become entrepreneurs and to develop family firms. The outcome was not big steel plants, railroads, and petrochemical complexes built within a single nation-state, but rather trading and financial networks that crossed national borders and generated extensive commercial linkages (Hamilton, 1996). This pattern has long been associated with the ethnic

---

3. For my own views, see Pempel 1999.

Chinese businesses driving much of the economic successes of Singapore, Hong Kong, and to a lesser extent Thailand, Malaysia, and Indonesia.

Broadly speaking, the Japanese model is nationalistic, capital intensive, large scale, oligopolistic, and politically driven. The Chinese model is personal and familistic, small scale, niche oriented, regional, and market driven. These two traditions have paralleled, competed with, and intersected each other at different times. And in parts of Asia today, most notably in the South China–Hong Kong–Taipei nexus, they overlap in important ways. But their separate historical path dependence must be acknowledged, along with the fact that they represent quite different "models of Asian capitalism." This chapter focuses almost exclusively on the Japanese industrial model of capitalism, but it is essential to remember that any effort to think comparatively about Asian capitalism requires a sensitivity to both traditions.

ASIAN INDUSTRIAL CAPITALISM IN COMPARATIVE PERSPECTIVE

There are several ways in which capitalism in Japan, South Korea, and Taiwan are broadly different from the capitalist patterns in the United States and continental Europe. Four points are essential.

First, Asian industrialization began much later than it did in the United States or Western Europe. Among other consequences, political democratization and the role of elections and political parties became far more integrally interwoven into the capitalisms of continental Europe and the United States than they did in Asia. At the same time, conservative as Asian capitalism has been overall, it has also been marked by a high degree of egalitarianism. Second, all three Asian countries had small state bureaucracies that were largely meritocratic and separated from the politics of clientelistic patronage. Third, the socioeconomic coalitions that have undergirded capitalism in Japan, South Korea, and Taiwan have been fundamentally different from those in the capitalist countries of Europe and North America. Fourth, and finally, all three Asian regimes have been intimately and bilaterally linked, for strategic reasons, to the United States. Appreciation of the role of labor and welfare policies demands at least a schematic understanding of each of these differences, particularly in any efforts to assess the "transferability" of the Asian experiences to other parts of the world.

Late industrialization and late democratization allowed political and economic elites in Japan, Taiwan, and South Korea the comparative luxury of pursuing economic transformation with only minimal sensitivity to populist pressures. Japan, Asia's earliest industrializer, introduced a parliament in 1890, and universal male suffrage came only in 1925. Truly universal suffrage came only after World War II. South Korea and Taiwan were Japanese colonies until after World War II, and both had authoritarian regimes until well into the 1980s. Their democratization came vastly later than that of Japan.

Capitalism in all three thus developed with far fewer political and electoral constraints than in Europe or North America. The authoritarian regimes of Germany, Austria, Italy, and even Vichy France provide collective experiences far closer to those of these Asian countries than do, say the Scandinavian, British, or American models. Furthermore, even the European authoritarian regimes had earlier and more comprehensive experiences with democratization than did those in Asia.

All three Asian industrial capitalist countries have also had small but activist state bureaucracies that have been largely meritocratic and relatively free from the bloat of political patronage. Thus, the United States has a civil service divided between careerists and political appointees that generates a "government of strangers" (Heclo 1977). In Italy, more than one-half of the civil service positions are exempt from competitive examinations, and there are over 1000 parastatals, including such huge operations as the ENI (Ente Nazioale Idrocarburi) with a focus on energy and IRI (Instituto per la Ricostruzione Industriale) concentrated in heavy industry. State-owned enterprises accounted for 38 percent of the workforce and 45 percent of the sales in industry and services in the 1980s, making the Italian state a major stakeholder in the national economy (Samuels 1996). Almost all state-owned enterprises have extensive patronage responsibilities (Posner 1977, 238–39). In the corporatist capitalist countries of Northern Europe, public sector employment has been extremely high and has played a vital role in maintaining low unemployment.

Such patterns are virtually absent from Japan, South Korea, and Taiwan. All have tiny state governments with budgets that comprise small portions of the national GNP; all have highly meritocratic civil services. Japan began this process in the late nineteenth century and continued it with little change into the postwar period. Until the end of the 1990s only two (or in some cases three) political appointees sat atop the essentially exam-based, careerist civil service.[4] Japan's civil service, meanwhile, and its level of government spending are about half the size per capita of those in the United States or the United Kingdom and even smaller than those in Scandinavia.

Meanwhile, Japan, through colonialism, transferred this broad pattern to both Korea and Taiwan (Cumings 1984). In contrast to the imperialisms of

---

4. For a more comprehensive treatment of the Japanese civil service, see Kim et al. 1995.

Britain, France, Belgium, Italy, and the United States, Japan's armies and bureaucrats brought with them industry, commerce, transportation, and communications, creating strong, well-educated, local bureaucracies in their two colonies. Under Japanese occupation, the Korean state was highly centralized and burrowed down to every village in the form of a police force and an agricultural extension service (Amsden 1989, 34). Similarly in Taiwan, the reach of the state was long and pervasive: cadastral surveys, railroads, ports, schools, and scientific agricultural improvements were a positive face of the strong state, paralleled by the often less welcome police, tax collectors, and military. Though Japanese colonialism was no less self-serving than that of the other major imperial powers, the Japanese pattern relied on an elaborate state apparatus open to locals, elaborate educational and financial networks, and an extensive communications and transportation infrastructure.[5] Moreover, in both of its colonies, Japan rather unusually also developed heavy industry, including steel, chemicals, hydroelectric facilities, metallurgy, and transportation (Cumings 1984, 55–56; Ho 1978, 70–90). The result was a legacy more conducive to subsequent development than that left behind in South Asia, Africa, or the Middle East.

Not surprisingly, Japan, South Korea, and Taiwan emerged in the postwar periods with "strong states" having highly trained technocrats in well-institutionalized government offices as well as with the makings of an industrial infrastructure. Government bureaucrats in all three were drawn from a highly educated technocratic elite. In both Korea and Taiwan the bureaucracies were fused with extensive military influence, both in personnel and as the model for emulation. The result was what Hagen Koo called the "hypermilitarization" of both countries' bureaucracies and their controls over society (Koo 1987, 172).

At the same time, the number of civil servants per 1000 remained far smaller in Korea and Taiwan than even in Japan; also smaller were both government budgets as a ratio of GNP.[6] All three countries have resisted any major inclination toward demiurge or toward major public spending programs. Consequently the costs of, and transfer payments by, the national government remained low while far more capital was available for use by the private sector.

Too easily, such a focus suggests that a depoliticized, socially disembodied, rational civil service, reminiscent of Max Weber's "idealized" civil service has driven Japanese, Korean, and Taiwanese development (see Gerth

5. It is useful in this regard to note that in Korea and Taiwan during this period the colonial state did indeed stand rather apart from Korean and Taiwanese societies.

6. On Korea, see Woo-Cumings 1995, 452–53.

and Mills 1958, 196–244). The question remains: Where do the architects of the developmental state get their marching orders? Or perhaps more meaningfully, even if government agencies do make their own rules, with whose interests in mind are these rules developed and enforced? To answer this question, it is necessary to turn to the third key difference from European and North American capitalism, namely the socioeconomic coalitions underlying the Asian capitalist regimes.

The underlying socioeconomic coalition in all three countries has linked three key sectors—big business, smaller businesses, and agriculture. Systematically excluded was organized labor. The distinctiveness of this exclusion and its role in Asian capitalism was most conspicuous in Japan. In the period since World War II, such an alliance was quite unusual for any industrialized country. More typically, in the other industrialized democracies, labor and business had reconciled the most extreme of their differences, achieved a substantial liberalization of trade, and "even while providing generous death benefits, presided over domestic agriculture's demise" (Rogowski 1989, 99). The few notable exceptions to this pattern involved land-rich countries such as the United States, Australia, New Zealand, and Canada where major agricultural exporters, heavily dependent on world markets, often allied with business. But in these cases too, the alliance focused on (selective) free trade and (relatively) open markets.

No such labor-business alliance emerged in the three Asian countries; rather, business and agriculture forged antilabor alliances that resulted, not in the free trade that typically comes from a business-labor accord, but rather in relatively closed mercantilist hothouses, largely devoid of countervailing pressures from labor, consumers, or other popular sectors. It is not that organized labor was completely irrelevant in the three countries. What was critical, however, was that organized labor never acquired the political muscle to give significant shape to the national economic agenda, or to provide a political counterweight to management's powerful bargaining position at the factory level. More will be said about this point in the specific treatment of labor and welfare; for the moment it is simply important to realize the fundamentally different socioeconomic basis on which capitalism rested in Asia and how this differed from the socioeconomic roots of North American or Western European capitalism.

Agriculture in all three countries was driven by small-scale, privately owned farms, not plantation agriculture. All three countries underwent massive land reform programs during the years immediately after World War II. Industrialization thus proceeded without strong opposition from powerful landowners resistant to industrialization and manufacturing.

Yet the conservative colorization of Asian capitalism was not so comprehensive as to create societies that sharply bifurcated rich and poor. Rather, Asian capitalism remained relatively egalitarian, particularly in comparison to those capitalist regimes that have a generally conservative and nonpopulist political base. Japan has a Gini index comparable to that of social democratic Sweden or Norway, rather than to more conservative countries such as the United States, Britain, Canada, and Germany. And in contrast to Latin American countries such as Brazil or Argentina with Gini index figures around .60, Taiwan's has been low and falling to just below .30 while South Korea's, although it has risen slightly, has been in the range of .33–.35 since the mid-1960s (see Haggard 1990, 226; Koo 1984, 1029–37; and Evans 1987, 217–20).

Finally, postwar Japanese, South Korean, and Taiwanese capitalism was intimately linked to American capitalist markets. As an outgrowth of the cold war the United States sought to develop a pro-Western, conservative, pro-capitalist order in Asia. All three countries benefited as a result. Various forms of military assistance provided technology and capital for industrial development projects; regional trade was kept distorted as a means of isolating China and generating Asian models that could be held up as counterexamples to China's state-led economic development. U.S. markets were kept open to exports from all three countries (and to most of pro-Western Asia generally) with few, and/or late, demands for reciprocity. As a result, all three countries had relatively low rates of foreign direct investment as well as trade patterns more heavily dependent on the U.S. market than is true of any other capitalist countries.

In short, the broad sweep of capitalism in Japan, South Korea, and Taiwan has several key characteristics that separate them in fundamental ways from the capitalisms of the United States or Europe. These differences in turn are important in the particular ways in which labor and welfare policies have consequently evolved in Asia.

LABOR AND WELFARE IN ASIAN CAPITALISM

Asian approaches to both labor and welfare are logically critical to their broader patterns of capitalism. During the earliest years of their industrialization, all three countries followed roughly similar trajectories involving massive labor repression and minimal state provision of welfare services. Such welfare services as were available came largely through the firm, not the state.[7] As politics became more democratic and labor gained greater legitimacy, state welfare services were expanded. But even Japan, which has moved the furthest along this trajectory, has remained highly resistant to the introduction of anything approaching a full-fledged West European–style welfare state; indeed, in the mid-1950s it trimmed back even its minimal state services in response to fiscal pressures and political opportunities.

Japan's systematic moves toward industrialization began in the last third of the nineteenth century. The effort to create "a rich country and a strong army," not surprisingly, led to the aggressive suppression of unions while state programs for social welfare were minimal. Instead, welfare was presumed to be the responsibility of the family and the firm. The only significant government effort nationwide involved a minimalist poor-relief plan, modeled on the Poor Laws of England, introduced in 1874 and revised in 1931 (Okamoto 1991).

The government was also selectively involved in pensions, but only in the form of lump-sum payments for government employees. Naval and army pension plans were enacted in 1875 and 1876 respectively while a civil service pension plan was begun in 1884. All three were integrated in 1923. At that date, however, social spending had still not reached one percent of Japan's net domestic product.

Such welfare as existed was delivered primarily through the workplace. Both government and business sought to promote a version of labor-management harmony linked to Japan's allegedly historical "beautiful customs" (*bifu*) involving close, paternalistic relations between worker and employer. Light industry, most notably textiles, was then driving Japanese capitalism, and workplace paternalism was easily justified and economically rational.

As heavy industry began to replace light industry as the locomotive of the Japanese economy, a shortage of skilled labor developed. Large firms in shipbuilding and iron and steel introduced various techniques to secure skilled labor: so-called lifetime employment, seniority-based wages, and enterprise welfare. Also begun were retirement allowances and mutual-aid credit, along with industry-wide blacklists of workers who quit one firm in search of a better job or were otherwise troublesome. All kept worker welfare closely linked to their employers and workplace.

Retirement allowances became a core element of enterprise welfare in response to the recession of the 1920s. Western-style unemployment insurance

7. On the provision of occupational welfare, see Shalev 1996.

was rejected by both government and business in favor of semimandatory layoff payments by firms. The retirement allowances were introduced as gratuities rather than as labor's right. They remained ultimately subject to management's discretion. Not surprisingly, throughout the prewar period, there were huge differentials by firm size in the provision of such retirement and dismissal allowances (Yamazaki 1988).

In addition to providing lump-sum retirement payments, large factories began as early as 1919 to set comparatively young ages for retirement. By the mid-1920s over 50 percent of the factories in Japan had some form of mandatory retirement for skilled and semiskilled workers (Toshi 1991, 281).

State involvement came in two important exceptions to the predominantly private provision of welfare, namely the National Health Insurance Law in 1938 (Sudo 1991) and the Employee Pension System Law in 1941. No ideological conversion in favor of broad social welfare provisions was under way, however. The first law dealt with the problems of tuberculosis, which was having a growing and deleterious effect on Japanese soldiers. The latter generated funds for munitions and the military through obligatory contributions to a program that would not provide benefits for decades.

Meanwhile a host of regulations provided government controls over labor. The Police Regulations of 1900 banned any actions to "instigate" or "incite" workers to participate in collective actions. The Peace Preservation Law of 1925 prohibited activities that challenged private ownership. Thus the highest prewar unionization ratio remained only 7.9 percent in 1931.

If labor was politically weak in Japan during the prewar period, it was even weaker in postwar South Korea and Taiwan. Virtually none of the limited benefits enjoyed by Japanese labor were available to its Asian counterparts. As late as the 1990s unionization levels reached only about 10 percent in South Korea; there were no minimum-wage standards, strikes and closed shops were outlawed. As one description suggested in the 1980s, "The labor movement had always been subject to various state controls, through limits on organization and strike activity, through informal penetration, and through government participation in the settlement of disputes; under the new [Chun] government, the system of industrial relations became even more repressive" (Haggard and Moon 1990, 220).

In Taiwan, the incoming Chinese nationalist government brought with it most of the repressive labor legislation enacted in the mainland context during the protracted civil war (Deyo 1987, 184). As in Korea, strikes and collective bargaining were illegal, and the existing unions were under strong Kuomintang controls, including party control over leadership selection and all union activities (Johnson 1987, 150). Like Japan, however, oppressive political conditions were mitigated in both countries by firm-level paternalism. Again it is important to note, such paternalism rarely translated into collective political influence.

The Japanese left and organized labor gained considerable strength and long-term potential from the early years of the U.S. Occupation into at least the late 1960s. Pro-left radicalism was widespread among important segments of the Japanese population; electoral support for the socialists rose rapidly (Watanuki 1991, 50–51). Meanwhile, Japanese labor unions engaged in sustained and frequently violent strikes.

Electoral demographics appeared to favor labor and the progressives, since the conservative base was composed of rapidly dwindling social groups. Indeed, Ishida Hirose, an important member of the LDP and a labor minister in the Ikeda cabinet, in an extremely influential article offered a series of socioeconomic projections to suggest how electorally ominous socioeconomic conditions were for the conservatives. If current demographic trends continued without shifts in the voting orientations of major blocs, Ishida warned, the LDP would be ousted from power by 1968 (Ishida 1963).

That warning elicited a threefold response. First, Japan's more radical unions were subjected to severe pressures from the government, and firms created and recognized more moderate "second unions" within their plants in efforts to marginalize the more radical unions. Throughout the 1950s and into the early 1960s, Japanese unions remained highly militant and strike rates were high. But with the defeat of labor in the Miike Coal Mine strike of 1960, the tide clearly turned. From then on, Japanese enterprise unions in the private sector (though not fully in the public sector for another two decades) came to identify their interests with those of the firm and its long-term profitability.

Second, occupational welfare was expanded at the firm level. Many Japanese firms spend considerable sums to create, if not cradle-to-grave socialism, at least its hiring-to-retirement equivalent. Many large firms provide subsidized housing, housing allowances, and/or downpayment loans for new homes; transportation allowances; medical facilities for employees and their families; in-plant canteens, barber shops, nurseries, and discount shopping centers; organized company vacation spots at ski lodges or hot springs resorts; childcare allowances and often on-site nurseries; as well as company picnics, athletic clubs, cultural clubs, and libraries. In addition, the best programs provide generous insurance schemes and retirement plans. Those working under such conditions had little personal or political incentive to demand state-generated nationwide social benefits. Most of their basic needs were met by their employers. Employment-related perks became an crucial salary supplement for those whose skills were in high demand.

Yet while such benefits became common in some Japanese firms, far more Japanese employers provided few, and in some cases, almost none of these amenities, a fact conveniently ignored by those lauding the alleged cultural inexorability of Japan's presumed proclivity toward generous workplace welfare schemes.

In addition to direct attacks on militant unions and the expansion of firm-level benefits within large firms, Japan's conservative government co-opted some of the appeal of the left from a third direction, namely by introducing small-scale government medical and retirement programs. The Employees Pension System (EPS) and the National Pension System (NPS) were established in 1954 and 1959 respectively. These were paralleled by the National Health Insurance (NHI) and Employee Health Insurance (EHI) programs. The two "employees" programs (EPS and EHI) were linked to job status; the "national" programs (NPS and NHI) provided government safety nets. Thus, unlike in numerous Western European systems, healthcare and retirement benefits were not treated as "rights of citizenship."[8] Instead, the public programs remained small and residual, providing low benefits, and in the case of the pension system, requiring a long period of contributions before eligibility.

Public welfare expenditure in Japan during the early 1960s thus accounted for only 7.0 percent of GDP, while the comparable figure was 17.0 percent in France, 16.5 percent in Germany, 13.6 percent in Italy and Sweden, 12.6 percent in the United Kingdom, and 10.3 percent in the United States. Income maintenance expenditure also showed no substantial change throughout the 1960s. Japan spent 2.1 percent of GDP for income maintenance programs in 1962 and 2.8 percent in 1972, both of which were only a third of the OECD average (OECD 1976, 25, 36).

Retirement pensions for the noncontributing elderly were minuscule (Campbell 1992, 139–41). Only about 3.4 million Japanese were eligible for benefits as recently as the early 1970s. Japan emerged as the industrial democracies' most conspicuous "welfare laggard." Meanwhile, South Korea and Taiwan had begun no significant government programs in even those fields where Japan was taking its initial embryonic steps. Only in the late 1980s did Korea begin to introduce embryonic social welfare measures.

---

8. The contrast here is most explicitly with the Scandinavian concept of complete entitlement as citizens to a variety of social programs. See Esping-Andersen 1990. See also Tanabe 1997.

Japanese labor market policies provided one of the least immediately visible stimulants to economic policy during the 1950–70 period as well as an important link to social welfare policies. Government policies were designed neither to provide unemployment checks nor to create public relief jobs (Kume 1995, 312–13). Instead a proactive labor market policy fused government and business in the provision of market-oriented job training policies. These in turn helped sustain relatively full employment and, more important, avoided measures that would otherwise have resulted in a permanent or semipermanent underclass of unemployed. Japan's national unemployment rate thus remained among the lowest in the industrialized democracies, while costly government programs of income-maintenance and unemployment payments were virtually nonexistent.

A major change in Japanese labor relations took place in response to the breakdown of Bretton Woods and the first oil shock. As noted, Japanese labor-management relations had been marked by high levels of conflict during the early postwar years and successful repression by business and government during the late 1950s and early 1960s. By the 1970s, strike rates had fallen sharply, and private sector unions increasingly came to identify their economic interests less with the working class and far more with the bottom-lines of their specific companies. As the national labor supply began to shrivel and as manufacturing productivity soared, however, workers in such private plants began to gain increased bargaining power and substantial wage hikes.

Clearly, the externally induced inflation of 1973–74 tied to the first oil shock gave labor both the incentive and the power to demand large wage hikes aimed at offsetting rapidly rising domestic costs. Doing so, however would have seriously undermined the price competitiveness of Japanese manufacturing exports and thereby undercut national economic growth. Quickly, a three-way "de facto incomes policy" was arranged, under which private sector labor moderated its wage demands in exchange for business guarantees of long-term job security and job retraining programs, along with government guarantees of low taxes, anti-inflationary policies, and financial support for worker retraining and industrial reorganization (Shinkawa 1984; Kume 1997).

This arrangement enabled Japan quickly to stem its wage-price inflation and become the first industrial country to snap back economically. There was barely a glitch in Japan's overall growth or export competitiveness. Government resources, managerial concessions, and labor linkages to firms were key ingredients in allowing a bargain that warded off what might have been a severe challenge to national and company export competitiveness.

Perhaps even more important, the agreement strengthened existing ties between unionized blue-collar workers and management in large private firms, eroding latent class appeals of the union movement and the political left. And it did so in ways that did not seriously challenge the privileges of long-time conservative supporters. Private sector unions became even more politically and economically moderate, ultimately reorganizing into Rengō, a single peak federation with a largely nonpolitical, economic agenda (Tsujinaka 1987). As well, the electoral behavior of blue-collar workers shifted, and significant numbers became supporters of the LDP (Sato and Matsuzaki 1986; Miyake 1985).

When conservative electoral fortunes seemed problematic in the early to mid-1970s, the government also took steps to change the long-standing orientation on social welfare. Even Japan's larger businesses, whose beneficial position through occupationally based welfare would be partially undercut by any new government programs, urged government action to increase welfare programs as a way to ward off potential conservative electoral defeats.

Social welfare took top priority in the drafting of the 1973 national budget, the "first year of the welfare era." Free medical care for the elderly, initiated earlier by progressive local governments, was introduced at the national level. The proportion of medical expenses paid by the two public insurance programs was increased, pushing the average increase in medical costs upward, from 17.2 percent between 1966 and 1972 to 27.3 percent between 1973 and 1975.

In addition, payouts in both the Employee Pension System (EPS) and the National Pension System (NPS) were substantially enhanced (Fujita 1984, 30). The employees pension benefit was almost doubled to about 45 percent of the average employee's income; the national pension was increased proportionately. More important still, indexation was introduced for both systems.

These measures came, obviously, from a conservative government anxious to forestall electoral challenges rather than from a socialist government anxious to institutionalize citizen rights. As such, they were more Bismarckian than Beveridgite. As both a proportion of the national budget and as a proportion of GNP, spending on social welfare measures increased steadily from 1973 until the early 1980s. Even so, as late as 1980, social security transfers in Japan remained relatively low compared to the other OECD countries at 10.9 percent of GNP (compared to 22.9 percent in France, 15.3 percent in Germany, and 15.8 percent in Italy) (Noguchi 1987, 188). Modest as they were, these still contributed to a positive electoral upswing in conservative support.

If this "era of welfare" had lasted for a decade or more, Japan's welfare mix might have moved decisively toward an "institutionalized" welfare state based on citizenship rights. Occupational welfare might simultaneously have diminished in significance. This, in turn, might well have weakened management's control over employees and the wide differentiation in access to social welfare by different groups.

Welfare reforms, however, came face to face with a return to fiscal austerity beginning in the middle of the 1980s. Conservatives introduced welfare programs with the expectation that Japan's twenty years of dramatic economic growth would continue, thereby providing the needed funding for the new programs. But the very first year of Japan's new "welfare era" coincided with the oil crisis. Suddenly, Japan's growth was reduced to more normal proportions. Slower growth and lower government tax revenues, combined with the weakening political position of the LDP, led to funding the new programs through deficit budgeting. Japan's deficit dependency ratio had been just over 4 percent in 1970; for 1971–74, it rose rapidly to the 11–16 percent range, continuing up to just below 30 percent in 1976 and 1977, hitting 37 percent in 1978, and peaking in the next year near 40 percent (Yamamura 1985, 497–98).

Deficit financing had the obvious advantage of being far less immediately visible and painful to the general public than one based on major hikes in taxes or on employee contributions. But as public deficits mounted, the idea of emulating Western-style welfare programs came under withering attack, particularly from the business sector and the Ministry of Finance. Furthermore, the preemption of the opposition's ability to exploit pollution or welfare as issues to attack the LDP had been partially accomplished. The LDP, in the famous "double election" of 1980, reversed its seemingly inexorable electoral decline, and the opposition parties were brushed to the sidelines. The resulting conservative electoral dominance in turn allowed a return to prior fiscal restraint.

Conservative intellectuals developed an extensive campaign arguing that excessive welfare service led to outbreaks of "advanced-country disease," or the "English disease." Expansion of public services, they contended, encouraged people to depend excessively upon the state, discouraged their desire to work, and weakened their incentives to invest and improve productivity. Furthermore, Japan, which demographic models had already shown was undergoing rapid aging, was destined to become an even bigger spender. Steps had to be taken to reverse past trends (Koyama 1978; Kanbara 1986, 118–43). Drawing on the theme that Japan was different from other advanced democracies and that welfare should be left primarily to the family and the firm, these conservatives advocated building a "welfare *society* with vitality" and creating a "Japanese-style welfare *society*."

Contending that free medical care for the elderly had turned hospitals into "old people's salons" (*Asahi Nenkan* 1983, 440), the government passed an Old People's Health Bill in 1982 introducing copayments and pressuring local governments to reduce their initiatives to improve medical care for elderly patients. In addition, in 1985 the Employees Pension Plan was revised to slow down benefit increases, raise contributions, and reduce government subsidization. The pension system was made two-tiered with a base pension for all citizens topped by a wage-linked pension tied to one's occupation (Kato 1991, 165–84). Pensions to government employees were similarly slashed.

In all these ways, government contributions were slowed, or actually reduced, reversing the trend that had begun in the 1970s and re-institution-alizing the wide differentials in the retirement benefits of those in different sized firms and different industrial sectors. The changes also meant an effective capping of the previously geometrically climbing expenditures for social security and medical care. These plateaued at about 27 percent of the national budget during the decade of the 1980s, while actual spending for health and income security dropped slightly from 18 percent in 1982 to 16.3 percent in 1990 (Keizai Koho Center 1992, 80). The minimalist welfare and lifestyle programs that had barely been introduced were quickly rolled back.

It was within this context that administrative reform began under the Suzuki cabinet in the early 1980s. Administrative reform was delegated to the Second Provisional Administrative Reform Commission (Rinchō), created by then-director general of the Administrative Management Agency (and subsequently prime minister) Nakasone Yasuhiro in March 1981.[9]

Most fundamentally, administrative reform involved appeasing business and bureaucratic agencies upset at the radical jumps in government costs, the potential for even greater deficits through automatic entitlement programs, and the challenge to worker linkages to the firm and fear that the "unique Japanese national character" would be undermined.

Rinchō was strict in its cutbacks on budget deficits and government entitlements. Until the 1970s, Japanese government expenditures had been stable in the low 20 percent range of GNP; during the decades of the 1970s this had expanded to nearly 35 percent (Provisional Commission 1984, 1).

---

9. On administrative reform, see, inter alia, Noguchi 1981 and Gyōsei Kanri Kenkyū Center 1979.

The bond-dependency ratio rose sharply as a result; massive debt-servicing costs became a natural and built-in part of the annual budget. Debt servicing rose from 0.12 percent of GNP in 1966, to 0.39 percent in 1970, to 1.56 percent in 1978, and to 2.94 percent in 1982.[10] To check this expansion, national budgets during 1982–84 were kept at zero, low, or negative rates of growth thereby dramatically reducing program expansion and costs, as well as civil service growth.

Beyond its budgetary focus, Rinchō also embarked on substantial privatization of the railways, the telecommunications industry, the tobacco and salt monopolies, and parts of Japan Airlines and other public corporations, further reducing the size and scope of Japanese governmental activity and cost. Not at all incidentally, these privatization measures dramatically undercut the political and economic power of the few remaining militant public sector unions (see, inter alia, Ōtake 1994, chaps. 2–5).

It was not until June 1994, in the wake of LDP collapse and four years of recession that Japan got a government that included representatives of organized labor. And that coalition government actually eviscerated most of the original left-of-center agenda. As a result, by the later 1990s, Japanese capitalism continued to be shaped by the long-term exclusion of organized labor from government programs and by the relatively low levels of state welfare programs. Low levels of unemployment, broad social equality, and extensive occupational welfare (at least in larger firms) softened many of the human aspects of limited welfare. But overall, Japan stood as the exemplar of a strikingly different form of capitalism than was prevalent in either the corporatist versions of continental Europe or the revised conservative capitalisms of the United States or Britain.

The Taiwanese and South Korean experiences were broadly similar to those of Japan up to the point when Japan began to introduce more moderate policies toward labor and some social welfare programs. These, as noted, came in response to electoral pressures. Not surprisingly when Korea and Taiwan began to open their political systems, labor militance increased, and the governments of those countries undertook some social welfare measures. This was most notable in South Korea where the labor laws were revised in 1987. Strikes expanded dramatically, and a wave of antigovernment labor unrest was unleashed.

Partly in response to labor militance and demands for enhanced social welfare programs the South Korean government included social welfare as a

10. Japan Economic Planning Agency, *Yearbook of National Account Statistics* (Tokyo: Government Printing Office, annual), as cited in Noguchi 1987, 196.

goal in its economic plans. Its 1982–86 economic plan was relabeled an "Economic and Social Development Plan." Medical insurance was expanded to cover 92 percent of the population (versus only .06 percent in 1970). Similarly, government expenditures on social and welfare services rose from about 25 percent of total government spending in 1976 to about 40 percent in 1990 (Kim 1997, 175).

Overall, however, neither South Korea nor Taiwan moved to follow any model of capitalism widely different from that pursued by Japan. And if they do, it in no way will negate the broad similarities among the three countries in their historical evolution of capitalism, a version of capitalism quite different from those in North America and Western Europe.

CAN EAST ASIA SERVE AS A DEVELOPMENTAL MODEL?

Japan's economic success and the subsequent high growth of the Asian NICs and near-NICs captured widespread interest throughout the 1980s and into the 1990s. The conviction grew that Asia could serve as a model for developing economies in other parts of the world.

The analysis above suggests several very positive lessons that might be drawn from the Asian experience by developmentalists. Four are particularly noteworthy. First, economic development is obviously a politically constructed project rather than the passively generated consequence of numerous uncoordinated and invisible hands. Asian economic success highlights the ways in which political power, if mobilized and wielded astutely, can enhance a nation's economic success. Asian capitalism also presents a serious alternative to popular, but intellectually squishy, "explanations" of Asian economic performance based on notions of national culture such as "Confucianism," "the Confucian ideal of rule," "post-Confucianism," "samurai Confucianism," and the like (Pye 1985; Calder and Hofheinz 1982; Morishima 1982; Chan 1990). The analysis in this chapter makes it clear that economic development does not require a commitment to Confucianism so much as it does a commitment to labor suppression and low levels of social welfare.

Asian capitalism also shows that there is more than one single historical path to economic success. In line with Gerschenkronian scholarship showing how early and late developers differ in their political and economic institutions, the Asian case clearly evolved, particularly during the postwar period, in ways that underscore the possibility of alternative historical paths to similar goals.

Third, while it was not a focus of this chapter, Asian capitalism suggests a particularly important connection between economic success and international market forces. Robert Wade is explicit in demonstrating such links through what he calls "governed markets," namely, the "synergistic connection between a public system and a mostly market system, the outputs of each becoming inputs for the other" (Wade 1990, 5). Japan, South Korea, and Taiwan long had hothouse economies, but most products that thrived in the hothouse did so as the result of competition or collusion with one another for intra-hothouse sales; those that flourished outside the protected glass walls meanwhile did so because of their international competitive capabilities. Asian capitalism thus offers little endorsement for the often popular developmental strategies of "national champions," import substitution, or nationally owned conglomerates.

Finally, the Asian cases suggest that far more options exist for developing countries than are implied by the pessimistic predictions of modernization theory, dependency theory, or world systems theory.[11] In fact, one of the most striking options that emerges is that business and government can collude in ways that co-opt labor, rather than capitulate to it. Most class-based critiques of capitalism seek to tie labor's long-term interests to a redistributive project. But the recent experiences of unions and workers in Europe and North America suggest that any business-labor redistributive project may well founder on the shoals of a firm's or a sector's declining international competitiveness. In contrast, the Asian experience suggests that tripartite collusion at the plant level—based on job guarantees and occupational welfare—might well allow the simultaneous advance of profits and worker lifestyles. Quite obviously, such an assertion remains to be tested at least against long-term economic problems throughout Asia, but it is at least one possible conclusion to consider based on the analysis given here.

Weighted against such contributions, however, are two counter lessons that are also clear. First, without question state bureaucrats played an important role in national economic success in all three Asian countries. Government agencies at different times have frequently been in the economic driver's seat. However, the role of the national bureaucracy should not be taken as evidence that development is the simple outgrowth of a depoliticized, socially

11. It is important to recognize that there have been several waves of dependency theory and world systems theory, including some that are sensitive to various possibilities for improved economic conditions in less-industrialized countries. See, e.g., Peter Evans's notion of "dependent development" (Evans 1979) or Henderson's notions of globalized production (Henderson 1989).

disembodied, rational civil service, reminiscent of Max Weber's "idealized" civil service (see Gerth and Mills 1958, 196–244).

To do so is to ignore the socioeconomic sectors that underpin any set of governmental institutions. What are the relative resources and power bases of such diverse groups in different countries prior to any effort at economic development; how do these relative power capabilities interact; what are the politics of socioeconomic coalition formation; and how have such coalitions enhanced or retarded the capacity of state bureaucrats to act autonomously? Bureaucrats were important to national economic development in Asia, but so too were the coalitional freeze-out of organized labor, the fusion of policy connections among farmers and big and small business, and the generation of a policy profile that could mobilize key social sectors in pursuit of a common agenda.

Asian economic successes were the consequence of Asian capitalism in its full complexity—a mixture of institutions, coalitional arrangements, and public policy profiles. It was not just the outgrowth of state structures and actions. Not all state steamrollers move in the same political direction, and understanding how Asian capitalism developed requires a sensitivity to the more comprehensive characteristics of entire regimes.

A second caveat involves the international political environment within which Asian success was achieved. The developmental focus on Asia is too often exclusively domestic. Developmental hurdles are seen to lie in business organization; allocation of scarce capital, energy resources, and technology; tax credits; budgetary incentives; mass education; labor regulations; foreign direct investment; and the like. All are important, but a focus on them ignores the power distributions and the strategic goals of major international powers; trade, investment, energy, and environmental regimes; the actions of multinational corporations and transnational nongovernmental organizations; foreign aid; and so forth.

Development involves the improvement of a country's economic conditions *relative to other states*. Hence, it is critical to situate Asia's developmental success within the broader context of the world and international system within which it occurred. That success was intimately tied into the cold war, bilateral relations with the United States that generated low-cost security, and a big and open export market for the goods of America's allies.

The cold war has ended; bilateral trade and investment frictions between Asia and the United States have risen; U.S. officials are far less willing to allow countries like South Korea or Taiwan to replicate the Japanese economic experience through undervalued currencies, protected home markets, and easy access to the U.S. market. In short, potential imitators of Japan are likely to face far less amenable international conditions in the next fifty years than Japan faced in the last fifty, and those who try to follow Korea or Taiwan will have even less of a window with which to succeed.

Nothing made Asia's changing international vulnerability more clearcut than its financial crises. Japan's problems were heavily shaped by domestic miscalculations, but the loss of government control over the value of the yen, the need to meet Bank of International Settlements standards to lend internationally, the pressures from international ratings agencies like Moody's and Dow Jones, U.S. pressures for deregulation, the diminished power of the Ministry of Finance and the Bank of Japan to control Japanese capital movements, and a host of other external forces make it clear that Japan no longer enjoys the nurturing international climate from which it benefited during the cold war.

Similarly indicative of international vulnerabilities were the massive attacks by currency speculators on the currencies of Thailand, Indonesia, South Korea, and Malaysia; their dependence on external investment capital; the declining abilities of their central banks to control externally induced inflation; and the harshness of conditions imposed on the first three of these countries as contingencies for loans from the International Monetary Fund.

Asian capitalism and Asian development are by no means irrelevant to potential imitators. But the complex socioeconomics and the integral links between the Asian experience and the international environment within which it occurred should make it clear that economic development is far more complicated than simply creating more MITIs and more industrial policies.

REFERENCES

Amsden, A. 1989. *Asia's Next Giant: South Korea and Late Industrialization*. New York: Oxford University Press.

Calder, Kent E., and Roy Hofheinz Jr. 1982. *The Eastasia Edge*. New York: Basic Books.

Campbell, John Creighton. 1992. *How Policies Change: The Japanese Government and the Aging Society*. Princeton: Princeton University Press.

Chan, Steve. *East Asian Dynamism: Growth, Order, and Security in the Pacific Region*. Boulder, Colo.: Westview.

Cumings, B. 1984. "The Origins and Development of the Northeast Asian Political Economy: Industrial Sectors, Product Cycles, and Political Consequences." *International Organization* 38, no. 1:1–40.

Deyo, Frederic C. 1987. "State and Labor: Modes of Political Exclusion in East Asian Development." In F. Deyo, ed., *The Political Economy of the New Asian Industrialism*. Ithaca: Cornell University Press.

Esping-Andersen, Gøsta. 1990. *The Three Worlds of Welfare Capitalism*. Princeton: Princeton University Press.

Evans, Peter. 1979. *Dependent Development: The Alliance of Multinational, State and Local Capital in Brazil*. Princeton: Princeton University Press.

———. 1987. "Class, State and Dependence in East Asia: Lessons for Latin America." In F. Deyo, ed., *The Political Economy of the New Asian Industrialism*. Ithaca: Cornell University Press.

Frieden, Jeffry A., and David A. Lake. 1995. *International Political Economy*. 3d ed. New York: St. Martin's Press.

Fujita Sei. 1984. *Fukushi Seisaku to Zaisei*. Tokyo: Nihon Keizai Shinbunsha.

Gerschenkron, Alexander. 1962. *Economic Backwardness in Historical Perspective*. Cambridge: Harvard University Press.

Gerth, H. H., and C. W. Mills, eds. 1958. *From Max Weber: Essays in Sociology*. New York: Oxford.

Gyōsei Kanri Kenkyū Center. 1979. *Gyōsei Kaikaku no Bijon* [A vision of administrative reform]. 3 vols. Tokyo: Gyōkankyū Center.

Haggard, Stephan. 1990. *Pathways from the Periphery*. Ithaca: Cornell University Press.

Haggard, Stephan, and Chung-in Moon. 1990. "Institutions and Economic Policy: Theory and a Korean Case Study." *World Politics* 42, no. 2 (January): 220.

Hamilton, Gary. 1996. "Overseas Chinese Capitalism." In Tu Wei-ming, ed., *Confucian Traditions in East Asian Modernity*. Cambridge: Harvard University Press, 328–342.

Heclo, Hugh. 1977. *A Government of Strangers: Executive Politics in Washington*. Washington, D.C.: Brookings Institution.

Henderson, J. 1989. *The Globalization of High Technology Production: Society, Space and Semiconductors in the Restructuring of the Modern World*. London: Routledge.

Ho, Samuel. 1978. *The Economic Development of Taiwan 1860–1970*. New Haven: Yale University Press.

Ishida Hirohide. 1963. "Hoshu Seitō no Bijon" [A vision of the Conservative Party]. *Chūō Kōron* 78, no. 1 (January): 88–97.

Johnson, Chalmers. 1982. *MITI and the Japanese Miracle: The Making of Industrial Policy, 1925–75*. Stanford: Stanford University Press.

———. 1987. "The Government Business Relationship in Japan, South Korea, and Taiwan." In Frederick C. Deyo, ed., *The Political Economy of the New Asian Industrialism*. Ithaca: Cornell University Press.

Kanbara Masaru. 1986. *Tenkanki no Seiji Katei*. Tokyo: Sogo Rodo Kenkyusha.

Kato Junko. 1991. "Seisaku Katei Kenkyū no Riron to Jissho: Koteki Nenkin Seido Kaikaku to Iryo Hoken Seido Kaikaku no Kesu wo Megutte" [A theoretical and empirical study of the policymaking process: Analysis of the reform processes of the public pension and health insurance systems]. *Rebaiasan* 8:165–84.

Keizai Koho Center. 1992. *Japan 1992: An International Comparison*. Tokyo: Keizai Koho.

Kim, Eun Mee. 1997. *Big Business, Strong State: Collusion and Conflict in South Korean Economic Development, 1960–1990.* New Paltz: SUNY Press.

Kim, Hyung-ki, Michio Muramatsu, T. J. Pempel, and Kozo Yamamura, eds. 1995. *The Japanese Civil Service and Economic Development: Catalysts of Development.* Oxford: Oxford University Press.

Koo, Hagen. 1984. "The Political Economy of Income Distribution in South Korea: The Impact of the State's Industrialization Policies." *World Development* 12:1029–37.

———. 1987. "The Interplay of State, Social Class, and World System in East Asian Development: The Cases of South Korea and Taiwan." In F. Deyo, ed., *The Political Economy of the New Asian Industrialism.* Ithaca: Cornell University Press.

Koyama Kenichi. 1978. *Eikokubyo no Kyokun,* Kyoto: PHP Kenkyujo.

Kume, Ikuo. 1995. "Institutionalizing the Active Labor Market Policy in Japan: A Comparative View." In Hyung-ki Kim, Michio Muramatsu, T. J. Pempel, and Kozo Yamamura, eds., *The Japanese Civil Service and Economic Development: Catalysts of Change.* Oxford: Oxford University Press.

———. 1997. *Disparaged Success.* Ithaca: Cornell University Press.

Miyake Ichiro, ed. 1985. *Seitō Shiji no Bunseki* [An analysis of political support]. Tokyo: Shokubunsha.

Morishima, Michio. 1982. *Why Japan Has 'Succeeded': Western Technology and the Japanese Ethos.* Cambridge: Cambridge University Press.

Mouffe, Chantal. 1987. "Hegemony and Ideology in Gramsci." In Tony Bennett et al., eds., *Culture, Ideology and Social Process.* London: Open University.

Noguchi Yukio. 1981. *Gyōzaisei Kaikaku* [Administrative and financial reform]. Tokyo: PHP.

———. 1987. "Public Finance." In Kozo Yamamura and Yasukichi Yasuba, eds., *The Political Economy of Japan: Vol. 1 The Domestic Transformation.* Stanford: Stanford University Press.

OECD. 1976. *Public Expenditure on Income Maintenance Programs.* Paris: OECD.

Okamoto Takiko. 1991. "Kyuhin Seido no Hensen." In K. Yokoyama and H. Tada, eds., *Nihon Shakai Hosho no Rekishi.* Tokyo: Gakubunsha.

Ōtake Hideo. 1994. *Jiyūshugiteki Kaikaku no Jidai.* Tokyo: Chūō Kōronsha.

Pempel, T. J. 1993. "Of Dragons and Development." *Journal of Public Policy* 12, no. 1:79–95.

———. 1999. "The Developmental Regime in a Changing World Economy." In Meredith Woo-Cumings, ed., *The Developmental State.* Ithaca: Cornell University Press.

Posner, Alan R. 1977. "Italy: Dependence and Political Fragmentation." In Peter J. Katzenstein, ed., *Between Power and Plenty.* Madison: University of Wisconsin Press.

The Provisional Commission on Administrative Reform. 1984. *The Fifth Report on Administrative Reform—The Final Report.* Tokyo: Institute of Administrative Management.

Pye, Lucian W. 1985. *Asian Power and Politics: The Cultural Dimensions of Authority.* Cambridge: Harvard University Press.

Rogowski, Ronald. 1989. *Commerce and Coalitions: How Trade Affects Domestic Political Alignments*. Princeton: Princeton University Press.

Samuels, Richard J. 1987. *The Business of the Japanese State: Energy Markets in Comparative and Historical Perspective*. Ithaca: Cornell University Press.

———. 1994. *"Rich Nation Strong Army": National Security and the Technological Transformation of Japan*. Ithaca: Cornell University Press.

———. 1996. "Great Forces and Great Choices: Italy and Japan in Comparative Perspective." Paper delivered at the American Political Science Association Annual Convention, August 29–September 1.

Sato Seizaburo and Matsuzaki Tetsuhisa. 1986. *Jimintō-Seiken* [LDP power]. Tokyo: Chūō Kōronsha.

Shalev, Michael, ed. 1996. *The Privatization of Social Policy? Occupational Welfare and the Welfare State in America, Scandinavia and Japan*. Oxford: Oxford University Press.

Shinkawa Toshimitsu. 1984. "Senkyūhyaku Nanajūgonen Shuntōto Keizai Kiki Kanri" [The 1975 Shunto and the management of economic crisis]. In Ōtake Hideo, ed., *Nihon Seiji no Shoten* [Problems in Japanese politics]. Tokyo: San ichi Shobō.

Sudo Midori. 1991. "Shakai Hosho Seido no Ayumi." In Yokoyama K. and Tada H., eds., *Nihon Shakai Hosho no Rekishi*. Tokyo: Gakubunsha.

Tanabe, Kuniaki. 1997. "Social Policy in Japan: Building a Welfare State in a Conservative One Dominant Party State." In Michio Muramatsu and Frieder Naschold, eds., *State and Administration in Japan and Germany*. Berlin: DeGruyter.

Toshi, Kii. 1991. "Retirement in Japan." In J. Myers and Jill Quadagno, eds., *States, Labor and the Future of Old-Age Policy*. Philadelphia, Temple University Press.

Tsujinaka Yutaka. 1987. "Rodokai no Saihen to Hachijurokunen Taisei no Imi" [The significance of the reorganization of labor relations and the 1986 system]. *Leviathan* 1:47–72.

Wade, Robert. 1990. *Governing the Market: Economic Theory and the Role of Government in East Asian Industrialization*. Princeton: Princeton University Press.

Watanuki, Joji. 1991. "Social Structure and Voting Behavior." In Scott C. Flanagan et al., eds., *The Japanese Voter*. New Haven: Yale University Press.

Woo-Cumings, Meredith. 1995. "Developmental Bureaucracy in Comparative Perspective: The Evolution of the Korean Civil Service." In Hyung-ki Kim, Michio Muramatsu, T. J. Pempel, and Kozo Yamamura, eds., *The Japanese Civil Service and Economic Development: Catalysts of Change*. Oxford: Oxford University Press.

World Bank. 1993. *The East Asian Miracle: Economic Growth and Public Policy*. New York: Oxford University Press.

Yamamura, Kozo. 1985. "The Cost of Rapid Growth and Capitalist Democracy in Japan." In Leon Lindberg and Charles Maier, eds., *The Politics of Inflation and Economic Stagnation*. Washington, D.C.: Brookings Institution.

Yamazaki, H. 1988. "Kōsei Nenkin Seido no 'Bappon Kaitei.'" In Tokyo Daigaku Shuppankai, ed., *Tenkanki no Fukushi Kokka 2*. Tokyo: Tokyo Daigaku Shuppan.

PART THREE

Models of Capitalism in Advanced Industrial Societies

European Welfare State Regimes: Configurations, Outcomes, Transformations

JOHN D. STEPHENS

In this chapter, I analyze the structure and performance of European welfare states using this volume's "Models of Capitalism" framework as a point of departure. Since the publication of Esping-Andersen's *Three Worlds of Welfare Capitalism* (1990), it has become commonplace to analyze welfare states in advanced capitalist democracies through the lens of a typology of three or four types of "welfare state regimes." In later work, Esping-Andersen and Kolberg (1992) argue that welfare state regimes are interrelated with different labor market regimes. My coauthors and I argue that these welfare state and labor market regimes are in turn interconnected with "production regimes" as identified by Soskice (1999) (Kitschelt et al. 1999; Huber and Stephens 2001). These welfare state / labor market / production regimes are essentially what is captured with the concept of models or types of capitalism.

I begin by elaborating the version of welfare state regime typology I believe is most consistent with the evidence available. I then briefly discuss the interrelationship between these welfare state regimes and labor market and production regimes. In the second section, I show that these different welfare state regimes are associated with and arguably causally related to very different distributive outcomes and levels of poverty. They are also associated with different levels of economic growth and unemployment. Having reviewed the extensive literature on neocorporatism and industrial policy and having conducted my own research, I contend that the performance of the different welfare state regimes on these two conventional indicators of economic health is a product of their associated labor market and production regimes. In the third section, I analyze the changes in welfare state policy and their causes since 1980 in what might be termed the era of retrenchment.

WELFARE STATE, LABOR MARKET, AND PRODUCTION REGIMES

In his path-breaking work on social policy regimes, Esping-Andersen breaks with previous work which classified welfare states along a single dimension

This chapter draws heavily on chapter 4 in Huber and Stephens 2001. I gratefully acknowledge permission to use this material from the University of Chicago Press.

of generosity. Esping-Andersen argues that (1) welfare states vary along multiple dimensions and (2) they cluster around three distinct regimes. While subsequent work on the welfare state has disputed varying aspects of Esping-Andersen's argument, such as the number and type of regimes, the classification of various countries, and the degree to which countries cluster into the three (or four) distinct groups, his typology has proved to be a highly useful heuristic explanatory device. In this chapter, I will adopt Esping-Andersen's typology with a few modifications. First, following Castles and Mitchell (1993), I distinguish an Antipodean type of "wage earner welfare states." While this essay focuses on Europe, it is important to distinguish this group from the liberal welfare states on Europe's northwest periphery (Table 10.1a and 1b). Second, I label his conservative/corporativistic group "Christian democratic." This labeling is consistent with the "liberal" and "social democratic" labels in that it indicates the conformity of welfare state characteristics with the basic preferences of major political tendencies, Christian democratic, secular center and right, and social democratic parties, respectively. More important, the label gets away from the misleading implication of Esping-Andersen's work that the "conservative" welfare states of continental Europe reinforce inequalities created in the market and thus preserve the stratification system. Though there is no question that Christian democratic welfare states preserve gender stratification, they are quite redistributive across income groups, though not as redistributive as social democratic welfare states, as we shall see. Finally, I leave it as an open question how clearly countries cluster into four distinct types. I do contend that within a given country, different aspects of the welfare state "fit" together and the welfare state regime as a whole "fits" with the labor market and production regimes. The groups themselves vary in their homogeneity, with the Scandinavian social democratic group being the most homogenous and the continental Christian democratic being the most heterogeneous. I have divided the Christian democratic group into three subgroups.

The data in Table 10.1a and 1b outline the basic differences between the policy configurations in the different types of welfare states. All data are for 1980 or the closest possible year and thus represent a cut in time before the recent era of retrenchment. The first two columns document—in conjunction with the implicit absent category—years of secular center and right cabinet, and the differences in the political underpinnings of the groups.[1]

1. Political differences are not the only factor that distinguishes the groups. Size of the domestic economy, market structure, and export orientation, among other factors, have shaped the associated labor market and production regimes, which in turn have a feedback effect on the welfare state regimes (e.g., see Stephens 1979, Katzenstein 1985, Hall 1986, and Wallerstein

Table 10.1a Welfare State Regimes, ca. 1980

	(1) Left cabinet years	(2) Christian Democratic cabinet years	(3) Social security expenditure	(4) Transfer payments	(5) Total taxes
Social Democratic Welfare States					
Sweden	30	0	31	18	56
Norway	28	1	20	14	53
Denmark	25	0	26	17	52
Finland	14	0	17	9	36
Mean	24.3	0.3	23.6	14.5	49.4
Christian Democratic Welfare States					
Austria	20	15	21	19	46
Belgium	14	19	21	21	43
Netherlands	8	22	27	26	53
Germany	11	16	23	17	45
France	3	4	25	19	45
Italy	3	30	20	14	33
Switzerland	9	10	13	13	33
Mean	9.6	16.4	21.6	18.4	42.5
Liberal Welfare States					
Canada	0	0	13	10	36
Ireland	3	0	19	13	39
United Kingdom	16	0	17	12	40
United States	0	0	12	11	31
Mean	4.7	0.0	15.2	11.5	36.5
"Wage Earner" Welfare States					
Australia	7	0	11	8	31
New Zealand	10	0	16	10	—
Japan	0	0	10	10	28

SOURCES (by column number):

(1) Left Cabinet: Scored 1 for each year when the left is in government alone, scored as a fraction of the left's seats in parliament of all governing parties' seats for coalition governments from 1946 to 1980 (data from data set in Huber, Ragin, and Stephens 1997).

(2) Christian Democratic Cabinet: Religious parties' government share, coded as for left cabinet (Huber, Ragin, and Stephens 1997).

(3) Social security benefit expenditure as a percentage of GDP (ILO; cited in Huber, Ragin, and Stephens 1997).

(4) Social security transfers as a percentage of GDP (OECD; cited in Huber, Ragin, and Stephens 1997).

(5) Total taxes as a percentage of GDP (OECD; cited in Huber, Ragin, and Stephens 1997).

Table 10.1b Welfare State Regimes, ca. 1980

	(6) Public HEW employment	(7) Health expenditure % public	(8) Spending on non-aged	(9) Decommodi- fication index	(10) Support for mothers' employment
Social Democratic Welfare States					
Sweden	20	92	12.7	39	62
Norway	15	98	8.5	38	43
Denmark	18	85	11.5	38	64
Finland	9	79	10.5	29	66
Mean	15.5	88.5	10.8	36.2	58.8
Christian Democratic Welfare States					
Austria	4	69	4.1	31	—
Belgium	6	82	10.2	32	59
Netherlands	4	76	12.6	32	34
Germany	4	79	8.0	28	36
France	7	79	7.5	28	53
Italy	5	84	3.4	24	36
Switzerland	5	68	—	30	—
Mean	5.0	76.7	7.6	29.3	43.6
Liberal Welfare States					
Canada	7	75	5.7	22	35
Ireland	—	92	6.8	23	—
United Kingdom	8	90	9.2	23	22
United States	5	42	4.5	14	14
Mean	6.7	74.8	6.6	20.6	23.7
"Wage Earner" Welfare States					
Australia	7	62	2.8	13	22
New Zealand	—	84	3.1	17	—
Japan	3	71	2.4	27	—

SOURCES (by column number):
(6) Public health, education, and welfare employment as a percentage of the working age population (Welfare State Exit Entry Project, Science Center-Berlin). Canadian figure provided by
John Myles on the basis of Statistics Canada data.
(7) Public health expenditure as a percentage of total health expenditure (OECD; cited in
Huber, Ragin, and Stephens 1997).
(8) Spending on the non-aged as a percentage of GDP (OECD 1996b, 107).
(9) Decommodification index (Esping-Andersen 1990, 52).
(10) Support for mothers' employment (Gornick et al. 1997).

The Scandinavian countries are distinctive in terms of their years of social democratic governance. Finland is the lowest on this indicator and is also lowest on all of the indicators of welfare state generosity. In the mid-1960s Finland experienced a "system shift" marked by the coming to power of a coalition led by the social democrats and including the communists and other parties, and by unification of unions and the development of a corporatist social pact with the employers. In the subsequent two and a half decades, Finland caught up with her Nordic neighbors in terms of welfare state generosity (Stephens 1996; Huber and Stephens 1998). For instance, between 1980 and 1990, Finland moved from last to first among the Nordic countries on Esping-Andersen's decommodification index (column 11).[2]

Liberal welfare states are characterized by the absence of Christian democratic government and, with the exception of Britain, little or no influence of social democracy in government. The British Labour Party was in office relatively frequently before 1980, and this is reflected in the indicators of social policy, where it appears as more generous than other liberal countries, especially in the area of health care, one of the key elements of the policy initiatives of the first postwar Labour government (see column 7).[3] Keep in mind that the figures in Table 10.1 (and Tables 10.2 and 10.5) cover years quite early in the first Thatcher government and thus do not indicate the effects of her cutbacks.

The "wage earner" welfare states are characterized by strong labor parties, which nonetheless were narrowly defeated in most elections between 1945 and 1980, and by strong unions (see Table 10.2). Earlier in the century, interventionist labor courts awarded Antipodean workers many wage and nonwage benefits that elsewhere were products of welfare state legislation. The postwar political situation reinforced the tendency of the Antipodean labor movements to rely on "social protection by other means," that is, through highly regulated labor markets (Castles 1985).

Since the Christian democratic welfare states are the most heterogeneous, I have broken them down into three subgroups, which will play some role in my subsequent discussion. The first "group" contains only Austria. It is the only Christian democratic welfare state in which social democracy has been more influential than Christian democracy. Both its production regime

---

1990). It is beyond this chapter to trace these links. Evelyne Huber and I do this elsewhere (Huber and Stephens 2001).

2. Olli Kangas, personal communication, 1996.

3. Until separation, Irish policy was made in London and thereafter social policy innovations in Ireland tended to follow the British lead. Thus, the policy patterns in the two countries are much more similar than one would predict given their social and political characteristics.

and to a lesser extent its labor market regime are closer to the social democratic model than to the Christian democratic one. In the comparative political economy literature, it is often classified with Sweden as the most "corporatist" political economy among the advanced industrial democracies. In the next group—Belgium, Netherlands, and Germany—social democracy has been influential but not as influential as Christian democracy. Along with Austria, these countries also are more generous than the other three Christian democratic countries on most of the welfare state indicators in Table 10.1. These countries also share labor market and production regime characteristics with the Nordic economies, which set them off from the other three countries in the Christian democratic group.

As one can see from the table, both the Christian democratic and social democratic welfare states are much more generous than the other groups in terms of their social expenditure (columns 3, 4, 7). Indeed, it would appear that the Christian democratic welfare states actually provide more generous transfer payments than the social democratic welfare states. While it is true that they spend more on transfers, and they are "transfer heavy" as compared to the "service heavy" social democratic welfare states (Huber, Ragin, and Stephens 1993; Huber and Stephens 2000), the transfer spending figures in Table 10.1 for Christian democratic welfare states are high in part because the target populations were large. Unemployment was high, thus expenditure on unemployment compensation was correspondingly high; and in addition, many of these countries dealt with unemployment problems by putting workers on early pensions or disability payments.

Esping-Andersen's decommodification index (column 9) is a better indicator of the generosity of transfer entitlements than the transfer expenditure figure. It is a composite measure of the characteristics of three income transfer programs (pensions, sick pay, and unemployment compensation); the components are various measures of qualifying conditions and benefit duration and income replacements for two categories of workers, a "standard production worker" and those qualifying for only minimum benefits (Esping-Andersen 1990, 49, 54). One can see from the index that social democratic welfare state transfer systems are more generous than the Christian democratic ones.

While not all of the data on which this index is based, the Social Citizenship Indicators Project at the University of Stockholm, are public yet, it is apparent from what is available and parallel data from other sources that a principal reason for the difference between the social democratic and Christian democratic welfare states on the index is that income replacement rates among those with minimum qualifying conditions are much better in the Nordic countries (Palme 1990; Kangas 1991; Carroll 1994; OECD 1994). Palme's data on minimum and standard pensions for this period show that minimum replacement rates in the Nordic countries are considerably higher than in all other countries except Austria and Netherlands, which achieve parity with the Nordic countries (Palme 1990). Indeed, the Christian democratic countries as a group, even with Austria and Netherlands included, actually come out worse than the liberal welfare states on this measure. The reason for this is obvious: all the Scandinavian countries have (or had as of 1980) a basic flat rate pension that goes to all citizens when they reach retirement age, an earnings-related pension dependent on years of work and income, and a supplement for all those with low or no earnings-related pensions. Most of the continental countries lack the citizenship pension or its equivalent. By contrast, income replacement rates of the "standard production worker" are only slightly higher in the social democratic countries than in Christian democratic countries, and in both groups, they are considerably higher than in the liberal welfare states. In the case of unemployment insurance, OECD (1994) figures show a similar pattern; there is a much larger difference between the Christian democratic and social democratic welfare states in replacement rates for the low income workers than for workers with the average wage.

It is not in the structure of transfers that the social democratic welfare states and Christian democratic welfare states differ most, though. As Evelyne Huber and I have shown in an analysis of pooled times series data, the most distinctive feature of the social democratic welfare state is the public funding *and* delivery of social services (Huber and Stephens 2000). While in all welfare states the government is the primary provider of education, only in the social democratic welfare states does the government provide a broad range of social services. One can see the dramatic differences in this regard from the figures for public health, education, and welfare employment as a percentage of the working-age population in column 6 of Table 10.1. In the case of health care, it is clear from the figures in column 7 that other welfare states pick up the tab for health but are not the primary deliverers of it. Outside the Nordic countries, only three other countries, the United Kingdom, New Zealand, and from 1978, Italy, had national health services, and in two of these (the United Kingdom and New Zealand), they were products of social democratic governments.

It is apparent from the very great differences in public social service employment (column 6), that the social democratic welfare states are virtually alone in providing a wide range of services in addition to education, and in the three countries just mentioned, health care. The expansion of these programs—day care, elder care, job training programs, temporary employment programs in the public services, and afterschool programs, to name a few examples; along with improvement of maternal and parental leave programs—were the main areas of welfare state innovation in the Nordic countries in the 1970s and 1980s. The differences in the level of public social services are the reason why taxation levels in social democratic welfare states are significantly higher than in the Christian democratic welfare states, averaging close to 49 percent of GDP compared to 42 percent in the latter group (Table 10.1, column 5) despite the fact that transfer payments are actually lower on the average in the social democratic welfare states.

Two distinctive features of the social service intensiveness of the social democratic welfare states are worth underlining. First, they are "women friendly" and have promoted the expansion of women's labor force participation. This is reflected in the index in column 10, which measures the extent to which a wide range of social provisions facilitate the entry of mothers with young children into the labor force. Second, they are aimed at the non-aged, as can be seen from the OECD figures on spending on the non-aged as a percentage of GDP in column 8 of Table 10.1.[4] In both cases, these distinctive features involve investment in human capital and in the mobilization of labor.

Table 10.2 outlines some of the parameters of the labor market regimes associated with the welfare state types. Given that at least some strands of the literature on corporatism consider social democratic government to be a precondition for corporatism, it is not surprising that social democratic welfare states are highly corporatist as indicated by Lehmbruch's (1984) scale of corporatism (column 4). The Christian democratic welfare states, particularly the four countries of the northern tier, are also highly corporatistic. Union organization is very high in the social democratic countries. While union density is lower in the Christian democratic countries, coverage of union contracts is quite high because of agreements between employers and unions that extend union agreements to nonunionized workers or government legislation that achieves the same end. Wage setting is also very centralized in the social democratic welfare states and very decentralized in the liberal welfare states, with the Christian democratic welfare states falling in

---

4. These figures underestimate the differences between the social democratic and Christian democratic welfare states because they include spending on early pensions and disability pensions, which were employed as means of labor force reduction in a number of the Christian democratic welfare states at this time.

between. As a result of the differences in union organization, bargaining centralization, wage setting, and union contract coverage, wage dispersion is much greater in the liberal welfare states than in the social democratic welfare states, again with the Christian democratic welfare states falling in between, but in this case clearly closer to the social democratic group.[5] In fact, other than in Austria, wage dispersion in the northern tier countries is remarkably similar to that in the Nordic countries, which is surprising given the absence of explicit Nordic-type wage compression policies on the part of the unions in these countries.[6]

The social democratic welfare states are very different from the Christian democratic welfare states, including those of the northern tier, in terms of women's labor force participation and, as a result, in the levels of total labor force participation of the working-age population. The high level of women's labor force participation is both a result and a cause of the Nordic welfare state / labor market pattern (Huber and Stephens 2000). As of 1960, the Nordic countries were not distinctive in the level of public social service employment and, with the exception of Finland, in the level of women's labor force participation. By the mid-1960s, vigorous growth in all of the economies of northern continental Europe (Austria, Switzerland, Germany, France, and Benelux) and Scandinavia had produced high rates of male labor force participation and very low unemployment among males. Unlike the northern continental countries, in part because of the influence of the strong union movements, the Scandinavian countries limited recruitment of non-Nordic foreign labor, which provided greater job opportunities for women in the private sector.

This growth of women's labor force participation stimulated demands by women for the expansion of day care and other social services, which, along with social democratic governance, helped fuel the growth of public social service sector employment. These public social service jobs were filled very disproportionately by women, so this in turn stimulated a further expansion of women's labor force participation. As a consequence, by the mid-1970s, all four Nordic countries were already characterized both by high levels of women's labor force participation and by high levels of public health, education, and welfare employment. This feedback cycle between left/union strength, women's labor force participation, and public service employment continued to the late 1980s when the employment crisis hit Sweden, Finland,

5. The wage dispersion figures are the 90–10 ratio, that is, the wages of a full-time employee at the 90th percentile of the wage distribution are expressed as a multiple of one at the 10th percentile.

6. For a discussion of Austria's outlier status in this regard, see Pontusson 1996.

Table 10.2 Labor Market Regimes, ca. 1980

	(1)[a] Female labor force participation	(2)[b] Union density	(3)[c] Union coverage	(4) Corporatism index	(5) Centralization of wage setting	(6)[d] Wage dispersion	(7)[e] ALMP spending
Social Democratic Welfare States							
Sweden	74	82	83	4	60	2.0	75
Norway	62	59	75	4	57	2.0	26
Denmark	71	70	—	3	60	2.1	20
Finland	70	73	95	3	—	2.5	18
Mean	69.3	71.1	84.3	3.5	59.0	2.2	35
Christian Democratic Welfare States							
Austria	49	66	71	4	20	3.5	8
Belgium	47	72	90	3	34	2.4	10
Netherlands	35	38	60	4	47	2.5	10
Germany	51	40	76	3	20	2.7	10
France	54	28	92	—	20	3.3	7
Italy	39	51		2	40	2.6	4
Switzerland	54	35		3	—	2.7	23
Mean	47.0	47.0	77.8	3.2	30.2	2.8	10
Liberal Welfare States							
Canada	57	31	38	1	9	4.0	6
Ireland	36	68		3	—	2.8	9
United Kingdom	58	48	47	2	28	2.8	6
United States	60	25	18	1	6	4.8	4
Mean	52.8	43.0	34.3	1.8	14.3	3.9	6

Table 10.2 Labor Market Regimes, ca. 1980 (*continued*)

	(1)[a] Female labor force participation	(2)[b] Union density	(3)[c] Union coverage	(4) Corporatism index	(5) Centralization of wage setting	(6)[d] Wage dispersion	(7)[e] ALMP spending
"Wage Earner" Welfare States							
Australia	53	51	80	1	40	2.8	5
New Zealand	45	59	67	1	—	2.9	20
Japan	54	31	21	—[f]	16	3.0	6

SOURCES (by column number):

(1) OECD; cited in Huber, Ragin, and Stephens 1997.

(2) Huber, Ragin, and Stephens 1997; Visser 1996.

(3) Traxler 1994.

(4) Lehmbruch 1984.

(5) Wallerstein 1999.

(6) OECD 1996a.

NOTES:

[a] Percentage of women aged fifteen to sixty-four in the labor force.

[b] Union membership as a percentage of total wage and salary earners.

[c] Union contract coverage as a percentage of total wage and salary earners.

[d] The wages of a full-time employee at the 90th percentile of the wage distribution as a multiple of the wages of one at the 10th percentile. The data for Belgium, the Netherlands, and New Zealand are from the mid-1980s; the data for Switzerland, from 1991.

[e] Active labor market spending as a percentage of GDP divided by the percentage of the labor force unemployed. Computed from data in Nickell 1997 by David Bradley.

[f] Concertation without labor.

and to a lesser extent, Norway. Indeed, as we pointed out, one of the main areas of welfare state innovation in all four Nordic countries was in the area of gender relations, particularly policies enabling women to enter the labor force, not only through services such as day care, but also through transfers, such as paid parental leave.

The continental Christian democratic welfare states followed a quite different trajectory. The labor migration issue was handled differently as foreign labor was imported in large numbers, arguably because of a combination of Christian democratic emphasis on the traditional male breadwinner family and weaker union influence on labor recruitment policies. Moreover, in these countries, union contracts cover a large proportion of the labor force, which prevented the expansion of a low-wage service sector, a source of employment for women in liberal welfare states (Esping-Andersen 1990). As a result women's labor force participation is the lowest in the continental Christian democratic welfare states of the four welfare state types, despite the fact that social policy is more "working mother friendly" in the Christian democratic welfare states (compare column 1 of Table 10.2 with column 10 of Table 10.1).

As a result of these labor market configurations, then, neither social democratic nor Christian democratic welfare states produce the dualist labor markets with a low-wage sector, largely though not entirely in services, a characteristic of the liberal welfare states.[7] This "fits" with the generous welfare states of these countries and with an overall "high road" economic strategy and thus with the type of production regime these countries have. Soskice adopts the term "production regime" from Hollingsworth, Schmitter, and Streeck (1993) to refer to what he termed "national institutional frameworks of incentives and constraints," a no doubt clumsier but more descriptive phrase (Soskice 1999).

Soskice contends that different production regimes are critically shaped by employer organization. In his view, employer organization takes three distinctive forms: coordination at the industry or subindustry level in Germany and in most Northern European economies (industry-coordinated market economies); coordination among groups of companies across industries in Japan and Korea (group-coordinated market economies); or absence of coordination in Anglo-American countries (uncoordinated market economies). In coordinated economies, employers are able to organize collectively in train-

---

7. Italy does have a low-wage sector in the blackmarket, and Spain and Portugal have yet larger blackmarket and informal sectors.

ing their labor force, sharing technology, setting product standards, and bargaining with employees. The capacity for collective action on the part of employers shapes stable patterns of economic governance encompassing a country's financial system, its vocational training, and its system of industrial relations.

In the industry-coordinated market economies of Central and Northern Europe, initial labor skills are effectively organized in companies or with strong company and union involvement in public schools. Unions are organized mainly along industrial lines and play an important cooperative role in organizing working conditions within companies and in setting wage levels for the economy as a whole. Either banks and industries are closely linked, providing industries with preferential sources of long-term credit; or the state plays a major role in bank ownership and performs a similar role in preferential credit provision for industry. In uncoordinated market economies, however, training for lower-level workers is not undertaken by private business and is generally ineffective. Private sector trade unions are viewed as impediments in employer decision making, have little role in coordinating their activities, and are weak. Ties between banks and industry are weak, and industries must rely on competitive markets to raise capital.

Together, these institutions—relations among employers, the organization of the financial system, vocational training, and industrial relations—comprise a country's production regime, a deeply embedded set of institutions that is relatively impervious to short-run political manipulation. While Soskice's analysis focuses on innovation in manufacturing, these institutional frameworks can be seen as national/economy wide (see Kitschelt et al. 1999). With this extension, one can distinguish a Nordic pattern in which there is economy-wide bargaining and a large state role in economic management from the continental pattern, in which bargaining is generally carried on at the industry level and the state's role is more muted. This extension also allows us to extend the notion of production regime to governmental policies designed to achieve growth and employment, such as macroeconomic policy, trade policy, and financial regulation (Huber and Stephens 1998, 2001). In the social democratic welfare states and the northern tier of Christian democratic welfare states, the combination of strong unions and dependence on competitive exports necessitated a policy of wage restraint and the centralization of unions, employers' organizations, and the bargaining process has made such a policy possible. The unions' "side payment" for wage restraint has been full employment and the development of the generous welfare state described above.

In the case of the Nordic countries and Austria, fiscal and monetary policies were moderately countercyclical and backed up by occasional devaluations, except for Finland where these policies tended to be procyclical. The core of the long-term growth/employment policy, however, and this cannot be overemphasized, was a combination of supply-side and tax policies which themselves largely affected the supply side. The supply-side policies extended beyond general supply-side policies (such as education, infrastructure, cheap credit policies, and generalized support for R and D) to selective policies (such as active labor market policy, credit policies favoring industrial borrowers over consumers and speculators, regional policies, and subsidies or subsidized credit to selected industries). Tax policies heavily favored reinvestment of profits over distribution. Interest rates were kept low through credit rationing, state supply of cheap credit, and public sector surpluses. These policies were predicated on financial controls. Accordingly, fiscal policy was generally austere. These countries usually ran budget surpluses (see Table 10.3). The demand side of the social democratic growth/employment models was only in part internally generated; it was also a result of demand for exports created by the vigorous postwar growth in the core advanced capitalist economies of North America and Europe.

In the context of this volume with its intent on drawing comparative implications for models in Latin America, it is worth underlining that economic models of the Nordic and most of the northern tier countries were characterized by (1) fiscal conservatism, (2) emphasis on supply-side measures, (3) wage restraint, (4) openness to trade, and (5) financial regulation. In Latin America, governments pursuing redistributive reforms in the past usually pursued the opposite policies on points 1–4; and indeed, it is generally assumed that if a country is constrained to follow policies 1–4, as all countries undergoing structural adjustment are, social democratic redistributive reform is impossible.[8] The European experience shows that this is not the case. While financial deregulation does eliminate an important tool of economic management used by social democratic governments in the past, that alone does not make social democratic reformism impossible. Of course, neoliberalism, insofar as it prescribes indiscriminate state shrinking, is incompatible with social democratic reform, but governments that successfully follow policies 1–4 will not be constrained by external forces to shrink state activity.

A frequent criticism of Esping-Andersen's typology is that he assumes, not only that most if not all of the advanced industrial democracies can be

8. However, see Bresser Pereira et al. 1993.

Table 10.3 Export Dependence and Budget Deficits

	Exports as a percentage of GDP			Budget surplus as a percentage of GDP		
	1960–73	1974–79	1980–89	1960–73	1974–79	1980–89
Social Democratic Political Economies						
Sweden	22	29	33	2.8	−0.4	−3.1
Norway	40	43	43	3.3	1.4	4.9
Denmark	30	29	35	1.4	0.6	−3.4
Finland	22	27	30	2.0	1.1	−1.0
Mean	28.5	32.0	35.3	2.4	0.7	−0.7
Christian Democratic Political Economies						
Austria	27	33	38	−0.1	−2.3	−3.7
Belgium	38	50	67	−1.8	−4.2	−8.8
Netherlands	46	49	57	−0.3	−5.7	−6.9
Germany	21	27	32	0.3	−1.6	−2.6
France	13	20	22	−0.3	−2.5	−3.8
Italy	15	20	20	−3.2	−9.2	−11.6
Switzerland	30	34	36	4.6	3.7	3.7
Mean	27.1	33.3	38.9	−0.1	−3.1	−4.8
Liberal Political Economies						
Canada	20	24	27	−1.6	−3.3	−6.2
Ireland	35	45	54	−3.8	−9.2	−11.7
United Kingdom	20	27	27	−1.8	−5.8	−3.7
United States	5	8	8	−1.7	−3.6	−4.3
Mean	20.0	26.0	29.0	−2.2	−5.5	−6.5
Antipodean Political Economies						
Australia	15	15	16	1.4	−2.9	−3.4
New Zealand	23	27	30	—	—	—
Japan	11	13	15	1.5	−3.3	−2.5

SOURCE: OECD; cited in Huber, Ragin, and Stephens 1997.

classified into three distinct types, but also that the countries "cluster." This problem is further aggravated when one attempts to add characteristics of the production regime to the analysis. So, for instance, while most of the Christian democratic welfare states of continental Europe are coordinated market economies, Soskice points out that the Netherlands, Italy, and France only partly fit this designation. Rather than abandoning the typology, our solution is to treat the types as ideal types to which countries more or less conform. Moreover, we would contend that within each country, the aspects of its welfare state, labor market, and production regimes do "fit" each other. Statically, this fit would appear to be "functional"; dynamically and historically, the policies and practices making up the overall regime were initiated and adjusted to fit, and on the margin transform, the existing regime.[9]

THE PERFORMANCE OF REGIMES

The combined labor market and welfare state regimes along with the production regime underpinning them result in very large differences in the distributive outcomes in the three groups of welfare states, as one can see from Table 10.4.[10] The differences in income distribution after direct taxes and transfer payments between the social democratic welfare states and the northern tier of Christian democratic welfare states and the other countries are particularly striking (column 1). These differences are in part a result of the wage bargaining system outlined above and shown in Table 10.2, column 5, and in part the result of the redistribution effected by direct taxes and transfers (column 2). While figures in column 2 (the percentage reduction in inequality after direct taxes are levied and transfers are paid) overstate the redistributive effect of taxes and transfers,[11] neither they nor the figures in column 1 include the distributive effect of free or subsidized public goods and services, which would increase equality in all welfare states (Saunders 1991), but particularly in the social democratic welfare states.

Columns 4–6 of Table 10.4 document differences in poverty levels in countries with different welfare state regimes. Poverty is defined as less than 50 percent of median income in the country in question. Again, it is clear that the social democratic welfare states did very well in combating poverty and the liberal welfare states very poorly. One also observes a difference between the northern and southern Christian democratic welfare states.

9. This is not meant to imply that any of the historical actors necessarily had to have an accurate picture of how the total regime fit together.

10. All of the figures in Table 10.4 are from Luxembourg Income Surveys; calculations by David Bradley.

11. Gøsta Esping-Andersen (personal communication, 1994) points out that Mitchell's figures overestimate redistribution because many retired people, particularly in countries in which public pension systems are generous, will have little or no pre-transfer income, thus exaggerating the degree of pre-transfer income inequality. Note that though this would raise the level of pre-transfer income inequality; it would not affect post-tax and transfer inequality. Thus, the figures in column 1 of the table are accurate and, given the methodology of the LIS surveys, comparable measures of inequality in disposable income.

However, the southern Christian democratic welfare states appear to lie between the social democratic and northern Christian democratic welfare states on the one hand, and liberal welfare states on the other, on these measures, rather than much closer to the liberal welfare states, as they are in the income distribution/redistribution data in columns 1–3.

Without embarking on a detailed primary analysis of the LIS data, it is difficult to pinpoint with precision which policies have been most responsible for the pre-post tax/transfer reduction in inequality and the crossnational variations in disposable income inequality. Crossnational differences in disposable income inequality are in part a product of variations in market income inequality, and these in turn are in large part a product of wage dispersion and unemployment levels. From Tables 10.2 and 10.5, one can see that part of the reason for egalitarian outcomes in the social democratic welfare states and the northern tier of Christian democratic welfare states is that, in the early 1980s, these countries had compressed wage differentials or low unemployment or both.

As to the redistribution effected by taxes and transfers, on the basis of Korpi and Palme's (1998) analysis, one can say with some confidence what the impact is of various types of overall policy configurations on crossnational differences in the reduction in inequality. They demonstrate that the systems which combine "basic security," usually transfers with flat-rate benefits, and "income security," transfers with earnings-related benefits, have the greatest redistributive impact. The Nordic pension systems, which combine a flat-rate citizenship pension and an earnings-related supplement, are good examples of this type, and Korpi and Palme point out that most other programs and thus the Nordic welfare states as a whole have this structure. What is very surprising, so surprising that Korpi and Palme (1998) term it the "paradox of redistribution," is that these welfare states are more redistributive than systems which rely on heavily "targeted" benefits, benefits for which there is an income or means test. While the use of targeted benefits is common among the liberal welfare states, it is the Antipodean "wage-earner welfare states" which carry this principle the furthest. Most transfers in these countries, including public pensions, are designed to exclude upper income groups.

In contrast to the social democratic welfare states, entitlements in the Christian democratic welfare states are almost entirely employment based and earnings related. They generally lack the basic security tier; the task of meeting the needs of those outside the labor market falls to means-tested benefits. Perhaps even more surprising than Korpi and Palme's paradox is that the Christian democratic welfare states with their great reliance on

Table 10.4 Welfare State Outcome, ca. 1980

	Year of LIS survey	(1)a Post-tax transfer GINI	(2)b Redistribution resulting from taxes and transfers	(3)c Post-tax transfer GINI-aged	(4) Percentage of group in poverty	(5)	(6)
					25–59d	Agede	Single mothersf
Social Democratic Welfare States							
Sweden	1981	.20	52	.16	4.8	0.3	7.7
Norway	1979	.22	40	.26	3.7	4.7	12.1
Denmark	1987	.26	36	.24	4.8	9.2	4.5
Finland	1987	.21	38	.22	3.0	3.0	4.8
Mean		.22	41.4	.22	4.1	4.3	7.3
Christian Democratic Welfare States							
Austria	1987	.23	—	.25	2.3	6.0	13.3
Belgium	1985	.23	46	.23	4.4	6.0	14.2
Netherlands	1983	.28	38	.27	6.7	3.9	6.6
Germany	1981	.25	38	.29	4.2	10.0	6.0
France	1984	.33	34	.37	15.9	18.9	22.8
Italy	1986	.31	28	.30	10.5	8.3	17.5
Switzerland	1982	.32	21	.37	6.1	15.2	22.4
Mean		.28	34.2	.30	7.1	9.8	14.7
Liberal Welfare States							
Canada	1981	.29	24	.31	10.3	9.3	42.0
Ireland	1987	.33	35	.32	10.9	4.9	15.4
United Kingdom	1979	.27	33	.26	5.5	4.8	10.8
United States	1979	.31	26	.34	11.9	21.8	42.3
Mean		.30	29.4	.31	9.7	10.2	27.6

Table 10.4 Welfare State Outcome, ca. 1980 (*continued*)

	(1)[a] Post-tax transfer GINI	(2)[b] Redistribution resulting from taxes and transfers	(3)[c] Post-tax transfer GINI-aged	(4)(5)(6) Percentage of group in poverty		
Year of LIS survey				25–59[d]	Aged[e]	Single mothers[f]
"Wage Earner" Welfare States						
Australia	1981	.29	29	.29	9.3	5.3	44.8

SOURCES: All data in Table 10.4 are from Luxembourg Income Surveys. The calculations were done by David Bradley with household adjustments and other definitions such that the figures are consistent with those in Mitchell 1991, Atkinson et al. 1995, and those periodically updated at the LIS website (http://lissy.ceps.lu).

[a] Gini index for disposable household income.

[b] Redistribution: Percentage reduction in the Gini index for pre-tax and -transfer income caused by taxes and transfers (Mitchell 1991).

[c] Gini index for disposable household income among the aged.

[d] Poverty—Age 25–59: Percentage of households in which the household head is between twenty-four and sixty with a disposable income below 50 percent of the average disposable household income

[e] Poverty—Aged: Percentage of households in which the household head is over sixty-five with a disposable income below 50 percent of the average disposable household income

[f] Poverty—single mothers: Percentage of single mothers with disposable incomes below 50 percent of the average disposable (post-tax and post-transfer) household income

employment-based, earnings-related benefits are more egalitarian in their impact than the liberal welfare states with their greater reliance on programs targeted to the needy. That this is true can be readily seen from Table 10.4. Part of the explanation, following Korpi and Palme's logic, is that the Christian democratic welfare states are simply much larger. Though their benefit structures are less egalitarian, they more than make up for it in greater expenditure. In addition, where benefits are generous, they tend to squeeze out private alternatives (see Kangas and Palme 1994 and Stephens 1995). As Kangas and Palme show in their analysis of LIS data on the income of the aged, these private alternatives are *invariably much less egalitarian* than the least egalitarian of public pension systems (the Finnish).[12]

As to the policy measures which are most effective in combating poverty, we can give more precise answers, particularly with regard to the two groups most vulnerable to poverty, the aged and single mothers. Palme's (1990) data on minimum pensions for the early 1980s make it abundantly clear that the level of minimum pensions is the main factor which accounts for the international differences in poverty levels among the aged. The income replacement rates for this group are highest (around 50 percent) in the Nordic countries and Netherlands and France, the five countries with by far the lowest levels of poverty among the aged.

As for single mothers, a complex of labor market characteristics and transfer payments would appear to explain the pattern across welfare state regimes as well as outliers within the types.[13] The employment levels among single mothers and thus policies supporting mothers' employment are certainly very important, but low levels of wage dispersion, which indicate the absence of subpoverty full-time work, certainly contributed to the comparatively very low levels of poverty among single mothers in the Nordic countries. What is surprising, given the low overall level of women's labor force participation in Christian democratic welfare states, is that labor force participation among lone mothers in these countries was higher than in the liberal welfare states and only a bit lower than in the social democratic welfare states. This almost certainly was due to the stronger supportive policies for

---

12. This begs the question of why targeted welfare states (and targeted welfare policies within welfare states) are so ungenerous. The answer generally given in the comparative welfare states literature is that precisely because they are targeted, they have a narrow support base and thus few supporters and many opponents.

13. Aside from the data in Tables 10.4, cols. 1–3, the following data were consulted for the generalizations made in the next two paragraphs: labor force participation among single mothers—Bradshaw et al. 1993; social assistance—Gough et al. 1997; family allowances—Wennemo 1994; unemployment compensation—OECD Jobs Study replacement rate data, Carroll 1999, and Esping-Andersen 1990.

mothers' employment in Christian democratic welfare states (Table 10.1, column 10; Gornick et al. 1998). The intermediate levels of wage dispersion in the Christian democratic welfare state should also have contributed to the intermediate levels of poverty among single mothers.

In terms of transfer payments, family (child) allowances were clearly of great importance, especially for low income families, since they were flat rate or means tested and never income related. On the average, family allowances were higher in Christian democratic welfare states than in social democratic welfare states, with liberal welfare states again ranking on the bottom (Wennemo 1994). Social assistance and unemployment compensation, especially for low-paid workers, reinforced the overall pattern, since the Nordic welfare states provided the most generous transfers followed by Christian democratic welfare states and then the liberal welfare states.

Given the demonstrated effectiveness of minimum pensions and flat-rate child allowances as antipoverty measures, it is important to inquire into the conditions under which effective minimum pension systems in the form of flat-rate, tax-financed citizenship pensions were first introduced. One can then ask whether these conditions were in any way comparable to those in Latin America at present. Of course, these pensions, entitlement to which is based on citizenship and not employment, and which are financed out of general revenue, not contributions from employers or the insured, could theoretically have been set so low as to leave recipients below a subsistence minimum, which is the case for social assistance pensions in the Latin American countries that have them. However, that was neither the intention of the legislators nor the demand of their support bases, and it was not the outcome of citizenship pensions either. The best case for comparison with Latin America is Finland, since it was the least developed of the Nordic countries in the 1950s. Finland introduced citizenship pensions in 1956, when its Real Gross Domestic Product per capita, expressed in constant 1985 U.S. dollars, was at $4,600; the comparable figure for Chile, for instance, in 1992 was $4,890.[14] Finland in 1956 had still a very large agricultural population, and the agrarian party was the dominant political force. It was precisely this constituency of small farmers who had an interest in tax-financed, flat-rate pensions, and the agrarian party formed an alliance with the social democratic party to introduce them. The social democrats alone would not have been strong enough to pass a pension system, and organized labor was comparatively weak and internally divided. The point is that this type of scheme

14. These figures are from the Penn World Tables, the best source for comparable data. They are available at www.nber.org/pwt56.html.

is affordable at the stage of development of the more advanced Latin American countries, and that it is appropriate in a context where a large proportion of the population is not in formal-sector-dependent employment.

Table 10.5 outlines the performance of the different welfare state regimes on growth and employment. Here it is impossible to embark on even a brief summary of the vast literature on the comparative economic performance of advanced industrial societies, not to speak of presenting my own view of the state of this debate. Though this is of obvious importance for the broader concerns of this volume, it is beyond the scope of this chapter to embark on this task. Let me make a few points of relevance to the current social policy discussion in Latin America. First, as Table 10.5 indicates, it is difficult to maintain that the generous social democratic and Christian democratic welfare states have been a clear drag on economic growth or unemployment levels. A more complex argument might be made in which it is claimed that generous social policy and high taxes produce microlevel disincentives that are a drag on growth, but then the associated labor market and production regimes provide contrary incentives that more than make up for them.[15] In any case, there is no evidence from the postwar record of Europe that the same regime cannot simultaneously and successfully promote growth and redistribution, something that Hirschmann (1979) has observed no Latin American regime has done successfully.

Second, both the social democratic and Christian democratic welfare states were built in economies very open to trade (see Table 10.3) and, especially in the social democratic welfare states, around the interests of the export-sector workers, whose unions were the dominant force within their respective union movements. These workers and unions had and have strong interests in the competitiveness of the export economies of their countries. While it is true that demographic change and rises in unemployment have put severe pressures on the welfare state, it is not true even now that entitlements have made export industry uncompetitive. For example, at the same time as the Swedish welfare state was going through a serious crisis in the mid-1990s, Swedish export industry had several consecutive spectacular years. On the basis of my work with Evelyne Huber (Huber and Stephens 1998, 2001), I contend that there is very little evidence to support the thesis

15. Agell (1996) claims that micro disincentives were a serious problem in Sweden, while Korpi (1996) and Dowrick (1996) argue the aggregate growth figures do not sustain the view that the welfare state is a drag on growth. What I am pointing out in the text is that both assertions could be true. In fact, a recent comprehensive review of the empirical literature on the work disincentives of taxes and social benefits reveals that the studies to date yield very contradictory findings (Atkinson and Mogensen 1993).

that the increasing volume of world trade has made generous welfare states uncompetitive. As the discussion of the welfare state / labor market / production regimes of the European core, especially the social democratic welfare states and the northern tier of Christian democratic welfare states should have made clear, these countries are occupying a high-road niche in the world economy based on highly skilled and educated labor, cooperative production, and capital-intensive production techniques, which is compatible with both high wages and generous social benefits.

RETRENCHMENT IN THE POST-1980 PERIOD

Rollbacks in welfare state programs have been a universal phenomenon in the past two decades.[16] The timing and severity of such rollbacks demonstrate that they were largely unemployment driven. The countries where unemployment rose early (Denmark and the Netherlands) initiated cuts in the mid-1970s; the countries where unemployment rose late (Sweden, Norway, and Finland) continued to expand welfare state entitlements until the late 1980s. The countries where unemployment levels remained very high for a long time (e.g., the Netherlands) made deeper cuts than the countries where they remained more moderate (e.g., Norway). This is not to say that all the policy changes were somehow dictated by economic constraints; perceptions and beliefs about the effectiveness of different policies in achieving certain goals did play a role. Thus, the rising hegemony of neoliberal doctrines certainly contributed to the rollbacks.

These rollbacks in most cases did no more than reduce the increase in welfare state expenditures. In fact, if one looks at the aggregate data for the different welfare state types, the average annual increase in most indicators of welfare state expenditures in the 1970s was higher than it had been in the Golden Age of postwar capitalism (i.e., 1946–73), and they continued to increase in the 1980s, though at a slower pace than in the previous two periods. Essentially, in the 1970s governments countered the deteriorating economic situation with traditional Keynesian countercyclical policies, but by the 1980s they had all realized that the rules of the economic game had changed and demanded new approaches. Still, the increase in claimants of benefits kept pushing up expenditures.

Retrenchments began virtually everywhere with lags in adjustments of benefits to inflation and increased copayments for welfare state services,

16. This section summarizes the findings of Stephens et al. 1999.

Table 10.5 Unemployment and Growth

	Unemployment					Growth				
	1960–73	1974–79	1980–89	1990–94	1995–98	1960–73	1973–79	1979–89	1990–94	1995–97
Social Democratic Welfare States										
Sweden	1.9	1.9	2.4	5.2	7.6	3.4	1.5	1.8	−1.6	2.2
Norway	1.0	1.8	2.7	5.6	4.3	3.5	4.4	2.3	2.0	3.8
Denmark	1.4	6.0	8.1	10.9	6.3	3.6	1.6	1.8	1.0	2.7
Finland	2.0	4.6	5.1	12.3	14.2	4.5	1.8	3.2	−3.6	4.5
Mean	1.6	3.6	4.6	8.5	8.1	3.8	2.3	2.3	−.6	3.3
Christian Democratic Welfare States										
Austria	1.7	1.6	3.3	3.9	4.1	4.3	3.0	1.9	1.0	1.9
Belgium	2.2	5.7	11.3	10.7	12.5	4.4	2.1	1.9	.1.2	2.0
Netherlands	1.3	5.0	9.7	6.2	5.8	3.6	1.9	1.1	1.2	3.3
Germany	.8	3.4	6.7	7.8	9.0	3.7	2.5	1.7	2.1	1.3
France	2.0	4.6	9.1	10.6	12.0	4.3	2.3	1.6	.2	1.5
Italy	5.3	6.3	9.3	10.6	12.1	4.6	3.2	2.4	.7	1.5
Switzerland	.0	.4	.6	2.7	3.9	3.0	−.1	1.8	−.8	.4
Mean	1.9	3.9	7.1	7.5	8.5	4.0	2.1	1.8	.8	1.7
Liberal Welfare States										
Canada	5.0	7.2	9.3	10.3	9.2	3.6	2.9	1.8	−1.0	1.2
Ireland	5.2	7.6	14.3	14.9	10.5	3.7	3.3	2.7	4.8	9.4
UK	1.9	4.2	95.	8.4	7.4	2.6	1.5	2.2	−.3	2.5
USA	5.0	7.0	7.6	6.6	5.1	2.6	1.4	1.5	.8	3.3
Mean	4.3	6.5	10.2	10.1	8.1	3.1	2.3	2.1	1.1	4.1
"Wage Earner" Welfare States										
Australia	1.0	5.1	7.5	9.6	8.4	3.2	1.5	1.8	.3	2.2
New Zealand	.2	.8	4.4	9.2	6.6	2.2	.2	−1.4	.6	.7
Japan	1.3	1.8	2.4	2.3	3.5	8.3	2.5	3.4	2.2	1.7

SOURCES: OECD various years

particularly health care. The data on the public share of total healthcare expenditures reflects these economizing measures; the average annual increase in the public share was already lower in the 1970s than in the earlier period, and in the 1980s the public share declined. Increases in waiting days for benefits, decreases in the length of time for which the most generous benefits could be claimed, and decreases in replacement rates followed. Eligibility criteria for a variety of programs were stiffened, particularly for unemployment and disability benefits. Only rarely were entire programs abandoned or radically changed, such as the maternity and death grants and the child benefit in Britain. Nevertheless, the cumulation of all these changes meant in some cases a significant reduction of entitlements.

From a Latin American perspective, one of the most notable trends has been for governments to deal with the crisis of pension systems, a crisis which is largely demographically driven, by moving away from a pay-as-you-go system with defined benefits to a system in which benefits depend on contributions accompanied by the institution of or an increase in advance funding. In social democratic and Christian democratic Europe, this falls far short of the transformation of the public system to a statutory, compulsory, privately administered, and fully funded pension system along Chilean lines. However, in some cases in which the public system did not provide high earnings-related income-replacement rates, something like the Chilean system has developed via collective bargaining. For instance, in the Netherlands and Denmark, the labor market partners have negotiated earnings-related contributory pension schemes which have been legally extended to other employees and thus cover 70 percent of the workforce.[17] Note that in none of these cases has the pension system as a whole been "Chileanized," since they have provisions—such as flat-rate, tax-financed citizens pensions, minimums built into contributory basic public pension schemes, or pension-tested supplements—which provide a floor for those with little or no pensions under the contributory, earnings-related schemes. In addition, the pension funds are managed as collective, not individual accounts, which reduces individual and cohort risks.

In the United Kingdom in 1985, the Thatcher government passed legislation that, while maintaining the governmental earnings-related supplementary pension systems (SERPs), created a system in which there are strong incentives for people, particularly for younger people, to opt out into private schemes. By the mid-1990s, when participation in SERPs was already

17. I thank John Myles and Paul Pierson for the information on recent changes in the Dutch, Danish, and British pension systems contained in this and the following paragraphs; see Myles and Pierson 2001.

down to 18 percent, additional legislation furthered this process. Thus most British employees are now covered by a system that combines a governmental basic system and a statutory contributory earnings-related system along Chilean lines.

Data analyses carried out by Evelyne Huber, Leonard Ray, and myself show a sharp decline in partisan effects on welfare state expansion/retrenchment, with one important exception, public social service employment (Stephens et al. 1999). Curtailment of entitlements, or at best defense of existing entitlements, was on the agenda everywhere. The right was constrained in its ability to cut by the popularity of most of the large welfare state programs, and the left was constrained in its ability to raise taxes to keep the programs on a sound financial basis by the economic slowdown. The exception was the expansion of the public social service sector in Scandinavia, which continued throughout the 1980s. Given the high concentration of social democratic rule in Scandinavia, this showed up in statistical analyses as a partisan effect on public sector employment.

There were only a few cases of large-scale ideologically driven cuts. The most dramatic were those by the Thatcher government in Britain and the National (conservative) government in New Zealand (it is pertinent that both of these countries have political systems that concentrate power and make it possible to rule without a majority of popular support). This is not to say that there have not been significant differences in the rhetoric of political parties with regard to desirable welfare state reforms, but simply that electoral constraints worked against radical departures from established welfare state models. Only in Great Britain and New Zealand could one speak of an actual system shift from welfare state regimes that used to provide basic income security to welfare state regimes that are essentially residualist, relying heavily on means-testing.

Despite these common trends to retrenchment and the rarity of ideologically motivated rollbacks, there were very important differences between welfare state types in how they handled the higher unemployment. These differences become visible if one looks at activity rates. The well-developed Christian democratic welfare states attempted to deal with unemployment by decreasing the labor supply. Older workers were helped into early retirement or provided with disability pensions. Labor force participation among male workers in the age group 60–64 fell from around 70 percent to 22 percent between 1973 and 1991 in the Netherlands (Hemerijck and Kloosterman 1994); in Germany this rate was 31.5 percent in 1986 (Hinrichs 1991). In the well-developed social democratic welfare states, in contrast, active labor market policies were used to keep up employment.

If we look at total activity rates, including women, the differences become even more pronounced. As noted above, the only significant welfare state expansion in Europe in the 1980s was the expansion of public social services in Scandinavia. Since most of these jobs were filled by women, female labor force participation continued to expand during this decade. This expansion was facilitated by other social reforms, such as expanded parental leave provisions. As a result, by 1993 an average of 72 percent of women worked in the Scandinavian countries, as opposed to only 54 percent in the countries with Christian democratic welfare states. This made for much more favorable ratios of total working to nonworking population in the former compared to the latter.

Given the crucial role that unemployment and activity rates play for the viability of a generous welfare state, we have to seek to understand the reasons for the dramatic increases in unemployment in the 1980s and early 1990s. Of particular importance is the question whether globalization, specifically the internationalization of commodity and capital markets and of production, is responsible for these increases and makes it impossible to return to significantly lower levels of unemployment.[18]

In the first section of this chapter, I underlined the importance of controls on financial markets for the coordinated market economies, particularly the Nordic countries and Austria. Internationalization of financial markets made it more difficult—though not necessarily impossible—for governments to ensure the availability of cheap credit for investment. Since deregulation of external capital flows was linked to deregulation of domestic financial markets, governments have not been able to rely on regulations but have had to provide actual subsidies or tax incentives. This imposes higher costs, which are particularly difficult to absorb in periods of stagnation. Moreover, most subsidies are illegal under EU rules, and many are illegal under GATT rules after the Uruguay Round. Paradoxically, the new international financial environment requires the use of more selective policies, precisely as the dominant economic doctrine has influenced many governments to abandon such policies in favor of a more market-driven allocation of resources.

Internationalization of production heightened the ease with which firms can move across borders, which has caused a shift in bargaining power away from governments and labor toward capital. It has also reduced the incentive for capital to support corporatist arrangements designed to forge compromises with strong labor movements and governments on wage,

18. It is important to note here that, contrary to the commonplace "jobless growth" view, employment creation since 1973 has actually been quite impressive, given the lower growth rates. It has absorbed the rise in women's labor force participation, which has occurred everywhere.

macroeconomic, and social policies. Centralized bargaining is an essential component of corporatist institutions, and as capital's interest in these institutions declined, pressures for decentralization of bargaining intensified. These pressures were particularly strong where centralized bargaining was used to bring about compressed wage differentials between labor with different levels of skill and education, most prominently in Sweden. The decline in centralized bargaining in turn has made it much more difficult to obtain wage restraint in exchange for policies that support employment.

Again, there are significant differences among countries in the extent to which they have been affected by these trends. On the one end, there are countries like Norway and Austria, where governments have traditionally played a very important role in the economy and domestic capital has been weak. There, selective policies to promote investment as well as centralized bargaining have remained comparatively strongest and unemployment lowest. On the other end is Sweden, where the important export firms became increasingly internationalized and employers came to perceive that corporatism worked to the advantage of labor. In this case, bargaining was decentralized, and selective investment promotion was weakened. These developments probably contributed to the rise in unemployment to levels unprecedented since the Depression, though this was primarily a product of policy mistakes of both social democratic and bourgeois governments. Subsequently, corrective measures by the social democratic government succeeded in bringing unemployment down to below 5 percent by 2001.

In the light of the Latin American discussion, it is appropriate here to make some comments on the decentralization and privatization of social services in Sweden, the country that is often pointed to as exemplary for what is good—or bad—about the social democratic welfare state. The first point to note is that decentralization affected only the delivery of welfare state services, not their financing. It entailed a relaxation of central administrative regulations and greater autonomy for municipal governments in choosing methods to achieve objectives and experimenting with greater user influence in the provision of social services, such as child care, elder care, school, and cultural activities (Olsson 1990, 277). The second point to note is that general regulations remained in force to maintain equal access to and uniform quality of these services. Private nonprofit providers were allowed to compete with the public sector in some services, but they received the same financing as their public sector counterparts and were prohibited from levying additional charges and being selective of their clientele. In other words, central regulations prevented the emergence of a two-class educational and social service system, with more affluent people procuring their services from private and the less affluent from public providers.

CONCLUSION

In the initial section of this chapter, taking the works of Esping-Andersen and Soskice as points of departure, I argued that it is heuristically useful to view the political economies of advanced industrial societies as falling into one of four types of welfare state / labor market / production regimes, three of which have two or more representatives in Western Europe. Indeed, the crossnational data I presented on the welfare state and labor market regimes and their outcomes support the view that it is not only heuristically useful, but also that there is empirical evidence that the distinct types exist, even if they do not cluster as cleanly as sometimes implied. Moreover, the regime types are clearly rooted in different political constellations as the labels social democratic, Christian democratic, and liberal imply, though other structural and historical causal factors, such as size of the domestic economy and export dependence, would have to be brought in to provide even a relatively parsimonious account of their origin.

The data on outcomes provided very strong evidence that these regime types are associated with, and arguably causally related to, quite different distributive outcomes and levels of poverty. Students of the comparative social policy of advanced industrial societies will not be very surprised to learn that the social democratic and liberal welfare states exhibit the opposite outcomes. What may be more surprising to at least some of these scholars, given the characterization of the Christian democratic welfare states as "conservative" and "reinforcing market outcomes," is how redistributive they in fact are. In fact, the four countries I have referred to as the "northern tier"— Austria, Germany, the Netherlands, and Belgium—are strikingly similar to their Nordic neighbors in these outcomes as well as in many aspects of their welfare state, labor market, and production regimes.

In terms of the labor market and production regimes, Kitschelt, Lange, Marks, and I have noted some tendency for the Nordic type to converge with the continental type, best represented by Germany. On a somewhat more speculative vein, I would project the emergence of a "Northern European mode of production" in Austria, Benelux, Germany, and Scandinavia, which given its economic clout and, with the entry of Austria, Sweden, and Finland into the European Union, its numeric representation, might become tone-giving for the European Union.[19] In any case, the countries clearly share an egalitarian, high-wage, high-skill, high-labor-productivity, high-capital-intensity niche in the world economy. The data on past growth indicate that these positive developments have not been bought at the expense of growth, and recent developments notwithstanding, there is little indication that these countries have lost their export competitiveness in the world economy.

This is not to say that these welfare state regimes have not been under stress. Demographic change, increased unemployment, and the lower growth that has plagued all industrial societies since 1973 (see Table 10.5) had, by the mid-1980s, by and large halted the expansion of welfare state entitlements and ushered in an era of retrenchment across industrial societies. Outside of pension system change, where past and expected future growth of the aged population has been a key stimulus to reform, the rise in unemployment is by far the most important immediate cause of retrenchment. Quite simply, as unemployment rises, the number of people dependent on the welfare state rises and the number contributing to it declines. Once it is perceived that increased levels of unemployment are more or less permanent, then either cuts in entitlements or increases in taxes become necessary. Neither alternative is popular, but with relatively slow growth and already high tax rates, cuts in entitlements have born the brunt of adjustment. Despite retrenchment, none of the social democratic or Christian democratic welfare states have gone though anything like a regime shift in the their welfare state regimes. In fact, on the balance, they are more generous now than they were in 1973.

The view of the problems of the welfare state propagated in the European conservative and liberal newspapers is that "more is worse" and thus that the Scandinavian welfare states are in the worst position to respond to the challenges of the global economy. This view appeared to find confirmation in the recent economic difficulties of Sweden and Finland. However, as Evelyne Huber and I have shown elsewhere, the problems of these economies are largely caused by conjunctural swings in the economy aggravated by poor, inadvertently procyclical economic management on the part of the governments and, in the Finnish case, by the collapse of Soviet trade (Huber and Stephens 1998), a finding further supported by their recovery in the late 1990s.

Though it is unquestionable that the high level of taxation gives the Scandinavian governments less flexibility in their attempts to restructure the wel-

19. Please note the "might." This ignores collective action problems and the institutions of EU decision making.

fare state, the configuration of their welfare state regimes gives them important advantages over the Christian democratic ones in other regards. First,
the Christian democratic welfare states are much more transfer heavy with
more expenditure directed at the aged. By contrast, the social democratic
welfare states invest more in youth, improvements in human capital, and
labor mobilization. Second, in large part as a direct product of the foregoing, women's labor force participation rates are much higher in Scandinavia than on the continent. As a result, the total ratios of the working
population to the nonworking population are not only much more favorable in the social democratic welfare states than in the Christian democratic,
the ratios are actually improving through time, in sharp contrast to the ratio
of working-age population to the aged, which is so often cited with concern
in discussions of the future of the welfare state. Third, because of the labor
force participation ratio and because fewer entitlements are tied to employment, the division between privileged labor force "insiders" and excluded
"outsiders," above all youth, is less severe in Scandinavia than on the continent (Esping-Andersen 1997).

By contrast, one of the two liberal countries in Europe, the United Kingdom, has undergone very significant changes, more in its labor market
regime than its welfare state regime, but the changes in the welfare state
regime have been quite significant. While it is perhaps not quite correct to
label the changes a "regime shift" because the United Kingdom was already
a liberal regime, it is true that the British welfare state shed most of its social
democratic characteristics (with the important exception of the National
Health Service) during the Thatcher-Major period. From the point of view
of this volume, that is, from the point of view of the future of Latin American social policy, an important and unanswered question is whether it was a
"functional necessity" for the United Kingdom to move in this direction,
given the nature of its economy, an "uncoordinated market economy."[20]
That is, with increased international competition, did the United Kingdom
have to adjust its labor market regime and welfare state regime to allow for
the growth of a low wage economy? As Kitschelt, Lange, Marks, and I point
out, it is true that the liberal market economies have moved much more
strongly in a liberal direction in the past two decades than the two European types of coordinated market economies (Kitschelt et al. 1999). Moreover, the Antipodean type, which grafted a liberal production regime hiding
behind protectionist barriers to a highly regulated labor market providing

20. In their excellent essay on the Reagan and Thatcher governments, King and Wood
(1999) appear to imply this without really saying it.

a high degree of social protection "by other means," did move in a strongly liberal direction once it was perceived that countries could not live from rents collected from primary sector exports. Thus, these countries also moved not only in a liberal direction but also toward a greater "functional fit" between their production, welfare state, and labor market regimes. In addition, both of them did so initially under labor governments, so attributing the change to purely political motives, as one might be inclined to do in the British case, is difficult.

However, in closing, I would like to express some reservation about this line of argument. It implies that these liberal economies are dependent on not only flexible labor markets (which is implied by Soskice's analysis of manufacturing innovation in these countries) but also on low wage markets (which is not implied by his analysis) to maintain and develop international competitiveness. To my knowledge, there is little evidence that these advanced liberal economies have or even could compete in world markets on the basis of low wage exports. Most of the low wage job creation in these countries is in services, most of which are not tradable. How much one can raise the minimum wage directly or indirectly either by increasing employer social benefit contributions or by raising the reservation wage through an increase in entitlements without increasing unemployment is still hotly debated in these societies (see, for example, Card and Krueger 1995).

Of course, the Latin American economies do compete in part on the basis of low wages in the export sector. My discussion of production and welfare state regimes would appear to imply that, in order to have generous social policies, they must move to an (export) production regime in which a country moves up the product cycle by upgrading labor productivity and increasingly competing on the basis of higher quality, higher-skill labor, and more capital-intensive production. While I would argue that, in the long run, the successful development of Latin America depends on that, I would also argue that in the short to medium run, the production regime–welfare state regime link is not absolute: there are variant social policy regimes that are compatible with different production regimes. For instance, Denmark relies much more on small to medium-sized firms for export than do the other Scandinavian countries, yet it has developed a social democratic welfare state regime. The Danish adaptation has been to rely much more on general taxation, above all income taxes and value-added taxes, rather than employer payroll taxes to finance its welfare state, arguably because of the labor cost burden on small employers that the latter would entail. In a different way, the pair contrasts between the United States and Canada and

New Zealand and Australia point in a similar direction. Each of these pairs has an essentially similar production regime but different types of social policy that do make a difference for poverty and inequality. In all four countries, the direction of social policy has been to maintain or create the development of a low wage market. However, Canada and Australia have tried to cushion the impact of this low wage work with compensating social policy, such as negative income taxes or subsidies to the working poor, a sort of "neoliberalism with a human face." Combining my observations on the Danish, Canadian, and Australian cases, one might argue that the short-term "humane" path for Latin American countries is to subsidize the working poor via social policies financed by general taxation.[21] On a theoretical level, the conclusion one can draw from these comparisons is that an uncoordinated production regime does not make the construction of a coherent and redistributive social policy regime impossible, just more difficult. Thus, in the long run, a successful strategy is more likely to be one that includes reforms in both the production and welfare state regimes.

REFERENCES

Agell, Jonas. 1996. "Why Sweden's Welfare State Needed Reform." *The Economic Journal* 106, no. 439 (November): 1760–71.

Atkinson, Anthony B., and Gunnar Viby Mogensen. 1993. *Welfare and Work Incentives: A North European Perspective.* Oxford: Clarendon Press.

Atkinson, Anthony B., Lee Rainwater, and Timothy M. Smeeding. 1995. *Income Distribution in OECD Countries: Evidence from the Luxembourg Income Study.* Paris: Organization for Economic Co-operation and Development.

Bradshaw, Jonathan, John Ditch, Hilary Holmes, and Peter Whiteford. 1993. "A Comparative Study of Child Support in Fifteen Countries." *Journal of European Social Policy* 3, no. 4:255–71.

Bresser Pereira, Luiz Carlos, Jose Maria Maravall, and Adam Przeworski. 1993. *Economic Reforms in New Democracies: A Social Democratic Approach.* New York: Cambridge University Press.

Card, David, and Alan B. Krueger. 1995. *Myth and Measurement: The New Economics of the Minimum Wage.* Princeton: Princeton University Press.

Carroll, Eero. 1994. "The Politics of Unemployment Insurance and Labor Market Policy." Paper presented at the International Sociological Association Meetings, Bielefeld, Germany, July.

21. The pitfall of this strategy is obvious: it subsidizes low-wage work and thus encourages investment in low-wage production rather than in investment in upgrading labor productivity. Therefore, strengthening unions is an important complement to this strategy.

———. 1999. *Emergence and Structuring of Social Insurance Institutions: Comparative Studies on Social Policy and Unemployment Insurance.* Doctoral Dissertation Series, No. 38. Stockholm: University of Stockholm, Swedish Institute for Social Research.

Castles, Francis G. 1985. *The Working Class and Welfare.* Sydney: Allen and Unwin.

Castles, Francis, and Deborah Mitchell. 1993. "Three Worlds of Welfare Capitalism or Four?" In Francis G. Castles, ed., *Families of Nations: Public Policy in Western Democracies.* Brookfield, Vt.: Dartmouth University Press.

Dowrick, Steve. 1996. "Swedish Economic Performance and Swedish Economic Debate: A View from Outside." *The Economic Journal* 106, no. 439 (November): 1772–79.

Esping-Andersen, Gøsta. 1990. *The Three Worlds of Welfare Capitalism.* Princeton: Princeton University Press.

———. 1997. "Welfare States at the End of the Century: The Impact of Labour Market, Family, and Demographic Change." In *Family, Market, and Community: Equity and Efficiency in Social Policy.* Paris: OECD.

Esping-Andersen, Gøsta, and Jon Eivind Kolberg. 1992. "Welfare States and Employment Regimes." In Jon Eivind Kolberg, ed., *The Study of Welfare State Regimes.* Armonk, N.Y.: M. E. Sharpe.

Gough, Ian, Jonathan Bradshaw, J. Ditch, Tony Eardley, and Peter Whiteford. 1997. "Social Assistance in OECD Countries." *Journal of European Social Policy* 7, no. 1:17–43.

Gornick, Janet, Marcia K. Meyers, and Katherin E. Ross. 1997. "Supporting the Employment of Mothers: Policy Variation Across Fourteen Welfare States." *Journal of European Social Policy* 7:45–70.

———. 1998. "Public Policies and the Employment of Mothers: A Cross-National Study." *Social Science Quarterly* 79, no. 1 (March): 35–54.

Hall, Peter. 1986. *Governing the Economy: The Politics of State Intervention in Britain and France.* New York: Oxford University Press.

Hemerijck, Anton C., and Robert C. Kloosterman. 1994. "The Postindustrial Transition of Welfare Corporatism." Paper delivered at the Conference of Europeanists, Chicago, March 31–April 2.

Hinrichs, Karl. 1991. "Public Pensions and Demographic Change." *Society* 28, no. 6 (September/October): 32–37.

Hirschmann, Albert. 1979. "The Turn to Authoritarianism in Latin America and the Search for Its Economic Determinants." In David Collier, ed., *The New Authoritarianism in Latin America.* Princeton: Princeton University Press.

Hollingsworth, J. Rogers, Philippe Schmitter, and Wolfgang Streeck. 1993. *Governing Capitalist Economies: Performance and Control of Economic Sectors.* New York: Oxford University Press.

Huber, Evelyne, and John D. Stephens. 1998. "Internationalization and the Social Democratic Model: Crisis and Future Prospects." *Comparative Political Studies* 31, no. 3 (June): 353–97.

———. 2000. "Partisan Governance, Women's Employment, and the Social Democratic Service State." *American Sociological Review* 65:323–42.

———. 2001. *Development and Crisis of the Welfare State: Parties and Policies in Global Markets.* Chicago: University of Chicago Press.

Huber, Evelyne, Charles Ragin, and John D. Stephens. 1993. "Social Democracy, Christian Democracy, Constitutional Structure and the Welfare State." *American Journal of Sociology* 99, no. 3:711–49.

———. 1997. Comparative Welfare States Data Set, Northwestern University and University of North Carolina (http://www.lis.ceps.lu/compwsp.htm).

Kangas, Olli. 1991. *The Politics of Social Rights.* Stockholm: Swedish Institute for Social Research.

Kangas, Olli, and Joakim Palme. 1994. "Class Politics and Institutional Feedbacks: Development of Occupational Pensions in Finland and Sweden." In Michael Shalev, ed., *Occupational Welfare and the Welfare State in Comparative Perspective.* New York: Plenum Press.

Katzenstein, Peter. 1985. *Small States in World Markets.* Ithaca: Cornell University Press.

King, Desmond, and Stewart Wood. 1999. "The Political Economy of Neoliberalism: Britain and the United States in the 1980s." In Herbert Kitschelt, Peter Lange, Gary Marks, and John D. Stephens, eds., *Continuity and Change in Contemporary Capitalism.* New York: Cambridge University Press.

Kitschelt, Herbert, Peter Lange, Gary Marks, and John D. Stephens, eds. 1999. *Continuity and Change in Contemporary Capitalism.* Cambridge: Cambridge University Press.

Korpi, Walter. 1996. "Eurosclerosis and the Sclerosis of Objectivity: On the Role of Values Among Economic Policy Experts." *The Economic Journal* 106, no. 439 (November): 1727–46.

Korpi, Walter, and Joakim Palme. 1998. "The Strategy of Equality and the Paradox of Redistribution." *American Sociological Review* 63, no. 5 (October): 661–87.

Lehmbruch, Gerhard. 1984. "Concertation and the Structure of Corporatist Networks." In John H. Goldthorpe, ed., *Order and Conflict in Contemporary Capitalism.* Oxford: Clarendon Press.

Mitchell, Deborah. 1991. *Income Transfers in Ten Welfare States.* Brookfield, Australia: Avebury.

Myles, John, and Paul Pierson. 2001. "The Political Economy of Pension Reform." In Paul Pierson, ed., *The New Politics of the Welfare State.* New York: Oxford University Press.

Nickell, Stephen. 1997. "Unemployment and Labor Market Rigidities: Europe vs. North America." *Journal of Economic Perspectives* 11, no. 3:55–74.

OECD (Organisation for Economic Co-operation and Development). 1994. *The OECD Jobs Study: Evidence and Explanations.* Paris: OECD.

———. 1995. *Historical Statistics, 1960–93.* Paris: OECD.

———. 1996a. *Employment Outlook,* July 1996. Paris: OECD.

———. 1996b. *OECD Economies at a Glance: Structural Indicators.* Paris: OECD.

Olsson, Sven E. 1990. *Social Policy and Welfare State in Sweden.* Lund, Sweden: Arkiv.

Palme, Joakim. 1990. *Pension Rights in Welfare Capitalism: The Development of Old-Age Pensions in 18 OECD Countries, 1930 to 1985.* Stockholm: Swedish Institute for Social Research.

Pontusson, Jonas. 1996. "Wage Distribution and Labor Market Institutions in Sweden, Austria, and Other OECD Countries." Institute for European Studies, Cornell University, Working Paper No. 96.

Saunders, Peter. 1991. "Noncash Income and Relative Poverty in Comparative Perspective: Evidence from the Luxembourg Income Study." Paper delivered at the conference on Comparative Studies of Welfare State Development, Helsinki, Finland, August 29–September 1.

Soskice, David. 1999. "Divergent Production Regimes: Coordinated and Uncoordinated Market Economies in the 1980s and 1990s." In Herbert Kitschelt, Peter Lange, Gary Marks, and John D. Stephens, eds., *Continuity and Change in Contemporary Capitalism.* New York: Cambridge University Press.

Stephens, John. D. 1979. *The Transition from Capitalism to Socialism.* Urbana: University of Illinois Press.

———. 1995. "Preserving the Social Democratic Welfare State." *Nordic Journal of Political Economy* 22:143–62.

———. 1996. "The Scandinavian Welfare States." In Gøsta Esping-Andersen, ed., *Welfare States in Transition.* London: Sage.

Stephens, John D., Evelyne Huber, and Leonard Ray. 1999. "The Welfare State in Hard Times." In Herbert Kitschelt, Peter Lange, Gary Marks, and John D. Stephens, eds., *Continuity and Change in Contemporary Capitalism.* New York: Cambridge University Press.

Traxler, Franz. 1994. "Collective Bargaining: Levels and Coverage." *OECD Employment Outlook,* July, 167–94.

Visser, Jelle. 1996. *Unionization Trends. The OECD Countries Membership File.* Amsterdam: University of Amsterdam, Centre for Research of European Societies and Labor Relations (CESAR).

Wallerstein, Michael. 1990. "Centralized Bargaining and Wage Restraint." *American Journal of Political Science* 34, no. 4 (November): 982–1004.

———. 1999. "Wage Setting Institutions and Pay Inequality in Advanced Industrial Societies." *American Journal of Political Science* 43:649–80.

Wennemo, Irene. 1994. *Sharing the Cost of Children: Studies on the Development of Family Support in the OECD Countries.* Doctoral Dissertation Series, No. 25. Stockholm: University of Stockholm, Swedish Institute for Social Research.

How to Design a Liberal Welfare State: A Comparison of Canada and the United States

JOHN MYLES

The end of the cold war and the demise of East European socialism have dramatically altered the intellectual agenda of the social sciences. Now that capitalism has won, so to speak, the new debates turn on the issue of what kind of capitalism (Albert 1993; Esping-Andersen 1990)? Much more heed is being paid to the strikingly different ways capitalism has, and is, being practiced in North America, Europe, and Japan.

The debate has several foci: (1) national differences in the organization of business and the relations between capital and labor; (2) national differences in the *extent* of state involvement in the economy; and (3) national differences in the *type* of state involvement in the economy. The outcomes of interest are also several: (1) which models are more effective at the business of capitalism, namely the accumulation of capital; and (2) which models are more effective at the distribution of social, economic, and political welfare among their respective populations.

My aim in this chapter is to contribute to an understanding of one of these models, variously referred to as the *liberal* or *neo-American* model, by considering two national variants, the Canadian and the American.

- Without going into too much history, I will describe the welfare state institutions that developed in Canada and the United States during the golden age of postwar expansion.
- Second, I will describe the actual performance of these welfare state institutions as they matured and in the face of the changed economic circumstances that began to appear from the mid-1970s on.
- Third, I will consider the policy responses made by legislators during the 1980s and 1990s as they tried to adjust to (or to create) a new political and economic environment.

This is a revised version of a paper by the same title published in *Social Policy and Administration* 32, no. 4:341–64. Support for this project was provided in part by the Robert Schuman Centre, European University Institute, Florence. I am grateful to Gøsta Esping-Andersen, Evelyne Huber, and the participants in the *Models of Capitalism* project for comments on an earlier version of this paper. Portions of the section "Why the NIT Design Has Prospered" are drawn from Myles and Pierson 1997.

- And finally, I will attempt to evaluate the implications of these policies and strategies mainly with respect to their capacity to satisfy the consumption needs of their respective populations.

The presentation is organized around the important distinction between welfare state *regimes* and welfare state *design*. The regime approach, most frequently associated with Esping-Andersen's (1990) division between liberal, conservative, and social democratic regimes, is useful, since it takes us beyond the narrow world of social spending and turns our attention to the larger institutional complex in which this social spending takes place (Castles and Mitchell 1992). More specifically, regimes are distinguished by the explicit or implicit principles and rules that regulate transactions between the three institutional nuclei from which individuals derive their welfare in modern capitalist societies: the state, the market, and the family. Liberal welfare regimes are characterized by a preference for market solutions to welfare problems. As a result, the volume of social spending in these nations is low and inequality is higher. High levels of inequality, however, are not just a function of social spending. Inequality is high in Canada and the United States because inequality in the distribution of primary (market) incomes is high, a result of relatively unregulated labor markets, on the one hand, and high inequality in the distribution of human capital, on the other.

Countries with otherwise similar welfare state *regimes* differ dramatically in *program design,* however, that is, in the models they use to finance and distribute benefits. The design of old age pensions in Canada, for example, more closely resembles that of Sweden than of the United States. And U.S. Social Security is more similar to the Bismarckian design of continental Europe than to that of Canada or the United Kingdom. One of my main purposes is to show that differences in programmatic design matter a great deal in understanding distributional outcomes. While both Canada and the United States have faced similar distributive challenges since the 1970s, a result of changes in the labor market and in family structure, differences in program design have produced very different distributive outcomes. At least until the 1990s Canada's tax-transfer system successfully offset the effects of rising inequality in labor market earnings and new family forms so that the final distribution of income and poverty rates remained stable.[1] In the United States, in contrast, family income inequality grew substantially as did child poverty.

---

1. Preliminary results for 1995 show an increase in Canadian poverty levels. Whether this indicates the beginning of a secular trend and the reasons for it remain to be determined.

At first glance, it might seem that while a mean-spirited Reagan-Bush administration was busy dismantling America's (already modest) welfare state, Canadian legislators were moving in the opposite direction, opening the treasury doors in response to rising need. In 1980, the United States spent 4.5 percent and Canada 5.5 percent of GDP on transfers to nonelderly households. By 1990, U.S. spending had fallen to 3.5 percent of GDP, while Canadian spending had risen to 7.6 percent, approximately the OECD average (OECD 1994). In fact, retrenchment politics have dominated the social policy agenda in both countries. Indeed, in the face of rising deficits, serious retrenchment efforts began in Canada as early as 1978 under the Trudeau government. In 1984, the Progressive Conservatives were elected to office and initiated a profound restructuring of Canadian social policy. The results of this retrenchment exercise—relative stability in the final distribution of income in Canada and rising inequality in the United States—were the product of two increasingly divergent models of social spending (Banting 1997). Since the 1970s, the model of choice for the redesign (and retrenchment) of Canadian social spending has been the so-called negative income tax (NIT) or guaranteed income (GI) first proposed many decades ago by Milton Friedman, a model that the United States has also pursued but much less aggressively (Myles and Pierson 1997).

Policy design is important not simply because it shapes the distribution of transfers in the short run but also because of the way it shapes the direction of policy reform in the long run. Initial policy designs play a central role in determining the range of possible policy designs that can be implemented in the future. Choices made by legislators early in the process of developing welfare states have profound implications for the choices available to subsequent generations of legislators. As we will show, the design choices made by Canadian and U.S. legislators during the age of expansion played a key role in shaping the retrenchment strategies available to legislators in the 1980s and 1990s. Policy divergence in the two countries since the formative 1960s are not just the result of differences in the ratio of mean spirits to warm hearts on the two sides of the border.

The first section of this chapter locates Canada and the United States within Esping-Andersen's now familiar typology of welfare *regimes*. Here I highlight the broad institutional similarities between the two countries. In the sections that follow, I turn to the question of differences in programmatic design and how these differences subsequently shaped both the pattern of retrenchment in the two countries and the distributive outcomes of these changes.

MODELS OF WELFARE I: WELFARE STATE REGIMES

The now standard starting point for identifying the distinctive social policy models of Canada and the United States is Gøsta Esping-Andersen's (1990) division between liberal welfare state regimes of the Anglo-American democracies on the one hand, and the conservative and social democratic social policy models of continental and Northern Europe, on the other.

In *liberal* welfare states citizens are constituted primarily as individual market actors. There is a reluctance to replace market relations with social rights, and citizens are encouraged to seek their welfare in the market, for example, through subsidies for private welfare benefits. Basic security schemes are more likely to be means tested and social insurance benefits modest. The main exemplars are the Anglo-American democracies.

The second regime type goes under a variety of labels—conservative, corporatist, and more recently, Christian democratic—depending on the characteristics emphasized. It is *conservative* in the classic European sense of the term, highlighting its precapitalist origins in the dynastic elites of continental Europe (Kerr et al. 1960). It was decidedly antiliberal in origin, concerned not at all with market efficiency, but deeply concerned with maintaining an organic-hierarchical social order inherited from the past. Social rights are extensive, and there is only a marginal role for private welfare arrangements (the market). It is *corporatist* in the sense that, in their origins at least, these rights and privileges were differentiated on the basis of class and status and redistribution was marginal or nonexistent. These states were also strongly influenced by *Christian Democratic* (i.e., Catholic) doctrines rejecting the primacy of the market, on the one hand, but insisting on principles of subsidiarity and the primacy of the family as the locus of social welfare, on the other. Hence, while social spending in these nations is considerably higher than in liberal welfare states, the emphasis is on income transfers sufficient to cover the income needs of the male breadwinner while social services such as child care that facilitate women's employment are modest. The main exemplars are the continental European countries.

Social democratic welfare states (found mainly in Scandinavia) represent a model of society characterized by extensive social rights and a marginal role for private welfare provision (as in continental Europe). But rights are universalistic rather than corporativistic, emphasizing equality of citizenship rather than preservation of status differences. Hence, unlike the continental model, there is considerable emphasis on redistribution and providing all with high levels of basic security. Women's place is in the labor market; thus the welfare state is service intensive as well as transfer intensive, providing

Table 11.1 Means-Testing, Private Welfare, and Social Spending, 1980

	Means-tested benefits as a percentage of social expenditure	Private pensions as a percentage of total pensions	Private health expenditure as a percentage of total health expenditure	Social expenditure as percentage of GDP
United States	18	21	57	13
Canada	16	38	26	15
OECD (18)	6	13	22	20

SOURCES: Adapted from Esping-Andersen 1990, table 3.1; OECD 1994, table 1a.

both employment for women and the services required to allow women/parents high levels of participation in the labor market.

Some of the features that highlight the liberal character of Canadian and U.S. welfare policy, circa 1980, are presented in Table 11.1. Liberal welfare states rely on more intensive use of means-tested (residual) forms of welfare, on the one hand, and more private, market-based insurance, on the other. Greater reliance on means-testing and private insurance means a smaller share of national income flows through the public purse and aggregate social spending is smaller as a result.

A distinguishing feature of the regime approach is that welfare states acquire their distinctiveness not simply in terms of the volume of social spending but also in terms of their adoption of qualitatively different approaches to questions of income security and equality. An identical input of expenditure may lead to quite different outcomes as measured by poverty and inequality.

Having said this, however, it is also true that the level of spending matters a great deal in the construction of Esping-Andersen's regime types (Bonoli 1997). For example, three elements figure in the construction of his decommodification index for old age pensions: (1) the level of benefits for the covered population; (2) the share of the elderly population covered; and (3) the distribution of benefits within the covered population. While the effect of the shape of the distribution (3) on total spending is indeterminate, both benefit levels and coverage unambiguously increase the total size of the welfare state. Extensive social rights—whether conservative or social democratic—result in the *decommodification* of labor, allowing individuals to survive independently of the market. Implicit in the three worlds of welfare is a claim that big welfare states matter. Why?

To illustrate, it is helpful to ask why so-called *conservative* welfare states can be considered more decommodifying than *liberal* welfare states, when in fact the former tie benefits more closely to labor market earnings than the latter, that is to say, spending is *less* redistributive in conservative than in liberal welfare states. The general answer is that conservative welfare states spend a lot while the more redistributive (means-tested) liberal regimes tend to spend rather little. The result is that social transfers constitute a much larger share, and market incomes a smaller share, of the final distribution of income in conservative than in liberal regimes. Assuming the distribution of transfer income is more equal than the distribution of market income (which is always the case), income inequality (and poverty rates) will inevitably be lower in big (conservative) than in small (liberal) welfare states. The implication is that the private/public mix in old age income—the sheer size of the public sector—can be equalizing even in transfer programs that involve little explicit redistribution.[2]

The first lesson, then, is that *big* welfare states do matter in determining the final distribution of welfare. The point is illustrated for the *nonelderly* population in Table 11.2 where we show the level of family income inequality (measured by the ratio of adjusted family income at the 90th percentile to family income at the 10th percentile) and social spending on the nonelderly as a percentage of GDP.

It would be a profound error, however, to conclude that inequality in the final distribution of income (column 1) is merely a function of the level of social spending (column 2). The principle source of income of most people, most of the time, is the labor market. If inequality in labor market incomes is very high (as it is, for example, in the United States), welfare states will have to redistribute vastly larger sums to achieve levels of equality comparable to those countries where earnings inequality is low. Underlying the comparatively high levels of inequality found in the United States and Canada are correspondingly high levels of labor market inequality (Table 11.3). Low income earners in Canada and the United States earn about 40 percent of the median wage compared to an average of 63 percent in eleven other OECD nations.

2. To formalize the argument Pedersen uses the decomposition of Gini formulated by Lerman and Yitshaki (1985). The contribution of any given component of income (Q_k) can be partitioned into three factors: the Gini coefficient for the component (G_k), the share of the component in the overall income package (S_k) and the correlation between the component and the overall income package (R_k) so that:

$$G = Q_k = \Sigma \times S_k \times R_k$$

which simply stated means that overall inequality is determined by the concentration of the component itself, its share in the overall income package, and its covariation with the remaining income components. Assuming the Gini for public pensions is smaller than the Gini for private pensions, then as the share (S) of public pensions rises, overall inequality must fall. This result is reinforced by the fact that the correlation (R) is not independent of the share (S). As S_k rises, so does R_k.

Table 11.2   Inequality in Family Income and Social Expenditures for Nonelderly Households as a Percentage of GDP, Selected Countries

	Family Income Inequality	Social Expenditures as a Percentage of GDP
Norway	2.8	13.9
Sweden	2.8	14.4
Netherlands	2.9	13.1
Germany	3.0	9.6
France	3.5	8.3
New Zealand	3.5	6.3
United Kingdom	3.8	8.1
Canada	3.9	7.6
Australia	4.3	4.3
United States	5.6	3.5

SOURCE: Family income, Luxembourg Income Study; Social Expenditures, OECD 1994.
NOTE: Ratio of family income at the 90th percentile to family income at the 10th percentile.

Inequality in labor market incomes is related to the structure of welfare *regimes* in at least two ways. The first concerns the institutional regulation of wages and earnings. The second concerns the organization of education and training, that is to say, the production and distribution of human capital that underlies the wage distribution.

Union density levels (membership as a percentage of the labor force) in the United States have fallen dramatically since their peak in the 1960s. Canadian rates have remained comparatively stable but are somewhat below the OECD average. Much more significant than membership rates, however, are coverage levels. In most OECD nations, the majority of workers are *covered* by union wage agreements even if they are not union members (Table 11.4). Traxler (1996) divides national bargaining systems into inclusive and exclusive labor systems based on the level at which bargaining takes place, the extent of bargaining coordination, and the degree of extension practices. The exclusive systems where there is little extension are found only in Canada, the United States, Great Britain, and Japan. The average coverage level in these four countries is 31.5 percent of workers. In the remaining fourteen, inclusive, systems the average coverage level is 79 percent.

National systems of education and training, a neglected dimension of welfare *regimes,* can also play a critical role in shaping the distribution of welfare. If the distribution of human capital, the skills and capacities individuals bring into the labor market, is very unequally distributed, then other things being equal, we would expect higher wage inequality. The United States and Canada have traditionally focused training resources on the top

Table 11.3   Ratio of Lower (First) and Upper
(Ninth) Earnings Deciles to the Median, 1990

	d1/d5	d9/d5
United States	0.4	2.2
Canada	0.42	1.85
OECD (11)	0.63	1.74

SOURCE: OECD 1993, table 5.2.

third of the labor force who attend university and do relatively little in developing the human capital resources of the other two-thirds. As a result, both countries have comparatively large segments of their populations who are only semiliterate. This is dramatically illustrated by the results of the 1994 International Literacy Survey (Organization for Economic Development and Statistics Canada 1995). The survey instrument required respondents to extrapolate information from three types of texts: a prose text, a documentary text, and a text containing numerical information. Table 11.5 shows the percentages in six countries included in the study who scored at the very lowest literacy level. Approximately a fifth of American adults are functionally illiterate and between 16–18 percent of Canadians. Remarkably, the OECD results indicate little or no improvement in literacy rates among younger generations of Americans, unlike the pattern in other countries.

The low level of wage regulation in Canada and, especially, the United States means that wage rates are comparatively free to fluctuate in response to market processes of supply and demand. A large pool of relatively unskilled labor and high inequality in the distribution of human capital means that, left on its own, the market will tend to produce high levels of earnings inequality and large numbers of workers with very low earnings. These tendencies are somewhat more muted in Canada by virtue of higher minimum wages, a larger unionized sector, and a somewhat more efficient system for education and training. Nevertheless, both countries experienced a large increase in earnings inequality in the 1980s. The proximate cause of this increase is still under debate. The consensus position in the economics literature is that the main culprit is technical change that has radically changed the demand for skilled and unskilled labor. However, the *fact* that changes in demand and supply were translated into higher levels of earnings inequality is usually attributed to the absence of labor market institutions that regulate the wage structure (Freeman 1993), thus allowing wages at the bottom of the labor market to fall to market-clearing levels. The effects

Table 11.4 Union Density and Union Coverage,
1990 (as a percentage of the labor force)

	Density	Coverage
United States	15.6	18
Canada	35.8	38
OECD (18)	40.0	68

SOURCE: Traxler 1996.

were mainly experienced by younger adults (under thirty-five) and especially by young adult males. Since, however, most young children are in households headed by young adults, they too were exposed to a higher risk of poverty.

Although labor market regulation and income transfers fall broadly into the liberal mode in both countries, they differ dramatically in the delivery of public services, notably in health care.[3] The United States does provide national health insurance (albeit with large deductibles) for the elderly (Medicare) but only means-tested health insurance for the poor (Medicaid) for the working-age population. Both physician care and hospital services are provided on a universal basis for all Canadians. And Canada is remarkable even by European standards for the virtual absence of private provision of healthcare services. As I show below, the result of this difference has generated a remarkably different (nonliberal) trajectory of welfare state reform in the two nations.

The notion of welfare state *regimes* is useful, then, because it turns our attention from the narrow world of social spending to the larger institutional complex in which this social spending takes place. If we were to transfer the German system and German levels of social spending to the United States, poverty and inequality would no doubt decline but not nearly to German levels. In the absence of German institutions that regulate both the wage-setting process and the production of human capital (notably the apprenticeship system), American inequality and poverty levels would continue to soar above German levels.

Having said all this, however, it would be equally egregious to conclude that the narrow world of social spending *per se* does not matter. We have already made the point that the overall *level* of social spending matters. In

3. Public education also differs dramatically in the two countries. Few primary or secondary students in Canada attend private schools. All Canadian universities and colleges are public.

Table 11.5   Percent Low Literacy, 1994

	Prose scale	Document scale	Quantitative scale
United States	21	24	21
Canada	17	18	17
Germany	14	9	7
Netherlands	11	10	10
Sweden	8	6	7

SOURCE: OECD/Statistics Canada1996.

the following section, I take up an equally important point: *How* welfare states spend also matters a great deal. And here, the power of the contrast between Canada and the United States is especially useful.

MODELS OF WELFARE II: THE DESIGN OF WELFARE STATES

Esping-Andersen's regime approach provides an analytical window that allows us to find our way through the chaotic web (Pedersen 1995) of both apparent similarities and trivial differences that make up the minutia of welfare state designs. Parts take on their meaning from their place in the whole. Identical pension rules, for example, will produce very different outcomes where female labor force participation is low than where it is high, where employment policy and labor market institutions keep earnings inequality low, and so on.

Esping-Andersen's holism, however, is also the source of many of the criticisms directed at the typology: it is a typology of welfare *regimes,* not of welfare *programs.* Although liberal regimes all require workers to depend more on the market for their welfare, they differ fundamentally in programmatic design, that is, in the models they use to finance and distribute benefits. To take account of this complexity, a number of competing typologies have been advanced (see Bonoli 1997, Castles and Mitchell 1992, Ferrera 1993, and Palme 1990). Thus, for different reasons, both Palme (1990) and Castles and Mitchell (1992) argue that there are at least four worlds of welfare capitalism. Some "liberal" welfare states provide high levels of basic security for all citizens despite weak programs of income security for average wage earners (Palme). Some means-tested welfare states (e.g., Australia) are designed to exclude the "rich" rather than to confine benefits to the "poor" (Castles and Mitchell).

For our present purpose, whether there are four, five, or eighteen variants of welfare capitalism is beside the point. Rather, the lesson to be drawn is that within otherwise similar *regimes* there are significant variations in *how* welfare states raise and distribute funds and in turn these differences have significant consequences for shaping distributional outcomes. And significantly, as Pierson (1994) shows, *programmatic design* plays a decisive role in shaping subsequent pathways of policy reform. I will illustrate both claims in the context of the comparison between Canada and the United States.

In liberal welfare states, the average worker is expected to rely much more on the market than elsewhere. However, among liberal welfare states there are sharp differences in what happens to individuals and families who fail in the market. The reasons for these differences are not difficult to identify. Liberal welfare states differ modestly in spending levels but differ substantially in the way spending is financed and distributed. Postwar social programs were designed around three basic building blocks: (1) a residual *social assistance* model of means-tested benefits for the poor inherited from the prewar era; (2) the industrial achievement model of *social insurance* based on labor market performance; and (3) a *citizenship* model of universal flat-rate social benefits.

Each of these designs have both a juridical and a technical calculus embedded within them, an understanding of the grounds on which claims to a benefit are justified, on the one hand, and, on the other, an understanding of how a benefit system ought to be designed. Traditional social assistance programs designed in the poor law tradition were based on *social condition,* that is to say, indigence. Public provision was an act of charity and was stigmatized by a close examination of individual circumstances to distinguish the "deserving" from the "undeserving" poor. The transition toward a *citizenship* model of social protection—a universal right based on permanent residence—changes the criterion of indigence to that of membership in a national community. The rhetoric of charity is replaced by a rhetoric of social rights and is usually associated with the transition from the Elizabethan model of poor relief to the so-called Beveridge model of universal flat benefits. This was roughly the pathway followed by the Scandinavian and most Anglo-Saxon welfare states, outside the United States, from the beginning of the century through the early postwar years. Many, though not all, countries that followed the Beveridge path subsequently developed a mixed model of social provision, supplementing their universal flat benefit schemes with earnings-related social insurance schemes.

In contrast, the continental European tradition that originates with Bismarck was built on a (more or less) strong analogy with private insurance (hence the *social* insurance model) with emphasis on redistributing income over the life cycle and a (more or less) close correspondence between contributions and benefits. Social insurance is directed at wage-earners (not citizens) and aims to provide earnings replacement rather than basic security against the risk of low income in old age, illness, and periods of unemployment.[4]

Both Canada and the United States began their welfare state development early in the century in the poor law tradition, providing means-tested mother's allowances to indigent women with children. Canada added a means-tested old age pension in 1927, and the United States followed in 1935 (OAA). Thereafter, the Canadian trajectory of program design closely resembled the Scandinavian. Universal flat-rate benefits for children were added in 1944 and old age benefits in 1951. Universal hospital coverage came in 1958, followed by universal health insurance in 1965. As in Sweden, earnings-related schemes were added to cover unemployment (1941) and sickness and maternity leave (1971) and to supplement the basic flat-rate old age pension (1965). By the end of the period of welfare state reform in the early 1970s, the programmatic design, if not spending levels, of the Canadian welfare state was remarkably similar to that of Sweden. And like Scandinavia, the welfare state became closely identified with a political culture of social citizenship reflecting the underlying core of universal entitlements financed from general revenue rather than payroll contributions.

The American trajectory was very different. Unlike the Scandinavian and other Anglo-American democracies, the universalistic citizenship model, discussed briefly and rejected in the 1930s, never took hold. Programs introduced in the New Deal reforms of 1935 were a mix of traditional means-tested programs for the elderly (OAA) and the children of indigent women (ADC) and social insurance programs for the elderly (OAI) and the unemployed (UI). The reforms of the 1960s and early 1970s did little to change this mix. Medicare health insurance for the elderly could be considered the exception, since it covers approximately 99 percent of the American elderly and is financed in part through general revenue. Other old age programs were also substantially upgraded and modernized in the 1960s and 1970s. Replacement rates in the earnings-related Social Security scheme rose dramatically and were indexed to inflation. OAA, the means-tested program, was abolished and replaced with Supplemental Security Income (SSI), which

4. The association of these types with the names of Beveridge and Bismarck is somewhat misleading and misses important differences within types. Ironically, the actual Beveridge model for some flat-rate benefits (e.g., pensions) was not based on citizenship but on contributions. The Bismarckian earnings-related schemes conflate the corporatist design with universal state-administered schemes for all wage and salary workers.

set national rather than local (that is, state) standards for qualifying conditions and benefit levels.

For the working-age population, in contrast, the reform years of the 1960s were largely a story of what did *not* happen. Rather than universal health insurance, the United States introduced Medicaid, a means-tested program firmly embedded within the poor law tradition. Unlike in Canada, the unemployment insurance created in 1935 was not reformed, thus benefits remained low, replacing, on average, about 35 percent of average wages. Control of the program was left in the hands of the states and, after 1970, coverage rates declined significantly. By the end of the 1980s less than 30 percent of the officially unemployed were actually receiving benefits. Disability insurance was added in 1955 but sickness insurance, family allowances, and maternity and parental leave benefits all remain unknown in the United States. Rather, welfare politics for the working-age population both in the 1960s and in the decades that followed remained firmly locked on to a set of small but politically charged programs for the poor: means-tested cash benefits (Aid to Families with Dependent Children), and in-kind benefits (food stamps).

In sum, the design of the American welfare state created from the 1930s through the 1970s could be thought of as a social insurance welfare state for the elderly, albeit of modest proportions, and an unreformed poor law or means-tested welfare state for the working-age population. Canada, by comparison, created a mixed welfare state model combining traditional means-tested benefits and a Beveridgean core of universal benefits based on citizenship, supplemented by social insurance for retirement, unemployment, and sickness.

There are several reasons why the United States fell behind Canada in developing the welfare state, particularly for working-age adults. Crucial among them, as Quadagno (1994) has compellingly argued, is that during the critical era of welfare state expansions—the 1960s—the struggle for civil rights and political rights took primacy over and diverted attention from the struggle for social rights. The War on Poverty meant breaking down barriers to entry into the labor and housing markets, not new cash benefits or services for working-age families. In the 1970s, Nixon's plans to build a Republican base among the working class by expanding and improving social insurance programs, including health and family benefits (FAP), were derailed by Vietnam and Watergate. As Maioni (1998) has demonstrated for the case of health insurance, systemic differences also matter. Canadian political institutions, particularly parliamentarism and the existence of disciplined parties, no doubt made it easier to pass wide-ranging reform legislation than U.S. political institutions did. The intriguing, if unanswerable, question is whether absent Vietnam, Watergate, and the struggle for political and civil rights, a struggle long since completed elsewhere, the U.S. trajectory would have more closely resembled that of other OECD nations.

During the period of welfare state expansion of the 1960s and early 1970s both countries also debated a radically new design, quite different from the three traditional formulas, for providing benefits. This was the Negative Income Tax (NIT) or Guaranteed Income (GI) initially proposed by Milton Friedman in 1943 and based on a relatively simple idea: in good times workers would pay taxes to governments and in bad times governments would pay taxes to workers. Eligibility would be determined exclusively by income reported in a tax return, and assets are excluded from the test. There is no surveillance of beneficiaries or administrative discretion beyond that normally associated with the auditing of tax returns. Unlike traditional social assistance programs, tax back rates on earnings and other sources of income are always *much* less than 100 percent. One result is that benefits can reach into the ranks of the middle class, albeit at a diminishing rate. Since such programs are not (or need not be) for the poor alone, they are in principle able to generate sustaining political coalitions. One can usefully think of the NIT/GI design as the reverse image of yet another traditional welfare program in the United States, the home mortgage interest deduction, which provides large benefits to high income earners with high marginal tax rates, modest benefits to low income earners, and none at all to those with no taxable income. NIT/GI programs, in contrast, provide the largest benefits to low income earners, benefits decline as other income rises, and they disappear altogether at higher income levels.

Proposals to create a NIT/GI type program for families emerged almost simultaneously in the two countries. In Canada, a proposal to establish a Family Income Security Plan (or FISP) was brought to Cabinet in April 1970 by the minister of health and welfare, John Munro, where it was rejected as too costly.[5] In the United States, the prospect of a national Guaranteed Income became reality under Richard Nixon. In an effort to construct a base among traditional Democratic constituents (the "working poor"), Nixon advanced the Family Assistance Plan in 1969. The bill was passed by the House by a margin of 243 to 155 in April 1970. Two years later, however, a revised version of the bill was defeated in the Senate by a vote of 52 to 34.

5. FISP would have been partially financed by cutting universal family allowances for middle- and upper-income families. Protests from the women who would have been adversely affected also played a role in defeating the proposal.

Table 11.6 Selective Expenditures as a Proportion of Total Income Security, 1960–1992 (%)

	1960	1965	1970	1975	1980	1985	1990	1992
Canada	20.8	27.6	30.8	29.3	37.4	35.5	47.5	52.0
United States	20.4	18.8	22.8	24.3	20.9	16.7	16.3	17.8

SOURCE: Banting 1997.

Both countries succeeded, however, with two other, almost accidental and originally modest, initiatives. In February 1966, Canada's Special Senate Committee on Aging chaired by Senator David Croll, proposed the introduction of a Guaranteed Income Supplement for the elderly poor designed along NIT lines.[6] The proposal was initially resisted by both Cabinet and by federal officials but was finally adopted as a "temporary measure" in the face of enormous pressure from opposition parties, the New Democratic Party (NDP) in particular, to bring down old age poverty by dramatically raising the universal old age demogrant (OAS) to $100 per month (Haddow 1993, 70). In 1974, the United States introduced, virtually unnoticed, the Earned Income Tax Credit (EITC), a modest wage subsidy for working poor families with children.

The significance of the new design, however modest at the beginning, is this: over the subsequent two decades while the three traditional models of social provision came under attack, the NIT model won supporters and flourished in both countries. Beginning in 1978, Canada slowly began to refashion its entire cash transfer system along NIT lines. Canada's adoption of the NIT design as the model of choice for the distribution of cash benefits is highlighted by the remarkable findings reported by Banting (see Table 11.6). While the share of targeted cash benefits as a percentage of total income transfers in the United States held steady at around 20 percent between 1960 and 1992, in Canada, selective (targeted) benefits rose from 21 percent to 52 percent of income transfers, rising most rapidly after 1975. Overwhelmingly, these Canadian trends reflect the expansion of income-tested supplements, rather than traditional social assistance programs.

In the United States, the Earned Income Tax Credit (EITC), a modest wage supplement for the working poor established in 1973 and costing only

6. Croll's role in Canadian politics is similar to that of American New Deal Democrats such as Claude Pepper, who cut their political teeth in the 1930s. Like Pepper, Croll headed numerous commissions and committees related to old age and poverty well into his eighties. In an interview with one of the authors, he reported that his key motive for advancing the GIS design in 1966 was his hatred of the dole of the 1930s traditional means-tested welfare. Croll wished to establish a guaranteed income as a political right.

Table 11.7   Federal Spending on EITC
and AFDC, 1980–1996 (in $U.S. billions)

	EITC	AFDC[a]
1980	2.0	6.4
1981	1.9	6.9
1982	1.8	6.9
1983	1.8	7.3
1984	1.6	7.7
1985	2.1	7.8
1986	2.0	8.2
1987	3.9	8.9
1988	5.9	9.1
1989	6.6	9.4
1990	6.9	10.1
1991	10.6	11.2
1992	12.4	12.3
1993[b]	13.2	12.3
1994[b]	19.6	12.4
1995[b]	22.8	12.8
1996[b]	25.1	13.2

SOURCE: United States House of Representatives 1994, 389, 700.
[a] AFDC expenditures exclude state-level spending and administrative costs.
[b] Projections.

$2 billion dollars as recently as 1986 has grown exponentially since then, reaching $25 billion in outlays a decade later. In 1986, EITC benefits went to some 7 million families. By 1996, the figure was approaching 19 million families. The differential fates of the traditional means-tested AFDC and the income-tested EITC since the 1980s are highlighted in Table 11.7.

The resiliency of the new design appeared in bold relief in the United States in 1996, when the Earned Income Tax Credit, which fits the new framework, survived the Republican onslaught against federal poverty programs intact, while the traditional means-tested program of AFDC did not.[7] In Canada, social assistance rates have been falling during the 1990s, while the new style income tested benefits for families have continued to be enriched.

---

7. We should note that just as it has led the way toward the NIT/GI alternative, Canada led the way in ending welfare as we know it. The 1995 Canadian federal budget, which replaced the Canada Assistance Plan (CAP) with the Canada Health and Social Transfer (CHST), anticipated many of the features of the 1996 Personal Responsibility Act passed in the United States with respect to block grants and weaker national standards for provincial social assistance programs.

To bring our stylization of the two countries forward to the mid-1990s, then, we could say that the welfare state models look something like this.

1. *Income Transfers for the Elderly:* The United States relies on a mix of social insurance (Social Security) and traditional social assistance (SSI) for income transfers. Canada relies on a mix of social insurance (the C/QPP), flat benefits (OAS), and NIT-style transfers (GIS).
2. *Income Transfers for the Nonelderly:* The United States relies mainly on social assistance supplemented by a small and declining social insurance model for unemployment and a small but expanding NIT (EITC). Canada has a mix of social assistance and social insurance programs, which are declining, and a comparatively large and expanding set of programs based on a NIT design.

These differences in design, especially the more extensive use of NITs in Canada, are critical for understanding distributional outcomes in both static and dynamic terms. In the cross-section, they explain why poverty levels among the elderly and nonelderly populations are higher in the United States than in Canada. Because a politics of austerity tends to favor the NIT design over the alternative models—social insurance, social citizenship, and social assistance—Canada's more extensive adoption of NIT-style programs is likely to sustain and expand the Canadian-U.S. differences into the near future. In the conclusion, however, I will raise some reservations about the capacity of the NIT design to sustain these distributional outcomes in the longer run.

WHY THE THREE TRADITIONAL DESIGNS ARE FAILING

Since the 1970s the three traditional designs for social transfers—social assistance, social insurance, and citizenship benefits—have been subjected to continuing criticism. As a result, all three types of benefits have stagnated, been reduced, or been eliminated altogether. More critically, these designs have rarely if ever been used to meet new and emergent social risks. It is instructive to consider why.

Social Assistance: The reasons for the vulnerability of traditional means-tested benefits for the poor such as the American AFDC are well known. First, precisely because they are targeted at a minority (the poor) with little political influence, they lack significant political coalitions to support them, especially in periods of austerity and retrenchment. Added to this is the strong work disincentive created by high tax-back rates of 100 percent (or more). This was perceived as less of a problem when mothers were expected to remain at home with their children. Now, however, they are expected to work. In the United States the relative value of AFDC benefits for poor families with children declined continuously since the 1970s and then was replaced altogether in 1996 with the Personal Responsibility Act imposing both work requirements and time limits. Canadian social assistance rates remained constant or even grew somewhat in the 1980s. Since then, however, they have been on a downward trend.

Citizenship Benefits: Canada's model of universal flat benefits, once thought invulnerable, has all but disappeared, except for health care and some social services. The critique of universality was that scarce transfer dollars were being wasted on wealthy bankers and their wives. Their vulnerability also seems to be in part caused by the absence of the quasi-property rights associated with contributory schemes. Their resilience in the area of services and especially health is the result of two features. First, they enjoy immense political support, especially for health care.[8] Second, governments and corporations recognize that a single-payer model for the provision of health care permits much greater control over prices and supply and much lower administrative costs than the private insurance model of the United States

Social Insurance: The earnings-related benefits financed from payroll contributions on a pay-as-you-go basis was the model of choice in many countries in the postwar years for a variety of reasons. A major one, however, was ease of financing. One way to think about this is to recognize that the tax base for social insurance benefits in a pay-as-you-go system is today's wage bill, the average wage multiplied by the number of wage earners. The standard assumption of actuaries is that the implicit rate of return in such a design is equal to the percentage change in average wages multiplied by the percentage change in the number of employed. This meant that the 1960s were very favorable for such designs. As Brown (1996, 9) shows, given the economic and demographic variables prevailing at the time, the projected costs of pay-as-you-go schemes were considerably lower than funded plans. By current standards, real interest rates (returns to capital) were low, and annual increases in real wages (returns to labor) were high. While the decline in fertility (the baby bust) was not unknown, old age dependency ratios much lower than those projected today continued to be used in actuarial models well into the 1970s. The dramatic change in these

---

8. Public dissatisfaction grew dramatically during the 1990s as a result of spending cuts that reduced the supply of health services. However, the dissatisfaction has been expressed in demands for increased funding rather than adoption of some alternative design.

variables during the 1980s—declining real wage growth, higher real interest rates, and higher projected dependency ratios (a result of slower than expected expansion of the labor force and higher than expected gains in longevity)—dramatically changed the long-term viability of this model. The combination of low real wage growth, slower growth in the labor force, and high real interest rates inverted the advantages of the pay-as-you-go scheme over funded plans.[9] Under these conditions, contributions to finance social insurance schemes must increase faster than the wages of active workers to finance benefits, opening concerns about the impact on real living standards of the nonelderly and equity between generations.

Since demography is largely a given (or must be assumed to be so) and central banks are committed to slow, non-inflationary wage growth, the social insurance design faces major difficulties everywhere. The difficulties are compounded by the fact that high payroll taxes are considered to be an obstacle to employment creation. The concern is less with the level of payroll taxes than the projected rate of change so that even where payroll taxes are very low (e.g., Canada) this concern exercises a constraint on the social insurance design.

WHY THE NIT DESIGN HAS PROSPERED

NIT-like designs for the welfare state have typically been proposed as a universal guaranteed income for all citizens, either as an alternative to traditional social insurance programs (e.g., Friedman), as an addition to them, or in some mix of the two. In practice, however, almost all NIT programs are selective in the populations they target—the elderly and families with children in Canada, the working poor in the United States.[10]

Nothing in traditional welfare state theory tells us very much about the conditions likely to favor the *expansion* of income-tested programs of the

9. Financing pay-as-you-go schemes funded from payroll taxes depends on real growth in total wages and salaries, which in turn is the product of the rate of growth in average real wages and the growth of the labor force. A recent report by Canada's Department of Finance (Finance Canada 1996) illustrates the problem nicely. During the 1960s total wages and salaries grew at 5.1 percent per year, in the 1980s by 2.1 percent, and since the beginning of the nineties at 0 percent. In contrast real interest rates averaged 2.4 percent in the sixties, 6.3 percent in the eighties, and 4.6 percent since 1990.

10. In the countries of southern Europe, including France, where traditionally almost all social benefits were employment-based, modest basic incomes have been implemented (France, Spain, Portugal) or are under discussion (Italy) for those with no connection to the labor market. Britain has developed a program for working poor families, Family Credit, which resembles the EITC.

sort that has occurred in both Canada and the United States in the past two decades. We use the term "expansion" in a double sense: first, to refer to the growth of NIT-style testing as the model of choice for social transfers as compared to social insurance, social assistance, and citizenship programs; and second, to refer to the real growth in benefits within these programs. Indeed, there is precious little welfare state theory of any sort that leads us to expect this result. The reason is simple: virtually all welfare state theory is theory *about* the long historical trajectory of welfare state growth from the nineteenth century through the "golden age" that ended symbolically with the first great oil shock of 1973.[11] The NIT/GI model comes into its own after this age has passed, when the welfare state enters a period of containment and retrenchment.

Although NIT-style blueprints had been discussed since the 1940s, serious consideration of Milton Friedman's proposal for a Guaranteed Annual Income (or negative income tax) emerged in both Canada and the United States during the late 1960s, a period of major social policy innovation in both countries. These initial attempts, however, were soundly defeated. It would be another decade—around the late 1970s—before Friedman-style programs began to expand in both countries.

The reversal of fortune of these programs, from failure in the late 1960s to success from the late 1970s on, is telling. *NIT programs are the progeny of austerity.* At a time of budgetary stress, NIT-style reforms possess a number of attractive features that allow them to compete effectively both with traditional means-tested programs and, at times, with more universal ones. There are two broad reasons why this is so. The first is that these programs provide potential common ground for a powerful political coalition. This coalition includes public and private actors interested in controlling public expenditure, those with an interest in increasing labor market flexibility, and those seeking to increase the incomes of poor and near-poor households. Because these programs are much more targeted than universal programs, they offer hard-pressed public officials (and sympathetic private sector actors such as those in the financial community) the promise of expenditure restraint. At the same time, the structure of gradually phased-out benefits is widely considered to be more effective than traditional means-tested programs in sustaining work incentives—a matter of considerable importance to many employers.

---

11. Esping-Andersen's important welfare state typology is a case in point. His is a *historical* typology derived from actual welfare states as they developed in the postwar decades. It does not exhaust the possible range of welfare states forms, and hence is less useful for identifying new and emergent models of welfare state provision.

Political actors on the left are likely to be more ambivalent. Labor unions have generally been opposed. Crucially, however, this opposition has become less important as the political influence of organized labor has declined. Moderates and liberals, including advocacy groups for the poor, may have mixed feelings when the *quid pro quo* for expanding these targeted programs is cutbacks in other transfers. Yet they may see such cutbacks as probable in any event, and the possibility of increasing real benefits to those with low incomes will often lead them to support such initiatives, or at least serve to mute their opposition. One might question the clout of such groups in comparison with the influence of employers and finance ministries. In a context where austerity threatens to generate a popular outcry, however, such groups can provide essential political cover. In contexts where it is difficult to assemble legislative majorities (such as the United States), these groups may also have some influence with moderate politicians who control crucial swing votes.

This points to the second major advantage of NIT-style programs, which is their capacity to limit the popular reactions against welfare state reform which make other kinds of programmatic initiatives difficult. The contemporary politics of the welfare state has become the politics of blame avoidance (Weaver 1986). Austerity means that reforms almost always require painful cutbacks in existing programs, which are not only backed by entrenched interests but generally command widespread public support. In this context, operating through the tax system greatly increases policymakers' flexibility. Shifting to this arena partly circumvents the traditional interest group networks that support existing social programs. The rules governing reform of taxes are often looser than those governing changes in social programs. Perhaps most important, the intricacy of the tax system makes it easier for governments to present changes as relatively technical, or as part of large and complex package deals, or to phase in changes incrementally to minimize public outcry. Complexity and opacity facilitate a politics of stealth which make it harder for opponents to mobilize support among mass publics (Battle 1990).

The reasons why the NIT/GI design has become virtually hegemonic in Canada and more hesitantly adopted in the United States have been extensively reviewed elsewhere (Myles and Pierson 1997). One key to explaining the success of such a strategy lies, paradoxically, in the possibilities opened up by the policy legacies of Canada's traditional cash benefit system of *universal* flat benefits financed from general revenue and with only citizenship and residency as qualifying conditions. Since benefits are in no way linked to contributions, beneficiaries do not have the pseudo-proprietary claims to benefits associated with contributory programs such as Social Security. Indeed, citizenship entitlements have proven vulnerable to income-testing not just in Canada but also in virtually every other nation with a tradition of citizenship entitlements. Since the 1980s, partial or total clawbacks of universal flat-rate pensions from middle and upper income earners have been implemented in Australia, Denmark, Finland, Holland, Iceland, Sweden and especially, New Zealand (Myles and Quadagno 1997). In contrast, proposals to income-test contributory schemes such as Social Security in the United States have been thus far unsuccessful and have rarely reached the political agenda.

DISTRIBUTIVE OUTCOMES

Based on an understanding of traditional means tests, it has long been social science lore that the shift from universal to selective benefits will, in the long term, make the poor worse off. Have, as the conventional view suggests, the "poor" in Canada suffered as a result of growing selectivity based on NIT principles? In the intermediate term, at least, the answer is no. Income-testing of social benefits for families with children has reduced social transfers directed at middle income groups while raising benefits for those at the bottom of the income distribution. This proved to be especially important in light of a sharp rise in earnings inequality during the 1980s. Until recently, the Canadian system of social transfers has been successful in stabilizing the final distribution of family incomes and containing child poverty (Picot and Myles 1996). In the United States, changes in social programs exacerbated rather than offset market trends, with the result that between 1970 and 1986 the Canadian poverty rate (measured by U.S. standards) moved from 6.9 points *above* the U.S. level to 4.5 points *below* it. The story for the elderly is even more dramatic. In the mid-1970s, old age poverty rates in Canada were well above U.S. levels. By the mid-1990s, poverty rates among Canadian seniors had fallen to 5 percent, among the lowest in the OECD, compared to 20 percent in the United States (Smeeding and Sullivan 1998; Myles 2000).

Does the Canadian trajectory and two decades of expansion in the once modest U.S. EITC imply a similar destiny for the U.S. welfare state? Such a prospect is unlikely for several reasons. In Canada's universalistic welfare state universal benefits are financed from general revenues, a fact that provided a natural bridge to the NIT design. The United States has no comparable set of programs to reform. Expanding the EITC to nonworking poor families would be a firm step onto the traditional land mine of American politics, namely race. Since EITC is restricted to the working poor, it does not threaten to raise the reservation wage of workers in those regions of the country (especially the South) whose economic fortunes hinge critically on the protection of their low wage labor markets from upward pressure. A more expansive NIT (such as Nixon's failed Family Assistance Plan) would change all this.

Assuming these obstacles were overcome, however, what would be the likely long-range outcome?

So far, Canadian developments have confounded critics (including this author) who have maintained that targeted programs will never sustain the political support needed to be effective. In part because they reach well into the middle class, the new income-tested programs in Canada have remained popular. There is no question that as a purely technical exercise, a NIT/GI array of social expenditures can be designed that is more progressive and does more for the poor than those currently available in either country. The problem is a political, not a technical, one.

The expansion of the NIT/GI design is a product of an era of transition and retrenchment. The unanswered question is: what happens when the transition is over? The Achilles heel of the entire system is the fact that the process can only happen once. Now that the benefits of higher income Canadian families have been reduced or eliminated, they are no longer available to finance future expenditure growth for low income families. Should the number of such families rise as a result, say, of continued growth in earnings inequality, the additional costs could only be met through a process of welfare state expansion, not retrenchment. Similarly, now that the benefits that used to go to higher earners are gone, they are no longer available to absorb further cuts in the social budget. Instead, by necessity, future cost-cutters will have to look to the very NIT programs produced during previous retrenchment exercises and to other programs for the poor to reduce expenditures. Whether a NIT/GI design can stabilize at a level that achieves the income security and redistributional aims of the old system while also being politically sustainable is an open question.

CITIZENSHIP PRESERVED: THE CASE OF HEALTH CARE

In the immediate postwar years Canada and the United States had virtually identical health care systems (Maioni 1994): private fee-for-service care, voluntary nonprofit hospitals, private insurance, and philanthropic charity care for the poor. In 1957, Canada parted ways with the United States, introducing national insurance to cover hospital services. In 1965, national health insurance was extended to include physician services. In contrast, American reforms and the introduction of public insurance in the 1960s were targeted on the poor and the elderly. Between 30 and 40 million Americans are without health insurance, and many more remain underinsured, that is, insured for only part of their potential health care costs.

As the Canadian system matured in the 1970s and 1980s, its advantages over the American design soon became apparent: coverage and cost. The former made the program wildly popular among the mass public; the latter won the support of private sector as well as public sector elites. For individuals and families, most healthcare expenditures are removed from the market. Under the so-called single-payer system, all that is required at the time of service is to submit one's healthcare card. There are no copayments or deductibles. Poll after poll since the 1970s have persuaded political elites that the system is immensely popular, and anyone who threatens it faces political oblivion.

Equally, and perhaps more, important for the system's viability are considerations of cost. In 1960, Canada and the United States were both spending just over 5 percent GDP on healthcare expenditures. By 1991, Canada was spending 9.9 percent of GDP on healthcare; the United States, 13.4 percent. The differences are a result of the much lower administrative costs of the single-payer model and the capacity of governments to regulate both prices and supply. In contrast, by the 1990s, healthcare expenditures in the United States were widely recognized as being out of control. No one recognizes these large cost differentials better than the large manufacturers who produce on both sides of the border and must absorb the much larger costs of providing private insurance in their U.S. plants. In this area, at least, a welfare state is widely recognized as being a source of comparative advantage for Canadian producers.

Issues of cost and coverage led the Clinton administration to seek a major overhaul of U.S. health care in 1993. By then, history had preempted the possibility of the single-payer model: by the 1990s the health insurance industry was too large and significant a player to be destroyed with a single piece of legislation, a classic instance of path dependency in policymaking. Instead, Clinton proposed mandatory employer coverage and healthcare subsidies for the nonemployed. Costs, it was hoped, would be controlled by the introduction of some degree of competition among insurers and providers. The principal opponents of the plan, small employers and the insurance companies, eventually succeeded in attracting allies to their cause while the

Clinton administration slowly eroded its bases of support in the business community and the general public with the result that the plan came to nought.[12]

CONCLUSION: DESIGNING WELFARE STATES

Among the families of nations (Castles 1993) that make up the developed capitalist democracies, Canada and the United States (along with the other Anglo-Saxon countries) give pride of place to the market as the site from which individuals and families are expected to draw their welfare. Within this set of countries, however, there are large differences in the way benefits and services are financed and delivered. My aim here has not been to explain these differences but to consider their consequences.[13]

Building on a legacy of universal benefits financed from general revenue, Canada has managed to pass through an era of retrenchment and cost-cutting that was comparatively successful at stabilizing though not reducing poverty rates. Failure to transcend the poor law tradition in the formative years of the U.S. welfare state foreclosed this option. Early decisions have profound consequences for later ones. When they were created, universal flat benefits provided a comparatively inexpensive method of supplementing the incomes of target populations facing a high risk of poverty (the elderly, families with many children). They were favored as much for the ease and low cost of administration as they were for their ostensibly egalitarian objectives. Relative to earnings-based programs, they won support from the then large sectors of the labor force (especially farmers) who were not wage earners and from those outside the labor force altogether (especially women). As technology, bureaucratic capacity, and especially the efficiency of the tax collection system (the *sine qua non* for a NIT-style design) improved, the transition to a more systematically targeted but, relative to the United States, effective benefit system became a natural one for Canada. The healthcare example offers a similar lesson. National health insurance faced stiff opposition from entrenched interests in both Canada and the United States when the idea was first proposed in the 1940s and 1950s (Maioni 1997). But after three more decades of expansion and maturation of a large and sophisticated health insurance industry, the Clinton

12. The debate over the reasons for the failure of the plan are still being debated. For one insider's view, see Starr 1995.

13. For a review of the sources of difference in Canadian and American welfare state policy, see Myles 1996.

administration faced even stiffer opposition. Early decisions profoundly limit later ones.[14]

Designing welfare states is much like designing a city. A large investment in any particular design makes adopting a new design very difficult. It is extremely difficult if not impossible to introduce mass transport into the low-density cities designed around the automobile and superhighways constructed in postwar America. The radical redesign of mature welfare states is equally problematic.

REFERENCES

Albert, M. 1993. *Capitalism Against Capitalism*. London: Whurr Publishers.

Banting, Keith. 1997. "The Social Policy Divide: The Welfare State in Canada and the United States." In K. Banting, G. Hoberg, and R. Simeon, eds., *Degrees of Freedom: Canada and the United States in a Changing World*. Montreal: McGill-Queens University Press.

Battle, Ken [Grattan Gray, pseud.]. 1990. "Social Policy by Stealth." *Policy Options* (March): 17–29.

Bonoli, Giulian. 1997. "Classifying Welfare States: A Two-Dimensional Approach." *Journal of Social Policy* 26, no. 3:351–72.

Brown, Robert. 1996. "Reforming Canada's Retirement Income System: Is Prefunding the Answer?" *Canadian Business Economics* 4:3–12.

Castles, Fran. 1993. *Families of Nations: Patterns of Public Policy in Western Democracies*. Aldershot, U.K.: Dartmouth Publishing.

Castles, Francis, and Deborah Mitchell. 1992. "Identifying Welfare State Regimes: The Links Between Politics, Instruments and Outcomes." *Governance: An International Journal of Policy and Administration* 5:1–26.

Esping-Andersen, Gøsta. 1990. *The Three Worlds of Welfare Capitalism*. Princeton: Princeton University Press.

Ferrera, Maurizio. 1993. *Modelli di Solidarieta*. Bologna: Societa Editrice Il Mulino.

Finance Canada. 1996. *An Information Paper for Consultations on the Canada Pension Plan*. Ottawa: Department of Finance.

Freeman, Richard. 1994. *Working Under Different Rules*. New York: Russell Sage Foundation.

Haddow, Rodney. 1993. *Poverty Reform in Canada, 1958–1978: State and Class Influences on Policy Making*. Montreal: McGill-Queen's University Press.

Katz, Michael B. 1986. *In the Shadow of the Poorhouse: A Social History of Welfare in America*. New York: Basic Books.

Kerr, Clark, John Clark, Frederick Harbison Dunlop, and Charles Myers. 1960. *Industrialism and Industrial Man*. New York: Oxford University Press.

14. This observation, of course, begs the question of why Canada was able to introduce universal health insurance in the 1960s and the United States was not. For an excellent analysis of the institutional differences and political forces that shaped the development of health care policy in the two countries, see Maioni 1997.

Lerman, Robert, and Shlomo Yitshaki. 1985. "Income Inequality Effects by Income Source: A New Approach and Applications to the United States." *The Review of Economics and Statistics* 67:151–56.

Maioni, Antonia. 1994. *Divergent Pasts, Converging Futures? The Politics of Health Care Reform in Canada and the United States.* Orono, Me.: Canadian-American Center, University of Maine.

———. 1997. "The Development of Health Insurance in Canada and the United States, 1940–65." *Comparative Politics* (July): 411–31.

———. 1998. *Parting at the Crossroads: The Emergence of Health Insurance in the United States and Canada.* Princeton: Princeton University Press.

Myles, John. 1996. "When Markets Fail: Social Welfare in Canada and the United States." In G. Esping-Andersen, *Welfare States in Transition.* London: Sage.

———. 2000. "The Maturation of Canada's Retirement Income System: Income Levels, Income Inequality and Low Income Among Older Persons." *Canadian Journal on Aging* 19:287–316.

Myles, John, and Paul Pierson. 1997. "Friedman's Revenge: The Reform of Liberal Welfare States in Canada and the United States." *Politics and Society* 25:443–72.

Myles, John, and Jill Quadagno. 1997. "Recent Trends in Public Pension Reform: A Comparative View." In K. Banting and R. Boadway, eds., *Reform of Retirement Income Policy: International and Canadian Perspectives.* Kingston: Queen's University School of Policy Studies.

OECD (Organisation for Economic Co-operation and Development). 1993. *Employment Outlook.* Paris: OECD.

———. 1994. *New Orientations for Social Policy.* Vol. 12. Paris: OECD.

Organisation for Economic Co-operation and Development and Statistics Canada. 1995. *Literacy, Economy and Society.* Paris and Ottawa: OECD and Statistics Canada.

Palme, Joakim. 1990. *Pension Rights in Welfare Capitalism: The Development of Old-Age Pensions in 18 OECD Countries, 1930 to 1985.* Stockholm: Swedish Institute for Social Research.

Pedersen, Axel West. 1995. *Pension Systems and Income Inequality in Retirement: From Institutions to Outcomes.* Florence: European University Institute.

Picot, Garnett, and John Myles. 1996. "Social Transfers, Changing Family Structure and Low Income Among Children." *Canadian Public Policy* 22:244–67.

Pierson, Paul. 1994. *Dismantling the Welfare State? Reagan, Thatcher and the Politics of Retrenchment.* Cambridge: Cambridge University Press.

Quadagno, Jill. 1994. *The Color of Welfare: How Racism Undermined the War on Poverty.* New York: Oxford University Press.

Smeeding, Timothy, and Dennis Sullivan. 1998. "Generations and the Distribution of Economic Well-Being: A Cross-National View." Luxembourg Income Study Working Paper, no. 173.

Starr, Paul. 1995. "What Happened to Health Care Reform?" *The American Prospect* 20:20–31.

Traxler, Franz. 1996. "Collective Bargaining and Industrial Change: A Case of Disorganization? A Comparative Analysis of Eighteen OECD Countries." *European Sociological Review* 12:271–87.

United States House of Representatives, Committee on Ways and Means. 1994.
   Where Your Money Goes: The 1994–95 Green Book. Washington, D.C.:
   Brassey's.
Weaver, R. Kent. 1986. "The Politics of Blame Avoidance." *Journal of Public Policy*
   6:371–98.
Wilson, William Julius. 1987. *The Truly Disadvantaged: The Inner City, the Under-
   class, and Public Policy*. Chicago: University of Chicago Press.

Work, Training, or the Dole? Active and Passive Labor Market Policies in Western Europe

THOMAS JANOSKI AND ANTONIO ALAS

Among advanced industrialized countries, Sweden and the United States represent contrasting and sometimes antagonistic approaches to the labor market. Sweden has been and continues to be the world leader in active labor market policies. Two Swedish economists—Gøsta Rehn and Rudolf Meidner—were responsible for formulating the active labor market approach with their articles in *Tidens* in the late 1940s. The United States has generally avoided direct government intervention into labor markets with the exception of the mid-1960s to early 1980s. Despite the popularity of employment programs during recessions and oil crises, the dominant economic approach to the labor market in the United States has not strayed too far from the Chicago school of economists, who emphasize the efficiency of markets and the ineffectiveness of government regulation of employment. But as somewhat extreme cases, the economies of Sweden and the United States are difficult to emulate. Two other European countries—the United Kingdom and Germany—are not so committed to either extreme, but nonetheless exhibit a clear preference for one strategy over the other and can pursue their own courses under specific institutional and economic constraints. This chapter examines their approaches to solving the European employment crisis in the context of sixteen other OECD countries.

The United Kingdom experienced industrialization and acquired trade unions and a labor party before other countries. For most of the 1980s and 1990s, it has experienced restructuring and Margaret Thatcher. The United Kingdom is a country very much in need of innovative labor market policies, but it has only moderate political forces and weak institutions to support them. As a result, labor market interventions have been intermittently funded, involved with a number of different and complex institutions, and in some ways, oriented toward U.S. market-based models.

We thank Günther Schmid for his support in developing the data base for this study. We thank Matthew Sargent and Matthew Moore for research assistance. This chapter has benefited by research funded by NSF grant 92-10437, the Wissenschaftszentrum in Berlin, and the Swedish Bicentennial Fund. Please direct correspondence to Thomas Janoski, 1571 Patterson Office Tower, Department of Sociology, University of Kentucky, Lexington KY 40506-0027; e-mail: tjanos@uky.edu.

As a late but strong industrializer, Germany has had strong Social Democratic Party power, moderate unionization, and some restructuring under Helmut Kohl's more muted market strategies. Germany employs a strong employment service with effective funding for programs of job placement, job training, and job creation. It is not the strong and perhaps unattainable case that Sweden displays; nonetheless, it has been an effective user of selected Swedish labor market strategies.

These two countries also have some similarities. They have both faced high unemployment in the last ten to fifteen years, especially in the northern and midland areas of the United Kingdom, and the Ruhr and the "neue Bundesländer" of the East in Germany. Both the United Kingdom and Germany have also experienced strong gravitational pulls toward pan-European norms and policies. Membership in the European Union has strongly affected economic policy, with the implementation of a unified European currency being a major sign of this, and labor and social policies are also coming under increasing attention. Though weaker in direct authority, a second transnational political force is the Organizational for Economic Cooperation and Development (OECD), which has had a strong advisory effect on labor market practices with its major policy campaigns in the 1960s and again in the 1990s.

The purpose of this chapter is to present the contexts of labor market policy in the advanced industrialized countries, and then look at the labor market policy mix in Britain and Germany. We will look at the advanced industrial countries in terms of Esping-Andersen's (1990) three worlds of welfare capitalism—social democratic, traditional, and liberal regimes—because these clusters of countries structure labor market policy responses among eighteen countries and illustrate different models of capitalism (Janoski 1994, 1998). In the next sections, we will define active and passive labor market policies, look at economic institutions and policies, and then go into the two country cases in more detail.

WHAT ARE ACTIVE AND PASSIVE LABOR MARKET POLICIES?

Active labor market policy (ALMP) is not simply a set of Keynesian spending programs. In fact, the original Swedish conception of ALMP in the late 1940s—the Rehn-Meidner model—was never fully implemented, mainly because politicians thought that its anti-inflation controls would be unpopular. Consequently, the version of the model that was implemented was mainly oriented toward controlling unemployment and, to some degree, excessive wage growth.

ALMP consists of state intervention into the labor market through job placement, job training, and job creation policies in order to prevent or lessen unemployment (Janoski 1990, 7–8). The "active" in ALMP means that the state employment service or a more specialized organization will work with firms and trade unions to initiate early planning to prevent unemployment. Such programs are still considered active when they are in reaction to already existing unemployment, since they do not subsidize unemployment. Passive programs like unemployment compensation may be seen as doing just that. Another way to look at ALMP may be to contrast it to Esping-Andersen's concept of "decommodification" (1990, 21–23). ALMP does not keep people out of the labor market, but instead, it is a "recommodification" policy that gets people into jobs. The three major aspects of ALMP—job placement, training, and creation—are active in and of themselves. Job placement is the most direct of the three, since it involves finding appropriate jobs for people who are out of work or seeking new jobs. Job training targets people who need jobs and positions that are subject to labor supply bottlenecks. Job creation concerns a government's attempt to create work either indirectly through tax incentives, or directly by creating new positions in government services. In addition to these three, there are many others that might be on the borderline between ALMP and other policies.

Passive labor market policy (PLMP) can include a wide array of different programs and initiatives; however, the main PLMP of concern in this chapter will be unemployment insurance, job security and maintenance measures, and minimum wage legislation.

OVERVIEW OF EUROPEAN APPROACHES TO LABOR MARKET POLICY

Supranational mandates on labor market and unemployment policies have been important environmental aspects of domestic policy in Western Europe. While the European Community has only a small amount of formal power in this area and the OECD has none, these two groups make policy recommendations that set the tone for employment and many other policies. Their mandates have occurred in two waves during the post–World War II period. In the 1960s, the OECD made a strong effort to promote Swedish-style ALMP based on the Rehn-Meidner model. Multinational teams made visits to European and North American countries until the early 1980s to interview labor market officials and to appraise their labor market policies (e.g., OECD 1964, 1970, 1974). Although the OECD had no formal authority, some of its member states were persuaded to implement more ALMP.

The later 1970s and early 1980s brought the oil crisis and high unemployment throughout the Western world. The OECD and European Union took somewhat contradictory positions at this time. The OECD was backing away from social spending but not totally abandoning ALMP. Nonetheless, after an initial flurry of ALMP spending, most countries kept close to budgetary constraints and controlled ALMP spending. Unlike the OECD, the European Economic Commission used its Social Fund to back labor market policies in some of the poorer states and declining regions in Europe (e.g., Ireland and the Ruhr region of Germany have qualified to varying degrees for such programs). However, its resources were limited.

In the late 1980s and 1990s, the OECD promoted ALMP again with "The OECD Jobs Strategy," which was a new and improved version of the 1960s strategy but with the experience of high unemployment and an emphasis on flexibility and restructuring (OECD 1994a, 1994b, 1995, 1996a). It supported specific and carefully targeted interventions by the state into the labor market. Following up on the white paper of 1993 (EC 1993), the European Council in its Essen strategy promoted a similar belt-tightening policy but nonetheless stressed the transformation of passive into active policies. They recommended the transformation of (1) unemployment compensation into job creation or training subsidies; (2) tired bureaucratic services into more individualized and user-friendly interactions in a stronger and more flexible employment service; (3) unemployed and isolated workers into lifelong learners connected to new skills and firms, and even entrepreneurs working in individual or community programs; (4) restless youth into involved employees in workshop schools, internship programs, and stronger apprenticeship programs (often through a job guarantee program); (5) bored workers into interested employees learning many skills through job rotation; and (6) firm-level strikes and confrontations into cooperative tripartite wage negotiations (i.e., labor, management, and the state bargaining over a larger number of employees and firms) (EC 1997a).

European approaches to PLMP have not had as much emphasis as ALMP. Passive policies are generally portrayed as necessary but sometimes counterproductive. In the 1990s, the negative aspects of passive policies were pointed out in two ways. First, payments for passive policies were roughly double those for active policies in the OECD/EC area. Some of this was unavoidable perhaps because of record levels of unemployment. But it certainly doesn't lend credence to the rhetoric of turning passive policies into active ones. Second, fiscal constraints have brought belt-tightening. The replacement rate for unemployment compensation has consistently been reduced in most countries, and after an initial flurry, job maintenance programs have generally been criticized. The OECD Jobs Strategy consistently criticizes job security or maintenance programs because they reduce employer flexibility. The insider-outsider theory has grown out of this basic problem of employers refusing to hire new workers because they know how difficult it will be to lay them off (Lindbeck and Snower 1988).[1]

Welfare reform has taken off in a number of countries where public assistance rolls have been high. This reform has led to a much higher emphasis on work and has increased the pressure on recipients to find jobs. It generally takes place in countries that have weak ALMP and strong reliance on PLMP and other social policies. In a sense, aspects of welfare reform are ALMP through the back door with a heavy dose of moralistic preaching and political rhetoric. Nonetheless, welfare reform has provided a number of functionally equivalent ALMP programs, though training is often frowned upon as a way to avoid work.

LABOR MARKET CONDITIONS AND EXPENDITURES

Europe experienced low unemployment and high economic growth after rebuilding its way out of the rubble of the last world war. From 1960 to the early 1970s, unemployment was consistently lower in Europe than in the United States, and economic growth somewhat higher. As most countries experienced high unemployment with the oil shocks of 1974 and 1980, nearly all the OECD countries experienced difficulties. Coming out of the last oil shock, countries that used ALMP and combined it with reasonable investment and sometimes currency devaluation policies were able to keep their unemployment low.[2] For instance, in the latter part of the 1980s, Sweden and Norway still had unemployment rates of 2.3 and 3.0 percent, which is below what many economic theorists consider a natural rate of unemployment. However, these employment levels were sometimes attained at the cost of high inflation, which was nearly guaranteed by periodic currency devaluations in Sweden. These unemployment, growth, investment, and inflation rates from 1985 to the mid-1990s can be seen in Table 12.1.

1. The insiders who are usually older workers have the jobs and decent pay, while the outsiders, who are usually teenaged and younger, suffer the highest levels of unemployment.
2. The United States is an exception in that jobs grew extensively without ALMP interventions.

Table 12.1 Economic Conditions in Advanced Industrialized Countries (percentages)

Country and regime type[a]	(1) Standardized unemployment rates			(2) Long-term unemployment rates (>1 yr.)			(3) Rate of economic growth in real GDP			(4) Rate of Inflation (change in consumer price index)			(5) Average growth in private capital investment (nonresidential)		
	1985–89	1990–94	1995–96	1983	1990	1993	1985–89	1990–94	1995–97	1985–89	1990–94	1995–96	1985–89	1990–94	1995–97
Germany	6.4	6.0	8.6	42	47	40	4.9	6.8	1.8	2.0	3.7	1.7	5.2	1.6	0.8
United Kingdom	9.9	9.2	8.5	46	34	43	9.6	5.3	2.5	5.3	4.6	3.0	11.0	-2.9	6.7
Neocorporatist															
Denmark	6.8	8.7	7.0	44	30	25	6.4	4.1	2.6	4.3	2.1	2.1	5.3	0.2	10.3
Finland	5.0	11.4	15.8	19	9	30	9.9	1.0	4.1	4.9	3.3	0.9	8.5	-14.4	14.2
Netherlands	7.8	6.3	6.6	49	49	52	3.7	4.8	2.6	0.7	2.9	2.0	7.0	-0.5	5.6
Norway	3.0	5.7	5.0	6	19	27	12.8	4.1	4.0	6.6	2.7	2.1	-2.1	0.0	8.8
Sweden	2.3	6.0	9.6	10	5	11	9.1	4.5	2.2	5.7	6.0	1.5	9.0	-5.2	10.8
Traditional															
Austria	—	3.9	4.1	—	13	17	5.2	6.0	1.5	2.2	3.4	2.5	7.7	3.2	4.1
Belgium	9.4	7.9	9.8	65	69	53	6.4	4.7	1.8	2.4	2.8	1.7	10.4	-3.4	4.4
France	10.0	10.6	12.0	42	38	34	7.2	3.7	2.0	3.6	2.6	1.6	7.0	-1.1	1.0
Ireland	16.2	14.7	12.0	37	66	59	8.4	6.7	—	3.7	2.7	1.9	4.0	-0.1	14.6
Italy	9.5	9.7	12.0	58	70	58	10.5	6.6	1.5	6.2	5.2	3.7	6.5	-1.9	5.3
Liberal															
Australia	7.5	9.6	8.6	25	22	37	11.5	4.5	3.7	7.8	3.0	2.5	7.2	-2.1	11.6
Canada	8.8	10.2	9.6	10	6	14	7.9	3.0	2.6	4.3	2.8	1.8	8.9	-0.1	7.2
Japan	2.6	2.4	3.3	13	19	17	5.9	3.7	2.4	1.1	2.0	0.6	10.3	0.1	6.4
New Zealand	5.2	9.2	6.2	—	19	33	12.8	4.1	2.5	11.3	2.6	2.4	2.7	5.2	7.7
Switzerland	—	3.2	3.7	—	—	—	5.5	4.1	0.1	2.1	3.9	1.0	6.5	-3.4	2.3
United States	6.2	6.6	5.5	13	6	12	6.9	5.0	2.7	3.6	3.6	2.7	2.0	2.1	9.4

SOURCES (by column number): (1) OECD 1998, 246; (2) ibid., 10; (3) OECD 1995; (4) OECD 1998, 240; (5) ibid., 230.

[a] See Esping-Andersen 1990.

The United Kingdom, however, had higher unemployment and lower growth from the 1960s to the mid-1980s than most of the OECD countries. By 1985 it started to come out of this slump with some periods of higher investment (11 percent from 1985 to 1989) but unemployment was still high. Germany had exceptionally low unemployment rates in the later 1950s and 1960s, but it was slowed down considerably by the oil crises. Unemployment rates rose to very high levels as capital investment began a slow but steady decline. Inflation, however, remained low under a policy with strong historical roots in the hyperinflation of the Weimar republic.

Governments have varied in their responses to unemployment. Some countries like Sweden and Germany have been leaders in ALMP, while others, such as the United Kingdom, have been followers. Sweden spent near or over 1 percent of GNP on ALMP from 1965 to 1979, more than any other country at the time, and nearly 3 percent of GNP in the 1990s. As a whole, social democratic countries have spent more on ALMP, but some traditional countries (e.g., France, Ireland, Belgium) and even liberal Australia have spent much more from 1985 to the present (see Table 12.2). Germany has often been far behind Sweden. It began spending over 1 percent of GNP on ALMP in the late 1970s, and reunification has brought expenditures to an even higher level. The United Kingdom reached its peak of expenditures in the 1980s but has never spent more than 1 percent on ALMP/GNP.

Most countries spend more money on PLMP than on ALMP. It is often a policy goal of many countries to shift expenditures from the passive to the active side, but this is not as easy as it sounds. Active measures involve much more in the way of service arrangements with training requiring instructors, job creation needing managers, and job placement using employment counselors. PLMPs are income transfers that require a bureaucracy to verify employment conditions and then print a check. Sometimes the unemployed may have had little or no contact with this bureaucracy for months at a time. Also, PLMP is generally seen as the last policy of self-respect before public assistance. Table 12.3 shows the PLMP expenditures in industrialized countries, and in many ways, they match up with ALMP expenditures in the social democratic countries (i.e., those who spend on ALMP also spend heavily on passive measures). In other words, during periods of high unemployment there is no trade-off between active and passive measures, though in better economic times, trade-offs may exist. Both Germany and the United Kingdom spend a moderate amount of money over GNP on passive measures, but this is much less than many of the social democratic countries and even Belgium and Ireland. However, Germany spends more than the United Kingdom, which can be explained by their higher benefit levels.

Table 12.2 Active Labor Market Policy (ALMP) Divided by GNP at Factor Cost (%)

Regimes/ Country	1995– 1996	1990– 1994	1985– 1989	1980– 1984	1975– 1979	1970– 1974	1965– 1969
Germany	1.59	1.64[2]	1.11	1.00	0.81	0.63	0.33
United Kingdom	0.51	0.67	0.86	0.79	0.53	0.15	0.07
Sweden	2.61	2.99	1.81	1.94	1.75	1.40	0.95
Finland	1.93	1.77	1.09	1.23	0.44	0.23	0.21
Denmark	2.35	1.96	1.42	1.37	0.44	0.23	0.14
Norway	1.45	1.29	0.83	0.50	0.52	0.22	0.22
Netherlands	1.49	1.35	0.58	0.59	0.32	—	—
Neocorporatist average:	*1.97*	*1.87*	*1.51*	*1.13*	*0.69*	*0.52*	*0.38*
France	1.51	1.28[2]	1.43	1.10	0.88	0.42	0.30
Ireland	2.21	1.94[1]	0.95	0.67	0.37	0.22	0.19
Belgium	1.59	1.34	0.59	0.49	0.29	0.10	0.10
Austria	0.43	0.38	0.31	0.21	0.18	0.18	0.10
Italy	1.25	1.38[2]	0.23	0.26	0.13	0.07	0.06
Traditional average:	*1.40*	*1.26*	*0.70*	*0.54*	*0.37*	*0.20*	*0.15*
Australia	0.89	0.73[2]	0.45	0.25	0.20	0.01	—
Canada	0.52	0.61	0.44	0.53	0.50	0.57	0.50
New Zealand	0.91	1.04	1.02	0.88	0.27	0.06	0.06
United States	0.13	0.16	0.21	0.23	0.38	0.18	0.15
Switzerland	0.51	0.32	0.23	0.01	0.02	0.001	0.002
Japan	0.12	0.11	0.10	0.10	0.09	0.09	0.12
Liberal regime average:	*0.51*	*0.59*	*0.41*	*0.33*	*0.24*	*0.15*	*0.17*

SOURCES: All figures are computed from national sources from Janoski 1996, 713, except the last two periods which are adjusted to GNP at factor cost from OECD 1997c figures.
[1] This figure is for three years of the five-year average.
[2] This figure is for four years of the five-year average.

Unemployment policies in advanced industrialized countries fall into three categories. First, Austria, France, Germany, and to a lesser extent Sweden and the United Kingdom have unemployment help or supplementary unemployment benefits in addition to unemployment compensation. Unemployment help is a way station for comparable benefits to insurance before someone might fall into public assistance. Second, New Zealand and Australia have means-tested unemployment compensation that is more similar to public assistance. It may last for a long time but it pays relatively little. And third, a number of countries rely mainly on unemployment insurance, which runs out after a specified period. Belgium, Ireland, Denmark, Finland, Switzerland, and Norway have longer benefit durations and generally higher payments, while Italy, Canada, Japan, and the United States have shorter durations and lower payments.

Table 12.3 Passive Labor Market Policy (PLMP) as a Percentage of GNP (passive labor market policies include unemployment compensation and early retirement measures for labor market reasons)

Countries grouped by regime type	1995–97	1990–94	1985–89
Germany	2.14	2.05	1.80
United Kingdom	1.45	1.52	0.90
Sweden	2.60	1.60	1.40
Finland	4.05	3.93	2.25
Denmark	4.56	5.01	4.70
Norway	1.10	1.35	1.15
Netherlands	3.06	2.60	2.30
Neocorporatist regime average:	*3.074*	*2.898*	*2.360*
France	—	—	—
Ireland	3.33	3.25	2.99
Belgium	3.01	2.90	2.75
Austria	1.44	1.33	1.08
Italy	1.45	1.03	0.88
Traditional regime average:	*2.308*	*2.128*	*1.925*
Australia	1.64	1.85	1.80
Canada	1.32	2.09	2.28
New Zealand	1.25	1.88	1.95
United States	0.39	0.58	0.60
Switzerland	1.25	1.02	0.36
Japan	0.35	0.30	0.26
Liberal regime average:	*1.033*	*1.287*	*1.208*

SOURCES: All figures are computed from OECD 1983-98.
ALMP/PLMP Calculations & Tables.
Germany/National Employment Plan 1998.
UK/National Employment Action Plan 1998.

Germany spends more on PLMP than the United Kingdom because German benefits are much higher. Maximum payments in Germany on unemployment compensation are eight times higher than in the United Kingdom, and minimum payments for unemployment assistance are even higher than the maximum payment for unemployment compensation in the United Kingdom (see columns 1 and 2 in Table 12.4). However, this is also because the average wage in Germany is much higher than similar wages in the United Kingdom. The replacement rate—unemployment compensation benefit payments as a percentage of average wages—is actually higher in the United Kingdom (76 percent in the United Kingdom compared to 73 percent in Germany). Nonetheless, Germany spends more on PLMP than the United Kingdom (2.1 percent compared to 1.5 from 1995 to 1997) because unemployment assistance payments are high and last a long time.

Table 12.4 Rules and Benefits Concerning Passive Labor Market Policies (PLMP)

Countries grouped by regime type	(1)	Unemployment compensation (2)			Employment protection			Minimum wages (6)	(7)	
		1972	1980	1990	(3)	(4)	(5)		1975	1994
Germany	1.0+ᵃ	.74	.64	.42	2/1	Yes	1.0	Industrial bargainingᵈ	—	45
United Kingdom	1.0	.43	.28	.16	3/3	No	1.0	Wage councilᵈ	—	—
Neocorporatist										
Denmark	2.50	—	.60	.47	0/1	No	0.5	—	—	—
Finland	1.92	.32	.50	.61	2/2	No	1.0	—	—	—
Netherlands	3.00	—	.93	.75	3/3	Yes	3.0	Legislation	—	—
Norway	1.54	.18	.32	.39	1/1	Yes	2.0	Central bargaining	—	—
Sweden	1.15	.31	.49	.64ᶜ	1/1	Yes	1.0	Central bargaining	—	—
Traditional										
Austria	0.58+ᵃ	.55	.57	.57	0/12	No	2.0	—	—	—
Belgium	5.0ᵇ	.83	.73	—	3/3	No	2.5	Legislation	66	58
France	2.50	.34	.41	—	1/1	No	2.5	Legislation	45	49
Ireland	1.25	—	.43	.45	3/3	No	—	—	—	—
Italy	0.50	.11	.14	.08	0/0	No	2.0	—	—	—
Liberal										
Australia	5.0/0ᵇ		very low		3/3	—	—	Arbitrationᵈ	—	—
Canada	0.96	—	.37	.47	3/3	—	—	Legislation	52	43
Japan	0.50	.31	.36	.20	1/1	—	—	None	—	—
New Zealand	5.0/0ᵇ		very low		3/3	—	—	Arbitrationᵈ	60	44
Switzerland	0.50	—	—	—	1/1	—	—	None	—	—
United States	0.58	.36	.36	.36	0/0	No	0.0	Legislation	45	38

Table 12.4 Rules and Benefits Concerning Passive Labor Market Policies (PLMP) (*continued*)

HEADINGS AND SOURCES BY COLUMN NUMBER:

(1) Maximum duration of unemployment compensation in years in 1989. OECD 1993a, 105.

(2) Replacement rates: unemployment benefit as percentage of average wage. OECD 1993a, 105.

(3) Minimum months notice required, blue/white collar. OECD 1993a, 96.

(4) Consultation required with union or works council. OECD 1993a, 96.

(5) Protection index (a measure derived from the sum of five items: written notice, statement of reasons, required consultation, administrative authorizations, and severance pay). Calculated from OECD 1993a, 96.

(6) Institution authorizing minimum wage. OECD 1993b.

(7) Minimum wage as a percentage of average wage. OECD 1997d, 13.

[a] Both Austria and Germany have *Arbeitslosebnihlfe* or *Notstandhilfe*, which are means-tested unemployment compensation administered by the employment service but not public assistance. It can last for years and is about 92 percent of unemployment benefits (Winter-Ebrren 1998, 33–36; Janoski 1990). The extension through these programs are noted by the +, which means durations are longer than what is listed.

[b] Belgium, Australia, and New Zealand have benefits listed as indefinite. These have been scored as 5.0, but it is also noted that Australian and New Zealand benefits are very low.

[c] Swedish replacement rates go up considerably when children are involved. For more specific figures on the Swedish system, see OECD 1997d.

[d] Minimum wages in Germany vary according to industry but they are roughly equivalent to French ratios (Symes 1995, 177). The United Kingdom has no minimum wage now, but previously wages councils set minimum wages for catering and agricultural work. Australia and New Zealand had wage tribunals that engaged in arbitration, but that system was abandoned in the 1990s.

Various sorts of employment protections are part of PLMP. This involves redundancy payments and rules involved in protecting people dismissed from their jobs. There are minimum levels of notice and requirements of consultation with trade unions or works councils (see columns 3, 4, and 5 in Table 12.4). The minimum months listed in the table range from none to two months, but the maximums depend on seniority and can sometimes get as large as six to twelve months. The social democratic countries have the highest protections on average, though France, Japan, and Switzerland are also high. Germany has moderate and the United Kingdom somewhat low protections. Italy and the United States have no protections at all on either notice or consultation with unions, though increased protection may be negotiated in union contracts.

Minimum wages are hard to compare in advanced industrialized countries because minimums are set by diverse institutions such as legislatures, collective bargaining, wage councils, or arbitration tribunals. Although the evidence is sketchy (see column 6 in Table 12.4), the United States appears to have lower minimum wages as a percentage of average wages in 1994. Minimum wages in Germany are determined in industry level bargaining and extended to a large portion of the economy through bargaining coverage laws. Minimum wages as a percentage of average wages are about 45 percent, but this clearly varies according to industry. In the United Kingdom, bargaining is less centralized and doesn't create an economy-wide minimum wage. In low wage industries (e.g., catering and agricultural work) minimum wages had been set by the wage councils (Edwards et al. 1992; Robinson 1996, x), but these councils were disabled by Thatcher, which contributes to the fact that the United Kingdom often has the lowest average pay in the EC.

One should be careful in reading the relationship between PLMP and ALMP and unemployment and economic growth. In general, ALMP reduces unemployment, but countries tend to use more ALMP when their unemployment rates go up. Consequently, there is the puzzling question of which effect dominates. The results are different in terms of time and space. In time within one country, ALMP reduces what the unemployment rate might have been but there is no measure of what unemployment might have been. Over time, a high correlation between unemployment and ALMP may result. In cross-national analyses, countries with high expenditures on ALMP generally have lower unemployment rates (Zetterberg 1995; Layard et al. 1991; Forslund and Krueger 1994). Consequently, this seemingly simple relationship is complex and should be interpreted carefully (Janoski et al. 1997).

POLITICAL AND INSTITUTIONAL CONTEXTS OF LABOR MARKET POLICY IN TWO COUNTRIES

Political Parties

The political and institutional support for labor market policies differs quite markedly in the United Kingdom and Germany. The German Social Democratic Party has been a consistent supporter and reformer of ALMP over the years, especially from the mid-1960s to the mid-1980s. But the Christian Democratic Party, especially in its small but significant trade union wing, also initiated strong ALMP measures in the 1950s and during Helmut Kohl's long term of office.

British politics from 1945 to 1951 were dominated by building an extensive welfare state with a national health service and defending the Empire or Commonwealth. The welfare state envisioned at this time was relatively passive in terms of labor market policy. The country was rebuilding and soon was booming. Immigration increased, and the government was recruiting workers from throughout Europe while New Commonwealth immigrants thronged ashore for the first time (Paul 1997). The Labour Party probably supports ALMP as much as the Social Democratic Party in Germany; however, the Conservative Party tends to let employment policy languish and sometimes attacks it outright. The neocorporatist innovations by Labour in the 1960s and 1970s with the Manpower Services Commission are a case in point. From the right, Thatcher eliminated many programs in the United Kingdom in the 1980s and 1990s, while Kohl was careful not to dismantle labor market policy programs or institutions.

Trade Unions and Collective Bargaining

In Germany, trade union membership has declined from 36 percent of the labor force in 1980 to 29 percent in 1994, but the bargaining coverage of negotiated contracts still extends to slightly more than 90 percent of the labor force. Trade unions are highly centralized in eleven industrial unions and a major trade union federation—the Deutsche Gewerkschafts Bund (DGB); employers in Germany are equally well organized, belonging for the most part to a single federation—the Bund der Deutschen Arbeitgeber (BDA). These two federations—the "social partners"—can strongly influence policy through their centralized bargaining at the industry/region level and by means of participation in tri- or bipartite policy boards in the welfare state (OECD 1997b, 71; Janoski et al. 1997).

Trade unions have traditionally been strong in the United Kingdom, but they are very decentralized, and the shop steward is famed for his or her power in the plant. Trade union density dropped from 50 percent in 1980 to 39 percent and 34 percent in 1990 and 1994. All of these figures are higher than in Germany, but the bargaining coverage of this decentralized system is 21 to 40 percentage points less than in Germany in all three periods (see column 2 in Table 12.5). The Trade Union Council (TUC) tries to coordinate collective bargaining, sometimes in cooperation with government guidelines, but it has only very little power over the hundred or so unions in its federation (Edwards et al. 1992, 20–21). The Confederation of British Industry (CBI) and other employer organizations exist, but they play a small role in the predominant form of single-employer bargaining.[3] Consequently, even with higher trade union density, British bargaining coverage is much less than the more centralized system in Germany. Bargaining centralization and coordination are weak, and the system has often been portrayed as one with delays, confusion, and unpredictable strikes (Lane 1989, 211–12; Crouch 1993, 247). Not having works councils (worker-elected councils at the workplace) and codetermination (worker representatives on boards of directors) may also contribute to this confusion. The power of the trade unions was a major bone of contention with the Thatcher government, and she was able to pass industrial relations acts to weaken them. The new Blair government has kept its distance from the trade unions, which sometimes dominated previous Labour governments.

Education Systems

Educational systems in these two countries differ drastically in their structure, and this has consequences for youth training and unemployment. In Germany, the educational system is much more attuned to labor market realities than in many other countries. The system of higher education is quite good, and enrollments are growing. The apprenticeship system in Germany has a strong state and employer basis of cooperation. The dual system of the state-supported *Berufschulen* and the employer-provided apprenticeship system has covered half of teenage school enrollments in the 1960s. It has contracted some since then to around 40 percent, but it still supplies a large number of highly skilled workers, who receive the equivalent of a journeyman's card when they pass their final exams and graduate. This

---

3. The Confederation of Business and Industry is engaging in more industry level bargaining as the level of bargaining in general decreases (Edwards et al. 1992; Armstrong 1984).

gives German firms an advantage in having a highly trained workforce emerging out of their secondary schools (Janoski 1990, 51–54, 109–21). Evidence of this system can be seen in the fact that over 90 percent of teenagers fifteen to nineteen are in some type of schooling, whereas only 70 percent of British teenagers are so engaged. Further, 33 to 35 percent of German youths aged twenty to twenty-four are in training, while 10 percent less are so involved in Britain (EC 1997b, 83, 109). One partial result of this is that youth unemployment rates for German teenagers has ranged from 7 to 8 percent, while the British unemployment rate for youths fifteen to twenty-four has been 16 to 18 percent.

The British system of higher education is quite well respected, and recent reforms by the Thatcher government have added business schools to the classical traditions of the Oxbridge universities. But in training the noncollege workforce, Britain has faced a severely declining apprenticeship sector and high rates of school leaving (i.e., teenagers dropping out of school). In the 1980s and early 1990s, this fact was played up by a series of articles from the National Institute of Economic and Social Research comparing British vocational education in a single occupation to the same training offered in Germany or France (Prais 1981, 1995; Prais and Wagner 1988). They revealed one devastating lack of British skills after another. The general impact of education for noncollege students has a negative impact on ALMP because these school-leavers do not fit as well into high-level vocational retraining as the similarly situated German workers do (Janoski 1990). In the postwar period, the British state's reform of education, especially at the vocational level, has been confused and usually ineffective.

Overall Results of Institutional Contexts and Policies

Labor market institutions, including the structure of the trade unions and consequent collective bargaining procedures, produce a contentious and somewhat disorganized industrial relations system in Britain. The ratio of collective bargaining coverage to trade union membership is about 3.2 in Germany and 1.4 in the United Kingdom, which means that Germany gets about 3 percentage points of coverage for a single percentage of membership, while the United Kingdom gets about 1.5 points per each percent of membership. As a result of this and an overall difference in competitive edge, wages and benefits are much higher in Germany, though both have been growing recently in the United Kingdom. The result is an interorganizational system of labor union and employer confusion in Britain, and unity in Germany. In the United Kingdom, these institutional differences prevent

Table 12.5 Collective Bargaining Institutions, Coverage, and Structure

Country / Regime	(1) Trade union density (%)	(2) Bargaining coverage (%)	Centralization score	(3) Coordination score	Bargaining institutions
Germany					
1980	48	91	2.0	3.0	IND
1990	41	90	2.0	3.0	IND
1994	35	92	2.0	3.0	IND
United Kingdom					
1980	50	70	2.0	1.5	WC, COS, IND
1990	39	47	2.0−	1.0+	WC, COS, IND
1994	34	47	1.5	1.0	COS, IND
Neocorporatist					
Finland					
1980	70	95	2.5	2.0+	CORP
1990	72	95	2.0+	2.0+	CORP
1994	81	95	2.0+	2.0+	CORP
Denmark					
1980	76	69	2.0+	2.5	CORP
1990	71	69	2.0	2.0+	CORP
1994	76	69	2.0+	2.0+	CORP
Netherlands					
1980	35	76	2.0	2.0	PILL
1990	26	71	2.0	2.0	PILL
1994	26	81	2.0	2.0	PILL
Sweden					
1980	80	86	2.0+	3.0	CORP
1990	83	86	2.0	2.0	CORP
1994	91	89	2.0	2.0	CORP

Table 12.5 Collective Bargaining Institutions, Coverage, and Structure (*continued*)

Norway				
1980	57	2.0	2.5	CORP
1990	56	2.0+	2.5	CORP
1994	58	2.0+	2.5	CORP
Traditional				
France				
1980	18	2.0	2.0−	CORP
1990	10	2.0	2.0	CORP
1994	9	2.0	2.0	CORP
Belgium				
1980	56	2.0+	2.0	PILL
1990	51	2.0+	3.0	PILL
1994	54	2.0+	3.0	PILL
Austria				
1980	56	2.0+	3.0	CORP
1990	46	2.0+	3.0	CORP
1994	42	2.0+	3.0	CORP
Italy				
1980	49	2.0−	1.5	CORP
1990	39	2.0−	1.5	CORP
1994	39	2.0	2.5	CORP
Liberal				
Australia				
1980	48	2.0+	2.0+	TRI
1990	41	2.0+	2.0+	TRI
1994	35	1.5	1.5	TRI, COM
Canada				
1980	36	1.0	1.0	COM
1990	36	1.0	1.0	COM
1994	38	1.0	1.0	COM

Table 12.5 Collective Bargaining Institutions, Coverage, and Structure (*continued*)

Country / Regime	(1) Trade union density (%)	(2) Bargaining coverage (%)	Centralization score	(3) Coordination score	Bargaining institutions
New Zealand					
1980	56	67	2.0	1.5	TRI
1990	45	67	1.5	1.0	TRI
1994	30	31	1.0	1.0	COM
Switzerland					
1980	31	53	2.0	2.0+	IND
1990	27	53	2.0	2.0+	IND
1994	27	50	2.0	2.0+	IND
United States					
1980	22	26	1.0	1.0	COM
1990	16	18	1.0	1.0	COM
1994	16	18	1.0	1.0	COM
Japan					
1980	31	28	1.0	3.0	COM
1990	25	23	1.0	3.0	COM
1994	24	21	1.0	3.0	COM

SOURCES: All figures computed from OECD 1997a, 71. Centralization descriptions come from a wide variety of national sources.

Table 12.5 Collective Bargaining Institutions, Coverage, and Structure (*continued*)

ABBREVIATIONS:

IND = Industry collective bargaining at the national or regional level.

WC = Wages council for industries without collective bargaining. In the United Kingdom, these councils set minimum wages until they were more or less disabled by Prime Minister Thatcher (Edwards et al. 1992, 14).

CORP = Neocorporatist bargaining at a relatively centralized level.

PILL = The pillarization form of neocorporatist bargaining, which is sometimes called consociationalism. The social partners are determined by religion, ethnicity, or language, rather than by membership in labor and management.

COM = Collective bargaining at the company or plant level between management and unions.

COS = Collective bargaining at the work group level between management and union stewards.

TR = National arbitration boards or tribunals on wages in Australia and New Zealand. These tribunals are in the process of devolving into company-level bargaining, but more so in New Zealand than in Australia.

Table 12.6   Youth Unemployment and Training (1993–1995 averages)

Country	(1) Standardized unemployment rates	(2) Youth unemployment rate	(3) Teenagers 15–19 in training (%)	(4) Young adults 20–24 in training (%)	(5) Long-term unemployed with low education (%)
Germany	8.2	8.5	91.4	34.6	44.4
United Kingdom	9.6	16.9	71.1	22.9	63.4
Austria	3.9	6.9[a]	80.6[a]	30.9[a]	46.5[a]
Denmark	8.5	11.6	86.0	45.8	29.7
Finland	16.9	32.3	86.4[a]	42.7[a]	42.2[a]
Netherlands	6.9	11.8	90.0	48.2	31.6
Sweden	9.5	21.5	68.6[a]	26.5[a]	32.6[a]
Belgium	9.6	23.5	93.0	38.1	59.1
France	11.9	27.8	92.3	40.6	55.2
Ireland	14.1	22.5	80.9	25.7	72.9
Italy	11.2	32.0	73.6	32.8	58.0
Spain	23.3	43.6	78.3	40.1	67.2
OECD Average	7.8				
EC Average	10.9				

SOURCES (by column number):
(1) OECD 1998, 246.
(2) OECD 1996b, 42.
(3), (4), and (5), European Commission 1997a, 65–110.

[a] 1995 values only.

the effective coordination of labor market policies and the implementation of new programs. Another factor is that the vocational education system in Germany feeds into active job training programs, while the British system for noncollege students makes job training programs work all the harder to just get to entry-level training. Thus, no matter what ALMP and PLMP may be in each country, different industrial relations and labor market contexts will make implementing ALMP much more difficult in the United Kingdom than in Germany.

As a result of these institutional strengths, countries with more central-ized bargaining, effective ALMP, and rigorous education systems for all stu-dents will have higher average wages and more income equality. For instance, Sweden and the Netherlands have greater income equality than all other countries, as indicated by their low Gini indexes in columns 1 and 2 of Table 12.7. Their ratios of the top 10 percent of wages to the bottom 10 percent of wages are the only ones that drop below the 2.00 level (see columns 6, 7, and 8). For instance, in Sweden in 1985 and Norway in 1990 the richest 10 percent only made less than double than the poorest 10 percent, while the richest in Canada and the United States often make four times the income of the poorest.

Germany and the United Kingdom do not differ a great deal on Gini indexes of income inequality; however, the richest in the United Kingdom generally make more in comparison to the poorest than in Germany, and this difference increased from 1980 to 1990. The picture can be made clearer by looking at class wage gaps (see columns 3, 4, and 5). While the United States has the most massive ratio of average CEO to blue-collar wages (26 to 1), the United Kingdom is second among seven countries (16.9 to 1), Germany, the lowest (10.6 to 1). The United Kingdom has the second highest average managerial wage to blue-collar wage (6.2 to 1), Germany, the second lowest (4 to 1). And the United Kingdom has the highest white-collar to blue-collar wage ratio (2.9 to 1), and Germany's is much lower (1.6 to 1). The CEO, manager, white-collar to blue-collar wage ratios show that the lack of institutional unity among the working class in the United Kingdom results in some real wage and income inequalities. These inequalities are due to institutional differences, welfare state policies, and to some degree, to labor market policy, to which we now turn.

LABOR MARKET POLICIES IN GERMANY

In 1927, the Weimar Republic created the *Reichsanstalt fur Arbeitsvermitt-lung und Arbeitslosenversicherung* (Corporation for Labor Placement and Unemployment Insurance). It coordinated ALMP, unemployment compensation, and many other payments and services (Janoski 1990, 82–92). The Reichsanstalt was administered at the national, state, and local levels with tripartite bargaining conducted by equal numbers of trade union, employer, and government representatives. It had strong funding from employee/employer contributions that created a relatively large agency compared to others, a monopoly over job placement that required firms to report their employment vacancies, and numerous other powers. The depression exhausted the Reichanstalt's revenues, but it did manage to implement some job creation programs before Hitler dismantled it and set up his own authoritarian labor market programs (Janoski 1990, 37–45). But in the postwar rubble of Germany, the Federal Labor Placement and Unemployment Insurance Law of 1952 reestablished the employment service on the Weimar model. The principle was to involve the social partners and the state in the administration of

Table 12.7 Inequalities of Income and Wealth in Advanced Industrialized Countries

Country and regime type	Income inequality measured by Gini index		Class wage gaps			Richest to poorest[a]		
	(1) 1974	(2) 1987	(3)[b]	(4)[c]	(5)[d]	(6) 1980	(7) 1985	(8) 1990
Germany	.386	.257	10.6:1	4.0:1	1.6:1	2.39	2.36	2.31
United Kingdom	.327	.260	16.9:1	6.2:1	2.9:1	2.51	2.90	3.24
Neocorporatist:								
Sweden	.271	.220	—	—	—	2.14	1.97	2.14
Netherlands	.264	.240	—	—	—	2.06	2.16	2.29
Norway	—	—	—	—	—	2.06[e]	2.16[e]	1.97[e]
Traditional:								
France	.417	—	16.0:1	6.3:1	2.1:1	3.27	3.32	3.44
Italy	—	—	14.7:1	7.0:1	1.9:1	2.10	2.06	2.08
Austria	—	—	—	—	—	2.64	2.70	2.76
Liberal:								
Australia	—	—	—	—	—	2.02	2.13	2.24
Canada	.348	.270	11.9:1	3.8:1	1.4:1	3.47	4.04	3.98
Japan	.336		11.4:1	5.4:1	1.2:1	2.61	2.75	2.86
United States	.369	.385/.320	26.0:1	5.8:1	2.1:1	4.81	5.58	5.63

SOURCES (by column number):

(1) Sawyer 1976.

(2) Brickhauser, Frick, and Schwarze 1997 (Germany and the United States, after-tax income in 1987) and Jantti 1997 (Canada, Netherlands, Sweden, and the United Kingdom, 1986).

(3), (4), and (5) Computed from Bryant 1999 based on Towers Perrin data; however, also see Aboud and Bognanno 1995 and Abraham and Houseman 1995.

(6), (7), and (8) OECD 1995, 14.

Exceptions on year correspondences, columns (6), (7), and (8):

	1980	1985	1990
Austria	—	1987	1989
Canada	1981	1986	—
Germany	1983	—	—
Italy	—	—	1987
Japan	1979	1987	—
Netherlands	1987	—	—
Norway	1981	1986	1991
Sweden	1981	—	1991
United States	—	—	1989

[a] Ratio of top 10 percent of incomes to bottom 10 percent of incomes for male workers.

[b] Average CEO to blue-collar-worker wage.

[c] Average manager to blue-collar-worker wage.

[d] Average white- to blue-collar-worker wage.

[e] Figures are for both sexes.

labor market policies. Just after the war, the Germans spent a great deal of money on active policies, unlike countries like the United States and United Kingdom. But as unemployment gave way before the economic miracle, the employment service tended toward passive unemployment insurance policies (Janoski 1990). Nonetheless, the tradition of a strong institutional network ready to combat unemployment was established.

With rising Social Democratic Party power, the Labor Promotion Act of 1969—*Arbeitsförderungsgesetz* (AFG)—renamed the employment service as the *Bundesanstalt für Arbeit* (Federal Labor Institute) and replaced the unemployment insurance approach of the earlier agency with much more active policies. The ALMP programs of the Bundesantalt focused on job placement, retraining, and job creation, especially in the Ruhr Area where declining steel and coal workers needed help. However, Helmut Schmidt reacted to the economic decline of the early 1970s with retrenchment. And under the impact and stress of the oil shocks in 1981, the Labor Market Consolidation Act was passed to tighten up the budgetary controls on the employment service and reduce ineffective policies.

Helmut Kohl took over the chancellorship in 1982 and held it for the next seventeen years. In the first Kohl government, the Christian Democratic Party approach to labor market policy was only a moderate change from that of the previous administration. Budget tightening had already begun, and the oil crisis had been ridden out. Nonetheless, the right/centrist government continued most ALMP from the previous administration.

In the second Kohl government, from 1988 to 1997, Kohl engineered German reunification using two policy responses. First, the vast majority of nationalized industries were closed in the East and the *Treuhandanstalt* (Trusteeship Administration) sold off as many as possible. These closings put millions of people out of work.[4] Massive PLMP and ALMP programs were then put to work in the East as Bundesanstalt expenditures tripled from 1989 to 1993. In the 1993 recession, the government not only had to subsidize the Bundesanstalt budget but it had to borrow the funds to do so.

---

4. The *Treuhandanstalt* had a difficult time for three reasons. First, before the law was passed, a number of private corporations were created by former communist officials, including some STASI leaders. Second and most important, the *Treuhandanstalt* tried to get what was considered to be fair market value for their properties. For some it did, since many properties were bought up by West German firms, but for many others, sales were extremely slow. As properties lingered on the market, the *Treuhandanstalt* started modernizing some properties and selling them. Many properties went for drastically reduced prices. And third, the second director Detlev-Karsten Rohwedder was assassinated by terrorists, but the new director Birgit Breuel saw the Anstalt's mission through to its conclusion (Conradt 1996, 236–37, 249).

At this time, half of all unemployment benefits went to the East, although the East had only a fifth of the German population.

In the third Kohl government, the difficulties of absorbing and transforming the East German economy became more evident. When East German wages were brought up to West German levels through the bargaining process and its extension to nearly all the labor market, the competitive advantage of the East was severely impaired in comparison to other former communist countries. Berthold and Fehn conclude that "the main cause of the unemployment problem in Germany is that unions and employers have pursued the wrong wage policy in the face of changing economic conditions" (1997, 184). Labor market policies were made more flexible and restrictions on private employment offices were loosened by the Amendments to the Employment Promotion Act of 1994 and by the AFG Reform Law of 1997.

Although these regime changes were not unlike those which occurred in the United Kingdom in terms of the alternation of political party power, it is remarkable that employment policy has been so stable and one institution has led throughout the period. Rose and Page show that while Britain ended over 55 percent of its employment policies from 1971 to 1987, only 5 percent of similar policies were stopped in Germany (1990, 71–73). Similarly, while the Bundesanstalt administered policy from 1952 to the present in Germany, the British have gone through the labor exchange, the Jobcentres, the employment service, and an alphabet soup of other administrative agencies (e.g., ITB, MSC, TEC, LEC, and TC). In the United States, a country somewhat similar to the United Kingdom on labor market policy, this sort of organizational and programmatic confusion has led to serious breaks in the provision of labor market services (Janoski 1990).

Employment Service and Job Placement

From the initial law in 1952, the employment service in Germany has been strongly funded, and its many offices have done a reasonably good job in placing workers. The employment service has a number of features that make it strong but also constrain it in some ways. It is funded by contributions from employers and employees and, as such, constitutes an insurance program. This gives it a procyclical funding base that is spent in a countercyclical way; in good times, less money is spent and these savings are available during recessions when more spending is needed. However, long recessions generally exhaust the trust fund base, and the government has to provide additional money from general revenues to keep many programs funded. The employment service is an *Anstalt*, an independent "public service corporation." This means that the government gives it general guidelines through ministry interpretations of law but otherwise permits it to implement the programs it chooses. It is governed in a tripartite fashion at the national, state, and local governing councils. This means that trade union and employer federations each supply a third of the representatives on each of the governing councils, with the final third coming from the national, state, and local governments.

The powers of the German employment service are much greater than those in liberal English-speaking countries. The employment service has had a monopoly until recently over job placement. This means that there are very few private employment agencies to skim off the top of the pool of job candidates. For instance, instead of having a college placement office run by a university in the United States, college students go the employment service office located at or near the university. Employers are also expected to report vacancies to the employment service, and as a result, the Bundes-anstalt receives a large number of vacancies and makes a large percentage of placements. Although most Germans find jobs through personal networks and other informal means, the Bundesanstalt is expected to help everyone else.

The employment service was reoriented toward ALMP in 1969 with the Labor Promotion Law. The occupational composition of the employment service itself went through a hiring replacement program where lawyers oriented toward insurance were replaced by labor economists more interested in ALMP. After these changes, the employment service started to implement a wide range of programs, including more job retraining and job creation for the economically disadvantaged (Janoski 1990; Blankenberg 1976). The success of this reorientation can be seen in the easy transition from school to work in Germany compared to other countries.

In the 1990s, the Bundesanstalt tried new and more entrepreneurial approaches to getting people to work. The monopoly on job placement began to be questioned, and the Bundesanstalt was seen as being somewhat stodgy.[5] In the 1990s, Germany started to allow more private and temporary employment services to operate, hence ending the official monopoly powers of the employment service. These were not a tremendous success,

5. In the 1980s, Sweden put employment representatives on subway platforms and opened computer files jobseekers.

but they may have helped some (Walwei 1998). In 1992, the Job Information Service or *Stellen-Informations-Service* was set up in the East to allow self-service access to computer listings of employer job requests (EC-MISEP 1993). The Bundesanstalt also set up twelve new European career advice centers to help European Union citizens to find out about careers and specific job openings (EC-MISEP 1993). However, the internet portends even greater changes.

Job Training Policies

Job training in Germany is built upon the strong institutional base of apprenticeship and the Berufschule. The flow of workers into apprenticeship programs associated with state-run occupational schools and employer-supervised work training is fully institutionalized in a network that includes both the state and employers as active participants.

The Bundesanstalt coordinates initial training, retraining, and advanced training. Initial training tends to be the smallest program of the three, since the apprenticeship program provides the initial training for the vast majority of those who enter the labor market without first attending college. Initial training is for the very small number of dropouts, some immigrants, and women entering the workforce. The two largest programs are for retraining and advanced training. Retraining has traditionally targeted the workers in the declining industries in the Ruhr area, especially in the coal and steel industries. Retraining has also been used for some immigrants and especially in East Germany. A new job training program in the Eastern states is the "Training Program East," which provided DM 500 million from the federal government and matching funds from the states. Some of these funds have also been subsidized by the European Social fund (EC-MISEP 1993).

Job training in Germany differs from that in the United Kingdom and the United States. It has tended not to focus on youth unemployment because youths are effectively trained in the apprenticeship system. Also, the Bundesanstalt job training programs have high visibility and status among blue-collar workers because they are seen as an avenue to social mobility. For instance, in 1970 only 11 percent of workers entering public training programs were unemployed. However, by the time the oil crisis had hit, job training had been refocused on the unemployed and 66 percent of new entrants in 1983 were unemployed (Disney et al. 1992, 79–80). Despite the recent changes, the Bundesanstalt programs are not stigmatized like unemployment offices in other countries.

Job Creation Policies

Job creation policies in Germany have focused on two unique and sometimes expensive programs that have continued from the 1950s and 1960s. One is "short-time work," where the Bundesanstalt provides subsidies for companies who might lay off workers to put these and other workers on a work-sharing arrangement. Thus, perhaps twice the number of workers who would be laid off work part time at near full pay. The logic of the program is to help companies get over a short slump without losing workers, but it is not a long-term solution. The other program is a "winter work subsidy" to foster year-round employment in the construction industry. These subsidies help construction firms to operate in the winter when costs are higher and work is slower.

But the biggest job creation program was started just after the AFG was put into place. It is the Work Promotion Measures program, which provides jobs for the long-term unemployed. These programs have been in operation from 1970 to the present, becoming a greater part of the budget in periods of economic crisis. The jobs created tend to be longer-term than those created by British job creation programs, but success is slightly higher, with 38 to 41 percent of participants finding jobs within thirty-two months after leaving the program and 3 to 5 percent going into training (Disney et al. 1992, 103–4; Blau et al. 1996, 149–68). However, even at their peak enrollment in the German program job creation programs have been only about half that of similar British programs.

As unemployment in the Eastern and Western parts of Germany reached unheard of levels, spending on active and passive policies increased considerably. Although the Work Promotion Law already provides a considerable array of job placement, job training, and job creation programs, a number of new ones were developed. The Companies for Labor Promotion, Employment, and Structural Development (ABS companies) are liaisons between training organizations and employers. The ABS companies often deal with dismantling bankrupt company assets, preparing industrial sites, and getting involved in new construction. The Bundesanstalt and other agencies provide support, sometimes by bending regulations. In regions where unemployment is over 30 percent, these measures reduce unemployment and provide needed services for economic redevelopment (Widmaier and Blancke 1997, 32–33).[6]

---

6. A related program is the Alliance for Jobs, which was started by IG Metall chairman Klaus Zwickel. The program is essentially voluntary and negotiated in collective bargaining contracts. As such, it is not a government-sponsored job creation program (Bastain 1998).

Another innovation—START—is a corporate initiative of the North-Rhine-Westfalian government, the Bundesanstalt, the DGB, employer associations, chambers of commerce, and communities. Under the Contract Labor Act, which provides for agreements between START and the unemployed, the company created twenty-two offices which cooperate closely with the Bundesanstalt in order to establish regional networks. The intent is to provide a way station for the long-term unemployed to be trained or socialized into the work process when they are close to going back to work. It also gives employers a look at employees in a temporary work situation where employers do not have to face heavy dismissal payments or restrictive job security rules (Widmaier and Blancke 1997, 33–34).

Unemployment in the East was a major problem as businesses were closed and resold. Although not really an ALMP program, the Bundesanstalt offered an expensive early retirement option to workers who were older and not really ready to start a new career. Passive policies, including unemployment compensation, have been reduced somewhat, and the replacement rate for unemployment compensation has gone down from 74 percent to 42 percent in the last twenty-five years. Nonetheless, new programs have increased passive policies. For instance, ethnic German immigrants (*Aussiedler*) entering Germany receive transitional benefits.

LABOR MARKET POLICIES IN THE UNITED KINGDOM

The British developed a much narrower institution called the National Employment Exchange in 1909 under the Board of Trade headed by Winston Churchill. Lloyd George had set the stage, and William Beveridge fleshed out the details of organization (King 1995; Janoski et al. 1997). With the National Insurance Act of 1911, the employment service came to administer unemployment compensation. These labor exchanges never had a monopoly on job placement, and Churchill and others were able to avoid the vague references to state, employer, and trade union participation in the authorizing legislation (King 1992, 38–40).

Britain has been imprinted by weak labor market institutions.[7] The employment service / labor exchange has not had the powers or the funding of the German employment service. The training institutions for workers have seen the gradual weakening of the apprenticeship system, which was never institutionalized to the extent that it was in Germany. Most of the

---

7. "Imprinting" is a common term used in the political and organizational literature on institutions.

over-fifty labor market programs started during this period were discontinued and replaced by newer programs. Employment service, training schools, and governing bodies have come and gone with great regularity. While Rose and Page (1990, 71–73) see this as evidence of the greater flexibility and power of the British government, it more accurately reflects an inability to build strong labor market institutions that can implement and deliver ALMP.

The following section looks at the three major labor market policies as they have moved through (1) the period of low unemployment of the 1950s and early 1960s, (2) the neocorporatist attempts to establish training and promote job placement in the later 1960s and early 1970s, and (3) the emphasis on training and job search contracts in the 1980s and 1990s.

Employment Service and Job Placement

The original employment service established by the Labour Exchange Act of 1909 continued into the post–World War II period. But job placement policies in the United Kingdom have been haunted by a "fragmented and centralized" labor exchange. They were "inaccessible and unattractive," and job placement was buried under the weight of administering unemployment compensation. Since the United Kingdom pursued little in the way of unemployment reduction policies during the Great Depression, the labor exchange became the "unemployment office" where workers went "on the dole" (Lewis 1978, chap. 2, p. 2). The employment service was an executive agency without trade union cooperation, employer notification requirements, or monopoly powers in the labor market.

Unlike Germany after the Second World War, Britain had a labor shortage and low unemployment, and a strong program of ALMP did not seem necessary. Yet productivity, growth, and wages were relatively stagnant. The Industrial Training Act of 1964 established industrial training boards to promote training. But with increasing unemployment toward the end of the 1960s, many people became dissatisfied with the employment service and the low levels of training.

The intermittent labor governments of the late 1960s and early 1970s set out to reduce unemployment by creating neocorporatist institutions to regulate employment policy. The Employment and Training Act in 1973 brought the tripartite Manpower Services Commission into existence in 1975 as an umbrella organization in the labor market. In 1973, the Employment Agencies Act separated the employment service from unemployment insurance, which many thought would revitalize the agency, and this eventually led to the more focused Jobcentres. But the Jobcentres as an employment service were never the center of labor market policy. Training was handled by a separate Training Services Agency and then by the employer-dominated Training and Enterprise Councils. The Employment Subsidies Act of 1978 promoted the hiring of new workers, and the Employment Protection Act of 1978 brought about considerable employment rights, especially requiring employers to justify dismissals and making redundancy payments to those let go. This act also included requirements for employers to notify the employment service of large layoffs (EC-MISEP 1988, 19).

But the employment service has been unable to escape the image of the dole. When one says 'the employment service' in the United Kingdom, one is referring to a much smaller agency and very restricted set of labor market policies compared to those in Germany. In the 1970s, placement activities were extended into the compulsory schools, and offices were created and made more attractive, but this was not enough. From 1973 to 1979 the Manpower Services Commission provided a form of tripartite administration; however, this was a short-lived experiment. According to an employment service index constructed for eighteen countries, the employment service in Germany is two to three times more powerful than the employment service in the United Kingdom, although the employment services in many of the liberal countries (e.g., the United States and New Zealand) are weaker than those in the United Kingdom (Janoski et al. 1997, 247). Nonetheless, the British employment service is the weakest in Europe, and it is such without the usual excuses that exist in liberal countries (e.g., a small tax base, weak civil service, or low regard for the government).

Under Thatcher-inspired policies, the employment service was reintegrated with unemployment benefits by 1986, and a battery of policies prefaced with "job" were started to put the unemployed to work more quickly (EC-MISEP 1988; Sanders 1996). "Jobclubs" offered help and peer support with job searches, and the "Job Interview Guarantee" offered enhanced job placement services, including preparation for actual interviews. "Job Search Seminars" offered advice, and "Job Review Workshops" offered two-day courses that aimed to broaden the range of jobs in the search. "Work Trials" encouraged employers to take people on a temporary basis, and "Jobplan" and "Workwise" offered even more intensive job search assistance. Unemployment assistance was linked to many of these different types of programs, and after two years of unsuccessful and/or unenthusiastic searching the unemployed would be referred to "Restart Courses" that would remotivate their search. "Jobfinder's Grants" and "Jobmatch" offered financial assistance of various sorts (Robinson 1996, 68–69). By 1995 the "Jobseekers Allowance," which replaced unemployment compensation and other job search supports, made these connections between active and passive policies more formal. But receipt of this benefit required entering into a Jobseeker's Agreement in which each unemployed person promised to follow specific plans to find work (1996, 66–67). All of these policies reflected the Thatcher government's policy to get people directly into private sector jobs rather than engage in other labor market policies that they thought were expensive and uncertain.

Job Training Institutions Change Three Times

The educational training system for workers in the United Kingdom has been in a continual state of flux. In the 1950s and 1960s, an attempt was made to improve apprenticeship training after the Carr Report in 1958, but to little effect (OECD 1970, 187). The apprenticeship system was left to the employers with little or no government involvement. The Industrial Training Act of 1964 created a system of Government Training Centers, but these efforts at training did not make a significant dent in the problem either. The Training Centers themselves could just barely handle the skilled trades; the semiskilled and other occupations were beyond their reach (OECD 1970, 69–80, 191, 183–204).

The main ALMP program initially emphasized under the Thatcher regime was job training. The Industrial Training Act of 1982 made provisions for industrial training for persons over sixteen, and established Industrial Training Boards, which combined labor and management in the planning of training. It specifically imposed a levy on employers. This training was later governed by the tripartite Manpower Services Commission and the more employer-dominated Training Commission (EC-MISEP 1988, 37–38). The government's role was to stimulate training by awareness campaigns, subsidies to employers, and improving training methods.

Training was intended for two groups based on age and experience. For youths, the Technical and Vocational Training Initiative was created in 1983 to train fourteen-to-eighteen-year-olds in a more effective manner. It was not specifically targeted for the unemployed and was probably more like secondary school. Second, the Youth Training Scheme (1985 to 1988) was a comprehensive and diverse training program of vocational training, apprenticeships, and work experience to prepare young people for work. It provided one year, and then in 1986, two years of training (EC-MISEP 1988, 38). OECD described it as a group of "large-scale undifferentiated training programmes of mixed quality" (1997b, 92). But by 1992 only 9 percent of sixteen-to-seventeen-year-olds entered apprenticeships in the United Kingdom, a quarter of the rate in Germany (Robinson 1996, 80). In 1994, the government intensified its effort with "Modern Apprenticeships," and aimed for a higher standard than the Youth Training Scheme, that is, at National Vocational Qualification level 3 or above rather than level 2 under the earlier program.

For adults, the Training Opportunities Program (1972 to 1985) provided full-time training for unemployed adults in short-term courses. This was followed by the New Job Training Scheme, which offered occupational training to improve or extend the skills of the unemployed over eighteen, but especially eighteen-to-twenty-four-year-olds who had been unemployed for six months to a year. Training for three months to a year was provided in schools and on the job. The Wider Opportunities Training Program added full-time but shorter courses for a larger clientele. Reviews found that about half of the Wider Opportunities graduates went into jobs or further training and 70 percent of the New Job Training graduates did so (Disney et al. 1992, 175–76).

With the merger of the education and employment departments in the 1990s, training was put under new organizations with little or no input from the trade unions. After the Manpower Services Commission and the Training Commission (later called the Training Agency), eighty local employer-led Training and Enterprise Councils were established in England and Wales, and twenty Local Employer Councils in Scotland. Both were modeled after the Private Industry Councils in the United States, and they ran Employment Training programs and a number of other voluntary programs. The intent of Employment Training was "training workers without jobs for the jobs without workers," and as such offered a mix of programs for unskilled workers (Disney et al. 1992, 177). Trainees also had "training agents" who assessed their needs and drew up a "Personal Action and Training Plan" for each worker. Each applicant was then assigned to a "training manager," who provided a package of about 60 percent OJT and 40 percent school training. Training placement was with employers doing community projects. In keeping with the "job"-prefaced programs, these job training programs were closely monitored, but results showed that they were not as successful as expected, and their number was cut in 1991 and 1992 (Disney et al. 1992, 180).[8]

Job Creation Policies in the United Kingdom

Oddly enough, the country that produced John Maynard Keynes did not engage in job creation policies during the Great Depression or to any great

---

8. There is also a Training for Work Scheme that provides Career Development Loans from £200 to £8000 that can be used to pay for vocational training (Robinson 1996, 69, 81).

extent during the oil crisis (Gourevitch 1986, 130). Nonetheless, two types of policies have existed: temporary job creation measures and wage subsidy programs. Temporary job creation measures have included the Job Creation Program (1975 to 1978), the Special Temporary Employment Program (1978 to 1981), the Community Enterprise Program (1981 to 1982), the Community Program (1982 to 1988), and the Employment Action Program (1991 to 1996). The Community Program was the largest, and it targeted the long-term unemployed for temporary work that would restore work habits and improve future prospects for obtaining work. Projects included environment, energy conservation, and some forms of community care. Evaluations showed that 21 to 37 percent of participants got regular jobs within eight months and 4 to 7 percent went into training (Disney et al. 1992, 165–68). Since the jobs were community oriented and not likely to be done by private industry, substitution effects were minimal and the program was five times as cost effective as welfare spending. Even though 48 to 54 percent of the participants remained unemployed afterward, this was a relatively effective program by job creation standards (Disney et al. 1992, 168, 172).

The Wage Subsidy measures have existed for (1) job preservation—the Temporary Employment Subsidy from 1975 to 1979 and the Temporary Working Scheme from 1979 to 1984; (2) small firms—the Small Firms Employment Subsidy from 1977 to 1980; (3) targeted programs—Adult Employment Subsidy from 1977 to 1978, New Workers Scheme from 1987 to 1988, and Jobstart Allowance from 1986 to 1991; and (4) general employment often for local community projects—the Enterprise Allowance Scheme from 1982 to 1996. While not massive and late in coming, these job creation programs were still higher in funding and enrollment than German efforts.

Evaluating Labor Market Policies and Institutions

Evaluation research in the area of labor market policy has gone through unsettling changes since the 1960s. Research in the 1960s often focused on the gross number of jobs created, and calls were made for more emphasis on net measures that would take into account deadweight, substitution effects, and other factors.[9] In the 1980s and 1990s, a lively debate ensued

9. Deadweight loss refers to an ALMP program producing the same result that would have occurred without the program. For example, a program places an unemployed person in a firm that was going to hire an unemployed person anyway. In other words, the program wasted both effort and money. Substitution effects occur when an unemployed worker hired through an ALMP program replaces a worker who would have been hired and thus makes that person unemployed. Consequently, substitution effects simply replace an employed worker with a formerly unemployed worker. The end result is nil. Displacement effects are very similar

on the virtues of experimental assessments with control groups with similar concerns about selection and randomization biases (Heckman and Smith 1993, 1996; Björklund and Regnér 1996; Snower 1997). The United States was at the forefront of pushing these kinds of evaluation methods, while much of Europe was focused more on improving the internal functioning of many programs (Janoski 1990; Wilensky 1985).

The oddest feature of this type of research has been the continued discrediting of previous research findings and the advocacy of new types of methods that are not quite perfected, or too costly or intrusive to implement. The tendency to throw the baby out with the bath water has not disappeared in this area, and most evaluation research still has a very high obsolescence rate. Nonetheless, the importance of evaluation research remains, and some countries have laws requiring evaluation research on all new programs.

Evaluation of ALMP programs is usually conducted at the macro-level and the program-level. At the macrosocial level, ALMP has been examined in cross-sectional and pooled formats. Layard, Nickell, and Jackman (1991) show that ALMP spending, union coordination, and employer coordination reduced unemployment for twenty countries from 1983 to 1988. Zetterberg also finds that ALMP expenditures reduced unemployment in nineteen countries from 1985 to 1991 (Forslund and Krueger 1997, 288). But these results are sensitive to historical periods. Forslund and Krueger find strong results for ALMP expenditures over GDP and much stronger results for ALMP expenditures over total labor market expenditures in twenty countries from 1983 to 1988, but the opposite effect for 1993 (1997, 290). If one covers a substantial period of time (e.g., Europe from the 1960s to the 1990s), ALMP will show strong effects of reducing unemployment. If one confines the analysis to an upturn in unemployment (e.g., Europe in the 1990s), then ALMP increases will be chasing unemployment, which makes it look like ALMP causes unemployment.[10]

---

to substitution effects and could even be considered a specialized form of substitution. For instance, a firm with subsidized workers produces and sells more of its product, but another firm making the same product must lay off workers, since they lose sales by a similar amount. Another specialized case is fiscal substitution/displacement, which occur when federal governments subsidize local governments in providing services that they would have already provided. The substitution here is of money in two different budgets rather than people. Each of these effects presumes that employment is in a zero-sum situation, and what is induced by policy results in a reduction elsewhere (Fay 1996, 43).

10. By analogy, in a short period of time (e.g., hours) taking antibiotics might seem to be highly correlated with a disease, and one might even think that the drug might cause the disease. In a longer period of time (e.g., a few weeks), the drugs have enough time to operate, and one could conclude that they eradicate the disease.

It would seem that the problems of macroanalysis could be solved at the program level; however, the opposite complexities exist of treating one program within a larger system. The state may give an unemployed person a job, but is another person bumped out of a job as a result or is the money spent on the program taken away from private sector investment that would have created various other jobs?

The results of many American job training program evaluations (MDTA, CETA, JTPA, and demonstration projects) show that earnings have been strongly increased for adult women in all programs, moderately increased for adult men in most programs, and weakly increased for youths in only about half the programs (Friedlander, Greenberg, and Robins 1997, 1831–32). Job creation programs are often more successful by definition, that is, people are placed in jobs so they are no longer unemployed (Lindbeck 1997, 1309); however, substitution or displacement in the public sector (governments hiring people who displace workers in the private sector) and deadweight in the private sector (firms hiring people they would have hired anyway) substantially reduce the significance of this success. The United States no longer funds much in the way of job creation programs, especially after the employment boom of the 1990s, but studies done in the 1970s showed substitution effects in the 20 to 30 percent range, and in the 1980s, higher substitution effects of 40 to 50 percent were found. When CETA was retargeted on the disadvantaged and long-term unemployed, substitution and deadweight effects had much less effect on these programs. Job placements after job creation efforts were in the 40 to 80 percent range, and earnings gains tended to parallel job training gains (Janoski 1990, 158–61). In Sweden, Forslund and Krueger estimate displacement effects of 36 to 69 percent (1995, 278–79), but most of this occurred with public road construction, and health and welfare workers exhibited little or no displacement of private sector workers. Roughly estimating these displacement, substitution, or deadweight effects to be about 50 percent, one might conclude that two created jobs produce one real job.

In terms of job placement in the United States, the percentage of vacancies registered at the employment service is about 12 percent, the number of persons placed out of all vacancies is about 6 percent, and the percentage of placements made from vacancies on file is about 45 percent. These rates are probably typical for countries with weak employment services like the United Kingdom. In the German Bundesanstalt, vacancies registered at this agency average about 30 percent of all openings, successful job placements of all vacancies are about 20 percent, and job placements out of vacancies on file at the agency are about 60 percent.

In a review of over 100 evaluation studies, Meager and Evans conclude that these results are much less complete compared to the U.S. and Swedish studies. They also question the interpretation of the studies and "which specific measures work better than others, and under which circumstances?" (1998, pt. 4, 1). Consequently, despite the many evaluations undertaken, a variety of factors—methodological differences, data deficiencies, and different institutional and macroeconomic contexts—make it difficult to come to "firm conclusions about policy effectiveness." Nonetheless, twenty-six of thirty-two studies listed in Table 12.8 show some positive results.

In a study of nineteen countries, the OECD shows that ALMP can be much more effective than PLMP in areas with high and persistent unemployment. Job security measures for white-collar and blue-collar workers and the duration of unemployment benefits increase both long-term and short-term unemployment. But the greater the amount spent on ALMP (by the ratio of ALMP/PLMP), the lower the long-term unemployment rates and incidence (OECD 1993a, 106; Compston 1997). The same ratio has a smaller positive effect on short-term unemployment, but this is good because it is in effect promoting security in the labor market to allow workers enough flexibility to change jobs.

With the methodological bar raised so high, there are no decisive evaluation results for labor market policies. Nonetheless, one may conclude that spending on effective job placement programs and carefully targeted training programs can be quite effective. Both programs must be attuned to technological developments with job placement especially amenable to information diffusion on the internet. Spending on job creation programs can be quite expensive and somewhat inefficient (producing about one real job for each two created), but they have a more certain result in getting an unemployed person directly into a job.

New Deals and Future Developments

Both Britain and Germany have recently elected left-centrist governments, and ALMP is important to both their agendas. Since the 1998 election, the policy thrust of the new German government headed by Gerhard Schröder is still developing. Employment policies will probably favor ALMP expenditures, but a radical change is not expected. Ottmar Schreiner, the deputy chair of the SPD caucus, outlined the SPD proposal to guarantee a job or vocational training position to every young person without work for six months or more. This will cause a considerable increase in ALMP expenditures. Job creation measures, which are about 25 percent of current

Table 12.8 Evaluation Results Programs Targeted on the Long-Term Unemployed in Germany and the United Kingdom

Measures and evaluators	Evaluation method	Results
1. Job placement / job counseling		
a. Germany		
None	—	—
b. United Kingdom		
Atkinson 1994	Survey of individuals and trainers	32% with job-search training got jobs, 26% of those without such training
Bellman and Lehmann 1990, 1993	Aggregate impact analysis	Restart decreases unemployment and long-term unemployment, but increases very short-term unemployment
White and Lakey 1992	Random experiment with control group	Restart had a small but positive effect
Dolton and O'Neill 1996	—	Short-term effects stronger than long-term effects
2. Job training		
a. Germany		
Bellmann and Lehmann 1991	Aggregate impact analysis	No significant impact on long- or short-term unemployment
Bellmann and Lehmann 1990	Aggregate impact analysis	Reduces short-term employment, but no significant impact on long-term employment
Disney et al. 1992	Individual data and aggregate impact analysis	Fail to reach the most disadvantaged, employment outcomes better for OJT. Post-training employment decreases with age. Less successful than direct job creation in aggregate analysis
b. United Kingdom		
Payne et al. 1996	Individual survey with matched control groups	Greater probability of getting a job: 3% after 1 year, 15% after 2 years, 22% after 3 years. Training better than job creation
Payne 1990	Individual survey with matched control groups	Significant positive effects on subsequent earnings compared to control group
3. Job creation schemes		
a. Germany		
Bellman and Lehmann 1990	Aggregate impact analysis	Significant reduction in short-term unemployed, but not long-term unemployed
Spitznagel 1989	Individual data	After ABM, 22.4% employed but increases to 42.4% after 32 months

Table 12.8 Evaluation Results Programs Targeted on the Long-Term Unemployed in Germany and the United Kingdom (*continued*)

Measures and evaluators	Evaluation method	Results
b. United Kingdom Jackman and Lehmann 1990, Bellman and Lehman 1990	Aggregate impact analysis	No apparent effect
Haskel and Jackman 1988	Aggregate impact analysis	Strong effect for 18–24 year olds and older workers, but not 25–54 year olds Substitution and deadweight not assessed
Disney et al. 1992 Crimes 1996, McGregor 1996	Aggregate impact analysis Individual data, cost-benefit analysis	No statistically significant effect Participants have better employment probabilities than other training programs. Substitution and deadweight claimed to be low
Payne et al. 1996	Individual survey with matched comparisons	Employment probability decreased by 1% in first year, but increased by 4% after 3 years

4. Job creation subsidies, private sector

a. Germany Bellmann and Lehmann 1990	Aggregate impact analysis	No significant reduction of unemployment
Schmid 1979	Aggregate impact analysis	75% displacement/substitution effects
Schmid 1982	Aggregate impact analysis	Deadweight very significant for young people. Elderly and long-term unemployed hard to place but stable after being placed
b. United Kingdom Atkinson and Meager 1994	Employer survey	New and partial jobs, 29% Substitution and deadweight 28–43%
NERA 1995	Employer and employee surveys	New jobs 27%, deadweight 16–20%

5. Self-employment

a. Germany Kaiser and Otto 1990, IAB 1991, Meager 1993	Participant surveys and aggregate impact analysis	Deadweight less than 20% but long-term survival rates in question
b. United Kingdom Bellmann and Lehmann, 1990, Lehmann 1993	Aggregate impact analysis	Reduces unemployment
Johnson et al. 1988	Aggregate impact analysis Participant surveys	Weak affect on aggregate unemployment

Table 12.8   Evaluation Results Programs Targeted on the Long-Term Unemployed in Germany and the United Kingdom (*continued*)

Measures and evaluators	Evaluation Method	Results
14 Different enterprise allowance scheme studies	Participant surveys	Deadweight high (50-70%) Displacement high (over 50%) Indirect job creation small (35 jobs for 200 participants after 2 years)
	6. Cross-program studies	
a. Germany Hubler 1997	Individual data with control groups for selection bias	Traditional training less effective than firm training measures (OJT or apprenticeship)
b. United Kingdom White 1997	Individual data, matched comparison control group	All three job placement programs have short-term employment impacts net of deadweight Work trials have the highest, Jobclubs next, and job interviews the least
Gardiner 1997	Evaluations of evaluations	Training measures cost the most, job search less Job creation has no clear evidence

SOURCE: Meager and Evans 1998. The Evaluation of Active Labour Market Measures for the Long-term Unemployed ILO, Employment and Training Department. Geneva: ILO. (See http://www-ilo-mirror.who.or.jp/public/english/60empfor/publ/etp16.htm#). The extensive references cited above are not contained in this chapter, but see the Meager and Evans article for complete citations.

unemployment-related costs, may be doubled with expenditures on unemployment compensation being transferred to ALMP. At the moment, SPD coalition plans are still developing (TWIG 1998).

With a two-year head start, the British government's policies under Prime Minister Blair are not only clearer but portend major changes. His "centrist-labor" government came into power in late 1996 with an emphasis on education and what Blair called the "New Deal." The New Deal of the Welfare to Work Program of January 1998 emphasized gateways for employment for young teenage and adult workers (DfEE 1999, 2000). First, the New Deal for Young People channels youths aged eighteen to twenty-four into registration, sessions with a personal adviser, and education, training, child-care, health care, housing, and/or jobs for those who can work. Four options are especially advised: (1) a job with a subsidy of sixty pounds a week, (2) work in the voluntary sector with a grant, (3) work on an Environmental

Task force with an allowance, or (4) up to twelve months of further entitlement to support for those lacking qualifications. Second, the New Deal for those over twenty-five involves advisory interviews, intensive help finding jobs, and a variety of employer subsidies. Education and training are also possible, as are employment zones, the New Deal for Lone Parents, and the New Deal for Partners of Unemployed People.[11]

The employment service is to implement these programs with the active cooperation of business and voluntary groups, and is to provide a motivational core in terms of service to job seekers. This involves applications for a Jobseeker's Allowance (i.e., unemployment insurance) with a signed contract or Jobseeker's Agreement that specifies the conditions for receiving the allowance and a job search plan. The contract is monitored by employment advisers in interviews once every two weeks. After thirteen weeks the job seeker must open up his or her job search to a wider range of jobs (i.e., lower pay in jobs more remotely connected to their training). After six months, interviews are arranged to refresh their search (not unlike Jobrestart under Thatcher). The employment service has gone through a resocialization process on values and has brought information technology to bear on their counseling and placement activities. Although considerable success has already been claimed, time will tell how this mini-revolution fares.[12]

CONCLUSION

The world of labor market policy in Britain and Germany is filled with optimists and cynics. For the moment, the politicians are optimists with elaborate plans for starting new programs and increasing the amount of funding to be spent on ALMP. In Britain and the United States, the emphasis is on "getting off the dole" and welfare. The evaluation researchers, who want scientifically valid control groups and macroeconomic adjustments to discover various sorts of displacement and substitution effects, tend to be cynics. While attending to both the political and scientific worlds, OECD is more moderate in its assessments. Many of the recent recommendations of

11. The New Deal for Young People started in January 1998 and the New Deal for Adults over Twenty-Five, in June 1998. The New Deal for Lone Parents in October 1998, with pilot programs being started for these and other programs about six months earlier (DfEE 2000, chaps. 26–32; 1999, chap. 3.1).

12. The general education measures in Prime Minister Blair's plans are highly ambitious and touch on vocational education in many different ways, but the most important factor for labor market policy is his intention to upgrade standards for graduates (DfEE 2000, chaps. 8–24; 1999, chaps. 2.1, 2.2).

the OECD Jobs Strategy focus on targeting on what kinds of policies work, and the ones that work best are targeted to the needs of particular kinds of unemployed workers. Broadly based or shotgun policies that try to reduce unemployment for the masses are much more likely to waste money. Another important trend is to monitor or even micromanage the progress of job seekers and to change the passive culture of employment services and unemployment insurance to a much more active job search or nearly entrepreneurial culture with jobseekers allowance payments. Nonetheless, there are limits to ALMP, and labor market policy certainly cannot do the work of investment policy, monetary regulations, trade policies, and R and D programs that otherwise fuel growth.

Although often overlooked, institutions are important. Strong labor market institutions such as those in Germany with tripartite participation of labor, management, and government provide the basis for labor market cooperation. High-quality vocational education in the secondary schools will constitute the shoulders that job retraining policies may stand upon. While not without problems, Germany's strong labor market institutions make ALMP easier to implement and increase the likelihood that it will be successful. Britain is in the midst of changing its labor market institutions and educational system, but institutions are not built in a day, a week, or even a few years. It will be interesting to see how far the ambitious British reforms can progress in changing their culture of work in the next decade.

Neoclassical economists often disdain strong institutions, and indeed, Teulings and Hartog (1998, 1) say that many economists believe that in Europe "labour market institutions are responsible for the persistently high unemployment level relative to" the United States. Now this may be true for job maintenance or job security programs that make personnel policies inflexible, and it may be true for PLMP that creates a drag on growth. However, ALMP promotes the flexible use of employees through placement measures and advanced training. Further, cooperative institutions embodied in "neo-corporatist bargaining" promote policies that bolster economic growth, especially in international markets. And while most economists may prefer "competition over corporatism" (reversing the title of Teulings and Hartog's *Corporatism or Competition?*), the United States is creating ALMP through the back door in its job search services within welfare reform measures. In the end, ALMP programs that are effectively managed within strong institutions can bring worker, employer, and state interests together into one policy package. Thus, when ALMP is used in a targeted fashion with institutions strong enough to implement them, ALMP can be a powerful and complementary alternative in any nation's tool box.

REFERENCES

Abowd, John, and Michael Bognanno. 1995. "International Differences in Executive and Managerial Compensation." In Richard Freeman and Lawrence Katz, *Differences and Changes in Wage Structure*. Chicago: University of Chicago Press.

Abraham, Katharine, and Susan Houseman. 1995. "Earnings Inequality in Germany." In Richard Freeman and Lawrence Katz, *Differences and Changes in Wage Structure*. Chicago: University of Chicago Press.

Anglo-German Foundation. 1988. *Local Labour Market Policies in Britain and Germany.* London: Anglo-German Foundation.

Armstong, E. G. A. 1984. "Employers Associations in Great Britain." In John Windmuller and Alan Gladstone, *Employer Associations and Industrial Relations.* Oxford: Clarendon Press.

Barside, W. R. 1990. *British Unemployment, 1919–1939.* Cambridge: Cambridge University Press.

Bastain, Jens. 1998. "The Institutional Architecture of an Alliance for Jobs." In Jens Hölscher and Anja Hochberg, *East Germany's Economic Development Since Unification.* London: Macmillan.

Berthold, Norbert, and Rainer Fehn. 1997. "Reforming the Welfare State: The German Case." In Herbert Giersch, ed., *Reforming the Welfare State.* Berlin: Springer Verlag.

Björklund, Anders, and Håkan Regnér. 1996. "Experimental Evaluation of European Labour Market Policy." In Günther Schmid, Jacqueline O'Reilly, and Klaus Schönmann, eds., *International Handbook of Labour Market Policy and Evaluation.* London: Edward Elgar.

Blankenburg, Erhard, Günther Schmid, and Hubert Treiber. 1976. "Legitimäts- und Implementierungsprobleme 'aktive Arbeitsmarktpolitik.'" In Rolf Ebbinghausen, ed., *Burgerlicher Staat und politische Legitimation.* Frankfurt: Sührkamp Verlag.

Blau, Harald, Herbert Hofmann, Wolfgang Meyerle, Sonja Munz, and Kurt Vogler-Ludwig. 1997. *Labour Market Studies—Germany.* Luxembourg: European Union, Employment and Social Affairs.

Bryant, Adam. 1999. "American Pay Rattles Foreign Partners." *New York Times,* "Week in Review," January 17, pp. 1 and 4.

Burkhauser, Richard, Joachim Frick, and Johannes Schwarze. 1997. "A Comparison of Alternative Measures of Economic Well-Being for Germany and the United States." *Review of Income and Wealth* 43, no. 2 (June).

Calmfors, Lars. 1994. "Active Labor Market Policy and Unemployment: A Framework for the Analysis of Crucial Design Features." *OECD Economic Studies* 22:7–47.

Calmfors, Lars, and P. Skedinger. 1995. "Does Active Labour-Market Policy Increase Employment? Theoretical Considerations and Some Empirical Evidence from Sweden." *Oxford Review of Economic Policy* 11:91–109.

Compston, Hugh. 1997. "Union Power, Policy Making and Unemployment in Western Europe, 1972–1993." *Comparative Political Studies* 30, no. 6:732–51.

Conradt, David P. 1996. *The German Polity.* 6th ed. White Plains, N.Y.: Longmans.

Crouch, Colin. 1993. *Industrial Relations and European State Traditions*. Oxford: Clarendon Press.

Department of Employment and Education (DfEE). 1999. *New Deal for Young People and Long-Term Unemployed People Aged 25+: Statistics*. London: DfEE.

———. 2000. *Second Chances: A National Guide to Adult Education and Training Opportunities*. London: DfEE [www.dfee.gov.uk/scondchance/home.html].

Disney, Richard, Lutz Bellman, Alan Carruth, Wolfgang Franz, Richard Jackman, Richard Layard, Hartmut Lehmann, and John Philpott. 1992. *Helping the Unemployed: Active Labour Market Policies in Britain and Germany*. London: Anglo-German Foundation.

Edwards, Paul, Mark Hall, Richard Hyman, Paul Marginson, Keith Sisson, Jeremy Waddington, and David Winchester. 1992. "Great Britain: Still Muddling Through?" In Anthony Ferner and Richard Hyman, eds., *Industrial Relations in the New Europe*. Oxford: Blackwell.

Esping-Andersen, Gøsta. 1990. *The Three Worlds of Welfare Capitalism*. Princeton: Princeton University Press.

European Commission (EC). 1993. *Growth, Competitiveness, Employment: The Challenges and Ways Forward into the 21st Century, White Paper*. Bulletin of the European Communities, Supplement 6/93. Luxembourg: Office for Official Publications of the European Communities.

———. 1997a. *The Way Forward: The European Employment Strategy*. Luxembourg: Directorate-General for Employment, Industrial Relations, and Social Affairs.

———. 1997b. *Social Europe: National Seminars on Implementing the European Employment Strategy: A Summary*. Supplement 6/96. Luxembourg: Directorate-General for Employment, Industrial Relations, and Social Affairs.

———. 1997c. *Commission Draft for the Joint Employment Report, 1997*. Directorate-General V, Employment, Industrial Relations and Social Affairs, Brussels, September 30.

European Commission-MISEP. 1979–98. *Employment Observatory*. Maastricht, Luxembourg, and Berlin: MISEP.

———. 1987. *Employment Policies Germany*. Luxembourg: EC-MISEP.

———. 1988. *Employment Policies United Kingdom*. Luxembourg: EC-MISEP.

Fay, Robert. 1996. "Enhancing the Effectiveness of Active Labour Market Policies: Evidence from Programme Evaluations in OECD Countries." OECD Section on Labour Markets and Social Policy, Occasional Papers, no. 18 (OECD/GD96-111).

Forslund, Anders, and Alan B. Krueger. 1994. "An Evaluation of the Swedish Active Labor Market Policy: New and Received Wisdom." In Richard Freeman, Robert Topel, and Birgitta Swedenborg, eds., *The Welfare State in Transition*. Chicago: University of Chicago Press.

Friedlander, Daniel, David Greenberg, and Philip Robins. 1997. "Evaluating Government Training Programs for the Economically Disadvantaged." *Journal of Economic Literature* 35 (December): 1809–55.

Gourevitch, Peter. 1986. *Politics in Hard Times: Comparative Responses to International Economic Crises*. Ithaca: Cornell University Press.

Heckman, James, and J. Smith. 1993. "Assessing the Case for Randomized Evaluation of Social Programs." In K. Jensen and P. Madsen, eds., *Measuring Labour Market Measures*. Copenhagen: Ministry of Labor.

———. 1996. "Experimental and Non-experimental Evaluation." In Günther Schmid, Jacqueline O'Reilly, and Klaus Schönmann, eds., *International Handbook of Labour Market Policy and Evaluation*. London: Edward Elgar.

Janoski, Thomas. 1990. *The Political Economy of Unemployment: Active Labor Market Policy in West Germany and the United States*. Berkeley and Los Angeles: University of California Press.

———. 1994. "Direct State Intervention in Labor Markets." In Thomas Janoski and Alexander Hicks, eds., *The Comparative Political Economy of the Welfare State*. Cambridge: Cambridge University Press.

———. 1996. "Explaining State Intervention to Prevent Unemployment." In Günther Schmid, Jacqueline O'Reilly, and Klaus Schönmann, eds., *International Handbook of Labour Market Policy and Evaluation*. Cheltenham: Edward Elgar.

———. 1998. *Citizenship and Civil Society*. Cambridge: Cambridge University Press.

Janoski, Thomas, Christa McGill, and Vanessa Tinsley. 1997. "Making Institutions Dynamic in Cross-National Research: Time-Space Distancing in Explaining Unemployment." *Comparative Social Research* 16:227–68.

Jantti, Markus. 1997. "Inequality in Five Countries in the 1980s: The Role of Demographic Shifts, Markets, and Government Policies." *Economica* 64:415–40.

King, Desmond. 1995. *Actively Seeking Work? The Politics of Unemployment and Welfare Policy in the United States and Great Britain*. Chicago: University of Chicago Press.

Lane, Christel. 1989. *Management and Labour in Europe*. Aldershot, U.K.: Edward Elgar.

Layard, Richard, Stephen Nickell, and Richard Jackman. 1991. *Unemployment: Macroeconomic Performance and the Labour Market*. Oxford: Oxford University Press.

Lewis, Janet. 1978. *Labor Market Administration in the UK*. Berlin: Wissenschaftszentrum.

Lindbeck, Assar. 1997. "The Swedish Experiment." *Journal of Economic Literature* 35:1273–319.

Lindbeck, Assar, and Dennis Snower. 1988. *The Insider-Outsider Theory of Employment and Unemployment*. Cambridge: MIT Press.

Meager, Nigel, with Ceri Evans. 1998. "The Evaluation of Active Labour Market Measures for the Long-Term Unemployed." Geneva: International Labour Office, Employment and Training Department.

National Employment Action Plan—Federal Republic of Germany. 1998. Brussels: Report to the European Council, May 28.

Organisation for Economic Development and Co-operation (OECD). 1964. *Manpower Policy and Programmes in the United States*. OECD Reviews of Manpower and Social Policies. Paris: OECD.

———. 1970. *Manpower Policy in the United Kingdom*. OECD Reviews of Manpower and Social Policies. Paris: OECD.

———. 1974. *Manpower Policy in Germany.* OECD Reviews of Manpower and Social Policies. Paris: OECD.

———. 1983–98. *Employment Outlook.* Paris: OECD.

———. 1993a. "Long-term Unemployment: Selected Causes and Remedies." *Employment Outlook.* Paris: OECD.

———. 1993b. "Active Labour Market Policies: Assessing Macroeconomic and Microeconomic Effects." *Employment Outlook.* Paris: OECD.

———. 1994a. *The OECD Jobs Study.* Paris: OECD.

———. 1995. *The OECD Jobs Study: Implementing the Strategy.* Paris: OECD.

———. 1996a. *OECD Jobs Strategy, Technology, Productivity and Job Creation. Analytical Report.* Vol. 2. Paris: OECD.

———. 1996b. "Recent Labour Market Developments and Prospects." *Employment Outlook.* Paris: OECD.

———. 1997a. "Economic Performance and the Structure of Collective Bargaining." *Employment Outlook.* Paris: OECD.

———. 1997b. "Implementing the OECD Jobs Strategy." *Economic Survey, United Kingdom.* Paris: OECD.

———. 1997c. "Implementing the OECD Jobs Strategy." *Economic Survey, Germany.* Paris: OECD.

———. 1997d. *Benefit Systems and Work Incentives.* Paris: OECD.

———. 1998. *OECD Economic Outlook.* Paris: OECD.

Paul, Kathleen. 1997. *Whitewashing Britain: Race and Citizenship in the Postwar Era.* Ithaca: Cornell University Press.

Prais, Sig J. 1981. "Vocational Qualifications of the Labour Force in Britain and Germany." *National Institute Economic Review* 98 (November): 47–59.

———. 1995. *Productivity, Education and Training: An International Perspective.* Cambridge: Cambridge University Press.

Prais, Sig J., and Karin Wagner. 1988. "Productivity and Management: The Training of Foremen in Britain and Germany." *National Institute Economic Review* 123 (February): 34–47.

Robinson, Peter. 1996. *Labour Market Studies—United Kingdom.* Series No. 1, December. Luxembourg: European Commission, Employment and Social Affairs.

Rose, Richard, and Edward Page. 1990. "Action in Adversity: Responses to Unemployment in Britain and Germany." *West European Politics* 13, no. 4:66–84.

Sanders, David. 1996. "New Labour, New Machiavelli: A Cynic's Guide to Economic Policy." *The Political Quarterly* : 290–302.

Sawyer, Malcolm. 1976. "Income Distribution in OECD Countries." *OECD Economic Outlook.* Occasional Studies, July, pp. 1–36.

Snower, Dennis. "Evaluating Unemployment Policies: What Do the Underlying Theories Tell Us?" *Oxford Review of Economic Policy* 11:110–35.

Symes, Valerie. 1995. *Unemployment in Europe: Problems and Policies.* London: Routledge.

Teulings, Coen, and Joop Hartog. 1998. *Corporatism or Competition? Labour Contracts, Institutions and Wage Structures in International Comparison.* Cambridge: Cambridge University Press.

TWIG. 1998. *This Week in Germany.* New York: German Information Center; Washington, D.C.: Embassy of the Federal Republic of Germany.

United Kingdom Employment Action Plan. 1998. Brussels: Report to the European Council, September 16.

Walwei, Ulrich. 1996. "Improving Job-Matching Through Placement Services." In Günther Schmid, Jacqueline O'Reilly, and Klaus Schönmann, eds., *International Handbook of Labour Market Policy and Evaluation.* London: Edward Elgar.

———. 1998. "Job Placement in Germany." Labour Market Research Topics, no. 31. Nuremberg: IAB.

Widmaier, Ulrich, and Susanne Blancke. 1997. "Germany." In Hugh Compston, ed., *The New Politics of Unemployment.* London: Routledge.

Wilensky, Harold. 1985. "Nothing Fails Like Success: The Evaluation-Research Industry and Labor Market Policy." *Industrial Relations* 24:1–19.

Winter-Ebmer, Rudolf. 1998. "Potential Unemployment Benefit Duration and Spell Length: Lessons from a Quasi-Experiment in Austria." *Oxford Bulletin of Economics and Statistics* 60, no. 1:33–45.

Zetterberg, J. 1995. "Unemployment, Labor Market Policy and the Wage Bargaining System." In J. Johannesson and Eskil Wadensjö, eds., *Labor Market Policy at the Crossroads.* Stockholm: Ministry of Labor.

Governing Labor Markets: The U.S. Model

DAVID BRIAN ROBERTSON

In the 1980s, U.S. leaders actively promoted the notion that the U.S. labor market had become a prolific job creation machine (McKenzie 1988; Brodsky 1994). Over the next decade, many foreign observers urged their national policymakers to borrow U.S. labor market policies and introduce them in their nations ("Europe Hits a Brick Wall" 1997; Heise 1997). Government did not meddle as much in U.S. labor markets, it was said. As a result, U.S. labor markets could adapt much more quickly and efficiently to global competition and rapid technological change. Most European nations, in contrast, had hung on to hopelessly inflexible worker protections. These countries consequently suffered high unemployment. If only European nations were more like the United States, some suggested, they too could turn into "jobs machines."

But U.S. labor market policy is much harder to borrow, and its success is much more ambiguous, than this popular view suggests. Though the United States has used many of the labor market tools that other nations use, U.S. policymakers have protected employers' freedom to hire, fire, and control the terms of employment to an unusual extent. Its unique institutional, economic, ideological, and historical circumstances account for the exceptional autonomy that the United States allows its employers. Even if U.S. labor market policy were easy to transfer abroad, foreign policymakers have reason to hesitate to adopt the U.S. model. Beneath the spectacular appearance of its job growth statistics, serious problems of economic efficiency, security, and fairness underlie U.S. labor markets at the beginning of the twenty-first century.

GOVERNING LABOR MARKETS

In the last twenty years, policymakers in many countries have questioned the value of government intervention in labor markets. Neoclassical economic theory generally views such government interference as more harmful

Thanks to Evelyne Huber, Eric Hershberg, Gary Marks, John D. Stephens, John Myles, T. J. Pempel, Peter Lange, David Finegold, and Bruce Western for suggestions, comments, and additional than beneficial for optimum economic performance. In the neoclassical view, each person's labor is a commodity, and free markets are the most efficient mechanism for allocating and pricing labor (as they are for any other commodity). When employers and workers freely adjust to consumer demand, labor's price—wages and salaries—will reach an equilibrium. In this happy state, unemployment will not exist. All jobs will be filled. All job seekers will find work. Workers' earnings will reflect their effort and their skills. Prolonged joblessness, under these ideal conditions, is impossible (Thurow 1986, 194–97). Neoclassical economics concedes that events such as recessions upset this equilibrium and displace workers. In this view, however, episodes of unemployment since World War II have been modest, temporary, and aberrant (Samuelson 1989).

In neoclassical economic theory, employers must control hiring, firing, and wages to adjust to changing markets as quickly as possible. Government or trade union interference with the going rate of wages or with dismissals will cause the economy to perform less efficiently.[1] From this perspective, then, excessive public controls on jobs and excessively generous benefits for the jobless have strangled employer control of the labor market. Many European nations in particular are said to suffer from "Eurosclerosis," a sort of hardening of labor market arteries that makes labor markets too inflexible to allow for dynamic job creation (Balls 1993; "Is the Model Broken?" 1996).[2]

Governments initially began to govern labor markets, however, for powerful moral and practical reasons that transcend economic efficiency. Jobs are a primary source of survival and prosperity for most citizens. Wages and salaries provide personal security as well as status, economic power, and achievement. The "creative destruction" of free market forces may benefit the economy in the long run by shifting industries and investment to more productive uses, but long-term aggregate growth offers little immediate consolation to fired workers and devastated families. Involuntary joblessness remains a root cause of destitution, hunger, ill health, and squalid living conditions.

---

readings that improved the analysis in this chapter. Thanks also to Rowan and Littlefield Publishers for granting permission to use a substantial amount of material from chapter 10 of my book, *Capital, Labor, and State: The Battle for American Labor Markets from the Civil War to the New Deal* (Lanham, Md.: Rowman and Littlefield, 2000).

1. Government intervention in markets may promote economic efficiency if it can supply goods and services that markets underproduce, such as education and training (even then, government inefficiency may result in greater cost than benefit).

2. Conservatives warn that recent legislation and court decisions gradually have imposed the kinds of restrictions on employer prerogatives that portend creeping "Eurosclerosis" even in the United States (Henderson 1993).

Pragmatic interests have prompted all governments to turn these diffuse moral claims into practical programs for governing labor markets. Because most citizens are wage earners or depend on wage earners, there exists a potentially huge political constituency in every nation for laws protecting wages, limiting hours, and setting workplace standards. Trade unions have been the strongest advocates of more extensive worker protections. When competition is intense, however, even employers sometimes lobby government to set labor standards that limit competitors' labor advantages. The fear and resentment sparked by uncertain employment and shrinking wages can undermine political stability. Unemployment, strikes, and lockouts periodically disrupt the economy. Even if a particular distribution of income or of jobs is economically justifiable, such problems as child labor, long working hours, and dangerous workplaces challenge governments to maintain the social fabric.

Public officials have used four types of policy instruments to govern labor markets: trade union laws (Figs. 13.1), regulation (Fig. 13.2), management (13.3), and work insurance (primarily workers' compensation and unemployment insurance). A hundred years ago, the most industrially advanced capitalist nations implemented few of these instruments, leaving employers with virtually unlimited discretion. At the turn of the century, however, most industrializing nations began to implement these tools much more extensively. By the 1920s, labor market policy had significantly circumscribed employer autonomy in many nations (Robertson 2000).

Trade union laws have had the greatest impact on the balance of employer and worker power in the labor marketplace. In the nineteenth century, many European nations suppressed trade unions. When they later relaxed constraints on unions, these governments tacitly conceded trade unions' legitimate right to counterbalance employers' labor market power. By creating special mechanisms for resolving disputes, governments institutionalized a role for unions and collective bargaining. After World War II, many governments extended unions' influence by creating tripartite institutions for negotiating wage and price agreements, regulations, social insurance levels, and other issues. Some nations provided that collective bargaining agreements would extend to unorganized workers in the bargaining unit or even industry-wide. Several European nations enacted codetermination laws that mandated the participation of organized labor in corporate management (Slomp 1990; Adams 1993).

Government support for collective bargaining can curb employers' labor market autonomy substantially. If strong trade unions organize most of the labor force, they can establish wages, hours, benefits, and other worker

---

Trade Union Law

- Legalization of trade unions
- Arbitration, mediation, and conciliation
- Collective-bargaining protections
- Secondary boycott and picketing rules
- Codetermination laws
- Extension of collective-bargaining agreements to unorganized workers.

Fig. 13.1   Trade Union Law

protections for most workers through collective bargaining. Where collective bargaining terms are extended to most of the workforce, unions are the chief determinants of worker security. Indeed, union agreements may substitute entirely for certain kinds of worker protections, such as legal minimum wages (Traxler 1996). Moreover, trade unions are the most politically important advocates for the adoption, extension, and retention of other labor market policies. Unions also can play a major role in policing policy implementation. Swedish unions, for example, monitor job health and safety regulations, manage unemployment benefits, and contribute to active labor market policy (Rothstein 1992, 1996). Without extensive centralized bargaining, then, worker protection will be of more limited extent and will depend more heavily on regulation, active labor market management, and public work insurance.

In the late nineteenth century, industrializing nations began to govern labor markets directly by regulating working conditions. Initially, these nations regulated female and child labor. These regulations then expanded to include dangerous industries such as mining and rail transport and low-wage "sweatshop" industries such as the garment trades. In the 1890s Australian states and the British government initiated minimum wage regulations for unorganized workers in low-wage industries. After the Second World War, European nations strengthened legal protections against dismissal and other labor regulations. By the early 1970s, most nations were also regulating occupational health and safety and limiting employment discrimination against women, minorities, older workers, and other groups. Most nations reacted to the economic downturn of the 1970s by expanding work regulation, such as advance notice of mass layoffs and plant closings (Commons et al. 1918 and 1935; Rattner 1980; Kelman 1981; U.S. DOL 1986; OECD 1991, 1994b, pt. 2).

Periods of massive joblessness and spurts of industrial unrest prompted governments to intervene more actively in labor markets. A century ago, pub-

```
┌─────────────────────────────────────────┐
│           Labor Market Regulation          │
│                                             │
│   • Restrictions on hiring and firing       │
│   • Rules governing factory conditions      │
│   • Wage floors and hours ceilings          │
│   • Vacation and leave rules                │
│   • Occupation health and safety laws       │
│   • Antidiscrimination and equal-pay laws   │
│   • Rules governing mass layoffs            │
└─────────────────────────────────────────┘
```

Fig. 13.2   Labor Market Regulation

lic labor statistics bureaus began to provide data about joblessness, wages, prices, and specific employment problems. Free public employment exchanges attempted to match jobless workers with unfilled jobs. German apprenticeship initiatives received credit for the nation's growing industrial strength, and other nations advanced apprenticeship and vocational education initiatives (Douglas and Director 1931; Palmer 1978). The U.S., German, and Swedish national governments developed employment-creation projects of unprecedented scope during the depression of the 1930s. After World War II, Germany and Sweden established national labor market boards with sweeping responsibilities for active labor market management. Enthusiasm for coordinated and extensive employment and training programs peaked in the 1960s and 1970s, with Sweden serving as a model (U.S. Senate 1974). As economies turned sluggish in the 1970s, most nations offered public service employment to shore up the slackening demand for workers. Governments also began to offer subsidies to induce more hiring in the private sector (Casey and Bruche 1985; Wilensky and Turner 1987; Janoski 1990).

Around the turn of the century, industrializing nations began to replace the patchwork of court awards for work injuries with workers' compensation plans. These industrial accident compensation programs often constituted the initial social insurance programs of the welfare state. Unemployment insurance programs followed the establishment of work injury insurance and old age pensions. Governments substantially liberalized eligibility, coverage, and benefits for these income insurance programs between the end of World War II and 1960. Unemployment insurance also expanded in many countries after the economic slowdown beginning in the mid-1970s. Social insurance expenditures tended to grow rapidly into the 1970s. New entitlements and popular early retirement plans prevented work insurance programs from shrinking in the 1980s (Commons et al. 1918 and 1935; Flora and Alber 1981, 57; OECD 1994b, 176).

> Labor Market Management
>
> • Labor statistics agencies
> • Apprenticeship programs
> • Vocational education
> • Public labor exchanges
> • Immigration laws
> • National labor market boards
> • Job training programs
> • Public employment programs
> • Employment subsidies

Figure 13.3   Labor Market Management

EMPLOYER AUTONOMY IN U.S. LABOR MARKET POLICY

In the 1890s, no industrializing nation was using these labor market instruments in a way that substantially limited employer autonomy. The United States was no exception. It is true that Britain had more advanced factory legislation, that Australia and New Zealand had initiated minimum wage laws and arbitration laws, and that Germany had instituted social insurance. The United States, however, also had initiated pathbreaking labor market programs, such as state bureaus of labor statistics, state public employment offices, and general eight-hour laws. Labor leaders fought passionately for these programs on the grounds that they would advance the workers' protection. Some of the United States's most industrialized states had instituted labor regulations comparable to those in Britain. U.S. courts had tolerated unions earlier than other nations, and the United States did not overtly repress unions in the way Germany had done before 1890.

By the 1920s, however, nations economically comparable to the United States were setting significant boundaries on employer autonomy, and permitted labor markets to determine outcomes within these more limited boundaries. These boundaries tightened further over the course of the century. By the end of the 1970s, most of the industrialized democracies pursued protective labor market policies (OECD 1991, 52–53). Sweden was using labor market instruments actively to increase the bargaining power of workers, to equalize incomes, and to improve labor market efficiency (see Rothstein 1996).

By the 1920s, the United States clearly had departed from comparable nations and established a unique model for governing labor markets, one that protected employers' autonomy to an exceptional extent. Even though the U.S. government has employed nearly all of the labor market policy instruments in Figures 13.1, 13.2, and 13.3, U.S. programs have posed a much more limited challenge to employer autonomy than programs abroad.

Trade Union Law. U.S. trade union law helps to fragment and decentralize union power, limiting unions' ability to contest employers' autonomy on a broad scale. Though the United States did not legally suppress trade unions at the turn of the century, its courts responded positively to employer lawsuits and limited unions' use of strikes, picketing, and boycotts. The National Labor Relations Act of 1935 created a comparatively explicit set of rules to formally guarantee the process of union representation and collective bargaining. The law mandates specific steps in establishing union recognition and the bargaining process in a firm. Though the administration of the law tended to encourage unionization in the late 1930s, the Taft-Hartley amendments of 1947 created provisions that restored some of the bargaining position of employers.

Most continental European laws regulating collective bargaining have been more supportive of unions than the American system (Bellace 1993; Gross 1974, 130–48; Rogers 1990, 117–23). Under U.S. law today, workers must participate in a special election process to certify union recognition in a given workplace. In such elections a majority of votes for a union conveys exclusive bargaining rights to a union. This process makes it difficult to expand union gains won in a single plant to workers across an entire industry, and it excludes most American workers from the protections won in union contract negotiations. American employees instead must rely on employer-provided benefits and statutory law for labor market protection. At the beginning of the 1990s, collective bargaining agreements covered fewer than one in five American workers. This percentage constituted less than half that of any other major OECD nation except for Japan. The U.S. legal framework for union representation and collective bargaining has contributed to the decline of collective bargaining coverage in the United States (Rose and Chaison 1985; Freeman 1994). Continental European collective bargaining tends to be more centralized, and therefore tends to provide security to a large majority of workers. European officials often play a more active role in brokering conflicts between employer associations and unions and in extending agreements industry-wide (Blanchflower and Freeman 1992; Traxler 1996).

The U.S. labor relations system advantages employers in many other ways. First, the United States allows state governments the discretion to make organizing unions much more difficult by enacting "right to work" laws. These laws, now in effect in twenty-one states, ban unions requiring employees to join a union in order to retain employment (Meltz 1985;

Crandall 1993, 74–76). Second, the system permits employers legally to resist and to evade unions. A number of U.S. employers have redoubled their efforts to evade unionization in recent decades with tactics such as firing employees who are organizing unions, intimidating nonunion employees, hiring labor consultants who specialized in union avoidance, mounting elaborate anti-union publicity campaigns prior to union certification elections, contracting work to nonunion outside suppliers, disinvesting in unionized plants, and relocating production to nonunionized plants (Estlund 1993; Kochan, Katz, and McKersie 1994). Third, the United States's complex legal procedures cause extraordinary delays in settling disputes, such as unfair labor practice controversies. The process of litigation can drag on for years and invites employers to use delaying tactics to postpone unionization or grievance settlement indefinitely (Summers 1991; Gross 1995). Fourth, U.S. labor law provides for an unusually close and intrusive government oversight of internal union affairs. The federal government supervises the process of union organization and requires financial and other reports from unions. U.S. employers, in contrast, need not file reports on the use of consultants hired to help them indirectly resist or break unions. European governments tend to ignore internal union affairs (Taylor and Whitney 1987, 584–622; Cella and Treu 1998).

Compared to similar nations, then, American trade unions play a much smaller role in ensuring worker security. Indeed, union agreements abroad may substitute entirely for certain kinds of worker protections, such as legal minimum wages (Traxler 1996). Moreover, trade unions are the most politically important advocates for the adoption, extension, and retention of other labor market policies. Unions also can play a major role in policing policy implementation. Swedish unions, for example, monitor job health and safety regulations, manage unemployment benefits, and contribute to active labor market policy (Rothstein 1992, 1996). Labor courts, works councils, and codetermination laws, which institutionalize worker rights and collective bargaining, are common abroad but absent in the United States (Aaron 1971; U.S. DOL 1992; Hancock, Logue, and Schiller 1991).

Regulation. Though U.S. governments impose many regulations on employers, these regulations limit employers' autonomy less than regulations abroad. In those areas where the letter of the law is stringent, as in civil rights laws and occupational safety and health, the implementation of the law often is much weaker than the letter.

The employer's right to hire and fire a worker is his most indispensable tool for workplace control, and a worker's greatest vulnerability. Most industrialized nations limit employers' right to hire and fire workers, and provide workers with a basic property right in their jobs. U.S. law, in contrast, rests on the doctrine of "employment at will." This principle means that employers completely control hiring and firing when no labor contract limits that power. Though state laws and court decisions limited the "employment at will" doctrine in forty-five states in the 1980s, the principle dominates in U.S. law. The United States clearly provides less protection against arbitrary dismissal than any other industrialized nation (Bok 1971; Kruger 1991; OECD 1994b, pt. 2, p. 74).

By the end of the 1970s Canada, France, Sweden, West Germany, the United Kingdom, and Japan had enacted laws that required private employers to notify their employees before a large layoff. The United States did not enact a similar law until 1988. The U.S. law required employers to provide much shorter notice than foreign laws, it exempted more employers from the law, and it did not (as other nations) require employers to compensate dismissed employees (U.S. DOL 1986, 32; Abraham and Houseman 1993).[3]

The United States Fair Labor Standards Act establishes a legal, nationwide minimum wage that covers virtually all workers. The FSLA, however, offers very limited protection for wage earners' purchasing power. In the 1960s, the U.S. minimum wage represented 54 percent of the average private sector wage, but this percentage had fallen to 35 percent of average earnings by 1990; the minimum wage was restored to about 40 percent of the average private sector wage in the mid-1990s (U.S. Census Bureau 1996, 429). Belgium, Greece, France, and the Netherlands maintain a minimum wage that is about one-half of the average (OECD 1997, 11–14), while in other countries union wage bargains are extended to cover unorganized workers. Other labor market regulations, such as equal opportunity laws, do not interfere with the employers' control of wages above the legal minimum (Weiler 1986).

The legal limit for a normal workweek is much the same in the United States as in other industrialized nations, but other regulations for working hours and leaves are largely absent. Unlike most other industrialized nations (except Italy and the United Kingdom), the United States does not require employers to grant an annual vacation (Mishel, Bernstein, and Schmitt 1997, 413). Unlike most other nations (except for Canada, Japan, and to some extent the United Kingdom), the United States does not enforce rules of equal pay and employment security for part-time workers, though their numbers are growing (Thurman 1990, 158). The United States enacted its Family and Maternal Leave Act in 1993, several years after every other

---

3. France subsequently repealed its notification law.

OECD nation. The U.S. law permitted fewer weeks of leave than did other nations, provided for no income replacement, and permitted employers to deny leave to their highest salaried workers (OECD 1990, center insert, 8).

Some U.S. regulations of the 1960s and 1970s were very strict and even adversarial. The Civil Rights Act (1964) included far-reaching limitations on labor market discrimination on the basis of race, sex, age, and handicap. Sweden and Britain drew on U.S. law in developing employment discrimination regulations (Jain 1979; Rattner 1980). The Occupational Safety and Health Act (OSHA) of 1970 provided for strict and extensive regulation of workplace safety (Kelman 1981; Noble 1986). Insufficient long-term enforcement of all labor market regulations, however, has permitted American employers more latitude than such statutes imply. In the 1980s the U.S. Employment and Training Administration, the Labor Standards Administration, the Occupational Safety and Health Administration, the Equal Employment Opportunities Commission, and the National Labor Relations Board, all headed by officials supportive of employers, reduced their efforts on behalf of workers. General Accounting Office studies in the late 1980s revealed that "sweatshops" and child labor were reemerging as a serious problem throughout the United States, and that the U.S. Labor Department could not assess penalties large enough to deter labor law violations (Maier 1985, 219–21; U.S. GAO 1988).

Labor Market Management. The United States puts less effort into managing its labor markets than comparable nations. American workers depend heavily on their own initiative, their employers' efforts, and private labor market institutions to improve their job prospects.

The United States provides little direct training for the labor market, despite its tradition of free public schooling and postsecondary education for higher-status occupations. There is less coordination between formal secondary education and employment in the United States than in nations such as Germany, Japan, and Sweden. Several nations had made labor market education (including workplace visits) a part of the classroom curriculum. U.S. public support for apprenticeship is minuscule. In 1990, U.S. apprenticeship programs registered less than one-quarter of one percent of the American labor force, and the United States funded about $140 per participant. Germany, in contrast, spent about $8500 per starting apprentice and provided apprenticeship training for about two-thirds of German youth hired by employers (OECD 1991, 41; U.S. GAO 1991, 10–11). Vocational training in American community colleges and private, for-profit vocational schools often are disconnected from labor demand. A recent study of government grants to students studying at for-profit vocational schools showed that many of the students were training for jobs in which there already existed at least twice as many workers as jobs (U.S. GAO 1997).

Public employment offices play a relatively small role in American labor markets, while private, fee-charging offices play a relatively large role. The United States spent a smaller percentage of GDP on public employment services and administration than Canada, Australia, or most nations in the European Union (with the exception of Italy, Spain, and Luxembourg; OECD 2000a, 223–30). While a few nations (notably Germany, Sweden, and Austria) have largely forbidden private, fee-charging employment agencies, these offices play a remarkably large role in labor markets in the United States. Most OECD nations provide for labor participation in office policy through tripartite supervisory or advisory boards, but the United States does not (OECD 1991, 26; see Janoski 1990; King 1995).

U.S. policymakers in the 1960s and 1970s claimed that new employment and training programs constituted a more active government approach to labor market management. The Area Redevelopment Act (1961), the Manpower Development and Training Act (1962), the Trade Expansion Act (1962), and the Economic Opportunity Act (the War on Poverty 1964) authorized job training and other services and benefits for jobless workers. The Comprehensive Employment and Training Act (CETA 1973) consolidated existing job training programs and established a public jobs program. In 1978 CETA provided nearly three-quarters of a million public jobs (Franklin and Ripley 1984).

Despite the bold rhetoric, though, these programs reinforced employer autonomy in U.S. labor markets. U.S. expenditures on active labor market programs such as employment and training only approached those of other nations as CETA expenditure was peaking in 1977. U.S. expenditures never approached the one percent of GDP spent on such programs by Sweden and Germany in the 1960s and 1970s and Britain in the mid-1980s. While other nations developed additional jobs programs and protections for workers in the late 1970s and early 1980s, the United States cut labor market programs significantly in the same period. By the late 1980s, then, the United States was spending substantially less than other comparable nations on labor market management (Fig. 13.3; see also Wilensky and Turner 1987, 55–64; Schmid, Reissert, and Bruche 1992, 184). In 1997, U.S. spending on active labor market measures (as a percentage of GDP) was about a quarter that of the OECD average (OECD 2000b, 214–15).

Moreover, those U.S. employment programs that do exist carefully protect employer predominance in labor markets. First, most of the employment and training initiatives have aimed to adapt workers to business needs

Table 13.1   Comparative Expenditure on Active and Passive Labor Market Policy, late 1980s

	Expenditure on active measures as a percentage of GDP	Passive income maintenance[a] as a percentage of GDP	Total
Australia	.30	.99	1.29
Austria	.29	.96	1.24
Belgium	1.18	3.05	4.23
Canada	.51	1.58	2.09
Denmark	1.20	4.51	5.71
France	.80	2.08	2.87
Germany	1.00	1.33	2.33
Italy	.80	.72	1.52
Japan	.15	.36	.52
Netherlands	1.13	2.64	3.77
Norway	.91	1.05	1.96
Spain	.78	2.36	3.14
Sweden	1.70	.69	2.38
Switzerland	.17	.19	.36
United Kingdom	.68	.94	1.62
United States	.24	.38	.62

SOURCE: OECD 1991, 52–53.
[a] Primarily unemployment compensation.

without interfering in managerial prerogatives. The Area Redevelopment Act and the Economic Development Act encouraged training to employer specifications as part of a package of economic development tools (U.S. DOL 1966, 23–31; Pressman and Wildavsky 1973). The U.S. Job Training Partnership Act (JTPA) of 1982, which replaced the CETA program, created local Private Industry Councils (PICs) to manage federally funded employment and training programs. JTPA explicitly guaranteed employer representatives a working majority on these PICs (Robertson and Waltman 1993).

Second, of the major industrial democracies, the United States had the least coordination of active labor market programs (Wilensky and Turner 1987, 25–28, 55–58; Rothstein 1985). Such laws as CETA delegated authority to "prime sponsors" (state or local governments), who then hired numerous nonprofit and private organizations to provide employment and training services. By 1980, federal officials no longer knew, within a range of 30 to 50 thousand, exactly how many organizations were ultimately receiving CETA funds (U.S. House of Representatives 1980, viii). The Job Training Partnership Act of 1982 reduced federal monitoring of local employment activities even further, even as other, small job training efforts developed independent of JTPA. In 1995, the federal government funded one hundred and sixty-three job training programs, located in ten cabinet departments and several smaller independent agencies (U.S. GAO 1995).

Third, U.S. employment and training programs are primarily part of the U.S. welfare system for poor adults, rather than part of a broader strategy for managing labor markets and increasing worker security. Employment programs under the Economic Opportunity Act of 1964, the revised CETA program of 1978, and the Job Training Partnership Act of 1982 all aimed primarily at the poverty population and sought to remove this population from the relief system. CETA enrollments were heavily weighted toward the employable poor. Though evaluations of CETA training programs were mixed, they consistently found that if CETA did nothing else, it provided income for the poor and disadvantaged. Welfare reforms enacted in the late 1980s and 1990s echo the federal WIN program of the late 1960s by requiring welfare recipients to register for employment and training services as a condition of remaining eligible for income support (Wilensky and Turner 1987, 56, 61; Robertson 1987). The U.S. Employment Service is an adjunct of an unemployment insurance system that makes job search a condition for receiving benefits. There is a striking contrast between the extensive and detailed labor force statistics that U.S. officials gather (particularly on those at risk of qualifying for income-maintenance programs) and the exceptional dearth of information collected about the openings that employers have available (Hammermesh 1993).

Work Insurance. American work insurance is less generous and equitable than work insurance in comparable nations. State governments bear most of the responsibility for workers' compensation and unemployment insurance. State laws, tax rates, and benefits vary enormously, with every state feeling competitive pressure to minimize the burden of its taxes on employers.

States historically provided less extensive coverage and benefits to injured workers than the British program on which most were modeled. In 1978, state workers' compensation programs replaced anywhere from 43 to 67 percent of the average disabled workers' income in the United States. In Britain the Industrial Injury benefit replaced 107 percent of the income for the average worker. British benefits were especially generous to workers who had low incomes before they became disabled (Haveman, Halberstadt, and Burkhauser 1984, esp. 128–33).

U.S. unemployment insurance differs from most Western European schemes in ways that strengthen employers' influence over the program. First, employers provide all the funds for the program (only Italy among the large OECD nations also relies on employer funding). Full employer funding maximizes employers' policy influence in the program. Second, most states use "experience rating" to set employer tax rates. Experience rating sets higher rates for employers with more unstable employment records. The original designers of U.S. unemployment insurance hoped that this provision would stabilize employment, but instead it provides incentives to raise eligibility standards to reduce the population of potential recipients. Experience rating and interstate competition also explain why states tightened eligibility requirements during the fiscal stresses of the 1970s and 1980s.

U.S. unemployment compensation consequently offers workers less protection against income loss. Benefits vary widely, though even the most generous are limited in comparison to similar nations. In many European states in the 1990s, replacement rates varied from 50 to 70 percent of lost income (Schmid, Reissert, and Bruche 1992; Reissert and Schmid 1994, 83–119). In the United States, average weekly jobless benefits in 1997 constituted 34 percent of weekly wages. This figure varied from 51 percent of average weekly wages in Hawaii and 41 percent in Arkansas to 24 percent in California and less than 30 percent in Alabama, Alaska, Arizona, Connecticut, the District of Columbia, Georgia, Louisiana, Missouri, New Hampshire, and New York (U.S. DHHS 1999, 336). U.S. unemployment insurance theoretically covers the entire workforce, but in practice states have increasingly limited coverage by restricting eligibility and the duration of benefits. While 75 percent of unemployed American workers qualified for unemployment insurance in the recession of 1974–75, only 38 percent qualified in the recession of the early 1990s (U.S. DOL 1986, 4, 30; Economic Policy Institute 1992). The percentage of unemployed receiving jobless benefits also dropped in Germany, the United Kingdom, and the Netherlands, but these nations provided alternative sources of support for the jobless that are unavailable in the United States The United States is the only wealthy OECD nation without a regular income safety net for the jobless who no longer qualify for unemployment insurance. U.S. collective bargaining agreements provide better coverage for employees, but as in the case of protective regulations such agreements cover a small and shrinking fraction of the workforce (Rein 1996).

In sum, U.S. labor market policy permits employers to exercise much more latitude in labor markets than is true abroad. This policy has made it more difficult for workers to organize into unions to counterbalance employer market power. Thus, unions offer benefits and protections to only a fraction of American workers. For the rest, according to Benjamin Aaron, a leading expert on comparative labor law, "unorganised workers have less constitutional and statutory protection against economic risks and unfair

treatment than do workers in most industrialized nations of the world"
(Aaron 1990, 256).

U.S. LABOR MARKET POLICY AS AN INTERNATIONAL MODEL

In the 1980s, many foreign policymakers sought to emulate the U.S. model.
Britain's Thatcher government explicitly undertook to borrow U.S. ideas
about governing labor markets. These British officials aimed to "price
workers into jobs" by systematically (if incrementally) reducing trade union
protections, encouraging wider wage disparities, and fostering wage earners' compliance with employers' decisions (U.K. DOE 1985, 1, 13, 19–20;
Robertson 1987). In the early 1990s, the OECD diagnosed the problem of
high European unemployment in fundamentally similar, though much gen-
tler, terms. Though the OECD conceded that U.S. labor markets had a number of problems, U.S. labor market change was occurring, in the OECD's
terms, "against a background of buoyant employment growth." The OECD
prescribed fewer public limitations on labor markets (OECD 1994a; 1994b,
pt. 1, pp. 55, 69; 1995) and "making work pay" policies that would reduce
public income support for the jobless and increase support for low-paid
workers (OECD 2000b, 7–10). Even Swedish employers attacked Sweden's
egalitarian policies (Pontusson and Swenson 1996; Balls 1993).

The U.S. job creation record made U.S. policy attractive abroad. From
1970 to 1990, total employment in the United States increased 40 percent,
compared to 10 percent in Germany, 8 percent in France, and 3 percent in
the United Kingdom. U.S. Bureau of Labor Statistics figures indicated that
private employment (not adjusted seasonally) rose from 88.5 million in
early 1992 to over 111 million at the end of 2000 (Bok 1996, 29; U.S. BLS
2001a).

If foreign policymakers import U.S. labor market policy, will their labor
markets also generate vast numbers of new jobs? Answering this question
involves three distinct issues. First, is U.S. labor market policy the cause of
its recent success in job creation? Second, is it possible for other nations to
import U.S. labor market policy? Third, would it be desirable for other
countries to borrow from the U.S. model even if they are able to do so?

It is extraordinarily difficult to draw firm conclusions about whether any
labor market policy has desirable effects. Unique circumstances rather than
policy choices seem to account for a large portion of the U.S. jobs that have
been created. Favorable import and oil prices, demographic developments,
the growth of temporary help agencies, and other circumstances helped to

lower the unemployment rate without stimulating inflation (Gordon 2000). The sheer growth of the U.S. labor force supported the growth of service sector jobs.[4] Fueled by relatively high birthrates and immigration, the U.S. labor force grew on average 1.3 percent a year from 1987 to 1997, and high U.S. divorce rates strongly encouraged divorced spouses to enter the labor market. Most Central and Western European labor forces grew at less than half the U.S. rate during this period (Wilensky 1992, 473–88; Brodsky 1994; OECD 1994b, 1–5; OECD 2000a, 14). Ostensibly lower U.S. jobless rates, however, also conceal a significant segment of jobless male workers who are in prisons. The population of prisoners grew by 300 percent from 1980 to 1996, to over a million and a half, a population that is a much larger percentage of the workforce than is true in comparable nations. If these individuals were counted in the labor force, U.S. male unemployment rates would be virtually indistinguishable from those in Western Europe (Western and Beckett 1999).

Can other countries replicate the U.S. job creation record by adopting the U.S. model of labor market policy? The small literature on policy borrowing suggests that there are many obstacles to borrowing another nation's public policy successfully (Rose 1993; Robertson and Waltman 1993). Contemporary U.S. labor market policy has developed under unique economic, ideological, and political circumstances that do not exist in most other societies. The size of the nation, including its vast domestic market and its self-contained natural resources, made it possible to develop self-sufficient production of nearly every type of good by the beginning of this century. Its geographical and economic size encouraged the development of large mass production firms. These large corporations altered the path of the U.S. political economy and, after midcentury, played an important role in providing labor market protections for workers in the primary labor market. American political culture emphasizes self-reliance and minimal government in a way that discourages more extensive worker protections and public labor market management.

Even more important, America's unique political institutions profoundly shaped the way strategies for governing labor markets evolved in the United States. Competitive American federalism continues to motivate state officials to limit jobless benefits, workers' compensation awards, labor regulations,

4. Among OECD nations, the share of employment engaged in the service sector has been converging in recent years. The OECD estimated that service sector employment constituted 74 percent of the U.S. workforce in 1998; the OECD average was about 64 percent, but several nations (France, the United Kingdom, Sweden, and Canada, among others) exceeded 70 percent of employment in the service sector (OECD 2000a, 83–85).

employment services, and trade union laws to ease the burden on employers (Karr 1997). Because U.S. labor market policy developed under decentralized conditions, substantial confusion, overlap, and inefficiency characterize U.S. labor market governance. Further confusion results from the multitude of private community-based training organizations, fee-charging private employment offices, state and local welfare agencies, and for-profit employment and training firms that are involved in U.S. labor markets. The separation of powers has compounded the difficulties of making effective U.S. labor market policy. U.S. legislatures, executives, and judges sometimes have acted as rivals who undermine the policy initiatives of other institutions. The complex implementation structure of U.S. labor market policy makes it costly and difficult to put initiatives into effect and hard to evaluate results. Litigation and contentiousness often flare up because these procedural safeguards introduce so much institutional rivalry into the implementation of public policy.

Even if policymakers abroad felt confident that they could borrow U.S. labor market policy successfully, they may have good reason to hesitate to do so. It is far from clear that U.S. labor market policy is successful even in terms of economic criterion of efficiency. Even if the U.S. model were proven unarguably successful at promoting economic efficiency, however, it may be accompanied by increasing social insecurity and inequality.

Research has revealed little conclusive evidence that employment protection laws, generous jobless benefits, or increased minimum wages actually increase unemployment as they are alleged to do (Brodsky 1994; OECD 1994b, pt. 1, p. 172; Card and Kruger 1995). The European Union's Directorate General for Employment and Social Affairs recently observed that "it is now much more widely accepted that employment problems are not caused by excessive labor market regulation" (Larsson 2000, 35). It may be that the expansionary fiscal and accommodating monetary policy of the United States had more impact on U.S. job creation in the 1980s than its labor market policy did. In the 1980s, when U.S. unemployment rates began to deviate downward from those in Europe, the federal government's tax cuts and military procurement constituted a rate of fiscal expansion unmatched by other OECD nations (ILO 1995, 142–43).

The nominal job creation success of U.S. labor market policy masks some potentially serious economic shortcomings. Skill training often has positive externalities for society (for example, higher overall productivity) that does not have a direct payoff for the individual employer who provides the training. U.S. and British employers tend to seek low-skilled workers. This approach permits individual employers to make short-term economic gains, though at a substantial cost to long-term, national economic productivity. Without additional public support for employment and training, then, private employers may undersupply skills training and, in turn, contribute to the underperformance of the economy as a whole (Finegold 1993). Poor information about job vacancies, job applicants, and training opportunities burdens the economy with higher than necessary transaction costs. Overlapping programs, the lack of relocation assistance, and the absence of centralized employment policy coordination may increase the cost and duration of unemployment. The result is a less efficient economy and unnecessarily prolonged involuntary joblessness. Such inefficiencies as "substitution" (in which an employer receiving a job subsidy hires someone the firm would have hired without the subsidy, in effect substituting public funds for those of the firm) or "creaming" (selecting the best-prepared applicants for training) may be more pervasive under U.S. circumstances, where employer autonomy is more pronounced.

U.S. labor market policy, then, may not be especially efficient, when these broader and longer-term issues of economic efficiency are taken into account. Its consequences for other social values, such as security and fairness, are even more debatable.

The perception of job insecurity has increased in nearly all industrialized nations since the 1980s. Despite the vaunted job creation record of the United States, American, British, French, and Japanese workers felt less secure about employment than workers in other OECD nations (where surveys were available). In 1997, Federal Reserve Board chairman Alan Greenspan argued that the labor market insecurity of workers had tempered their wage demands and made it possible for the United States to experience economic growth with low inflation (Uchitelle 1997). American workers' sense of insecurity follows from the real problem of obtaining income when one is jobless, and the reality that a laid-off worker's new job tends to pay less than her or his previous job. The U.S. Council of Economic Advisers (1996) reported that, for several years after a job loss, an average displaced worker's earnings remain roughly 10 percent below what they could have otherwise expected to earn. Clearly a lower jobless rate helps alleviate workers' concerns about income security. The OECD found, however, that a more extensive safety net—particularly in the form of broader and more centralized collective bargaining and more generous unemployment insurance—promotes an increased sense of economic security among workers (OECD 1997, 129–50).

Increased inequality in the American workforce suggests that the American job machine may be better understood as a job-sharing machine for low-wage workers. A much larger fraction of full-time American workers than European workers earn less than half or two-thirds of the median wage. This data is consistent with the view that wages for low-paid workers have remained low as the number of low-paid jobs expanded, creating in effect a work-sharing scheme among full-time workers at the low end of the U.S. labor market (OECD 1994b, pt. 1, p. 22). Average hourly earnings (in constant 1982 dollars) in the U.S. private sector dropped from $8.60 in early 1973 to $8.00 in late 1979 and $7.50 in 1990, and have risen to about $7.90 since 1997 (Freeman and Katz 1994; Lawrence 1996, 18–24; U.S. BLS 2001b).[5]

American workers receive widely unequal remuneration. A. B. Atkinson recently used data from the Luxembourg Income Study (LIS) to study trends in inequality in the United States and fourteen West European nations (including the relatively poorer nations of Ireland, Spain, Portugal, and Italy). The LIS is a comprehensive effort to develop comparable cross-national data on, among other things, disposable income. This measure includes cash transfer programs within nations (but does not take into account indirect taxes or public spending on health care, education, and other services). Atkinson found that American disposable income clearly became more unequal in the 1970s, and has continued to grow more unequal over time. The bottom 10 percent of income earners is much worse off in the United States than in any of the European nations, and this earnings disparity caused the United States to have a much less equal distribution of income by several different measures. The average income of the least well compensated fifth of Americans (that is, the bottom 20 percent) was substantially lower than the average income of earners in any of the European nations. Even if Europe were considered a single labor market, the distribution of compensation would be more unequal within the United States than in a common European labor market of 325 million people (Atkinson 1995).

At the beginning of the twenty-first century, the American model of governing labor markets has reanimated the classic debate between employer prerogatives and worker protection. The American model is more powerful as a symbol than a policy template, for it evolved under circumstances unique to its economy, political institutions, and culture and cannot easily be borrowed. Moreover, its consequences are far more complex and ambiguous

---

5. Lawrence uses compensation rather than earnings to measure changes in American workers' position over time because compensation includes health, retirement, and other benefits provided workers as a compensation package. Lawrence finds that, in contrast to earnings, American workers' compensation grew from 1979 to 1994, and grew about as much as output.

than the label "American jobs machine" implies. The American model's appeal is better understood as an ideological tool that offers powerful lessons—not to mention political and rhetorical weapons—to those who currently are trying to understand how economic efficiency, security, and fairness can and should be balanced in capitalist order of the twenty-first century.

REFERENCES

Aaron, Benjamin, ed. 1971. *Labour Courts and Grievance Settlement in Western Europe.* Berkeley and Los Angeles: University of California Press.

———. 1990. "Settlement of Disputes over Rights." In Roger Blanpain, ed., *Comparative Labour Law and Industrial Relations,* 1:256. Deventer, Netherlands: Kluwer.

Abraham, Katherine G., and Susan N. Houseman. 1993. *Job Security in America: Lessons from Germany.* Washington, D.C.: The Brookings Institution.

Adams, Roy J. 1993. "Regulating Unions and Collective Bargaining: A Global, Historical Analysis of Determinants and Consequences." *Comparative Labor Law Journal* 14:272–97.

Atkinson, A. B. 1996. "Income Distribution in Europe and the United States." *Oxford Review of Economic Policy* 12, no. 1.

Balls, Edward. 1993. "Europe's Jobs Crisis: A Labour Market 'Gripped by Eurosclerosis.'" *Financial Times,* June 21, p. 3.

Bellace, Janice R. 1993. "The State and Industrial Relations: A Strategic Choice Model." *Comparative Labor Law Journal* 14:249–70.

Blanchflower, David G., and Richard B. Freeman. 1992. "Unionism in the United States and Other Advanced OECD Countries." *Industrial Relations* 31:56–79.

Bok, Derek C. 1971. "Reflections on the Distinctive Character of American Labor Laws." *Harvard Law Review* 84:1394–1463.

———. 1996. *The State of the Nation: Government and the Quest for Better Society.* Cambridge: Harvard University Press.

Brodsky, Melvin M. 1994. "Labor Market Flexibility: A Changing International Perspective." *Monthly Labor Review* 117:53–60.

Card, David, and Alan B. Kruger. 1995. *Myth and Measurement: The New Economics of the Minimum Wage.* Princeton: Princeton University Press.

Casey, Bernard, and Gert Bruche. 1985. "Active Labor Market Policy: An International Overview." *Industrial Relations* 24:37–61.

Cella, Gian Primo, and Tiziano Treu. 1998. "National Trade Union Movements." In Roger Blanpain, ed., *Comparative Labour Law and Industrial Relations,* 6th ed. Deventer, Netherlands: Kluwer.

Commons, John R., et al. 1918. *History of Labor Legislation in the United States.* Vols. 1 and 2. New York: Macmillan.

———, et al. 1935. *History of Labor Legislation in the United States.* Vols. 3 and 4. New York: Macmillan.

Crandall, Robert W. 1993. *Manufacturing on the Move*. Washington, D.C.: The Brookings Institution.

Douglas, Paul, and Aaron Director. 1931. *The Problem of Unemployment*. New York: Macmillan.

Economic Policy Institute. 1992. *Unprepared for Recession: The Erosion of State Unemployment Insurance Coverage Fostered by Public Policy in the 1980s*. Washington, D.C.: Economic Policy Institute.

Estlund, Cynthia L. 1993. "Economic Rationality and Union Avoidance: Misunderstanding the National Labor Relations Act." *Texas Law Review* 71:921–92

"Europe Hits a Brick Wall." 1997. *Economist,* April 5, pp. 21–23.

Finegold, David. 1993. "The Changing International Economy and Its Impact on Education and Training." In David Finegold, Laurel McFarland, and William Richardson, eds., *Something Borrowed, Something Learned? The Transatlantic Market in Education and Training Oxford Studies in Comparative Education*. Washington, D.C.: The Brookings Institution.

Flora, Peter, and Jens Alber. 1981. "Modernization, Democratization, and the Development of Welfare States in Western Europe." In Peter Flora and Arnold J. Heidenheimer, eds., *The Development of Welfare States in Europe and America*. New Brunswick, N.J.: Transaction Books.

Franklin, Grace A., and Randall B. Ripley. 1984. *CETA: Politics and Policy, 1973–1982*. Knoxville: University of Tennessee Press.

Freeman, Richard B. 1994. "Lessons for the United States." In Richard B. Freeman, ed., *Working Under Different Rules*. New York: Russell Sage Foundation.

Freeman, Richard B., and Lawrence F. Katz. 1994. "Rising Wage Inequality: The United States Versus Other Advanced Countries." In Richard B. Freeman, ed., *Working Under Different Rules*. New York: Russell Sage Foundation.

Gordon, Robert J. 2000. "Neither Too Hot nor Too Cold: The U.S. Economy in the 1990s." In OECD, *Policies Towards Full Employment*. Paris: OECD.

Gross, James A. 1974. *The Making of the National Labor Relations Board*. Albany: State University of New York Press.

———. 1995. *Broken Promise: The Subversion of U.S. Labor Relations Policy, 1947–1994*. Philadelphia: Temple University Press.

Hammermesh, Daniel S. 1993. *Labor Demand*. Princeton: Princeton University Press.

Hancock, M. Donald, John Logue, and Berndt Schiller, eds. 1991. *Managing Modern Capitalism: Industrial Renewal and Workplace Democracy in the United States and Western Europe*. New York: Greenwood Press.

Haveman, Robert H., Victor Halberstadt, and Richard V. Burkhauser. 1984. *Public Policies Toward Disabled Workers: Cross-National Analyses of Economic Impacts*. Ithaca: Cornell University Press.

Heise, Arne. 1997. "A Different Transatlantic View: The American Job Machine." *Challenge* 40:50–56.

Henderson, David R. 1993. "The Europeanization of the U.S. Labor Market." *Public Interest* 113:66–81.

ILO (International Labour Organization). 1995. *World Labour Report, 1995*. Geneva: ILO.

"Is the Model Broken?" 1996. *Economist,* May 4, p. 17.

Jain, Harish C. 1979. *Disadvantaged Groups in the Labour Market and Measures to Assist Them.* Paris: OECD.

Janoski, Thomas. 1990. *The Political Economy of Unemployment: Active Labor Market Policy in West Germany and the United States.* Berkeley and Los Angeles: University of California Press.

Karr, Albert R. 1997. "States Lure Industry by Touting Low Unemployment Insurance Taxes." *Wall Street Journal,* February 11, A1.

Kelman, Steven. 1981. *Regulating America, Regulating Sweden: A Comparative Study of Occupational Safety and Health Policy.* Cambridge: MIT Press.

King, Desmond. 1995. *Actively Seeking Work? The Politics of Unemployment and Welfare Policy in the United States and Great Britain.* Chicago: University of Chicago Press.

Kochan, Thomas A., Harry C. Katz, and Robert B. McKersie. 1994. *The Transformation of American Industrial Relations.* Ithaca, N.Y.: ILR Press.

Krueger, Alan B. 1991. "The Evolution of Unjust-Dismissal Legislation in the United States." *Industrial and Labor Relations Review* 44:644–60.

Larsson, Alan. 2000. "Putting Europe to Work." In OECD, *Policies Towards Full Employment.* Paris: OECD.

Lawrence, Robert Z. 1996. *Single World, Divided Nations? International Trade and OECD Labor Markets.* Washington, D.C.: The Brookings Institution.

Maier, Kenneth J. 1985. *Regulation: Politics, Bureaucracy, and Economics.* New York: St. Martin's Press.

McKenzie, Richard B. 1988. *The American Job Machine.* New York: Universe Books.

Meltz, Noah M. 1985. "Labor Movements in Canada and the United States." In Thomas A. Kochan, ed., *Challenges and Choices Facing American Labor.* Cambridge: MIT Press.

Mishel, Lawrence, Jared Bernstein, and John Schmitt. 1997. *The State of Working America, 1996–1997.* Armonk, N.Y.: M. E. Sharpe.

Noble, Charles. 1986. *Liberalism at Work: The Rise and Fall of OSHA.* Philadelphia: Temple University Press.

OECD (Organisation for Economic Co-operation and Development). 1990. *OECD Observer,* no. 166 (October-November).

———. 1991. *Labour Market Policies for the 1990s.* Paris: OECD.

———. 1994a. *The OECD Jobs Study: Facts, Analysis, Strategies.* Paris: OECD.

———. 1994b. *The OECD Jobs Study: Evidence and Explanations.* Parts 1 and 2. Paris: OECD.

———. 1995. *The OECD Jobs Study: Implementing the Strategy.* Paris: OECD.

———. 1997. *Employment Outlook.* Paris: OECD.

———. 2000a. *Employment Outlook.* Paris: OECD.

———. 2000b. *Policies Toward Full Employment.* Paris: OECD.

Palmer, John L., ed. 1978. *Creating Jobs: Public Employment Programs and Wage Subsidies.* Washington, D.C.: The Brookings Institution.

Pontusson, Jonas, and Peter Swenson. 1996. "Labor Markets, Production Strategies, and Wage Bargaining Institutions: The Swedish Employer Offensive in Comparative Perspective." *Comparative Political Studies* 29:223–50.

Pressman, Jeffrey L., and Aaron B. Wildavsky. 1973. *Implementation: How Great Expectations in Washington Are Dashed in Oakland.* Berkeley and Los Angeles: University of California Press.

Rattner, Ronnie Steinberg. 1980. "The Policy and the Problem: Overview of Seven Countries." In Rattner, ed., *Equal Employment Policy for Women: Strategies for Implementation in the United States, Canada, and Western Europe.* Philadelphia: Temple University Press.

Rein, Martin. 1996. "Is America Exceptional? The Role of Occupational Welfare in the United States and the European Community." In Michael Shalev, ed., *The Privatization of Social Policy? Occupational Welfare and the Welfare State in America, Scandinavia, and Japan.* Armonk, N.Y.: M. E. Sharpe.

Reissert, Bernd, and Günther Schmid. 1994. "Unemployment Compensation and Active Labor Market Policy." In Günther Schmid, ed., *Labor Market Institutions in Europe.* Armonk, N.Y.: M. E. Sharpe.

Robertson, David Brian. 1987. "Labor Market Surgery, Labor Market Abandonment: The Thatcher and Reagan Unemployment Remedies." In Jerold L. Waltman and Donley T. Studlar, *Political Economy: Public Policies in the United States and Britain.* Jackson: University Press of Mississippi.

———. 2000. *Capital, Labor, and State: The Battle for American Labor Markets from the Civil War to the New Deal.* Lanham, Md.: Rowman and Littlefield.

Robertson, David Brian, and Dennis R. Judd. 1989. *The Development of American Public Policy: The Structure of Policy Restraint.* Glenview, Ill.: Scott, Foresman.

Robertson, David Brian, and Jeerold L. Waltman. 1993. "The Politics of Policy Borrowing." In David Finegold, Laurel McFarland, and William Richardson, eds., *Something Borrowed, Something Learned? The Transatlantic Market in Education and Training Oxford Studies in Comparative Education.* Washington, D.C.: The Brookings Institution.

Rogers, Joel. 1990. "Divide and Conquer: Further 'Reflections on the Distinctive Character of American Labor Laws.'" *Wisconsin Law Review* 1 (January/February): 1–147.

Rose, Joseph B., and Gary N. Chaison. 1985. "The State of the Unions in the United States and Canada." *Journal of Labor Research* 6 (Winter): 97–112.

Rose, Richard. 1993. *Lesson-Drawing in Public Policy: A Guide to Learning Across Time and Space.* Chatham, N.J.: Chatham House.

Rothstein, Bo. 1985. "The Success of the Swedish Labour Market Policy: The Organizational Connection to Policy." *European Journal of Political Research* 13:153–65.

———. 1992. "Labor-Market Institutions and Working-Class Strength." In Sven Steinmo, Kathleen Thelen, and Frank Longstreth, eds., *Structuring Politics: Historical Institutionalism in Comparative Analysis.* New York: Cambridge University Press.

———. 1996. *The Social Democratic State: The Swedish Model and the Bureaucratic Problem of Social Reforms.* Pittsburgh: University of Pittsburgh Press.

Samuelson, Robert J. 1989. "The Next Recession." *Newsweek,* April 17, p. 49.

Schmid, Günther, Bernd Reissert, and Gert Bruche. 1992. *Unemployment Insurance and Active Labor Market Policy: An International Comparison of Financing Systems.* Detroit: Wayne State University Press.

Slomp, Hans. 1990. *Labor Relations in Europe: A History of Issues and Developments.* Westport, Conn.: Greenwood Press.

Stinson, John F., Jr. 1997. "New Data on Multiple Jobholding Available from the CPS." *Monthly Labor Review* 120:3–7.

Summers, Clyde. 1991. "Patterns Of Dispute Resolution: Lessons From Four Countries." *Comparative Labor Law Journal* 12:165–77.

Taylor, Benjamin J., and Fred Whitney. 1987. *Labor Relations Law.* 5th ed. Englewood Cliffs, N.J.: Prentice-Hall.

Thurman, Joseph. 1990. "Working Time." In Roger Blanpain, ed. *Comparative Labour Law and Industrial Relations,* 1:133–66. Deventer, Netherlands: Kluwer.

Thurow, Lester. 1986. "Conflicting Theories." In Clark Kerr and Paul D. Staudohar, eds., *Economics of Labor in Industrial Society.* San Francisco: Jossey-Bass.

Traxler, Franz. 1996. "Collective Bargaining and Industrial Change: A Case of Disorganization? A Comparative Analysis of Eighteen OECD Countries." *European Sociological Review* 12:271–87.

Uchitelle, Louis. 1997. "Job Insecurity of Workers Is a Big Factor in Fed Policy." *New York Times,* February 27, C6.

U.K. DOE (Department of Employment). 1985. *Employment: Challenge to the Nation.* Cmnd. 9474. London: HMSO, 1985.

U.S. BLS (Bureau of Labor Statistics). 2001a. Data on National Employment, Hours, and Earnings, Total Private Employment, not seasonally adjusted, 1939–2000, Series EEU005000001, <http://stats.bls.gov:80/cgi-bin/surveymost> (accessed January 1, 2001).

———. 2001b. Data on National Employment, Hours, and Earnings, Total Private Average Hourly Earnings, 1982 dollars, 1964–2000, Series EES005000049, <http://stats.bls.gov:80/cgi-bin/surveymost> (accessed January 1, 2001).

U.S. Census Bureau. 1996. *Statistical Abstract of the United States 1996.* Washington, D.C.: GPO.

U.S. Council of Economic Advisers. 1996 (April 23). *Job Creation and Employment Opportunities: The United States Labor Market, 1993–1996.* <http://www.whitehouse.gov/WH/EOP/CEA/html/labor.html> (accessed January 1, 2000).

U.S. DHHS. (Department of Health and Human Services). 1999. *Social Security Bulletin, Annual Statistical Supplement, 1999.* Washington, D.C.: GPO.

U.S. DOL (Department of Labor). 1966. *Report of the Secretary of Labor on Manpower Research and Training under the MDTA.* Washington, D.C.: GPO.

———. 1986. "Secretary of Labor's Task Force on Economic Adjustment and Worker Dislocation." *Economic Adjustment and Worker Dislocation in a Competitive Society.* Washington, D.C.: GPO.

———. 1992. *Foreign Labor Trends: Germany.* Washington, D.C.: GPO.

U.S. GAO (General Accounting Office). 1988. *"Sweatshops" in the U.S.: Opinions on Their Extent and Possible Enforcement Options.* GAO/HRD-88-130BR. Washington, D.C.: GPO.

———. 1991. *Transition from School to Work: Linking Education and Worksite Training.* Report GAO/HRD-91-1-5. Washington, D.C.: GAO.

———. 1995. *Multiple Employment and Training Programs: Information Crosswalk on 163 Employment Training Programs.* Report GAO/HEHs-95-85FS. Washington, D.C.: GAO.

———. 1997. *Proprietary Schools: Millions Spent to Train Students for Oversupplied Occupations.* Washington, D.C.: GAO.

U.S. House of Representatives (Committee on Government Operations, Subcommittee on Manpower and Housing). 1980. Hearings on *CETA's Vulnerability to Fraud and Abuse.* Washington, D.C.: GPO.

U.S. Senate (Committee on Labor and the Public Welfare, Subcommittee on Employment, Poverty, and Migratory Labor). 1974. Hearings on *Labor Market Policy in Sweden.* Washington, D.C.: GPO.

Weiler, Paul. 1986. "The Wages of Sex: The Uses and Limits of Comparable Worth." *Harvard Law Review* 99:1728–807.

Western, Bruce, and Katherine Beckett. 1997. "How Unregulated Is the U.S. Labor Market? The Penal System as a Labor Institution." *American Journal of Sociology* 104:1030–60.

Wilensky, Harold L. 1992. "The Great American Job Creation Machine in Comparative Perspective." *Industrial Relations* 31:473–88.

Wilensky, Harold L., and Lowell Turner. 1987. *Democratic Corporatism and Policy Linkages: The Interdependence of Industrial, Labor-Market, Incomes, and Social Policies in Eight Countries.* Berkeley: Institute of International Studies, University of California, 1987.

Conclusion: Actors, Institutions, and Policies

EVELYNE HUBER

The reference in the title of this volume to models of capitalism reveals a tension in our intellectual enterprise, the tension between seeing models in a holistic way as integrally related sets of policies and institutions in a given historical context, and seeing them as analytically separable and potentially transferable institutions and policy designs. On the one hand, Pempel argues that the East Asian models of capitalism have to be understood as the product of specific combinations of political coalitions, institutions, policies, and world historical time. On the other hand, Myles points out that the comparison between the United States and Canada demonstrates that there is considerable room for choice in policy designs that make a difference, despite broadly similar political power distributions, economic conditions, and locations in world historical time. Thus the intellectual task before us is to identify successful policy designs and ask what the institutional preconditions are for these designs and how they might work under different world historical and local political circumstances, or what substitute designs and institutions might be constructed to achieve the same policy objectives.[1] For policymakers, it is not a matter of "imitating national models" but of creatively adapting policy instruments to local conditions and creating institutions through which to deploy these instruments.

As I pointed out in the Introduction, the comparisons with Northeast Asia and Southeast Asia are particularly relevant for Latin America because of the extraordinary developmental success of the former and the more moderate success but greater similarities to Latin America in terms of resource endowments and initial insertion into the world economy of the latter. The comparisons with advanced industrial democracies in the areas of labor market and social policies are relevant because there are wide contrasts among these countries in the degree of poverty elimination and reduction of inequality despite largely similar levels of affluence. These contrasts

1. I fully agree, then, with Enrique Iglesias, the president of the InterAmerican Development Bank, who states that "it is the responsibility of scholars and policymakers to examine the evidence of policies that have achieved particular development objectives, why they have worked, and what initial conditions are required for success in the context of changing social, political, and economic conditions" (Birdsall and Jaspersen 1997, vii).

demonstrate the imperfect relationship between economic growth and poverty and inequality. Whereas there is evidence that very high inequality is a fetter on growth, there is no evidence that growth automatically translates into greater equality.[2] Rather, a variety of economic, labor market, and social policies affect the primary income distribution, and this distribution in turn can be heavily modified by tax and transfer systems.

Now, despite the analytical need to disaggregate national models of capitalism into their constituent parts, it is still important to explore the interrelationships among institutions, actors, and policies. Various policies can be mutually reinforcing or work at cross purposes; different institutions can make the pursuit of certain policies more or less difficult; and various actors can improve collective outcomes through cooperation or make everybody worse off through confrontation. Importantly, growth- and equity-oriented policies can be mutually reinforcing. One such example of positive relationships among actors, institutions, and policies is offered by the coordinated market economies with social democratic labor market and welfare state regimes discussed by Stephens. Strong employer and labor organizations and an activist state work together to achieve high competitiveness of firms, high levels of employment, a high level of human capital, and a very generous social safety net. These actors work with medium- and long-term horizons and cooperate to maintain high levels of investment, technological upgrading, high-quality production, labor training and retraining, wage setting to safeguard competitiveness of exports, job placement, and so on. High-quality production allows for both high market wages and a high social wage in the form of high earnings replacement rates in unemployment, sickness, and pension insurance; provision of extensive public social services; and generous transfers to groups with a tenuous relationship to the labor market, particularly children and youths. In contrast, at similar levels of economic development, in uncoordinated market economies with liberal labor market and welfare state regimes the lack of cooperation among employer and labor organizations and the state results in more skewed distributions of human capital, a more dualistic economy with high and low productivity sectors and a dual labor market, a more unequal distribution of market wages, and a lower social wage, particularly in the area of transfers and services for the working-age population and their children.

In East Asia, there has been coordination, but between business and government only, under the exclusion of labor organizations. This coordination has been successful in achieving high investment rates, technological upgrad-

2. For an empirical analysis challenging the Kuznets curve, see Bowman 1991.

ing, high levels of human capital, and high levels of employment. Market and even more so social wages lagged behind for a long time because labor did not have the organizational strength to push for improvements. That distributional outcomes were nevertheless comparatively egalitarian is largely due to the redistribution of assets through the land reform and/or significant investments in the rural sector, the high level and relatively equal distribution of human capital, the low levels of unemployment, and the welfare functions of the extended family.

In Latin America, there has rarely ever been any general coordination between the government, employers, and labor unions.[3] Employer organizations have typically been weak, and individual businessmen sought direct and personalistic relations with government agencies. Relations between individual employers and labor organizations have generally been highly antagonistic. Governments, through their ministries of labor, were intimately involved in labor relations, but in mediating and adjudicating specific conflicts, not in seeking general cooperation at levels above the firm. Relations between governments and labor organizations were overwhelmingly antagonistic as well. Where they were not, they tended to be paternalistic; organized labor received material benefits but had to accept governmental controls over its activities. The absence of coordination and trust among government, business, and labor contributed to the comparatively low investment levels, slow and limited technological upgrading, low levels of human capital, and high levels of un- and underemployment. The resulting dual labor markets and low market and social wages, along with the historically very highly unequal distribution of assets, maintained poverty and inequality at comparatively very high levels.

Of course, institutional factors shape the degree of coordination between government, labor, and employer organizations to a significant extent. A Weberian bureaucracy, with hiring and promotion based on merit, with salaries adequate to attract highly qualified officials, and with an esprit de corps is a crucial asset for establishing continuity and credibility of government policies and eliciting cooperation from business and labor. Business and labor on their part need to have organizations that can speak and negotiate authoritatively for their members. The fewer these organizations in number, that is, the more centralized the organizations of both labor and employers, the easier it is to achieve cooperation and compliance on broad economic, labor market, and social policies. Finally, particularly in democracies, the

---

3. Only a few highly temporary exceptions can be found, such as under Perón in his first (1946–55) and second (1973–74) periods as president of Argentina, or in the Brazilian auto industry in the 1990s.

structure of political institutions proper which can concentrate or disperse political power, is important for the achievement of comprehensive legislation. Institutions like federalism, presidentialism, and bicameralism disperse political power and offer many veto points through which particularistic interests can obstruct reforms of a wide-ranging character. This applies both to reforms that enlarge governmental functions and those that reduce these functions. The strength and discipline of political parties can to some extent compensate for this dispersion of power, but in federal systems parties tend to be more fragmented and thus to aggravate it.

Still, within the context of broad similarities regarding the extent of coordination between government, business, and labor, as facilitated or obstructed by institutional factors, there are important differences in levels of poverty and inequality, attributable to different political coalitions and their policy choices. Among Latin American countries, Uruguay and Costa Rica have consistently done better than other countries. Similarly, within the category of coordinated market economies there are important differences between social democratic and Christian democratic welfare state regimes in terms of distributive outcomes, as there are in the category of uncoordinated market economies with liberal labor market and welfare state regimes. Across these different systems, generous minimum benefits in transfer programs—pensions, child allowances, unemployment insurance, or even means-tested social assistance—are effective in keeping poverty rates low. In the area of social services, public funding and delivery of health care provides more equal access and is cheaper than private alternatives. The existence of these differences points to room for meaningful choice in policy designs. In other words, welfare state and production regimes, though interrelated in some ways, are not inseparable packages or models; rather, specific policies can be made to fit in different contexts. Or to look at it in another way, even if a country cannot achieve the benefits of cooperation in all or even in many of the policy areas because of the nature of the actors and institutions, governments have the option of choosing policy instruments that will deliver some of the desired outcomes. Whether governments are likely to choose effective pro-growth and pro-equity policies, of course, depends heavily on their ideological commitments and perceptions of what is possible, and thus on the power distributions they are confronting, an issue I shall return to.

Another way to think about the problem of holistic models versus room for policy choice is in terms of the concept of path dependence (e.g., Pierson 1999). As just pointed out, synchronic comparisons show different combinations of policies within the framework of overall similarities in economic coordination and interventionism, which does support the argument that there is room for choice. In a dynamic view, though, prolonged pursuit of a given set of policies makes changes in any one of them more difficult because such policies can shape not only preferences of actors and their perceptions of what is possible but also the composition of the actors themselves (Huber and Stephens 2001). Seen in this light, we can say that the room for choice in Latin America remains considerable, because—as Sheahan makes clear—no particular models of capitalism have been pursued for long enough to become firmly institutionalized. This is even true of the currently heavily favored neoliberal model.

EMERGING MODELS OF CAPITALISM IN LATIN AMERICA?

The overall trend since the 1980s in Latin America has clearly been in the direction of neoliberal models. Sheahan's overview chapter as well as the policy-focused chapters clearly show the trend toward outward-oriented economic policies with increasing reliance on market mechanisms and private investors, both domestic and foreign, paralleled by state retrenchment in economic and social policies. The question is whether this model will be firmly institutionalized or whether it will generate a social and political backlash leading to significant modifications and thus continued instability in policies.

Despite significant domestic opposition against the neoliberal model, the constraints of a globalized economy make any radical departures from it unlikely. More likely than radical modifications of neoliberal economic and social policy patterns is the slow emergence of a new mix, with generally liberal economic policies but more interventionist social policies. Sheahan points to two examples, Brazil and Chile. One could add Uruguay and Costa Rica. These four cases illustrate two different routes to the new model. One route, exemplified by Chile, leads via rapid and radical liberalization, privatization, and deregulation in economic and social policies to a later, very partial and limited recuperation of state intervention in economic policy and a stronger recuperation of policies for poverty reduction. The other, exemplified by Brazil, Uruguay, and Costa Rica, consists of more selective and slower economic liberalization and an uninterrupted strong role for the state in social policy.

The problem for the Chilean route is political: once the private sector becomes the exclusive agent of accumulation, and once labor's organizational strength is emasculated, the economic and political power balance is highly unfavorable for enabling the government to raise the revenue necessary for the pursuit of effective antipoverty policies. The same danger is inherent in the second path, that is, an increasing imbalance between the state and the private sector, and between capital and labor, resulting from economic liberalization and privatization, can endanger the commitment to equity-oriented policies among the state elite, as demonstrated in the case of the Southeast Asian countries discussed by Welsh.

Political institutions, of course, are important factors mediating between the economic and political power balance and policy outcomes. Stephens demonstrates that there is a very strong relationship between long-term incumbency of different political parties and the distributive outcomes of labor market and social policy in advanced industrial democracies. In particular, dominance of social democratic parties is associated with the lowest levels of poverty and inequality. In addition, constitutional structures that disperse power are associated with lower levels of welfare state effort (Huber and Stephens 2000a, 2001). Taking these factors into account in analyzing recent political trends in Latin America renders a mixed picture of chances for the effective pursuit of equity-oriented policies. On the one hand, the sustained or growing strength of left-leaning or mildly social democratic parties, such as the Socialist Party and the Party for Democracy in Chile, the National Liberation Party in Costa Rica, the Workers' Party in Brazil, and the Broad Front in Uruguay, gives some room for optimism in the cases of these countries. On the other hand, their minority position combined with the power dispersion resulting from the authoritarian remnants in the Chilean constitution and from the extreme fragmentation of the party system in Brazil severely limits the room for maneuver of these parties. In most other countries such parties are either much weaker or absent altogether, and party system fragmentation makes consistent pursuit of any equity-oriented policies difficult.

INVESTMENT PROMOTION POLICIES

There is a long-standing consensus in the debate about the determinants of economic growth that high levels of investment in physical capital have a positive impact; more recently, a consensus has developed that investment in human capital has a positive impact as well (Schmidt-Hebbel, Servén, and Solimano 1996).[4] The next question to ask is what factors account for dif-

4. Central among other factors that have been emphasized as determinants of growth are technological innovation and expansion of exports. Several of the essays in Birdsall and Jaspersen 1997 review these debates.

ferences in investment levels. Several have been proposed, such as high savings rates, stable macroeconomic conditions, political stability, efficient supervision and regulation of the banking system, consistency in policymaking, favorable exchange rates, and access to foreign savings. The logical conclusion would be that governments should concentrate on policies that increase domestic savings, maintain macroeconomic and political stability, strengthen institutions and provide consistency in policymaking, adapt the exchange rate to the economy's changing position in international markets, and attract foreign savings. Yet caveats have been raised in several of these policy areas.

There is disagreement about the direction of the causal relationship between domestic savings and growth (see, e.g., Fishlow 1995; Page 1997 versus Gavin, Hausmann, and Talvi 1997; and the reviews by Schmidt-Hebbel, Servén, and Solimano 1996, and Kay, forthcoming), and about the level of inflation defining macroeconomic stability and being conducive to growth. There is also a recognition that an inflow of too much and unregulated foreign savings can have detrimental effects on growth (Ffrench-Davis and Reisen, forthcoming). Whereas no attempt can be made here to take a position in these disputes at a general theoretical level, what we can do is to look comparatively at the experiences of Northeast Asian, Southeast Asian, and Latin American countries and identify systematic patterns of variation in their performance on indicators accepted by the literature as related to economic growth. As an additional step, we can identify the policies that were pursued with the intent of improving the performance in these areas.

There is no doubt that both domestic savings and investment rates have been significantly and consistently higher in East Asia than in Latin America for the past three decades. As of 1965, investment and savings rates were roughly similar in the two regions, around 20 percent of GDP, but in the period 1970–80 investment grew faster in East Asia than in Latin America, and in 1980–91 it continued to grow at 7 percent a year, whereas it declined by 1.2 percent per year in Latin America. In 1991, the average investment rate for Latin America was 18 percent of GDP, for East Asia 35 percent; average savings rates stood at 22 percent and 32 percent, respectively (Jaspersen 1997, 83).[5] In East Asia, both private and public savings rates have been high; in Latin America, both of them have been lower. In fact, as Grosse points out, despite significant economic growth in Latin America in the 1990s, the average savings rate declined to 19 percent of GDP in the period 1993–96,

5. The Latin American countries included in this calculation are Argentina, Brazil, Chile, Colombia, Mexico, Uruguay, Venezuela, and Costa Rica; the East Asian countries are Japan, Korea, Singapore, Hong Kong, Thailand, Malaysia, and Indonesia.

from 21 percent a decade earlier. A strong banking system, stable interest rates, and private savings for retirement are often credited with keeping private savings rates high in East Asia. Chang offers an additional explanation, restrictions on luxury consumption through high tariffs, taxes, and outright bans; Fishlow (1995, 18) adds to this the emphasis on exporting industrial consumer goods that were not made readily available in the internal market. Most of these restrictions would be obviously extremely difficult to use in contemporary Latin America, both for political reasons and because of the Uruguay Round of GATT. However, the imposition of high taxes on luxury consumption—while politically difficult to implement—would not violate any international economic agreements.[6] Such taxes then could contribute to an increase in public savings and a slow recuperation of public investments, which fell to exceedingly low levels—with detrimental consequences for growth—during the period of structural adjustment.

An additional problem in Latin America has been the channeling of savings into productive investments; this is true for both domestic and foreign savings. The traditional explanation for this problem is the weakness of financial markets, and the prescription has been liberalization of financial markets and other areas of economic activity, and privatization of pension schemes. Grosse argues strongly that the shift to private pension funds has produced a boom in Latin American capital markets. However, others argue that privatization of pension schemes has at best been a contributing factor to the rapid development of capital markets in Chile, where the reform is old enough for its effects to be clearly visible (e.g., Barrientos 1998, 143). Moreover, at least so far, financial liberalization has not resulted in significant increases in savings and investment rates in Latin America.[7] On the contrary, financial liberalization has made capital flight, a historic problem for most Latin American countries, even easier, and it has introduced serious new vulnerabilities. In particular, the unregulated inflow of foreign capital into Latin America in the first half of the 1990s, mostly in the form of portfolio investment and therefore short-term funds, led to an expansion of internal credit, much of it going to consumption and real estate booms, an

6. The argument has been made that taxes on luxury consumption are invariably undermined in Latin America by contraband. There is certainly some truth to this argument, but it applies more to smaller items of luxury consumption, such as liquor, perfumes, and so on, than to large ones, such as luxury cars, boats, big-screen television sets, and the like. Luxury condominiums and homes are another form of luxury consumption that could be reduced through property taxes, with beneficial effects on private savings and on government revenue.

7. Edwards (1997, 135) argues that it is too early to tell how recent financial reforms will eventually affect aggregate savings, but he adds that recent evidence suggests that the results may not be as favorable as expected by early supporters of financial liberalization.

appreciation of the exchange rate, and the danger of abrupt and massive capital outflows requiring severe adjustment measures, as in the Mexican peso crisis of December 1994 (Ffrench-Davis and Reisen, forthcoming). It is important to note that Chile, the supposed model of neoliberal reforms, reimposed some controls after the financial crash of the early 1980s and kept controls in effect on short-term capital flows until 1998.[8] Thus, unlike Argentina for instance, Chile managed to escape the ramifications of the Mexican crisis, known as the "Tequila Effect." After 1995, the composition of capital inflows into Latin America changed, and by 1997 more than half of net capital inflows were FDI (ECLAC 1998). This was undoubtedly beneficial, since it reduced the negative effects in the form of increases in consumption, real estate prices, and appreciation of the exchange rate, and helped to keep the rate of private investment up. Nevertheless, financial liberalization meant that short-term capital remained important, and its rapid outflow in the second half of 1998, particularly from Brazil, as a result of contagion from the East Asian and Russian financial crises, again demonstrated the very high vulnerability of the Latin American economies to the strategies of external financial managers.

In fact, the experience of East Asia in the 1990s should caution against any uncritical advocacy of financial liberalization. As Radelet and Sachs (1998) have convincingly argued, the East Asian crisis was essentially a financial crisis, in large part caused by a boom of international lending followed by a sudden withdrawal of funds, as a result of rapidly escalating panic on the part of foreign investors. The repercussions of this sudden withdrawal of funds on the collapse of domestic financial institutions then imposed huge financial burdens on public budgets to bail out the failed institutions. Chang et al. (1998) agree that the panic in international financial markets was an essential ingredient of the financial crisis in Korea, and they argue that it was precisely the speed and mode of financial liberalization and the abandonment of traditional policies to coordinate investments that made Korea so vulnerable and contributed to the bankruptcies of some major firms. Welsh agrees that the enormous expansion of financial markets in the 1990s aggravated the vulnerability of Southeast Asian NICs.

---

8. In one sense, it would be more accurate to call these controls a tax on the basis of how they functioned, but the intent behind their imposition was less a collection of revenue than a discouragement of short-term speculative capital flows. Foreign investors were required to deposit 30 percent of the capital they were sending into Chile interest-free with the Central Bank. In case of withdrawal before twelve months, an extra tax was imposed on these funds, in addition to the loss of interest. In the context of the economic crisis of 1998, Chile abandoned this tax in an effort to attract foreign capital of any sort.

There is general agreement that FDI has more favorable effects on economic growth than portfolio investment; it increases productive capacity,
brings access to technology and markets, and has a weaker effect on the
appreciation of exchange rates (Stallings 1995, 11). Welsh emphasizes how
crucial FDI—particularly from Japan, Taiwan, and Korea—was for the rapid
industrialization of the Southeast Asian NICs. Grosse argues that economic
stabilization and liberalization together with specific policies to attract FDI,
such as equal treatment to domestic capital and the provision of special
incentives or debt-equity swaps, have shown the desired results and contributed to a significant increase of FDI into Latin America in the 1990s.
Nevertheless, the neoliberal arguments for unregulated inflows of FDI, or
even more so for undifferentiated use of incentives to attract FDI, can be
challenged on the grounds of both the Latin American (Evans 1979) and the
East Asian experiences (Welsh, this volume; Chang 1998). Evans demonstrated some two decades ago that FDI in Brazil had the most beneficial
effects on local production of inputs, technology transfers, and local R and
D where the Brazilian state had bargaining leverage and put pressure on foreign corporations. In fact, the most successful examples occurred in industries where joint ventures were formed between foreign corporations and
Brazilian state-owned enterprises (Evans 1979, 276–77). Welsh points out
that the Southeast Asian NICs were certainly highly open to FDI, but did
not pursue laissez-faire policies. Rather, they selectively promoted certain
sectors and built partnerships with foreign capital. Still their heavy reliance
on FDI left them very vulnerable to changes in the economies from where
the FDI originated. Chang (1998) notes that both Korea and Taiwan maintained strict regulation on entry and ownership of transnational corporations. In Korea in the early 1980s around 50 percent of all industries were
still closed to foreign investment, and only in about 13 percent of manufacturing industries was foreign ownership above 50 percent allowed. The
Korean government encouraged joint ventures and carefully monitored
technology transfers and imposed local contents requirements and standards of export performance. Of course, not all Latin American governments will have the same bargaining leverage, and this leverage will also
vary by industry. However, it would be a grave mistake of omission for
these governments to rely on the market alone to induce foreign capital to
make contributions to local productive capacity, and to fail to exploit bargaining leverage stemming, for instance, from the size of local markets,
location in relationship to other markets, the quality of the labor force,
resource endowments, and prospects for economic growth.

For foreign and domestic investors alike, predictability of future economic conditions is a key consideration in committing major investments to productive projects. Predictability rests on stability—stability of the rules of the game and of major economic parameters such as inflation, growth, and exchange rates. There is no question that political instability is a major disincentive to private investment, as are severe macroeconomic fluctuations. It is less clear what constitutes favorable levels (as opposed to changes) in inflation and exchange rates. Chang argues that inflation in East Asia was actually moderate, not low, by comparative standards during the periods of high growth. The implication is that excessive emphasis on low inflation might have costs in terms of investment and growth. From a Latin American perspective, with the recent experience of hyperinflation in several major countries, the issue looks very different. A return to even moderate inflation would be seen as a dangerous step on the slippery slope toward loss of control over inflation (Bresser Pereira 1996). Since inflationary behavior is so heavily determined by expectations, such a development might even become a self-fulfilling prophecy. In other words, what may be levels of inflation that are tolerable and supportive of high levels of investment in one historical context may not be in another. Or at the very least, the move from one level to another may not be tolerable under certain historical conditions.

Whereas favorable exchange rates have been mentioned as one condition of high investment rates, none of the chapters in this volume, or in a recent IDB volume (Birdsall and Jaspersen 1997), explicitly problematizes the issue of exchange rates. In peripheral comments, the stability of East Asian compared to the volatility of Latin American exchange rates is pointed out, along with the "realistic" level of the former, which favored export growth (see, e.g., Pack 1997, 245). One can certainly accept the argument that exchange rate policies in Latin America over the past twenty years have been inconsistent, and that the resulting unpredictability of exchange rates has worked as a deterrent to investment.

Further discussions of exchange rate policy should be set in the context of trade policy. The notion of "realistic" levels of the East Asian exchange rates referred to above conflicts with a political perception that Northeast Asian currencies were (unfairly) undervalued for years, which led to their revaluation under U.S. pressure through the Plaza Accords of 1985. Having an undervalued currency should stimulate investment in production for exports, as long as input prices are not a major factor in the calculation—or they are subsidized. The effect on investment in production for the domestic market would depend very heavily on the degree of protection of that market. In the new international economic environment where subsidies are largely illegal and protection greatly limited, having an undervalued currency should benefit countries with an already established productive structure that has a low dependence on imported inputs. Countries producing at lower levels of commodity chains, particularly those dependent on raw material exports where local labor costs constitute a relatively small percentage of production costs, would benefit less from having an undervalued currency.

TRADE POLICY

Trade liberalization in Latin America has been rapid and of great magnitude, but it has hardly fulfilled the promises made by its most ardent advocates. Trade has increased, but, as Baumann makes clear, in import penetration more so than in export growth. Moreover, diversification and upgrading of exports has been limited; natural resource based exports remain crucial. The argument that competition from imports along with lower prices for inputs would force companies to become more efficient and enable them to break into international markets turned out to be based more on ideology than on empirically grounded understanding. There are at least two major flaws in this argument. First, many companies were simply too weak financially, managerially, and technologically to make this adaptation rapidly and on their own; they went bankrupt and their installed production capacity was lost with them. Second, comprehensive trade liberalization, while obviously not a sufficient condition for export growth, is not even a necessary one. Rather, liberalization could be selective, aimed specifically at inputs for export production.

Thus, if the goal is export promotion, particularly a move toward higher value-added exports, selective protection may be an appropriate policy, along with a number of other policies, as will be discussed in the next section. The danger is, of course, that protective measures become permanent and do allow for inefficient production, as happened in many cases under the ISI policies in Latin America. Korea, Taiwan, Thailand, Indonesia, and Malaysia demonstrate that this is not a necessary feature of protectionist policies. As Chang shows, Korea used a combination of protection of infant industries with industrial policies, such as managed competition and technology policy and export promotion, and gradually increased the exposure of these industries to international competition. Welsh explains that the Southeast Asian NICs began with the promotion of light industry, much of it tied to the natural resource export sector, under strong tariff protection, and then gradually moved to an export-led growth model, with promotion of heavy in addition to light industry, and a gradual and selective liberalization of the trade regime.

Given the presence of excessive protection, there is no doubt that trade liberalization was necessary in Latin America. The problems lie in the speed and scope and erratic nature of liberalization and even more so in the neglect of complementary policies that should have preceded or accompanied trade liberalization. Gradual and predictable phasing out of protection, along with support for technological upgrading, investments in human capital, improvements in industrial relations systems, and provision of information about international market opportunities are all essential ingredients of a policy regime supportive of adaptation of companies to an open market environment. Of course, they require a more interventionist state than the neoliberal vision of the 1980s allowed. Though some of the costs incurred in terms of destroyed production capacity are irreversible, a resolute pursuit of such supportive policies could still be highly beneficial for expanding and upgrading export production.

In Latin America regional integration has clearly been important for the growth in trade. It has also been associated with an increase in foreign capital inflows, both from within and outside the region. Mexico's exports, which now account for about two-fifths of all Latin American exports, would not have grown to such an extent without NAFTA. Recently, Mercosur has become the most dynamic area and has attracted most of the FDI going into Latin America. Critics point out that regional trade expansion does not expose Latin American industries to the same competitive pressures for technological upgrading as export expansion to extraregional markets. Nevertheless, there is evidence that trade integration through Mercosur has strengthened the capacity of member countries to export to the rest of the world as well. The same is true for the Central American Common Market, even though at a very modest level (Bulmer-Thomas 1998, 36).

In any discussion of trade policy, the projected impact of the Uruguay Round of GATT and the WTO is crucial. It makes open trade barriers illegal, except in situations of impending balance of payments crises. There is more room for action in the promotion of industries, particularly at the local level. The use of tax breaks and direct subsidies is limited, with some exceptions in the case of regional development programs. However, it is by no means clear how consistently the rules can and will be enforced, particularly vis-à-vis the actions of local governments. Support for technological upgrading is crucial and can take many forms; the same is true for the provision of market information. This makes close cooperation between governments, business associations, and individual firms in designing appropriate policies and strategies for export promotion essential.

INDUSTRIAL POLICIES

In Latin America in the 1980s the view predominated that the state should do little more than protect private property and provide infrastructure. By the 1990s the realization set in that the state's role in promoting accumulation as well as providing social services and income transfers—at least enough thereof to ensure political stability—remains essential. This, of course, raised the question as to the appropriate policies for the promotion of industry. Since the official view of pre-1980 policies is one of undifferentiated failure, the initial answer to this question was "not the industrial policies of the past," but rather new horizontal, or neutral policies supportive of industrial development in general, not specific sectors. However, as Chang argues convincingly, the notion of horizontal industrial policies is misleading in a context of scarcity. Even support for R and D or skills upgrading of the labor force requires decisions about the types of research and the types of skills most likely to contribute to technological upgrading of production in growth sectors. Research and skills developed for the biochemical industry cannot easily be shifted to the information technology industry and vice versa.

Selective industrial policy has not only a sectoral dimension but also a local one. Restructuring of industries that are the main support of local economies makes targeted industrial policy necessary to dampen social disruption as well as upgrade productivity. Tokman emphasizes the importance of targeted sectoral and local industrial policy as an essential complement to labor market policy to promote high employment levels in medium to high productivity activities, which in turn are essential to reduce poverty levels.

Both Northeast and Southeast Asian NICs pursued selective industrial policies, and whereas there certainly were some failures and changes in course, such as the initiatives in automobiles in Malaysia and in aircraft manufacturing in Indonesia (Welsh), there is no doubt that both sets of countries were highly successful in achieving rapid industrial transformations. The traditional total package of industrial policies as pursued in Korea comprised import protection for infant industries plus managed competition to deal with the problem of economies of scale plus technology policies plus export promotion (Chang). The successful implementation of these policies required cooperation among enterprises, banks, and the government to assure long-term finance, a high-quality training system, and an industrial relations system that avoided disruptions. The achievement of such cooperation has become more difficult in Korea as large enterprises have gained more independence from the government, for instance through direct access to foreign financial markets. It has also become more difficult as trade unions have gained strength and autonomy in the course of political liberalization. It is even more difficult to establish in a context where enterprises developed without strong ties to the government as over the past ten to fifteen years in Latin America, and where labor relations have traditionally been highly antagonistic.

Industrial policy, particularly government support for technology upgrading, also becomes more difficult as industries are approaching the technology frontier. Technological learning is easier where an economy is attempting to catch up with more developed economies, but the closer the most advanced sectors come to the technology frontier, the more difficult technology transfer and the tougher the competition and pressures from advanced firms and countries become. This means that there should be sectoral differences in industrial policy. Traditional technology transfer policies may work well in more established mass production industries, whereas in the most advanced sectors new forms of industrial policy need to be developed, arguably with greater concentration on support for R and D in cooperation with the private sector. Still, such policies should be tied to export promotion policies for these most advanced sectors, such as arrangements for financing and the provision of market information.

As Peres argues, Latin American policymakers are highly skeptical vis-à-vis the idea of "picking winners" and developing new industries, preferring instead to strengthen already existing industries. To some extent, this is certainly reasonable; nobody would expect Paraguay to develop major production of personal computers or components. On the other hand, it becomes a matter of fine distinction what constitutes "already existing industries." Brazil, for instance, has a well-developed production of some components for the informatics industry, and several countries have firms that produce petrochemical and biochemical products and consumer electronics. How much production makes "an established industry" that deserves support, and how much weight should be given to the goal of upgrading export production and thus supporting branches that have still a small volume of production?

Recognizing these issues and devising strategies to deal with them is certainly preferable to pretending that they can be avoided by pursuing nonselective industrial policies. Moreover, even in this new "no industrial policy" environment, most Latin American countries are continuing to use policies that are not neutral with regard to resource allocation among industries.

Nonuniform tariffs advantage some industries over others, regionally targeted fiscal incentives do the same, and exemption of certain sectors from participation by private investors, such as oil in Mexico, constitute a form of preferential resource allocation.[9] Clearly, it would contribute to more rational policymaking if governments were to admit that they are necessarily engaged in some forms of sector-specific industrial policy, and if the various components were put into an explicit and coherent framework. Still other problems have to be overcome in order to develop effective industrial policies in Latin America. As with any other policy, a well-structured bureaucracy with highly qualified and motivated members is a crucial prerequisite. Peres points out that implementation of industrial policy often falters because of overlapping and poorly defined areas of responsibility. Moreover, the extent of political appointments in the bureaucracy means that there is little continuity and that industrial policies are typically designed and implemented with a time horizon of one period in office—hardly a basis for building the kind of long-term cooperation needed for success in this area.

LABOR MARKET POLICIES

The main tasks for labor market policies are promotion of high employment levels and low unemployment and underemployment levels; protection of labor rights; organization of wage setting; and promotion of cooperation for improvements of productivity. The actual creation of jobs cannot be assigned to labor market policy, or only to a very small extent in a contributory role. Rather, private investment decisions shaped by public investment policies and industrial policies are crucial for job growth. Labor market policies can make a contribution in the form of rules facilitating flexible working hours, job sharing, and so on, and in providing a qualified labor force that can make investments more attractive.

The main problems in Latin America are not only open unemployment but also underemployment, that is, employment in low-productivity sectors and low-wage jobs, mostly in the informal sector and thus without legal protection. The main focus of policy in the past fifteen years, though, has been on open unemployment, since the destruction of large numbers of jobs in manufacturing and the public sector was not accompanied by an adequate rate of job creation in the new growth sectors, even once economic

---

9. I am indebted to Victor Bulmer-Thomas for drawing my attention to these forms of de facto industrial policy.

growth resumed. Rather than being understood as structurally rooted in the new economic model, the lack of significant employment growth has been blamed heavily on labor market rigidities in wage setting and job protection. Accordingly, international financial institutions and many governments have called for more flexibility in wage setting and in hiring and firing, at the same time as the governments withdrew from an active pursuit of investment promotion and industrial policies. The international financial institutions and many neoliberal economists have pointed to the United States as a model of labor market policies worthy of emulation because of its presumed outstanding record in employment creation.

Robertson's chapter takes a closer look at the supposed model quality of U.S. labor market policy and points to the falling minimum wage, the high number of people who are working two jobs, and the less than stellar performance in unemployment once the huge prison population is taken into account. He suggests that other factors are responsible for the high rate of job creation, including the deficit spending of the 1980s. Moreover, despite the high rate of job creation, the expansion of the dual labor market has led to growing poverty and inequality in the primary income distribution. Robertson argues convincingly that U.S. federalism is an important factor keeping labor rights and strength restricted by fragmenting authority and creating veto points against protective legislation, as well as by setting states up in competition for investment through providing a favorable business climate.

As both Janoski and Alas's and Stephens's chapters make clear, more successful models in terms of poverty and inequality in primary income distribution are provided by the northern continental European and Scandinavian countries, even though employment growth there has been lower than in the United States over the past twenty years. The key there has been promotion of full employment and a reduction of inequality through a combination of supply-side industrial policies, investment in human capital, active labor market policy, centralized wage setting, and high contract extension. The internationalization and deregulation of financial markets has made the pursuit of traditional investment promotion and consequent job creation policies more difficult, but the other policies mentioned remain viable (Huber and Stephens 1998, 2001).

Active labor market policy in the form of initial training, retraining and relocation of redundant workers, and support for job creation has been a cornerstone of labor market policy in the Scandinavian countries and, to a somewhat lesser extent, in Germany. This type of policy is successful in the context of other employment promotion policies, but less so as an isolated set of temporary measures or even as a substitute for these other policies. Moreover, as Janoski and Alas make clear in the comparison of Britain and Germany, the successful pursuit of coherent active labor market policies requires the presence of strong, centralized organizations of employers and labor, willing to engage in cooperation with each other and the state. They argue that where such institutions are present, active labor market policies can be effective, pointing to evidence that unemployment levels are lower in countries where governments pursue such policies than in comparable countries where governments do not. They further point out that the ratio of spending on active to spending on passive labor market policies has a strong negative effect on long-term unemployment rates, and they argue that active labor market policies facilitate employment flexibility and labor mobility.

East Asian countries have not had extensive labor market policies outside of investment in human capital and labor training, but their investment promotion and industrial policies were most supportive of employment creation. The land reforms in Korea and Taiwan and the investments in the rural sector in Indonesia, Malaysia, and Thailand supported self- and family employment in the rural sector and productivity increases in the peasant economy, and fast industrial growth helped the absorption of the labor force into the urban sector (Pempel, Welsh, this volume). Labor rights remained minimal until the 1960s in Japan, the 1980s in Korea and Taiwan, and the present in the Southeast Asian countries. Even after that, only a minority fraction of the labor force, mostly middle-aged and older men, came to benefit from stable employment and company welfare in large firms in Japan, Korea, and Taiwan. In Japan, this fraction amounts to roughly one-quarter of the labor force. Women, younger people, and workers in small enterprises enjoy less stability and benefits. One of the reasons why inequality has remained relatively low despite this situation is the redistributive function of the extended family.

Wage restraint in the sense of keeping wages from rising faster than productivity is clearly an essential element of labor market policies. Even if unions in traded sectors realize the need to adjust their wage demands to the requirements of competitiveness in world markets, the problem remains how unions in nontraded sectors, particularly the public sector, can be prevented from driving up wages and exerting pressure on unions in the traded sector. Measures to ensure wage restraint can take very different forms. The polar opposites are labor repression combined with dictates of the ministries of finance in East Asia, and highly centralized collective bargaining with voluntary wage restraint on the part of unions in exchange for commitments of investments and social policies in the coordinated market economies of

Europe. In the United States and in Latin America since the 1980s wage restraint has largely been a result of restrictive labor legislation and significantly weakened unions.

Given these different experiences and the specifics of the Latin American situation, what would be desirable labor market policies for Latin America? Certainly in one area the diagnosis of rigidities and the call for greater flexibility in Latin American labor market policy was correct. Traditionally, Latin American countries have pursued little to no active or passive labor market policies like those analyzed by Janoski and Alas. The most common patterns were total neglect or denial of social protection, or active repression of labor. Where there was protective labor legislation at all, it protected not the right to employment and income maintenance in general but the right to a specific job through significant severance pay, which obviously was an obstacle to structural adaptation of enterprises to changing demand conditions. On the other hand, the lack of unemployment insurance has made loss of a job a near-catastrophic event. Thus a change in legislation to facilitate layoffs should be accompanied by a sustained effort to improve unemployment insurance protection. Moreover, changing the rules for layoffs caused by structural adaptation does not mean that protection against arbitrary firings should be relaxed. Employers in Latin America have traditionally fought unions, and firings of union organizers and supporters are potent weapons in that fight.

Another generally recognized problem in Latin American labor markets is the low average skill level of the labor force. Investment both in general education and specific skills training is the obvious solution. Yet despite general agreement on the diagnosis of the problem and the remedy, little has been done to advance in these areas. General education expenditures contracted in the 1980s and recovered only partially in the 1990s, and there is comparatively little being done by governments and the private sector to improve specific labor skills. One factor that works against private sector efforts is the extensive use of subcontracting and the unwillingness of small and medium subcontractors to invest in the upgrading of labor skills. In East Asia large contractors have often participated in the training of workers in those subcontracting enterprises with which they maintained long-standing relationships. In Latin America, governments could create a regulatory environment to make subcontracting relationships more stable and thus investment in training of the subcontractors' labor more attractive, and they could support labor training directly.

One of the major arguments against protective labor legislation in Latin America, of course, has been the size of the informal sector. The informal sector has grown, so the argument goes, precisely to avoid government regulation. While there is more than a grain of truth to this argument, the commonplace conclusion that a generalized reduction of government regulation and taxation is necessary and sufficient to reduce the size of the informal sector is unwarranted. Rather, intensified enforcement efforts could have the effect of drawing some of these enterprises into the formal sector. This raises the question of differences in the importance of various types of government regulations. Clearly, excessive red tape in getting permits to establish an enterprise, along with high payroll taxes, can discourage entrepreneurial activity, and enforcement of these regulations may lead to business closures. On the other hand, enforcement of basic labor rights and basic tax collection should be expanded to small and medium enterprises, along with better access for these enterprises to credit. The direct and indirect (via a stronger tax base) benefits in terms of workers' welfare would arguably outweigh the loss of substandard employment that might occur.

A central question in the debate about labor market polices in OECD countries as well as in Latin America is the presumed trade-off between greater downward flexibility of wages (and welfare benefits) and higher employment levels. Even in advanced industrial countries, it is highly questionable whether such a trade-off exists.[10] Certainly the British example suggests that simply lowering wages and taking away rights from the lowest paid does not necessarily create more jobs. In Latin America, wages are already abysmally low in the informal sector, particularly in personal services, and the central problem is precisely the prevalence of low-productivity, low-paid employment that leaves workers and their families way below the poverty line. Lowering formal sector wages might bring some of these jobs into the formal sector, but it would not alleviate the key problem of poverty. On the contrary, it might aggravate the problem by lowering the wages of those already employed in the formal sector. In addition, it would weaken the incentive for employers to invest in upgrading productivity.

The Chilean example is a case in point for the negative effect of excessively flexible labor markets on poverty. Díaz (1993) argues that precarious waged employment was the single most important element of poverty in Chile at the beginning of the 1990s. Forty-one percent of the two lowest

10. Blanchard and Wolfers (1999) suggest that differences in levels of employment across advanced industrial countries can be explained by the interaction of rigidities in labor market institutions and a number of shocks. However, data problems with time-variant measures of labor market institutions weaken these claims, particularly the fact that one of their most important institutional variables, benefits in unemployment insurance schemes, underwent major changes in the 1980s and 1990s.

income quintiles in the 1990 household survey were associated with formal urban employment, but many of them without any contractual arrangement. The growing practice of large firms to use subcontractors has led to a proliferation of small and medium-sized firms that employ workers at very low wages, for limited time periods, under poor working conditions, and with little access to training.

In Latin America a closely related debate is whether these economies can afford a meaningful minimum wage. One of the arguments that they cannot holds that the enforcement of a minimum wage would destroy formal sector jobs and push more people into unemployment or the informal sector and into poverty. Others emphasize that it would be of extremely limited benefit because it would only cover formal sector workers and hurt others by swelling the ranks of those in the informal sector and thus depressing wages there. Lustig and McLeod (1997) review these debates and conclude that the theoretical discussion is inconclusive and the matter is essentially an empirical one. They show in a regression analysis of changes in poverty in twenty-two developing countries that the levels of the minimum wage and of poverty are negatively related; an increase in the real minimum wage is accompanied by a fall in poverty. However, they caution against using the minimum wage as a tool to combat poverty, arguing that this might increase unemployment in the longer run. The InterAmerican Development Bank's 1996 Report finds that in country-level analyses "in general there is no evidence that raising minimum wages leads to greater unemployment" (IDB 1996, 203), presumably because those in charge of setting the minimum wage are taking the relevant conditions into account. So again, the issue of a tolerable level of the minimum wage in a given country is certainly an empirical one. Morley's (1995, 148–50) analysis of Costa Rica confirms the importance of the minimum wage as a tool to combat poverty. He shows that poverty could be reduced in Costa Rica in the 1980s despite very low economic growth in part because of the increases in the minimum wage, and that employment increased at the same time.[11] The two general conclusions one can draw from these studies are that a lowering of the minimum wage in Latin America would most likely increase the level of poverty, and that gradual increases in the minimum wage are an effective means to lower poverty, if used in moderation.

A final question concerns the desirable strength and role of unions. Outside of a few sectors in a few countries, organized labor in Latin America is

---

11. The other part of the reason for poverty reduction in the 1980s in Costa Rica was that the economic recovery was led by agriculture, where most of the poor were concentrated.

extremely weak. The combination of physical repression under the military regimes and loss of membership because of the destruction of jobs in traditionally well organized sectors is largely responsible for this state of affairs, but restrictive labor legislation is keeping labor from regaining strength in several of the democracies (Drake 1996). Opponents of changes in these restrictions argue that the East Asian example demonstrates that weak unions are good for development, whereas labor in Latin America has mostly had a negative impact on development by taking adversarial positions to capital, driving up wages excessively, and engaging in heavily politically motivated actions. There are several strong counterarguments to make. First of all, the Northern European experience demonstrates that strong labor movements can be good for development, or at the very least compatible with the development of highly competitive economies and very important for the equitable distribution of the benefits from economic growth. Second, given that labor in Latin America was either fought by employers and governments or met with paternalism and attempts at co-optation, but was rarely ever accepted as an autonomous partner, it is not surprising that unions sought help from sympathetic political forces and used strikes to demonstrate their strength and gain concessions where they failed to gain them in negotiations. Third, in Northeast Asia there was a strong drive for development, a sense of national purpose rooted in the pursuit of national security, which resulted in sustained high investment levels and a relentless search for technological progress, even in the absence of union pressure for higher wages. In Southeast Asia, the quest for national integration gave rise to a similar commitment to rapid development. Where this drive and national purpose are missing, as in contemporary Latin America, union pressure can be an important factor forcing employers to invest in technological upgrading and move production up the commodity chain. In contrast, in the absence of union pressure the incentive to compete on the basis of cheap labor and neglect technological upgrading is much stronger. As Tokman makes clear, a joint commitment of unions and employers to improvements in productivity is essential for growth and equity in Latin America.

The European experience, particularly the contrast between Scandinavia or Germany on the one hand and Britain on the other, also demonstrates that high degrees of centralization are conducive to coordination of union action and cooperation with governments and employer organizations in the interest of maintaining national competitiveness. A fragmented union movement is in a much more difficult position to restrain wages when needed and to seek compensation in other ways. Thus, whereas the restrictions on higher-level union organization in contemporary Latin America are certainly contributing to keeping labor weak, as their advocates desire, they are failing to lay the groundwork for the eventual emergence of a labor movement that could play a productivity-, growth-, and equity-enhancing role.

SOCIAL POLICY

The goals of social policy, of course, are contested terrain. A minimalist conception of social policy sees its role as promoting social order and political stability, a maximalist conception sees it as building a welfare state regime that provides every citizen or resident with an adequate share in economic and social resources as appropriate for the standards of a given society, so that every individual is able to participate in the life of this society and fully develop her or his capacities. If one adopts the maximalist conception, one needs to develop operationalizations to assess progress toward this goal. I would suggest that in the context of all the societies considered here, social policies that effectively reduce poverty, redistribute income, and improve the provision of free public services, particularly health care and education, can be considered as working toward this goal, as long as they are being promoted in a deliberate, coherent, and comprehensive manner. According to this operationalization, the deliberately technocratic solutions that are being promoted by the international financial institutions as complements to structural adjustment programs do not qualify as efforts to move toward a maximalist conception, because they take the form of targeted programs to alleviate the symptoms of poverty under exclusion of more comprehensive and coherent approaches to combat its causes, and they divorce these programs from the issue of redistribution.

The historic problems that are at the root of the widespread poverty in Latin America are high inequality in the distribution of wealth, income, and human capital; high population growth; low labor force participation, including female labor force participation; and a high proportion of the labor force in low productivity sectors.[12] The extent of these problems requires a broad attack on poverty from different angles. Comprehensive social policy, including both cash transfers and social services, is obviously central, but it needs to be complemented by labor market policies and the provision of infrastructure in both urban and rural areas. Moreover, as the East Asian experience demonstrates, redistribution of land and strong investment in the

12. For a comprehensive view of the roots of and responses to poverty and inequality in Latin America, see Tokman and O'Donnell 1998.

peasant economy are crucial factors for the reduction of poverty and inequality. Welsh further argues that in Southeast Asia price controls and subsidies for food and petroleum were an essential component of the social safety net.

As Filgueira and Filgueira point out, however, this is not how the problem was traditionally or is currently being defined and attacked in Latin America. Rather, with few exceptions, land reforms have remained very limited or were even rolled back, and small landowners rarely ever benefited from public investment. Price controls and subsidies for basic foodstuffs and petroleum were widely used up to the 1980s, and they did improve the situation of the urban lower classes, but by themselves were insufficient to keep people out of poverty. As part of the austerity measures to respond to the debt crisis of the 1980s, such controls and subsidies were largely abandoned. Traditional social policy has mostly focused on formal sector wage and salary earners, and the approach to transfer payments and social services has largely been based on the social insurance model. Social insurance schemes developed in a highly fragmented manner, and by the early 1980s the older ones among them were beset by financial problems already (Mesa-Lago 1989). These problems then were severely aggravated by the economic crisis of the 1980s and opened the way for profound reforms. In line with the neoliberal thrust of economic reforms, the dominant approach to social policy reform has been privatization, targeting, and decentralization (Huber 1996). However, there have been very important exceptions both in traditional forms of social policy and in contemporary approaches to reforms, such as in Costa Rica and Uruguay, which make it clear that social policy designs are a profoundly political question, shaped by power and interests, not a technical question of finding the most efficient design to achieve generally shared goals.[13]

In Latin America as a whole, the 1980s saw a severe deterioration of living standards; with rising unemployment, falling real wages, and cuts in social expenditures. The wage share in gross national income declined, and inequality increased except in Costa Rica, Colombia, Uruguay, and Paraguay (Morley 1995, 28). In general, the different governments' approaches to social policy reform corresponded closely to their vision of an appropriate

13. The literature on social policy reform in Latin America has been growing rapidly. For interesting collections of essays, see Barreto de Oliveira 1994 and Raczynski 1995. The Kellogg Institute at Notre Dame published a number of very interesting working papers: among them, Faria 1994, Draibe et al. 1995, C. Filgueira 1994, F. Filgueira 1995, Lo Vuolo 1995, and Raczynski 1994; Ippolito-O'Donnell, forthcoming, contains a number of papers presented at a conference on Social Policies for the Urban Poor at the Kellogg Institute at Notre Dame. The technical side has been investigated by Mesa-Lago 1989 and 1994 and Cruz-Saco and Mesa-Lago 1998.

model of the relationship between state and market, and state and civil society, and to the interests of their power base. Those who fully embraced economic neoliberalism also went furthest away from universalistic approaches to social policy and toward residualism, that is, toward a growing role of private insurance and private providers of services and a restriction of the role of the state to taking care of the poorest of the poor only. Chile under Pinochet went furthest in this direction, with a preferred role for the private sector in both pensions and health care and a residual role for the state in taking care of those with lower incomes and the very poor. Uruguay in contrast has retained a more universalistic approach with heavy reliance on the state, combining both public and private funds in the pension system. Several countries introduced mixed public/private schemes, often with competition between public and private components and incentives structured to the detriment of the public components (Barrientos 1998; Cruz-Saco and Mesa-Lago 1998).

Most of the reforms are of recent origin and their effects have not been thoroughly evaluated yet. However, a few statements can be made with confidence.[14] The oldest reform is the Chilean pension reform, and it has failed to solve two crucial problems, the extent of coverage and the high administrative costs. Coverage formally stands at about 80 percent of the labor force, but only roughly half of those affiliated are active contributors (Cruz-Saco and Mesa-Lago 1998, 389–408). Administrative costs are high, particularly for low income earners, mostly because of the high expenses for marketing and the imposition of flat fees in addition to commissions.[15] Moreover, we know from studies of welfare states in advanced industrial societies that public pension schemes are more egalitarian than private ones, even if the public ones have a strong earnings-related component (Korpi and Palme 1997). We also know that countries with private insurance and delivery of health care spend more of their GDP on health care and have more unequal access than countries with public insurance and delivery. In Chile, the private health system covered 30 percent of the population in 1995, the public one 70 percent; expenditures in the private system amounted to U.S.$310 per person, compared to U.S.$197 in the public system (Larrañaga 1997).

If we assume that effective large-scale poverty reduction is a desired goal, what can we learn from countries where this goal has been achieved about

14. For a comparative analysis and evaluation of pension reforms, see Cruz-Saco and Mesa-Lago 1998, and Huber and Stephens 2000b.

15. None other than the InterAmerican Development Bank (IDB 1996), a strong supporter of privatization schemes, found that as of the mid-1990s the administration of the Chilean pension system was the most expensive in Latin America.

the most effective policies? First, we have to recognize that large-scale poverty reduction is not possible without a redistribution of income through the tax and transfer system. As Stephens shows, the advanced industrial countries with the lowest poverty rates also have the lowest post-tax / post-transfer inequality, partly because of comparatively low inequality in primary income distribution achieved through labor market policies, and partly because of highly redistributive tax and transfer systems. The need for redistribution is much greater in Latin America, of course, given the much less equal primary income distribution. Thus the first and most important policy lesson is the need to establish an effective and progressive tax system. It is very clear that Latin America is significantly undertaxed compared to other regions. In 1991–95, the average tax burden in Latin American countries was 14.1 percent of GDP, compared to 16.8 percent among East Asian countries. That it is not impossible to collect higher taxes at the level of development of Latin American and Caribbean countries is demonstrated by the considerable variation among them, with Guyana, Barbados, Jamaica, and Trinidad and Tobago all having tax burdens of 24 percent and above (IDB 1996, 128). Tax reform has been on the agenda of most Latin American countries as part of their structural adjustment programs, but progress has been rather limited. Where there was progress, it was mostly in aggregate tax collection based heavily on value-added taxes; collection of income taxes from individuals remains very spotty (see, e.g., Berensztein 1998). This is a problem, not only because of lost tax revenue, but also because the income tax system can serve as a very effective and nonstigmatizing channel for income-tested transfers payments, as Myles's discussion of the Canadian example demonstrates.

Going back to the European experience, the countries with the lowest poverty rates have income transfer systems composed of (1) universalistic basic flat-rate benefits financed from general tax revenue, (2) public earnings-related benefits financed by employer and employee contributions, and (3) social assistance supplements financed from general tax revenue for those still in need. Universalistic basic pension benefits and child allowances are particularly effective in keeping vulnerable groups—the elderly, families with many children, and single mothers—out of poverty. As Stephens points out, universalistic flat-rate pension benefits were introduced at comparatively early stages of welfare state development, when these countries had reached roughly the same level of affluence that the more advanced Latin American countries reached in the 1980s and 1990s. These pension schemes were largely the product of a political alliance and compromise between the labor movement that pushed for social security programs and small farmers who opposed earnings-related benefits. Child allowances along with other family support programs were introduced later (Wennemo 1994). Universal flat-rate pensions and child allowances would be an appropriate approach in the Latin American context as well, where a large proportion of the population are not formal sector wage and salary earners. They have the additional advantage of being simple and cheap to administer. The most frequent argument against them is that they waste scarce resources on middle and upper income earners who do not need them. However, this argument loses validity in the context of an efficient and progressive tax system through which the benefits can be reclaimed. Universalistic programs have three more advantages. First, they acquire much larger political support bases than programs targeted at specific groups only. Second, they provide policy legacies that are more favorable for the maintenance of a redistributive and solidaristic thrust than particularistic and targeted schemes, as Myles's comparison between welfare state retrenchment in the United States and Canada makes clear. Third, they cannot be abused for patronage purposes because there is no bureaucratic discretion.

My general argument in favor of universalistic and against targeted schemes should obviously not be misinterpreted as an argument for the immediate abandonment of all targeted schemes in Latin America, particularly those nutritional and other health schemes targeted at poor neighborhoods and poor schools. Targeting individual families through household means tests has many problems; it is cumbersome and expensive administratively; it has a stigma attached to it; it gives much room for administrative discretion and thus clientelism and political manipulation; and—depending on program structure—it may be divisive by setting the poor up in competition with one another for benefits. The collectively targeted schemes, based on aggregate social indicators, can be very effective in alleviating some of the symptoms of poverty, even though they are also subject to the dangers of political manipulation. If they are channeled through schools in poor areas, they can also be useful to improve school attendance and thus human capital. What I am arguing against is governments concentrating on such targeted schemes as the essence of social policy and keeping off the agenda universalistic alternatives aimed at a comprehensive attack on the roots of poverty.

In addition to a universalistic income transfer system, the second major pillar of a comprehensive approach to improving the life chances of the majority of the population is the provision of high quality and universally accessible education and health care. Success in these policy areas is closely interrelated. Researchers have long argued that investment in education alone is not sufficient to improve the capacity of the poorest sectors, since children from poor families have more difficulties learning. Now there is systematic cross-national statistical evidence that inequality in income distribution is negatively related to absolute skill levels of the 20 percent of the population scoring lowest on comparable tests of literacy skills (OECD/ Statistics Canada 2000). In other words, in more egalitarian societies the bottom 20 percent have higher skill levels. Thus, since it is accepted that higher levels of human capital are conducive to economic growth, redistributive policies together with investment in quality education for all are not only compatible with, but in the longer run actually supportive of, economic growth.

That the state has an obligation to provide free public education, and even enforce school attendance, has long been a widely accepted premise in advanced industrial countries. Even in Latin America most governments rhetorically accepted this obligation, pleading resource constraints and lack of parental cooperation to explain the obvious gap between rhetoric and reality. In health care this obligation has been much more disputed, and the role of private delivery and financing of health care much more extensive, both in advanced industrial and in developing countries. The experiences of European and North American countries clearly show that public financing and provision of health care are vastly more egalitarian and also cheaper than private insurance and provision. The Costa Rican example demonstrates how successful an integrated approach to preventive and curative health care in a public health system can be in improving basic health indicators in the context of a developing country. The contrast with Brazil, for instance, which has a higher GDP per capita, is impressive. Brazil, of course, has made major efforts to strengthen the preventive and public parts of its health care system, but private hospitals, doctors, and drug companies have been formidable opponents in this struggle (Weyland 1996).

The reform thrust in many Latin American countries encompassed, not only efforts to privatize parts of the pension and health systems and move toward public provision of services for the poorest groups only, but also a decentralization of the responsibility for the provision of social services to subnational governments. Theoretically, advocates of decentralization have argued that it should make the providers of social services more responsive to the needs of the local population. In practice, the key issue remains financing. As long as the decentralization of responsibilities is accompanied by an adequate redistribution of resources from the central government, the outcome may well be better delivery of social services and more citizen input, as appears to have happened in Swedish municipalities. Where decentralization is mostly a means for the central government to reduce expenditures and to break the power of public sector unions, and therefore redistribution of responsibilities for service delivery also means redistribution of responsibilities for raising the funds to pay for them, the outcome is growing disparity in the quality of the services between poorer and more affluent local communities.

Decentralization bears additional dangers, particularly where institutions to enforce accountability are weak. In Brazil, for instance, some state governors used resources from the federal government designated for the improvement of public health services for other purposes (Weyland 1996, 174). Political manipulation of social services to strengthen the support base of power holders is every bit as likely at the local as at the national level. The degree of responsiveness to local needs depends very heavily on the organizational capacity of the local population, which implies that responsiveness is not likely to be greatest toward the neediest because of their lack of organizational capacity.

Change from one system to another, in transfer systems as well as social services, is always difficult. People who have paid into an earnings-related social insurance scheme are obviously extremely reluctant to accept a transition to a universalistic flat-rate benefits scheme. Private providers of health services sternly resist an expansion of government regulation of their compensation. Nevertheless, some of the changes in Latin America over the past fifteen years have been dramatic, and there is no a priori reason other than the interests and power of neoliberal and other opponents of universalistic and redistributive measures why these changes could not have gone in a different direction. If the earnings-related pension scheme is in such a financial crisis that it cannot pay adequate benefits and according to the government needs to be privatized, why would citizens naturally be more inclined to accept the promise that the government will provide some compensation to the individual private accounts for previously made contributions than the promise that the government will provide a basic tax-financed subsistence pension for all, to be supplemented by earnings-related benefits from a new scheme? In the case of health care reform, given the opposition from private providers and insurers to an expansion of public supervision, it is crucial that any new initiatives be directed toward strengthening public provision and financing of health services so as to gradually push private providers and insurers into a minority position.

Traditionally, financing of social security schemes in Latin America rested on employer and employee contributions, with employer contributions reaching very high levels. In protected economies this was acceptable to employers, since they could pass the costs on to their customers; in the new open economic environment, employers are opposing contributions to social security schemes as a problem for competitiveness. There is no doubt that such obligations are one factor affecting labor costs and that they need to be kept at internationally comparable levels. However, this does not mean at all that they need to be abolished, as they were in Chile. The vast majority of industrialized and industrializing countries do impose such obligations on their employers. Still, financing of income transfers and social services in Latin America needs to be shifted more toward general taxes. This is particularly appropriate to finance universalistic flat-rate pensions and child allowances and healthcare services. Employer contributions assessed as a percentage of remunerations paid can also be considered one form of corporate taxation and be channeled into the general fund for transfers and social services, rather than into one or more funds to finance specific entitlements of employees, thus strengthening the solidaristic aspects of social policy.

TRANSFERABILITY OF POLICIES

As Filgueira and Filgueira, Pempel, Robertson, and Stephens forcefully argue, if we want to understand the possibilities for transferring growth- and equity-promoting policies from one geographical-historical setting to another, we need to look primarily at institutions and actors, and at the distribution of interests and power among these actors. There are good reasons to discount cultural arguments as determinants of the feasibility of given policies. The argument about Confucianism and its promotion of discipline and harmony as a precondition for the success of East Asian industrialization is not at all convincing in the light of the harsh labor conflicts in Japan in the 1950s and 1960s and Korea in the 1980s. In the Latin American case, the argument about the Catholic and corporatist tradition and its impact on the acceptance of hierarchy and fatalism and thus the lack of entrepreneurial motivation is equally unconvincing in the light of the long tradition of popular protest and revolt and the flourishing of informal entrepreneurial activities. Rather, to understand the roles of the state, capital, and labor in the shaping of policies, we have to look at their relationship to each other and to other major social actors, as well as at domestic institutions and the international context in which they operate.

To begin with an examination of domestic institutions, the first precondition for making coherent policies is a considerable degree of centralization of political institutions, or in other words, the absence of numerous veto points. Centralization should by no means be equated with authoritarianism, however. Certainly, there was very high centralization of power under the authoritarian governments in Korea and Taiwan, but the example of the Scandinavian countries shows that democracies can act in a comprehensive and coherent manner as well. Federalism and presidentialism disperse political power and provide numerous veto points that make comprehensive approaches difficult. The effects are very visible, for instance, in welfare state policies in the United States and also in austerity and adjustment policies in Brazil.[16] In addition to providing veto points, federalism also bears the danger of setting subnational units up in competition with each other for investment, thus giving capital great leverage against both governments and labor to keep labor rights and the social wage restricted. Robertson makes this dynamic very clear in his discussion of the United States.

In the Latin American context, there is considerable concern with the dangers of high centralization of power in democracies, as the centralist tradition has long been associated with tendencies to authoritarianism. However, the key problem in Latin America is not constitutional concentration versus dispersion of political power, but the weakness of constitutionalism per se. In other words, the weakness of democratic institutions rather than their degree of centralization facilitates the overstepping of constitutional powers by chief executives and thus the emergence of what O'Donnell (1994) has so aptly called "delegative democracies." In the context of weak democratic institutions, decentralization can in fact have rather negative consequences also in the form of abuses of power by regional and local elites. What is needed for the effective pursuit of policies that promote the interests of underprivileged majorities is a strengthening of representative institutions and of accountability of policymakers, not power dispersion through multiple veto points.

Policy legacies constitute another aspect of institutional structure, whose importance is demonstrated by Myles in his comparison of social policy in Canada and the United States. Path dependency is clearly important in that it shapes conditions within which later changes have to be made; however, these conditions can gradually be modified through additional policies. Radical departures from established policy patterns are rare, but they are possible in perceived crisis situations. The radical departure from traditional economic and social policies in many Latin American countries under the

16. Immergut (1992) drew attention to this point initially, and Maioni (1998) demonstrates it very clearly in her comparison of healthcare policy in Canada and the United States. Huber et al. (1993) and Huber and Stephens (2000a and 2001) demonstrate the impact of power dispersion on social policy in a pooled cross-sections and time series analysis for advanced industrial countries.

impact of the debt crisis is a clear example. Under normal conditions, changes are easier where old structures are not firmly entrenched, that is, where they have not been in existence very long or where they are not affecting powerful actors or large sectors of the population. One key lesson to take into account for social policy in the stage of setting up programs is the danger inherent in relying on private providers of services and insurance. Private for-profit providers will always work according to the logic of markets and thus introduce more inequalities into transfers and services than public providers, who—if under the direction of progressive governments and subject to accountability by democratic institutions—are more likely to be working according to a political logic of universalistic access and uniform quality.

There is little disagreement that a key requirement for effective policy transfer in any area is an effective bureaucracy capable of implementing policies as designed. Emphasizing the Weberian characteristics of an efficient bureaucracy and its autonomy from particularistic interests does not entail ignoring the importance of the power distribution in society that shapes the overall design of policies; it simply directs attention to the capacity of the state apparatus to pursue policy goals in a consistent manner. Similarly, Evans's (1995) notion of the need for autonomy to be counterbalanced by embeddedness, that is, effectively functioning channels for ongoing interaction between the bureaucracy and the private sector, has been widely accepted as a precondition for the successful pursuit of developmental policies. This notion can be extended to the need for such channels between the government, business, and labor for the pursuit of labor market and social policies that are generous, comprehensive, and compatible with improvements in productivity and international competitiveness. In terms of specific state capacities, an efficient tax administration system is of primary importance, both for mustering the resources needed for growth- and equity-enhancing policies and for administering income transfer programs.

When we shift our focus from institutions to the distribution of power and interests among actors, we find that it is useful to discuss those in relationship to specific policy areas. The type of policies for promotion of investment and competitiveness that a government might successfully adapt depends to some extent on the leverage of the government vis-à-vis private investors based on the share of crucial resources controlled by the government. At one extreme is the situation in Korea and Taiwan in the 1950s and 1960s where the state controlled all external capital flows, much of it coming in the form of grants from the United States, and virtually the entire formal domestic credit system (e.g., Woo 1991); at the other extreme is the situation in Mexico in the 1990s where capital markets had been largely deregulated and private investors, domestic and foreign, could plunge the country into a financial crisis. In all countries, including Western European ones, government intervention in financial markets in order to stimulate productive investment has become much more difficult (if not impossible) today than before the mid-1980s, because financial deregulation has shifted control over funds away from governments to private investors (Huber and Stephens 1998).

In the area of industrial policies, the more dependent companies are on public support for R and D, technology licensing, and protection from competition, the larger is the government's room for action. As domestic corporations advance in competitiveness and size, and in capacity to deal with foreign corporations and enter foreign markets independently, they will become much more likely to challenge government's development plans and policies and pursue their own particularistic interests. As Evans (1995) points out for the Korean case, the very success of the developmental state tends to undermine its power base and thus its capacity to continue in the same role.

In Latin America we are dealing with a fundamentally different trajectory. Even in the heyday of the developmentalist state, the state never had the same amount of control over resources as the Northeast Asian states did. Though the state did take control over the foreign exchange system, it was never the recipient of grants to nearly the same extent as Korea and Taiwan; it remained dependent on private capital to generate the huge majority of foreign exchange inflows. Thus, private capital, both large domestic and foreign capital, enjoyed greater autonomy from the state and was capable of exerting more pressure for the protection of its interests. One policy area where this power distribution has remained important is in the use of industrial policies to move up the commodity chain in exports and thus get away from dependence on primary exports. The pursuit of such policies is very difficult where agribusiness and large landholders are powerful economic and political actors. In this situation, the forging of a countervailing political support coalition for industrial policies among export-oriented manufacturing and business service enterprises is an essential first step in the successful transfer of any kind of industrial policies.

Turning to the transfer of labor market and social policies, the question becomes who could be the carriers, the political support base for comprehensive and solidaristic social policy reform in Latin America? In Europe, social democratic and Christian democratic parties played the key political role, and these parties were particularly strong and effective where they had solid support bases in strong labor movements. These parties and the labor movements close to them needed to form alliances with additional allies at different times, principally small farmers and white-collar workers. Differential length of incumbency of social democratic and Christian democratic parties and different alliances resulted in social policy regimes with different distributive outcomes, as Stephens demonstrates. It was the alliance between labor, small farmers, and social democratic parties, for instance, that produced the basic flat-rate, tax-financed citizenship pensions. Christian democratic parties tended to respond to labor pressure more with employment-based, earnings-related social insurance schemes. It is important to point out here that with the exceptions of Britain and New Zealand, the welfare states shaped by these different political alliances in advanced industrial societies have retained their essential characters, despite the widespread need for austerity caused by rising unemployment in the 1980s and 1990s. Furthermore, whereas there has been a decline in partisan differences in social policy in these societies, these differences have by no means disappeared (see Huber and Stephens 2001). In other words, political power and political choices continue to matter in the new international economic context.

In Latin America both reformist parties and labor movements are much weaker, and dependence on allies is more pivotal. The large informal sector and the rural population are clearly potential allies in the struggle for basic flat-rate pensions and child allowances and universal public health care, since they would greatly benefit from such schemes. However, they are very poorly organized and thus difficult to forge into partners in powerful alliances. The leading role in forging alliances among different social actors falls by default onto democratic left or reformist parties. This presents another set of difficult prospects, given the weakness of parties and party systems in general and of reformist parties in particular. Nevertheless, the experience of the Workers' Party (PT) in Brazil and recent advances of democratic left parties in Uruguay, Argentina, and Mexico suggest that there is hope for political organizing efforts on the part of reformist forces to result in greater influence on policy. There are some additional signs of hope for the construction of alliances. Growing concern among the middle classes about the deterioration of social services and about social disintegration manifesting itself in rising crime rates could generate pressures for a resumption of greater state responsibility for social inclusion and the provision of quality services.[17] Finally, there is a growing recognition on the part

---

17. O'Donnell (1998) argues that the sectors in the middle of the middle, neither those in danger of falling into poverty nor those linked economically to the rich, need to play the leading

of some entrepreneurs that the quality of human capital is too low and that increased investment in education alone is not the answer, since this human capital deficit is at least in part a result of the widespread poverty and lack of medical attention. This suggests the possibility of an alliance between labor, business, and reformist parties to improve transfer schemes and social services while shifting more of the burden of financing from payroll taxes to other forms of taxation. Tax-financed programs, in turn, open greater room to maneuver for redistribution and for an extension of the schemes to the population outside the formal sector.

One question regarding possible sources of progressive forms of social policies that is being raised in Latin America is whether innovation could come from local governments that may be controlled by progressive forces, and then be adopted at the national level. Though decentralization of responsibility for social policies has gone quite far in various countries, such a scenario seems unlikely for at least two reasons. First, local governments typically do not have sufficient resources to experiment successfully with comprehensive social policies. Second, even if they did, the power constellation at the national level would still have to be favorable to shape national policy following the local example. In other words, progressive forces need to be able to extend their control over policymaking to the national level.

Pempel and Welsh emphasize the importance of the international context for the successful pursuit of growth-oriented policies in the East Asian economies: Pempel focuses on the cold war and the consequent favorable treatment of Korea and Taiwan by the United States, and Welsh on the integration of Southeast Asian economies into production networks of Japanese, Korean, and Taiwanese firms. Clearly, both global and regional influences shape the effects of economic policies (see Stallings 1995). Since the 1980s, the global context has made a variety of policy instruments more difficult to wield for governments everywhere. In Latin America, this difficulty has been aggravated by the regional hegemony of the United States. U.S. influence for a century has been working against progressive reform in Latin America at various levels directly and indirectly (see, e.g., LaFeber 1984 and Schoultz 1998). Most recently, the U.S. government and the international financial

---

role in forming a political coalition to combat poverty and inequality. He further argues that the potentially most successful strategy is to link the fight against poverty and inequality to the fight for an improvement of democracy. He is rather skeptical concerning the potential of unions to transcend the narrow self-interest of their members. At present, given the embattled state of unions, this skepticism is certainly warranted. However, with an expansion of the formal sector and of union membership, and with a strengthening of central labor organizations, unions may well adopt a more universalistic analysis and strategy, encompassing the interests of the un- and underemployed.

institutions under U.S. influence, like the IMF, the World Bank, and the InterAmerican Development Bank, have been pushing for neoliberal economic and social reforms, amounting to a general retrenchment of state involvement in the implementation of market-correcting policies, be they aimed at growth or equity. Social policy has been promoted mainly in the form of compensatory measures to smooth the economic adjustment policies, not as a coherent strategy to attack the problems of poverty and inequality. In addition, U.S. corporations are making the formation of influential reformist coalitions more difficult by opposing a strengthening of unions. There are two potential bright spots for Latin American reformist forces in the regional context, though; first, the possibility of mustering some support from regional branches of international organizations like the ILO or branches of the UN, such as the United Nations Research Institute for Social Development or the United Nations Development Program; and second, the growing recognition on the part of some sectors in the international financial institutions that excessive poverty and inequality are barriers to growth and thus need to be remedied.

The process of regional integration may stimulate growth, but it will not offer any support for equity-enhancing policies, since it is a process of pure market integration. There are even fewer efforts being made than by the European Union to coordinate social and labor market policy, since freedom of movement for labor is not on the agenda. On the contrary, regional integration can be expected to exert downward pressure on taxation and social protection as a result of greater competition among states for investment and firms forging strategies to take advantage of this competition.

The essays in this volume have highlighted in various explicit and implicit ways the importance of cooperation between the state, capital, and labor for both growth and equity. In East Asia public-private sector cooperation was highly successful in the pursuit of competitiveness policy and in the designing of infrastructure provided by the state. In contrast, the approach toward labor consisted in a combination of repression and enterprise-level co-optation, not coordination like in Western Europe with inclusion of organized labor at the enterprise and higher levels. This approach not only created a situation of stress that exploded in significant labor militancy in Korea, for instance, once political liberalization had set in, but it also provided less transparency of government–private sector interaction and thus less of a check on corruption. Of course, union corruption is also a well-known phenomenon, just to mention the Peronist unions in Argentina, the unions linked to the hegemonic Institutional Revolutionary Party (PRI) in Mexico, or the Teamsters in the United States, and inclusion of labor is not a panacea for the pursuit of particularistic interests over national policy goals. The point is simply that industry-wide or national-level tripartite bodies are less likely to leave corruption unexposed and thus more likely to reduce its incidence.

The example of Western European coordinated market economies demonstrates that cooperation at the national or sectoral level between government, business, and labor in training and wage setting can be beneficial to all parties in facilitating growth with high levels of productivity and employment and a generous social safety net. Cooperation between business and labor at the enterprise level is supportive of productivity increases. Tripartite cooperation makes it possible to sustain a labor market regime with an emphasis on active labor market policy, an adequate minimum wage, and health and safety protection, linked to other policies designed to stimulate investment and employment and to improve educational levels of the entire labor force, which in turn is most likely to be supportive of productivity increases and workers' welfare. Such cooperation also entails the acceptance of a well-functioning tax system, which in turn makes it possible to sustain a universalistic social policy regime, with adequate flat-rate minimum benefits and free health care, and thus effectively to combat poverty and inequality without damaging fiscal discipline and economic growth.

For Latin America, the achievement of such cooperation would require no less than a major institutional and behavioral transformation.[18] After the wave of neoliberal reforms Latin America is in a way further from cooperation than it was in the 1970s. The state apparatus has been stripped of legitimacy and partly of capacity to intervene in economic development with investment promotion and industrial policies; unions have been greatly weakened; and the successful businesses have adapted to a largely unregulated market environment. The hegemony of U.S. capital and the international financial institutions in the region have by and large taken tripartite cooperation and comprehensive approaches to industrial policies, labor market policies, and social policies off the agenda. Reversing this trend does not mean returning to the old patterns of cooperation and policymaking, which were often very particularistic and paternalistic and had many negative effects on growth and distribution; it does mean recovering the best of the developmentalist tradition in Latin America, widening cooperation and policy coverage to make it transparent and universalistic, and learning from policies that have proven successful in other countries. If this

18. That the consciousness of the need for such cooperation in Latin American countries is rising can be seen by ECLAC's call for a "fiscal covenant," that is, a "basic socio-political agreement that legitimizes the role of the state and establishes the areas and scope of government responsibility in the economic and social sphere" (ECLAC 1998b, 1).

volume can make a small contribution to this learning process, it will have achieved its purpose.

REFERENCES

Barreto de Oliveira, Francisco, ed. 1994. *Social Security Systems in Latin America.* Washington, D.C.: IDB, Johns Hopkins University Press.

Barrientos, Armando. 1998. *Pension Reform in Latin America.* Aldershot, U.K.: Ashgate.

Berensztein, Sergio. 1998. "The Politics of Tax Reform in Argentina and Mexico." Ph.D. diss., Department of Political Science, University of North Carolina, Chapel Hill.

Birdsall, Nancy, and Frederick Jaspersen. 1997. "Lessons from East Asia's Success." In Nancy Birdsall and Frederick Jaspersen, eds., *Pathways to Growth: Comparing East Asia and Latin America.* Washington, D.C.: IDB, Johns Hopkins University Press.

Blanchard, Olivier, and Justin Wolfers. 1999. "The Role of Shocks and Institutions in the Rise of European Unemployment: The Aggregate Evidence." Harry Johnson Lecture, Massachusetts Institute of Technology.

Bowman, Kirk. 1991. "Should the Kuznets Effect Be Relied on to Induce Equalizing Growth: Evidence from Post-1950 Development." *World Development* 25, no. 1:127–43.

Bresser Pereira, Luiz Carlos. 1996. *Economic Crisis and State Reform in Brazil.* Boulder, Colo.: Lynne Rienner.

Bulmer-Thomas, Victor. 1998. "El Mercado Comun Centroamericano: Del regionalismo cerrado al regionalismo abierto." In Victor Bulmer-Thomas, ed., *Integracion Regional en Centroamerica.* San Jose, Costa Rica: FLACSO.

Chang, Ha-Joon. 1998. "Globalisation, Transnational Corporations, and Economic Development—Can the Developing Countries Pursue Strategic Industrial Policy in a Globalising World Economy?" In D. Baker, G. Epstein, and R. Pollin, eds., *Globalisation and Progressive Economic Policy: What Are the Real Constraints and Opportunities?* Cambridge: Cambridge University Press.

Chang, Ha-Joon, Jae Park Hong, and Chul Gyue Yoo. 1998. "Interpreting the Korean Crisis: Financial Liberalisation, Industrial Policy, and Corporate Governance." Draft manuscript (Department of Economics, Cambridge University).

Cruz-Saco, María Amparo, and Carmelo Mesa-Lago, eds.. 1998. *Do Options Exist? The Reform of Pension and Health Care Systems in Latin America.* Pittsburgh: University of Pittsburgh Press.

Díaz, Alvaro. 1993. "Restructuring and the New Working Classes in Chile: Trends in Waged Employment, Informality and Poverty, 1973–1990." Discussion Paper no. 47. Geneva: United Nations Research Institute for Social Development.

Draibe, Sônia Miriam, Maria Helena Guimarães de Castro, and Beatriz Azeredo. 1995. "The System of Social Protection in Brazil." Working Paper no. 3, Democracy and Social Policy Series. Notre Dame: Kellogg Institute, University of Notre Dame.

Drake, Paul. 1996. *Labor Movements and Dictatorships: The Southern Cone in Comparative Perspective.* Baltimore: Johns Hopkins University Press.

ECLAC. 1998a. *Economic Survey of Latin America and the Caribbean.* Santiago: Economic Commission for Latin America and the Caribbean.

———. 1998b. *The Fiscal Covenant.* Santiago: Economic Commission for Latin America and the Caribbean.

Edwards, Sebastian. 1997. "Why are Latin America's Saving Rates So Low?" In Nancy Birdsall and Frederick Jaspersen, eds., *Pathways to Growth: Comparing East Asia and Latin America.* Washington, D.C.: IDB, Johns Hopkins University Press.

Evans, Peter. 1979. *Dependent Development: The Alliance of Multinational, State, and Local Capital in Brazil.* Princeton: Princeton University Press.

———. 1995. *Embedded Autonomy: States and Industrial Transformation.* Princeton: Princeton University Press.

Faria, Vilmar E. 1994. "The Current Social Situation in Brazil: Dilemmas and Perspectives." Working Paper no. 1, Democracy and Social Policy Series. Notre Dame: Kellogg Institute, University of Notre Dame.

Ffrench-Davis, Ricardo, and Helmut Reisen. Forthcoming. "Capital Flows and Investment Performance: An Overview." In Ricardo Ffrench-Davis and Helmut Reisen, eds., *Capital Flows and Investment Performance: Lessons from Latin America.* Paris: OECD Development Centre.

Filgueira, Carlos. 1994. "Heterogeneity and Urban Poverty in Uruguay." Working Paper no. 9, Democracy and Social Policy Series. Notre Dame: Kellogg Institute, University of Notre Dame.

Filgueira, Fernando. 1995. "A Century of Social Welfare in Uruguay: Growth to the Limit of the Batllista Social State." Working Paper no. 5, Democracy and Social Policy Series. Notre Dame: Kellogg Institute, University of Notre Dame.

Fishlow, Albert. 1995. "Future Sustainable Latin American Growth: A Need for Savings." *Review of Black Political Economy* 24, no. 1 (Summer): 7–21.

Gavin, Michael, Ricardo Hausmann, and Ernesto Talvi. 1997. "Saving, Growth and Macroeconomic Vulnerability." In Nancy Birdsall and Frederick Jaspersen, eds., *Pathways to Growth: Comparing East Asia and Latin America.* Washington, D.C.: IDB, Johns Hopkins University Press.

Huber, Evelyne. 1996. "Options for Social Policy in Latin America: Neoliberal versus Social Democratic Models." In Gøsta Esping-Andersen, ed., *Welfare States in Transition: National Adaptations in Global Economies.* London: Sage, United Nations Research Institute for Social Development.

Huber, Evelyne, Charles Ragin, and John D. Stephens. 1993. "Social Democracy, Christian Democracy, Constitutional Structure, and the Welfare State." *American Journal of Sociology* 99, no. 3:711–49.

Huber, Evelyne, and John D. Stephens. 1998. "Internationalization and the Social Democratic Model: Crisis and Future Prospects." *Comparative Political Studies* 31, no. 3 (June): 353–97.

———. 2000a. "Partisan Governance, Women's Employment, and the Social Democratic Service State." *American Sociological Review* 45:323–42.

———. 2000b. "The Political Economy of Pension Reform: Latin America in Comparative Perspective." Geneva 2000: Occasional Paper 7. Geneva: United Nations Research Institute for Social Development.

————. 2001. *Development and Crisis of the Welfare State: Parties and Policies in Global Markets*. Chicago: University of Chicago Press.

Immergut, Ellen. 1992. *The Political Construction of Interests: National Health Insurance Politics in Switzerland, France and Sweden, 1930–1970*. New York: Cambridge University Press.

IDB (InterAmerican Development Bank). 1996. *Economic and Social Progress in Latin America: 1996 Report*. Washington, D.C.: Johns Hopkins University Press.

Ippolito-O'Donnell, Gabriela. Forthcoming. *New Perspectives on Welfare Reform in Latin America*. Notre Dame: University of Notre Dame Press.

Jaspersen, Frederick. 1997. "Growth of the Latin American and East Asian Economies." In Nancy Birdsall and Frederick Jaspersen, eds., *Pathways to Growth: Comparing East Asia and Latin America*. Washington, D.C.: IDB, Johns Hopkins University Press.

Kay, Stephen. Forthcoming. "Pension Reform and Savings in Latin America." *Journal of Inter-American Studies and World Affairs*.

Korpi, Walter, and Joakim Palme. 1997. "The Paradox of Redistribution and the Strategy of Equality: On the Role of Welfare State Institutions for Inequality and Poverty in the Western Countries." Paper prepared for the conference "The Welfare State at the Crossroads," Sigtuna, Sweden, January 9–12.

LaFeber, Walter. 1984. *Inevitable Revolutions: The United States in Central America*. New York: W. W. Norton.

Larrañaga, Osvaldo. 1997. "Eficiencia y Equidad en el Sistema de Salud Chileno." Serie Financiamiento del Desarrollo. Santiago: Comisión Económica para América Latina y el Caribe.

LoVuolo, Rubén. 1995. "The Welfare State in Contemporary Argentina: An Overview." Working Paper no. 2, Democracy and Social Policy Series. Notre Dame: Kellogg Institute, University of Notre Dame.

Lustig, Nora, and Darryl McLeod. 1997. "Minimum Wages and Poverty in Developing Countries: Some Empirical Evidence." In Sebastian Edwards and Nora Lustig, eds., *Labor Markets in Latin America: Combining Social Protection with Market Flexibility*. Washington, D.C.: The Brookings Institution.

Maioni, Antonia. 1998. *The Emergence of Health Insurance in the United States and Canada*. Princeton: Princeton University Press.

Mesa-Lago, Carmelo. 1989. *Ascent to Bankruptcy: Financing Social Security in Latin America*. Pittsburgh: Pittsburgh University Press.

————. 1994. *Changing Social Security in Latin America: Toward Alleviating the Social Costs of Economic Reform*. Boulder, Colo.: Lynne Rienner.

Morley, Samuel A. 1995. *Poverty and Inequality in Latin America: The Impact of Adjustment and Recovery in the 1980s*. Baltimore: Johns Hopkins University Press.

Organization for Economic Development and Statistics Canada. 2000. *Literacy in the Information Age*. Paris: Organization for Economic Co-operation and Development, and Ministry of Industry, Canada.

O'Donnell, Guillermo. 1994. "Delegative Democracy." *Journal of Democracy* 5 (January).

————. 1998. "Poverty and Inequality in Latin America: Some Political Reflections." In Víctor E. Tokman and Guillermo O'Donnell, eds., *Poverty and*

Inequality in Latin America: Issues and New Challenges. Notre Dame: University of Notre Dame Press.

Pack, Howard. 1997. "The Role of Exports in Asian Development." In Nancy Birdsall and Frederick Jaspersen, eds., *Pathways to Growth: Comparing East Asia and Latin America*. Washington, D.C.: IDB, Johns Hopkins University Press.

Page, John. 1997. "The East Asian Miracle and the Latin American Consensus: Can the Twain Ever Meet?" In Nancy Birdsall and Frederick Jaspersen, eds., *Pathways to Growth: Comparing East Asia and Latin America*. Washington, D.C.: IDB, Johns Hopkins University Press.

Pierson, Paul. 1999. "Increasing Returns, Path Dependence and the Study of Politics." Harvard University, Center for European Studies.

Raczynski, Dagmar. 1994. "Social Policies in Chile: Origin, Transformations, and Perspectives." Working Paper no. 4, Democracy and Social Policy Series. Notre Dame: Kellogg Institute, University of Notre Dame.

———, ed. 1995. *Strategies to Combat Poverty in Latin America*. Washington, D.C.: IDB, distributed by Johns Hopkins University Press.

———. 1997. "Social Policies in Chile: Origin and Transformations." Paper prepared for the conference "Social Policies for the Urban Poor in Latin America. Welfare Reform in a Democratic Context." Kellogg Institute, University of Notre Dame, September 12–14.

Radelet, Steven, and Jeffrey Sachs. 1998. "The Onset of the East Asian Financial Crisis." Draft manuscript (Harvard Institute for International Development).

Schmidt-Hebbel, Klaus, Luis Servén, and Andrés Solimano. 1996. "Ahorro, Inversión y Crecimiento Económico: Una Revisión de la Literatura." *Pensamiento Iberoamericano* 29 (January-June): 107–54.

Schoultz, Lars. 1998. *Beneath the United States: A History of U.S. Policy Toward Latin America*. Cambridge: Harvard University Press.

Stallings, Barbara. 1995. *Global Change, Regional Response: The New International Context of Development*. New York: Cambridge University Press.

Tokman, Víctor E., and Guillermo O'Donnell, eds. 1998. *Poverty and Inequality in Latin America: Issues and New Challenges*. Notre Dame: University of Notre Dame Press.

Wade, Robert. 1996. "Japan, the World Bank, and the Art of Paradigm Maintenance: The East Asian Miracle in Political Perspective. *New Left Review,* no. 217:3–36.

Wennemo, Irene. 1994. *Sharing the Costs of Children: Studies on the Development of Family Support in the OECD Countries*. Doctoral Dissertation Series, No. 25. Stockholm: University of Stockholm, Swedish Institute for Social Research.

Weyland, Kurt. 1996. *Democracy Without Equity: Failures of Reform in Brazil*. Pittsburgh: University of Pittsburgh Press.

Woo, Jung-en. 1991. *Race to the Swift: State and Finance in Korean Industrialization*. New York: Columbia University Press.